JAZZ AGE CATHOLICISM:
MYSTIC MODERNISM IN POSTWAR PARIS, 1919–1933

Jazz Age Catholicism

Mystic Modernism in Postwar Paris, 1919–1933

Stephen Schloesser

UNIVERSITY OF TORONTO PRESS
Toronto Buffalo London

ISBN 0-8020-8718-3

Library and Archives Canada Cataloguing in Publication

Schloesser, Stephen
Jazz age Catholicism : mystic modernism in postwar Paris, 1919–1933 / Stephen Schloesser.

Includes bibliographical references and index.
ISBN 0-8020-8718-3

1. Catholic Church – France – Paris – History – 20th century. 2. Church renewal – Catholic Church – History – 20th century. 3. Catholic Church – France – History – 20th century. 4. Paris (France) – Church history – 20th century. 5. Religion and culture – History. I. Title.

BX1530.S34 2005 282′.4436′09041 C2004-907369-9

Jacket illustration: Georges Rouault, *The Crucifixion.* The Minneapolis Institute of Arts, Gift of the P.D. McMillan Land Company.

University of Toronto Press acknowledges the financial assistance to its publishing program of the Canada Council for the Arts and the Ontario Arts Council.

University of Toronto Press acknowledges the financial support for its publishing activities of the Government of Canada through the Book Publishing Industry Development Program (BPIDP).

For
John W. O'Malley
and
Mary Louise Roberts

Scholars, Teachers, Mentors, Friends

Contents

Acknowledgments

I would like to thank the Charlotte W. Newcombe Fellowship, the Georges Lurcy Fellowship, the Harris Fellowship, and the Mellon Foundation for financial support (and the Bourse Chateaubriand's offer of support) of this project when it was a doctoral dissertation for the history department at Stanford University. For additional support and time needed to transform the work into a book, I am grateful to the Erasmus Institute of the University of Notre Dame, especially Robert Sullivan, for a postdoctoral fellowship; to the Bannan Institute of Santa Clara University, especially Mark Ravizza, for a year-long resident fellowship; and to Boston College, especially Joseph F. Quinn, Dean of Arts and Science, Michael A. Smyer, Associate Vice President for Research, and T. Frank Kennedy, Director of the Jesuit Institute.

I am deeply indebted and enormously grateful to those in France who made this work possible. Isabelle Rouault graciously welcomed me into her home, providing access to the family archives as well as valuable insights into her father's life and work. Odile Weber, niece of the late Alice Espir Tournemire, also welcomed me into her home and shared with me Charles Tournemire's memoirs. René Mougel accommodated me with great warmth at the Maritain Archives in Kolbsheim. Richard-Isée Knowles shared his wealth of knowledge about the Tournemires and also documents from the Société Baudelaire archives. Étienne Fouilloux first helped me obtain the Bourse Chateaubriand and has remained constant in his encouragement of this project. Naji Hakim's support and information have been invaluable, and I look back with fondness on the way he and Marie-Bernadette Dufourcet extended themselves on my behalf both at La Sainte Trinité and at Notre-Dame-des-Champs. I would also like to thank Marie-Louise Langlais for introducing me to the Sainte-Clotilde organ and sharing her artistry with a demonstration of works by the instrument's legacy of musicians: César Franck, Charles Tournemire, and her late husband, Jean Langlais. Philippe Chenaux, Frédéric Gugelot, Pascal Ianco, Bernadette Lespinard, Christian Lesur, and Dominique Salin, S.J., have been most kind in their assistance.

Closer to home, Mary Louise Roberts has been, from the day we met until the present, a model of intellectual acuity, humane compassion, commitment to her students, and disarming wit. I feel honoured to have been her first dissertation student. My other readers at Stanford, Philippe Buc, Albert Gelpi, and James J. Sheehan, helped me articulate a project I usually felt I could not begin to understand. I am also deeply indebted to Brad Gregory, Paul Robinson, and J.B. Shank for their readings along the way. The project originated as a paper for Keith Baker and his enthusiasm propelled me to continue. I am also grateful to Gavin Langmuir and Kurt Mueller-Vollmer for medievalist and modernist training.

The process of turning the dissertation into a book relied on generous gifts of time and expertise from many friends and colleagues. Paul Breines, John O'Malley, S.J., Dominique Salin, S.J., Paul Spagnoli, and Robert Sullivan (along with Lou Roberts) did me the enormous favour of reading the manuscript in its entirety at different moments, offering corrections, suggestions, and encouragement. I have been consistently edified (and amazed) by the way in which scholars responded with graciousness (and speed) to my often frantic inquiries: my thanks to Lawrence Archbold, James Bretzke, S.J., M. Brady Brower, William Bush, Caroline Bynum, James P. Callahan, Gregory Carlson, S.J., James David Christie, Paul Crowley, S.J., Bernard Doering, Caroline Ford, Jane Fulcher, Martha Hanna, Ellis Hanson, Ruth Harris, Alain Hobbs, Jeffrey Howe, Dennis Hunt, Benjamin Ivry, Jeffrey H. Jackson, Mark Jordan, Soo Yun Kang, James Keenan, S.J., Ann Labounsky, Robert Sutherland Lord, Jo Burr Margadant, Franco Mormando, Philip Nord, Robert Rumbolz, David Schultenover, S.J., Robert Sholl, Susan Stewart, and Timothy Tikker.

For research assistance I would like to thank the generosity of the staffs at the Bibliothèque Centre Sèvres, most especially Marguerite-Marie Lenglet; the Archives Françaises de la Compagnie de Jésus, especially Robert Bonfils, S.J.; the Bibliothèque Saulchoir, Les Fontaines in Chantilly; The W.T. Bandy Center for Baudelaire and Modern French Studies at Vanderbilt University, especially Mary Beth Raycraft; the Medieval Institute in Toronto; and Hesburgh Library at the University of Notre Dame. In particular, I need to thank Sonia Moss and Mary Jane Parrine at Green Library, and Dan Benedetti at O'Neill Library; they went far beyond any call of duty in helping me, both while I was at home and abroad. I was lucky to have the help of undergraduate research assistants Davis Kessler and Michael Meng, whose dependability I greatly valued. I was also fortunate in obtaining Dick Lourie's editorial assistance. In addition to being wonderful friends both at Stanford and in Paris, Paul Fitzgerald, Caroline and Cyprien Godard, and Hervé Kieffel helped with translations on numerous occasions.

On a personal note, I want to express my deepest gratitude to the Jesuit communities at Santa Clara University in California and Centre Sèvres in Paris for the years during which they took me in as a guest, sharing their homes and lives. When I lost heart, Mark Ravizza restored it. My parents have wondered for many years what this project was all about, and I am profoundly grateful that they are here to see it realized.

Kind permission has been granted to reprint portions of this book that have previously appeared:

'"What of that curious craving?": Catholicism, Conversion and Inversion *au temps du Boeuf sur le Toit*,' *Historical Reflections / Réflexions Historiques* 30/2 (Summer 2004): 221–53.

'From "Spiritual Naturalism" to "Psychical Naturalism": Catholic Decadence, Lutheran Munch, *Madone Mystérique*," in *Edvard Munch: Psyche, Symbol, and Expression*, ed. Jeffrey Howe, 71–110 (Chestnut Hill, MA: McMullen Museum of Art, 2001).

'Maritain on Music: His Debt to Cocteau,' in *Beauty, Art, and the Polis*, ed. Alice Ramos, 176–89 (Washington, DC: American Maritain Association / Catholic University of America Press, 2000).

All scriptural quotations are from *The Holy Bible translated from the Latin Vulgate, diligently compared with the Hebrew, Greek, and other editions in divers languages: the Old Testament first published by the English college at Douay, A. D. 1609: and the New Testament first published by the English college at Rheims, A. D. 1582* (New York, Cincinnati, and Chicago: Benziger Brothers, 1899).

I have used and cited English translations of published works when available. Those translations have occasionally been altered. All other translations are mine.

JAZZ AGE CATHOLICISM

There is no beauty in him, nor comeliness:
and we have seen him, and there was no sightliness,
that we should be desirous of him.

Despised, and the most abject of men,
a man of sorrows, and acquainted with infirmity:
and his look *was* as it were hidden and despised,
whereupon we esteemed him not.

– Isaiah 53:2–3

Homo sum: humani nihil a me alienum puto.

– Terence

Il a prononcé alors distinctement, bien qu'avec une extrême lenteur,
ces mots que je suis sûr de rapporter très exactement:
'Qu'est-ce que cela fait? Tout est grâce.'

Je crois qu'il est mort presque aussitôt.

– Georges Bernanos

Introduction

A Refusal to Quarantine the Sacred

> If we face squarely the fact of the incarnation, which our faith testifies to be the fundamental dogma of Christianity, we must simply say: God can become something, he who is unchangeable in himself can *himself* become subject to change *in something else* ... It follows – and this truth is now situated on a profounder level than before – that the creature is endowed, by virtue of its inmost essence and constitution, with the possibility of being assumed, of becoming the material of a possible history of God.
>
> – Karl Rahner

> to bear in her womb
> Infinite weight and lightness; to carry
> in hidden, finite inwardness,
> nine months of Eternity ...
>
> – Denise Levertov[1]

In 1926, Jacques Maritain, the self-described 'anti-modernist' Catholic philosopher, and Jean Cocteau, the iconic figure of the postwar avant-garde, jointly published their *Letter to Jacques Maritain* and *Response to Jean Cocteau*. This collaboration between the representatives of two seeming incommensurable cultural positions caused a literary sensation. Moreover, it seemed to signal a new epoch and location for Catholicism in French intellectual society. The gloating review of one Catholic apologist conveyed the sense of having arrived: 'One result of this type of publication, in addition to many others, is that it loudly proclaims the stupidity of that state of mind which likes to say: "The Church is incompatible with everything that is modern; it is a power of the past."'[2] The Maritain-Cocteau joint venture seemed to symbolize a larger synthetic possibility: that Catholicism and modernity could be reconciled.

The apologist blamed the view that Catholicism was opposed to 'everything that is modern' on laicists[3] and their 'stupid state of mind.' However, the most succinct formulation of this apparently insurmountable opposition had been the work of a Pope, not laicists. The infamous 1864 *Syllabus of Errors* published by Pope Pius IX had explicitly defined Catholicism over and against modernity in a proposition it condemned: 'The Roman pontiff can and ought to reconcile and harmonize himself with progress, with liberalism, and with modern civilization.'[4] Certainly, the meaning of the word 'modern' was as vague in 1864 as it was in 1926 (and is even more so today)[5] – this murkiness in meaning was part of what made the term so versatile and useful. However, if we take the term as simply meaning an embrace of modernity – that is an embrace of temporal progress over unchanging tradition – we can recover the shock in the 1920s that the French aptly named 'The Crazy Years.' In 1864, Catholicism had been defined as irreducibly anti-modernist; in 1926, it actively sought out the avant-garde. How was this possible?

This is the story of postwar French Catholic revivalism, also known as the *renaissance catholique* or *renouveau catholique*. As a way of restoring meaning after the chaotic trauma of the Great War, a Catholic elite in Jazz Age Paris engaged in a revivalist effort. In reconfiguring traditional tropes of Catholic thought and practice as the ultimate expressions of postwar modernity, they seem to have been quite successful. As H. Stuart Hughes once observed, 'Only in France did Catholic thinkers – in large proportion converts to the faith – succeed in establishing their view of the universe at the center of intellectual and literary discourse.' Commenting on the last of the conversions to Catholicism by towering French intellectual figures, that of the philosopher Gabriel Marcel in 1929, Hughes wrote that its 'quiet effortlessness' was 'a sign that by the end of the 1920's the enrollment of a leading thinker in the ranks of Catholicism no longer gave cause for public scandal or jubilation; the new position of religious faith among France's intellectual elite had become accepted as a normal feature of literary life in the interwar years.' Yet, he writes, as opposed to Italy, Germany, and the United States, 'it was normal in France alone.'[6] The question remains: why? By telling the story of the *renouveau catholique*, a renovation of tradition simultaneously modernist and anti-modernist, I hope to answer that question.

Sacramentum et res: Catholic Dialectical Realism

My thesis is simple: after the Great War, Catholicism came to be imagined by certain cultural and intellectual elites not only as being thoroughly compatible with 'modernity,' but even more emphatically, as constituting the truest expression of 'modernity.' Its eternal truths were capable of infinite adaptation to ever-changing circumstances. In a decade that mourned the decimation of its youth, Catholicism could be forever young.

This reconception of the relationship between Catholicism and culture was a radical departure from the prewar epoch. From the mid-nineteenth century onward, the 'Pope and the Ultramontanists ... came to believe that there was an absolute dichotomy between Catholicism and the contemporary world.'[7] Ultramontanist Catholicism both imagined itself and was imagined by others as the antithesis of the dominant 'modern' cultural and intellectual ideologies: Liberalism in politics, Science (i.e., positivism) and historicism in thought, Realism and Naturalism in art. Ultramontanism looked 'beyond the mountains' of the Alps, beyond national churches, and most especially beyond Gallican Paris to the pope in Rome for the centre of a cosmopolitan 'Roman Catholicism' – transnational identity in the age of nationalism.[8] In opposition to the Heraclitean flow of modernity's ever-changing river, ultramontanism offered an alternative Parmenidean stasis: art, thought, and politics built on eternal values, unchanging truths, and supernatural forces. It was a culture war. In the wake of the Dreyfus Affair in France, it became a civil war between Catholicism and the Republic.

The postwar *renouveau* radically re-imagined this relationship and sought to move Catholicism from the margins of culture to its very centre. Rather than despairing over a vision of religion and culture as two opposing forces irreconcilably set against one another, Catholic revivalists reconceptualized both the 'eternal' and the 'modern.' The modern, with its hard nose for 'realism' (the things of this ever-changing world), could now be seen as this epoch's expression of the eternal. In a trope borrowed from the late-century symbolists, eternal and unchanging truths needed to be 'clothed' *à la mode*, that is, in up-to-date intellectual and artistic fashions. Catholicism and culture were now related to one another in a radically different way: as the eternal living Idea in need of an ever-changing wardrobe. Or, as Jean Cocteau once put it, in his neoclassical Jazz Age aphorism: 'Tradition appears at every epoch under a different disguise.'

What made this reconceptualization and re-valuation possible? It was the revivalists' skilful retooling – to suit their own modernist program – of three traditional Catholic ideas: hylomorphism, sacramentalism, and transubstantiation. The philosophical doctrine of hylomorphism, coming from the Greek words *hulē* [matter] and *morphē* [form], holds that all real things are composed of two elements: material stuff that is pure potentiality, and the actuality of 'form,' an unseen causal force that gives order, unity, and identity to matter.[9] The theological doctrine of sacramentalism holds that created things are a visible 'sign' [*sacramentum*] which both bears within itself and simultaneously points beyond itself to an invisible 'reality' [*res*] which is, in the final analysis, the Creator. This dialectical vision that sees created matter as the *visible sign* carrying an uncreated *invisible reality* underlies the fundamental Catholic practices of sacraments and sacramentals.[10]

Third, the substance-accident metaphysics inherited from Aristotle was most famously used by medieval scholastics to explain transubstantiation, that is, the divine presence of Christ effected at Mass in the bread and wine.[11] 'Substance' in this ontology, contrary to our modern notion of it as physical stuff, is rather the underlying deepest reality of a thing.[12] Similarly, what we now think of as the contingent characteristics of a thing that are more or less 'substantial' in their physical properties (e.g., size, quantity, weight, colour, odour) are the 'accidents' that exist not in themselves but as the contingent and non-necessary (i.e., *per accidens*, 'accidental') modifications of the substance. Thus, in the doctrine of transubstantiation (which became an identity marker for Catholics after the Reformation), the accidents or outward appearances of the bread and wine remain the same even as the substance changes into the substance of Christ's own body and blood. Like the related doctrines of Christ's incarnation (i.e., God assuming human nature) and human divinization through grace, transubstantiation holds out the promise of earthly reality's ability to transcend itself.

In sum, hylomorphism, sacramentalism, and transubstantiation all exemplify a vision of the world as a dialectical composite of two interpenetrating planes of reality: seen and unseen, created and uncreated, natural and supernatural.[13] As such, they offer an alternative way of imagining relationships. Two entities – God and world, divinity and humanity, even (for the protagonists of this study) Catholicism and culture – need not be seen as two extended bodies in competition with one another, jealously fighting over a limited amount of space. Dialectical images suggest other possible modes of interrelating: one thing can point to, participate in, bear within, carry, actualize, perfect, translate, transpose, transform – or even become – something else.

For modernists and ultramontanist Catholics alike, the dominant cultural realism (e.g., positivism and historicism; literary grotesqueries; pictorial prostitutes, beggars, and clowns; musical chromaticism, passions, and dissonance) had seemed incompatible with a religion defined in opposition to those elements. The modern world had excluded religious belief; Catholicism had excluded the modern world. However, by recovering and recasting its dialectical tradition – in other words, through using the Church's own heritage – Catholic revivalists could re-imagine the relationship between religion and culture. Catholicism and 'modern civilization' – eternal and avant-garde, grace and grotesque, mystical and dissonant – could now be seen in categories other than simple competition: form actualizing matter, grace perfecting nature, substance underlying surface.

Why would such a palingenesis (revivalists used the word in the 1920s) of inherited ideas have such appeal in the Jazz Age? What were the conditions that permitted a recasting of Catholic tradition as the avant-garde? In contrast to the extreme oppositions (e.g., church v. state, science v. religion, realism v. supernaturalism) that prevailed in the late nineteenth century up until the war, the postwar period was more susceptible to the possibility of synthesis. In the social-political sphere, the war's need for a sacred union of opposing factions had catalysed a 'rallying' of Catholics to the Republic. This broad mutual reconciliation of church and state, most symbolically formalized in the Third Republic's re-establishment of ties with the 'Vatican,' reflected profound changes in popular attitudes.[14]

More specifically, the intellectual-cultural sphere was marked by another kind of synthesis that I call 'dialectical realism.' Other scholars have noted (correctly, in my view) that 'realism' was the keyword embraced by the postwar generation.[15] However, left unqualified, the term can be somewhat misleading. The realism of the 1920s differed profoundly from the nineteenth-century positivism that had excluded by definition such non-empirical elements as idealism, utopia, magic, hallucination, and dreams.

Postwar realisms included surrealism, magical realism, socialist realism, and, to use Walter Benjamin's term, 'dialectical images.' All these realisms attempted to combine, in a dialectical synthesis, both the positivist's observed world as well as something else unseen. These dialectical realisms promised the postwar epoch new possibilities: that the logical and linear world of our waking state is not the deepest truth of our lives (surrealism); that there are forces for change that escape both our observation and control (magical realism); that societal progress towards utopian equality is a real possibility (socialist realism). Avant-garde realisms – synthetic unions of both a nineteenth-century modernist's embrace of reality as well as an anti-modernist yearning for something beyond – were ambivalent reactions to an imagined 'generation of 1885' whose liberal rationalism was held responsible for the war.[16]

Traditional Catholic ideas like hylomorphism, sacramentalism, and transubstantiation were also 'dialectical realisms.'[17] In the nineteenth-century context, the unseen or metaphysical part of the Catholic dialectic seemed to be mere superstition, radically incompatible with modern realism. In the postwar epoch, that same unseen element could be newly appreciated as one among a host of avant-garde promises: that appearances deceive; that the deepest reality may be hidden within; and that substantial change is possible. In this new context, Catholic dialectical realism seemed compatible with secular dialectical realisms, and could be reworked as being both anti-modernist and ultramodernist.

Rethinking the Jazz Age: A Time to Mourn

This hope that genuine transformation is possible in ways we cannot see suggests one answer to a stubborn question: *why* was Catholic culture able to become such a salient influence in postwar France? What were its preconditions of possibility? Historians have pointed to two powerful mechanisms behind that influence: trauma and memorialization. The Jazz Age has typically been portrayed as the carefree 'Roaring Twenties' and the 'Crazy Years,' an epoch of automobiles, aeroplanes, the wireless, and flappers. But these images tell only part of the story, and historians have recovered the primary fact of the postwar period: bereavement.

One can begin with the sheer volume of French losses:[18] 1.3 million men were killed at the front while another 150,000 died from war-related causes, without counting those dead from illness. Out of 8 million mobilized men, 6.45 million who had seen the horror returned home to radically altered everyday lives. At the home front, around 570,000 civilians died due to forced evacuations from their homes, occupation, bombardments, and, at the end, to the Spanish Flu. Soldiers' deaths left behind 600,000 war widows and 760,000 orphans.

Although the armistice gave France a military victory, it did not end suffering and disorder.[19] The human loss most visible on the streets was the large number of *mutilés de guerre*, men whose limbs had been severed and whose lungs and sight were impaired by gas.[20] 1.1 million survivors received disabled veterans' benefits, an estimated equivalent to having lost another 360,000 men. For non-combatants as well, suffering continued. France emerged from the war financially ruined: urban production had been shattered and eight million acres of rural land bombed into a devastated desert. With resources depleted, France had to import large quantities of raw materials and even foodstuffs. Worker unrest, which had begun as early as 1917, continued after the war into the so-called Red Years. Increasing strike activity and the founding of the French Communist Party provoked fears that the 1917 Bolshevik revolution would spread from Russia to France. Finally, the franc began a catastrophic fall in early 1919, after the Allies refused to support it, thus compounding the problem of shortages with spiralling inflation. Even after President Poincaré's 'stabilization,' the currency remained unstable throughout the decade.

In addition to human and material losses, France also needed to grieve its cultural loss, that is, the loss of prewar values, meanings, and self-identity as a 'civilized' society. Before the war, the French had not yet seen 'any reason for abandoning their former belief in progress and their often overly optimistic, complacent estimate of the strength of France. Outbreak of war was held to be improbable in the enlightened twentieth century and the trend toward greater political and social equality seemed irreversible.'[21] For liberal rational culture in the period of empire, 'civilization' represented the highest form of a perfectible humanity in all its moral achievement.[22] Civilization itself rested upon scientific progress: the belief that 'human beings could control their destiny through scientific rationalism and that social and moral progress were inevitable.'[23]

The most important characteristic of the Great War as compared with previous conflicts – that is, its enormous scale – could initially have been seen as the fruit of scientific progress.[24] Continuing a trend begun in the previous century, small armies of professional soldiers were replaced by mass conscriptions of huge populations, vast armies of 'hastily trained civilians for reasons that were never clear to them at the time.'[25] Into these civilian hands were placed technological marvels developed over a period of three industrial revolutions. Inventions such as the telegraph, sub-machine guns, mustard gas, railways, tanks, aeroplanes, dirigibles, and submarines were 'destined to revolutionize war even more completely than had the introduction of the horse in the third millennium B.C.'[26]

However, the irreversible march forward seemed to reverse course as civilization's highest achievements were deployed for uncivilized ends. As early as June 1913, Admiral Lord Fisher, writing about the submarine that had so recently been nothing but a fiction in Jules Verne's imagination, warned: 'There is nothing else the submarine can do except sink her capture ... it is freely acknowledged to be an altogether barbarous method of warfare ... [but] the essence of war is violence, and moderation in war is imbecility.'[27] In December 1914, five months into the war, the philosopher Henri Bergson 'accused the Germans of having made their barbarism "scientific."'[28] 'Scientific barbarism' would have seemed like an oxymoron in nineteenth-century terms, the logical equivalent of 'civilized barbarism' or 'barbarous progress.'

22 April 1915 marked a milestone in modernization: the first deployment of poison gas on the Western Front. After inhalation, the chlorine vapour required just seconds to destroy the respiratory organs; asphyxiation followed. In late 1916, Louis Mairet wrote from the trenches: 'Confronted by the spectacle of a scientific struggle in which Progress is used to return to Barbarism, and by the spectacle of a civilization turning against itself to destroy itself, reason cannot cope.'[29] The promise of technological progress, the fruit of positivism and realism, had seemed enormous; but the promise turned out to be a threat. The fruit was bitter.

The Jazz Age was thus primarily a time of bereavement. A postwar sense that 'civilized intelligence' itself had perished in the trenches led to a European-wide 'mood of numbed bewilderment.'[30] A tool for exploring this cultural bewilderment is the concept of 'national trauma,' which can usefully be defined as a collective encounter with chaos.[31] Like individuals, societies need to make meaning of serious dislocations by recovering continuity with the past.[32] Although the tradition may not have been initially able to absorb these traumatic ruptures, it must be reconfigured if the experience of chaos is to be accommodated and meaningful order re-established. By means of memorialization, a larger narrative is composed that is capable of giving disruptive events meaning.

Thus, memorialization is not a distant language of remembrance; it is the act of assigning meaning to an event whose significance we are still thinking through (and arguing over).[33] Moreover, memorialization does not happen only (or even primarily) in brick and mortar. Sites of memory and mourning (and hence, of self-identity: *lieux de mémoire*) can take many forms.[34] Literature, painting, music, film, and intellectual (e.g., philosophical and theological) movements can all be ways of thinking through and assigning significance to an event whose meaning lies open to debate.[35]

This recovered context also helps us situate another remarkable re-evaluation in post-1989 historiography: a rethinking of the avant-garde and of the notion 'modernism.' Were postwar intellectual, literary, and artistic movements a rejection of tradition or a nostalgic yearning for that tradition? This ongoing debate about the relationship between 'modernism' and 'tradition,' and whether the postwar avant-garde should be seen as an absolute rupture with the past or broadly continuous with the past, has destabilized the meaning of the words 'modernist' and 'modernism' themselves.

Rethinking 1922: 'Modernism is our antiquity.'[36]

Ezra Pound proclaimed 1922 as the revolutionary Year I of the post-Christian Era.[37] This implicit reference to the French Revolutionary calendar's violent purging of the past and regenerating humanity from a *tabula rasa* carried tremendous energy. Although Pound and his cohorts may have been speaking only about the English-language literary movement that became known as High Modernism, a broader sense grew throughout the twentieth century that 'modernism' (however one defined it) repudiated 'tradition' by definition. By 1970, Theodor Adorno could write in his *Aesthetic Theory* that 'today modernism negates the notion of tradition itself.'[38] His Marxist vision evaluated modernism negatively as a pursuit of abstract form over traditional representation or, in Fredric Jameson's words, as 'a way of avoiding social content ... of managing and containing it, secluding it out of sight in the very form itself.'[39]

More recently, Astradur Eysteinsson's survey of *The Concept of Modernism* provides a helpful working definition of 'how the concept has been made to signify' more broadly a 'rage against prevalent traditions': '"Modernism" signals a dialectical opposition to what is not functionally "modern," namely "tradition."'[40] Since I am not primarily interested in 'what modernism was' (if that can indeed be answered), this oversimplified yet functional notion of 'modernism' as the binary opposite of 'tradition' will suit present purposes. Taking 'modernism' simply in its functional role as a concept used to denote (by contrast) other discourses as being 'not-modern' or 'anti-modern' – and hence, devalue and delegitimate them as being irrational, childish, primitive, or antiquarian – I want to survey the effect that its destabilization in recent studies has had on rethinking works it once dismissed.

The Parisian avant-garde of the 1920s has been reinterpreted as having been ambivalently anti-modernist in its referring, consciously or not, to the Great War and its aftermath.[41] Already during the war, stoic and tragic forms of a classicist revival (endorsed by both the political right and left) seemed to offer 'invaluable moral solace to a nation in mourning.'[42] After the war, 'victory gave France the luxury of a *rappel à l'ordre* (call to order) whose political and cultural agenda was largely aimed at repressing the trauma of war'; instead of 'the *tabula rasa* predicated by high modernism, or even the celebration of the rowdy atmosphere of the famously Roaring Twenties ... we find a collective ethos driven toward the restoration of what had been *before* the war: a world stilled, and a vision infused ... by nostalgia and memory.'[43] This repression of trauma would explain the seeming 'silence of painters' in the face of the Great War.[44]

Moreover, this anti-modernist aspect of modernism was not limited to France. Jay Winter's survey of the vigorous European 'mining of eighteenth and nineteenth-century images and metaphors to accommodate expressions of mourning' leads him to judge as 'unacceptable' those theories which see 'the Great War as the moment when "modern memory" replaced something else, something timeworn and discredited' called 'tradition.' Winter follows Freud's classic distinction between mourning and melancholia. A bitterly ironic 'modern memory' could perhaps express 'melancholia' but could not facilitate 'mourning'; it could despair but not heal.[45] The 'universality of bereavement' in postwar Europe explains 'the enduring appeal of many traditional motifs' in the 1920s.[46]

This internal instability in the concept of the modern was not uniquely postwar. The ambivalence stretched back to the concept's nineteenth-century origins. For Charles Baudelaire, the question had been 'how to *represent* the eternal and the immutable in the midst of all the chaos?'[47] However, the eternal half of Baudelaire's equation was revisited for qualitatively new reasons in the 1920s. The 'trauma of world war and its political and intellectual responses ... opened the way to a consideration of what might constitute the essential and eternal qualities of modernity that lay on the nether side of Baudelaire's formulation.' The High Modernist Joyce framed his invented language within the traditional myth of Ulysses; the surrealist Louis Aragon also sought to write a novel 'that would present itself as mythology'; even the architect Le Corbusier sought 'to inform utility with the hierarchy of myth.'[48] From Pablo Picasso and Gertrude Stein to Josephine Baker and *Le Tumulte noir* to the syncopations of Stravinsky and 'Alexander's Ragtime Band,' postwar modernism was intrinsically linked with primitivism.[49] Viewed thus, the 'modern itself is an unstable category when the new, in literature and in fashion, comes into being in such close association with the ancient.'[50]

Feminist, gender, and post-colonialist studies have also destabilized the concepts of modernity and the modern. From a feminist perspective, an 'established view of modernity in terms of a polarized opposition between individual and society' needs to remember that the 'so-called private sphere, often portrayed as a domain where natural and timeless emotions hold sway,' is invisible but ever-present, 'radically implicated in patterns of modernization and processes of social change.'[51] Such critiques intersect with post-colonial ones[52] in perceiving an 'intellectual and political bankruptcy of the tradition/modernity opposition as elaborated in dichotomies of authenticity and alienation, nature and culture, timelessness and history, and so on.'[53] For example, the black Atlantic diaspora can be redefined as a 'counter-culture of modernity,' 'a non-traditional tradition, an irreducibly modern, ex-centric, unstable and asymmetrical cultural ensemble that cannot be apprehended through the manichean logic of binary coding.'[54] Taking feminist and African-American studies together, one sees that 'a canonized version of modernism' cannot accommodate 'Willa Cather, or even, under some circumstances, Virginia Woolf' and is also 'radically opposed to any adequate and accurate account of Afro-American modernism.' Ironically, the term modernism has 'thoroughly come to mean that which rejects everything progressive and challenging in the earlier twentieth century.'[55]

My own approach to modernity has been most significantly influenced by Svetlana Boym's *The Future of Nostalgia* (2001), a survey of the decade-old aftermath of the post-Soviet world. Prior to her discussions of particular places in the former Soviet Union and Eastern Europe, Boym considers the critical project of modernity more generally as a fundamentally ambivalent synthesis of past and present: 'Modernity and modernisms are responses to the condition of modernization and the consequences of progress. This modernity is contradictory, critical, ambivalent and reflective on the nature of time; it combines fascination for the present with longing for another time.'[56]

Boym coins a neologism – the *off-modern* – for this 'tradition of critical reflection on the modern condition that incorporates nostalgia.' 'The adverb *off* confuses our sense of direction; it makes us explore sideshadows and back alleys rather than the straight road of progress; it allows us to take a detour from the deterministic narrative of twentieth-century history.' Like the 'ex-centric' location of black Atlantic diaspora writers noted above, Boym's term more generally addresses the 'eccentric' position of all those the modern casts 'out of the center' and onto the margins. For 'off-modernists who came from eccentric traditions' – that is, 'those often considered marginal or provincial with respect to the cultural mainstream' – this 'creative rethinking of nostalgia was not merely an artistic device but a strategy of survival, a way of making sense of the impossibility of homecoming.'[57]

In sum, a survey of recent work on the meaning of the 'modern' as a category leads to an appreciation of Carl Schorske's observations: what 'the historian must now abjure, and nowhere more so than in confronting the problem of modernity, is the positing in advance of an abstract categorical common denominator ... Where such an intuitive discernment of unities once served, we must now be willing to undertake the empirical pursuit of pluralities as a precondition to finding unitary patterns in culture.'[58] We have identified the twentieth-century attempt 'to confront modernity in its own terms, free from the manacles of mind that history and historicism were now thought to impose' with the meaning of modernism itself. But this should not blind us to the fact that the nineteenth century's 'thinking with history' – 'a way of coming to grips with modernization by marshaling the resources of the past' – was thoroughly modern as well. 'To master modernity by thinking *with* history, to master modernity by thinking *without* history' are not mutually exclusive antitheses but rather aspects of modernity as a critical project in response to modernization.[59]

This book follows recent efforts to rethink Catholicism as one of several pluralities defining the Jazz Age.[60] Two revisionist contexts provide the necessary opening for cultural relocation: first, seeing the postwar epoch as a time of bereavement in need of creative synthesis of both tradition and present; and second, rethinking the 'modern' as ambivalently *off-modern* in its nostalgic futurism. Catholic revivalism became a salient influence in postwar France because it was an act of memorialization, an attempt to restore meaning and self-identity to a traumatized culture. Its actors accomplished this through a creative recasting of traditional Catholic tropes as the ultimate expression of postwar modernity. They self-consciously considered themselves to be off-modern: anti-modernist in their adhesion to tradition and ultra-modernist in their embrace of time's forward motion.[61]

Postwar Catholic Revivalism: A Mode of Cultural Expression

In this book, I examine the works of the philosopher Jacques Maritain, the painter Georges Rouault, the novelist Georges Bernanos, and the musician Charles Tournemire as various expressions of Catholic dialectical realism. My approach differs from earlier efforts in three ways.

First, rather than looking at four individuals within their particular disciplinary spheres, I approach them as expressions of one tendency, formulating traditional Catholic ideas in modernist guise. I do not claim, however, that they would have thought of themselves as members of a unified movement: they did not so imagine themselves. Only by looking back after nearly a century can we see them as the varied expressions of a single cultural-religious idea.

Second, rather than considering them apart from more general cultural-political influences, I study them within the context of the Great War and its aftermath. If they can be approached as together expressing one tendency, it is because of their common location in postwar France and their common uses of traditional Catholic ideas as modernist responses to cultural crisis.

Finally, for the three artists (Bernanos, Rouault, Tournemire), my primary focus is not on their artistic intentions or the works themselves. I emphasize, rather, their reception and analysis by critics. My sources are largely critical press reviews in print media both popular and specialized.

The *renouveau catholique* was not primarily an effort on the part of the Church's ecclesiastical institutions. Catholic revivalists created their own 'imagined community,' and this relocation from cultural margin to centre depended on the printed word.[62] These shifts in Catholic identity and self-understanding were thus produced for the most part by lay persons. Even the clerics associated with the movement exerted their influence not through the pulpit but via the publishing house.[63]

Moreover, non-Catholics, non-Christians, and non-believers played significant roles in Catholic revivalism. The success of Bernanos's *Under Satan's Sun* was largely due to a popularized notion of 1926 as the year of the 'Catholic novel' – an idea given cultural weight by Albert Thibaudet's essay published in the thoroughly secular *Nouvelle Revue française*. Similarly, Bernanos's reputation as a culturally central literary figure rested on reviews like that written by Gabriel Marcel (who had not yet converted to Catholicism) appearing in the same publication. It also depended on the activist advocacy of Frédéric Lefèvre, editor-in-chief of *Les Nouvelles littéraires*, the most influential postwar literary review. As the decade progressed, Maritain's own 'Thomist Circles' became increasingly influenced by Nicolas Berdiaeff's Russian Orthodoxy and Olivier Lacombe's specialization in Hinduism. One of the most astute interpreters (and fervent promoters) of Rouault was Waldemar George, a target of vicious attacks by anti-Semitic art critics. And one of Rouault's closest intellectual companions was the writer, poet, and essayist André Suarès, whose texts Rouault illustrated, and who would spend the Second World War outrunning first the Gestapo and then the collaborationist Milice.

In sum, cultural critics thought through philosophical, pictorial, literary, and musical productions using variations on peculiarly Catholic ideas such as hylomorphism. Whether they dismissed or embraced these categories, *they utilized them*. As an ironic result, the success noted above by H. Stuart Hughes – namely, that French Catholic thinkers succeeded 'in establishing their view of the universe at the center of intellectual and literary discourse' – depended upon factors and persons quite independent of Catholicism as an ecclesiastical institution.

What new interpretative insights does such an approach yield, unified around the sacramental idea, situated within the Great War's trauma, and substantiated by critical reviews? First, it recontextualizes the works of Maritain, Rouault, Bernanos, and Tournemire within a postwar crisis of mind. They appear as centrally engaged players in a cultural contest about what is ultimately real.

Second, as a corollary, it provides yet more evidence for understanding Catholicism as a mode of cultural expression, that is, as an attempt to produce ideas, values, and meaning. Catholicism's production of values and ideas in the modern period is often enough reduced or even dismissed as being incidental to socio-economic concerns.[64] However, Catholicism's meaning had changed in this period because the values and ideas of modernity changed, and its prior connection to liberal rationalism was severed as a reaction to a failed myth of progress. If modernism can be thought of as 'modernity against itself' written in the 'reverse lettering of this discredited myth,'[65] then Catholicism can also be located within a panoply of postwar avant-gardisms whose only common denominator was a rage against the modernity of liberal rationalism: surrealism, magical realism, and socialist realism, as well as Dadaism, High Modernism, neoclassicism, 'Asiaticism,' Fascism, and communism.

Finally, this *renouveau catholique*, as a modernist desecularization project, is yet another eccentric off-modernism further complicating an already complex picture of the modern matrix – modernization / modernity / modernism. Over the past two centuries, modernization gradually came to be understood as entailing 'secularization,' that is, rational modes of thought and forms of social organization superseding 'the irrationalities of myth, religion, superstition, release from the arbitrary use of power as well as from the dark side of our own human natures.'[66] During the 1960s, the 'secularization thesis' crystallized into accepted fact: modernization (i.e., industrialization and urbanization) necessarily entailed secularization. Since then, reflection on more recent historical events has suggested a new situation: the 'desecularization of the world.'[67] Recovering the largely forgotten story of the *renouveau catholique* offers a case study of one place and time in which modernity tried to recover the wondrous – the 'mystical' – that it had once eclipsed.[68]

This is a book about cultural Catholicism. In *Catholic Lives, Contemporary America*, Thomas Ferraro has offered a cautionary note on the word '*cultural* as a qualifier to *Catholicism*': it 'does not necessarily mean dilution or dissolution – a draining of the religious imagination into banal secularity – but can in fact signify the opposite, a form of transfigurative reenvisioning that refuses to quarantine the sacred.'[69] By 1914, prewar generations, both Republican laicists and Catholic ultramontanists, had created a world whose naturalist realism left no place for grace. Remarkably, their heirs in the Jazz Age who had seen the horrors of the trenches inverted that vision, imagining instead a synthetic world of graced realism. They refused to quarantine the sacred.

Prologue

Realism, Eternalism, Spiritual Naturalism

> If the average Catholic reader could be tracked down through the swamps of letters-to-the-editor and other places where he momentarily reveals himself, he would be found to be more of a Manichean than the Church permits. By separating nature and grace as much as possible, he has reduced his conception of the supernatural to pious cliché and has become able to recognize nature in literature in only two forms, the sentimental and the obscene ... He forgets that sentimentality is an excess, a distortion of sentiment usually in the direction of an overemphasis on innocence ... Sentimentality is ... an early arrival at a mock state of innocence, which strongly suggests its opposite.
>
> – Flannery O'Connor

> Nothing, no matter how vulgar or grotesque, need be discarded for fear of undermining the elevated style, for the weightiness of Christian representation depends upon the intense apprehension of an earthly drama whose meaning is fully realized in eternity.
>
> – Stephen Greenblatt[1]

The 1920s *renouveau catholique* depended upon a newfound capacity for synthesis. This synthetic mentality itself depended upon the Great War, which had necessitated the forging of previously unimaginable sacred unions for the sake of a common national effort against the Germans. In order to recover some of the shock that this new capacity engendered, we must return to the nineteenth-century origins of perceived oppositions, a time when the unifying of such incommensurable visions of reality seemed impossible. On the one hand, the dominant cultural vision was realist in excluding everything not visible to perception. On the other hand, the ultramontanist Catholic response was eternalist in its privileging of invisible verities. A third way, in its extremes condemned as heterodox, was 'spiritual naturalism' – a Catholic Decadent synthesis.

Nineteenth-century Origins: Naturalist Realism as Laicist Ideology

Realism had socio-political, intellectual-cultural, and literary-artistic aspects. Karl Marx theorized that all of human life is a violent struggle between social classes. Charles Darwin proposed that life, far from being a well-oiled machine maintained by a benevolent Providence, is a violent competition between species and races. Auguste Comte formulated his 'fundamental law' to which human intelligence is 'subjected from an invariable necessity': 'This law is that each of our principal conceptions, each branch of our knowledge, passes successively through three different theoretical states: the theological or fictitious, the metaphysical or abstract, and the scientific or positive.' Anyone who reflected on their own intellectual evolution would recall having been successively 'a *theologian* in childhood ... a *metaphysician* in youth, and a *physicist* in maturity.' Anyone who was 'truly of this century' – that is, the modern nineteenth century – could 'provide us with this easy proof.'[2]

In order to depict life's underdogs, both in violent moments at the barricades as well as during the duller stretches of everyday life, realist artists aimed at representing the 'reality' of this dark life with as much verisimilitude as possible, delighting in journalistic precision. Throughout the 1840s and 1850s, a discourse of art criticism about 'realism' evolved: as 'realism' and 'realist' were increasingly used to mean 'materialist' and 'naturalist,' their antonyms came to signify fanciful fictions – 'dream,' 'idealism,' 'fantasy,' and 'imagination.'[3] In 1856, Théophile Silvestre defined 'realism' simply as 'the negation of imagination' and 'the preeminence of visible and palpable truth.'[4]

The publication on 25 December 1861 of Gustave Courbet's open letter to his students in the *Courrier du dimanche* stands as a defining moment for French realism. In a positivist manner, Courbet suggested that an art come of age must put away the theological and metaphysical toys of youth: 'Above all, the art of painting can only consist of the representation of objects which are visible and tangible for the artist ... I maintain, in addition, that painting is an essentially *concrete* art and can only consist of the representation of *real and existing* things. It is a completely physical language, the words of which consist of all visible objects; an object which is *abstract*, not visible, non-existent, is not within the realm of painting.'[5]

These apparently innocuous aesthetic terms had politically and socially progressive overtones. Pierre-Joseph Proudhon explicitly compared Courbet to Comte: both exemplified Proudhon's own *Philosophy of Progress* (1853), namely, that 'absolutism was the antithesis of progress.' Once the imagination's preconceived absolute principles gave way to an unbiased empirical observation of what exists, society's natural tendencies would be revealed. Progress would inevitably follow.[6]

The same terms of subordinating imagination to scientific observation were applied to literature in theorizing the modern novel. The novel differed from earlier genres' portrayals of abstract and largely edifying religious, heroic, and aristocratic figures: Oedipus, Antigone, Christ, virgin martyrs, Beowulf, Parsifal, knights, and damsels in distress. The initial volumes of Honoré de Balzac's *la Comédie humaine* were gathered together and published as a unified collection in 1842. Although debate continues over just how 'realistic' Balzac's 'realism' was, his mammoth attempt to represent all of reality in a unified apprehension made him the genre's figurehead in France. Symbolically declaring its independence from the past as represented by Dante's *Divine Comedy*, Balzac's 'Human Comedy' and its imitators focused on concretely visible characters in everyday circumstances. Those circumstances came to be represented by realists in increasingly wretched terms.

Gustave Flaubert's ghastly descriptions in *Madame Bovary* (1857) stand as a benchmark of the movement. Dr Bovary's botched attempt at surgically correcting a club foot brings 'an awful spectacle' into view. 'The outlines of the foot disappeared in such a swelling that the entire skin seemed about to burst; moreover, the leg was covered with bruises caused by the famous machine. ... A livid tumescence spread over the entire leg, and a black liquid oozed from several blisters. Things had taken a turn for the worse.' Madame Bovary is revolted by her husband's incompetence and swallows poison, hoping to escape both her passionless marriage and her extramarital affair. The chemical's physiological effects provide horrific journalistic copy: 'Drops of sweat oozed from her face, that had turned blue and rigid as under the effect of a metallic vapor. Her teeth chattered, her dilated eyes looked vaguely about her ... She soon began vomiting blood. Her lips became drawn. Her limbs were convulsed, her whole body covered with brown spots, and her pulse slipped beneath the fingers like a stretched thread, like a harp-string about to break. After this she began to scream horribly.'

The bourgeois disaster ends on an ingenious note. Hovering over Madame Bovary's corpse, the priest Bournisien and the pharmacist Homais engage in their respective and opposed rituals of purification. 'Monsieur Bournisien sprinkled the room with holy water and Homais threw a little chlorine on the floor.'[7] Religion and Science struggle for the final word.

Flaubert's method came to be associated with the 'ugly,' a term that had already been used by earlier critics to describe Balzac's 'partial' (i.e., biased) vision of reality. In 'The Physiological Novel' (1860), Gustave Merlet reviewed *Madame Bovary* and proposed that this passion for ugliness be christened 'Bovarism': 'As for this thing that kills eloquence and poetry, sacrifices the man to the brute, rids oneself of both soul and heart, attempts to please us by a taste for depraved things, and the calumny of creation and society in pretending to see nothing but physical and moral ugliness – it is this I propose that we call from today forward *Bovarism*.'[8]

In 'The Ugly in the Arts' (1861), Edouard l'Hôte characterized the realistic method as 'the representation of vulgar things' and a desire 'to be passionate about what is common, to consecrate one's chisel, one's paintbrush or one's pen to the exaltation of the ugly.' In 1862, Anatole Claveau called realism the 'school of the ugly' and defined it as 'that which exaggerates the principle and searches for the truth only in ugliness.' In *Literary Studies for the Defense of the Church* (1865), Léon Gautier amusingly evoked the single-minded search of the Magi for the newborn Christ while describing the extraordinary measures realists endured in their quest: 'The Realist is in love with ugly reality and "uglifies" the beautiful in order to make it real. It is perhaps the first time in which one sees a whole crowd passionate for the ugly, walking, running, flying in search of it, shouting with cries of joy when discovering it, falling down before it in prostration and adoration.'[9] As mass production continued to transform French society, realism's 'ugliness' may have offended refined sensibilities, but it had a growing appeal for the crowd it aimed to represent.

After the publication of Darwin's 1859 *Origin of Species*, realism developed into naturalism. The naturalist movement reflected a growing interest in biology and evolution, especially with respect to mythologies of heredity: fears of bad blood impacting bourgeois fortunes via tuberculosis, alcoholism, and syphilis.[10] In the *Chronicles of the Rougon-Macquart Family* (1871–93), an epic twenty-volume history of a fictional Second Empire family, Émile Zola wanted to show how life obeyed the ironclad laws of genetic inheritance. 'It is especially important that I remain a naturalist, a physiologist,' he told himself in an 1868 memorandum entitled 'Differences between Balzac and me.' 'It will suffice to be a scientist, to describe what is by searching for what lies underneath. No conclusion, moreover. A simple exposé of the facts of a family showing the inner mechanism that makes it run.'[11] Among other social ills, his novels investigated alcoholism (*L'Assommoir: The Dram Shop*, 1877), prostitution (*Nana*, 1880), and shopping (*The Ladies' Paradise*, 1883), all with the realist precision of a journalist.[12]

Zola's *Germinal* (1885) typifies the naturalist novel. In this relentless story about the misery endured by coal miners – a story of poverty, illness, greed, oppression – nature works out its inexorable causal necessity, grinding down humans at every turn. As if life hasn't been bad enough for several hundred pages, towards the end of the novel the mine is about to flood, threatening to snuff out the miserable lives of those trapped in it. Étienne had felt compelled to murder Chaval: 'The need to kill seized him irresistibly, a physical need, like the irritation of mucus which causes a violent spasm of coughing. It rose and broke out beyond his will, beneath the pressure of the hereditary disease.' Chaval's death, like Madame Bovary's, offers the novelist a chance to indulge description: 'He fell, his face crushed, his skull broken. The brains had bespattered the roof of the gallery, and a purple jet flowed from the wound, like the continuous jet of a spring.' Later on, despite Étienne's and Catherine's attempts, Chaval's body keeps floating back as the flood waters swirl: 'It had not been worth while to knock his brains out, for he came back between him and her, obstinate in his jealousy.'

Catherine and Étienne finally consummate their passion not far from Chaval's corpse. Zola reports this last fleeting moment of physical passion:

> He shuddered to feel her thus against his flesh, half naked beneath the tattered jacket and trousers, and he seized her with a reawakening of his virility. It was at length their wedding night, at the bottom of this tomb, on this bed of mud, the longing not to die before they had had their happiness, the obstinate longing to live and make life one last time. They loved each other in despair of everything, in death.
>
> After that, there was nothing more.[13]

Sharing elements of Marxism and Darwinism, Zola's technique exemplified a positivist's duty to observe and accumulate facts in a fatalistic universe. The cumulative effect was both titillating and depressing: enormous unseen forces of an unjust society and pitiless nature colluded to make human lives seem as miserable and ultimately insignificant as possible.

In this age of increasing mass production, the naturalist novel was only one among many possible realistic spectacles that catered to a growing appetite for popular voyeurism.[14] Bourgeois patrons eagerly paid for excursions through the newly invented Paris sewer system, marvelling at the wondrous lack of foul odours.[15] The daguerreotype was used to capture urban architecture, blood under microscopes, and portraits of wealthy patrons, criminals, the insane, and colonial primitives – all with exacting precision.[16] Dioramas and panoramas allowed for three-dimensional immersion: not far from the Moulin Rouge, Alfred Grévin founded his wax museum, the Musée Grévin, whose exhibitions *L'Illustration* called 'the triumph of Naturalism.' Grévin vowed to Zola that the museum 'will be naturalist or will not be,' and he enshrined the gruesome climactic scene of *Germinal* in a diorama.[17] Here, the figures of Catherine and Étienne stood next to Chaval's corpse, soon to consummate their final act of love, frozen in timeless wax for mass consumption. Wood engravings of photographs enabled tabloids to mass-produce lifelike scenes with lurid details. Not content with print images, crowds thronged to view the corpses themselves, exhibited in morgue windows dressed like department store displays. In 1886, when about fifty thousand visitors came to view the bruised body of a four-year-old girl exhibited at a Paris morgue, vendors turned the quai de l'Archêveché into 'a genuine fairgrounds,' hawking 'coconut, gingerbread, and toys.'[18] Quite apart from larger philosophical considerations, naturalist realism's popularity pointed to a basic principle of consumer culture: sex and violence sell.

Scientific modernity in the forms of anthropology, psychology, and sociology also employed these tools of publishing, photography, and spectacle to promote a naturalist realism that implied materialist atheism. Anthropometry, craniology, and phrenology measured the shapes and sizes of skulls, hands, and beards, believing that these would reveal the subjects' mental capacities and moral dispositions.[19] Turin Professor Cæsare Lombroso's *Criminal Anthropology* (1895) was quite specific: pickpockets could be detected by their long hands and scanty beards; prominent jaws suggested the heart of a murderer. Joseph Conrad's novel *Heart of Darkness* (1899) captured the moment: as Marlow prepares to leave civilization for the African interior, his visit to the doctor produces a strange request. The doctor asks Marlow with 'a certain eagerness' if he can measure his head. 'Rather surprised,' Marlow consents, and the doctor produces 'a thing like callipers' and examines the 'dimensions back and front and every way, taking notes carefully.' 'I always ask leave, in the interests of science,' he explains, 'to measure the crania of those going out there.' 'And when they come back too?' asks Marlow. 'Oh, I never see them,' replies the doctor and adds ironically: 'the changes take place inside, you know.'[20] Anthropology's positivist reduction of interior states to exterior phenomena led to 'the end of the soul.'[21]

The new psychology was a second important form of scientific modernity. In France, it was symbolized by Jean-Martin Charcot, the 'Napoleon of neuroses' under whom Freud came to study in 1885.[22] A professor of neurological pathology at the Salpêtrière clinic, Charcot specialized in psychical research. Although for centuries physicians had traced the origins of 'hysteria' to an irritation of the uterus or a feverish imagination, Charcot insisted that it was a neurological disorder, the symptoms of which could be fully explained by accurate descriptions of surface phenomena.[23]

Thanks to the technology of photography, the massive two-volume *Photographic Iconography of the Salpêtrière* (1877–8) offered an audience far beyond the hospital's confines a glimpse of the gruesome yet delicious spectacle of hysteria's attack.[24] The camera's scientific gaze caught Charcot's model Augustine acting out the bodily contortions of hysteria's various species. Paul Richer's *Clinical Studies of Grand Hysteria* (1885) provided an encyclopedic compilation of every type of seizure.[25] A synoptic chart of hysterical postures strongly resembled Mendeleev's periodic table of the elements,[26] implying that Charcot had successfully mapped and categorized the psyche's every possible physical combination.

The new malady required a newly invented psychiatric profession for its treatment, scientifically displacing the former religious practitioners (i.e., priest-confessors and exorcists). Thus, the hysteria diagnosis took on political significance as it was used by anticlerical republicans to discredit religious beliefs and institutions.[27] *The Hysteric* (*L'Hystérique*, 1885), a ferociously anticlerical novel by Camille Lemonnier (a 'Flemish Zola') was likely inspired by Louise Lateau, a Belgian woman who was a famous instance of a stigmatic.[28] The phenomena registered on Sister Humility's unmanageable body present the possibility of two alternative readings. She could either be a 'mystic' (as the Catholic clerics insist), undergoing an interior supernatural event not accessible to positivist observation; or these stigmatic phenomena could be easily explainable manifestations of the hysterical attack, a physiological eruption subject to classification within scientific categories.

Charcot's *Demoniacs in Art* (1887) offered a historical overview of traditional religious iconography. Taking examples from centuries of artistic paintings depicting satanic possession and religious ecstasy, Charcot juxtaposed them with his own diagnostic figures: Bernini's 'Ecstasy of St Teresa' was thus reinterpreted as an example of a hysterical seizure.[29] The self-evident implication was that religion was irrational, neurotic, and (in the words of the brothers Goncourt) 'a part of the female sex.'[30] Quoting Paul-Maurice Legrain's 1886 work on *Delirium among Degenerates* (based on observations at the Sainte-Anne asylum), Max Nordau's *Degeneration* (1892) put the equation succinctly: 'Mystical thoughts are to be laid to the account of the insanity of the degenerate. There are two states in which they are observed – in epilepsy and in hysterical delirium.'[31] These discursive wars were political, social, and cultural. They were also gendered, and although the battle lines were mostly drawn on the privileged site of the female body, they also contributed to creating new notions of 'masculinity.'[32]

In addition to anthropology and psychology, the new sociology also functioned as an anti-clerical discourse, focusing much of its energy on the 'scientific' study of religion. Lucien Lévy-Bruhl's efforts at reintroducing Auguste Comte (who had died in 1857) to a new generation – *The Unpublished Letters of John Stuart Mill to Auguste Comte* (1899); *The Philosophy of Auguste Comte* (1900) – served a fin-de-siècle agenda.[33] In earlier times, 'The organization of Catholicism, "a masterpiece of political sagacity,"' had once 'established a body of beliefs which all minds accepted with complacent docility.' However, 'the decomposition of this great system' had 'produced the majority of the evils with which we are now struggling.' Thus, the 'theologico-metaphysical mind' – that is, the 'fictitious' – needed to be superseded by a positivist 'philosophy' – that is, a 'totalizing of experience' that would restore a sense of 'unity.'[34]

In *Ethics and Moral Science* (1904), Lévy-Bruhl lamented that there were 'very few persons among the so-called educated classes who do not complacently listen to stories of marvelous and inexplicable cures. How many accept,' he exclaimed, 'more or less openly, the hypothesis of a miraculous intervention of the Virgin or of a saint during the course of an illness!' In accepting 'so gross a contradiction,' intelligent persons easily agreed 'to a striking exception to biological laws, without perceiving that the miracle they accept necessarily implies several of those that they do not accept.'[35] Having little or no regard for this 'law of contradiction' was the centrepiece of *Mental Functions in Inferior Societies* (1910): the 'preological' and 'mystic' mentality found in the consciousness in colonial primitives was distinct from the modern mind precisely in not embracing the principle of non-contradiction. 'If I were to express in one word this general property of the collective representations holding so important a place in the mental activity of undeveloped peoples,' wrote Lévy-Bruhl,' I should say that their mental activity was a *mystic* one ... in the strictly definite sense in which "mystic" implies belief in forces and influences and actions which, though imperceptible to sense, are nevertheless real.'[36] *Primitive Mentality* (1922) expanded this analysis, devoting itself to 'mystic and invisible forces' and the 'mystic meaning of accidents and misfortunes.' The book's British translator promised that 'a colonizing country such as ours' would finally be able to make sense of a puzzling phenomenon, namely, 'the very real sense in which the primitive "participates" in the mystic nature of all that surrounds him, the way in which *he lives in the seen and the unseen worlds simultaneously* ...'[37] Lévy-Bruhl's sociological discourse about the mentalities of colonial primitives also served an anticlerical function: Catholic attributions of observable phenomena to invisible causes could be considered a vestige of prelogical and mystic mentality.

In sum, the scientific modernities of anthropology, psychology, and sociology all promoted a positivist totalizing principle: total phenomenal description yields total causal explanation. Although Comte had formulated his positivist philosophy in the mid-century, it only achieved its full force after the 1870–1 debacle of the Franco-Prussian War/Paris Commune and during the consequent Third Republic's formation. 'What we propose to do,' Léon Gambetta said famously of the new republic, 'is to apply positivism in the political order.' Positivism provided laicists with 'a consistent and complete set of ideas, a philosophical substructure, for their materialist and agnostic leanings. It supported their optimistic hope that men, through science, could remake the world.'[38]

However, as Zola's work amply demonstrates, this optimistic hope was shot through with fatalism as well. In 1885, the organic chemist Marcelin Berthelot announced the bittersweet terminus of scientific progress: '*Today the world is without mystery.* Rational conception claims to clarify and comprehend everything. It works hard at giving everything a positive and logical explication, and it spreads its fatal determinism all the way to the moral world.'[39] Jacques Barzun has summarized this paradoxical 'logic of progress': 'All events had physical origins; physical origins were discoverable by science; and the method of science alone could, by revealing the nature of things, make the mechanical sequences of the universe beneficent to man. Fatalism and progress were as closely linked as the Heavenly Twins and like them invincible.'[40]

Positivism might be a 'progressive' ideology, but it entailed a materialist world that left no place for human freedom and 'no place of grace.'[41] In response, Catholicism offered its counter-vision: eternalism.

Catholic Counter-Vision: Supernaturalist Eternalism as Ultramontanist Ideology

In opposition to modernity's embrace of constant change, ultramontanist Catholicism proposed a counter-vision that privileged things invisible and eternal. Although the nineteenth-century players would have called this 'supernaturalism' or 'spiritualism,' neither term works well today. 'Supernaturalism' too quickly conjures up images of ghost stories, monkey's paws, and extraterrestrials. 'Spiritualism' has come to designate a particular fin-de-siècle movement that included seances, extrasensory perception, and Theosophy. Thus, in order to underscore the central ultramontanist concern, I call their vision 'eternalism.'

If 'realism' privileged the unbiased observation of ephemeral facts, 'eternalism' emphasized the opposite: stasis, contemplation of the unchanging, and 'eternal peace' – *la paix de l'éternel*. Eternalism's intellectual and cultural expressions – in painting, music, philosophy, and poetry (but *not*, significantly, the novel) – all aimed at representing ultimate immaterial realities that could be neither perceived nor quantified. They were imagined to be universal and certain in their truth.

In several senses, eternalism might be seen as being anti-modernist since its opponents included realism, naturalism, liberalism, and socialism. However, its neo-medievalist use of the past (especially of the High Gothic and Romano-Byzantine Middle Ages) was thoroughly modern in its attempt to master modernity by 'thinking *with* history.' Contrary to caricatures promoted by both nineteenth-century liberalism and twentieth-century theories of modernization, the practice of inventing traditions (like Scottish kilts, Victorian state funerals, and Bastille Day) was not an element of 'traditional' societies but of 'modern' ones.[42] Cultural historicism was one way of 'coming to grips with modernization by marshaling the resources of the past.'[43]

Thus, eternalism was modern in its inventions of tradition and antimodern in the values and world-view it sought to realize. Set against an overall realist-naturalist hegemony, ultramontanist Catholicism was a marginal critical voice that functioned (to use the classical categories of Ernst Troeltsch) less like a 'church' and more like a 'sect.'[44] Given the history of French Catholicism exemplified in Gallicanism – which was, if anything, an over-identification of Catholicism and culture – this sectarian stance represented a significant departure from tradition. It also inverted the spirit of its post-Tridentine icon, Thomas Aquinas, the master synthesizer of Biblical faith and scientific reason.[45] As a trans-national outsider symbolically centred in the Roman Pope, nineteenth-century Catholicism did not see itself as a culturally central player, synthesizing and transforming elements of that culture. More often than not it saw itself as besieged, its eternalist values competing with hegemonic modernity.

Eternalism's artistic expressions looked back beyond the Gallican, Baroque, and even Renaissance epochs to an imagined medieval world when religious art had been uncontaminated by temporality, three-dimensional perspective, and 'sensuous worship.'[46] An 'aesthetics of ultramontanism' was one of 'the major transformations of Catholicism in nineteenth-century France.'[47] Employing two-dimensional surfaces, hieratic poses, idealized bodies, and a neo-Byzantine embrace of timeless perfection, it aimed at representing *la paix de l'éternel* – an absence of mundane motion, suffering, and (erotic) 'passions.' At the turn of the century, this neo-traditionalism converged with the neo-primitivist vogue to form an unlikely avant-garde.[48]

In 1838, E.J. Delécluze, a former student of Jean-Jacques-Louis David and a defender of classical art, gave an early summation of hieratic aesthetic values. The 'epithet *hieratic*' signified an 'exterior calm, an expressive sign for strength, force, power, and all of the attributes of divinity.' This calm created 'a predisposition to the exercise of thought, to the elevation of the soul and to the acquisition of knowledge of God and things divine.'[49] Delécluze did not believe that the style was particular to Christian art, and he saw no significant contrast between the *hieratic* found in '*classical*' works and the 'sacred monuments of all religions.'

However, others began to make distinctions. In 1841, the Société Libre des Beaux-arts, France's most important association of artists at the time, issued a report that distinguished between the 'historical' and the 'mystical.' 'A mystical composition,' reported the Société, 'is one located entirely within religious tradition and the true spirit of Christianity.' In 'the painting of history,' everything was supposed 'to be true and complete, ought to be represented with scrupulous concern for the authentic account.' In contrast, a mystical work expressed 'a symbol and not a material action; it is the interpretation of an idea and not the reproduction of fact.'[50] In the 1850s and 1860s, a 'mystical' aesthetic embracing eternal symbols and ideas would counter Courbet's 1861 denigration of the invisible.

Nineteenth-century Byzantine revivalism offered painters concrete historical models with which to express eternalist values.[51] Nostalgia for Byzantium was a thoroughly invented tradition that grew as the century aged. As late as 1837, a prominent archaeologist gave this negative opinion of nearly a thousand years of Byzantine art: 'religious thought ... rendered it immobile in order to render it sacred; one knows that in effect this art of the Byzantines remained captive in its hieratic prototypes, without giving, during almost ten centuries, a single ray of life, of liberty, or of movement ...'[52]

In the 1840s, however, Frédéric Ozanam, an early ultramontanist, founder of the Society of Saint Vincent de Paul, and a professor of literature, delivered a series of lectures at the Sorbonne that celebrated the Byzantine aesthetic. The 'great and resplendent image of Christ and of the celestial Jerusalem' had functioned 'to animate the hope of the faithful, in the midst of the perils of these bloody centuries.'[53] A highly publicized journey by two archeologists to Asia Minor resulted in a French work entitled *Manual of Greek and Latin Christian Iconography Translated from the Byzantine Manuscript, 'Guide to Painting'* (1845). When Ludwig I of Bavaria asked for the manuscript to be copied, the author Adolphe Didron offered his own copy to this 'enlightened prince to whom one owes the renaissance of Catholic art in Germany.' He expressed hope that it would further the building of 'Byzantine and Gothic monuments in Munich and the rest of Bavaria.'[54]

The neo-Byzantine vogue gained momentum in the 1850s. François Picot's mural painting for the church of Saint-Vincent-de-Paul in Paris (1853) employed this aesthetic of flat, hieratic, two-dimensional surfaces. Wearing the imperial dress of the Byzantine court, Christ the King was represented as the Pantocrator. The chasm between the temporal and eternal realms was emphasized by a dwarfed kneeling figure soliciting the ruler's patronage.[55] Two years later, Hippolyte Flandrin used the same style for the Church of Saint-Martin-d'Ainay in Lyon (1855), a Romanesque church that was restored in the 1840s. Flandrin had been affected by seeing Roman mosaics whose representation of God he described as 'truly immutable, eternal.'[56] The Christ-King, not seated on a throne but standing, was once again portrayed in a frontal pose against a gilded firmament, evocative of eternal peace.

Around 1860, Flandrin executed a mural painting of *The Crucifixion* for the Church of Saint-Germain-des-Près in Paris. This wholly unrealistic (or anti-realistic) representation illustrated Flandrin's agreement with Ingres's neoclassical dictum: the figure of Christ, even in his most grotesque moment of bodily torture, needed to reflect his being 'the most beautiful of all men.'[57] (Gerard Manley Hopkins summarized the tradition: 'There met in Jesus Christ all things that can make man lovely and loveable. In his body he was most beautiful.')[58] Viewed in contrast to Eugène Delacroix's stormy romantic *Christ on the Cross* (1853), a representation that ultramontanists would have associated with naturalism and social upheaval, Flandrin's Christ and followers formed a frozen tableau.[59] Whether enthroned in courtly glory or in death's agony, the ultramontanist Christ embodied eternal peace.

The spirit of Byzantium also expressed itself in architecture in the wake of the Franco-Prussian War/Paris Commune of 1870–1. Perhaps its most famous example is the Basilica of the Sacré Cœur in Paris, whose cornerstone was laid in June 1875. Built in 'reparation' to the Sacred Heart of Christ for the Communards' 'impieties' (including the assassination of the archbishop of Paris), it expressed a return to national order after military defeat and civil chaos.[60] The dome's massive interior image of the Sacred Heart, a fiery image once used by Jesuits against Jansenists in order to bring emotion and warmth back into classical Catholicism, now embodied cool passionless traits. The Basilica of Notre-Dame de Fourvière in Lyon, begun in 1872, was another Romano-Byzantine structure built in connection with the war. It fulfilled a vow made by the bishop to build a basilica if the city were spared Prussian occupation. Officials also chose this style, laden with mosaics, for the shrine at Lourdes' lower Basilica of the Rosary, begun in 1883.[61]

The ultramontanist program was so successful at equating the sacred with the hieratic style that even the Panthéon was completed in the neo-Byzantine manner. In 1881, the radical republican Edmond Turquet was put in charge of completing the laicist temple that would enshrine the remains of France's 'great men,' including Voltaire and Rousseau. Turquet cautioned Ernest Hébert, the artist commissioned to execute the apse's massive mosaic, against attempting to make the mosaic resemble an oil painting (as in modern Italian mosaics), instructing him rather to 'return to the elementary means employed by the mosaicists of Ravenna.'[62] In the 1890s, Maurice Denis, both Catholic and Nabi, declared that 'Byzantine painting is surely the most perfect type of Christian art.' Its formalist means expressed the 'magnificence of the immutable': 'its admirable relations signify transcendental truth; its proportions express concepts; there is an equivalence between the harmony of forms and the logic of Dogma.'[63]

If eternalism's suspension of time was capable of visual expression, it was even better represented by music, the art that requires temporal duration. Institutions like Solesmes Abbey, the Schola Cantorum conservatory in Paris, and the international Cecilian liturgical 'reform' movement all promoted a 'restoration' of Gregorian Chant.[64] An 1839 episcopal letter summarized the task: after a 'historic and artistic reaction' had finally restored ancient 'traditions of sacred architecture, the furnishings of the sanctuary, the hieratic types of Catholic painting and sculpture,' there remained but one task: 'to return to our ... Gregorian formulae.'[65] By 1846, Joseph d'Ortigue, a member of Lamennais's original 1830s ultramontanist circle, was making a distinction between 'music' and 'plainchant.' Whereas the 'tonal constitution' of music created 'a passionate and terrestrial expression,' the 'tonal constitution' of plainchant gave rise to 'a calm and contemplative state.'[66]

Not all were happy with this invention of tradition. When one of the most ardent promoters of Gregorian Chant published his *General History of Religious Music* (1860), music critic Paul Scudo's review assailed it as part of an ultramontane conspiracy aimed at religious and social oppression. 'Plainchant was altered more and more,' wrote Scudo, 'until it succumbed in this struggle of the spirit of liberty against the hieratic forms of the Church.' Arguing that there was no longer a need for a special liturgical aesthetic, Scudo concluded that plainchant was an 'insufficient form that no longer responded to the religious needs of our epoch.'[67] Hector Berlioz also attacked 'these Anabaptists of art,' denouncing this 'formation of a sect ... This innocent schism that says its end is to create true *Catholic* music, tends, in the religious service, to suppress music completely.' The formulas of d'Ortigue, complained Berlioz, did not even leave room in the church for 'the *Ave Verum* of Mozart, this sublime expression of ecstatic adoration, which has nothing to do with ecclesiastical tonality ...'[68] Such appeals to history and reason, however, could not withstand ultramontanism's force, especially as loyalty to the Pope grew after the 1870 dissolution of the Papal States.

Rival versions of Gregorian Chant emerged: since it was a modern imagination of what medieval chant might have sounded like, interpretations varied according to aesthetic sensibilities and commercial concerns.[69] In 1868, the publishing firm of Pustet of Ratisbon was granted a fifteen-year privilege as the Holy See's official printer of chant. Dom Pothier of Solesmes Abbey impugned Pustet's square-note typography as being too 'modern' in its fixed rhythms, and aimed at 'restoring' a more authentic Benedictine pedigree. His own invented tradition was published as the *Gradual Book Ordained by Saint Gregory the Great* (1883),[70] a collection of ritual chants following his deeply romantic approach to rhythm laid out in *Gregorian Melodies According to the Tradition* (1880): 'We feel it, the ears are deliciously affected by it, but we cannot say what it is.'[71] The Vatican would eventually settle matters and define a uniform standard of performance.[72]

If plainchant was eternalism's privileged genre, the pipe organ was its instrument. The French Revolution had left French organs and organists quite literally in ruins, and the state funded a revival of organ-building in order to restore the patrimony.[73] These new instruments, transformed by the invention of electricity which made possible a greatly expanded capacity for wind air pressure (and increased volume and velocity), became sites of an aesthetic feud. One organist, after discovering how technological advances made the key touch lighter and hence easier to play, disapproved of the modern convenience. He feared that the 'august instrument' would 'lose all its dignity' if organists started playing faster. They were already 'in the habit of playing too many notes.'[74]

In 1846–7, a heated exchange broke out in the *Revue de la musique religieuse, populaire, et classique*. The review's founder, Jean-Louis-Félix Danjou, an enthusiastic supporter of church music 'reform,' criticized the new organs being built by Aristide Cavaillé-Coll.[75] The new organs' attempt at 'the imitation of orchestral instruments' was an 'error' whose results would be 'disastrous for music.' The orchestra was merely 'effective for sensuous music, which is inappropriate in the Church.'[76] Cavaillé-Coll responded: since 'the same notes of the scale ... can be used to express a religious or a worldly idea,' the sacred or profane nature of the music must lie in the composition and not the instrument.[77]

Danjou countered with a neo-medievalist appeal. 'Mr. Cavaillé-Coll forgets that the organ is several centuries older than the group of instruments we call an orchestra,' wrote Danjou; 'he forgets that the organ sounded in our churches in the Middle Ages, that its majestic voice intoned our religious chants at a time when orchestras did not exist.' It had been made for 'worship,' not 'sensual' art. When organ builders grafted orchestral sounds onto the organ, its 'expression [was] made sensual,' and 'this virtuosity, this exquisite sensitivity, this lively yet tender expression' of worldly music was 'out of place' in a church. Religious music was eternalist: 'Calm, dignity, grandeur, majesty, and power are appropriate to the organ in the Catholic church. *Non in commotione Dominus*, say the holy books: the Lord delights not in turmoil or unrest.' Those who disagreed had not 'sufficiently considered the requirements of religious art; but organists come and go, while the laws of beauty are eternal.'[78]

As in Byzantine decoration, even secular authorities accepted ultramontanist categories when classifying music. In 1849, the new government of the Second Republic, continuing the practice of 'restoring' the organ patrimony of France, issued guidelines that imitated those values later institutionalized in the Cecilian movement. State officials condemned music that turned the faithful into 'spectators' and officially promoted the construction of instruments that would support Gregorian chant, the music it deemed 'most consonant with true religious architecture and the "primitive character" of the Roman liturgy.'[79]

The intellectual parallel to this aesthetic eternalism was the revival of medieval scholasticism, symbolically embodied in the figure of St Thomas Aquinas. Neo-scholasticism (also known as neo-Thomism) embraced eternal and unchanging verities, invisible entities inaccessible to sense perception. Catholic metaphysics opposed the positivism underpinning political republicanism. In Comte's theory, metaphysics represented the youthful or adolescent stage of human thought, eventually superseded by the 'positive state' of adulthood. The human mind in this final state, said Comte, 'recognizing the impossibility of attaining to absolute concepts,' would abandon 'the search for the origin and destiny of the universe, and the inner causes of phenomena.'[80] Against this empirical hegemony, neo-scholastic metaphysics held that ultimate realities were not only unseen but also unchanging – substances, essences, formal and final causes.

In his 1879 encyclical *Aeterni Patris*, Pope Leo XIII mandated the 'restoration' of neo-scholasticism and its teaching in all Catholic high schools, colleges, universities, and seminaries throughout the world.[81] Like neo-Gothic architecture, neo-Byzantine painting, and the chant of Saint Gregory the Great, neo-Thomistic philosophy was an invented tradition. Within Catholic ecclesiastical and educational institutions, the previous dominant influence had come from those indebted to post-Kantian idealism while those who advocated a systematic return to Thomas were a small, disruptive, and scorned minority. As late as 1865, a Jesuit provincial had written disparagingly of two Thomists: 'Those two members of the [Jesuit order], well known as uncompromising Thomists, suddenly rose in defense of that commonly rejected doctrine ... their way of feeling and of thinking implies a condemnation of the whole body of the Society and, which is worse, of the Episcopate.'[82] The Pope's mandate to teach only Thomism at the Jesuits' Gregorian University in Rome placed 'a severe strain on Jesuit obedience of the intellect' since many of the priest-professors were disciples of Suarez and Descartes.[83]

The Thomistic revival had originated as a refutation of rationalist, sceptical, and idealist assaults (of Descartes, Hume, and Kant) on the mind's ability to grasp reality as it is.[84] Whereas nineteenth-century neo-Thomism was built around a theory of knowledge, the medieval Thomas Aquinas built his epistemology on foundations of metaphysics and psychology.[85] This 'epistemologizing' of the works of Thomas resulted in a version distinctly modern in its anxieties and aims.[86]

A decade of coming to terms with the papal mandate produced institutional results. In 1893, the *Revue thomiste* appeared, one of many journals that would be dedicated to Thomistic scholarship. In 1894, Belgian Cardinal Mercier published an article entitled 'Neo-Scholastic Philosophy' outlining the aims of his Institut Supérieur de Philosophie to be established at the Catholic University of Louvain.[87] He wanted to approach Aquinas differently from the Roman method that embraced the thirteenth century in all its limitations. Mercier sought rather to recover the spirit of Aquinas and then apply it to contemporary culture. Louvain adopted a slogan: 'St Thomas must be for us a beacon not a barrier.'[88] His approach would deeply influence French Catholics and reach across the Atlantic to disciples at Harvard and Princeton.[89]

Maurice de Wulf, one of the Institut's founding professors and master expositors, situated Thomism as a middle-ground approach to 'realism.'[90] On the one hand, he rejected the 'naive realist' for whom reality is 'altogether independent of our knowledge of it, and our minds faithfully and accurately reflect things just as they are outside of us, in a merely passive way.' Here, de Wulf may have been consciously echoing – and criticizing – the realism of Stendhal: 'The novel is a mirror that strolls along the highway.' He also shared the concerns of idealists, symbolists, post-impressionists, and expressionists (like Stéphane Mallarmé, Gustave Moreau, and Parisian Wagnerites) in rejecting as 'too superficial' the total correspondence between the world of external reality and the world of consciousness.

On the other hand, de Wulf also rejected an idealism that views 'the known object [as] simply a product of our mental organization' and according to which 'we know directly only our internal or subjective modifications.' The problem with idealism, he asserted, is that 'the real object' – that is, the world outside our consciousness – plays no part in our knowledge. Idealism holds that we do not 'directly attain to reality' but simply to our own ideational constructions. Here de Wulf shared the concerns of realists: namely, that the mind's operations deform, distort, or disfigure reality.

In between these two extremes of naïve realism and idealism, de Wulf situated the position he imagined to be 'medieval scholasticism.' Knowledge is a 'complex phenomenon, the product of two factors.' One factor is the external object to be known; the other factor is the mind that knows. Scholasticism postulated a complicated process of mental abstraction that answered both concerns: against idealism, the object's form genuinely becomes a part of the knowing mind by informing it; against naive realism, 'the knower invests the thing known with *something* of himself' without disfiguring it.[91] In an epoch marked by positivism's despair of going beyond external observation, de Wulf's fundamental point offered great appeal: 'We directly attain to reality and being.'

The conflict between naturalist and eternalist world-views revolved around the meaning of that troublesome word: 'reality.' For naturalists, reality was the material of history, subject to constant change; their realism led to agnosticism or atheism. For eternalists, reality was form behind the matter, impervious to change; their realism led to metaphysical and theological truth. Realists and eternalists thus shared a dualistic view. They imagined the world as a struggle between enormous forces set in opposition to one another: Republic v. Church, Science v. Religion, Realism v. Truth (or Superstition). Each was marked by a melodramatic opposition between virtue and villainy, or a Manichean one between good and evil, or an apocalyptic one between light and darkness.[92] In this logic of an excluded middle, there seemed to be no possibility of a dialectical synthesis mediating the mutually exclusive poles.

Could the ugliness of everyday reality be imagined to be the outward expression of metaphysical or mystical forces? If one were restricted to the two orthodoxies of realism and eternalism, the answer would be no. One needed to choose between the base and the elevated. But in the fin-de-siècle, a heterodox third way would attempt to think through an apparent oxymoron: 'Spiritual Naturalism.' Joris-Karl Huysmans would synthesize the grotesque and the supernatural.

A Heterodox Third Way: Saint Hysteria

The nineteenth-century Catholic intellectual revival known as the *renouveau catholique* began to assume definitive shape in the 1880s.[93] The movement's 'Catholic literature' was an often-violent reaction to the period's dominant positivism, materialism, and naturalism. The first converts came to Catholicism via heterodox routes, attracted by fin-de-siècle forms of spiritualism: symbolist, orientalist, esoteric, Rosicrucian, and theosophical.[94] Not everyone appreciated this third way, as titles by a now-forgotten polemicist show: *Neo-Christianism and Religious Dilettantism* (1914); *Léon Bloy and the Feigned renouveau catholique* (1917); *The Process of the Feigned 'renouveau catholique' in the Court of Public Opinion* (1919); and *A Mystical Cythera: The Feigned renouveau catholique* (1920).[95] Nevertheless, this literary and artistic movement served many in the cultural elite by proving that one could be both Catholic and intellectual, and record numbers of converts to Catholicism passed through its doors over a period of fifty years. As Joséphin Péladan (a firm ultramontanist and self-appointed 'Sâr' of the Rose + Croix movement) remarked, the aesthetic state could be considered an 'interim period of faith,' since those who went to the Louvre often ended up at Notre Dame.[96]

The revival had its roots in the literary genre of the *fantastique*, introduced in France by Jean-Jacques Ampère with his 1829 translation of E.T.A. Hoffmann's *Fantasy Pieces in the Manner of Callot* (1814).[97] As opposed to the novel, the privileged genre of realism, the *fantastique* became associated with short stories and its use came to be almost obligatory in their titles. The *fantastique* referred to an admixture of realistic elements with fantastical ones – dreams and nightmares, drug-induced hallucinations, and 'supernatural' elements (ghosts, fairies, vampires, demons, spells). The *fantastical* story was new, not because of its content or message, 'but in the attitude toward storytelling' that it forced on the reader. It did not ask 'What happened?,' but instead exploited 'the very need inherent in reading to know what "really" happened.' For example, in Jacques Cazotte's 1772 work *The Devil in Love* (which nineteenth-century French critics considered the genre's beginnings on French soil), the reader was left unsure: 'was Alvare dreaming or did he really surrender to the devil?'[98]

As popular titles like Théophile Gautier's 'The Opium Pipe' (1838) and 'The Club of Hashish Smokers' (1846) demonstrate, the reader needed to propose alternative solutions to such quandaries based on mysticism, irony, madness, nightmares, or (especially) hallucinogenic drugs. (Hence, the evolution of an associated popular term, *hallucinatoire*.)[99] Qualitatively different from fairy tales or ghost stories, the *fantastical*'s introduction of indeterminacy into reality was not a simple case of attributing causality to a supernatural force. In ghost stories, the reader knew the cause and the narrative's conclusion was neatly closed. Rather, the *fantastical* left causality inconclusive and the reader's judgment insolubly uncertain. It was thus one particular expression of a wider desire to maintain a place for wonder in Berthelot's 'world without mystery.'[100]

The figure that later Catholic revivalists most looked back to for mythical origins was Barbey d'Aurevilly, the romantic writer who produced *A Married Priest* (1865) and *The Diabolicals* (1874). (It should be noted that *A Married Priest* was anathematized by the Archbishop of Paris and that the courts prosecuted d'Aurevilly for indecency in *The Diabolicals.*) D'Aurevilly greatly influenced his close friend Charles Baudelaire who in turn spent a huge effort translating the short stories of Edgar Allan Poe and publishing them during the 1860s. The influence of Poe's *fantastical* pieces can in turn be seen in the work of other early Catholic revivalists, such as Ernest Hello's *Extraordinary Tales* (1879), and Jean-Marie-Mathias-Philippe-Auguste Villiers de l'Isle Adam's *Cruel Tales* (1883) and *New Cruel Tales* (1886).

The first figures of the 1880s *renouveau catholique* were Léon Bloy, who converted in 1869 on account of d'Aurevilly (*The Revealer of the Globe* [1884], *The Desperate Man* [1886]); Paul Bourget (*The Disciple* [1889]); and Paul Claudel (*Golden Head* [1890]). They would soon be followed by Maurice Barrès, Joris-Karl Huysmans, Francis Jammes, and Charles Péguy. Those in the visual arts included Émile Bernard, Charles de Groux, Maurice Denis, and Jan Verkade. Painters associated with the Decadent movement (like Odilon Redon and Edvard Munch) were also influenced by the Catholic revival.[101]

The *renouveau catholique* owed a reciprocal debt to the Decadent movement.[102] The Decadents co-opted and exploited the mythologies of heredity that terrified bourgeois culture, enthusiastically embracing the neurasthenic and the hysteric as anti-heros.[103] Whereas positivists like Charcot embraced an ideology of order and insisted on a nature ruled by an observable, descriptive, and predictive reality, Decadents obsessed over 'natural disorder' in all its forms, including sexuality, sickness, insanity, crime, and poverty.[104] If social and psychological determinism in the new sciences excluded the supernatural by definition, Decadence restored the indeterminate by celebrating the perversion of nature.[105]

Literary Decadence arose within the broader context of 'spiritualist' movements sweeping through America, Britain, and the Continent.[106] An 1890 work promised that hypnosis was *a Key which will Unlock Many Chambers of Mystery*,[107] and its popularity spanned the century: from Mesmer's late eighteenth-century beginnings through the Marquis de Puységur in France to the figure of Svengali in Britain and the United States.[108] Like the hysteric, the hypnotized body and the seance became gendered sites of contest between science and mystery.[109] In Britain, the ability to fall under the influence of mesmerists was associated not only with the female body, but also with social or cultural 'primitiveness.' The colonized Bengalis, for example, were especially vulnerable, since their habits were 'sedentary,' their movements 'languid,' and their physiology 'feeble even to effeminacy.'[110]

Jews were also linked with mesmerism as well as neurasthenia and hysteria. George Du Maurier's novel *Trilby* (1894) invented the fictional Svengali as the 'hypnotizing Jew,' and Jews in England came to be represented as '"Svengalian" – ingratiating, seductive, dangerously alluring.' In France, Charcot insisted that Jews were disproportionately prevalent among those with degenerative diseases: hysterics, epileptics, neurasthenics, and diabetics. The *Revue de l'hypnotisme* claimed that the over-representation of Jews in the wards of Paris hospitals was not surprising given their 'propensity to neurosis.' By the century's end, 'argument raged as to whether patients who reliably succumbed to the entrancer were in fact biologically degenerate, hysterical, or both.'[111]

As psychical research tried to 'secularize the soul,' religious visions were not only popular but hotly contested.[112] Alleged apparitions of the Virgin Mary at Lourdes (1858) and Marpingen (1876) captured the popular imagination in both Bismarck's German Empire and the French Third Republic.[113] Zola's *Lourdes* (1894) tried to de-mystify the grotto with its depressing narrative of sick multitudes bereft of miracles. Catholic partisans celebrated its failure.[114] In the Anglo-American context, an ongoing debate continued to rage about whether the fits, trances, and visions (usually inscribed on the female body) were 'natural' or 'supernatural.' William James took the subject seriously and tried to account for it in his 1902 masterwork, *The Varieties of Religious Experience*.[115]

In sum, many varieties of spiritualism arose in reaction to scientific modernity, evolving into a self-described revolutionary (and revolting) nausea as the century's sun began to set. In America, an upper-class New York cosmopolite (and a graduate of both Yale and Columbia) described the period in apocalyptic tones: 'The immense nausea that is spreading through all lands and literature ... brings with it the signs and portents of a forthcoming though undetermined upheaval.'[116] In Europe, Emmanuel Goldstein wrote to Edvard Munch, 'All I have to do is think of Naturalism and Realism and all that other manufactured art and I get nauseous.'[117] Two journals appeared in 1886, the semi-monthly *Le Décadent litteraire et artistique* and the weekly *Le Décadence artistique et littéraire*. Anatole Baju, editor of *Le Décadent*, celebrated this point at which 'social evolution' had arrived and undermined the 'superimposed strata of classicism, romanticism and naturalism.' The epoch's manifestations included 'neurosis, hysteria, hypnotism, morphinomania, scientific charlatanism, Schopenhauerism to an excess.' A year later, Baju's *The School of Decadence* (1887) congratulated the movement for having achieved 'the honor of crushing Naturalism' while at the same time avoiding any 'contradiction with modern progress.'[118]

Between 1884 and 1907, Joséphin Péladan published *Latin Decadence*, a twenty-one-volume work, largely novelistic, unified by its call to save the 'Latin race.' As the titles of two volumes suggest (vol 8: *L'androgyne*; vol. 9: *La gynandre*), androgynous eroticism played a role in this purposeful attack on naturalism, blurring determinist sexual boundaries.[119] Drawing on the precedent of an ancient seventeenth-century fraternity, Péladan founded his 'Order of the Rose+Croix, of the Temple and of the Grail.'[120] The Salons de la Rose+Croix, organized between 1892 and 1897, exerted an important influence on painters. In addition to painting, Péladan also promoted Wagnerian symbolism in music (he published *The Complete Theater of Wagner* in 1894), thus unifying in his cult of the 'Ideal' disparate fin-de-siècle vogues: symbolism, spiritualism (especially in occult forms), and Catholicism.[121]

The most enduring Decadent influence on the *renouveau catholique* was Joris-Karl Huysmans. Huysmans would later define his conversion to Decadence as an essentially Roman Catholic revolt against the materialism of his age,[122] and his intellectual-aesthetic journey from positivism to mysticism became celebrated by Catholic revivalists as paradigmatic of religious-cultural conversion.[123] Initially a disciple of Zola and a master expositor of naturalism, Huysmans published four articles on Zola's novel under the title 'Emile Zola et *L'Assommoir*' in 1877. Appearing in the Belgian newspaper *L'Actualité*, headed up by his friend Camille Lemonnier (future author of *The Hysteric* [1885]), the study has been evaluated as 'an exposé and apology for Naturalism,' 'one of the most important manifestoes of the Naturalist movement,' and 'one of the best statements of the Naturalists' aims.'[124] Flaubert praised Huysmans's second naturalist novel, *The Vatard Sisters* (1879), for its naturalist's lack of 'falseness of perspective.'[125]

In 1881, suffering from nervous exhaustion, Huysmans retreated to convalesce, and his vision began to change. Choosing a bourgeois would-be writer as his protagonist in *Living Together* (*En ménage*), he wanted to provide a detailed description of the 'minuscule district of a soul.' But how could one naturalistically *describe* the invisible? Thinking through this problem led Huysmans to the metaphor of 'double lines,' a quasi-sacramental image.[126] In an 1882 letter to Edmond de Goncourt,

Huysmans praised a novel for its 'unique art of evocation, that is to say, *an art of double lines*. Under the line which is written and printed, there is another which is silent ... in an invisible and sympathetic ink.'[127]

The year 1884 marks the date of Huysmans's landmark novel, *À Rebours*, which Zola called 'a terrible blow to naturalism.'[128] Variously translated as *Against the Grain* or *Against Nature*, 'à rebours' commonly means 'on the contrary' or 'the wrong way.' The title implied an impish question: Was going against the rule of nature 'wrong way'? Or was anti-naturalist decline in fact true progress?

The novel's neurasthenic protagonist, Duc Jean Floressas des Esseintes, modelled largely on the symbolist painter Gustave Moreau, embodied the highly refined sensitivities of the urban dandy, including erotic fetishes that suggested male hysteria or at least neurasthenia.[129] Des Esseintes expresses his admiration for Charles Baudelaire: his poetry had plunged below surface appearances and 'descended to the bottom of the inexhaustible mine,' penetrating 'those districts of the soul where the monstrous vegetations of the sick mind flourish.' Baudelaire's pages are 'magnificent' precisely because 'exasperated by their powerlessness to express the whole truth.' The more Des Esseintes rereads his Baudelaire, the more he admires him: 'in days when verse had ceased to serve any purpose save to depict the external aspect of men and things, [Baudelaire] had succeeded in *expressing the inexpressible* ... the most fleeting, the most evanescent of the morbid conditions of broken spirits and disheartened souls.'[130] Later, Des Esseintes analyses a novel in terms of double-lines: 'underneath the written line peeped another visible to the soul only, indicated rather than expressed, which revealed depths of passion piercing through a reticence that allowed spiritual infinities to be defined such as no idiom of human language could have encompassed.'[131] Standing positivism on its head, Huysmans's metaphors in *À rebours* evoked older discourses of hylomorphism, sacramentalism, and transubstantiation.

In 1888, Huysmans saw Matthias Grünewald's *Crucifixion* at Colmar for the first time. This altarpiece had once stood behind the main altar in a hospital for victims plagued by ergotism. Christ's body, flowing with blood and erupting in grotesque sores, mirrored the bodies of the patients, diseased by ergot (rye-fungus), and manifesting gangrenous limbs, inflated bellies, and ulcerations.[132] Grünewald's violent representation offered those who contemplated it a God with whom they could identify, one who understood their passion because he had suffered it himself. Nothing could have been further from the ultramontanist aesthetic – that is, 'Christ was the most beautiful of all men' – than Grünewald's brutally hideous body of Christ.

The *Crucifixion* catalysed Huysmans's conversion. The 'ugly' body appealed to his naturalist's taste for realism, yet the sheer physical violence had been intended by Grünewald both to embody and point towards invisible redemption. Seeing it through the lens of his evolving theory of 'double lines' as well as the hysterical body as an ambivalent site, Huysmans discovered in Grünewald's brutal *Crucifixion* a 'spiritualization of the hysterical symptom.' Like Christ, the hysteric also experienced 'an irruption of the Real on the body' that forced the viewer to go beneath surface reality and consider occult causes. Thus, in Huysmans's later work, 'the irruption of the Real' was often represented as 'a religious spectacle of torture and murder.'[133]

By 1890, Huysmans had consolidated his vision. Writing to Jules Destrée, he declared that the Flemish primitives 'contained the whole of art, supernaturalism, which is the only true and great art.' His theory of double lines had evolved: 'absolute realism combined with flights of the soul, which is what materialistic naturalism has failed to understand.'[134] Unlike the symbolists, Huysmans had no intention of abandoning naturalism; rather, he wanted to fuse it with spiritualism in a new synthesis of nature and super-nature. That same year, in a letter to the satanist Abbé Boullan that later became famous, Huysmans coined a neologism for his double-vision: 'I want to confuse everyone – to create a work of art of *supernatural realism*, of *spirituralist naturalism*. I want to show Zola, Charcot ... that none of the mysteries which surround us are explained.'[135] Total description did not entail total explanation.

In 1891, Huysmans's literary expression of his new vision appeared in *Là-bas* [*Down There*], a novel reviewed by one contemporary in *Le Livre moderne* as packed with 'popular sorcery, mesmerism, spiritism, hypnotism [and] the oriental thaumaturgies of one sort or another that are so popular these days.'[136] In the opening chapter, the protagonist Durtal's internal monologue about Grünewald's *Crucifixion* serves as an aesthetic manifesto: 'This was the Christ of ... the early years of the Church, a common Christ, ugly, because he took on himself the sum of all the world's sins and assumed, in his humility, the most abject of appearances ... *Grünewald was the most fanatical of realists*, but as one looked at this Redeemer of whores, this God of the morgue, everything changed. From that ulcerated head emanated glimmers of light; a superhuman expression illuminated the gangrened flesh, the eclampsia of his features ... *Grünewald was the most fanatical of idealists.* Never had a painter so magnificently glorified the highest ... from the triumph of filth, extracted the purest cordial of love, the bitterest essence of tears ... No, this had no equivalent in any language ... this ideal of a supernatural realism ...' Durtal suddenly shakes himself and avoids slipping 'into the shadow of immutable dogmas': 'if I take this to its logical conclusion, I end up in the Catholicism of the Middle Ages, in a form of mystical naturalism [*naturalisme mystique*].'[137]

Although Durtal cannot go down this mystical route (at least, not yet), he also cannot deny the force of his friend Des Hermies's conclusions about naturalism's failure: 'You shrug your shoulders, but come, what has your Naturalism revealed to us about all those disheartening mysteries that surround us? Nothing. When it has to explain a passion of any kind, when it has to probe some trauma, to treat even the most innocuous of the soul's cuts and bruises, it puts everything down to the account of physical appetites and instincts.'[138] Ironically, the proof of naturalism's incapacity to explain mystery lay in one of its most celebrated figures, the hysteric. 'From the fact that numerous patients in the Salpêtrière are not possessed but hysterical, does it follow that other women who suffer from a similar illness must be too? ... it still remains to resolve this insoluble question: is a woman possessed because she's hysterical, or hysterical because she's possessed? Only the Church can answer, science can't.'[139]

Durtal's new aesthetic, formulated in response to this *fantastical* quandry, would serve as a manifesto for Catholic revivalists:

> 'One must preserve the documentary truthfulness, the precision of detail, the rich sinewy language of Realism,' he told himself, 'but one must also drive a well-shaft into the soul, and not feel the need to explain away its mystery in terms of diseases of the senses. *The novel, if possible, should divide itself into two parts – albeit welded together or rather commingled as they are in life – that of the soul and that of the body* ... In short, one must follow the great highway so profoundly excavated by Zola, but it would also be necessary to trace a parallel road in the air, an alternative route, so as to reach things both down here and beyond, to create, in a word, a spiritual Naturalism ...'[140]

Huysmans's reformulation of traditional Catholic ideas in novel terms – parallel routes, double lines, spiritualist-naturalism – allowed him to solve post-naturalist conundrums in a way that appealed to others en route to conversion. On the one hand, *total description* without any deformation of reality preserved the realist's ethical demand; on the other, one had to refuse the naturalists' conclusion of *total explanation* from *total description.*[141] In a 'world without mystery,' Huysmans stood against its eclipse: 'All this, you see, my friend, is as clear as a bottle of ink, mystery is all around and reason, as soon as it tries to take a step forward, stumbles in the shadows.'[142]

In 1905, after his conversion to Catholicism, Huysmans went beyond this fictional account in *Là-bas* and set out an analysis of Grünewald's works at Colmar more systematically in *Three Primitives*. He concluded:

> I find that his work can only be defined by coupling together contradictory terms ... [Grünewald] is, in fact, a mass of paradoxes and contrasts ... He is at once naturalistic and mystical, savage and sophisticated, ingenuous and deceitful ... he personifies still more the religious piety of the sick and the poor. That awful Christ who hung dying over the altar of the Isenheim hospital would seem to have been made in the image of the ergotics who prayed to him; they must surely have found consolation in the thought that this God they invoked had suffered the same torments as themselves, and had become flesh in a form as repulsive as their own; and they must have felt less forsaken, less contemptible ... His pestiferous Christ would have offended the taste of the courts; he could only be understood by the sick, the unhappy and the monks, by the suffering members of Christ.[143]

The 'suffering members of Christ,' a scriptural image as old as Saint Paul, neatly summed up Huysmans's vision of vicarious suffering.

Vicarious suffering was the principal theme of Huysmans's Decadent hagiography of *Sainte Lydwine de Schiedam* (1901), an early fifteenth-century Dutch mystic who offered her physical sufferings in expiation for the Church during the Great Western System and was canonized in 1890.[144] Even as Huysmans applied his journalist's attention to describing grotesque details, he portrayed them as physiological manifestations of interior mystical states. In language reminiscent of (and aimed at surpassing) *Madame Bovary*, Huysmans described Lydwine's sufferings:

> Soon, in addition to her other infirmities, her chest, until then unscathed, was also affected; she blew bloody mucus from her nose, which was filled with pustules and boils; the stones that had tortured her in her childhood and had disappeared returned, and she evacuated calculi the size of small eggs. Next her lungs and liver decayed; then a chancre dug a deep hole that spread throughout her body and devoured her flesh; and finally, when the

> plague ravaged Holland, she was its first victim and was afflicted with two buboes, one in the groin, the other near the heart. 'Two, that is well,' she exclaimed, 'but if it pleases Our Lord, I think three in honor of the Holy Trinity would be better!' and a third abscess formed in her cheek.
>
> She would have been dead twenty times over had these ailments been natural ...[145]

Lydwine's bodily grotesqueries were vicarious suffering – in Huysmans's words, 'mystical substitution' [*substitution mystique*] – a participation in the hideous passion of the body of Christ who was himself 'the first, the example of mystical substitution.' Since the earthly Christ could no longer suffer here on earth, and since he had wanted 'certain souls to inherit the succession of his sacrifice,' it must be 'in his Church, in the members of his mystical body [*corps mystique*].'[146] For Huysmans, Lydwine ideally expressed the ambivalent hysteric/mystic: a figure that has been called 'Saint Hysteria' and *la mystérique*.[147]

Huysmans's vision was never considered fully orthodox, and *À rebours* and *Là-bas* – especially the latter, filled with Satanic Black Masses, astral sex, child molestation, and murder – were condemned by the Catholic Church. Even after his conversion, his Catholic work was viewed with suspicion, as evidenced by a 1901 review of *Sainte Lydwine* appearing in the Jesuit journal *Études*: '[Huysmans] speaks of matters of piety, the miracles of saints, their ecstasies, the favors of which they are the object, their sufferings in a language worthy of the pages of *Là-bas*, a language of crudity and a realism which sometimes borders on immorality.'[148]

However, Huysmans won over a cultural and intellectual elite for whom ultramontanist Catholicism had little appeal. Although his critics might judge his Decadent aesthetic 'ugly,' he himself considered Catholic objects of piety – 'Saint Sulpician Art' (*l'art sulpicien*), the mass-produced religious goods sold in the quarter surrounding Saint-Sulpice in Paris – as genuine ugliness and the 'revenge of the devil.'[149] In *The Crowds of Lourdes* (1905), a response to Zola's *Lourdes* (1894), Huysmans had the devil speak to the Virgin Mary, admitting that she had conquered him through her Son, Jesus Christ. The devil then announced that he would avenge himself by plaguing her with 'religious art': 'I will set about in such a way that I will cause you to be insulted without relief by *the continuing blasphemy of ugliness*.'[150] Huysmans delighted in the irony: the author of works considered blasphemous turned the table on his pious foes. Not all would have shared his humour: only an elite could appreciate his denigration of pious objects as blasphemous and the endowment of his own spiritual naturalism with 'the distinction of taste.'[151] Huysmans's method suggests that the *renouveau catholique* succeeded in part due to an elitism that was at times overtly snobbish.

As the century's sunset and nighttime gave way to a new dawn, Decadence too faded away. However, Huysmans's groundwork would be stored away as a 'tradition' to which postwar literary and artistic critics would return in search of precedents. Against ultramontanism, a saintly life did not need to be a beautiful life; it could be thoroughly ugly. Against naturalism, grotesque descriptions did not entail nihilistic explanations; they might be symptoms of mystical causes. Huysmans had reconciled seeming oppositions, and a postwar generation seeking a faith that faced the facts would seek inspiration in Decadent Catholicism's sacramental vision.

When the Dreyfus Affair erupted in 1894, three discursive possibilities were in place: a hegemonic naturalist realism, a marginal ultramontanist eternalism, and an ambivalent spiritual naturalism. In the Affair's wake, the culture war between republicans and Catholics became increasingly political, culminating in the Act of Separation of Church and State in 1905. This was an act of 'repression' – literally, the 'throwing out' of mystical elements that did not seem commensurable with a simple laicist vision. As late as the war's eve in the summer of 1914, the French Prime Minister René Viviani boasted about the achievements of the anticlerical campaign: 'We have extinguished in the firmament lights that will never be rekindled.'[152]

Viviani was wrong. He could not have known that a mutilated France would need to mourn. This need to recover what had been repressed would usher in an epoch of synthesis, and the firmament would brighten in unexpected ways.

PART ONE

From Dualism to Dialectic

Chapter 1

Cultural Manicheanism: Apocalyptic Melodrama

> We may legitimately claim that melodrama becomes the principal mode for uncovering, demonstrating, and making operative the essential moral universe in a post-sacred era ... The ritual of melodrama involves the confrontation of clearly identified antagonists and the expulsion of one of them. It can offer no terminal reconciliation, for there is no longer a clear transcendent value to be reconciled to. There is, rather, a social order to be purged, a set of ethical imperatives to be made clear.
>
> – Peter Brooks

> The final paradox of the search for purity is that it is an attempt to force experience into logical categories of non-contradiction. But experience is not amenable and those who make the attempt find themselves led into contradiction.
>
> – Mary Douglas[1]

Between the years 1894 and 1914 in France, 'modernity' – understood in the political realm as laicism and in the cultural-intellectual realm as the Sorbonne's positivism/historicism – grew to be imagined as the dualistic opposite of Catholicism. Catholicism versus culture, religion versus realism, faith versus fact, eternal versus historical – such pairings represented two radically incompatible and mutually exclusive modes of envisioning the world. If we are to understand why the Great War came as a trauma in a particular way for Catholics, we must see what an inversion of imagination it entailed. As late as Easter 1914, a young Catholic revivalist used military imagery to describe the necessary struggle of a 'Catholic renaissance' against the dominant political and cultural institutions. Five months later, Catholic youth were sent to the trenches to die on behalf of those same institutions. Grasping the genuine shock of the wartime 'sacred union' in its 'holy war' against Germany depends on a sense of the earlier 'civil war' of Catholicism against the Republic. We must reimagine ourselves back into the turn of the twentieth century, a dualistic epoch marked not by reconciliations but rather by apocalyptic purges.

Civil War: The Radical Republic as External Enemy

The Dreyfus Affair brought a century of Catholic conflict with modernity to a head. From the outside, institutional Catholicism was assailed politically by external enemies in the radical Republic, and intellectually derided by its educational arms. From within its own educational institutions, theologians who have come to be known as the 'Roman Catholic Modernists' were perceived as having infiltrated the Church itself, undoing eternalist and transcendentalist elements of the faith by means of scientific and historicist methods of criticism. Ultramontanist Catholicism responded with 'integralism,' an attitude dictating acceptance of an integral whole or not at all: the ecclesiastical integralism of Pius X; the philosophical integralism of Thomism; and, eventually, the popular association of Catholic interests with the 'national integralism' of Charles Maurras's Action Française.[2] The combined effect would be, on the eve of the Great War, a multifaceted equation of Catholicism with anti-modernist forces.

The Dreyfus Affair's first act opened on 24 June 1894, when an Italian anarchist assassinated Sadi Carnot, the president of the Third Republic.[3] Later that summer, a French secret agent in the embassy of Italy's ally, the German Empire, discovered a one-page handwritten memorandum (*bordereau*) implicating a French traitor. After a brief inquiry, the investigation by French intelligence quickly narrowed its focus on half a dozen officers. One of those was an Alsatian Jewish artillery officer named Captain Alfred Dreyfus.

Like many other Jews from Alsace-Lorraine, Dreyfus had joined the military in order to help return his homeland to France and avenge the humiliating Prussian defeat of 1870. However, these patriotic motives were twisted by 1890s anti-Semites like Edouard Drumont into evidence of Jewish military infiltration. Drumont was the most powerful anti-Semitic voice of the fin-de-siècle: his *Jewish France* (1886) 'stood next to the Bible on the bookshelves of the most modest homes' and reached two hundred editions by the turn of the century;[4] his popular newspaper, *La*

Libre Parole (Free Speech) was founded in 1892. Two full years before the Carnot assassination, using metaphors of infectious disease both ancient and modern, Drumont launched his crusade to cleanse the French Army: 'The Semitic invasion is like the breeding of microbes: When the environment is not favorable, the growth process suffers. Though there have been some hints of weakness, the army has joined the combat with a remarkable strength of resistance. In undertaking this series of articles, we want to encourage the army in this holy struggle.'[5]

Captain Dreyfus's military superiors shared Drumont's popular anti-Semitism. They linked Dreyfus to the *bordereau* on an alleged analysis of handwriting styles and quickly indicted him. A source in the military's highest level leaked word of the indictment to Drumont, who in turn published the news on 1 November 1894. Prominently displayed beneath the masthead motto 'France for the French,' the *Libre Parole* headline read: 'High Treason: Arrest of the Jewish Officer A. Dreyfus.' 'He has committed the most abominable crime that an officer can commit,' wrote Drumont. 'He has, for venal ends, betrayed his fatherland ... But however painful that revelation may be,' he concluded, 'we have the one consolation of knowing that it is not a true Frenchman who committed such a crime!'[6] As a Jew, Dreyfus was not, as Maurice Barrès would say later, one of France's 'authentic citizens' – one of 'the children of Gaul and not of Judaea ...'[7]

In December 1894, a military court unanimously pronounced Dreyfus guilty of high treason, condemning him to perpetual deportation and a military court martial. Reporting the event for the Viennese *Neue Freie Presse*, the Austrian journalist Theodor Herzl – the founder of modern Zionism who would later declare that 'the Dreyfus case made me a Zionist' – recorded that 'Bloodthirsty cries filled the air.' As Dreyfus walked by, a group of officers alluded to the betrayal of Christ for silver as they shouted 'Judas! Traitor!'[8] Four months later, Dreyfus was transferred to Devil's Island to serve out his life sentence of solitary confinement.

After much cajoling over the next two years, the popular naturalist novelist Émile Zola was persuaded to take up a campaign in favour of Dreyfus's cause. On 13 January 1898, Zola published his famous 'J'Accuse!,' an open letter to the president of the Republic, in the Dreyfusard paper *L'Aurore*. The government brought Zola to trial, convicted him, and gave him the maximum sentence for libel. But Zola's conviction only fuelled the fires of political and social scandal, and the Dreyfus Affair galvanized France. On the left, literary figures such as Anatole France and Marcel Proust joined *L'Aurore* in calling for a retrial of Dreyfus. In

February 1898, Victor Basch, a Jewish activist, founded the Ligue des Droits de l'Homme et du Citoyen (League of the Rights of Man and of the Citizen). Six months later, Jean Jaurès founded the newspaper *La Petite République* and catalysed the recovery of progressive socialists who had been gradually emerging from their coma since the early 1880s.[9]

The Affair also energized political and religious forces on the right, who spun the case as a conspiracy of Jews and Freemasons to damage the military's prestige and destroy the Republic. On the very last day of December 1898, the Ligue de la Patrie Française ('League of the French Fatherland') was founded as a nationalist and anti-Dreyfusard answer to Basch's Ligue des Droits. The young Charles Maurras launched his program that would come to be known as 'integral nationalism,' a unification of right-wing forces into an integral whole. Maurras used the suicide of Colonel Henry – imprisoned on suspicion of having forged a key document condemning Dreyfus – to celebrate the protomartyr's 'precious blood': 'Know that along with your precious blood, the first French blood shed by the Dreyfus affair, there is not a single drop that does not still steam wherever the heart of the nation beats ... Given the current state of disorder among nationalist parties, we have not been able to arrange the grand funeral your martyrdom deserves ... even though the national sentiment is dispersed and divided against itself, and still incapable of action, it is nonetheless coming to life again. Wait, colonel, for it to awaken and reform.'[10] Seven years later, Maurras's Action Française movement would indeed 'awaken' with an astonishing strength.[11]

Although Maurras himself was not a believer, his movement would come to be embraced by influential Catholics who envisioned an integral union of Church and State.[12] Closer to home, the emotional and fanatical priests of the Assumptionist religious order used their daily newspaper *La Croix*, founded in 1882 and treated as gospel truth by many clergy, to wage a bitter campaign to strip all Jews of citizenship.[13] (Images in *Le Pélerin*, the Assumptionists' publication at Lourdes, also peddled an extremely violent and hateful racial anti-Semitism.)[14] Although most newspapers, read by a coterie of like minds, did not have great effect on mass opinion, *La Croix* had an influence disproportionate to its circulation numbers thanks to the clergy's disseminations of its ideas.[15] In spite of Church leaders who wanted to pursue the possibility of Christian democracy urged in Pope Leo XIII's encyclical *Au milieu des sollicitudes* (1892), the 'blundering conduct' of Catholics fatally compromised this first attempt at *ralliement*.[16]

In late June 1899, after Colonel Dreyfus had returned to France for a retrial, Prime Minister René Waldeck-Rousseau formed his 'government of the Republican Defense,' a left-wing coalition of radicals, socialists, and moderates.[17] When Dreyfus accepted the government's pardon, Waldeck-Rousseau seized the moment for a new anticlerical offensive. He directed his first blow at the Assumptionists, and then moved on to the other religious orders, which had grown to almost 200,000 members since 1880.[18] However, the parliament went further than Waldeck-Rousseau intended, and on 1 July 1901 it passed the landmark 'Law of Associations.' This law expelled all religious orders from France except those granted special authorization. In practice, few orders were exempted, and thousands of monks and nuns were sent to exile in Belgium, Spain, the United States, and elsewhere.

The law was first applied by Émile Combes, Waldeck-Rousseau's more radical successor, who formed a new Cabinet on 15 June 1902. Like Ernest Renan, Combes had been a seminarian who 'lost his faith.' ('Raised in the harem,' Combes quipped, paraphrasing Racine, 'I know its inner secrets.')[19] Having explicitly outlined his intentions in *A Laicist Campaign* (1904),[20] Combes turned his vision into reality with 'the most outrageous measure against freedom in education ever passed in public law,' directed specifically at the Brothers of the Christian Schools.[21] Meanwhile, Pope Leo XIII, having waged a successful campaign against Bismarck's *Kulturkampf* and been disappointed by the failure of *ralliement*, died in 1903. His successor took the name Pius X, harkening back to Leo's intransigent predecessor, Pius IX, and symbolically suppressing the intervening conciliatory reign.

Combes introduced a bill to repudiate the century-old Concordat established between Napoleon and the Holy See. On 9 December 1905, this Act of Separation of Church and State was published, severing all ties between the two institutions. Clergy were no longer paid by the state, committees of Catholic laymen were to administer parish affairs, and church property was confiscated as the state's own. The monks of Solesmes Abbey were expelled for the second time in the community's short history, this time not (as in 1880–95) into neighbouring French homes, but rather to Quarr Abbey on the Isle of Wight in the United Kingdom. Jesuits were expelled from their schools and exiled to Belgium and beyond. (Jesuit inculcation of bourgeois order in the Republic's African, Asian, and Middle Eastern colonies by means of education was apparently appropriate for natives abroad, even if domestically intolerable.) In retaliation, Pope Pius X excommunicated every French deputy who had voted for the separation act; he also forbade Catholics to participate in the new lay committees that would oversee parishes. Statistics from the Limoges area provide one example of the way in which separation speeded up France's ongoing dechristianization: between 1899 and 1914, the number of unbaptized children rose from 2.5 to 33.9 per cent; the number of civil marriages from 14 to 60 per cent; and the number of civil burials quadrupled. For France as a whole, the annual number of ordinations fell from 1,518 in 1904 to 704 by 1914.[22]

In sum, one catastrophic outcome of the Dreyfus Affair for the Catholic Church was its definitive divorce from the French Republic. A vehemently Manichean mindset took over as the new century increasingly came to be seen in apocalyptic oppositions: light versus dark, good versus evil, Catholicism versus modernity.

Inventing Integralism: Roman Catholic Modernists as Internal Enemies

In addition to this external crisis, the Church also underwent one internal to itself, known to history as the 'Modernist Crisis.'[23] Besides excommunicating the Catholic deputies who had voted for separation, the Holy See also placed five of the Abbé Alfred Loisy's books on the Index of Forbidden Books. Twenty-five years earlier, Leo XIII's encyclical mandating the restoration of Thomism in Catholic schools had linked rationalism with laicism: 'Many of those who, with minds alienated from the faith, hate Catholic institutions, claim reason as their sole mistress and guide.'[24] Now, as the radical Republican outcomes of the Dreyfus Affair intersected with the theological turmoil that marked the Roman Catholic 'Modernist Crisis,' events seemed to verify Leo's linkage of modern politics and thought.

In 1906, works by Lucien Laberthonnière and Edouard Le Roy, other French theologians who also used positivist and historicist methods in their approaches to scripture and dogma, were consigned to the Index's flames. On 3 July 1907, the office of the Holy Roman and Universal Inquisition issued the syllabus *Lamentabili Sane*. Like the *Syllabus* of Pius X's namesake issued fifty years earlier, it condemned sixty-five propositions expressing 'dangerous errors concerning the natural sciences, the interpretation of Holy Scripture, and the principal mysteries of the faith,' including #22: 'The dogmas the Church holds out as revealed are not truths which have fallen from heaven. They are an interpretation of religious facts which the human mind has acquired by laborious effort.' Finally, a papal encyclical titled *Pascendi* appeared two months later, offering a thorough catalogue of all that was to be condemned in the theses of 'modernists.' The Bishop of Dijon wryly observed, 'The Holy Father has given what I might call an encyclopedist description of the modernist, describing a person who, it must be admitted, does not exist. We know of no one writer covering a field as vast as the one described by Pius X and whose work shows all the aspects of the picture presented.'[25]

It retrospect, the bishop may have been correct: perhaps the 'Roman Catholic Modernist' was a phantom meant to terrorize, a rhetorical construction with no real reference. But it did instil terror, and Roman Catholicism evolved a new opposition: 'modernists' versus 'integralists,' that is, those who insisted on the 'integration' of all facets of life into an indivisible organic unity, hierarchically ordered beneath the Roman Pope. A simplistic metaphor with popular appeal, the term 'integralism' suggested a body that was integrally perfect and hence pure. If one held fast to the whole and did not question the parts, one could be guaranteed safety from polluted contaminants. Although the *intégristes* had never shown such enthusiasm for Leo XIII or his *ralliement*, they were ardent zealots for Pius X: 'We are integral Roman Catholics,' they boasted. 'That is, we set above all and everyone not only the Church's traditional teaching in the order of absolute truths but also the pope's directions in the order of practical contingencies. For the Church and the pope are one.'[26]

In the eyes of the *intégristes*, the Roman Catholic Modernists' application of scientific and historical criticism to scriptural and dogmatic texts ended up denying the existence of all unchanging truths. (Catholics were not alone; Jewish intellectuals also feared historicism's erosion of transcendental claims.)[27] The *intégristes*' primary intellectual weapon against this historicist erosion was Thomism, and particularly its promise of access to unchanging metaphysical truth. Thomas Aquinas's original medieval synthesis had reconciled Biblical revelation with the pre-eminent intellectual currents of his day – the Greek Aristotle, the Jewish Maimonides, and the Muslim Averroes.[28] Initially retrieved by Leo XIII as a hopeful tool for reconciling culture and Catholicism, French Thomism after the Dreyfus Affair was increasingly transformed into a sectarian discipline. Aquinas's dialectical method of synthesis now became a Manichean discourse pitting pure Catholicism against the contaminating currents of the new century. 'Medievalism' set itself against 'Modernism,' and neo-Thomism became the philosophical analogue of neo-Byzantinism: an intellectual expression of eternalism.[29]

In 1908, Pius X excommunicated Loisy for his 'Modernist' heresy.

Loisy responded in 1909 by riding triumphantly in an open car, cheered on by enthusiastic supporters, to his first class at the Collège de France as professor of the 'history of religions' – an appropriately historicist new discipline in line with the sociological vogue of Durkheim, Weber, and Lévy-Bruhl. That same year, a secret international anti-Modernist network was set up. Its Latin title, the *Sodalitium Pianum* ('S.P.,' i.e., 'Sodality of Pius V') was known in France by its code name *Sapinière*.[30] During this epoch, later dubbed by one historian the 'Stalinist era of the Vatican,'[31] Pius X both encouraged and subsidized the activities of this secret police. In 1910 the Holy See required all priests having pastoral charge to sign the 'Oath Against Modernism.' This oath included accepting an eternalist agenda: both the possibility of demonstrating the existence of God by rational means and the immutability of dogmas. During the years 1912–13, the very eve of the Great War saw the peak period of the integralist reaction.

Roman Catholic Modernism was yet another act in the more general nineteenth-century drama about 'realism': was the truly real 'natural' or was it 'eternal'? Changing or unchanging? Of nature or through grace? Rational or revealed? Although such metaphysical questions might seem abstruse, an elite group of impressionable Sorbonne students would see them as having extremely concrete consequences for their own existential situations. Two of these young students were Jacques Maritain and Raïssa Oumançoff.

Conversions from 'an accidental existence': Jacques Maritain and Raïssa Oumançoff

Jacques Maritain and Raïssa Oumançoff were members of a third wave of converts to Catholicism in France. Although the fortunes of the Catholic Church in France seemed dire at the turn of the century, conversions increased inversely to the institution's fortunes: it was 'at the very moment when the Church appeared to be a citadel under attack that intellectuals presented themselves at its doors.'[32] From 1885 to 1894, a first wave of high-profile conversions began as the Ferry Laws began to formalize the Third Republic's positivist ideology. A second wave from 1895 to 1904 – that is, during the period of the Dreyfus Affair and the radical Republic's anticlerical measures – expressed disenchantment with the Republic and its dominant ideology of progress. As one man of medicine who converted in 1901 put it, 'The prestige of our century fell singularly in my eyes, when I saw how moral progress was far from accompanying material progress, and I understood that one could speak of the bankruptcy of science.'[33] Most of these converts were drawn to Catholicism by a desire for order and tradition.

The largest number of conversions took place during a third wave between 1905 and 1915, a reaction to the 1905 Act of Separation. These converts reacted to the triumphant positivism of their elders and formed a group identity partly by opposing themselves to a litany of demons: on the German side, Immanuel Kant, Friedrich Nietzsche, and Richard Wagner; on the French side, Auguste Comte and Ernest Renan.[34] Yet the paths taken by these converts were winding and their stories more complex than caricatures might indicate. The stories of Jacques Maritain and Raïssa Oumançoff illustrate one such labyrinthine passage.

Jacques Maritain was born into a strongly political, Protestant, and freethinking household.[35] His grandfather, Jules Favre, had been prominent in the government of Napoleon III's Second Empire. Because of laws prohibiting divorce, Favre was never able to marry Jeanne Charmont (who had separated from her husband early on). As a consequence, when Charmont gave birth to Geneviève Favre (Maritain's mother), the old lawyer 'lost his head' and forged the civil papers in order to render her birth legitimate, a forgery he later had to confess before a tribunal.

When the Empire lost the Franco-Prussian War, Favre was given the humiliating task of negotiating the capitulation of Paris and the armistice with Bismarck. At 11:45 p.m. on 26 January 1871, when Geneviève was fifteen, Favre took her 'out on to the balcony of his office on the Quai d'Orsay, overlooking the Seine. In silence they listened to the final thunderous dialogue between the French and Prussian artillery. Midnight chimed and the clamour stopped.'[36] During the Commune that followed, Favre would sympathize with Adolphe Thiers and his bloody republican repression of the workers. Favre fell into popular disfavour, melancholically retiring from public life to his six-thousand volume library.[37] Identifying less and less with his earlier Catholicism, Favre reclaimed for himself a 'God of justice and reason' and became a pacifist Freemason.

Two years after the armistice, when Geneviève was seventeen years old, Jeanne Charmont died. Overwhelmed with bitter grief, Geneviève violently broke with her mother's fervent Catholicism in order to 'save the essential in myself, the independence of my soul.' When Favre remarried towards the end of his life, Geneviève in turn married Paul Maritain, who was completely devoted to Favre's work.[38] Favre died in January 1880.

Jacques Maritain was born on 18 November 1882. Three months later,

Geneviève submitted her first request for 'separation of body.' In contrast to the Catholic baptism of his sister Jeanne (born seven years earlier and named for Jeanne Charmont), Jacques was baptized Protestant. Paul Maritain's traditional Catholicism and Geneviève's adopted Protestantism had divided the household and contributed to an unhappy marriage. In July 1884, over and against violent Catholic opposition, the law re-establishing divorce was passed. On 8 December 1885, when Geneviève Maritain obtained her divorce and reclaimed her maiden name Favre, she became one of the first divorcées in France. She obtained custody of both Jeanne and the two-year-old Jacques, while Paul received visiting rights of two days a month. He retired from Paris into provincial life, distancing himself more and more from both politics and family. In his writings, Jacques mentioned his father Paul only once.

Jacques thoroughly absorbed his mother's socialist inclinations. Each evening he gathered with the husband of the cook to read Jean Jaurès's *La Petite République*. Graduating from the Henri-IV lycée, his thesis entitled 'What Are the Distinctive Traits of Human Nature?' took first prize in the general competition of 1900.[39] In this essay written at the age of seventeen, Jacques wrestled with the anxiety that would mark his thought and life for at least the next thirty years: namely, whether human beings possessed a freedom that made them qualitatively distinct from 'nature,' or whether they were one with 'nature' in a materialistically determined world.

Although human beings would like there to be 'a deep, essential difference' between them and nature, wrote Jacques, there is 'only a difference of degree that separates' the two. Human beings want to see that outside of us, nature presents us 'with the spectacle of the most rigorous determinism. Mechanical and inflexible laws reign over things; necessity is everywhere, in the human being is liberty.' To these difficult questions, Jacques offered his provisional judgment: 'We are not able to enter here into a profound discussion of free will; we would simply say that the arguments of the determinists, founded on the law of causality and the principle of sufficient reason, appear convincing; in our opinion, the belief that we have an absolute liberty of choice comes from a large number of motifs that we ourselves solicit ... as a consequence, none of them, as Auguste Comte says, is endowed with an "irresistibility" sufficient to our experiencing the feeling of necessity ...'[40] The young Maritain had thoroughly imbibed his culture's paradoxical naturalism: an optimistic fatalism. Anxiety over it would haunt him for years to come; a suicide pact was soon to follow.

Jacques enrolled at the Sorbonne that fall semester of 1900, attended lecture courses on Tolstoy and became an enthusiast for things both socialist and Russian. The following February 1901, he worked for a socialist candidate in the Parisian electoral campaign and formed a 'committee of solidarity' with Russian socialist students who were victims of Czarist repressions. Sometime during those first winter months of 1901, while collecting signatures, calling political meetings, and distributing pamphlets in the universities outside Paris, Jacques would meet the lasting love of his life – the Russian Jewish emigrée Raïssa Oumançoff.

Raïssa had been born on 12 September 1883, one year after Jacques's birth and two years after the assassination of Czar Alexander II. When his death was falsely attributed to a Jewish plot, a bloody campaign of reprisals sent several hundred thousands of Jews emigrating to Eastern Europe and the United States. For those who remained, mostly exiled from Moscow and St Petersburg into the Ukraine, severe restrictions were imposed, including quotas on the number of Jews allowed to attend Russian secondary schools and universities. This limitation of educational possibilities convinced Ilia and Hissia Oumançoff to exile themselves without hope of return for the sake of their daughter's education.

In 1893, Raïssa's father escaped Russia by naming New York as his final destination and taking a train for Paris. Two months later, after passing through complicated administrative red tape, his family was allowed to emigrate with him. As a ten-year-old refugee on the train from Berlin to Paris, Raïssa could only think that 'we would find papa again, and this was the great joy that carried us along, the hope that gave us all the strength we had.'[41] Thus the Oumançoff family arrived in Paris – a Paris which, only one year later, would be in an uproar over the arrest of the Jewish Colonel Dreyfus.

The Oumançoffs had left behind nation, folk, and family in order that their daughter Raïssa might be able to be educated, and their enormous sacrifice was repaid: seven years later Raïssa was a student at the Sorbonne in Paris. There, in the early months of 1901, as Waldeck-Rousseau's 'government of the Republican Defense' was debating the Law of Associations, she first met the young socialist Jacques Maritain. She later recalled the moment with great tenderness: 'One day, completely melancholic, I left a course of M. Matruchot, professor of plant physiology. I saw coming toward me a young man with a gentle face, with flowing blond hair, a light beard and a slightly bent over stride. He introduced himself to me, and told me that he was in the process of forming a student committee to support a protest movement among writers and French universities against the maltreatment suffered by Russian Socialist students in their country ... And he asked me my name for this committee. Such was my first encounter with Jacques Maritain ... We quickly became inseparable.'[42] Three months later, this eighteen-year-old son of a Republican political family and the seventeen-year-old daughter of Russian Jewish emigrés strolled through the Jardin des Plantes. The two customarily enjoyed walking to the garden after their classes, tearing off pieces of baguettes and feeding the 'innocent animals.' This particular day, however, their hearts were heavy.

They discussed what they were learning at the university and debated whether life's contingencies were malevolent, beneficent, or merely absurd.[43] For while the university had given them a good deal of 'particular knowledge' both scientific and philosophical, it was undermined by the 'relativism of the wise' and by the 'skepticism of the philosophers.' The wise, who 'only asked questions about that which was visible and measurable,' were content to refrain from 'reasoning about reason' – that is, about universal matters that might go beyond the particular. Raïssa later recalled this conflict in generational terms: 'We were no longer, those of us barely twenty years old, like [the older generation], clinging to skepticism and exhaling their *"que sais-je"?* like cigarette smoke, finding life otherwise quite excellent.[44] We were, with all our generation, their victims.'

This young couple pushed the positivist scepticism that an earlier generation had found liberating to its ultimate conclusions: being capable neither of 'thinking nor acting with dignity,' everything 'became absurd – and unacceptable – without even knowing what thing in us was able to refuse as well as accept.' One of them framed the problem in terms of universal norms of judgment: 'We cannot live simply according to prejudices, good or bad, we have a need to weigh justice and value – but according to which measure? What is the measure of everything?' The other responded in more existential terms: 'I want to know if existence is an accident, an act of charity or of bad luck. I despise the resignation and the renunciation of intelligence of which we have so many examples around us.' Raïssa summed up their despair: 'We no longer wanted *to will* without seeing; this "sublime" absurdity seemed a monster to us and gave us horror ... We did not want to accept any mask, any flattery from those great persons lulled to sleep by their false securities ... I did not want such a comedy. I could accept a sorrowful life, but not an absurd one.'

Before leaving the garden, they made a mutual pact. For a short time, they would 'extend credit to existence' and place their 'confidence in the unknown,' hoping that it might deliver them 'from the nightmare of a dark and useless world.' However, if this experience did not lead anywhere, they would commit 'suicide before the years would be able to accumulate their dust, before our youthful strength would be all used up. If it were impossible to live according to the truth we wanted to die by a freely-chosen refusal.' Exactly one year after Jacques's *lycée* thesis on determinism had won him the republican system's coveted honour, the same thoughts had brought him to the brink of suicide.

Immediately following this account of the mutual death pact, Raïssa wrote: 'Thus it was that the pity of God made us find Henri Bergson.' In the winter of 1901–2, the socialist writer and poet Charles Péguy, a close friend of Jacques's mother and a self-declared enemy of the Sorbonne, brought Jacques and Raïssa to hear Bergson lecture.[45] Bergson taught at the Collège de France located directly across the street from the Sorbonne. Even though it was, physically speaking, a mere matter of walking only 'a few footsteps' across the rue Saint-Jacques, the journey from the Sorbonne to the Collège was 'not as simple as one might believe.' For in fact, it was not a street but rather 'a mountain of prejudice and distrust' that stood between the disenchanted positivism of the Sorbonne and Bergson's re-enchantment of science and metaphysics.

Re-enchanting Reality: Henri Bergson's 'scientific metaphysics'

In turning to Henri Bergson for inspiration, Jacques and Raïssa would encounter a paradoxical figure: this Jewish philosopher was perhaps the main intellectual figure for Catholics during this high-water period of conversions after the Dreyfus Affair.[46] Unlike the Roman Catholic Modernists who found factual certainty in positivist approaches to scripture and dogmatics, Bergson offered a post-positivistic metaphysical system that promised access to deeper reality. Unlike the integralist Thomists, his metaphysics, far from being anti-modernist, was seen as scientific and culturally avant-garde. For university students disappointed by their elders' determinism (whether optimistic or pessimistic), Bergson promised that one could access an indeterminate and creative principle at reality's core.[47]

Human freedom was the central issue at stake for Bergson.[48] Like his American counterpart, the Harvard philosopher and psychologist William James, Bergson acknowledged a 'pragmatic' self responsible for scientific and technological modernization. According to Bergson, our pragmatic self is instrumental, largely operating by mechanical rote and dealing with surface impressions. It perceives objects capable of quantification and measurement, grasps things in their relations to our own needs, and serves the important purpose of making our way in the everyday world. Bergson called this surface self and its pragmatic instrumental relationship to the world 'intellect.'

But this surface self of intellect, he maintained, knew nothing of anxiety, fear, guilt, desire, or love. How could one possibly imagine that such an instrumental pragmatism could be entrusted with human freedom?[49] Thus Bergson postulated a second self, a 'deep self,' which he named 'intuition' as opposed to intellect. Intuition can directly apprehend 'reality' without the mediating (and distorting) filter of intellect. This was Bergson's first distinction: on the one hand, an intellect that analyses surface 'reality' for pragmatic purposes; on the other, an intuition that synthesizes a deeper 'reality' apprehended without mediation and without distortion.

This distinction permitted Bergson's second innovation: the redefinition of 'reality' as the constant becoming or 'duration' – *la durée* – that underlies what is seen. Extending the concept of biological evolution, *la durée* designated that Heraclitean flux of perpetual motion and endlessly creative novelty. Whereas *space* can be quantified and measured by intellect, the underlying reality of *time* (creative duration) cannot be so contained without distortion. Intuition can grasp duration immediately, but intellect 'spatializes' time, distorting what is fundamentally a creative process and freezing it into lifeless surface impressions. Intellect must always be, in Proust's formulation, *à la recherche du temps perdu*: in search of lost time.

The clearest metaphor that Bergson used to explain this difference was a thoroughly modern one: the recently invented marvel of the motion picture camera. When a camera takes what we call a 'moving picture,' it is, in fact, basically storing up a series of still pictures. When these are juxtaposed rapidly enough, we have the illusion of seeing temporal 'reality' reproduced before our eyes. However, it is only a ghostly shadow, and what it lacks is what is most crucial: *life itself – élan vital*. Similarly, the surface form spatialized by the intellect 'is only a snapshot view of a transition,' while the truly real is the continual underlying process of change. Thus, Bergson concluded, the pragmatic 'mechanism of our ordinary knowledge is of a cinematographical kind.'[50]

This distinction between the spatialized objects of intellect and *The Objects Given Immediately to Consciousness* (the title of his 1899 book) was Bergson's singular contribution: by means of science itself, he stood the nineteenth-century realist tradition on its head. The primary concern of the 'realists' going back to the early nineteenth century had been to represent life in as 'undistorted' manner as possible. For Balzac, Flaubert, and Zola, the aim had increasingly been to represent life as it is observed without the distorting lens that reason can impose in the act of interpreting data. For Bergson, too, the problem was to represent life as it is and not as it is 'transformed by the filter of reason.'[51] However, by the distortion of 'intellect' Bergson meant precisely the lifeless world of 'facts' gathered by observation: realism's 'reality' was dead and lifeless. Thus the true 'realism' for Bergson was the direct intuitive apprehension of the 'immediate objects of consciousness.' Like Freud's energizing psychology, Bergson's philosophy reconciled the apparently impossible: on the one hand, an epistemology 'modern' in its scientific rigour; on the other, a metaphysics 'traditional' in its privileging of unseen reality.[52] His scientific metaphysics recovered (in William James's words) nature's 'big blooming buzzing confusion.'

Bergson's closest analogue to pure philosophical intuition was aesthetic experience. Like Kant before him, Bergson thought of 'aesthetic' experience as that which regards objects in a 'disinterested' way – that is, without a pragmatic interest in what use-value they might have for the perceiver. As a passage from his 1900 work on *Laughter* demonstrates, when Bergson spoke about the ability of art and poetry to intuitively apprehend reality, his poetic rhetoric soared with a preacher's fervour:

> Between nature and ourselves, nay, between ourselves and our own consciousness a veil is interposed: a veil that is dense and opaque for the common herd, – thin, almost transparent for the artist and the poet ... From time to time, however, in a fit of absentmindedness nature raises up souls that are more detached from life ... Were this detachment complete, did the soul no longer cleave to action by any of its perceptions, it would be the soul of an artist such as the world has never seen. It would excel alike in every art at the same time; or rather, it would fuse them all into one. It would perceive all things in their native purity: the forms, colors, sounds of the physical world as well as the subtlest movements of the inner life.[53]

Bergson's elevation of art, poetry, and aesthetic experience over positivistic science as a privileged mode of unmediated access to reality would be his most lasting influence on Jacques and Raïssa Maritain.

In sum, human freedom was Bergson's central concern and his aesthetic notion of 'intuition' possessed a moral urgency. His philosophy looked back to Plato and forward to Sartre:[54] for only in those rare moments when we shake ourselves free of intellect's perceptive shackles and leave the cave for intuition's world of deeper reality – only then can we act in true human freedom. This was precisely its appeal for a youthful generation. Fifty years of fatalism, albeit optimistic, no longer seemed to offer answers to some pressing questions: Was human life determined? And if so, were horrors like Russian Jewish pogroms tragic or absurd? 'I could accept a sorrowful life,' Raïssa had said, 'but not an absurd one.' The problem, simply put, was 'how to act with dignity.'

Bergson preached a truth according to which Jacques and Raïssa could live. After the academic year 1901–2, their plans for suicide having been rendered unnecessary, Jacques and Raïssa became engaged. They were married two years later, on 26 November 1904. At this point, the Maritains stood as what we might consider to be archetypes of a generational elite in the early light of a new century: freethinking, Republican, socialist, Protestant / Jewish protégés of Bergson.

However, almost immediately after their marriage, the Maritains (like so many of Bergson's other disciples) grew restless for a religiosity beyond metaphysics. Paul Maritain, Jacques's father, had committed suicide earlier that year (on 20 February 1904), and one could speculate that this catalysed religious ruminations. (Jacques did not note the event in his diary.) Whatever the proximate cause, during the winter of 1904–5, the newlyweds began to read the works of Léon Bloy, the virulent pamphleteer. As will be seen, Bloy's extremely severe Catholicism would carry the Maritains to a location quite different from Bergson's eminently bourgeois respectability. In spite of these differences, Bergson and Bloy shared an important common belief in the power of art and literature. Even after Bloy, as the title for Maritain's 1953 A.W. Mellon lectures suggests (*Intuition in Art and Poetry*),[55] Bergson's fundamental notion of an 'intuition' providing unfiltered access to reality would remain a constant in the Maritains' thought for the next half-century.

Léon Bloy: Redemptive Suffering, Apocalyptic Martyrdom, Polluted Protagonists

The popularity of Léon Bloy, widely read by contemporaries on both the right and left and the symbolic centre of so many conversions during the post-1905 wave, can initially be somewhat difficult to understand.[56] What can account for the astounding appeal of this writer who was never capable of making a living from his writing and who lived as a beggar to the very end? The answer, in part, lies precisely in his poverty. Roger Shattuck's now-classic work dubbed this epoch as 'The Banquet Years,' a time marked by conspicuous consumption: 'a life of pompous display, frivolity, hypocrisy, cultivated taste, and relaxed morals' during which 'the untaxed rich lived in shameless luxury and systematically brutalized *le peuple* with venal journalism, inspiring promises of progress and expanding empire, and cheap absinthe.'[57] Poverty and suffering were Bloy's primary themes, and his anti-bourgeois polemic, both venomous and hilarious, offered a stark alternative to the reigning ideology.

Another part of the answer lies in Bloy's theology of suffering as a privileged mode of redemption, and in his corollary notion that those who suffer are religiously blessed. For Bloy, those who suffer, especially those considered to be polluted figures by self-righteous society – for example, the prostitutes and the Jews – are redeemed insofar as they are participants in the ongoing Passion of Christ. Certainly, this was an ancient established idea in both scriptures and tradition, and hardly unique to Bloy (or his friend, Huysmans). However, his creative retrieval of it in the wider context of an ultramontanist aesthetics – that is, one in which Christ, being divine, must have been 'the most beautiful of all men' – gave society's marginalized figures an alternative vision of holiness and beatitude. The ugliness of suffering and disfavour in the eyes of the majority need not lead to pessimism or despair; on the contrary, it might well be an indication of divine favour and an instrumental participation in the world's redemption. In his inversion of contemporary religious values, Bloy's retrieval of ancient images challenged a bourgeois Catholicism that set purity up over and against life's shadows and society's polluted members.

Bloy's life and writings were a complex intermingling of desires for both erotic companionship and meaningful order.[58] On the eve of the Franco-Prussian War, after a period of youthful drifting and thanks to Barbey d'Aurevilly, Bloy recovered his Catholic faith in 1869. In 1877 he met a young prostitute, Anne-Marie Roulé – later fictionalized as Véronique in his autobiographical novel, *The Desperate One* (1886) – and saw it as his personal mission to save her. As they became lovers, Anne-Marie too converted to Catholicism and began to have what she considered mystical experiences and revelations. As such, Anne-Marie was one in a long line of marginalized and humble figures – newly important in the nineteenth-century sites of La Salette, Lourdes, and Marpingen – who, precisely on account of their lowliness, were seen as privileged mystical visionaries.

Although Bloy initially hesitated to believe in the authenticity of his lover's visions, he later considered 1878–82 to be 'years of illumination' for him, with 1880 marking a state of 'mystical exaltation' for both himself and Anne-Marie. She had visionary premonitions of the coming of the 'Third Reign' – a belief in the imminent end of the fin-de-siècle worlds of both France and Russia – and throughout the rest of his life Bloy would cling tenaciously to this apocalyptic view of the world. Tragically, in 1882 Anne-Marie went entirely mad and had to be committed to an asylum named The Good Savior at Caen. She remained there until her death in 1907.

In 1883, the heartbroken Bloy met yet another impoverished prostitute, Berthe Drumont. Once again he fell in love; once again he felt a mission to redeem. She became his mistress, and the two of them lived together in wretched poverty until her death. Finally, in 1889 Bloy met Jeanne Molbech, daughter of the Danish poet, Christian Molbech. She converted from Protestantism to Catholicism and they were married in 1890. Although they too would live in absolute poverty and physical wretchedness, Bloy's love for Jeanne made him happier than he had ever been. The Bloys lived in the bohemian setting of Montmartre and the Moulin Rouge during its anarchic heyday.[59] Beginning in 1892, he would publish his daily journal in several volumes with the Mercure de France: *The Ungrateful Beggar* (1892–5), *My Diary* (1896–1900), *Four Years of Captivity with the Swine-on-the-Marne* (1900–4), *The Unsaleable* (1904–7), *The Old Man of the Mountain* (1907–10), *The Pilgrim of the Absolute* (1910–12), and *On the Brink of the Apocalypse* (1913–15). These provided a steady stream of reflections on contemporary life that would be Bloy's lasting legacy.

Already in November 1889, Bloy had intended to write a novel called *The Prostitute (La Prostituée)*.[60] It came to fruition in *The Woman Who Was Poor* (1897), a fictionalized account of his former lover Berthe Drumont as the protagonist Clotilde. In this revolutionary work, Bloy created a crucial category for the *renouveau catholique* by elevating the prostitute to the status of a Christ-figure, a true saint unrecognized and reviled by her bourgeois antagonists. Radically departing from neoclassical and ultramontanist notions that the sacred ought to be aesthetically perfect and integrally pure, in Bloy's hands the holy was marked most especially by fragility and fragmentation. Bloy's literature creatively synthesized both ancient and modern: the prostitute as the metaphor for urban modernity, and Christ's warning to the self-righteous: 'Amen I say to you, that the publicans and the harlots shall go into the kingdom of God before you.'[61]

The single most important idea for Bloy (as for his one-time friend Huysmans) was that of 'vicarious suffering.'[62] Again, the idea was not new: it had its origins in ancient Christianity's theology of the communion of saints and purgatory, and the practices of mass offerings, redemptions, and indulgences.[63] It was also a staple of nineteenth-century Catholic supernaturalism in the distorted teachings of the satanists Eugène Vintras and Abbé Joseph-Antoine Boullan.[64] Yet this notion of the inseparable interconnection of persons with one another took on a new significance within the changed context of the liberal republican individualist paradigm: human beings so closely relate to one another, that the sufferings in one life can make up for and redeem the sins in another. In an epoch marked by the transition from 'salvation to self-realization,'[65] vicarious suffering offered an attractive alternative for those seeking a radical religion.

Bloy's position was extreme: he made suffering not merely a *privileged* path to redemption, but in fact the *exclusive* mode of participation in the supernatural. As early as 1871, only two years after his return to Catholicism, Bloy wrote that if our 'spiritual *divinization*' is the result of God becoming a human being who can suffer, this 'implies for us as an invincible consequence, the inexorable necessity to be, in our turn, men and *men of suffering*.'[66] He made the claim even more exclusive: 'here below, the only supernatural thing is SUFFERING' while everything else is merely natural. Suffering, when we accept it, 'always' redeems: 'Every time we recommence the sacrifice of Calvary, we start the Redemption; our sufferings always redeem someone or something.' Suffering, far from being a mark of divine disfavour, was a certain sign of participating in redemption. A bourgeois society that disdained its marginal figures did so at its religious peril.

Bloy's use of words like 'suffering,' 'sacrifice,' and 'blood' had nineteenth-century Gothic and Decadent overtones. Writing about his desire to convert a friend's brother, Bloy said he was willing 'to purchase his conversion for the price of the longest and most sorrowful purgatory.' This would mean 'the most cruel sacrifice for a vain person like myself' – namely, the exchange of his reason for madness. Thus, he 'prayed to God to make an imbecile of me, an object of disgust' in order that he might accomplish 'this sacrifice of my thinking of which I am so proud.' We ought never to refuse suffering since '*We are made for that and for that alone*.' Human beings live in order to participate in Christ's ongoing passion that redeems the world: 'When we pour out our blood, it is on Calvary that it runs and from there across all the earth.'[67] As Maritain would later testify, Bloy saw himself as 'one of God's witnesses' and 'hoped that the martyrdom to which he aspired would be a bloody one.'[68]

The two most important expressions of Bloy's theology of suffering were Our Lady of La Salette and the 'Jewish race.' Whereas the masses may have been drawn to the more comforting image of Our Lady of Lourdes, the stern Lady of La Salette was the preferred object of devotion for the 'cultivated elite' of converted intellectuals like Bloy and Huysmans.[69] 'I do not sense any attraction,' wrote Bloy in *She Who Weeps* (1908), 'to an Immaculate Conception crowned with roses, white and blue, in sweet-smelling music and perfume.' Being 'too soiled, too far from innocence, too much the neighbor of stinking goats, too needy of pardon,' Bloy found it necessary to venerate a different kind of Virgin Mary: 'the Immaculate Conception crowned with thorns, My Lady of la Salette, the Immaculate Conception wounded by stigmata, infinitely bloody and pallid, distressed and dreadful, among her tears and chains, in her dark clothes of the Ruler of the nations, made up like a widow, crouched down in solitude; the Virgin pierced by Swords, such as she was seen during all the Middle Ages; a Medusa of innocence and of sorrows who changes those who see her crying into the stones of cathedrals.'[70] In this passage filled with neo-medieval and Decadent imagery, Bloy reversed both the aesthetics and theology of ultramontanism: the ideal expression of the Virgin's holiness was neither bodily perfection nor emotional calm, but rather hysterical grief, bodily wounds, and grotesque blood. Like Grünewald's Christ, the Virgin of La Salette was a bodily eruption, ambivalently hysterical and 'mysterical.' In order to save, the Madonna needed to repulse like Medusa.

In addition to the suffering Virgin, Bloy also venerated the suffering Jew. In his *Salvation by the Jews* (1892), Bloy offered an idiosyncratic vision of the Jewish people radically opposed to that propagated in Drumont's *Libre Parole* – that is, 'The Semitic invasion is like the breeding of microbes.'[71] He argued that, since the Jews had historically been the most abject of people, and since such suffering was necessarily redemptive, they must therefore be 'the *Race* out of which the Redemption comes forth (Salus ex Judaeis), *which carries visibly, like Jesus himself, the sins of the World* ... the race of Israel, which is to say of the Holy Spirit, whose exodus will be the marvelous wonder of Abjection.' Bloy capitalized the word 'Abjection' in order to refer it to its ideal referent in the abjection of Christ himself, described by the prophet Isaiah and read at the Catholic service every Good Friday: 'Despised, and the most abject of men, a man of sorrows, and acquainted with infirmity.'[72] The 'Jewish race' carried on the redemptive work of its most important son – Jesus Christ.

Bloy, like all other parties from Maurras to Zola, used Christian imagery to make sense of the Dreyfus Affair.[73] He saw Colonel Dreyfus's unjust prosecution as fulfilling the Jewish mission to save the world just as his ancestor Jesus had – namely, through his 'abjection,' his personal suffering echoing that echoed the suffering of his race. The historical Dreyfus Affair was partly apocalyptic for Bloy: the earthly apparition of an occult mystery. Parodying Zola's manifesto '*J'accuse!*,' Bloy wrote an essay against Zola entitled *Je m'accuse* ('I Accuse Myself').[74] Under 'the presumption of a known crime, for which he appears to be absolutely innocent and not responsible' – that is, espionage and treason – Bloy saw Dreyfus in reality being 'punished for an *unknown* crime' – that is, human sin. In apocalyptic imagery, outward appearances are signs pointing beyond themselves to a cosmic struggle between forces of light and darkness. In this sense the 'affair about which the whole world was speaking' was only 'an illusion': it was merely '*the human and hideous appearance of a DIVINE COURT CASE for which the moment has not yet come to be revealed in the light*.' By saying 'Je m'accuse,' Bloy accused himself of his own sinfulness for which Colonel Dreyfus' suffering was vicariously redemptive. Bloy judged this sacrifice 'very good.'

The appeal of Bloy's vitriol to those with progressive social leanings – like André Gide and the newly married Maritains – is not as strange as it might seem. His contempt for liberal bourgeois society and his polemical defence of the dignity of the poor during these banquet years of unprecedented affluence and conspicuous consumption found many sympathizers. Moreover, the paradoxical quality of Bloy's message was seductive: he attracted a largely intellectual elite in search of order, yet his images were shot through with Decadent disorder. His protagonists were the urban poor, Jews, and above all, prostitutes: all polluted figures who end up as privileged sites of grace. Seeing the Belle Époque as an affront to Divine Justice, Bloy celebrated worldly failure as the sign of otherworldly victory. His innovative creation was the Decadent 'aesthetic of failure' inflected with ironic and apocalyptic Gospel inversions: the last would be first and the first last; the blind saw while the sighted remained blind; unless the grain of wheat first die it could not bring forth life. Bloy's apocalyptic vision stirred the passions of a younger elite bitterly contemptuous of the received order in both politics and religion. As Maritain would later recall, Bloy felt that he was the voice of 'all those who are *abandoned or oppressed by the modern world,*' and that it was his mission to express their lasting lament.[75]

Integralist Conversion: The Maritains' Rightward Turn

Bloy's emphasis on suffering as redemption offered an existential answer to the disquieted heart of a Russian Jewish emigrée and, presumably, to her husband whose father, many years estranged, had recently committed suicide. Six months after having begun their reading of the controversial figure, the Maritains went to meet the Bloys on 25 June 1905.[76] Jacques's mother, Geneviève Favre, would be slow to forgive her son for his embrace of Bloy and the affront it brought to the family's republican reputation.[77]

As much as he might admire Bloy, however, Maritain could not shake his long-standing hatred for the Catholic milieu. He identified the Church with everything he rejected – the Army, the bourgeoisie, and conservatism; the condemnation of humanism, socialism, and progress. At the beginning of 1906, six months after first meeting Bloy, Jacques wrote in his journal: 'The Christians have abandoned the poor – and the poor among the nations: the Jews – and the Poverty of the soul: authentic Reason. They horrify me.' Although Bloy was a Christian, he was among them 'like a prophet' – that is, 'in a fury against his people. (But all the same, among the people.)' If one were to be baptized into the Church, he concluded, it would be necessary to live like a stranger 'come from outside,' fleeing 'the family of the satisfied who, in the name of their eternal salvation, have taken the part of those acting against the temporal salvation of the world.'[78]

If Bloy impressed the young couple, the influence was mutual: his own convictions about redemptive suffering and salvation from the Jews were influenced by meeting Raïssa, whom he came to love deeply. In February 1906, thanks to Jacques and Raïssa's financial underwriting of the publication costs, the penniless Bloy was able to reprint *Salvation by the Jews*.[79] Bloy dedicated the volume to the Jewish Raïssa herself.

Just as the book appeared, Raïssa, who would be sickly to the end of her life, very narrowly survived a life-threatening illness.[80] This traumatic event seems to have intensified the couple's religious quest, and soon after they asked Bloy to sponsor their entries into the Catholic Church. Their parents took it badly.[81] Ilya and Hissia Oumançoff considered their daughter's baptism a betrayal of the Jewish people and their suffering.

Although Jacques succeeded in appeasing them somewhat, the wound would last. He told his own mother over the mid-day dinner on 3 March and later noted that for her it was 'a catastrophe.' She herself reported in unpublished memoirs that the 'blow was so difficult that I did not believe I could ever pick myself up ... It seemed to me as though someone had taken everything that was good.' She saw Jacques as being doubly manipulated by both Bloy and Raïssa, gradually taken over by the 'Catholic spirit.' As a matter of fact, neither Jacques nor Raïssa seem to have known much of anything about Catholicism's essentials – an ignorance that amused Bloy when they mistakenly thought he would be the one baptizing them, sparing them 'contact with the institutional Church, which they mistrusted and feared.'[82]

On 11 June 1906, Jacques and Raïssa were baptized Catholics with Léon Bloy as godfather and his daughter Véronique as godmother. Soon afterward, nearly all of their Sorbonne friends distanced themselves from the couple. A harsh letter by the director of *La Tribune russe* (in which Jacques had published several articles in 1905) accused them of being 'afraid of life' and preferring to bury their heads in the sand. Geneviève complained to Ernest Psichari, Jacques's childhood friend: 'The sorrow that I am suffering in seeing my child bent before the yoke of his wife is unbelievable.'[83] However, more was to come as Jacques's sister Jeanne followed his example. Contrary to her husband's advice, Jeanne had their daughter Eveline baptized one evening in November 1906 at the church of Saint-Médard. Geneviève watched as her children reversed her father's and her own painful decisions to abandon Catholicism made a generation earlier.

On 25 August 1906, two months after their baptism, the Maritains moved to Heidelberg, Germany. Jacques had always been interested in biology, and he had received a grant to study with the vitalist biologist Hans Driesch, a key figure in promoting holism in 'reenchanted science.'[84] Driesch's embryonic experiments seemed to defy a mechanistic explanation of life, and he used Aristotle's hylomorphic principle of an *entelechy* to formulate a theory of life animated by teleological purpose. Maritain's studies with Driesch both conserved the past and looked forward to his future: the neo-vitalism continued what he had first found in Bergson's *élan vital*, while the retrieved Aristotelianism served as a foreshadowing of a thinker that Maritain was about to meet – Thomas Aquinas.

During their Heidelberg sojourn in 1907, three further events destabilized the Maritains' world. In January, Raïssa once again fell extremely ill, was rushed back to Paris, and, in expectation of imminent death, received the Catholic sacrament of Extreme Unction ('last rites'). Following Bloy's advice, the Maritains prayed fervently to Our Lady of La Salette. After Raïssa's recovery, they maintained their devotion to this strict and stigmatic version of 'She Who Weeps.'

Later that fall, on 8 September 1907, feast of the Birth of the Virgin Mary, Pope Pius X issued his encyclical letter *Pascendi Dominici Gregis* condemning the Roman Catholic Modernists. This letter coincided with a third event, yet another published work: Henri Bergson's masterpiece, *Creative Evolution*. Although many Catholic converts had depended upon Bergson's intellectual reconciliation of an evolutionary view of the world with a metaphysical one, his principle of an ever-flowing *durée* at the heart of reality did not mesh well with the Pope's explicitly static eternalism. They would have to choose between Bergson and the Pope. For the Maritains, traumatized by Raïssa's two near-death experiences and reception of the last rites, the choice was particularly poignant: Bergson had once saved their lives from suicide, and the Pope was integrally connected to another life-saver, La Salette. (As the Dominican Father Humbert Clérissac, their spiritual director, would tell Jacques, 'La Salette is a recall to integral Christianity, to the faith of the first centuries ... priests who do not desire sanctity are cesspools of impurity.')[85] The Maritains chose purity over possible danger.

As a result, during the years 1907–8 in Heidelberg, as Jacques completed his thesis on neo-vitalism, the Maritains' newfound lives as Catholic believers again lacked something. They needed an intellectual bridge from their now severed past to an unknown future. In 1909, under the influence of Clérissac, Raïssa began to read the works of Thomas Aquinas. She urged Jacques to study them as well and, having finished his thesis, he too began, in September 1910, to read the *Summa Theologica*. In 1911, again at the urging of Clérissac, the Maritains subscribed to *L'Action française*. The rightward turn had begun.

In October 1912, after eight years of marriage, the Maritains – along with Raïssa's sister Véra Oumançoff, who had been living with them since their Heidelberg days[86] – made a secret vow of perpetual chastity within their marriage. The three transformed their household into a small community of Benedictine oblates. Especially in the anticlerical context of the post-1905 years, this was regarded as 'a virtually lunatic act by those who found the Maritains' atemporal Catholicism incomprehensible, Jacques' mother included.'[87] Although Maritain's carefully composed explanation of this vow later on insisted that it had 'implied no scorn for nature,'[88] a certain Manicheanism in his vision of body and spirit seems undeniable, especially given his overall anxieties about naturalist determinism. A decade later, when Daniel Halévy called Maritain 'this new Tertullian' – that is, the ancient Stoic who believed (as Peter Brown notes) 'that abstinence from sex was the most effective technique with which to achieve clarity of soul' – he could not have known how accurate his analogy was.[89]

Thus, by November 1912, the Maritains were no longer as they had been on their wedding day in November 1904: freethinking, Republican, socialist, Jewish, and Protestant protégés of Bergson. After Raïssa's close calls with death had intersected with the stern visions of Bloy, La Salette, and Pius X, the Maritains grew to resemble the general type of the 'generation of 1914.'[90] This new taste for order, action, and Catholicism would be even more precisely typified, however, by Maritain's boyhood friend, Ernest Psichari.

Ernest Psichari: 'We Men of the Desert'

Ernest Psichari, born (like Raïssa) in September 1883, had been named after his maternal grandfather, Ernest Renan, a former seminarian who had become an Orientalist scholar of ancient languages and thought. Renan's historicist account of *A Life of Jesus* (1863), stripping Jesus of supernatural significance, had been a bestseller and cultural landmark; his long essay on *The Future of Science* (1848; revised 1890) further established him as an icon of republican positivist intelligence. 'The mere mention of Renan's name in fin-de-siècle France,' Robert Wohl has written, 'suggested the academic establishment, religious skepticism, and a mocking epicurean relativism that took pleasure in the contradictions of human thought and conduct and that despaired of establishing any absolute truths, whether religious or simply moral.'[91]

Ernest, one year younger than Jacques Maritain, had been a constant presence in Geneviève Favre's home. She treated Psichari as an adopted son, thinking it only right that the two powerful republican families descended from Jules Favre and Ernest Renan should be closely united.[92] Ernest and Jacques were the closest of friends at the Henri-IV *lycée*, sharing the progressivist passions of their strongly intellectual political families. Jacques's boyhood letters to Psichari were full of extravagant affection, each message a confession of adoration. 'I love you, I live, I think of you,' he wrote Ernest in December 1899, 'It is in you, in you alone that I live ...'; 'Without you I am nothing ... You are the Center, the

Fire, the Body, the Idea, Apollo. You are the light, I am the reflection. You are the Tree, I am the Shade. You are the Eye, I am the Look.' In eerily prescient words, he playfully asked: 'Do you want to leave with me for the Orient, down there, in India? We will be alone in a desert ... We will be saints. We will live a thousand years ...'[93] Raïssa later recounted that Psichari's 'friendship for Jacques was touching. Ever since high school he used to say, "Jacques and I are really only one. That which he thinks I think, that which he does I do, that which he feels I feel."'[94]

In 1903, the twenty-year-old Psichari had proposed marriage to Maritain's sister, Jeanne, whom he had known since childhood. Perhaps intuiting Psichari's homosexual inclinations, Jeanne declined Ernest's offer and married another man – undoubtedly disappointing her mother.[95] Deeply depressed, Psichari tried unsuccessfully to end his life. Foiled in his suicide attempt and determined to escape from what he considered the disorder of his life, he joined the army. A year later, this descendant of anti-militarist university professors found military life so attractive that he re-enlisted and transferred to the colonial artillery.

Psichari seems to have inherited some of his grandfather's Orientalist fascination: having been assigned to North Africa, he believed he had found natives who were 'uncorrupted' by 'civilization.'[96] Like Jean-Jacques Rousseau before him, Psichari imagined that these primitives found in a state of nature revealed what Europeans must have been like before the 'vices of decadence' had weakened them. In 1908, Psichari published a first-hand account of his experience entitled *Land of Sun and of Sleep*. Here, he explicitly used Rousseau's own imagery of civilization as a corrupt play of masks: 'In France we are caught in a social mesh; we play out our allotted, pre-established roles on the world's little stage, in conformity with what we possess and the environment in which we live. But over there [i.e., in Africa] our hearts rise up towards the highest thoughts imaginable. We are transported beyond ourselves. I am no longer a young middle-class Frenchman, getting on with my allotted tasks; I am a man, entirely given over to rough, primitive emotions.'[97] Psichari's attitude towards 'primitives' reflects the self-contradicting attitudes in colonizing Western societies views during the nineteenth and early twentieth centuries about 'civilization' and degeneration, a controversy extending at least as far back as Montesquieu's Persian harem and Rousseau's state of nature. Some identified Western civilization as the apex of masculinity while others (like Psichari) considered civilization's effects emasculating and believed that colonizers could co-opt the vigorous energies of 'primitives' to 'restore an ebbing masculinity.'[98] For Psichari, bourgeois society was artificial, inauthentic, and soft; the primitive desert, on the other hand, was authentic, healthy, and masculine. Colonial service allowed one to transcend the decadent relativism of Europe: it 'makes us better; it exalts us, raises us above ourselves, in a tension of the soul *where dream and action interpenetrate and become one.*' Upon his return to Paris, Psichari announced that he had 'conquered a belief' and hoisted his dream 'above all doubt and relativities.'[99]

On 17 November 1909, Psichari dined with the Maritains and the topic of religion inevitably dominated conversation. 'No obstacle to grace, inclined towards faith,' Jacques recorded, and then added bitterly, 'Péguy told him as he told my mother, that he had sent me to the Isle of Wight [i.e., Solesmes Abbey in exile] in order that I might get in touch with Catholics of better quality than Léon Bloy.' As Psichari left the Maritains for a second round of African duty, he took with him gifts that were markers of integralist Catholicism: a copy of *The Dolorous Passion of Our Lord Jesus Christ* by Anne Catherine Emmerich, and a 'miraculous medal' from the Rue du Bac convent (at which Catherine Labouré was said to have seen the Virgin Mary in 1830).[100]

During Psichari's second tour, the shock of an encounter with Islam crystallized the young freethinker's movement towards Catholicism.[101] In the early summer of 1912, awestruck by the technological wonder of an electric motor powering a telegraph station, Psichari told his Muslim guide that the 'Moors' would be fools to resist conquerors as powerful as the French. His guide, Sidïa, replied that while his French masters might possess 'the kingdom of the earth, the kingdom of heaven belonged to Moslems like himself.' This was a traumatic encounter with the Orientalist 'other' that Psichari's grandfather would not have anticipated: it resisted domination. Deeply shaken, the officially unbelieving Psichari immediately wrote the Catholic bishop of Senegambia, enclosed a donation towards the construction of a cathedral, and emphasized that it was essential for France 'to impress her Moslem subjects with a firm display of religious belief.' Later that summer of 1912, he wrote Jacques saying, 'I am, if I can say this absurd thing, a Catholic without faith.'[102] Since their 1909 dinner with Psichari, the Maritains had discovered Aquinas, subscribed to *L'Action française*, and just made their vow of chastity that October. They welcomed him back to France late that year.

In January 1913, Psichari brought his friend Henri Massis, an enthusiast for Maurras's Action Française, to meet the rediscovered friend of his youth. One month later, on 4 February 1913 – while the rest of the Catholic world ate and drank to excess on the *Mardi Gras* preceding Ash

Wednesday – Ernest Psichari converted to Catholicism. Standing in front of a mournful statue of Our Lady of La Salette in the Maritains' private chapel on the rue de l'Orangerie, Ernest read out his profession of faith and made his first confession. Four days later he received the oils of Confirmation anointing him a 'soldier of Christ' from the hands of the Bishop of Versailles, ancient seat of the absolutist throne. The next day, the First Sunday of the Lenten season of penitence and repentance, he made his first communion in the chapel of the Holy Childhood in Versailles. Not coincidentally, Massis's own conversion soon followed.

In 1876, Ernest Renan, symbol of modern scepticism, had written, 'We live on the shadow of a shadow. On what will one live after us?' In 1913, his grandson gave his answer by returning 'to the most ancient of French communities: the army and the church.'[103] Psichari became an instant celebrity, and his highly publicized conversion coincided with the 1913 appearance of his quasi-autobiographical novel written during his tour in Mauritania. Militantly entitled *The Call of Arms*, it was the story of a young man named Maurice Vincent enticed into joining the army by tales of colonial campaigns told by a veteran, Captain Timothée Nangès. The 'call to arms' was a call to moral conflict: a struggle against bourgeois republican life back in France. 'We remain morally above it,' says Nangès, adding (in a line worthy of the Decadents), 'The nation is not like us: it is drowning in progress.'[104]

After being wounded in Mauritania, Maurice's masculinity seems destabilized as he must return to Paris with his mutilated body no longer *intégrale* – he is a *mutilé de guerre* – and thus, by implication, perhaps no longer masculine.[105] Nostalgically remembering his carefree days as 'a barbarian, able to move freely' in Africa, Maurice finds his office job in Paris confining and suffocating. Civilization does not liberate but rather limits freedom. The veteran Nangès emphasizes the suffocation metaphor even more strongly: 'I am not really made for living in France. A sick person does not suffer from the fetid smell of his room. But if a healthy man comes in from outside, he will choke and vomit. That is what we experience, we men of the desert, when we come back to civilization.'[106]

Psichari's military adventures, widely disseminated through his literary talents, enabled him to become the ideal model of a 'new generation's' self-described preference for action, asceticism, discipline, and renunciation. Among his many promoters was Péguy, Geneviève Favre's close friend, to whom Psichari had written letters from the desert 'like a son to his father.' For Péguy, the young Ernest was the living incarnation of his own grandfather's generational theory in which youth and old age were difficult but fertile times, while middle age (one's forties) was a time of irremediable sterility. Thus, the youthful 'brown beards' and the aging 'white beards' needed to unite against the 'grey beards' – of whom, incidentally, Péguy was now one.[107] Within this generational context, Péguy saw Psichari's love for action the ultimate revolt of youthful belief against middle-aged paralysis. It was precisely against this middle-aged abandonment of any felt conviction – in Péguy's words, this process of *démystification*, substituting the *politique* for the *mystique* – that the militant generation of Renan's grandson called for revolt.[108]

The idea of a 'new generation' in search of a 'Catholic Renaissance' would be most persuasively constructed by Psichari's friend, Henri Massis. For Massis as for Péguy, Psichari stood as the ideal model of a 'new generation' and its modern taste for action, asceticism, discipline, and renunciation.

Une Renaissance catholique: Integralism, Apocalypticism, and the 'Generation of 1914'

In 1912, Henri Massis, working with Alfred de Tarde, conducted a newspaper survey for the Parisian daily *L'Opinion*.[109] In 1913, they published their results as a book with a title that outlined their thesis: *The Young People of Today. The Taste for Action. Patriotic Faith. A Catholic Renaissance. Political Realism.*[110] The work redefined both youth and modernity by constructing an activist younger generation in opposition to 'the generation of 1885' they defamed. Amplifying their recent work attacking the dominant intellectual trends in the university – *The Spirit of the New Sorbonne. The Crisis of Classical Culture. The Crisis of French.* (1911)[111] – Massis and Tarde accused the '1885 generation' of having perverted the Sorbonne by forming its fundamental orientation out of imported German historicism and idealism. Renan's generation had been 'pessimistic, self-doubting, morally flabby, overly intellectual and introspective, relativistic, incapable of energetic action, lacking faith, obsessed with decadence, and ready to accept the defeat and eclipse of their country.' All these traits converged in a debilitating 'dilettantism' which Massis defined as 'the unconcentrated being in whom the bundle of energy relaxes; it is the inability to choose or to put it better, it is the lack of love.'

In contrast, the young people of 1912 were turning their backs on their Sorbonne professors and putting away all such decadent self-doubt. They were patriots, prepared 'and even eager to give up' their lives – especially if that sacrifice would lead to throwing off the 'German yoke' and the regeneration of France. Tired of relativism, they hankered after moral 'absolutes' and joined in a *renaissance catholique* that offered *order*: a basis for both discipline and coherent action. In sum, whereas the 1885 generation had created 'disorder and ruins' in 'all matters,' a new generation created 'order and hierarchy.'[112]

An essay entitled 'Toward a Catholic Renaissance,' published in April 1914 in the Catholic journal titled *La Vie Nouvelle* (New Life), provides a striking example of this youthful phenomenon. The article appeared in a journal whose title obviously alluded to the Christian doctrine of bodily resurrection; it appeared at Easter, the ancient rite of spring celebrating that resurrection; it was an article about a Catholic *renaissance* or 're-birth'; and its subject was a resurrected body politic of France. Such rich layers of metaphor surely did not escape the anonymous but talented writer.

He proposed a plan of action that would be at the service of both those 'young people' who, hearing 'the call of *the New Life*,' would enter into 'the ranks' and fulfil 'their tour of combat,' as well as of those sympathizers who had kept enough 'moral reserve' in order to 'salute across the clouds of the French sky the radiant aurora of the youth who [were] preparing for the future ...'[113] This was a call to arms to resurrect a fragmented body: 'We wish, in effect, to restore order to our country ... "To group all the Catholic forces of French youth with a view to cooperating in the re-establishment of the Christian social edifice." All of our efforts converge there.'

This April 1914 call to enter the 'ranks,' fulfil a 'tour of combat,' and 'salute the radiant aurora of youth' was a call to a kind of civil war against the Republic and its perceived disorder. A few months later, when these same Catholic 'young people of today' would be called up to fight a war *on behalf of* that same Republic against the German menace, they would be forced to quickly rethink both their Catholicism and their Republicanism. In the meantime, on the eve of the catastrophe, the young activist could write with certainty: 'One word stands out in the platform of this program: the word *Order*.'

Jacques Maritain the Anti-modernist

One of many 'opinions' reproduced in *The Young People of Today* was Jacques Maritain's.[114] Asked to explain why 'the elite of French youth' were turning to 'face the Catholic light, and to ask of the Church this substantial truth' that stood in such contrast to the 'vast and carnal [*charnelle*] modern futility,' Maritain said there would be no end to compiling 'an enumeration of the secondary causes.' Nevertheless, he did venture some: 'Disgust with pseudo-science, with sad materialism and of the foolish German doctoral system, fallibility of humanitarian religion and of democratic idealism, revolt of the Intelligence against Idiocy; incredible stupidity of the free-thinking workforce; the necessity to sense little by little the re-establishment of order in oneself.'

The vitriolic text shows just to what an extent the young socialist had reversed course in a half-dozen years, adopting the nationalistic tropes and proto-Fascist rage of the Action Française. Yet, there is also continuity since both left and right shared a hatred of bourgeois culture. Curiously, in using the word '*charnelle*' to describe 'modern futility,' Maritain might simply have meant 'fleshy' or 'earthly.' But given its specific overtones of sexual desire, and given the vow of lifelong celibacy that he and Raïssa had so recently made to one another, its use suggests deep anxieties and the need to divide the world into absolute oppositions: the pollution of the 'futile modern' world versus the purity of 'Catholic light.'

Moving on to the 'primary cause' for the recent wave of conversions, that is, grace, Maritain's imagery reflected Bloy's apocalyptic influence. 'Will the conversion movement of contemporary youth,' Maritain asked, 'remain limited to a cultivated elite? In the end, God wants to send the *apostles of the end-times* to his poor, announced by Our Lady of La Salette ... and who will separate him from those whom he will choose?' Maritain continued in the same horrific vein, using imagery from the *Apocalypse*: 'But the masses taken as a whole: will they be – as it has been predicted by and will be effected by the words of Our Lady of La Salette – will they be hardened more and more in blasphemy and hatred of God, until that time when the expected convulsions [i.e., earthquakes] and the desired martyrdoms will come?' The present moment was the brink of catastrophe, a crisis posing an either/or choice that all needed to make.

With such cosmic ultimates at stake, Maritain's proposed solution seems almost a *non sequitur*: the pressing task of these end-times was the study of Thomistic philosophy. Concluding his 'opinion,' the integralist Maritain used the words 'cultivated elite' to mean not recent Catholic converts but rather wayward Catholic Modernists: if they continued to maintain their 'taste for Bergson, for Laberthonnière and for Le Roy,' then the unlettered masses would arrive at truth before the 'elite.' In short, the 'cultivated elite' needed to 'study with all its heart the doctrine of Saint Thomas, and let itself be penetrated by this beautiful light, which ... sovereignly regulates action.' Taken as a whole, Maritain's opinion for *The Young People of Today*, though probably written very quickly and hence not very coherent, expresses the dominant influences on him in 1913: Bloy's apocalypticism, Maurras's proto-Fascism, and Roman Catholic integralism.

In a series of lectures at the Institut Catholique of Paris in April-May of that year, Maritain increased his bitter attack on his old master, Bergson, and the virulence of his remarks scandalized a number of listeners who questioned his lack of moderation. Later that October, undeterred by criticism, Maritain published an extended version of these lectures as his first book, *Bergsonian Philosophy* (1913). (Since Raïssa had done much of the book's research, Jacques later remarked that the 'book should have appeared under our two names' had he 'not been so *grob*.')[115] Charles Maurras – whose *L'Action française* had been engaged in an anti-Semitic campaign against the popular Bergson since 1910 – took the opportunity to draw the attention of Cardinal Pacelli (the future Pius XII) and of the Pope himself to this 'brilliantly renowned young Catholic philosopher.' In early January 1914, Cardinal Merry del Val delivered Pope Pius X's personal blessing to Maritain for his vigorous defence of Aquinas. In February, Bergson was elected to the Académie française (and was even more violently attacked by Maurras). On 8 June 1914, thanks largely to Maritain's efforts, Bergson's three major books were put on the Index of Forbidden Books.[116] The problem, as Jacques had noted four years earlier after visiting Bergson, was that the philosopher of the *élan vital* could not imagine Being as unchangeable. 'The immutability of God is an idea of the ancient philosophers, a Greek prejudice,' said Bergson. 'Who says life, says change.'[117]

In April–May of 1914, Maritain delivered another series of lectures under the title of 'The Spirit of Modern Philosophy.' The first of these attacked Descartes as being the root cause of the dualisms that marked modern thought and modernity itself.[118] (Since they were published later that summer after war broke out with Germany, Maritain revised the text in order to trace modernity's original sin not to Descartes but rather to Martin Luther.) In June 1914, thanks to the intervention of Cardinal Lorenzelli, Maritain – anti-Bergsonian and neo-Thomist – was appointed adjunct professor (he still lacked a doctorate) of the history of modern philosophy at the Institut Catholique of Paris.

Significantly, the Roman appointment went over the head and objections of the Institut's rector, Monsignor (later Cardinal) Alfred Baudrillart. Baudrillart, a professor of modern history, was descended from an aristocratic line: his grandfather, Samuel de Sacy, had been a senator in the Second Empire, editor-in-chief of the *Journal des débats*, and a member of the Académie Française. Baudrillart himself had been educated in France's most elite quarters – his classmates at the École normale supérieure included the socialist leader Jean Jaurès and Bergson himself. Maritain, from a younger generation, a less stable family line, a less prestigious education, and a vitriolic Catholicism, gave Baudrillart pause. Seen from across the mountains, however, Maritain was the ideal anti-modernist bulwark.[119]

In sum, by the time Maritain assumed the professorship in June 1914, he was entangled in a thick web of 'anti-modernist' associations. A favourite of the ultramontanist Solesmes monks, Maritain was invited by the abbot to come and spend a month on the Isle of Wight (where the abbey had been in exile since the 1903 expulsion). On 1 August 1914, as the Germans invaded Belgium, Jacques and Raïssa left the fatherland for their sojourn in England until summer's end – a voyage about which Jacques's mother complained: 'At this moment, no one has any right over us except the *Patrie*.' As the Maritains settled into their abbatial quarters, a general declaration of war plunged France into what would become the Great War. Being absent from Paris, they did not bid farewell to Péguy and Psichari who would never return from the front.[120]

Two weeks later, Raïssa's diary noted the death of Pope Pius X, Maritain's integralist advocate, on 20 August.[121] With all of Europe's attention focused on the unanticipated slaughter of the first twentieth-century war, his successor, Pope Benedict XV, quietly dismantled Pius's secret intelligence apparatuses; the Roman Catholic Modernist crisis ended with a whisper, not a bang. The 'civil war' between Catholics and laicists gave way to a 'sacred union,' formed to wage 'holy war' against the common German enemy.

French society from 1894 to 1914 was riven by binary oppositions, Manichean dualisms, and apocalyptic images of cosmic struggles. If we imagine a body politic frightened of pollution, we can see the efforts on all sides to rigidify boundaries and purge their respective camps of the unclean. Extreme concerns with purity and pollution characterize discourse and sometimes create the imagery: infectious and pestilent Jews; the absolute (and chaste) separation of Church and State (engineered by no less than a former inhabitant of the seminary 'harem'); the historicist desire among both Solesmes monks and Roman Catholic Modernists to jettison centuries of accretions and get back to *urtexts*; a global secret papal police network set up to purge the Church of internal corruption. As late as July 1914, the anxiety to contain contamination had ended up in bitter oppositions between realism and supernaturalism, culture and Catholicism, modernism and integralism.

This was all about to change. As an unthinkable chain of events unfolded, significances would need to be reassigned and the terms of the war inverted. They would indeed be called to tours of duty and salute the French sky, not in a civil war against the Republic, but rather in a holy war on behalf of that same Republic. What had yesterday been reviled would tomorrow be most precious. Apocalyptic dualisms would no longer make sense. Future survival would depend upon forging sacred unions.

Chapter 2

Trauma and Memorial: Repatriating the Repressed

Now in what consists the work which mourning performs? The testing of reality, having shown that the loved object no longer exists, requires forthwith that all the libido shall be withdrawn from its attachments to the object ... This struggle can be so intense that a turning away from reality ensues, the object being clung to through the medium of a hallucinatory wish-psychosis ... Why this process of carrying out the behest of reality bit by bit, which is in the nature of a compromise, should be so extraordinarily painful is not at all easy to explain in terms of mental economics. It is worth noting that this pain seems natural to us. The fact is, however, that when the work of mourning is completed the ego becomes free and uninhibited again.

– Sigmund Freud

We'd simply lost the last of the parts out of which we could fashion a living whole. There would be no new memories of him. The only stories we could tell now were the ones we already had.

– Jonathan Franzen

nostalgie n.f. – 1759, in medicine; medical Latin, *nostalgia* (1678); composite of Greek *nostos* 'return home' and of suffix *–algie* [pain]. 1. Psychopath. Depressive state linked with an obsessive regret over one's homeland, of the place where one lived for a long time; homesickness. *Nostalgia of emigrés, exiles, prisoners of war ... The true peasant dead of nostalgia far from the field that saw his birth.*[1]

France's 1914–18 'sacred union' of the Republic's monarchist right and socialist left was only the first of various 'impossible' reconciliations that the war would effect. As the conflict dragged on into 1915–16, France's traumatic encounter with chaos necessitated making new meanings out of an increasingly senseless situation. A process of mourning would involve recovering and reconciling elements that peacetime's luxury had allowed to be disregarded. If the war would be traumatic for the nation as a whole, it was from its outbreak particularly so for Catholics. Only yesterday they had been fighting against the Republic; today they were fighting on its behalf. How could one make sense of such a confusion of former meanings? This would be the task of the *renouveau catholique*'s memorialization – a creative reconstruction of collective memory.

From Civil War to Holy War: Catholic Cultural Trauma

On 31 July, just as the Germans were mobilizing for the next day's invasion of Belgium, the socialist leader Jean Jaurès was assassinated. Jaurès had been organizing resistance to the oncoming war, assuring workers that their internationalist brethren in the German proletariat would never take up arms against their French comrades; his assassin may have been a right-wing nationalist angered by the anti-war rhetoric.[2] The Republic's president had a potentially disastrous problem: the divorce between republican liberals and socialist progressives had been irreconcilable since the bloody betrayals of the Commune. The assassination only exacerbated this divide. How could the Republic get those whom it had marginalized – workers on the left and monarchists/Catholics on the right – not only to resist the temptation to seize the moment and overthrow the regime, but actually to fight on its behalf?

On 4 August 1914, four days after Jaurès' assassination and two days after the beginning of hostilities, President Poincaré declared to the National Assembly that France would be 'heroically defended by all her sons for whom nothing [would] break the sacred union [*l'union sacrée*] against the enemy ...'[3] By the term 'sacred union' he meant an implicit oath by which 'The Socialists agreed not to exploit the murder of Jaurès and the Right agreed not to conspire against the civil government of the Republic. It was an agreement "not to shoot the pianist."'[4]

In preparation for his military deployment, Charles Péguy gave his house to the Bloys and moved his wife and children in to live with Maritain's mother, Geneviève Favre. Ernest Psichari marched off with his father-figure Péguy on behalf of their beloved *patrie*. Both were killed within the first few weeks of the conflict. Maritain eulogized his heroic friend in *La Croix*: 'He died, his rosary beads wrapped around his hand, in the evening of 22 August 1914 ... As he went back to his gun, after having carried the wounded Captain Cherrier to the first aid post, a bullet struck his temple.'[5] Two weeks later, Péguy – a towering figure in Catholic revivalism even though he had remained unbaptized on the doorstep of the Church – died an equally heroic death. The novelist Julien Green later recalled the scene: 'There he stood in his red and blue uniform, a living target in the blazing sun, telling his men to shoot at will, then running ahead of them to lead them on ... A bullet struck him in the forehead and he fell with a groan as his men ran to victory.'[6] On 22 September 1914, Alain-Fournier, author of *The Wanderer, or The End of Youth* (*Le grand Meaulnes*, 1913), a close friend of both Péguy and Jacques Rivière, was reported missing in action.[7] The deaths of this trio took on significance as blood paid by Catholics for the Republic.[8]

Meanwhile, on 26 August 1914, a German atrocity that shocked the world bore added significance for French Catholics. Violating the neutrality of Belgium in order to move its troops to Paris, the Germans encountered unexpected resistance at Louvain, home to the four-hundred-year-old Catholic University of Louvain (the 'Catholic Oxford' of Belgium) and, incidentally, to Cardinal Mercier's Institut Supérieur, symbolic centre of Thomism. The Germans slaughtered citizens and levelled the city. On 31 August Richard Harding Davis reported in the New York *Tribune*:

> London, August 30 – For two hours on Thursday night I was in what for six hundred years has been the city of Louvain. The Germans were burning it, and to hide their work kept us locked in the railway carriages. But the story was written against the sky, was told to us by German soldiers incoherent with excesses; and we could read it in the faces of women and children being led to concentration camps and of citizens on their way to be shot.
>
> ... The Town Hall was very old and very beautiful, an example of Gothic architecture, in detail and design more celebrated even than the Town Hall of Bruges or Brussels. It was five hundred years old, and lately had been repaired with great taste and at great cost ... Opposite was the Church of St. Pierre, dating from the fifteenth century a very noble building, with many chapels filled with carvings of the time of the Renaissance in wood, stone, and iron. In the university were 150,000 volumes.
>
> Outside the station in the public square the people of Louvain passed in an unending procession, women bareheaded, weeping, men carrying the children asleep on their shoulders, all hemmed in by the shadowy army of gray wolves ... These were on their way to be shot ... You felt it was only a

> nightmare, cruel and uncivilized. And then you remembered that the German Emperor has told us what it is. It is his Holy War.[9]

Louvain symbolized French-speaking Catholicism, both because of its ancient treasures and because of its modern refuge for priests, nuns, and monks exiled by the radical government. By levelling it in these initial weeks, the Germans had transformed what might have been just another Franco-Prussian conflict into a 'holy war.'

As in the Dreyfus Affair two decades earlier, religious imagery (holy war, sacrifice, martyrdom, blood redemption) was employed by French people of all religious perspectives (including non-believers) in order to make sense of the war.[10] Jacques Rivière, long-time friend of Gide and secretary of the *N.R.F.*, had converted to Catholicism in 1913. Bereft of his close friend Alain-Fournier and now a prisoner of war, Rivière gave lectures at the Koenigsbrück internment camp, trying to convince his fellow inmates that this war had a larger purpose. 'Man goes to war for a certain way of seeing the world,' he reasoned. Thus, 'all wars are wars of religion. And indeed, who would not rather die than see good and evil, beauty and ugliness, through our enemies' eyes?'[11] Rivière's Catholic vision was echoed by the prominent Jewish intellectual, Victor Basch, founder of the Ligue des Droits de l'Homme et du citoyen after the Dreyfus Affair. In his 1915 report *The War of 1914 and the Law*, Basch concluded: 'This war is the struggle of free peoples, desirous of freedom, against militarism, against imperialism ... That is how this terrible war can become a holy war.'[12] This ability of religious language to unite previously incompatible discourses was graphically captured in a painting by the Jewish artist Lucien Lévy-Dhurmer. In this scene, based on an actual incident, the Rabbi Abraham Bloch of Lyons offered a crucifix to a dying Catholic soldier; in his turn, Rabbi Bloch in fact later died cradled in the arms of a Jesuit priest, Father Jamin.[13] 'Sacred union' made possible a 'holy war.'

Catholics thus shared not only the trauma of the rest of the nation, but their own peculiar confrontation with chaos as well. All citizens of the Republic had to face an unexpected catastrophe; but those who had been so recently opposed to the Republic had an added burden: how to make sense of sacrificing themselves in unimaginably large numbers on behalf of what had been just yesterday their enemy? Abandoning its hostility to the Republic, Catholic discourse would refashion its ancient tropes in order to fulfil its role in the 'sacred union' against the German barbarians and, implicitly, to make meaning of the senseless deaths of Catholic youth.

Maritain and Massis: *Le Sacrifice*

The rapid adaptation of Jacques Maritain's language to the new circumstances provides a prime example of this Catholic refashioning. In late September 1914, a group of German intellectuals published a manifesto entitled 'Appeal to Civilized Nations' that denied, among other things, the truth of charges of atrocities in Louvain.[14] In response, Maritain, who had studied with Driesch in Heidelberg during 1907–8, published an essay in the 25–6 October 1914 issue of *La Croix* entitled 'German Science.' Maritain called German science an 'intellectual monster' whose production would have been impossible without the 'German pantheism that adores the divinized ego.' Both were sustained only by the 'brute force and material domination' of 'German imperialism.'[15]

Several weeks later, Maritain published another piece in *La Croix*, this one a testimonial to his fallen boyhood friend. Identifying himself as 'the oldest and most intimate friend of Ernest Psichari,' Maritain said that he did not want to fail 'this very pure memory.' Maritain used the opportunity to make Catholic peace with the memory of Ernest Renan. If it was true that Psichari had 'hoped in some manner to "redeem his grandfather,"' wrote Maritain, 'it was not in order to grant him amnesty.' Psichari had not seen his grandfather as a criminal; rather, he had 'kept for his grandfather the respect prescribed by the law of God and a sort of compassionate tenderness.'[16] Maritain skilfully gave Psichari's death a redemptive significance for Catholic collective memory – a reconciliation of grandfather and grandson as well as of Republic and Church.

One month later, Maritain embarked on a series of twenty-two lectures given at the Institut Catholique de Paris under the title 'The Role of Germany in Modern Philosophy.'[17] *La Croix* published the first lecture in its entirety, and after that resumés prepared by Maritain himself. For reasons of time, as Maritain concluded in the first lecture, 'We will study only several essential moments, in insisting on the principles, focusing ourselves most of all ... on *Luther* and on *Kant*.'[18] In laying the fault of modern philosophy's errors at the feet of the Germans, Maritain was seriously revising what he had said in lectures given earlier that year – that is, before the start of the war. Then, the original sin had been committed not by a German but by a Frenchman: the rationalist Descartes.

Among the intriguing cultural notes to be found in this massive undertaking was this small item: although German intellectuals liked to claim Beethoven for themselves, 'Beethoven to be precise was Belgian.' The Beethovens, moreover, were 'originally from the surroundings of Louvain,' and 'the grandfather of Beethoven was a chorister at the church of Saint-

Pierre de Louvain.' Though Maritain left unmentioned the recent atrocities there, including the destruction of the fifteenth-century Saint-Pierre, his audience would certainly have made the connection with horror. 'Thus Beethoven, by his genealogy and by his race (if not by his music), is Belgian and not German.'[19]

On 4 August 1915, almost one year to the day after the guns had commenced, Maritain concluded nine months of lectures with a final one dedicated to 'The German Influence in France during the 19th Century.' Asserting that one could already find the 'illusion of German idealism' personified in Mme. de Staël, he noted that she, 'Protestant [and] Genevan in origin,' had referred to herself as having been '*born French with a foreign character*.' This writer of uncertain cultural pedigree had celebrated Germany as 'the country of idealism, of philosophy, of poetry, of depth,' and the French nineteenth century followed her lead.[20] Her infidelity had been preceded by that of Louis XIV: although he had 'perceived the Prussian danger very well' at the end of his life, 'he was too late,' and one could today see 'the final fruit of this long infidelity of Christian kings to the supernatural vocation of France.'

Characteristically, Maritain's proposed solution for the salvation of France was a recovery of Thomas Aquinas: 'It follows from all this, finally, that in order to save our race and intelligence, we must come back to a civilization purely and integrally Catholic. And with respect to that which concerns philosophy in particular, it is not Victor Cousin, nor Auguste Comte, nor Descartes that we must take for our masters, but rather Saint Thomas. *Saint Thomas against Kant!*'[21] Although Maritain's Maurrasian anti-German rhetoric resonated with wartime sentiments, his integralist vitriol intensified his public image as an extreme anti-modernist.[22] Raïssa noted in her journal for mid-November 1915: 'Someone has slandered Jacques to Canon Gaudeau, denouncing him, both him and Bloy, as a *Satanist*. A good cross.'[23]

In the middle of the war, when victory seemed a distant possibility, Henri Massis tried to make sense out of the horror in *The Sacrifice, 1914–1916* (1917).[24] In this work, Massis's entry dated 8 September 1914 reflected on the recent deaths of Péguy, Alain-Fournier, and his dear friend Psichari: 'There are few generations who entered into life with such a feeling of renunciation, of humility. [This generation] knew far in advance and for what reason it was born: and thus the sense of these words that one of us said one day: "*We are*, he said, *a sacrificed generation*."'[25]

Massis divided his book into five chapters: (1) A Sacrificed Generation; (2) The Witness of Charles Péguy; (3) The Life of Ernest Psichari;

(4) Impressions of War (i.e., Massis's own notes from his short tour of duty); (5) The Holocaust. The epigraph quoted Péguy's couplet: 'France is necessary, Christianity must necessarily continue.' How could France and Christianity be reconciled? The answer was to be found in the holocaust offered by the 'sacrificed generation.' Massis made this connection explicit in the interpretation he offered for his friend Psichari's death: 'But God himself already knew the mission for which he had destined his son and the sacrifice for which, in his pity for France, he had reserved this soldier, the son of St. Dominic. Soon after the vows of Ernest Psichari had been made, God laid a claim on him to realize the double vocation which shared his heart: *to immolate himself in the land of his fathers, and to redeem it by this act of reparation.* Because the gift which Ernest Psichari went to offer for the service of the *Patrie* is at the same time a witness rendered to God, an authentic holocaust, "freely consented to and consummated in union with the sacrifice of the altar."'[26] This grisly theodicy had its source in the Bible: God tested Abraham's obedience by ordering him to offer up his only son Isaac as a burnt offering – a holocaust. The British poet Wilfred Owen used the same image in 'The Parable of the Old Man and the Young' to express outrage and bitterness at a generation that sacrificed its sons instead of its Pride. But in Massis's Catholic hand, the visible sacrifice of Psichari, 'united with the altar' of the Mass, was a sacrament – a sign of the invisible sacrifice of Christ. Out of pity for a France in need of redemption, God himself had chosen the victims for the necessary atoning sacrifice. Psichari 'immolated' himself as an 'authentic holocaust,' 'redeeming' the land of his fathers by his act of reparation. He served the Fatherland at the same time that he rendered a 'witness' (the Greek term is *martyros*, i.e., 'martyrdom') to God. Like the high-priest Christ himself, Psichari freely consented to and consummated this holocaust in union with the redemptive sacrifice of the Catholic altar – a sacramental understanding of his life-offering.

Psichari's own words would acquire new meaning as prewar tropes were read in the context of a holy war. He had written a novel before the war (which would be published only posthumously), *The Voices Crying in the Desert*, the title alluding to St John the Baptist: 'For this is he that was spoken of by Isaias the prophet, saying: *A voice of one crying in the desert, Prepare ye the way of the Lord, make straight his paths.*'[27] Psichari had transformed his colonial 'men of the desert' into nomadic prophets proclaiming the end-times, and his image of sacrificial blood had carried a very specific meaning: 'France's political crimes are atoned for, and in full, by the blood we spill in the colonies. It is an image of the Redemption.'[28] In 1913, Psichari meant blood that would atone for the Republic's 'crimes' against the Church. But since the book appeared only after the war, these lines seemed to prophesy the blood to be spilled not in the colonies but in trenches on France's own soil – spilled in a war of religion, not against the enemy Republic, but rather in a holy one on that same Republic's behalf.

The ancient idea of sacrifice, employed to put meaning back into a chaotic encounter, would be used not only by elites like Maritain, Massis, and Psichari, but shared by many others, including young Catholic soldiers themselves.

Testimony from the Trenches: *Le Renouveau catholique: Youth During the War*

Letters from these Catholic soldiers were gathered and published for public edification in the fervent work of the Abbé Louis Rouzic. As a chaplain at a Jesuit school for young Catholic men of the upper classes being prepared for the Grandes écoles, Rouzic wrote many books in which he rhetorically appealed to the 'elite.' Evident in his own writing, as well as in the letters written to him, is an implicit understanding: these privileged young men were trained to imagine themselves as a French Catholic vanguard called to regenerate the nation. Like many other soldiers sending the *lettres de poilus* from the trenches, these bright and articulate men wrote Rouzic from the front lines and P.O.W. camps, sharing their experiences and asking advice of their former chaplain.[29] Certainly, being students at a school from which the Jesuit teaching faculty had earlier been expelled – Rouzic was a diocesan priest, not a Jesuit[30] – these young soldiers would have been immersed in Catholic sentiment with respect to the Republic. Yet, as Rouzic's collection of excerpted letters clearly shows, they saw themselves as involved in a great and holy cause, destined to bring about the religious regeneration of their country.

Rouzic had planned a three-volume work entitled *The Renouveau catholique* and subtitled *Youth Before the War*, *Youth During the War*, and *Youth After the War*. In 1919, the first two volumes were realized and functioned as a memorial.[31] In *Youth Before the War*, Rouzic summarized pre-war Catholic revivalism and its struggle against the dominant culture. Quoting the nineteenth-century chemist Berthelot, Rouzic complained that positivistic science proclaimed the necessity of observation and limited itself solely to 'facts and the relations between facts ... the indefinite prolongation of life; the total domination of nature; scientific morality giving everything at once a rule of conduct, a sociology, and a politic; an understanding of the future equal to that of the past; the conquest of happiness, finally realizing all the aspirations of human nature; in brief, paradise on earth. In conformity with these results and these expectations, the motto of scientism, formulated by Berthelot, was: "From now on the world is without mystery," because the mystery which still remains today will evaporate tomorrow.'[32] The narrative was a standard one, a history of fall and decline from supernaturalism into positivist realism and its eradication of 'mystery' during the nineteenth century.

But Rouzic's narrative of mystery's eclipse acquired moral urgency from his second volume containing excerpts from letters that soldiers had sent him from the front.[33] Within this poignant setting, the pre-war complaint against positivism's refusal to ask ultimate questions took on a new wartime meaning. For the reader would have understood that a good many of these authors, having died in the trenches, would have to hope for their paradise, if anywhere, in a mysterious beyond. The abstract metaphysical discourse suddenly took on a horribly concrete character as these alumni, some still adolescents, attempted to discern meaning in and draw significance from their war experience.

The alumni soldiers drew upon two sources of inherited religious tropes: on the one hand, the call for renaissance, regeneration, and 'a new life' had already been issued during that now-distant Easter of 1914. On the other hand, an ancient vocabulary of sacrifices, holocausts, and redemptive blood offerings – making sense of the blood shed by Catholics for the Republic – provided new reasons demanding conversions to compensatory forms of life. Taken together, these discourses composed a theology of blood demanding justification in the form of a resurrected France.

Rouzic framed the theme of blood offerings as the means of national regeneration by quoting from Father Pierre Olivaint, S.J., a graduate of the École normale supérieure who later converted to Catholicism, a great educator who left teaching to work with the poor. Olivaint was one of five Jesuits massacred along with about fifty other hostages on 26 May 1871 at the end of the Paris Commune. Dragged through the streets by a mob from their prison to Belleville, the hostages were 'shot in screaming chaos, "like rabbits," as one witness put it, running in all directions ... one body had been peppered with sixty-nine bullets.'[34] Before his death, Olivaint had written: 'The blood of a God is precious indeed, but precious also is the blood of man, in spite of original sin. Learn "to honor your blood." Blood has been given to you to serve your soul. It gives the most generous life possible to your organs, by way of your heart. It has been given you in order to serve your family, sacrificing yourself for family, maintaining its nobility and honor. This is your vocation, on earth and in heaven. *Blood has been given to you for the regeneration of France* ...'[35] Olivaint most certainly knew Tertullian's ancient proverb: *sanguis martyrum semen christianorum* – The blood of the martyrs is the seed (literally: *semen*) of new Christians.

Olivaint's theology of martyrdom had been internalized by students at the Jesuit school.[36] A certain H. de V. wrote, 'I hope that this new year will give us victory and will see, finally, a planting in France of a harvest of grace which all the sacrifices allow us to hope for, which all the heroic blood will water. So that at the end of this war, France, by its living and by its dead, will be close to God.' Another alumnus, Albert, awaiting demobilization, quoted his chaplain who told his charges 'it was necessary that the blood which had to flow in expiation was pure, for only in this way can it be associated with the redemptive blood of Jesus Christ. The best have fallen so that those who survive might become the best.' Albert added: 'May it be so.'

The use of the word 'pure,' especially in the linkage of blood with fertilization, is multivalent: adolescent sexual virtue, instilled in the religious school, evoked connotations of both ancient Christian virgin-martyrs as well as primitive expiatory sacrifices (cf. Stravinsky's *The Rite of Spring*, 1913). Moreover, 'pure blood' suggested fears of 'mythologies of heredity' familiar to the bourgeoisie, terrors over degeneration through tainted blood, especially via the loss of 'vital fluids.'[37] Only unpolluted blood, shed by society's 'best,' would enable those who survived also to become an elite. Rouzic contributed his own thoughts along these lines. 'But if a young man, forgetful of these truths and these obligations, descends into corruption and turns this force given for fecund conquests into a murderous will, where then is the utility of his blood? *Quae utilitas in sanguine meo, dum descendo in corruptionem?*'[38]

Not only did the blood need to be uncorrupted, but the reborn nation itself had to be 'ideal,' free of all contingent imperfections. René de R. declared his 'courage and confidence in an ideal France regenerated by all the sacrifices.' Robert added that 'the victory and birth of a new France,' glimpsed in 'a future more or less drawing near,' was 'the consolation of those who fall.' In contrast to a bitterly 'modern' sense of irony found in other writings of Great War soldiers,[39] the utter disproportion between what had been expected and what was eventually experienced induced not irony but apocalypse in these young French Catholic soldiers. The sacrifices made being irredeemable in this world, the only possible just outcome had to be eschatological: the blood 'pure,' the remnant an 'elite,' the nation 'ideal,' 'a new heaven and a new earth.'

One also senses what we might call, in retrospect, a 'survivor's guilt': if the best had been killed, what did that mean for those who had been spared? How could such a slaughter of the best and the brightest be redeemed? 'This miraculous war is opening up a marvelous future for us,' wrote Lieutenant Antoine to his young comrades of the First Division. 'You may give free reign to your youthful exuberance: you will never be able to dream dreams beautiful enough to give you an idea of the reality of tomorrow.' However, he also tempered his enthusiasm with a call to future duty: '*Postards*, the Fatherland has already asked a great deal of you. Be assured that it will ask much more of you ... France no longer asks you to die for her; she asks you to be Christians.' In this strange hyperbole – that being asked to live a genuinely Christian life is somehow commensurate with being asked to die – feelings of guilt for having survived into the joyful future are assuaged. Antoine (perhaps the same Lieutenant) made this sense of expiation explicit: 'I am not the first to say that the best were the ones who died. They fulfilled in their own manner the mission of renewal which has been allotted to each *Postard*. As for the others, it must be fulfilled by their word and by example.' What better hope could one have for the new year than that the alma mater would 'play its role in the re-Christianization of France.'

Some writers show a keen sense of being part of an elite within an elected 'race.' 'The French race,' wrote André, 'has demonstrated too many beautiful virtues in the course of this war not to comprehend that these virtues alone are true and fecund: that order, discipline, and conscience alone permit a society to live. And all those who have made war will know well, I believe, how to make others comprehend the same.' Writing in the new year of 1919, Octave also hoped for 'a year of order, a year of reorganization, a year of union' on which the very life of France depended. Marcel too felt that 'order' needed to be the postwar mission, but it was an order filled with futuristic dynamism: 'Energy, energy, that must be the word of order. Fertile energy, the desire to create something; whatever that might be, let's hope that it will be something which will serve the life of the nation, its material or spiritual life.' Asking himself 'what profound influence will these 4 years of war leave upon our race?' Marcel answered, 'I believe the country leaves the war with confidence in itself, with its pride (in the best sense of that word) increased ten-fold. We can be proud of ourselves. The metal of our race has undergone the heaviest of tests. After everything, no one has found the flaws that others had hoped to see there.' After the war, it would be necessary for this action to 'prolong and maintain itself, to form the men who are necessary to us, if we do not wish France to die from its 1,500,000 dead!'

Indeed, the war's outcome afforded these young French Catholics (unlike their Austrian-German counterparts) the luxury of interpreting victory as flowing from the fundamentally religious character of its soldiers and leaders. 'What beautiful days we are living in! and with what *élan* the soul constantly sings the *Te Deum* in spirit!' exclaimed Xavier, alluding to the ancient Christian hymn of thanksgiving, *Te Deum laudamus*: 'We praise thee, O God: we acknowledge thee to be the Lord... The noble army of Martyrs praises thee.' God had 'not permitted the triumph of injustice,' and France's victory was 'due to the sacrifice of all those élites, that is, to the incessant prayer of Christians of all ages.'

But perhaps even more, the outcome was due to the Republic's military having been led by 'great Christians like Pétain and above all Foch.' The 'Holy Spirit [had] particularly inspired' them, and for their part, they had 'never ceased imploring divine light and assistance.' Perhaps every nation-state associates its will with the divine will, but the startling character of the French identification of God's will with Pétain's and Foch's can be grasped when contrasted with the theology of the vanquished, best illustrated in Karl Barth's 1922 *The Epistle to the Romans* (*Der Römerbrief*). 'The Gospel proclaims a God utterly distinct from men,' declared Barth (inflecting the 'Protestant principle' via Kierkegaard). 'We who stand in this concrete world know nothing, and are incapable of knowing anything, of that point above, and the corresponding discerning of it from below ... Therefore the power of God can be detected neither in the world of nature nor in the souls of men. It must not be confounded with any high, exalted force, known or knowable ...We mistake time for eternity. That is our disobedience ...'[40]

At the end of 1918, the postwar task had only just begun. 'The War is finished, but France is not saved,' wrote an unnamed student. 'Having vanquished her enemies, it is against herself that we must now defend.'[41] M.A. agreed: the 'victory' was 'above all the victory of France against the demon. [Since] the two victories, the one against the Demon and the other against the Kraut, are one in solidarity, the two battles must also be united as one. *Postards* must be both in their mind: Christians and French.'[42] Rouzic set these letters within an overall frame appealing to

Catholic veterans who would go to the Grandes écoles and continue the work of Christianizing the nation. Quoting Charles Péguy (as Massis had in *The Sacrifice*), Rouzic argued that the postwar mission included the reunion of Catholicism with the nation: '"It is necessary that France continue; it is necessary that Christianity continue" – from beyond the tomb the eloquent and patriotic voice of Péguy still cries out to us. But France cannot continue without Christianity, and Christianity, which does not come from us, can nevertheless only continue by us.' Using a hylomorphic metaphor of the organism informed by an *entelechy*, Rouzic imagined the two as interpenetrating: 'France and Christianity, it is all one, and Catholicism is an integrating part of the French soul [*une partie intégrante de l'âme française*]. It is by Christians above all that France will live and prosper.' To the testimony of Péguy, Rouzic added Bishop Jacques-Bénigne Bossuet, the seventeenth-century Gallican absolutist: 'Didn't Bossuet formulate this law of survival for modern nations: "Peoples will only endure if there are an elect who will pull the multitude along"?' Rouzic drew this conclusion for those in the Grandes écoles: 'Well then, think how necessary it is to propagate among ourselves the race of the elect.'[43]

In sum: the discourse of a 'call to order' and 'a new life' for France was already present by Easter 1914. Four years later, the organic and integralist language remained the same but its meaning had been utterly changed: before the war, the fragmentation of the body politic was owed to warring civil factions; now, its fragmentation was due to the heavy mutilations suffered from an external enemy. Since bodily mutilation as reality and metaphor showed up everywhere in the *mutilés de guerre*, 'integrity' would remain a key word in post-war France. In a 1918 essay reflecting on the repatriation of lands lost since 1870 in the Franco-Prussian war, René Doumic wrote in *La Revue des deux mondes*, 'Since the day when Alsace-Lorraine was taken away from her, [France] was unable to return to health. Healed at last of the wound that has been so grievously suffered, *re-established in her integrity*, made greater by four years of heroism, [France] rediscovers her balance and reclaims her rank among nations.'[44] Paradoxically, France's integral health, restored by the return of such metaphorically amputated bodily parts, had been accomplished only by the literal mutilation of her soldiers.

In this context, the prewar call to order would become a mode of memorialization and a vehicle of mourning – an attempt to make sense out of and even justify the slaughter of so many Catholics in a 'war of religion' fought on behalf of the same Republic. Writing in the *Echo de*

Paris and reflecting on the fallen, Paul Deschanel expressed the problem for survivors: 'we will be truly worthy of the Patrie saved by your courage only if we hold our souls up to the level of your virtue.'[45]

France's salvation had come at the price of a generation; the postwar task was 'to save it again in order to be worthy of the war's sacrifice.'[46] Perhaps no one exerted as great an effort to make France seem worthy of the name 'Catholic' than Monsignor Alfred Baudrillart, rector of the Institut Catholique.

Monsignor Baudrillart: The 'Catholic Committee of French Propaganda'

Not only at home but abroad, too, there was the serious task of refashioning a 'Catholic France' in order to rally the support of foreign Catholics. German-speaking Catholic propaganda efforts had convinced coreligionists in countries outside France, especially in neutral countries like the United States, that France was a bitterly 'atheistic' and anti-Catholic state. Implicitly, they were urged to cast their sympathies with the Catholic Austro-Hungarian Empire and its German ally. In response to this serious problem, Maritain's superior, Monsignor Baudrillart, rector of the Institut Catholique de Paris, found his own life suddenly altered. As he would later recall in his diary, his 1907 installation as rector had been 'in the midst of open war between Church and State.' No one at that time could have 'predicted the role that these greats events' of the war would lead him 'to play in the defense of the *patrie*.'[47]

In addition to his personal production of a truly astonishing number of wartime works in a propaganda effort on behalf of the Republic – including *The Soul of France at Reims* (1914), *Joan the Liberator* (1915), and *Jerusalem Delivered* (1917)[48] – Baudrillart also founded the Comité Catholique de Propagande Française à l'Étranger (Catholic Committee of French Propaganda Abroad). The committee's objectives and method were best summarized in the 1915 work, *The German War and Catholicism*, published simultaneously in English, Italian, Spanish, Portuguese, Dutch, and German translations. The book was prefaced by a letter from Cardinal Amette, the Archbishop of Paris, who wrote: 'In this hour ... all [France's] sons must desire to defend the justice of her cause and her titles to the esteem of the civilized world, before the eyes of the nations not engaged in the struggle.' Readers from neutral nations would be convinced that France remained 'faithful to her ancient role of Guardian of Right and Protectress of Civilization,' and that in spite of her faults and errors, she had not 'ceased to be worthy of the title which the Popes, from Anastasius down to Leo XIII, Pius X and Benedict XV have bestowed on her.' She remained 'the eldest Daughter of the Church.'[49] We can surmise that France's claim as 'Eldest Daughter' found a more sympathetic reception abroad than 'protectress of civilization.'

Baudrillart also wrote an introductory essay for the book, happily calling it a 'book of French propaganda ... addressed especially to the Catholics of the neutral countries.' He admitted to being among 'the first to deplore' those 'certain exterior acts' (presumably the Act of Separation) that had led others to 'believe that France has ceased to be a Christian and Catholic nation.' They had also been 'deceived' by the untrue declarations of France's enemies into imagining that 'Germany and Austria, now alas! the satellite of Germany, represent in the world the cause of order, authority, religion,' and that a Central Powers' victory, rather than France's, 'would be favourable to the sacred interests of Catholicism.'[50]

Baudrillart produced a formidable list of Catholic notables in both political and ecclesiastical spheres in order to reassure readers that churchgoing Catholics played key roles in the most influential places of the French state. Then he curiously signed this introduction, not as the rector of the Institut Catholique de Paris but rather as 'Recteur de l'Université catholique' (in the French edition) and 'Rector of the Catholic University' (in the English). Since the title 'Catholic University' had been outlawed by the Ferry Laws of the 1880s, for nearly thirty years the Francophone l'Université catholique had referred primarily to the Catholic University of Louvain. Perhaps Baudrillart meant his signature to evoke the destruction of Louvain; or perhaps it was his unilateral reversal of anticlerical legislation.

The book was a collection of essays ranging over many topics, including Christian just war theory, the German destruction of churches, and roles that clergy played in the French military. In 'The Catholic Role of France in the World,' a writer signed 'A Missionary' suggested that Otto von Bismarck, 'having experienced that religious strife in a country is an inexhaustible source of dissensions and weakness,' had injected France 'with this virus' that had 'poisoned and disfigured' it, leading Catholics abroad to say, 'Look at these atheists, these degenerates!'[51]

The missionary countered this impression: 'As soon as the cannon's powerful voice was heard at the frontier, the Sacred Union was formed' and the country's 'official label' of atheism was torn off. The world could then see that 'beneath an artificial France apparently in decay' lay 'another France' that had been 'partly hidden' but which 'represented the country' more faithfully. 'All of a sudden the old race returned to itself and revealed to the surprised world what lay concealed in the depths of her children's baptized souls.' Joan of Arc, concluded the missionary, 'must have recognized her blood!'[52]

In another essay, the anticlerical legislation was recast as an act of Providence – a kind of Trojan horse brought into the city centre that would lead to the re-Christianization of France. The anticlericals had recalled exiled clergy to serve not only as chaplains but also as stretcher-bearers and nurses. As the wounded soldier came into 'contact with the orderly-priest,' he would have 'the impression of being understood, loved, comforted ... the whole saturated with confidence in God and a supernatural atmosphere.' The writer exclaimed: 'How Providence loves to baffle all human calculations! The politicians never guessed that the law of the *curés sac au dos* [priests with knapsacks] was going to give the priest's ministry a new field of action and means, hitherto unknown of, by which to reach souls ... [This gives] one of our firmest reasons for hoping that God will give us the victory and bring back the whole of France to its Christian traditions.'[53]

In addition to convincing Catholics *abroad* that the soul of France remained religious, Baudrillart knew that Catholics on the home front needed conversion as well. In 1918, his Propaganda Committee published a large volume entitled *Catholic Life in Contemporary France*. Not translated into other languages, its French text was intended for domestic consumption. Its organization was panoramic, providing articles on multiple aspects of 'Catholic life' in social, cultural, and intellectual spheres: 'Religious life,' 'The Family,' 'The Social Catholic Movement,' 'Religious Sciences,' 'The Renaissance of Christian Philosophy,' 'Literature,' and 'Christian Art in the Confines of the 19th and 20th Centuries.' The book aimed at demonstrating that Catholicism really was the animating principle of the nation, pulsating with life in every conceivable reach of the body politic.[54]

In his contributed essay, Abbé Georges Michelet, professor at the Institut Catholique of Toulouse, proclaimed a 'Renaissance of Christian Philosophy in France.' In their 1912 work *The Young People of Today*, Massis and de Tarde had associated fin-de-siècle Sorbonne relativism with German idealism. Following their lead, Michelet too passed over in silence his French compatriots Comte, Taine, and Charcot, concluding that 'this universal relativism' had been a foreign import. 'German subjectivism, Kantian doctrines above all, came to know a new period of triumph over French thought' bringing a 'great wave of idealism, of relativity and subjectivism.' This intellectual wave posed grave challenges to genuine realism – 'the real, the objective, the metaphysical.' Alluding to the completely devastated French countryside of 1917, Michelet hyperbolically concluded that the intellectual waste had been even worse than the physical: 'This new German invasion, under the form of idealism and of subjectivism, has come to pile up as many ruins – and these less reparable – than the brutal invasion by the army.'[55]

In this new context, since German aggression seemed to have verified all the ominous predictions of the past century, old Catholic arguments about the nature of realism could seem newly relevant. 'Each new generation turns itself toward different idols,' continued Michelet, and after the industrial advances of the 1840s, the epoch of 1860–80 had fostered a 'cult' of the *Religion of Science* in science, history, and psychology. Positivism in science had exalted 'the fact before everything, the fact alone, the exclusion of all causes and of substances, a horror of rationality, the disappearance of the great problems which have tormented humanity for such a long time; in its place, Science – the scientific fact, the scientific law, key to all mysteries, the foundation of all hopefulness. The program was simple, in fact, it had a puerile simplicity.'[56] Since science could never ask metaphysical questions about 'why' the world was as it was, but only empirical ones about 'how' it worked, 'positivism seemed to be only an expression of positive science when it was in fact the deformation of science.' Although positivism pretended to be an 'apparent neutrality affirming a universal relativity,' in reality it was exclusive: 'everywhere the same atheistic and materialistic metaphysics underlying everything. And in defiance of French common sense, almost never enunciated.'[57] As for psychology, the creation of a psychology-without-a-psyche meant a sleight of hand: physiology masquerading as psychology, explaining all inner experience by means of materialist interpretations.

Michelet's essay bridged the past and the future: it discredited the old anticlerical regime by tracing its source to the German enemy; and it mapped out a topography in which Catholic questions of meaning, causality, and mystery could once again have significance in a postwar – and post-positivist – world. History was on his side: Einstein and Freud, prophets of the new modernism's occult indeterminacy, were about to begin their reign in 'The Invisible Century.'[58]

In his preface to this volume, Baudrillart explicitly referred to it as the third of his committee's trilogy: *The German War and Catholicism* (1915), *Germany and the Allies before Christian Conscience* (1916), and *Catho-*

lic Life in Contemporary France (1918). After one had read this third work, it seemed to Baudrillart that 'one would have to arrive at the conclusion that, in spite of the faults of official France, there is not a country in the world where Catholic life is more intense, more rich, and more fruitful in its works.'[59] Both at home and abroad, Baudrillart's skilful use of the publishing house made an enormous contribution to reimagining French Catholicism as something both thoroughly patriotic and vital to the *patrie*. The nation's élite would reward Baudrillart after the war by electing him to its pantheon of immortals.

'*Réconciliations nécessaires*': Baudrillart and the Académie Française

The French celebrated Bastille Day in July 1919 with a mid-summer 'Festival of Victory.' The centrepiece was to be a festive parade down the Champs-Élysées, which suddenly became a procession of the mutilated: 'one thousand of France's *mutilés de guerre*, horribly wounded and disfigured veterans, led the victory procession ... assisted by an assortment of canes, crutches, prosthetics and small vehicles.'[60] As these fragmented bodies filed in front of young women from the repatriated lands of Alsace-Lorraine, the veterans' missing limbs provided a symbolic representation of France's repatriated parts. Maurice Barrès made sense of the ironic spectacle by locating it within the larger context of the sacred union: 'The socialist deputy Brunet, pointing out a badly wounded chaplain being helped by another wounded man, said to me, 'There is the symbol of our union."'[61] Clearly, the war had changed France: former antagonisms had lost their salience, the body politic needed integration, and the Church was yet another part of the *patrie* in need of 'repatriation.'

Within this larger context, the 10 April 1919 reception of Monsignor Alfred Baudrillart as an 'immortal' into the Académie française can be viewed as one of the first postwar acts of restoration. The choice of Baudrillart to fill the seat vacated by the death of Comte Albert de Mun was highly symbolic, for his predecessor had also been a reconciler: a Catholic who had tried to implement Leo XIII's social teachings by organizing workers' associations, and a fervent nationalist politician in the Third Republic.

Marcel Prévost's discourse welcoming Baudrillart to the Académie underscored the rector's gift for reconciliation: tracing Baudrillart's life from childhood to the present, Prévost noted especially the cleric's dual faithfulness to both papacy and Republic during the Modernist Crisis, the Act of Separation, and the Great War. By founding his Propaganda Committee, Baudrillart had begun his 'wonderful campaign as French priest and patriot.' Until then, German Catholics 'had been able to freely poison their co-religionists throughout the entire world' with their 'ferocious propaganda.' However, in the committee's work and Baudrillart's own *The German War and Catholicism* – which, Prévost noted, the German bishops tried (unsuccessfully) to have Pope Benedict XV condemn! – the 'French spirit of clarity did not waste any time in triumphing over the impudent Germanic hodgepodge.' Thus, Baudrillart had proven himself a man cast in his predecessor's mould, another 'fervent Catholic' who simultaneously 'understood the necessities of modern society.' It was not a question of wanting modernity 'to blindly dominate' Catholicism; rather, it was 'necessary to bring them into accord' with one another. Albert de Mun had been 'one of the great workers of reappraisal, *of necessary reconciliations*.' This mantle, 'heavy with duty, heavy with hope,' was now passed on to Baudrillart.[62]

Baudrillart's life history had effected in his own person the very syntheses making him the ideal candidate for this postwar task. His personality was a product of 'the École Normale, of the University, of liberalism in the laicist sense of the word'; yet, 'at the very same time,' he was a product of 'the Catholic faith, of Scholastic philosophy, and of Vatican discipline.' Prévost pleaded with the cleric to extend this personal synthesis to his fatherland: 'You who are a bourgeois of Paris and have become a dignitary of Rome – will you not come to the aid of those around you and bring peace to [those oppositions] which in the end reached accord within you?' Two powers were dividing France: on the one hand, the Catholic Church said confidently, 'I have before me eternity'; on the other hand, 'democracy, which has just won the war,' could not make 'a claim quite as long' as eternity, but it was 'still able to count on a long future.' 'Oh! Monsieur,' exclaimed Prévost, 'for the peace of the world, for the happiness of generations both present and future, aid them in their reconciliation! You have access close to the representatives of each one of these two worldly forces: tell them that it is necessary to lay down their arms, to understand each other, to support one another.'[63]

Using overtly Catholic language, Prévost concluded his discourse with an appeal to this embodiment of France's national laicist *esprit*: 'Let us all make our examination of conscience, and, with a soul sincere and without venom, let us march, reconciled Frenchmen, toward the peace promised to men of good will!'[64] 'Examination of conscience' is the technical term for the internal review one undergoes before receiving Catholic sacramental confession; the 'reconciled soul' alludes to the absolved penitent; the 'peace promised to men of good will' quotes the Christmas gospel. Although there likely lingered a good deal of 'venom' at that ceremony, nevertheless the halls of the Académie française itself, protector of the purity of the French language, echoed with the continued employment of religious language made ubiquitous by the war.

The Vatican Vote: Restoring 'Relations Which Should Never Have Been Broken'

In November 1920, two years to the month after the armistice, the 'Vatican question' – that is, whether France's diplomatic relations with the Holy See should be restored – was being debated in the Chamber of Deputies. Ultimately they were restored, due in part to the rightist *bloc national* that had been voted into parliament just after the armistice. Many contemporaries, viewing it within the long-term picture of Church-State conflict, must have seen it as a regressive and nostalgic embrace of tradition, a devolution from the laicist advances of 1901–5. However, viewing the debate within a more acute context of trauma and bereavement, we can see it as one element of mourning and memorialization.

Headlines from the *Petit Parisien* during the week of the tumultuous parliamentary debate demonstrate to what extent the war was far from over: questions over the 'right to work' for the *mutilés de guerre*; controversy over the proposed tomb for the Unknown Soldier to be place at the Arc de Triomphe; reports of money laundered through Dutch banks for Hohenzollerns in exile; accounts of coal rationing as the cold winter approached; a milk shortage in Paris blamed on the cows that Germany had 'kidnapped from us'; the National Loan drive underway to pay off the war debt; and two articles concerning French bodies on foreign soil – one pointing out the problem of reclaiming those buried in Germany, the other suggesting the creation of monuments as sepulchres for those bodies.[65] In other words, the debate over restoring relations with the Vatican took place within a context of ongoing misery: bodies needed to be recovered and buried; the marble business boomed as memorials were built; and everyday trials of shortages, rampant inflation, unemployment, and unrest prolonged the sufferings of the war into the present. Within this context, a discourse of monuments and the need to repair memory were not mere nostalgia or regression, but a vehicle for the fight among factions over how to assign significance, wholeness, and ultimately, identity, to the nation's fragmented self. France, a *mutilé de guerre*, had much to grieve. In shaping its present for the future, it needed to reincorporate its past.

In its coverage of the deputies' 'tumultuous debate' on the 'Vatican Question,' the *Petit Parisien* reported that members of both the right and left contributed to a 'lively, passionate, and sometimes stormy' discussion. Léon Daudet, the virulent monarchist and editor-in-chief of *L'Action française*, cried out amid a 'deafening pandemonium' that the laicist laws of 1901–5 had been 'a Kraut politics!' An outraged member of the left responded: 'You are letting yourself say that the politics of the republican governments were a German politics?' Daudet repeated his charge: 'I said that the anti-clerical politics were a politics of German origin. Everyone knows that they were the politics of Bismarck in France, and that the pages written in denunciation [of the Church] were at the same time pages written in treason.'[66]

On 1 December 1920, in spite of such open hostilities, the deputies voted to restore relations with the Vatican by a margin of 397 to 209. The delegates were largely persuaded by the 'testament of a deceased' as it was delivered by Deputy Georges Leygues. Addressing his 'colleagues of the extreme left,' Leygues invoked the name of Albert Thierry, 'dead for France at the battle of Arras.' Thierry, 'a man who taught, an *instituteur*, socialist, syndicalist, [and] laicist,' had 'desired that his final thought be made public': namely, that the state 'must, after the war, take care of the churches like monuments precious to its heart and re-establish with the Catholic International of Rome those relations which should never have been broken. (Loud applause from the center, the right and among diverse rows in the left.)' Thierry's legal instruction carried the gravest possible weight: 'Laws have always been given to the people from the summits of mountains,' Leygues recalled. And who had 'climbed higher than our dead? (Loud applause from numerous rows.).'[67]

As part of a complex process of bereavement and memorialization, the monuments Thierry referred to can be seen both literally and metaphorically. The literal monuments were the church buildings confiscated as state property in the law of 1905. The metaphorical 'monument' was the restoration of France's place within the wider 'Catholic International' and, conversely, the repatriation of the severed Church to the French body politic. The Act of Separation had been published on 9 December 1905. Fifteen years later, dualistic polemic had lost much of its force. Only by weaving the seemingly meaningless loss into the pattern of a new larger story could the intervening sacrifice be assigned significance. The

Vatican restoration was, in the end, an act of making meaning: bereavement, mourning, memorialization, and monument building.

Paul Doncoeur: 'France has thrown us out' – Never again.

Four years later, Father Paul Doncoeur, S.J., made the same sort of blood-price argument for synthesis rather than division. In 1924, domestic and diplomatic crises challenged the recently elected left-leaning coalition [*Cartel des Gauches*] governed by the radical Prime Minister Edouard Herriot. Thinking that anticlerical measures might help rally the fractured left, Herriot sought to extend the laws of 1905 to the now-repatriated lands of Alsace, and even suggested the re-expulsion of members of religious orders according to the 1901 Law of Associations. Doncoeur, a Jesuit priest who had lived as an exile before the war, served at the front, and survived as a decorated *mutilé de guerre*, was also a gifted writer and editor at the Jesuit *Études*. In August 1924, actively associated with the DRAC (Ligue de défense des droits des religieux anciens combattants / League for the Defense of the Rights of Religious Veterans), Doncoeur used his literary skills to assist in a widespread counter-offensive against Herriot.[68]

The most celebrated document of this effort was Doncoeur's open letter to Herriot entitled *For the Honor of France ... We Will Not Leave!* First appearing on 23 October 1924, the letter was timed to follow the Herriot government's recent decision to grant amnesty for wartime deserters, and to appear just prior to the 11 November ceremonies that would commemorate the sixth anniversary of the armistice. It was soon republished in multiple venues, including *Peuple de France*, *La Victoire*, *La Croix*, *L'Écho de Paris*, and *Les Débats*. Taking charge of the publicity campaign, the DRAC had posters printed on 9 November: beneath giant letters proclaiming WE WILL NOT LEAVE was Doncoeur's letter, accompanied by an illustration of a seriously wounded military chaplain, missing one leg and leaning on his cane. With financial assistance provided by a fund-raising campaign launched by *Le Nouvelliste* of Lyon, the posters went up on walls all over the country on 10 November, just in time for the armistice commemorations.

Doncoeur's prose oozed sarcasm: Herriot had made the 'grand gesture of opening wide the two arms of France, still dripping with blood.'[69] He had granted amnesty to all the 'deserters and traitors' through this 'open door,' and Doncoeur applauded this healing act if it meant that the guilty would come back to serve and pay reparations to the nation. However, Herriot had now proposed to 'show this same door' to all the 'poor devils of religious orders' who had been recalled from exile 'on 4 August 1914 for battle.' Defiantly, Doncoeur issued his response: 'And so, no, we will not leave. Not a man, not an old man, not a novice, not a single woman is going to cross those borders once again.'

Doncoeur reminded his readers that France had called religious members back from their exile for the most callous of reasons: it needed male bodies at the front. He himself had been one of those: 'In 1901, when the infamous law was voted, I was an extremely young Jesuit; – it had only been four years since my father, an officer who had served in Africa, drove me to the novitiate of Saint-Acheul.' Doncoeur 'did what all the others did' and went into exile in Belgium, 'filled with shame.' From the age of twenty-two to thirty-four, Doncoeur lived 'all of my life as a man' in exile – for this, he said to Herriot, 'I pardon you.'

But that all changed at four in the morning on 2 August 1914. Even though he had been declared unfit for service, he said to his religious superior: '*Tomorrow is the war, my place is in the fire.*' With his superior's blessing, he 'headed with the cannon all the way to Verdun.' At daybreak on 20 August (incidentally, the day Psichari was killed), 'thirty paces away' from the German post, Doncoeur was 'enveloped by the crackle of twenty rifles' and saw his 'comrade completely stretched out, across from me, on the road, his head crushed.' At this moment, he sensed that 'my heart was protecting my entire country. Never had I breathed in the air of France with this pride, nor had I ever set my foot upon its soil with such assurance.'

In contrast to Doncoeur, Herriot had not served in the War – a point made abundantly clear as Doncoeur offered a travelogue of the battlefields on which he served while Herriot never showed up at the front. As one of the 'soldiers of Verdun,' Doncoeur had not succumbed to any 'fear of bullets, nor of gas, nor of the bravest German soldiers.' He was most certainly not now 'going to have any fear of political ambushes.' Thus, he concluded, 'I am going to tell you now why we are not leaving':

> We are not going because we no longer want a Belgian, or an Englishman, or an American, or a Chinese, or a German – encountering us one day far from our country – to pose to us certain questions to which we must respond, as we did before, while lowering our heads [in shame]: 'France has thrown us out.'
>
> For the honor of France – do you understand this term as I understand it? – for the honor of France, *never* will we say such a thing again to a foreigner. Therefore, we are all staying.
>
> This we swear on the tomb of our dead.

Doncoeur signed his letter as an 'Officer of the Legion of Honor. Former Chaplain of the 14th Division.' His letter embodied the discourse of bereavement, an attempt to make sense of the chaos. Arguing against a return to the old dualisms and invoking both the literal monument ('the tomb of our dead') and the metaphorical 'monument' of France's self-identity, his manifesto pointed to synthesis as the way out of fragmentation.

The defiant gesture had a success that went far beyond anything its organizers could have hoped for. In the end, Herriot's attempts failed: the religious were never expelled, and the laws of 1905 have never been extended to Alsace – it remains to this day a repatriated limb frozen in amber, embodying pre-1870 France. Herriot's own left wing had bigger fish to fry with internal struggles over Leninism after 1917, and they remained largely unmoved by the anticlerical lure. Unexpectedly, the episode led instead to a consolidation of the centre and right that enabled a 'second *ralliement*' of Church and State. 'Time and the wartime *union sacrée* had done their work,' concludes Gordon Wright; 'the extreme right had accepted the secular republic, the Moderate right-center was prepared to meet it halfway.'[70]

However, more than time was at work. In each of these post-war discourses – Prévost's plea to Baudrillart, the invocation of Thierry's last will and testament, Doncoeur's remembrance of blood-sacrifices – we see the underlying presumption that France, if it was to be healed and move on, needed to reconcile itself with a Catholic portion that had been partly lost, repressed, or destroyed. Herriot's attempt to recover old dualisms was the very type of a 'melancholic' or 'apocalyptic' imagination – in Freud's terms, an act of repression or 'foreclosure' (*Verwerfung*) and the disavowal or 'casting out' (*verwerfen*) of unacceptable material in service of a false sense of a unitary self. However, the work of grief (*Trauerarbeitung*) requires rewriting narratives that make peace with lost parts of oneself. France needed to grieve, and a dualistic imagination cannot mourn.[71]

A new generation imagined itself as capable of dialectically reconciling what had earlier been impossible: of being both *réaliste* and *mystique* at the same time. The time of severing and purging was over. It was a time for synthesis.

Chapter 3

Mystic Realism: A Faith That Faced the Facts

What is wanting, apparently, is the tragic imagination that, through communal form or ceremony, permits great loss to be recognized, suffered, and borne, and that makes possible some sort of consolation and renewal. What is wanting is the return to the beloved community, or to the possibility of one ... Without that return we may know innocence and horror and grief, but not tragedy and joy. Not consolation or forgiveness or redemption.

– Wendell Berry

I am sometimes afraid to call a spade a spade ... No, things ought to be called by their proper name. If they can't stand it, then they have no right to be. We try to save so much in life with a vague sort of mysticism. Mysticism must rest on crystal-clear honesty, can only come after things have been stripped down to their naked reality.

– Etty Hillesum

... I have seen
not behind but within, within the
dull grief, blown grit, hideous
concrete façades, another grief, a gleam
as of dew, an abode of mercy,
have heard not behind but within noise
a humming that drifted into a quiet smile.

– Denise Levertov[1]

For the postwar generation, the keyword was 'realism': the attempt to strip away what was false and ornamental and to grasp a sure and lasting reality. And yet it was a complicated realism, for perhaps the most distinctive self-expression of this postwar epoch was *sur-réalisme* – a hybrid of waking reality and a more authentic reality: the world of dreams, hopes, and hallucinations. And though surrealism was the most prominent, there was a broad array of such attempts to forge various hybrid realisms: neoclassicism, magical realism, socialist realism, and dialectical images. This cultural project of forging dialectical realisms marks what is essential in the history of France in the 1920s: 'a dialectic between a visceral desire for a return to the past in order to forget the war, and the practical impossibility of that return due to the fact of the upheavals caused by the conflict ...'[2] Within this larger spectrum of new realisms, a self-identified 'postwar generation' of Catholics could find a niche for their own retrieval of ancient dialectics, variously called 'Christian realism, 'integral realism,' or 'mystic realism.'

Une Génération réaliste: Born on 2 August 1914

Perhaps the single work most representative of those who had fought in the Great War was Jean Luchaire's *A Realist Generation* (1929). The word 'generation' carried intellectual significance and moral value. First, 'generation' implied a group that was 'natural' in a biological sense (i.e., born within a certain chronological period) and therefore transcended allegedly 'artificial' groups within it (e.g., class, party, religion). Other groups divided; a generation united.

Second, as conceived in the eighteenth century, 'generation' also suggested the natural (i.e., evolutionary) superseding of outmoded ideas and values. Condorcet's 1793 text of *The Declaration of the Rights of Man* proclaimed that 'a generation has no right to subject any future generation to its laws.' Saint-Just summed up the meaning of French revolutionary measures: 'You have therefore decided that one generation cannot place another in chains.' Jean-Jacob Fazi claimed to have invented the word 'gerontocracy' in the early nineteenth century for his work assailing the moral failings of an older generation: *On Gerontocracy, or, the Abuse of Wisdom of the Old Men in the Government of France* (1828).[3] Having abused their power, a geriatric generation forfeited their legitimacy. Third, this particular 'generation of 1914' acquired moral weight as a 'sacrificed generation.'

Luchaire's definition of his own 'generation' included all three meanings: 'A generation is a group of individuals born in the same period of fifteen or twenty years, influenced by the evolution of the same circumstances at the same moment. "Our generation" possesses a more precise landmark. It was born to collective life on the same day. This day was 2 August 1914.' On that day, a group of 'young people ... still practically virgins ... rudely made contact with the exterior world.' This 'unity of departure' meant an 'equality and unanimity of reaction' for 'all the youth of all social classes.'[4] All other distinctions melted away in the face of this primary self-identity: they were members of 'a realist generation.'

This concept reached its zenith during the 1920s in both France and Germany. As seen above, Henri Massis and Alfred de Tarde had already exploited the notion in *Young People of Today*, their 1913 book concretizing the image of youthfulness doing battle with the 'generation of 1885.' In *The Sacrifice* (1917), Massis transformed those young people into a 'sacrificed generation.' Just after the war, in 1919, the designation appeared again in Alphonse Mortier's *Testimony of the Sacrificed Generation* (1919). In 1920, although the historian Lucien Febvre dismissed the idea of a 'generation' as an *artefact* in 'Générations,' François Mentré theorized in *Social Generations* that a 'generation' was 'a new way of feeling and understanding life, opposed to or at least different from what went before.' Jacques Maritain's *Antimoderne* (1922) called his friend Ernest Psichari the 'leader of the generation of the sacrificed.' Responding to *Antimoderne*'s appearance, Georges Valois wrote a letter to Léon Daudet: 'Your publication of praise to Jacques Maritain is of no meager satisfaction for those of my generation who regard Jacques Maritain as the first among them ...' In 1924, Valois published his own work, entitled *From One Century to Another. Chronicle of a Generation (1885–1920).*

Martin Heidegger put the concept at the centre of his existentialist reflections in *Being and Time* (1927): 'The fact of living in and with one's generation concludes the drama of human existence.' In *Our Inquietude* (1927), Henri Daniel-Rops reflected with bitterness: 'Born under the sign of inquietude, this generation' had been formed in an 'atmosphere heavy with cynical lies' told by its elders.[5] In 1928, Karl Mannheim published his epic sociological study on *The Problem of Generations* as 'one of the fundamental factors in the unfolding dynamic of history.' The epigraph of Erich Maria Remarque's *All Quiet on the Western Front* (1929) read in part, 'This book ... will try simply to tell of a generation of men who, even though they may have escaped shells, were destroyed by the war.'[6] Thus, by the time Luchaire published his book in 1929, the word 'generation' had become a postwar site of memory / *lieu de mémoire*. Talking about 'generation' made sense of the war's absurdity in part by portraying elders as having victimized an innocent youth.

In this context, Luchaire's other term – 'realist' – can be seen as an aesthetic and epistemological program that was also deeply ethical: 'realism' was 'the word of order, the keyword of these angry young people who intended by it a repudiation of the old myths.' Until 1914, in spite of Massis and Tarde having constructed it otherwise, a movement of youthful 'realist' opposition to the generation of 1885 might have been perhaps nothing but a 'classic conflict' of youthful rebellion. But after the trenches, the survivors attacked their elders not merely for clinging to 'obsolete ideas,' but out of moral outrage over the slaughter. By 'their attachment to outmoded myths' the older generation had permitted an 'unjustifiable massacre.' The new generation wanted 'to see the world in its reality, pushing back all the prisms of outmoded ideologies.'[7]

Luchaire said that the war had given the youth of his day 'a passionate heart and a lucid spirit, a precise notion of and an immense and fiery desire to realize those conditions' which '*needed*' to be realized in the 'modern epoch.' In addition, the 'violence of the postwar disappointment' had transformed 'the romantics of yesterday' into 'the realists of today.'[8] A realist generation's avant-garde explorations would be aesthetic, artistic, and epistemological – but most especially, profoundly ethical.

A Sur-realist Generation: 'two distant realities juxtaposed'

And yet this generation's realism might look anti-realist, for perhaps the most significant cultural invention of this generation was *sur-realism*, a term coined in 1917 by Apollinaire. In 1924, André Breton's first *Surrealist Manifesto* clearly laid out the problem with traditional realism: 'By contrast, the realistic attitude, inspired by positivism, from Saint Thomas Aquinas to Anatole France, clearly seems to me to be hostile to any intellectual or moral advancement ... It constantly feeds on and derives strength from the newspapers and stultifies both science and art by assiduously flattering the lowest of tastes; clarity bordering on stupidity, a dog's life.'[9]

Breton had been deeply affected by his wartime experience working in psychiatric wards. Having studied medicine in his early years and having read Freud, Breton attempted to psychoanalyse his frequently shell-shocked patients. He wrote an introduction to the *Letters of War* (1919) published by one of his patients, Jacques Voche; Voche committed suicide later that same year. Thus, Breton's challenge to the dominant rationalist ideology in his first *Manifesto* emerged from close personal observation of (and being personally affected by) traumatized soldiers during the war. That 'part of our mental world which we pretended not to be concerned with any longer – and, in my opinion by far the most important part – has been brought back to light,' he declared. Having gone to meet Freud personally in 1921, Breton acknowledged his debt in 1924: 'For this we must give thanks to the discoveries of Sigmund Freud.'[10]

'We are still living under the reign of logic,' complained Breton. 'Under the pretense of civilization and progress,' society had 'managed to banish from the mind everything that may rightly or wrongly be termed superstition or fancy,' forbidding 'any kind of search for truth' which was not 'in conformance with accepted practices' of empiricism. Thus, the 'absolute rationalism' that still ruled permitted his generation 'to consider only facts relating directly to our experience' while forbidding the pursuit of any 'logical ends.'[11]

But Breton posed this question: 'Can't the dream also be used in solving the fundamental questions of life?' Ever since the Enlightenment, the dream had found itself 'reduced to a mere parenthesis, as is the night,' between the rationalist hours of the waking life. However, having examined the 'waking state,' Breton concluded that he had 'no choice but to consider it a phenomenon of interference' with the dream state's superior capacity to access reality. Breton then issued his surrealist call to overcome the Enlightenment legacy and forge a new kind of modernity, reincorporating into a new synthesis what had so long been repressed: 'we may hope that the mysteries which really are not [mysteries] will give way to the great Mystery. I believe in the future resolution of these two states, dream and reality, which are seemingly so contradictory, into a kind of absolute reality, a *surreality* if one may so speak.'[12]

In addition to taking the word from Apollinaire, Breton freely acknowledged that he had borrowed his dialectical model from the poet Pierre Reverdy. Quoting lines that Reverdy had written in 1918, Breton drew on the past (Baudelaire) and pointed to the future (Benjamin): '*The image ... cannot be born from a comparison but from a juxtaposition of two more or less distant realities. / The more the relationship between the two juxtaposed realities is distant and true, the stronger the image will be – the greater its emotional power and poetic reality ...*'[13] Breton's use of Reverdy's lines sounded much like a secularized version of sacramentalism, substituting the dream's free play for that of grace.

Breton admitted some ambivalence over exactly what word to use in order to express his essential point of 'juxtaposition.' 'We could probably have taken over the word SUPERNATURALISM,' he wrote. Gérard de Nerval had used it as a descriptive adjective: 'this SUPERNATURALISTIC dream-state, as the Germans would call it.' A footnote suggested two other possibilities: 'Natural Supernaturalism' as used by Thomas Carlyle, and 'Ideorealism' [*L'Idéoréalisme*] – the juxtaposition of idealism and realism – by Saint-Pol-Roux. More important than the term itself was the notion of a dialectical 'reunion' of realism with something beyond realism in service of serious problem-solving: 'Surrealism is based on the belief in the superior reality of certain forms of previously neglected associations, in the omnipotence of dream, in the disinterested play of thought. It tends to reunite, once and for all, all other psychic mechanisms and to substitute itself for them in solving all the principal problems of life.'[14]

Although surrealism is sometimes caricatured as frivolous play, Breton's own belief in its capacity for 'solving the fundamental questions of life' and 'solving all the principal problems of life' suggests the deeply serious and anxious postwar program of his dialectical vision. His personal encounters with traumatized soldiers, especially those suffering shell-shock (associated with 'male hysteria' and homosexuality), led him to share with his generational peers a loss of faith in earlier ideals of 'civilization' and 'progress.' Not surprisingly, then, in a 1928 issue celebrating the fiftieth anniversary of Charcot's 'hysterics' of 1878, Breton attacked the positivist treatment of the fin-de-siècle 'hysteric' in his journal *La Révolution surréaliste*. 'Hysteria is not a pathological phenomenon,' he asserted, 'and may, in every regard, be considered as the supreme means of expression.' A cover cartoon assembled the profiles of famous men of the older generation and attached a caption attributed to Hegel: 'WHAT ALL THESE MEN LACK IS DIALECTIC.'[15] For Breton, the *Surrealist Revolution* was a generational 'revolution' against a non-dialectical, one-dimensional gerontocracy whose day had passed.

More Dialectical Realisms: Magical Realism, Synthetic Realism, Dialectical Images

A 'dialectical generation' would innovate in countries outside of France as well. A year after Breton's manifesto in France, Franz Roh, who had survived military service as a German field officer, published *Post-Expressionism, Magical Realism* (1925).[16] It is perhaps because Roh's work was quickly translated into Spanish as *Realismo mágico* (1927) that we have come to associate the term most immediately not with German but rather with Latin American literature. Moreover, since the movement's primary journal, Massimo Bontempelli's *900*, was published in both Italian and French, Roh's notion influenced these three major national centres of Romance languages (and Catholic culture).

Like Reverdy and Breton, Roh wanted to foster a new aesthetic in terms of two juxtaposed distant realities. He too considered several alternative titles: 'Ideal Realism,' 'Verism,' 'Neoclassicism,' 'Superrealism,' and 'Mystic Realism.' However, by using 'the word "magic," as opposed to "mystic,"' he wrote, he wished 'to indicate that the mystery does not descend to the represented world, but rather hides and palpitates behind it ...'[17] Not coincidentally, Freud had just published his work on 'uncanny' or 'un-homelike' [*unheimlich*] feelings in 1919, after the postwar dissolution of his ancient homeland, the Austro-Hungarian empire. In the postwar German-speaking world, 'home' – what had once seemed most familiar – now filled one with an eerie sense of the unfamiliar, unexpected, and un-homely.[18] Magical realism, like uncanniness, has been characterized as projecting 'a mesmerizing uncertainty suggesting that ordinary life may also be the scene of the extraordinary' and offering 'a utopian, if evanescent, promise of transfigured perception, the hypnotic renewing of everyday existence.' Ott Dix, for example, wanted to get to the uncanny truth [*die unheimliche Wahrheit*] that lay behind his subject.[19] It was a *nostalgia*, that is, homesickness [*das Heimweh*], but one now filled with a quiet dread that home was not as it seemed. (In 1927, Heidegger explicitly connected the experiences of anxiety and the uncanny with the state of 'unhomelikeness' [*die Unheimlichkeit*] or 'not-being-at-home' [*das Nicht-zuhause-sein*]: 'When in falling we flee *into* the 'at-home' of publicness, we flee *in the face of* the 'not-at-home'; that is, we flee in the face of the uncanniness which lies in Dasein ...')[20] Down to the present day, 'magical realism' maintains its associations with both surrealism and Freudian concepts: 'The oxymoronic combination of *realism* and *magic* captures the artists' and the authors' efforts to portray the strange, the uncanny [*unheimlich*], the eerie, and the dreamlike – but not the fantastic – aspects of everyday life.'[21]

Walter Benjamin extended the terms of 'surrealism' and 'magical realism' in his investigation of 'dialectical images.' Influenced by the surrealist novels of both Louis Aragon (*The Peasant of Paris* [1926]) and Breton (*Nadja* [1928]), Benjamin formulated his own theory of dialectical realism in his essay 'Surrealism – The Last Snapshot of the European Intelligentsia,' begun in 1927 and published in 1929. However, dissatisfied with surrealism's failed promise to enchant, Benjamin searched for an alternative way to achieve his pedagogical aim: to 'educate the image-making medium within us, raising it to a stereoscopic and dimensional seeing into the depths of historical shadows.'[22] He proposed instead a method of 'dialectical images' – a 'literary montage' in which disparate elements would be juxtaposed and grasped in a 'profane illumination.' 'The true creative overcoming of religious illumination, wrote Benjamin, 'resides in a *profane illumination*, a materialist, anthropological inspiration.'[23] In re-creating Baudelaire's Paris as the 'capital of the nineteenth century,' Benjamin shared and endorsed Baudelaire's own nostalgic off-modernist desire to see within forgotten historical ruins a fleeting 'illumination' of the depths covered over by surface appearances.[24]

In a final example of dialectical realism, a discourse of 'synthetic realism' emerged during the years 1927–8 in the Soviet Union. The newborn state's earliest days had been accompanied by an exciting explosion of abstract futurism and constructivism, attempts to sever the past in a definitive way and construct a future in an ideal way. However, the materialism that undergirded official Marxist ideology was not easy to square with a radical utopian abstraction from representations of reality, and Soviet theorists' attention to 'factography – "the conquest of the literature of facts"' – led to the near-triumph of realism. In 1928, Mayakovski announced: 'I amnesty Rembrandt.'[25]

Yet, an inverse exclusive attention to the 'fact' was also highly problematic for a revolutionary ideology that sought not merely to represent what existed but rather to overthrow it in service of a future vision. Tretyakov put the ambivalence succinctly: 'For us, *faktoviki* (fact-people), there can be no facts as such. There is the fact-effect and the fact-defect. The fact that strengthens our socialist position and the fact that weakens it. The fact-friend and fact-enemy.'[26] An aesthetic that was both documentary and utopian required some synthesis of descriptive realism and visionary idealism.

The dialectical term 'synthetic realism' was employed by Ivan Matsa in an exploratory essay entitled 'Towards the Question of a Marxist Formulation of the Problem of Style' (1927). A year later, Matsa gave the main paper at a Moscow conference on 'Art in the USSR and the Tasks of Artists' staged by the Communist Academy. Attacking 'traditional ("petty-bourgeois") forms of realism,' Matsa argued (in strikingly hylomorphic terms) for a new kind of realism: it need not necessarily detail 'the exterior of the proletarian' but rather 'demonstrate his historic class essence.' More official pronouncements in 1928 moved to refine earlier notions of 'heroic realism' in line with prevalent notions of art as necessarily 'synthetic.' The 'perfected realist form' needed to synthesize the outward appearances with 'the communication of an inner dynamic, psychological expressiveness, an acute and synthetic depiction of nature, a striving to convey thingness, the extreme materialisation of the model, represented not in isolation from the social fabric of the surrounding milieu, but conditioned by it.' From about 1928 onward, critics called for painting to approach a 'dialectical' or 'dialectical materialist' outlook by presenting the heroic 'model' or ideal (whether a person or an object) 'in interaction with and illuminated by its social context.'[27]

The attempt to formulate a 'dialectical' realism that would be compatible with a 'dialectical materialist' view of the world would continue to occupy Soviet theorists. A 1930 textbook for use in art schools concluded with a section entitled 'On the Paths to a New Realism' in which the author, Em. Beskin, used the terms 'constructive realism, synthetic realism, dialectical realism.' That same year, Pavel Novitski rejected 'the vulgar realism of imitators, the realism of stagnant individual life, passively contemplative, static, naturalistic realism' while at the same time embracing 'proletarian realism ... a dynamic realism, showing life in movement, in action, revealing systematically the perspectives of life, a realism that makes things, that rationally reconstructs the old life.'[28]

After the USSR finally became socialist in the 1930s, the term 'socialist realism' would acquire its official status. In 1934, Maksim Gorki's speech to the 1934 writers' congress summed up the dialectical aims: on the one hand, the writer wanted to 'extract the basic meaning from the sum of *what is given* in reality and give it form – thus we get realism.' On the other hand, if to what is given the writer added '*what we desire*,' it was 'possible to further enrich the image we have created' that enabled writers 'to arouse a revolutionary relationship to reality, a relationship that in practical terms alters the world.' Scholars have noted a kinship between socialist realism and surrealism, especially that of Salvador Dali. They both shared this dialectical synthesis of 'what is given' by factual reality and 'what we desire' but do not yet possess.[29]

To summarize: all these dialectical forms of realism synthesized two elements. On the one hand, they retained the nineteenth-century's ethical sense that a realistic portrayal of everyday experience was a moral demand. They thought it an ethical imperative not to escape, and they did not turn to one-dimensional abstraction or pure formalism. They faced the facts. On the other hand, they also sensed that realist aesthetics privileging 'notions of representation modeled on visual reflection' – what might be called 'mimetic realism' or 'mimetology' – was no longer possible after the war.[30] To be 'realistic' is 'generally to settle for what one can have in some given circumstances – while the circumstances themselves are not necessarily questioned.' (Theodor Adorno put it more poetically: realism takes part in 'weaving the veil with which repression cloaks the circumstances involved.')[31] A new generation saw itself as facing this quandary: it did not want to escape reality and yet it was not willing to settle for what was given in reality.

Luchaire's generation was indeed a 'realist generation,' but it was realism with a twist. Unlike nineteenth-century modernity, it rejected naturalism; unlike 1920s High Modernism, it rejected abstractionism. (Since it rejected High Modernism, formalism, and abstraction – all extremely popular with other members of this age group – Luchaire's 'generation' should be considered less a biological entity [i.e., sharing a common birth date] and more a way of seeing the world [i.e., embodying a paradigm shift].)[32] Dialectical and not one-dimensional, the realist generation forged a different kind of 1920s modernity: a synthesis of what was given and what was dreamed of.

A *Génération Mystique*: Realist in Religion

It is within this wider framework of dialectical synthesis that we can situate the 1920s *renouveau catholique* as a religious realism. Pat Barker's novel entitled *Regeneration*, a fictionalized account of actual Great War encounters, nicely illustrates both the problem and promise of inventing 'religious realism.' In one scene (likely inspired by Wilfred Owen's poem 'At a Calvary near the Ancre'), Siegfried Sassoon tells the young Owen of his disgust with 'all those Calvaries' – that is, the crossroad memorials portraying a large crucified Christ, sometimes mourned by his friends. They were, says Sasson, 'just sitting there waiting to be turned into symbols.' He recalls his sacrilegious friend Potter who used every undamaged crucifix he could find for target practice. 'You could hear him for miles,' recalls Sassoon. '"ONE, TWO, THREE, FOUR, Bastard on the Cross, FIRE!" There weren't many miraculous crucifixes in Potter's section of the front.'

At this moment he hesitates, for he fears that Owen might be a believer: 'But perhaps I shouldn't be saying this? I mean for all I know, you're – .' Owen replies with his shell-shocked stutter: 'I don't know what I am. But I do know I wouldn't want a f-faith that couldn't face the facts.'[33] The traumatic encounter with the trenches did not necessarily mean that faith had to be abandoned; it did mean, however, that future faith would need to take into account the facts.

This young soldier's real-life counterpart was the young Pierre Villard.[34] Villard was a wealthy bourgeois who had taken a course on German philosophy from Maritain at the Institut Catholique, maintained a written correspondence with him as a soldier, and received much-needed sustenance from him. In a letter in January 1918, Villard wrote Maritain that the 'conditions of existence' in military life had made a realist out of him. 'I do not wish to fall into idealism,' he worried. 'I do not feel any taste for a Christianity cut off from reality.'[35] On the evening of 29 June 1918, Villard made his sacramental confession, and he was killed in action the next day, as reported to the Maritains by Abbé Charles Rolin. 'Sir, I have just fulfilled a very painful mission,' wrote Rolin, 'one of the last wishes of your friend Pierre Villard had been that you be informed in case of accident. This sad event has just taken place. Pierre was struck mortally ... by the fragment of a shell. His body rests now near a bit of the earth of France recently regained from the enemy by our regiment.'[36]

In religion as in other spheres, this was a realist generation; yet here too, it was realism with a twist, in this case, a synthesis of realism and 'mysticism' – a catch-all term that included supernaturalism, miracles, and the mysterious, as well as personal spirituality and orthodox religion. In the era of nineteenth-century secularization, 'mysticism' had a negative connotation: 'the progress of truth consisted in the light of science invading dark chambers inhabited by mysticism, until at last no darkness should be left.'[37] But the war's collective encounter with chaos and incomprehensibility gave new value to the language of *la mystique*. On 12 March 1915, Pierre-Dominique Dupouey wrote a letter in which he called the war-front *la grande ligne mystique* – the 'great mystical line all along which flows so much blood.' This wartime interest in *la mystique* endured through the end of the war and continued into the next decade.[38] On 27 February 1917, as we have seen, Jacques Rivière led a discussion group at the Koenigsbrück internment camp. Notes made for the discussion included this claim: 'Only miracles convert. And so I must track down the portion of my life that is a miracle ... Yes, it is indeed a miracle, of the same species as the healing of the possessed ... Tracking down the trails of God.' These lines would have a wide audience throughout the late 1920s and 1930s. After Rivière's brutal death from typhoid fever in 1925, Paul Claudel collected his friend's unpublished writings and published them with the *N.R.F.* as *On the Trail of God*. By 1937 it had gone through thirty-one editions.[39]

Henri Ghéon, another friend (and former paramour) of Gide, published his conversion story in 1919 with the *N.R.F.* and called it *The Man Born out of the War. Testimony of a Convert (Yser-Artois 1915)*.[40] When astonished friends asked Ghéon why, if he had felt the need to convert to Christianity, he had not chosen the liberty of Protestantism rather than Catholicism, he replied: 'I don't give two pins for a religion that gets rid of the miracle ... It was starting off with a miracle that brought my new faith to the point of hearing the voice that preaches love.'[41] One did not have to agree with the hyperbolic claim made in 1915 by the *Journal de la Grotte de Lourdes* – 'Never since the time of Joan of Arc has it been clearer that the supernatural governs the world' – to see that, even among representatives of France's intellectual elite, the experience of war had engendered a yearning for the miraculous.[42]

In his 1917 essay 'Mysticism and Realism,' a Catholic revivalist named Pierre de Lescure wrote about the dialectical character of his own 'mystic generation': 'The mystic generation is realist in religion ... It will be realist in the action determined by its religious vision.[43] In 1920, Jules Sageret published *The Mystical Wave*, a long investigation of 'mystical' currents in philosophy and science, including Bergsonism, neo-Thomism, and '*Énergétisme*.'[44] During the war, Bloud et Gay, the firm that published works by Baudrillart's 'Catholic Committee for Propaganda Abroad,' had begun a projected eleven-volume work by Abbé Henri Bremond (a former Jesuit whose works had been condemned as Modernist heresy) entitled *A Literary History of Religious Sentiment in France from the End of the Wars of Religion to Our Own Time* (1916). Now they continued to publish those volumes as they emerged, including *Devout Humanism* (whose dialectical title summarized Bremond's own mystic realism), *The Mystical Invasion, 1590–1620*, and *The Mystical Conquest* (vols. 3–6). Bloud et Gay's 1922 *French Catholic Almanac* devoted a full-page advertisement publicizing Bremond's history of the 'mystical': 'The reawakening [*réveil*] of Mystical Studies is one of the most significant facts of the postwar,' it declared. 'The best book of Religious History since 1914 was a history of mystical literature ... The Académie Française awarded it one of the highest prizes it gives out: A prize of ten thousand francs was give to the work of M. l'abbé Henri Bremond.' Listing the five volumes that were for sale, the typeset evoked an overwhelming wave: L'HUMANISME DÉVOT. L'INVASION MYSTIQUE. LA CONQUÊTE MYSTIQUE. LA CONQUÊTE MYSTIQUE . LA CONQUÊTE MYSTIQUE.[45]

Bloud et Gay also published Paul Archambault's series of *Notes for the New Day*, a journal produced by a brilliant group of friends gathered around the philosopher Maurice Blondel. The title of an early issue, appearing directly after one entitled *The Testimony of a Generation* (No. 2, 1924), asked, *What is the Mystical?* (No. 3, 1925). Later volumes pointed to the other half of the dialectic: *Where to Look for the Real?* (No. 9, 1927) and *Toward an Integral Realism: The Philosophical Work of Maurice Blondel* (No. 12, 1928).[46] This last bore an epigraph that echoed Massis: 'TO THE YOUTH OF TODAY, who desire realism and must desire it *intégral*.' Archambault's project used Blondel's philosophy of idealism united with 'action' in order to forge a Christian democratic union of Catholicism and politics, and provided Catholic intellectuals with a genuine alternative to Action Française.[47] In this left-leaning use of *intégral*, propounded by Blondel (who, like Bremond, had been attacked by integralists during the Modernist Crisis), idealist mysticism and realist action needed to be united in a synthetic whole. Otherwise, they would be insufficient for 'today's youth.'

Like surrealism, magical realism, and synthetic realism, a postwar 'Christian' or 'mystic' realism dialectically synthesized what was given and what was desired. Perhaps no one articulated this new possibility as well as Jacques and Raïssa Maritain. The war's traumas, including the deaths of Psichari, Péguy, and Villard, had forced them to re-imagine a faith that faced the facts.

Raïssa Maritain on Art: No Timidity. No Prudery. No Manicheanism.

The academic year beginning in September 1918 was a time of important transition for the Maritains as they left a segment of their lives behind and looked ahead to new paths. In June 1917, Jacques had finished his studies and received his diploma of Doctor of Scholastic Philosophy; in November, Léon Bloy had died. Jacques received a sabbatical year off from the Institut Catholique and had planned to write his *General Introduction to Philosophy* and the *Small Book of Logic*. These plans were complicated by unexpected sickness in the Maritain home: Raïssa's journal entry for 13 October records her sister Véra's serious illness and the terrifying possibility that it was a strain of the epidemic Spanish Flu. Fortunately for their household, Véra recovered and the Maritains turned their attention to the other world-event of late autumn 1918 – the armistice. 'The end of the war's nightmare, finally!' Raïssa exclaimed. 'On the feast of Saint Martin. Everything has gone miraculously fast since our offensive of 18 July.'[48] With the end of an era, the Maritains reflected on what the devastation of the war had meant for France, 'civilization,' and Catholicism, and what would be needed for reconstruction.

Beginning in February 1919, amid entries about the Versailles Peace Conference, Raïssa recopied 'several brief notes on art (1917)' originally made two years earlier. These were the germ of an aesthetic theory that would allow the reformulation of Thomistic language as a kind of postwar modernism. 'Art is an intellectual virtue,' she wrote, employing the

Aristotelian/Thomistic language of virtue and habit; 'strictly speaking, it is the faculty of creating *a new form, an original being*, capable in its turn of moving a human soul.' By utilizing the scholastic notion of 'form,' Raïssa employed traditional language for the avant-garde purpose of criticizing representational art: 'Merely to imitate, in the sense of *copying* nature, is to be outside the pale of art ... Thus cubism can be regarded as an effort to escape from the crude sensibility of the impressionists. It is abstract sensibility somewhat as mathematics could be regarded by some (such as Auguste Comte) as abstract natural sciences.'[49] A Catholic metaphysical attention to unseen forms had been reactionary during the nineteenth century. Now, in the world of Kandinsky, Mondrian, and Picasso, 'abstract sensibility' was newly fashionable.

More notes appearing one month later on 10 March 1919 demonstrate the soul-searching undertaken by the Maritains as they re-evaluated their place in a post-war culture – from the margins to the centre.[50] 'It is an error to isolate oneself from humanity just because one possesses a clearer view of the truth,' Raïssa reflected. 'If God does not call one to such solitude, it is necessary to live with God in the multitude; to make God known there, and to make God loved.' If one lived one's life 'in the public sphere [*cité*],' it would be necessary not 'to walk its streets with hands in the pockets' but rather to '*take part in the life of the public sphere*' and seek (quoting an encyclical of Pius X) to 'establish all things in Christ.'

In the recent past, there had too often been for 'pious Catholics' a 'turning up of the nose at activity'; but this only meant that the public sphere had been abandoned 'to those who understand neither its principle nor its end.' Catholics had 'too often been the servants of that which is the least worthy of being served,' namely, only invoking '"order" for their own interest.' This constant association of 'order' and Catholicism had made people 'a little too conscious' of Christianity as a static 'force which makes for order' but not enough as 'a dynamic driving force, in virtue of the charity and zeal which animate it.' The order that Christianity established and guaranteed was not meant to be marginal to the rest of society, 'not for the good of a small number.' It was rather something meant to animate the whole of society: 'it is for the good of the greatest number: the common good.' Throughout this passage, Raïssa implicitly contrasted two visions of Catholicism and culture: one saw Catholicism as a reactionary group endorsing a stuffy 'order.' The other saw Catholicism in the dynamic terms of hylomorphism: an *entelechy*, that is, the 'driving force' that energetically orders all of an organism's functions into a unified whole, serving as both its beginning principle and final purpose.

From here Raïssa's thoughts turned to a tired trope: namely, that insofar as 'modern art' from Flaubert to Gide concerned itself with (sexual) 'passions,' it was incompatible with Catholicism. Raïssa, wanting to reconcile the possibility of Catholicism and modern art, carefully distinguished between *pudeur* ('modesty') and *pruderie* ('prudery'). 'Modesty and prudery are opposed to one another and in inverse ratio to one another,' she claimed. A soul that had the 'spiritual instinct' of 'modesty' knew (with *Genesis*) that 'God has done all things well.' Seeing all things in their relation to 'the wisdom of God,' the modest person could not be a prudish one, that is, could not be 'ashamed of any of the things that God has made.' Prudery was a 'conventional' (and false) vision of spirit's superiority over flesh. Modesty, on the other hand, revealed 'the *real* superiority.'

Thus far, Raïssa had arrived at three understandings: insofar as modern art paid attention to form and not outward representation, it was eminently compatible with Thomism; insofar as Christianity was meant to be the dynamic form ordering society, Catholics needed to play their role at the centre; and a true distinction between modesty and prudery enabled the genuine Catholic to embrace without shame or apology even art that portrayed the passions. Drawing these principles allowed her to proceed towards the Maritains' genuine innovation: using art and aesthetic theory as a means of making Catholicism culturally central.

'Art draws all its objective value from its civilizing power,' Raïssa began, '– it contributes to spiritualizing humanity, to making it more ready to receive the natural and supernatural contemplative life ...' Since God 'did not create nature for the purpose of despising her powers,' and since (drawing on the traditional Catholic principle that 'grace builds on nature') the Creator liked to make 'nature as the collaborator of his omnipotence,' critics erred in not seeing the essentially spiritualizing function of art. 'The Catholics of today' might be 'all-embracing [*intègres*] in doctrine,' but as a rule they were 'narrow-minded as regards the proper domain of art and its civilizing function, the function it has in humanity of natural spiritualization.' In short, Catholics were 'hard on artists.' And it was understandable if artists asked themselves in turn, when confronted with such Catholic animosity, 'whether their natural gifts' were a sign of being blessed or rather of 'being among the reprobate.'

Thus it was time for Catholics to recover their catholicity. Alluding to the ancient aphorism of Terence – 'Nothing human is foreign to me' – Raïssa formulated her own manifesto: 'It seems to me that Catholics must possess a genuinely informed doctrine *concerning everything that is human*, a doctrine that conforms to truth, taste and intelligence. No timidity. No pharisaism. No ignorance. No prudishness. No Manicheanism. But rather Catholic doctrine luminous and total.'

Having disposed of Catholic prudery, Raïssa continued to think through the idea of 'purity' in her journal notes for 25 March 1919. Although some people might think that 'devoutness is enough in itself to make a Christian artist,' they were wrong: what was 'necessary to the artist' was 'purity of intention.' Catholics needed to 'realize exactly what pure and genuine art demands': the artist has 'moral obligations' and 'strict duties' to art that required the greatest self-denial. Here Raïssa left Christ's command untranslated: '*abneget semetipsum*' – 'If any man will come after me, *let him deny himself* ...' (Luke 9:23).

The lines following indicated that by this date (25 March 1919), the Maritains had been deeply influenced by two encounters: their conversations with the painter Georges Rouault and their reading of Jean Cocteau's just-published manifesto for a neoclassicist aesthetic, *The Cock and the Harlequin* (1918). 'An artist with integrity [*intègre*] as an artist' was 'very near to being a moralist. He has the feeling of a certain purity in himself.' This line she attributed to Rouault, and then offered for comparison the following aphorism from Cocteau: 'Cf. Cocteau's *Cock and the Harlequin*. This angel of whom the artist must be the guardian is precisely his rectitude as an artist.'[51]

By late March 1919, Raïssa and Jacques had reasoned through all the major intellectual moves that would soon be published as a landmark work refashioning Thomism as the most appropriate aesthetics underlying modernist art. But one task remained: Thomism had come to represent eternalism. Any change in perfection logically meant a devolution from an ideal state, and the idea of eternal forms 'progressing' over time seemed self-contradictory. How could Thomism be reconciled with modernity's fundamental notion of *time* and its corollary, *progress*?

On 5 April 1919, Raïssa solved this dilemma by imitating Aquinas's own syllogistic method: 'All our values depend upon the nature of our God ... God is Spirit ... In the scale of values, Spirit will therefore be first. And matter, bodies, will be last. To progress, therefore, is to go from matter to spirit ... To civilize is to spiritualize ... Art, like the sciences, draws its social value from its civilizing power. It is also an indicator of civilization.' For the Maritains, 'Art' functioned as the mediator between God and 'spiritual progress.' In contrast, 'material progress' meant not evolution but rather devolution from civilization: 'a return to barbarism, that is to animality, to matter, to chaos.'[52]

In the scheme of prewar oppositions, 'progress' had been 'material' modernization, and it had seemed to entail secularization, that is, the purging of the 'spiritual' in the sense of the 'eternal.' Raïssa's reasoning inverted this relationship: the spiritual was dynamic, not static, an evolution away from chaos towards order, and from barbarism toward civilization. (Bergson's influence had not been completely suppressed: the spiritual was creative evolution, the activity of a life principle.) Since art was the primary means of progress towards God, even the most modern art of the Jazz Age – especially insofar as it repudiated the crude naturalist aims of the previous century's 'modernists' – was 'spiritualizing.' This was an 'integralist' vision, but one with a distinctly postwar twist: a new civilization in which Catholicism could finally become 'catholic,' sacramentally informing every aspect of cultural and intellectual modernity, aiming at 'human and divine good through virtue, work, politics, the sciences, the arts, sanctity.' In mid-July 1919, Raïssa enthusiastically exclaimed, 'Know your religion, Catholics, know your greatness!'[53]

Jacques Maritain: *The Universal Review*

In late September 1919 the Maritains finally returned home from sabbatical to Versailles. Reflecting on the long year in seclusion, from September 1918 to September 1919, Raïssa wrote that she felt as if she had 'spent a year in Purgatory. My poor soul is quite shattered; it seems without life, without zest, without emotion ... Now I am slowly emerging from this dreary torpor.'[54] Writing this without knowing that she and Jacques were on the threshold of unforeseen success and popularity, the metaphor was more apt than she could have imagined: the previous year had been an unexpected period of purification by fire, an interim period of re-tooling themselves as they consolidated various strands – Bergson, Bloy, Driesch, Aquinas, Rouault, and Cocteau – into a new synthesis. As the secluded purgation ended, a flurry of activity in the *cité* was about to begin.

This activity was immediately catalysed by Henri Massis's July publication of his manifesto calling 'For a Party of Intelligence' in response to a similar manifesto on the left by Henri Barbusse.[55] In May 1919, Barbusse, whose *Fire* (1916) had been the most famous novel of protest during the war (and won the Prix Goncourt), had sent out a plea to aid in the formation of his *Clarté* movement, an 'International of thought' whose absence was felt even 'more gravely than ever in this hour of universal mistrust and universal calamity.'[56] As opposed to this internationalist movement, Massis's manifesto (heavily influenced by Maurras) envisioned a nationalist sacred union that would form around the Catholic Church. 'In this hour of inexpressible confusion, in which the future of civilization is in play,' he wrote, 'our salvation is of a spiritual order.'

Those signatories (including Maritain) who were 'believers,' said Massis, would 'judge that the Church is the only legitimate moral power and that it alone can form morals.' For others who were 'unbelievers, yet preoccupied by the fate of civilization' (like Charles Maurras), 'the Catholic alliance' would appear 'indispensable.' In order to accomplish the 'work of reconstruction that makes us unite,' no one would be surprised at the necessary association with 'Catholic thought.' For one of the 'most obvious missions of the Church, throughout the centuries, was the protection of intelligence against its own errors, the prevention of the human mind's self-destruction ...' Reworking a theme as old as Chateaubriand's *Genius of Christianity* (1802), Massis argued that Catholicism was the historical guarantor of civilization itself, and the postwar reconstruction of French intelligence depended on its return to the *patrie*.

In the September 1919 *N.R.F.*, Jacques Rivière, having become director of the review after returning from battle, delivered a scathing attack on the new party: 'intelligence' simply meant for them 'to "classify," to place in hierarchical order, to impose on what is real a form that has been chosen and decreed once and for all.'[57] Although Maritain would later feel enormous regret and embarrassment for not separating himself immediately from Massis, he did not oppose him publicly, and followed up the manifesto with responses published in *Les Lettres* – one to the editor, Gaëtan Bernoville, and another responding to a certain 'Colonel R. ...'[58] These clarified his own ideas about the 'action' necessary to Catholics in the wake of the war – 'action' that was about to lead him into a closer association with Action Française and, as Abbé Henri Bremond warned him at the time, put him in danger of 'a tour on a casserole grill in Purgatory.'[59]

On 9 January 1920, Charles Maurras proposed that he and Maritain use part of a bequest from Pierre Villard – Maritain's former student who wrote just before he died that he had 'no taste for a Christianity cut off from reality' – to found a new journal entitled *La Revue universelle*.[60] The idea had been suggested before the war by the Maritains' late spiritual director Father Clérissac. The Dominican had hoped that the three friends – Massis, Psichari, and Maritain – would collaborate on a 'universal review,' the title evoking Maurras's notion that French national genius embodied 'universal' humanity. Villard's bequest now made this dream a possibility: 'a sounding board for the ideas and principles of

Action Française in political and social activity, on the one hand, and on the other hand for Christian and particularly Thomist thought in religion and philosophy.'[61]

One week later, Raïssa noted with pride and joy in her journal that Jacques was working at the office of the newly founded review as its philosophical editor. 'Extraordinary thing,' she exclaimed, 'this review which Père Clérissac so much wanted, which he spoke of to Massis, Jacques and Ernest ... well! the project having been completely abandoned, now the review is being launched, and, as it happens, with Massis and Jacques on the staff. It is the first time Thomist philosophy has had such a wide entry into the world of culture.'[62] Psichari's name absent from the staff lent an unspoken poignancy: although Thomism would now have 'a wide entry' into the wider culture, the price paid for this integration had been high.

Yet another week later, on 26 January 1920, Jacques went to the Catholic University of Louvain – whose ancient library the Germans had torched in the war's first days – to lecture at Cardinal Mercier's Institut Supérieur de Philosophie. The faculty and students who gathered to hear Maritain's lecture 'On Several Conditions of the Thomistic Renaissance' were undoubtedly prepared for a presentation of relatively abstruse metaphysical distinctions. They must have been taken aback, then, only a little more than a year after the armistice, when the metaphysician introduced his remarks with a tragically concrete image from the war. Maritain recalled that he had originally been scheduled to come and speak to them about the philosophy of Bergson – the subject of his vitriolic 'antimodernist' first book – during the winter of 1914. However, those plans had never been realized. 'Between that date and the one today,' said Maritain, 'there have been torrents of blood. And it is in that blood that the dearest companion of my youth, Ernest Psichari, has preceded me on your Belgian land, where he waits for me in the peace of the resurrection.'[63]

Rhetorically speaking, this homage to Maritain's martyred friend made for a brilliant overture, and it must have deeply moved his audience. More importantly, it signalled that for all those gathered in traumatized Louvain, the war had profoundly changed things – especially the grandson of Jules Favre. The 'Thomist Renaissance' for which he was about to become the leading figure was not going to be like his pre-war attacks on Bergson had been: an intramural Catholic affair, marginal to the culture at large. The postwar renaissance was instead going to animate and regenerate every aspect of French culture. As such, Catholic revivalism would be both a monument to and a memorialization of the sacrifices paid in the war.

The philosophical revival of 'Thomistic realism' would answer the desires of a generation both 'mystic and realist,' and it would find a niche within an overall variety of dialectical realisms. Concretely speaking, it would be disseminated and popularized through the creation of a very particular institution of literary production and criticism – a literary 'Christian realism.'

1921–1926: Christian Realism and *la Semaine des Écrivains Catholiques*

The revival and popularization of Catholic philosophy would succeed largely because it was one aspect of a much larger effort on the part of Catholic publishing houses and presses that had been in existence for some time. Ironically, this fertile and varied landscape was due to the anticlerical legislation of 1901–5 directed at the Church's ecclesiastical institutions. After the expulsions of the religious congregations, lay persons came forward 'with vigor and competence' to own and manage a Catholic press that was 'inventive and prosperous.'[64] Released from its ecclesiastical environment, Catholic thought reached into a wider intellectual world via the press. This was the ground that had already been prepared since the turn of the century upon which postwar strategists could build. It would be the means by which persons of all religious beliefs (and non-belief), whether as supporters or critics, would contribute to the widening sphere of Catholic revivalism.

In the years 1919–20, various articles appearing in the journal *Les Lettres* (directed by Gaëtan Bernoville) criticized the fragmentation of Catholics in the political, social, and intellectual spheres. As a solution, they suggested an annual meeting that would give Catholic writers the chance to know one another and begin to speak in unified terms. At the beginning of 1921, Bernoville proposed the organization of a 'Catholic Writers' Week' and formed a committee of eighteen members (including Maritain) to spearhead the project.[65] The first annual 'Writers' Week' took place in mid-May 1921 and, in Bernoville's words, the gathering aimed at unifying 'a certain number of writers who represented the new Catholic intellectual generation.' As a response to the question 'What is the Catholic Writers' Week?' made explicit, its ambition was nothing short of the re-establishment of Christianity as the animating principle of France (and consequently the world): 'It consists of gathering together, in both scholarly sessions and friendly discussions, writers coming from horizons that are the most different and even sometimes the most opposed to one another – philosophical, esthetic, political, and social – but who, overtly professing the same religious faith, are searching together for a formula of practical union that would express the identity of their Catholic aspirations and their firm will to rechristianize France, *to reconstitute Christianity in the world.*'[66] This new generation of Catholic intellectuals – including Paul Archambault, Henri Ghéon, René Johannet, Jacques Maritain, Henri Massis, René Salomé, and Robert Vallery-Radot – had gathered in a 'genuine atmosphere of enthusiasm.' The event conveyed 'the impression that a new era of reconciliation, concord, and of work in common had been inaugurated for a whole brilliant intellectual Catholic elite.' The following year, *Études* reported that the event had collected some groups of presenters 'markedly superior to that of last year, so much so that one or two particularly brilliant sessions in the great hall of the Institut Catholique could barely contain the packed rows of auditors.' All this happened, noted the review, in spite of lowered expectations: during the second year it was to be anticipated that an event's 'repetition ordinarily attracts fewer numbers than a novelty.' In addition, 'to the extent that the memories of the war' distanced themselves from the present, it would require 'a greater effort to maintain, even among Catholics, a certain unanimity of spirit in the inevitable diversity of views and opinions ...'[67]

In 1922, Monsignor Baudrillart launched the *French Catholic Almanac*, yet another publishing venture aimed at shaping a vision of a widely Catholic France. Among the myriad other chapters devoted to giving an encyclopedic overview of Catholic life, the *Almanac* dedicated several pages to an essay by Jean Morienval entitled 'Catholic Literature Today.'[68] In using dialectical expressions like 'Catholic novel' and 'Christian realism,' Morienval and other Catholic revivalists reinvented the accepted meanings of terms by inverting their values.

Since the nineteenth-century novel had been (by definition) a 'realist' genre, excluding the metaphysical, supernatural, or mystical, the idea of a 'Catholic novel' – 'Christian realism' – had seemed self-contradictory. As late as 1920, André Bellessort wrote that, insofar as a book was a novel, it could freely range through 'the empire of the passions'; but insofar as it was 'Catholic,' it could only venture forth into this realm 'with scruple and trembling.' He concluded dramatically: the 'Catholic novel seems as difficult to realize as a squared circle.'[69]

Morienval inverted these meanings and made 'realism' Christianity's truest expression. In his subsection entitled 'Le réalisme chrétien,' Morienval appealed to the late critic Jean Lionnet, who had expressed his view syllogistically. If Christianity was true, and if 'the method of modern novelists' was 'to put as much truth as is possible in the novel,' then, 'by this very fact,' the modern novel was 'that which is best suited to Christianity.' Morienval glossed Lionnet's claim: 'One may thus conceive of a "Christian realism" which, avoiding a novelistic realism that consists in attaching itself particularly to the very worst in humanity, will find in it the exact truth of [humanity's] nature.' A 'Catholic novel' was not only possible; it was the ultimate logical expression of a true realism.

In order to legitimate this new twist, Morienval appealed to the authority of J.-K. Huysmans. Even after his conversion, Huysmans had 'noted and studied the passions, the phases of his religious life' with the same technique he had used in his naturalist works. Christianity delivered 'spiritual forces which are real' and thus, 'to a certain extent,' were capable of being 'observed and marked.'[70] Of course, Morienval left unspoken Huysmans's trademark fascination with Satanism and androgynous eroticism, aspects that had led to official Church condemnation of his most popular work. By this time, Huysmans's personality had been reshaped as an iconic figure for revivalism, and the invocation of his precedent made 'Christian realism' seem rooted in primordial traditions.

During the second annual 'Catholic Writers' Week' in 1922, the novelist Émile Baumann thoroughly domesticated Huysmans' heterodoxy as the reigning orthodoxy. 'Realism and supernaturalism,' declared Baumann, 'are one thing.' Baumann illustrated his sacramental literary theory with metaphorical horizons: since the Christian sees not only what is visible but also that which lies 'behind the horizon' of perception, it was difficult to represent this 'enlargement of earthly things' as seen within an infinitely larger yet still invisible horizon. Only the 'contemplative,' the 'artist with faith,' or the 'visionary' [*voyant*] was capable of seeing 'the infinite converging in the poor spark of our lives.' And yet, it was precisely this synthetic vision that suggested 'the immense possibilities of Christian art.'[71]

The Writers' Weeks continued to grow in success, and they were part of the Catholic organization called for by Baudrillart. On 3 November 1922, in his capacity as rector of the Institut Catholique, Baudrillart gave his seventeenth annual sermon for the traditional Mass of the Holy Spirit. Alluding to the Spirit's arrival at Pentecost in the form of tongues of fire, he entitled his sermon 'So that the *renouveau catholique* might endure.

The Sacred Fire!' Saying that it was not necessary to 'abandon our temperament' – that is, the 'excessive individualism' that distinguished 'all of us Latin peoples' – the rector nevertheless urged his faculty and students to 'ameliorate' this individualism. 'Catholics, you can, you must, and you will become the Super-French [*superfrançais*].' They had to 'renounce the sad mode of *each one for themselves*' and instead 'participate in the life of the body to which you belong, to the life of this University, to the life of the great associations to which you give your name.' One could not say, 'I can perfectly well manage without this assistance by remaining faithful to my belief and to my principles.' One thing alone was certain: 'that Catholic France absolutely cannot manage without this common action. It is by constituted groups that we will act. Isolated, *we will remain in our past powerlessness* and we will be once again the victim of adversaries who know how to walk and act as an ensemble.' Baudrillart concluded with a rhetorical flourish that explicitly linked the need for Catholic organization to sacrifices made in the war, especially implying the deaths of the students' older brothers: 'Take hold of it: it is the flame of Christian civilization that is menaced today, of this civilization for which so many of those older than you have died and to the service of which you must live. Let it be so!'[72]

By 1926, the discourse of the annual 'Week of Catholic Writers' had become established. *Les Lettres* was proud to report that, although the 'de-Christianization of the masses' might be progressing, 'the elite of the country, above all the intellectual and most brilliant elite' was either 'returning to Catholicism' or manifesting 'a growing sympathy for it.' A 'genuine renaissance' was translating this Catholic attitude into 'the various terrains of thought, of literature, and of art.' On the one hand, this *renouveau* expressed itself in critical essays and published works that demonstrated a 'new French blossoming'; on the other hand, it responded 'directly to the anti-Christian offensive.'[73]

During this Writers' Week, in addition to three panels devoted to 'The Anti-Christian Offensive,' three others addressed 'Catholicism and Literature': the first panel, on 'Saints in Modern Literature,' was to be reported by the Jesuit Father Paul Doncoeur. The second panel, 'Catholic Criticism and Contemporary Literature,' had Abbé Jean Calvet, professor of literature at the Institut Catholique, as its reporter. The third, devoted to 'The Novel and Catholic Inspiration,' was to be reported by Madame Jean Balde and presided over by Robert Garric, professor of French literature at the Sorbonne, director of *La Revue des jeunes*, and founder of the Équipes sociales. Various military honors were cited in the printed program: Father Marie-André Dieux was listed as having been a 'prisoner of war' and having received the *Croix de Guerre*; Father Paul Doncoeur was listed as an *Ancien Combattant* and a 'prisoner of war in Germany.' His cited publications included references to postwar crises: 'The Spiritual Reconstruction of the Country' (in the Jesuit journal *Études*), and the 1924 open letter to Prime Minister Herriot, 'We Will Not Leave.'[74] Bernoville's publicity for the event referred to France's having being 'drained of nearly all its blood,' and associated 'the eternal forces of our Catholic Renaissance' with a new generation: a 'vigorous and young movement which is trying to restore contemporary literature and art under the sign of the eternal.'[75] Thus, eight years after the end of hostilities, organizers continued to link their literary revival explicitly with the war. The movement consciously saw itself as justified and demanded by the price Catholics had paid, a rejuvenation of a fragmented body politic.

The movement from pulpit to publishing house was a self-conscious relocation from margin to centre, seeking to 'engage the question of Catholicism's penetration into the modern world of thought, of letters and of the arts.' Notes explaining the Writers' Week's after-dinner sessions show how shrewd the organizers were about the necessity of networking and forging concrete alliances. These sessions had been included so as 'to put writers of the Catholic Renaissance' [*Renaissance Catholique*] in friendly contact with one another and with 'their editors, their publishing houses, and their public.'[76] 'Christian realism' might have been a highly theoretical concept, but it was created and propagated by means of concrete institutions throughout the postwar decade and into the 1930s: the advertising and distribution efforts of publishing houses (themselves dependent on both journals and almanacs for circulation), the reviews published in response, scholarly studies, and collected anthologies.

In 1920, the 'Catholic novel' had seemed as difficult to realize as a 'squared circle.' In 1926, it had become mainstream. No less a figure than Albert Thibaudet, a paradigm of literary criticism in his day, published a piece in the *N.R.F.* entitled 'Reflections on Literature. The Catholic Novel.' Thibaudet remarked that, in the year in which he was writing, 'the Catholic novel, Catholic literature' seemed to have taken for themselves 'a privileged place' in French intellectual discourse.[77] The remark, coming from a non-sectarian author and appearing in the *N.R.F.* demonstrated that the *renouveau catholique* had effected an astonishing reversal in half a decade.

'A Crazy Need for Synthesis'

The synthetic principle of 'Christian realism' spilled over from literature into social action, politics, and reflections on science. In 1924, *La Revue des jeunes* published details from the 4–9 December 'Social Week of Students' held in Paris, a week of meetings for students involved in social action. Opening the week's lectures, one young activist defined a new breed of 'Social Catholics': 'neither pragmatists nor pure idealists,' these new youth were 'rather *realists* who have found in the teachings of the Church a marvelous richness of doctrine.' In the light of these teachings, 'after having *rigorously observed the facts* of the social situation,' these students would seek reforms 'with a view to making justice reign there and saving the social order.'[78] As distinct from pragmatism, authentic realism had something of the idealist in it – a dialectic significantly owed to Blondel and his promotion by Archambault.

In the same issue of *La Revue des jeunes*, René Salomé's article 'On the Brink of the New Europe' also spoke of the need to infuse idealism with realism. When 'the *idea* breaks with the real,' he observed, two disastrous things can happen. If the ideal is overwhelmed by the real, then an idea becomes nothing but 'the emotional and fraudulent projection of the appetites.' Conversely, if the real is obliterated by the idea, there results 'the predominance and despotism of ideologies marked by pathos, and the servitude of thought to the affections.' The future of the New Europe thus depended on a new generation that could synthesize the ideal with the real.[79]

In addition to social action and politics, revivalists also engaged the philosophy of science. In 1924, the Jesuit philosopher Pedro Descoqs published a long monograph entitled *A Critical Essay on Hylomorphism.* Descoqs went to great lengths elucidating the consequences of various theories of informed matter advanced by a number of contemporary scientists and philosophers (including Maritain). Unlike the theory of hylomorphism, scientific theories that considered their models of reality to be merely 'representative' or 'symbolic' had no intention of suggesting that their representations 'reached the basis of reality as such.'[80] Yet, for thinkers like Descoqs, this was precisely what was desired in science: a model that accurately reflected reality. Maritain made contributions to ongoing discussions on the work of Einstein, and *The Philosophical Revolution and Science* (1924) by Jules Sagaret (author of *The Mystical Wave*, 1920) explored Bergson and Einstein among others.[81] Echoing emerging concerns about the distance of mathematical models from the experienced life-world, revivalist critiques of science expressed yet another variation on realist anxieties and hence another aspect of Thomism's appeal.

The year 1926 has been represented as an experiential rush of inventions – of airplanes, automobiles, bars, elevators, gramophones, movie palaces, ocean liners, telephones, and more – in which people felt they were 'living at the edge of time.' In March 1926, the German magazine *Die Tat* described France's *renouveau catholique* as one of these ultramodern energies: 'Without a doubt, Catholicism is advancing; it is ... in the position of conqueror ... More and more, Catholicism is becoming a movement with its own art, economic beliefs, and responsibility for the world.'[82]

During the same month the German article appeared, Maritain was interviewed by a Polish journal sceptical of any such 'renaissance' in France. Asked whether he saw 'a difference in the Catholic youth before the war and after the war,' Maritain responded that 'the destruction of many of the false gods and by the disappearance of all sorts of illusions' had led youth to turn back to God and the Church. 'Postwar French youth, as in other countries,' displayed more of 'a sense of realities than the preceding generation' and had 'a lively aversion to empty discourse and hollow words.' When asked to supply some names in literature who formed part of this movement, Maritain responded that Bloy, Péguy and Psichari had been important before the war, and Claudel's influence endured. Those after the war included the dramatist Henri Ghéon, Jacques Copeau, founder of the 'Vieux Colombier' theatre, the poet Max Jacob, and Jean Cocteau. He added, 'I note that I am only citing here the most important names.'[83]

In the early summer of 1926, two essays by Gonzague Truc appeared – 'What is Thomism and Why it is Being Reborn' and 'Thomism and the Future of Thought' – and they remain noteworthy for their poignant clarity. Since the dominant culture considered it 'vain to ever interest itself in the *why* of things,' Truc asserted, it contented itself 'in knowing their *how*.' Modern thought did not want to 'separate itself from the sensible,' and instead 'catalogue[d] laws and facts.' From this Truc drew a conclusion evocative of Henry David Thoreau: restricted to a world of facts and incapable of asking questions of purpose, 'the majority of people die without ever having asked why they lived.' Thomism's rebirth could be attributed to people's desire for putting 'things back into their place' – that is, situating them within a wider horizon of reality.[84] This was its synthetic appeal: the possibility of interrogating life's *pourquoi* and *comment*.

Later that fall, a group of students at the Catholic University of Louvain identifying themselves as members of the 'postwar generation' founded a new review called *la Nouvelle Équipe* (The New Team). In their first issue's opening manifesto, the editors declared that this journal would be 'reserved to young people,' for they felt the 'necessity' of an organ of opinion where 'all of a generation would feel at home with itself ... become self-aware of its power,' and coordinate all its activities 'toward a Catholic end.'[85] Like Jean Luchaire, they too could point to a unifying moment of birth: the war, 'coinciding with our adolescence, revealed to us the conception of life in a world completely thrown off its axis.' They were thinking about *reconstruction* – especially the reorganization of civic life.

They envisioned their new journal as a rallying centre [*centre de ralliement*] wherein Catholicism and 'general culture,' the only two serious opponents to the forces of fragmentation, could join as one. At the *Nouvelle Équipe*, 'young intellectuals, whatever the domain in which they specialize might be,' would be grouped together as one. 'All of us work with a concern for synthesis and we hope, in this spirit, to cooperate – let it be humbly! – in this restoration of intelligence which manifests itself on diverse sides.' In a culture increasingly fragmented by specialization, everyone seemed to 'wade around in the details.' But this group wanted something more: 'we have a crazy need for synthesis!'

For a synthetic frame, they invoked the master: 'The work of Thomas Aquinas, to be precise, presents this imposing synthesis.' They concluded by locating themselves within a genealogy: by founding Louvain's Institut Supérieur de Philosophie, Cardinal Mercier had begun the work; more recently, Jacques Maritain was 'widening the way and tracing it out well.' A new generation now needed to pursue Aquinas out of their crazy need. Maritain himself wrote a short letter to congratulate the students on their new effort and reaffirm their diagnosis of the problem. 'The kind of agony all across the world renders the duties of Catholics – in particular young Catholics – more heavy, more urgent, more difficult than ever. You have taken account of the gravity of the hour, you are directing yourselves, under the sign of Saint Thomas, toward the *immense work of restoring spiritual unity*. This is what seems in my eyes the importance of your effort.'[86]

In 1926, the *renouveau catholique* was receiving international attention for its success. There were many reasons for this, but most significant is the way revivalists connected their movement to the war. 'The *renouveau catholique* is a gift from heaven to France,' wrote one in May 1926. 'It is at once both recompense and promise: recompense for the sacrifice of the very best, a promise of resurrection.'[87]

1927: Reviewing a Decade of Palingenesis

In 1927, Abbé Jean Calvet, professor of literature at the Institut Catholique de Paris, published *The Renouveau catholique in Contemporary Literature*, a panoramic view looking back over nearly a decade of postwar revivalism. In what had now become a standard trope of *renouveau* publications and conferences, Calvet's study underscored 'young people' and 'youthfulness.' For example, he noted that after the war the Dominicans had changed the name of their earlier journal to *La Revue des jeunes* [*Review of the Youth*] in order to express Catholicism's desire for 'young people, for young ideas, for young talents,' and to carry out their mission of 'counseling and directing, the new generations.' When Calvet listed the writers for the *Revue* – Louis Bertrand, Paul Claudel, Robert Garric, Henri Ghéon, Jacques Maritain, and Léontine Zanta, a list that had itself become a standard trope of the *renouveau* – he emphasized the way in which they continued 'to collaborate at the journal side-by-side with the very youngest writers.' The journal *Les Lettres*, revived in 1919, could also count among its 'brilliant group of writers' both 'already illustrious masters' like Henri Bremond and Louis Bertrand and 'all the good writers of the young generation' like Ghéon and Maritain.[88]

However, in 1927, neither Ghéon (fifty-two years old) nor Maritain (forty-five) belonged literally to a 'young generation.' For Calvet, the codeword 'generation' did not signal a biological artifact of common birthdates so much as an intellectual paradigm shift – that is, a vision or a collective way of interpreting the world that had arrived to replace an outworn one.[89] Unlike their fin-de-siècle elders, who pursued progress without any regard for tradition, this new generation of 'the very youngest writers' wanted instead to 'apprentice themselves to the tradition before transmitting it.' Noting that classical Greek writers, Enlightenment philosophers, and even modern scientists acknowledged the existence of 'climacteric' years – fundamental physical and moral turning points in an organism's life – Calvet interpreted the postwar period as one such climacteric in the life of France. To make his point, he quoted no less an authority than the nineteenth-century literary giant, Charles Sainte-Beuve. 'There are decisive times in the life of individuals,' Sainte-Beuve had written a decade after the 1830 revolution, in which 'their physical or moral constitution suddenly undergoes serious changes and re-founds itself once again, in which one must 'bail them out' so to speak, in a certain style and under certain conditions, with one's ideas and with the means at hand. There are, in a word, years of *climacteric* as ancient medicine called them, *palingenesis* as the modern philosophers call them. Such critical periods may be found equally well during the life of an epoch ... Are we not ourselves, in both a moral and literary aspect, in one of these moments ...'[90] With the hindsight afforded by his own decade, Calvet interpreted France's postwar moment as a climacteric: a generational crisis, dangerous to pass through, demanding both physical and moral regeneration. 'The young generation,' he said, had been 'mutilated and instructed by the war.' It had been up to them to plant a cultural harvest, to take up the 'work upon a terrain' whose 'undergrowth of scientism' had 'already been cleared away' by predecessors such as Bloy, Huysmans, and Péguy.

Moreover, they had needed to forge a future by a creative inheritance of the tradition – by a palingenesis, with its connotations of physical regeneration, organic metamorphosis, and even bodily resurrection. In Sainte-Beuve's time, palingenesis had been an early nineteenth-century biological theory about the supposed production of new life from putrescent animal matter. (Like the theory of spontaneous generation, it held out the hope of 'absolute desiccation without losing the faculty of resurrection,' and was refined after Darwin to mean the 'appearance of inherited characteristics from distant ancestors which are not found in immediate predecessors.')[91] As used by Calvet, it expressed what might be called 'futurist nostalgia' or 'avant-garde traditionalism' – a critical evolutionary moment in which older characteristics return after a period of absence, are inherited by a new generation, and are reproduced in some kind of new organic synthesis.

'*Now or never*,' Calvet wrote of 1918, '*was the time for a palingenesis, for a new birth*. It was necessary to put away the old timidity which had for a long time paralyzed the Catholics and the thinkers in their turn.' Calvet turned the tables on Ernest Renan's visionary program of a complete 'intellectual and moral reform': 'We had to risk thinking, risk judging, risk revising the judgments of laicist thought and completely reform the grid of values [*la table des valeurs*]' – the phrase evoked Mendeleev's periodical table based on patterns of combining 'valency'[92] – 'by reclassifying ideas and men.' Calvet's astute insight accords with recent historical reflections: so long as Catholics continued to think within schemes of perception and appreciation that had been imposed by dominant groups, they internalized those same symbolic relations of force. Symbolic violence, as Pierre Bourdieu (influenced by Antonio Gramsci) has suggested, can only succeed insofar as the subjected persons are predisposed to accept the imposed categories and 'recognize' the violence. As Calvet understood, postwar Catholics needed to reject (and even invert) inculcated principles and imposed identities that perpetuated (and guaranteed) their marginal status.[93]

This mammoth undertaking could not be the particular province simply of clerics or theologians: 'In order to reconstruct the *table des valeurs*, it was no longer a question of being inspired by a vague philosophy,' even if it was 'itself derived from the Gospel.' Nor, with 'all due respect to theology,' could the effort be one of theological exploration 'simply in order to deepen our understanding'; that was 'the role of specialists.' Rather, this reform program would take theology's conclusions as a 'point of departure' as it moved into the wider public sphere and '*searched for ways to integrate art and life*.' The moment demanded a radical reformation: 'the time had come to insist on *pure Catholicism, integrally accepted and lived out*.'[94] Calvet's play on the variations of the word *intégral*, itself a clever example of discursive palingenesis, draws our attention to the many ways in which bodily fragmentation and redemption are implied in postwar discourse.[95] Before the war, an 'integralist' Catholicism meant an anti-Modernist intellectual assent to the correct theological propositions. But for Calvet, this 'ghetto-ized' attitude had ill-served its adherents: while Catholics were bloodying one another over intramural struggles, mainstream French thought and art had gone its own way.

So, in this postwar effort at renewal, the Catholics of 1918 had done things differently: they were 'not simply pleading for doctrine ... not continuously being on the defensive' as if they were 'always under indictment,' and not making themselves satisfied with their 'status as beggars.' Instead, they 'staked out [their] claim,' namely, that Catholicism could enrich 'modern thought whose destitution,' whether knowingly or not, was begging 'for this kind of nourishment.' In the final analysis, it had been a matter of *refusing to recognize* the hegemony, a matter of 'Catholic thinkers taking the place of privilege which belongs to them and presenting themselves as benefactors of the new world.'[96]

The conditions of the Great War brought about a radically new relationship of forces which made possible within the ranks of Catholic intellectuals the movement from an oppositional 'eternalist' stance to a hylomorphic one: coming in from the *banlieue* to the *cité*, they had assumed the role of an *entelechy* animating the body politic. The reason for their success is suggested by the metaphorical appeal of palingenesis: 1920s modernism, we now see, was generally *off-modern* – a mixture, hybrid, or dialectical synthesis of futurism and nostalgia. This need to retrieve traditional traits in service of repairing a war-torn self-identity marked not just Catholics but French postwar society and mentality in general. As one part of this wider cultural thrust, the *renouveau catholique* succeeded remarkably. In a decade marked by dialectical realisms, 'Christian realism' appealed to a 'generation' *réaliste* yet *mystique*. Their 'crazy need for synthesis' typified 'the Crazy Years.'

PART TWO

Jacques and Raïssa Maritain: Cultural Hylomorphism

Chapter 4

Ultramodernist Anti-modernism: Neoclassical Catholicism

> In former days the artist remained unknown and his work was to the glory of God. He lived and died without being more or less important than other artisans; 'eternal values,' 'immortality' and 'masterpiece' were terms not applicable in his case. The ability to create was a gift. In such a world flourished invulnerable assurance and natural humility ... Today the individual has become the highest form and the greatest bane of artistic creation ... The artist considers his isolation, his subjectivity, his individualism almost holy ... Thus if I am asked what I would like the general purpose of my films to be, I would reply that I want to be one of the artists in the cathedral on the great plain ... Regardless of whether I believe or not, whether I am a Christian or not, I would play my part in the collective building of the cathedral.
>
> – Ingmar Bergman

> True realism consists in displaying the surprising things
> which habit conceals under a dust cover and prevents us from seeing.
>
> – Jean Cocteau

> Classicism is Memory and Sorrow ...
>
> – Vincent Scully[1]

In Jacques Maritain's landmark *Art and Scholasticism* (1920), two personified virtues – Art and Prudence – represented forces previously thought incompatible: modern artists and neo-scholastic philosophers, immoralists and men of order, bohemians and bourgeois, culture and Catholicism. The work's title nicely summarized Maritain's appeal to a culture in chaos: the reconciliation of former foes. To a 'realist generation,' he offered three tantalizing propositions: first, privileged and infallible access to what is real: that is, certain, unchanging, and eternal forms. Second, he showed that what is real not only *could* but even *ought to be* clothed in avant-garde matter, the most modern Jazz Age productions. Finally, he proposed important equivalences allowing him to refashion Catholicism: the artistic imitation of the underlying 'form' was an imitation of divine creation. As a corollary, the true artist performed that imitation with infallible rectitude. Hence, the artist was always in some way participating in a divine act. This application of ancient hylomorphism made it possible to reimagine the relationship of Catholicism to culture as one of form to matter.

Jean Cocteau's Neoclassicist Realism: An Off-modern *Avant-Garde*

In his project of making neo-scholasticism a postwar avant-garde, Maritain would rely heavily upon Jean Cocteau, an ultramodernist figure whose neoclassicism also privileged eternal forms. The Maritains had first encountered Cocteau's work through the composer Georges Auric, a member of Cocteau's musical Group of Six. They had met Auric in 1916 at the Montmartre home of Léon Bloy. In the summer of 1918, Auric read them Cocteau's long poem, *The Cape of Good Hope* (1918). As is clear from Raïssa's diary entry for 25 March 1919, citing Cocteau, the Maritains had also received a copy of Cocteau's *The Cock and the Harlequin* (1918), either from Auric or from Père Charles Henrion, a priest much involved in the arts.[2] Cocteau's anti-modernist theory of the avant-garde would provide Maritain with just the ambivalent possibilities that his own project needed.

Cocteau's talent for refashioning found materials as something new predated the war, and it was not initially seen as an unmitigated good. Henri Ghéon published the first review of Cocteau in the celebrated *N.R.F.* in the autumn of 1912.[3] (Ghéon, André Gide's closest friend and later a prominent figure in Catholic revivalism, had a colourful past. His 'innumerable homosexual exploits' with Gide included 'an extraordinary six-month long, three-cornered affair' with Jean Schlumberger's eighteen-year-old brother.)[4] Ghéon's stinging review of the poems in *The Dance of Sophocles* (1912) asserted that Cocteau's reputation had been manufactured by 'all the dispensers of instant glory' and questioned his originality. 'But to determine which of his gifts are authentic, which ones borrowed, would require the most patient analysis. *He discovers and he rediscovers*.'

While Cocteau appeared to be 'extraordinarily gifted,' he was also 'extremely youthful,' and even his most successful work lacked 'the necessary moral homogeneity' to have any cohesion or depth.[5] Deeply wounded, Cocteau retreated from the Parisian public eye and spent 1913 recovering and retooling at Igor Stravinsky's family home in Leysen, Switzerland.

The war that came the following year ushered in an epoch that valued the capacity for sacred unions – for combining apparently incompatible elements and making the old seem young again. The French literary left, which had long called for reconciliation with the Germans, found itself in the position of having to prove its patriotism. Members of this tendency, to whom Cocteau had attached himself – including colleagues like Guillaume Apollinaire and surrogate fathers like André Gide and Marcel Proust – all suddenly found themselves on the defensive. The circulation of Maurras's *L'Action française* skyrocketed as Apollinaire, Gide, Proust, Rodin, and many others took out wartime subscriptions to 'integral nationalism's' daily newspaper.[6] Like socialism itself, anything international in scope and extending beyond the *patrie*'s frontier came to be seen as 'German.'[7] This included Pablo Picasso's cubism, whose geometrical abstraction, in spite of its execution by a Spaniard in Paris, lack the 'Latin' subject matter that would make it French.

On the aesthetic right, the florid effusions of Russian exoticism and impressionistic symbolism now seemed to represent anarchic and decadent disorder. Stravinsky's *The Rite of Spring* (whose premiere on 29 May 1913 had caused riots) had been a neo-primitivist celebration of primeval instincts and sexual passions and represented human sacrifice in pagan Russia. But now France was engulfed in a horrific slaughter of its own youth.[8] Cocteau had been closely associated with Stravinsky and also with Diaghilev and Nijinsky of the Ballets Russes. He now turned away from the 'Orient,' issuing a 'call to order' and a restoration of France's 'Latin' roots.

With cubist abstraction and exotic decoration both being attacked, Cocteau seized the opportunity to co-found the journal *Le Mot* ('The Word') in September 1914. In his now-classic study of the Parisian avant-garde, Kenneth Silver has noted that Cocteau's 1914–15 collaboration on the journal already showed his 'working method: his hesitation between self-consciously modernist culture and anti-modernist reaction will be transformed into an aesthetic of ambiguity; what had been equivocation will become pluralism, and will put Cocteau in the ideal position to influence the course of events in the Parisian art world.'[9] On the one hand, *Le Mot* sought in March 1915 to save 'leftist' strains of 'cosmopolitan' art such as Picasso's cubism: by indiscriminately throwing 'shoddy goods from Munich and the masterpieces of the pure French tradition' into the 'same sack' for grain, confusion was already arising and young painters were being 'reproached for Berlin influence.' Cocteau urged discretion: 'Ah! let us safeguard the treasure of France ... let us be careful not to throw away the good grain with the bad.'

On the other hand, the journal defended the 'rightist' anti-modernists as well – those who refused to give up the great German masters of romanticism and symbolism. 'Wagner is indigestible but brilliant,' wrote Cocteau. Although it was true that 'Munich is atrocious,' nevertheless 'a pure French return to sublime simplicity' demanded that Germany not be rejected altogether. 'I will no longer brush my teeth with Odol, but I will not deprive myself of Schubert, Bach, or Beethoven.'

In short, *Le Mot* situated itself as being neither right nor left. Rather, it offered a self-imagined voice of moderation positioned in the centre, resisting wartime hysteria. *Le Mot* begged its 'devoted readers to follow it, believe in it, and have confidence in it.' It hoped to become, 'little by little, the organ of common sense, equilibrium, and intellectual order.'[10] French rationality was capable of accommodating both the abstract cubism of Montmartre and the sensuous excess of Bayreuth.

Cocteau had an opportunity to realize concretely this conciliatory vision after his own tour of military duty. On 18 May 1917, he opened his production of *Parade* as a patriotic benefit for the *mutilés de guerre* (wounded veterans) of the eastern Ardennes region. Both the aesthetic left and right collaborated on the production: Picasso created the sets and costumes while Diaghilev staged the production. Cocteau wrote the story for Erik Satie's musical score.[11]

Cocteau meant *Parade* to be 'the first great public and monumental example of the new avant-garde neoclassicism,' a manifestation of the postwar 'reawakening' of the 'French spirit.' Apollinaire would later define this 'new spirit' as 'a particular and lyric expression of the French nation, just as the classical spirit is a sublime expression, *par excellence*, of that nation.'[12] Cocteau intended the work as a 'realist ballet' that would be 'more real than the real' and hence redefine the real. To convey this ultra-realism, Apollinaire coined the term *sur-réalisme* for the program notes and announced that *Parade* was to be 'the point of departure of a series of manifestations of the *Esprit nouveau*, which will not fail to seduce the elite and which promises to transform arts and manners in universal exhilaration.'[13]

The word *parade* means 'sideshow,' that is, the tent one would find at a circus. By means of this metaphor, the ballet's narrative redefined the 'real' as something surprising and hidden beneath the exteriors we habitually perceive without notice. The barkers outside the sideshow tent try everything they can to tempt Sunday strollers to step inside and see the real show going on under the tent. But the audience, convinced that the real show is outside and that 'realism' is to be read on the surface of things, cannot be lured in to see what lies beneath the cloak of the circus tent.

Life imitates art. The audience at the ballet, like the audience within the ballet, could not be persuaded to accommodate this sacred union: 'the radicalization of Diaghilev and the *embourgeoisement* of Pablo Picasso.'[14] *Parade* turned into a debacle that failed to seduce as promised, managing only to scandalize. After twenty minutes, the audience jeered, hooted, and took to fist-fighting while shouting jingoist epithets (all this at a benefit for *mutilés de guerre*): Krauts! Wops! Treason! German Art! Cocteau recalled overhearing one man remark, 'If I had known it was going to be so stupid, I would have brought my children.' Gide's journal records his backstage visit with Cocteau: 'He knows very well that Picasso created the sets and the costumes; Satie composed the music, but he wonders if Picasso and Satie are not by Cocteau.'[15] Ghéon's 1912 review of Cocteau had echoed a letter of Gide; now Gide's assessment echoed Ghéon's: '*He discovers and he rediscovers*.'

In an effort to reaffirm his patriotism, Cocteau immediately began writing *The Cock and the Harlequin* (1918), a book of musical 'neoclassicist' aesthetics shot through with a nationalist polemic.[16] It served as a manifesto for the postwar neoclassical movement, and in particular as an apologia for the musical Group of Six: Georges Auric, Louis Durey, Arthur Honegger, Darius Milhaud, Francis Poulenc, and Germaine Tailleferre.[17] Its jingoism appeared immediately in the dedication to Georges Auric explaining the book's title: 'I admire the Harlequins of Cézanne and Picasso,' he wrote, 'but I do not like Harlequin. He wears a black mask and a costume of all colors.' Like German art, Harlequin's mask allowed him to pass for French art. But he dissimulated; he was a traitor. Cocteau alluded to the Gospel scene in which Peter, confronted around a campfire, disguised the fact that he was a follower of Christ. Hearing the predicted cock's crow at the sun's rising (whose light uncovered the darkness), Peter was revealed as a traitor. 'After denying the cock's crow,' Cocteau continued, Harlequin 'goes away to hide. He is a cock of the night.'

On the other hand, the Gallic Cock did not dissimulate. 'I like the real cock ... The cock lives on his *own* farm.' The book was dedicated to Auric because he had '*escaped from Germany.*' Italicized in the original, Cocteau meant to discredit other musicians (especially Claude Debussy) who could not escape writing 'German' music under Wagner's romantic spell. But a new age had dawned, and a musician of Auric's age proclaimed 'the richness and grace of a generation that no longer grimaces, or wears a mask or hides or shirks, and is not afraid to admire or to stand up for what it admires. It hates paradox and eclecticism ... It also shuns the colossal. That is what I call escaping from Germany. Long live the Cock! Down with Harlequin!'[18]

The rest of *The Cock* was a call for an allegedly Latin, neoclassical, and 'French' aesthetic: 'The music I want must be French, of France,' Cocteau demanded, sounding suspiciously like the masthead slogan for Drumont's *La Libre Parole* – 'France for the French.'[19] *The Cock and the Harlequin* consisted largely of aphorisms lampooning Germans and Russians. For example: 'Socrates said: "Who is that man who eats bread as if it were a good full meal and splendid food as if it were bread?" Answer: The German musical enthusiast.' Cocteau also lashed out at those who had ridiculed *Parade* and called it 'Kraut' music. Turning the tables, he associated those who were incapable of appreciating the 'new spirit' with German decadence: 'The opposition of the masses to the élite stimulates individual genius. This is the case in France. Modern Germany is dying of approbation, carefulness, application and a scholastic vulgarization of aristocratic culture.'[20] As Silver has noted, all of this was extremely close to the anti-modernist xenophobia in Léon Daudet's *Out from Beneath the German Yoke* (1915). 'As Cocteau demonstrated so well, the turgid, narrow, and boring cultural theories of the extreme Right could, with a bit of wit and ironic distance, seem fresh again.'[21]

Cocteau exalted the lonely genius of the misunderstood avant-gardist whose innovations offend the uncomprehending masses. *The Cock*, intended partly as a defence of the music of Erik Satie, apologized for having dragged Cocteau's friends away from the élite surroundings of the café-concert to the low-brow theatre more popular with the masses: 'THE CAFÉ-CONCERT IS OFTEN PURE; THE THEATRE IS ALWAYS CORRUPT.' Cocteau added: 'Let us keep clear of the theatre. I regret to have felt its temptation and to have introduced to it two great artists [Picasso and Satie].' He did not 'regret it because of the scandal; the full realization of my idea would have created the same scandal' in any setting whatsoever. But by having staged *Parade* in a popular setting, he had put it in 'a sphere where the public, a hundred years behind the times, cannot possibly be taken into consideration.'[22]

In another comparison illustrating the speed at which the artist advances ahead of the masses, Cocteau lampooned the public's transport: 'It is the artist who is really rich. He rides in a motor car. The public follows in a 'bus. How can we be surprised if it follows at a distance?' In trademark capitals, he summarized this elitism in another aphorism:

WHEN A WORK OF ART APPEARS TO BE IN ADVANCE OF ITS PERIOD,
IT IS REALLY THE PERIOD THAT HAS LAGGED BEHIND THE WORK OF ART.[23]

None of this avant-gardism was genuinely new. One aphorism, however, stood out from among the rest as being an innovation: a neoclassical rewriting of the avant-garde as being the surface disguise of underlying unchanging tradition.

TRADITION APPEARS AT EVERY EPOCH UNDER A DIFFERENT DISGUISE,
BUT THE PUBLIC DOES NOT RECOGNIZE IT EASILY
AND NEVER DISCOVERS IT UNDERNEATH ITS MASKS.[24]

Cocteau had imagined *Parade* as a 'ballet-réaliste,' 'more real than the real.' In order to discover it, one needed to look beneath the tent and the masses resisted all lures. But what was to be discovered? What treasures did the avant-garde have to reveal? Cocteau's answer would be extremely significant for postwar Catholicism: *tradition*. Unchanging tradition lay hidden beneath the mask of ever-changing fashion.

Cocteau's image was genial: one might presume that the masses, always lagging behind, would be clinging to 'tradition.' However, the opposite was true. Since 'the public likes to "recognize" what is familiar ... hates to be disturbed ... [and] is shocked by surprises,' it is incapable of discovering tradition. Hence, the worst that could 'happen to a work of art is to have no fault found with it so that its author is not obliged to take up an attitude of opposition.' This was the motto that every artist needed to get 'well into your head': 'Cultivate those qualities in you for which the public blames you: they are Thyself.'[25] On the final page of *The Cock*, Cocteau expressed this sentiment in evocative language:

WE SHELTER AN ANGEL WHOM WE SHOCK WITHOUT CEASING. WE MUST BECOME GUARDIANS OF THIS ANGEL.

Shelter well your virtue of performing miracles because 'if they knew that you are missionaries, they would have torn out your tongue and fingernails.'

These are the words that Raïssa Maritain would paraphrase in March 1919: 'This angel of which the artist must be the guardian is properly speaking his own rectitude as an artist.'[26]

Cocteau's anti-modernist / avant-garde appeal for the Maritains was at least threefold: the function of art was to bring to light the deeper realities that remain hidden in everyday life; those deeper realities were in fact a tradition that assumed modern garb; and paradoxically, an élite vanguard was required to penetrate the surface tent and rediscover antiquity. Ancient Catholic ideas like sacramentalism and hylomorphism had found their avant-garde expression in Cocteau's sideshow.

Form and *Déformation*: 'The truth is never in the copy.'

In the 10 March 1920 issue of *La Revue des jeunes*, two months after Maritain's pilgrimage-homage to Psichari at Louvain, yet another account of his and Raïssa's aesthetics appeared as 'Notes on Saint Thomas and the Theory of Art.'[27] After noting that he had already tried to set out his theory in *Les Lettres* during the past autumn, Maritain specified that the present article would revisit a special chapter in that study, 'and show how the principles of Saint Thomas allow us to reconceptualize' an ancient problem that preoccupied 'modern artists: that of *imitation* in art.'[28] Maritain's key to reconciling the antique and the modern would turn on the hylomorphic notion of 'form.' By showing that both ancient and avant-garde aesthetics advocated the 'de-formation' of surface representations in order to express a deeper sense of 'form,' Maritain united past and future in their opposition to *imitation* as understood by nineteenth-century naturalism.

Maritain began with Aquinas's idea of the beautiful as a 'bursting forth of the *form*, – of a form in the *metaphysical* sense of this word, which is to say of an immaterial radiation, – a created derivation of the first bursting forth, – which gives to each thing the seal of being.' Moreover, it was the apprehension of the 'splendor of the form' – Maritain preserved the Latin: *splendor formae* – which gave intelligence its joy in the face of beauty, a joy which 'art can only bring to the intelligence by means of the *intuition of the sense*.'[29] The exact meaning of Maritain's paradoxical notion of 'intuition' – that is, an immediate apprehension of a non-material form by means of physical sensation – has kept students of his work busy ever since.[30] For present purposes, it is simply important to recall Maritain's earlier influences and underline the continuity: the conjunction of 'form' as internal *entelechy* (and not 'outward shape') with the notion of artistic *intuition* as privileged access to the real drew on

Bergson's vitalism and Driesch's embryology.

This double influence let Maritain negotiate his dialectical realism as something neither strictly realist nor strictly idealist: 'the *imitation* proper to art does not consist in copying a sensible appearance, as realism likes to do, nor an ideal archetype, like platonic idealism would like.' Artistic imitation was rather the use of 'sensible signs' in order to 'express or manifest' what 'Aristotle called a *form*, which is to say a principle of intelligible determination, a spiritual radiation present in things.' The artist's special gift – here Maritain owed Bergson's *Laughter* (1900) a large debt – was the capacity to 'discern' this form, which 'sometimes shines for him only, in the very depths of the real, in the midst of the exterior or of the interior world.'

Having established that for both Aristotle and Aquinas the true form is the invisible form, Maritain could now repudiate representational art of every kind and simultaneously reconcile the most abstract of modern art with the most ancient of Catholic texts. In order 'to manifest this form, and therefore to be perfectly *docile* and *faithful* to the invisible Spirit who plays in nature,' the artist was not only permitted – the artist was *required* – to abstain from exact representation: 'even necessarily must, deform, reconstruct, and freely transfigure the material appearances of nature.' Art indeed imitated nature, but 'not in a servile or material way, as does for example photography or casting a mould' – this kind of 'servile imitation is the destruction of art pure and simple.' Instead, art imitated nature 'with filial spiritual devotion ... not its exterior aspects, but those very processes that ... are only a participation in and a derivation of the divine Art itself in things.' Perhaps realizing that such an embrace of the avant-garde might sound implausible, he concluded this passage with the magisterial Latin of the scholastics: '*ars imitatur naturam* IN SUA OPERATIONE' – *art imitates nature* IN ITS OPERATIONS. Art imitated nature, but in nature's *internal* – or (synthesizing Aristotle, Bergson, and Driesch) *vital* – processes of animating a particular material organism. Along with this ancient authority Maritain invoked a modern as well, quoting Cézanne's post-impressionist condemnation of naturalism: 'there is a horrible resemblance.'[31]

Thus, the true artist was implicitly a 'religious' artist simply by being 'perfectly docile and faithful to the invisible Spirit' whose operation of nature was both a 'participation in and a derivation of the divine Art itself.'

Aquinas provided the ancient integralist authority; the modern was now provided by the post-impressionists Paul Gauguin and Maurice Denis (whose avant-gardist 'neo-traditionalism' was newly popular after the war). These two 'reflective and very conscious artists' would both tell you (in the words of Denis) that 'the thing which must be deplored the most ... [is] this idea that art is the *copy* of something.' Maritain glossed: 'to believe that art consists in *copying* or in reproducing things exactly is to pervert the meaning of art.'[32]

If the post-impressionists were Maritain's heros, Ingres and Rodin, both of whom had Romantic appeal in their own ways, and both 'more passionate and with less sharp intelligences,' provided the foil. Ingres said it was necessary '*to copy* quite simply, quite stupidly, to copy slavishly that which one has before one's eyes'; Rodin declared himself 'in complete obedience to nature and never pretending to be in command of it. My only ambition is to be slavishly faithful to [nature].' Maritain objected that the words '"copy" and "slavish"' were used here 'in a very improper sense.' Imitating nature was not a matter of 'slavishly imitating the object.' Rather, it meant 'to manifest with the greatest fidelity, at the price of employing all the "deformations" that might be necessary, the *form* or the radiant intelligibility whose bursting-forth is seized in the real.'[33]

So, for Maritain, the most ancient (Aquinas) and the most modern (Denis) were thoroughly in accord with one another, whereas the real discord was to be found in an illegitimate interregnum (Ingres, Rodin), that is, the 'realist' period from the Renaissance through nineteenth-century naturalism. 'Medieval art was naturally, instinctively, protected against naturalism ... by the hieratic traditions which came to it from the Byzantines': it did not 'copy the materiality of nature,' nor did 'it copy immoveable supersensible exemplars,' being rather 'astonishingly indifferent to material regularity and geometrical correctness.'[34] Whether or not Maritain knew enough art history to know that Romanesque artists eschewed mimetic resemblance in an attempt to get at the *res* – that is, *the thing itself*[35] – he genially used the medievals in service of his own quasi-Bergsonian project. Art, and especially twentieth-century formalist and abstract art, provided privileged and immediate access to the most truly *real*.

Maritain ended this largely metaphysical essay with an ode to medieval artisans that associated them with military heroes. Artisans had been 'faithful to the point of heroism' with respect to 'the vital necessities of intelligence.' Their 'liberty of the mind' had been 'overflowing with spirituality' that was 'daring, rash, inventive,' and – 'like the metaphysics of Saint Thomas' – was 'in love with being ... receptive to all the aspects of sensible reality, but dominated by the supernatural realities present at its heart.'[36]

Maritain's final sentence (misquoted and without attribution) included a fragment from Dante's *Inferno*. Just as Cocteau's wartime *Le Mot* had featured Dante on one of its covers with the words 'Dante on Our Side'[37] – that is, the symbol of 'Latin genius' on the side of both France as well as Cocteau's call to order – so Maritain used Dante to trace his genealogy back to Latin forms and the 'Catholic' Middle Ages. Praising the 'art of the Middle Ages, true child of God,' Maritain quoted Dante – *Sicchè l'arte vostra a Dio e nipote* – and lauded his 'divinely glorious – and so profoundly human as well! – illustration of the great ideas of Saint Thomas on art and on beauty, *resplendentia formae super partes materiae proportionatas*.'[38] Letting Aquinas's untranslated formula serve as the ultimate verification of appeals to symbolist, Decadent, and formalist artists (Baudelaire, Redon, Cézanne, Gauguin, and Denis) underscored Maritain's key point: moderns expressed timeless values in fashionable ways.

In this seminal essay appearing in March 1920, we see the genius of Maritain's postwar project in germ. It was, to use a phrase of Michel Foucault, 'the reversal of a relationship of forces, the usurpation of power, the appropriation of a vocabulary turned against those who once used it.'[39] This translation of antiquity as modernity was made possible by Maritain's central innovation: the use of hylomorphism to insist that 'art imitating nature' meant *not* the slavish copy of outward shape but rather the imitation of the 'form' as *entelechy*. Catholicism and culture were eminently reconcilable – both had rejected the modernity of naturalism.

A Sacred Union: *Art et scholastique*/Art and Prudence

Two months after this essay in *La Revue des jeunes*, *Art and Scholasticism* appeared as a small monograph on 25 May 1920. A work of modest proportions, purporting to be a philosophical treatise on scholastic aesthetics, the book's success was both unexpected and phenomenal. Translated into languages all over the globe, it would refashion Thomism's cultural location and establish Maritain's reputation.[40] *Art and Scholasticism*'s singular novelty was implicit in its title: it hybridized a traditionally anti-modernist Catholic metaphysics with the postwar avant-garde. It offered a postwar promise: Catholicism and modernity had been reconciled.

This fusion was not found primarily in the narrative of the main text, whose style resembled in every way a standard work of scholastic philosophy. The innovation lay rather in the endnotes: Maritain's legitimating sources came not only from the expected medieval masters, but also from moderns (who often conflicted with themselves).[41] For example, in notes 152/3 and 154, Maritain juxtaposed Aquinas's *Summa Theologica*, the most canonical Catholic urtext, with Cocteau:

> 152. *Sum. theol.,* I-II, q. 43, a.3. «Cum igitur homo cessat ab usu intellectualis habitus, insurgunt imaginationes extraneae ... corrumpitur intellectualis habitus».
> 153. *Ibid.,* q. 42, a.3.
> 154. JEAN COCTEAU, *The Cock and the Harlequin*[42]

The juxtaposition would have surprised some and appalled others. The untranslated Latin conveyed the 'universal timelessness' of the passage – a text equally relevant (or irrelevant, depending on one's point of view) to any historical time and place. Cocteau's *The Cock* showed that neo-scholasticism really was forever young in another sense: it could accommodate even the avant-garde.

Another unlikely set of notes juxtaposed Maurras and Gide:

> 142. M. ANDRÉ GIDE EXCELLENTLY WRITES: 'By nationalizing itself a literature takes its place and finds it significance in the concert of humanity ... What more Spanish than Cervantes? More English than Shakespeare? More Italian than Dante? More French than Voltaire or Montaigne, than Descartes or Pascal? ... and what more universally human than these writers?' (*Reflections on Germany*, Nouvelle Revue française, 1 June 1919)

Maritain amplified Gide's observations with Maurras's:

> 143. Of the people of Athens Charles Maurras has written: 'The philosophical spirit, quickness to conceive the Universal permeated all their arts ... The classical, the Attic, is the more universal in proportion as it is more austerely Athenian–Athenian of an epoch and a taste better purged of all foreign influence.[43]

Both the proto-Fascist and the 'immoralist' made the same postwar jingoistic point: what was most 'particularly nationalistic' could, in fact, be what was most 'universally human.' Such juxtapositions were, to use the metaphor that ran throughout the book, the union of two virtues that modern culture desperately needed: anti-modernist 'Prudence' and ultramodernist 'Art.' This was the innovative genius of hybridizing 'art and scholasticism.'

Descended from a long tradition of France's *mission civilisatrice* (civilizing mission), the notion that a thoroughly particular French culture had universal relevance for all of humanity was a postwar site in which former antagonists could find reconciliation.[44] Maritain's own gloss elucidated a particularist / universalism that could be written by Maurras, Massis, Gide, or Cocteau: 'The most universal and most humane works are those that bear most openly the distinguishing mark of their fatherland [*patrie*].' The works of 'Pascal and Bossuet' that had established the French language in its classical form, making it the *lingua franca* in diplomatic circles around the globe, were written during the absolutist monarchy, 'an age of vigorous nationalism.' (Maritain did not mention that Bossuet's Gallican absolutism and Pascal's Jansenist anti-monarchism would have shared little in common besides their linguistic artistry.)

Reach back even further to the time of the Abbey of Cluny's 'amazingly peaceful victories' that had created a transnational culture, and to 'St Louis's reign,' one could see that cosmopolitan Christendom had been imbued with 'an intellectual radiance most authentically French.' At precisely the time when French culture was most particular, 'the world knew the purest and freest International of the mind, and the most universal culture.' Thus, Maritain concluded, 'a certain kind of nationalism – *political and territorial nationalism* – is the natural safeguard of ... the very universality of intelligence and art.'[45] A year earlier, Barbusse had called for an 'International of thought'; Massis responded with his call for a 'Party of Intelligence' particularly French and Catholic. Like Cocteau, Maritain seemed to unite left and right in his call for a particular French culture that would 'safeguard' an 'international' of intelligence and art.

As a rhetorical device, Maritain personified the 'virtues' of Art and Prudence. This allowed him to propose a diagnosis for postwar distress (i.e., the modern 'divorce' of these virtues) as well as a prescription for recovery (i.e., their reconciliation). On the one hand, at the 'time of the Italian Renaissance,' in a 'civilization solely inclined to the *Virtù* of the Humanists,' Prudence had been 'sacrificed to Art.' In a culture that endorsed art for art's sake, this 'turn away from Wisdom and Contemplation' that aimed 'lower than God' became 'the first cause of all disorder' in a 'Christian civilization.' On the other hand, nineteenth-century bourgeois moderates [*bien pensants*], 'inclined solely to Respectability' – and implicitly prudery – had subordinated Art to Prudence. This 'ungodly divorce between Art and Prudence' was noticeable in times when Christians had 'lost the strength to bear the integral fullness [*intégrité*] of their riches.'[46]

Focusing on the Renaissance as the beginning of religious art's decline into sensual representation had been common coin in the ultramontanist aesthetic. Maritain appropriated this language but for a different purpose: by discrediting realism he could closely link medieval and contemporary non-representational art with one another. To the line seen above in the 'Notes on Saint Thomas' – 'Medieval art was naturally, instinctively, protected against naturalism ... by the hieratic traditions which came to it from the Byzantines' – Maritain now added this gloss: 'the art of the Renaissance on the contrary allowed itself *to be gravely contaminated.*'[47] Bodily metaphors of purity and pollution (nudity, virginity, chastity, perversion, contamination) recurred in Maritain's writings on art throughout this decade. Art was about restoring organic integrity to a fragmented body politic.

Maritain also located the Renaissance as the moment when the artisan's *métier* became corrupted into the artist's *beaux-arts*, and he concluded in a way consonant with his boyhood socialism: 'The divorce was a consequence of the changes which had taken place in the fabric of society and in particular of the rising of the bourgeois class.'[48] The Italian Renaissance had divorced art (as Machiavelli had divorced politics) from ethical concerns, and in the nineteenth century, they had sacrificed true Art for naturalist representations, satisfying bourgeois tastes. (The angry ghost of Bloy haunts these pages, but the code words – *civilisation*, *désordre*, *l'intégrité* – had distinctly postwar overtones.)

In the postwar crisis, Christians needed a certain kind of heroism: the 'strength' to bear the heavy *intégrité* of their riches. As both contemplative artists and prudential persons, Catholic citizens needed to immerse themselves in the *cité*. For Maritain, the ideal postwar Christian seemed to be the creative artist – or at least, someone who could appreciate the modern artist's work. Seen within the wider context of the immediate postwar period – widespread food, milk, and coal shortages, spiralling inflation, *mutilés de guerre* crowding the streets, and the practical business of burying and mourning the dead – Maritain's diagnosis and prescription seem a bit bizarre. However, his primary promise to unite apparently irreconcilable differences – Art and Prudence, art and scholasticism, culture and Catholicism, Gide and Maurras, modern and antimodern – had tremendous appeal for a culture in need of synthesis. The medium was the message: in the juxtaposition of apparently contradictory sources, Art and Prudence had been demonstrably reconciled in the text itself.

The Infallibility of Art and Its Authority over Prudence

Maritain wished to frame his aesthetic so as to establish the intrinsic 'infallibility' (and hence independence) of Art from the sometimes fallible moral judgments (lapses in Prudence) of its practitioners. As seen above, Raïssa recorded the couple's ruminations about this concern in the winter/spring of 1919 and solved the problem by distinguishing between *pudeur* and *pruderie*. It is also instructive to recall that Maritain's boyhood literary hero had been Charles Baudelaire. Did a Catholic convert need to renounce a passion for Baudelaire, prosecuted on charges of immorality? (With seventeen citations, Baudelaire was *Art and Scholasticism*'s most frequently cited source after Aquinas [forty-nine] and Aristotle [twenty-eight]. The Maritains would soon become members of the Société Baudelaire.) Could the odes to Lesbos in *The Flowers of Evil* be poetically infallible regardless of the poet's hashish addiction and his horrific suffering (and eventual death) from syphilis? Could *The Immoralist* (1902) by a towering figure in French intellectual life be infallibly correct independently of Gide's own moral location?

Questions like these show the tremendous cultural appeal of what might seem like an impossibly abstract (and perhaps irrelevant) method: Maritain wanted to overcome the oppositions of the fin-de-siècle that had hermetically sealed 'pure' eternalist Catholics from contamination by the polluted *cité*. 'When he disapproves of a work of art,' wrote Maritain, 'the prudent man, securely based on his moral virtue, is firmly persuaded that he is defending against the artist a sacred good, the good of making; and he looks upon the artist as a child or a lunatic.' Conversely, the artist, perched 'upon his intellectual *habitus* ... is sure that he is defending a good no less sacred, that of Beauty ... The prudent man and the artist therefore find it hard to understand each other.'[49]

In this regard, being a scholastic philosopher helped Maritain, since scholasticism, which preceded the invention of the idea of 'fine arts,' did not actually have a theory about them. At the book's very outset, Maritain stated the obvious: 'The Scholastics composed no special treatise with the title "Philosophy of Art."'[50] Maritain turned what might be a deficit for a less creative thinker into an asset: he gave himself convenient permission for what we might call a 'fishing expedition' into scholasticism's wide range of topics, seeking the bits and pieces that suited his purpose – from the 'art of the shipwright to the art of the grammarian and the logician.' He could then go on to pick and choose for his aesthetic theory whatever ideas would strengthen his proposals for a much larger cultural program. Maritain made his present-day project explicit, expressing hope that this treatise would not only 'draw attention to the utility of having recourse to the wisdom of Antiquity' but also 'to the possible interest of an exchange of views between philosophers and artists.' Such an exchange would be necessary in order to escape from 'the vast intellectual confusion bequeathed to us by the nineteenth century.'[51] In the age of Eliot, Joyce, and Pound, antiquity and the avant-garde joined forces against an outmoded modernity.

Maritain began by asking: 'How does Prudence, at once an *intellectual and moral* virtue, differ from Art, which is an *intellectual* virtue?'[52] Art's being only one kind of virtue whereas Prudence seemed to be more complex suggested that Art played second fiddle to Prudence (and thus modern art's 'passions' would be subject to the judgment of *pruderie*). (In fact, the widely distributed American translation made an understandable but unjustified addition of the word 'merely': 'How does Prudence ... differ from Art, a merely *intellectual* virtue?')[53] Whether explicit or implied, by the time Maritain finished his argument, those chairs would be switched, and Art's infallibility would not be subject to the judgment of Prudence.

Employing the standard scholastic method, Maritain began by carefully distinguishing the virtue of 'Prudence' from 'Making' (i.e., *poesis*). The moral virtue Prudence denoted the conformation of a person's will 'to the law governing all human acts and the true end of human life.' The person acting with prudence was 'also good, purely and simply.' Since Prudence was a virtue both intellectual and moral, one judged two things: the act and the actor.

However, since Making was not a practical virtue, one did not judge the artisan who acted. Making was self-enclosed, an intellectual process ordered to 'a definite end, separate and self-sufficient.' A butcher made good cuts, a baker made good bread, a smithy made good horseshoes. The virtue of Making related not to the 'perfection of the one making' but only to the perfection 'of the work made.'[54] As long as the 'making' was good, the artistry could be judged good, regardless of whether the artisan was morally good or a scoundrel.

The work of art could thus be viewed as 'infallible' – surely the metaphor was intended to evoke papal pronouncements – certain and necessary in its correctness regardless of the moral standing of the one pronouncing. Maritain's syllogistic logic went like this: if Art was 'a *virtue of the practical intellect*, and if every virtue brings itself exclusively to the good,' then it was 'necessary to conclude from this that Art as such (I say Art and not the artist who frequently acts against their own art) never makes a mistake, and that it comports an *infallible rightness*.' Maritain emphasized the deductive certainty of this conclusion from the terms' initial definitions: 'If this were not true, it would not be a virtue [*habitus*] properly speaking, solid by means of its very nature.'[55] His scholastic defence of the artistic work's infallible authority paralleled Cocteau's smug aphorism: 'In art, every value which can be proven is vulgar.'[56]

Surely Maritain recognized that this would sound like a sleight of hand to sceptical 'men of prudence.' So he inserted an extended line without translation – not unusual for him in the notes but unusual in the text – from Aristotle: 'Art, on the contrary, which has for its material something to be made, proceeds by *certain and determined routes*, "imo nihil aliud ars esse videtur, quam certa ordinatio rationis, quomod per determinata media ad determinatum finem actus humani perveniant." The scholastics constantly affirm this after Aristotle, and they make of this possession of certain rules an essential property of art as such.'[57] Compounding the weight of this authority, he immediately paraphrased the scholastic John of St Thomas affirming Aristotle's point: Art held onto 'its airtight certainty [*fermeté*] by means of its rational and universal rules and not of *consilium*' – that is, contingent discussion and consensus. The 'rightness of [Art's] judgment' was not taken, 'as in the case of Prudence, from circumstances and occurrences, but rather from the certain and determined routes which are its own.' This passage too was authoritatively cited in Latin.[58] Once again, the medium was the message. Whether or not Maritain's popular readership was able to sight-translate the ancients, his textual pastiche was masterful, conveying its own infallible aura of authority both ancient and modern.

Appealing to mathematics, the most certain kind of thinking (because the most abstracted from existence), Maritain compared the artist to a geometer: the moment the artist 'work[ed] well,' he was as unerring in judgment as the Geometer demonstrating universal and eternal truths. Aquinas used the comparison himself: 'It makes little difference whether [the geometer] be in a good temper or in a rage [*Sum. Theol.*, I–II, q. 57, a.3].' If the Geometer was angry or jealous, his sin was 'the sin of a human being, not the sin of an artist [*Ibid.*, q. 21, a.2, *ad* 2].' (In the 1927 revision of *Art and Scholasticism*, Maritain bolstered Aquinas's authority with a *bon mot* from Oscar Wilde: 'The fact of a man being a poisoner is nothing against his prose.')[59]

Maritain's fundamental point was that a practical virtue depends on accidental contingencies whereas an intellectual virtue does not. From this crucial distinction it followed that the rightness of Art's judgment was not historical, accidental, or open to discussion, dependent on a consensus resulting from a prudential deliberation over particular 'circumstances and occurrences.' Art's judgment was instead certain, determined, and necessary, simply because in order to *make* something good one needed to follow fixed rules. Maritain had switched the chairs and inverted the accepted order: Art has gone from implicitly being 'merely' intellectual to now being 'more exclusively intellectual than Prudence.' Art had been shorn of material contingencies and circumstances. Art was less like statecraft and more like science in its apprehension of universal truth. Since every virtue carried the actor to the good, and since the good 'in the case of an intellectual virtue is the *true* [*vrai*],' the virtue of Art was infallibly true.[60]

This allowed Maritain to arrive at the point intended all along: an absolute claim of independence for the artist vis-à-vis the prudish bourgeois. Maritain acknowledged that there were 'many conflicts between the prudent man and the artist with regard to, e.g., the representation of the nude' and then settled the contest. 'The Prudent Man as such, judging everything from the angle of morality and in relation to the good of humanity, is absolutely ignorant of everything that has to do with art. Without a doubt he can, and he ought, to judge the work of art insofar as it is of interest to morality. He has no right to judge it as a work of art.'[61]

Twenty years earlier, the Maritains had considered suicide in a world without certainties. Bergson had offered them a way out by imagining 'intuition,' best exemplified by art and poetry, as providing unmediated access to that most deeply real. Two decades later, the Maritains' own aesthetic theory, even more airtight than Bergson's in its identification of the most deeply real not with a never-ending *durée* but rather with static and eternal truths, allowed them to pass this confidence on to a new generation.

Manly Humility: Against Bourgeois Individualism

In addition to these two postwar promises – Art's infallible access to truth and its corollary authority over Prudence – *Art and Scholasticism* offered a third: an image of the artist as a holy monk and heroic warrior. The 'despotic and all-absorbing power of art,' wrote Maritain, had an 'astonishing power to bring about peacefulness' – or, more literally, 'appeasement' [*d'apaisement*]. Following Bergson (who followed Kant), Maritain thought of the 'aesthetic' as a vision of things in themselves and not in relation to their possible use-value for the viewer. Since art freed the one contemplating it 'from every human care,' it established 'the *artifex*, artist or artisan, in a world apart, cloistered, defined and absolute.' A kind of secular monk, the artist could 'devote all his manly strength and his manly intelligence to the service of the thing' being made. In a period of social, economic, and cultural upheaval, Maritain pictured the artist's studio as a postwar refuge for troubled souls: 'the ennui of living and willing ceases at the door of every *atelier*.'[62]

In addition, Maritain's use of 'manly' [*d'homme*] to qualify the artist's 'strength' and 'intelligence' subtly inverted common associations of artists with 'effeminacy.' As the Wilde trial in England had demonstrated, 'the physicality of the artistic male was considered particularly suspect. Being cultured was just a step away from being effeminate.'[63] Maritain recast the artist as a chivalrous knight – or perhaps a trench soldier – whose single-minded service of something larger than himself overcame bourgeois individualism's *ennui* and kept him in the line of fire. In order to keep the artist's self 'always in the direct line of Action' – the capitalization was Maritain's: *la droite ligne de l'Agir* – and not 'sacrifice his immortal substance to the devouring idol in his soul,' artistry would 'require a measure of heroism.' 'Truthfully speaking, such conflicts' between self-regard and service of another could 'only be abolished on condition that a deep humility make the artist unconscious, so to speak, of his own art, or if the all-powerful unction of wisdom imbue everything in him with the sleep and the peace of love' – *la paix de l'amour*.

Maritain fused these images drawn from Kant, Bergson, monasticism, and the battlefield with one taken from ultramontanism: Fra Angelico, the nineteenth-century icon transformed by Denis into the patron of avant-garde neo-traditionalism. (The means to restoring painting, Denis believed, was 'to restore to honor the aesthetic of Fra Angelico, who alone is truly Catholic; who alone responds to the aspirations of the pious, mystic souls who love God.')[64] Referring to the deadly allure of fame, Maritain offered avant-garde artists a model who had been artist, monk, and soldier of Christ: 'Undoubtedly, Fra Angelico felt none of these interior contradictions.'[65]

Maritain's call for the artist's heroic lack of self-concern underscored one of the most continuous lines of his thought from the 1910s through the 1930s: a contempt for bourgeois-capitalist individualism, the aspect of 'modernity' he most despised.[66] A victorious France needed to repudiate Descartes's egoistic legacy of the *Cogito* and return to the Middle Ages, a time when 'more beautiful things were created and there was less self-worship.' In that golden age, before anonymous artisans became artistic celebrities, 'the blessed humility in which the artist was situated exalted [both] his strength and his freedom.' Humility reconciled the artist's uninhibited freedom with the need to act prudently; it enabled the artist to know his place in an organic, integral, and hierarchical community. 'In the powerful social structure of medieval civilization, the artist had only the social rank of an artisan, and every type of anarchic development was forbidden to his individualism, because a natural social discipline imposed certain limiting conditions on him from the outside.'[67]

In this ideal medieval world that had preceded the Renaissance turn to art as consumption and commodification, an artisan did not work for 'the art dealers, but rather for the people of faith': the artisan's mission had been 'to shelter [*abriter*] prayer, to instruct intelligence, to make both soul and eyes rejoice.' Building to a climactic exclamation, Maritain's anti-bourgeois sentiments, unchanging from his youthful leftism to post-conversion integralism, spilled over into purple prose: 'Oh incomparable time, when an ingenious people was formed in beauty without even perceiving it, like the perfect religious must pray without knowing that they are praying! when professors and image-makers lovingly taught the poor, and when the poor appreciated their teaching, because they were all of the same royal race born of water and of the Spirit.' But then came the turn to ego, self-regard, and the cult of celebrity: 'The Renaissance was destined to drive the artist mad and make him the most miserable of men ...'[68] *Art and Scholasticism* concluded that now was the time to undo the divorce that had brought modernity to its present individualistic fragmentation.

Cultural Hylomorphism: Catholicism as *Catholicity*

Catholicism stood 'alone in its ability to reconcile perfectly Prudence and Art.' The reason stemmed from Catholicism's 'universality ... the very *catholicity* of its wisdom that *embraces everything that is real*.' (Jacques's reformulation of Raïssa's play on Terence's dictum – 'Catholics must possess a genuinely informed doctrine *concerning everything that is human*' – significantly substituted 'real' for 'human.') Catholicism occupied a middle position between Protestantism and humanism: Protestants accused Catholicism of 'immorality' and humanists accused it of 'rigorism,' a double assault 'symmetrically rendering witness to the divine superiority of [Catholicism's] point of view.'[69] 'What is morally and mentally magnificent about Catholicism,' d'Aurevilly had written, 'is that it is wide, comprehensive, and unbounded, embracing human nature whole and in its diverse spheres of action, and that, above what it embraces, it unfurls still the great maxim: Woe to him that taketh scandal! In Catholicism is nothing prudish, priggish, pedantic, fidgety.'[70] Raïssa echoed d'Aurevilly off-stage: 'No ignorance. No prudishness. No Manicheanism. But rather Catholic doctrine luminous and total.'

Maritain's Catholicism could reconcile these seeming opposites because he applied his hylomorphic conception of reality to culture itself. Catholicism could universally accommodate any form of cultural representation whatsoever precisely because it was a broader application of the more limited principle of art: it did not demand imitation of a 'shape' limiting it to a particular culture and historical location, but was rather the *entelechy* capable of informing and animating any culture whatsoever. This was its essential *catholicity*.

To return to the beginning: like Bergson, Maritain offered an uncertain generation the promise of access to the deepest reality. If 'the joy of the beautiful work comes from *some truth*,' this did not mean that it came from 'the truth *of the imitation as reproduction of things*.' Rather, joy came from 'the perfection with which the work expresses or manifests the form, in the metaphysical sense of this word; it comes from the truth *of the imitation as manifestation of a form*. This is what is meant by the *"formal"* aspect of imitation in art: the expression or the manifestation, in a work harmoniously proportioned, of some principle of intelligibility which shines forth. It is this act of expression which gives art its *joy of imitation*. This is also that which gives art its value of *universality*.'[71] Maritain's cultural hylomorphism depended on this notion of 'form' and on art as the imitation of this form. The form to be imitated was not the outward shape of something – 'The essential is not that the representation be exactly conformed with a given reality' – since this would limit Catholicism to a certain place and time. Catholicism's capacity for catholicity depended on the interior form's ability to take on the clothing of any epoch whatsoever: 'it is rather that, through the material elements the beauty of the work, the clarity of a form should clearly shine, supreme and whole – of a form, and thus of *some truth*.'

Art and Scholasticism offered several postwar appeals: infallible access to truth; the independence of Art's making; the artist as both monk and warrior; the catholicity of Catholicism. It accomplished these by its anti-representational theory of art, a theory made possible by retrieving Aristotelian-Thomistic hylomorphism. In Maritain's scheme, the only true ultramodernity was the anti-modern – eternal forms whose transcendence allowed for universal incarnation. This logical conclusion would be made more explicit in the revolutionary assertions of *Antimoderne*.

1922: Anti-modernist Ultramodernity

For High Modernism, 1922 marked the revolutionary 'Year I' of the post-Christian Era: Ezra Pound declared it so, and Eliot's *Wasteland* and Joyce's *Ulysses* seemed to provide ample evidence.[72] However, in Baudrillart's *French Catholic Almanac* of 1922, Christianity was far from dead, and it seemed to be taking a significantly new direction with its 'Christian realism.' This hybrid realism, allowing for the unpredictable and unseen, caught the moment's vogue: 'In this summer of 1922,' wrote a reviewer for *Études*, 'in those circles where one's curiosity is piqued to know, the talk of the town has been Einstein. Last winter it was Freud, and it's persisting.'[73] Into this complex mêlée Maritain issued his manifesto defiantly entitled *Antimoderne* (1922).

Like coffee table books that lie unexamined beyond their alluring covers, this book's brazen title has been referred to more often than its contents have been actually explored. As recently as 1990, one author could write, 'The title of a book of Jacques Maritain, *Antimoderne*, sums up the spirit of a generation, [or, to be] more exact ... that of the converts ... By underlining the monolithic, intransigent and immutable character of Catholicism, it created a complex to be taken or rejected in its integral wholeness.'[74] Yet, one has only to read Maritain's short *avant-propos* to the work to find what André Laveyssiere revealed in his 1923 review for *La Croix de Marseille*: 'When such a word ["Antimodern"] stands out against the cover of a volume, it seems that we will necessarily find within a concise, virulent indictment, against all ideas called modern ... This conception is too simplistic and demands an intellectual effort arrested in mid-stream. In addition, this cannot be the position that a Jacques Maritain takes when he makes use of the word "antimodern," for doesn't he rightly say that he could just as well have given his work the title "Ultramodern."'[75]

This astute reviewer was alluding to Maritain's challenge found within the first few pages:

> That which I call here *anti-modern* might just as well be called *ultra-modern.*
>
> It is well known, in fact, that Catholicism is as *anti-modern* on account of its immoveable attachment to the tradition as it is *ultramodern* on account of its bold ability to adapt itself to the new conditions erupting suddenly in the life of the world.[76]

In this bold declaration, Maritain embraced the fundamental mark of 'modernity' – that is, a positive valuation of temporality and historical change. (Or, as Raïssa would later write: 'How stupid he is, [Paul] Morand, with his "anti-modern" Catholicism. You can tell him that the *modern* is *Nothing other than time.*')[77] In doing so, Maritain appropriated the vocabulary of his adversaries (both modernist and anti-modernist) and turned their meanings against them.

To an earlier generation, Maritain's qualification of 'Catholicism' as 'adaptive' would have seemed completely absurd. As the intellectual expression of integralist Catholicism against both republican positivists and (later) the Roman Catholic Modernists, Thomism was consciously intended to stand for unchanging ideas and values. Yet Maritain explicitly repudiated as 'absurd' the nineteenth-century neo-medievalist project: 'We love the art of the cathedrals, of Giotto and [Fra] Angelico. But we detest the neo-Gothic and pre-Raphaelism. We know that the course of time is irreversible; as much as we admire the century of Saint Louis, we do not want *to return to the Middle Ages* on that account, along an absurd path which certain penetrating critics generously accuse us of.'[78] (Or as he had written in *Art and Scholasticism*: 'The medieval architects did not restore "in the style," after the manner of Viollet-le-Duc. If the choir of a Romanesque church was destroyed by fire, they rebuilt it Gothic and thought no more about it.')[79] Just as Maritain's anti-naturalist theory of art detested making 'copies' of nature, so he dismissed neo-medievalism's desire to 'copy' the outward forms of ancient art.

Maritain's transformation of Thomists into ultramodernists was one of the most important catalysts for the 1920s neo-Thomistic revival.[80] What factors played into his ability to think through Catholicism and modernity as commensurable? The first factor, seen already in *Art and Scholasticism*, was Maritain's novel insights into the implications of hylomorphism. In hylomorphic theory, forms did not exist without a particular historical instantiation in matter: thus, what is transcendent and lacking all concrete specifications *is itself capable of assuming any of them.* Precisely by reason of its lack of historical particularity, transcendence possessed a 'boldness' or 'daring' which allowed it to wear the latest fashions of whatever epoch in which it was incarnate. By exploiting the potential in hylomorphic language, Maritain reconfigured the discourse so that he could innovate – not *in spite of* the tradition *but rather precisely because* he maintained the tradition.

Since the 'forms' did not change, Catholicism could still be considered 'anti-modern' by reason of its ahistorical and unchanging 'attachment' to the tradition. There was a fixed core, an immutable positive content in which Maritain believed standing steadfast against time's erosion. However, just as Maritain reinterpreted 'art imitating nature' to mean the imitation of an interior formal cause, so in *Antimoderne* he reinterpreted the 'retrieval' of the Middle Ages as the retrieval of an inner spirit or principle. 'We hope to see the spiritual principles and the eternal norms which medieval civilization has given us returned/reproduced in a new world, informing a new matter.'[81] (Cocteau echoed here: 'TRADITION APPEARS AT EVERY EPOCH UNDER A DIFFERENT DISGUISE ...') One might justifiably object that the Middle Ages had been one of civilization's 'best epochs, in a particular historical realization, superior in quality' to other epochs 'in spite of their enormous deficiencies.' Nevertheless, it was time to admit that history had moved on: the Middle Ages were 'definitely in the past' [*définitivement passée*].[82]

The image of the Gothic cathedral helpfully distinguishes two models of Catholicism's relationship to culture and prompts us to ask, what allowed Maritain to innovate as he did? There are at least three sources for his innovation: philosophical hylomorphism, theological incarnationalism and sacramentalism, and Baudelairean aesthetics.

Maritain emphasized hylomorphism's historicity more than his predecessors had. In the oppositional model of the fin-de-siècle, as we have seen, eternalism's reading of 'forms' as eternal disembodied entities confronting historical culture produced a model that was dualistic, apocalyptic, and melancholic. Maritain's quite different reading of the 'form' as always instantiated in some historical matter allowed him to spin hylomorphism as a model that was dialectical, synthetic, and 'mournful' (in Freud's sense of the term). Not stuck in the past, it did not need to cling to the outward 'shapes' of past – as did Viollet-le-Duc's gargoyles or the vogue for recreating Byzantium. Rather, when art imitated the inward 'form' – 'spiritual principles and eternal norms' in the sense of a formal cause – it was free to realize that form within whatever outward shapes seem appropriate – from Severini to Kandinsky to Cocteau.[83] In solving the problem of modernity by 'thinking without history,' Maritain's modernism was less Viollet-le-Duc than Le Corbusier – distinctly twentieth-century in his structuralist approach to significance.[84]

In addition to philosophical hylomorphism, Maritain's theory of culture also reverberated with theological overtones of sacramentalism and incarnationalism. For Maritain, ultramodernist Catholics could say 'we love the new' precisely because they claimed to 'adhere to a philosophy whose proper character is to be perennial, and which therefore is as much a thing of today as it is of yesterday.' But there was 'this condition: that the new truly *continue* the old, and that it add, without destruction, to the substance acquired.'[85] The phrase bore a striking resemblance to language Maritain would have studied in his catechism. In trying to explain the fundamental problem of the Incarnation – that is, how the one person of Jesus Christ could be both fully human and divine – the ancient Church had turned to Greek philosophical terminology and declared the definition at Chalcedon: Christ was 'the same one in being (*homoousios*) with the Father as to the divinity and one in being with us as to the humanity,' maintaining this one personal identity in two natures 'without confusion, without change, without division, without separation.'[86]

Employing similar language in his theory of culture, Maritain's 'substance acquired' was something old, traditional, and *eternal*; on the other hand, the 'new' or *modern* element was to be loved insofar as it did not destroy but rather *continued* the inherited substance. The integralist Catholic view of culture saw the 'modern' element as *replacing* or *destroying* the substance of Catholicism; it relied on an implicitly spatial metaphor: two 'substances' competing for a place on a limited amount of turf. But Maritain's theological view, neither spatial nor competitive, relied on the analogy of the Incarnation: the divine was capable of *becoming something else* without replacing it or destroying it, even as it remained itself without confusion. This was its capacity as a transcendent being.

The word 'substance' also reverberated with another theological overtone of the most distinctive strand of Catholic discourse – *transubstantiation*. This doctrine denoted the process by which the 'substance' of the bread and wine, even while retaining outward sensory appearances ('accidents'), was seen to be transformed at Mass into another reality (imperceptible to the senses) – namely, the body and blood of Christ. Although Maritain's model inverted this relationship – his eternal 'substance' remained the same even as the historical material 'accidents' changed – he retained a key element: the idea of *continuity* and organic outgrowth. Even as one thing *became* another, it did so *without destruc-*

tion or replacement: the original being (e.g., bread/Catholicism) had the dynamic capacity within itself to become another thing (e.g., body of Christ/modern culture). Maritain's innovation was to re-imagine the relation between two cultural forces not as a side-by-side 'con-substantiation,' but rather of a substance/accident transubstantiation. In the discourse of 'substance' and 'transubstantiation,' Maritain's philosophical and theological strands coalesced.

A third source of Maritain's thought was perhaps less obvious but nonetheless implicit: he read his Aquinas through the lens of his boyhood hero, Charles Baudelaire.[87] Maritain's ability to see in hylomorphism what his predecessors had missed – that is, the fundamental importance of the fashionable material element – was likely due to his immersion in Baudelaire's theory of modern art. For Baudelaire, living in the midst of Baron von Haussmann's destructive modernization of old Paris (for the sake of boulevards and the sewer system), the artistic question had been 'how to *represent* the eternal and the immutable in the midst of all the chaos?'[88]

Baudelaire's solution of the problem of 'modernity' famously defined beauty as being 'always and inevitably of a double composition ... made up of *an eternal, invariable element*, whose quantity it is excessively difficult to determine, and of *a relative, circumstantial element,* which will be, if you like, whether severally or all at once, the age, its fashions, its morals, its emotions.' Baudelaire amplified the terms: 'By "modernity," I mean the ephemeral, the fugitive, the contingent, the half of art whose other half is the eternal and the immutable ... This transitory, fugitive element, whose metamorphoses are so rapid, must on no account or be dispensed with. By neglecting it, you cannot fail to tumble into the abyss of an abstract and indeterminate beauty ...'[89]

As noted above, the 'trauma of world war and its political and intellectual responses' had 'opened the way to a consideration of what might constitute the essential and eternal qualities of modernity that lay on the nether side of Baudelaire's formulation.'[90] Walter Benjamin, Maritain's contemporary, used Baudelaire to formulate his own theory of dialectical images. Jacques and Raïssa became active participants in the Société Baudelaire (to be examined further below) during the 1920s. Baudelaire had preceded Aquinas in Maritain's life by almost two decades. Maritain read Aquinas through Baudelaire's vision of modernity expressing antiquity.

Maritain's task had been to figure out how an anti-modernist's attention to the eternal can end up as not just compatible with, but the very exemplar of the modernist's privileging of the materially ephemeral. A philosopher trained in biological vitalism, as late as 1921 Maritain was writing about the living form as *entelechy*.[91] He was aided by his conversion to Catholicism's theological heritage. But the longest-enduring influence was Baudelaire, the most-quoted authority in *Art and Scholasticism* after Aquinas and Aristotle. This allowed him to see the 'modern' with Baudelaire's (and implicitly, Bergson's) off-modern eyes: a never-ending *durée* of creative novelty, the immutable assuming the flesh of the fugitive.

Particularist Universalism: The *catholicité* of Catholicism

This hylomorphic reconfiguration of the universal and particular in non-competitive terms allowed Maritain to exploit yet another linguistic possibility: that of the particular 'Roman Catholic' as the truly 'catholic,' that is, *universal*. Integralist Catholics had distinguished between merely 'particular' sciences of the nineteenth century (anthropology, biology, geology) and the 'universal' science of metaphysics.[92] Particular sciences were inferior to the universal: whereas metaphysics can investigate the ultimate questions of human existence that transcend history and culture, particular sciences can only investigate microcosms from their limited standpoint. Again, the implicit model was spatial and the two were imagined as being in competition with one another: universal v. particular, eternal v. contingent, depth v. surface, Catholic v. Republican, anti-modern v. modern. In this model, the universal was in fact (though not in theory) just another particular.

In his appropriation and reversal of this tradition, Maritain drew on an essay entitled 'The Catholicity of Thomism' (1921) by H. Woroniecki published in the *Revue Thomiste*.[93] At first, Woroniecki continued an earlier integralist discourse: associating 'modern thought' with such 'particular' sciences as biology and chemistry, he underscored their empirical concern with observable 'facts' – they quantify, measure, calculate, and predict observable phenomena. None of them was capable, however, of true 'rationality' – that is, the possibility of considering questions of underlying causality, purpose, and therefore of meaning. (Heidegger himself would soon try to address this confusion in different but related terms: 'Ontological inquiry is indeed more primordial, as over against the ontical inquiry of the positive sciences.')[94]

But was Thomism just one more particularist system in competition with the rest? Woroniecki noted that modern thinkers were 'scandalized at the role the Church assigns ... in favor of the teaching of St Thomas Aquinas,' effectively edging out and displacing other systems. One could 'frequently hear' (presumably from critics within the Church itself) 'the complaint that Catholicism is becoming Thomist.' To this accusation Woroniecki responded by playing on the double-meaning inherit in the word *catholique*: 'Wrong! It is the contrary which is true. It is not Catholicism which is Thomist, but rather Thomism which is catholic; and it is catholic because it is universalist. – Because whoever says universalist says catholic.' Unlike other philosophical systems like Descartes's rationalism, Hume's scepticism, and Kant's idealism, Thomism was not 'the individual work of a single man, but rather the result of the social work of generations,' the one philosophy that had made 'an explicit profession of universalism.' What Thomism owed before all else to St Thomas, wrote Woroniecki, was this 'freedom with respect to every individual particularism' in matters of philosophical thought. His image was implicitly hylomorphic: Thomism was related to other philosophies as form informed materials.

By quoting Woroniecki at length, Maritain could draw on a mainstream authority to make a claim that might equally offend both anticlerical laicists and intransigent Catholics. In the future, asserted Maritain, Catholics would 'be able to and ... need to allow the *universalist* tendency, so admirably manifest in a St Thomas Aquinas, to play freely.' This universalism led 'Catholic thought, kindly and peacefully, to look everywhere for agreements rather than oppositions, for the fragments of truth rather than to overturn things, to build up rather than to disperse.'[95] Although particulars might always be necessarily competing with one another, Catholicism, by its very universalist nature, was not divisive but synthetic.

Catholicism needed to become catholic; this was its specific postwar task. 'Certainly, Catholics are not lacking for any work, and there is plenty there to tempt their spirit of initiative. For they must face a task of universal integration ...' If Catholics, 'in order to preserve their own being,' rejected 'those spiritual principles by which the modern world positions itself, places itself in opposition to, and specifies itself as *modern*,' it was not in order 'to destroy the modern world, but rather to conquer it and transform it.'[96] Maritain's call to abandon intransigence for involvement was echoed by his reviewer in *La Croix de Marseille*: 'Catholics are more frequently asked to leave their ivory tower in order to mix themselves in more and more with the life that surrounds them, that carries them like a whirlwind; but there is not only social and civic life, there is the life of the mind, the intellectual life; and it is to be hoped they will take for their guide ... [the mind of] Aristotle, afterwards re-clothed [*revêtue*] by this genius ... Aquinas.'[97]

Maritain's highly developed equation of the particular Roman Catholic and the universal catholic provided an intellectual framework by which the unthinkable became possible. 'By this same universality,' Thomistic doctrine infinitely overflowed 'the tightness of the present moment into the past as well as into the future.' It was 'not opposed to the modern systems as the past is related to the given present' in a competitive way, but rather related 'as the *éviternel* is related to the momentary. *Anti-modern* against the errors of the present time, it is *ultra-modern* for all the truths which are wrapped up in the time to come.'[98]

Maritain sarcastically asked, 'Is it necessary to remark, moreover, that today everything except Catholicism itself – even and perhaps above all those ideologies specifically modern (look at the Futurists, for example) – immediately appears to be old-fashioned and, as it were, a moon waxing full?' Futurism, a celebration of the rapidity of change, had fallen victim to its own values. Catholic catholicity, however, was eternally young, embracing every age: past, present, and future. In this appropriation and subversion of an old combative language, not only did the universal and the particular cease to be competitors: they actually needed one other. The eternal required the fashionable just as form required matter.

Returning to his provocative title, Maritain carefully distinguished his vision of culture from the integralists': if he was '*anti-modern*, it [was] not because of personal taste, certainly,' but rather because modernity's self-definition 'hates and holds in contempt the past while adoring itself, and because we hate and hold in contempt this hatred and this contempt and this spiritual impurity.' However, if the modern could be redefined and acted 'to save and to assimilate all the riches to be accumulated in these modern times ... to love the effort of those who are searching for them ... to desire their renewal [*renouvellement*] – well then, we desire nothing more than to be the *ultramoderns*.'[99]

Maritain's critics assailed his idea of 'adaptation' with vehemence. 'A nice daring indeed!' exclaimed *L'Internationale*. The true daring was Maritain's taking 'the old truths misjudged by the Church' (e.g., Galileo's heliocentric theory) 'whose revelation were endlessly postponed by reason of [the Church's] authority' and calling them 'new conditions' – this took some daring! 'The principle of adaptation – a little late on several occasions – of the holy Catholic, apostolic, and Roman Church is in fact well-known. It tries, most of all, to block scientific truths from coming to light, and for this it employs torture against scientists reckless enough to affirm truths contrary to the Scriptures ... And then, when these tortures have only slowed down the affirmations which the Church feared, then it adapts.'[100] Daniel Halévy also criticized the work, not because it was too optimistic, but rather because it was too dark. Maritain, this 'new Tertullian' who had adopted devotion to the 'tragic and menacing Virgin' of La Salette 'with ardor,' had not let himself 'become drunk with the positive results of the Catholic renaissance. He considers humanity, and he sees it in perdition.'[101]

However, another reviewer impishly deconstructed the word for his readers: 'Let us first of all recognize with the author that *Antimodern* does not necessarily signify "adversary of the telephone," nor moreover "monarchist, partisan of Philippe, or fear of automobiles."'[102] In *La Libre Parole*, Jean Morienval (author of 'Catholic Literature Today' in the 1922 *French Catholic Almanac*) also delighted in this Thomistic modernism. Noting the surprising extent to which 'the evolution of ideas' had 'modified its course' since the war's end, Morienval invoked the image of the nineteenth-century positivist historian: 'You can imagine as the funniest thing on earth a flabbergasted [Hippolyte] Taine standing before this young philosopher, renowned as one of the most solid minds today, who, tranquilly, serenely, and with a force of unshakeable conviction has just declared himself a disciple of Aristotle and of St Thomas Aquinas.' Rather than developing his own philosophical system, Maritain had instead 'devoted himself to showing how scholasticism, taken to its point of perfection in St Thomas, is sufficient to explain everything in the universe.'

This conviction that Aquinas's system was eternally valid was the antimodernist aspect of Maritain's thought. Yet, there was his modernist aspect: 'he also recognizes that the human spirit is in motion, and that there are new things.' Even as Maritain wished 'to enjoy these new things,' he believed that in the face of new problems, 'the necessary cerebral activity' would have 'all the better chance of reaching the truth the more that it is inspired by the principles of St Thomas. This is what M. Jacques Maritain has laid out with a quiet audacity in several studies which he collects today under the title: *Antimodern*.'[103]

Ernest Psichari: *Antimoderne* as Memorial

If *Antimoderne* was a supreme act of cultural synthesis, it was also a personal act of memorialization, a monument to Ernest Psichari. Not coincidentally, *La Revue des jeunes* simultaneously published *Antimoderne* with a posthumous biography of Psichari entitled *Ernest Psichari according to Unpublished Documents* (1922) for which Maritain wrote the preface.[104] The *Revue* advertised the two works by juxtaposing them on the same page, providing a poignant image of their friendship. Situated on top, the advertisement for Psichari read in part: 'Here is the first complete biography of the grandson of Renan ... The story of this life is nothing other than the conquest of integral order by a soul with an admirable rectitude.' The advertisement for Maritain directly below read: 'A vigorous philosopher, ignorant of none of the doctrines, tastes and tendences of our epoch, he knows how to present to our contemporaries that Thomism of which he has made himself the defender. His *Antimodern* might just as well have been called *Ultramodern*; for the thought of Saint Thomas that is its soul is a universal and enduring thought.'[105]

Antimoderne was framed by tributes to Psichari: the first chapter (the text of the 1920 address at Louvain) began with the allusion to his friend still waiting 'in peace for the resurrection' on 'your Belgian soil.' The final chapter was a lengthy homage simply called 'Ernest Psichari.' The book's entire message – its opening manifesto, the patient laying out of hylomorphic theory, and its call to synthesize Catholicism and secular culture – was inscribed within this larger story of sacrifice and the moral imperatives incumbent on the survivors. Maritain wove his reconfiguration of Catholicism within a larger narrative of trauma and memorialization.

In the final chapter, Maritain quoted from a letter of Psichari to Massis (who had in turn called Psichari the perfect 'holocaust'). 'Our generation,' Psichari had written, 'that which began its life of men with the century, is important. Onto our generation have come all the hopes and we know it. On our generation depends the salvation of France, and therefore that of the world and of civilization. Everything has been gambled on our heads. It seems to me that the youth obscurely sense, that they see great things, that great things will be done by them. They will be neither amateurs nor skeptics. They will not be tourists along the way of life. They will be those for whom we have been waiting.'[106]

Towards the end of the chapter, Maritain quoted from his own 1914 open letter to *La Croix*: '[Psichari] desired the truth for itself. He lived by the truth, he died for it, for he could not separate his love for France from his love for the Church, and his admirable death was not only the value of a gift offered for the service of the *patrie*, but even more [the value] of a witness offered to GOD, and of a true sacrifice freely consented to and consummated in union with the sacrifice of the altar [of the Mass].'

Antimoderne's final line read: 'We, we know that GOD loves the man who gives with joy, *hilarem datorem*; and it is thus that Psichari gave his life.'[107]

In the end, *Antimoderne*'s transformation of Catholicism into ultramodernism was a memorial to Psichari's self-donation. What could justify such a sacrifice? Nothing less than the regeneration of France. In order to become the larger culture's animating principle, Catholics needed to become truly catholic. Maritain's models gave Catholics a new way of imagining their self-identity and their relationship to culture. He reconfigured the language of overtly anti-modernist Thomism into a Catholic ultramodernism. By 1922, he had made the reconciliation of Prudence and Art a theoretical possibility. Beginning in 1923, his relationships with Jean Cocteau, Max Jacob, Raymond Radiguet and others would try to make that possibility a reality.

Chapter 5

Catholic Catholicity: Nothing Human Is Alien

> This is oddly expressed, I see; I mean / a being so intimately present as God is to other things would be identified with them were it not for God's infinity or were it not for God's infinity he would not be so intimately present to things.
>
> – Gerard Manley Hopkins

> One wanted, she thought, dipping her brush deliberately, to be on a level with ordinary experience, to feel simply that's a chair, that's a table, and yet at the same time, It's a miracle, it's an ecstasy.
>
> – Virginia Woolf[1]

Jacques Maritain's ability to make anti-modernism seem ultramodernist owed a debt to his reading of Cocteau's own ordered anarchism. Through unforeseen circumstances, he would meet Cocteau himself in 1924, and this joining in real life of what had been before personified virtues (Prudence and Art) would extend the reach of a universalist Catholicism into previously unanticipated regions. But this *entente cordiale* would engender anxiety in Cocteau and Maritain as well as their critics: the appeal of Catholic revivalists to homosexuals for their legitimating 'modernity' might mean they were only 'passing' as moderns; or, conversely, the panicked sense that they truly were *becoming* 'modern' and hence losing their Catholic identity. In spite of these questions and the conflicts they would provoke, Maritain's vision of a catholicity that was genuinely global was adopted by others, and his own circle of friends and associates – especially after the papal condemnation of Action Française in December 1926 – reflected that universality.

1923: Order Clothed as Anarchy

In the autumn of 1922, Maritain sent a copy of *Antimoderne* to Cocteau (and perhaps to his paramour, Raymond Radiguet, as well). The following spring, Radiguet reciprocated with a copy of *The Devil in the Flesh* (1923) inscribed 'To M. Jacques Maritain, an admirer of *Antimoderne*; asking for his indulgence. Raymond Radiguet.' Not to be outdone, Cocteau followed suit in May and sent a copy of *The Grand Écart* (1923) inscribed 'To Jacques Maritain, this antimodern – that is to say, sorrowful – book. His admirer Jean Cocteau.'[2] Maritain quickly responded to these gifts with the first letter of a correspondence that would span nearly four decades.

Maritain's biographer, Jean-Luc Barré, rhetorically poses this question: 'But why pay so much interest to Cocteau and engage in such solicitude if not because this friend of Picasso, Proust and Apollinaire seemed to crystallize the genius of his epoch ... in the time of the Boeuf sur le toit, of gin, Jazz and the Charleston, of the crazy white nights of the après-guerre?'[3] Le Boeuf sur le Toit (The Ox on the Roof), a bar located on the rue Boissy d'Anglas, had opened on 10 January 1922 and received its name from Cocteau's 1920 musical farce, *Le Boeuf sur le toit, ou, The nothing doing Bar*.[4] For many, this highly influential scene of both jazz and avant-garde – one of the bar's main attractions was the Jean Wiéner-Clément Doucet two-piano jazz team – became a symbol of the decade.

'The war had swept aside many social and sexual conventions, prejudices, and barriers,' writes James McNab, so that at Le Boeuf, 'one might find, at one moment, a play of contrasts, a juxtaposition of disparate elements, or a melting pot, which would have been inconceivable before World War I, in Proust's rigidly stratified society ... Here opium came out of its den, homosexuality was released from the closet and was in vogue, and there was an enervated desire to "try something new."'[5] Musically, this juxtaposition of elements was represented by Wiéner's 'salad concerts' tossing together pieces serious and popular, new and old: the first concert had jazz from the Billy Arnold Orchestra, followed by fragments of Stravinsky's *Rite of Spring* (with Stravinsky at the pianola), and concluded with a work by Milhaud, a member of The Group of Six.[6] Cocteau would accompany the jazz pianist on drums to the delight of 'Coco' Chanel, the Prince of Wales, and Arthur Rubenstein. Here Radiguet was said to have been introduced to opium by the mysterious Madame de Warkowska, who quizzically remarked, 'Opium? Why make so much fuss? They smoked at my first communion in Shanghai.'[7]

Barré rightly underscores Maritain's conscious efforts to access the iconic aura of this cultural symbolic centre. However, Maritain's successful courting of Cocteau also aimed at something narrowly focused: he wanted to draw on Cocteau's postwar genius for dressing up 'order' in the appealing garb of 'anarchy' – a *rappel à l'ordre* during *les années folles*. Part of this ability came from Cocteau's genius for 'finding and refinding.' But another part came from his being 'modern' in an unspoken yet understood way: he was homosexual.

Just as prostitution had been a metaphor for nineteenth-century modernity, so homosexuality came to represent the modern in the postwar epoch.[8] The ambiguous social location of a figure like Cocteau – a fragmented modern leading the charge in an integrating 'call to order' – allowed him to represent a privileged intersection of both 'anti-modernity' *and* 'ultramodernity' in an age of passing. If discourse about gender, as Catharine Stimpson has remarked, is always 'talking about gender and *something else again*,'[9] then that *something else* for Catholic revivalists was this sexual modernity's potential to forge new configurations, alliances, and hybridizations – like Cocteau and Radiguet as paradigms of a right-leaning avant-garde. By 1927, the very worst that Drieu la Rochelle could say about anarchic postwar France was that it had lost all 'natural' boundaries: 'This civilization has no sexes.'[10]

In this decade of passing, Catholicism too wanted to pass for modern.[11] This helps explain why the association of Catholicism and homosexuality in the 1920s became a common literary trope. In England, 'the notion of Anglo- and Roman Catholicism as a magnet for homosexuals had passed from a running joke to a simple fact by the 1920s.' Radclyffe Hall, both a lesbian and a convert to Rome, posed this rhetorical question in her 1928 novel *The Well of Loneliness*: 'And what of that curious craving for religion which so often went hand in hand with inversion?' In France, Henri Ghéon (with whom Gide had the three-cornered affair with Maurice Schlumberger), Julien Green, Max Jacob, Marcel Jouhandeau, and Maurice Sachs would all convert to Catholicism by the end of the decade – Gide himself was rumoured to be on the verge.[12] This discursive instability provided the cultural preconditions needed by Jacques Maritain. If aesthetic anarchists could simultaneously perform the roles of anti-modernists calling a culture to order, then perhaps Maritain could play a double role as well, reconfiguring anti-modernist Catholicism as a Jazz Age modernism.[13]

Cocteau had been introduced to Radiguet by the cubist poet Max Jacob. (Jacob had earlier given Pablo Picasso, a starving teenage painter, financial support that helped him survive, sharing with him room and board [and perhaps bed].) He converted from Judaism to Catholicism after seeing a vision of Christ in his room: 'It is on my wall, at no. 7, rue de Ravignan, that [Christ] appeared to me September 28, 1909, at 5 o'clock ... 5 o'clock in the afternoon.'[14] At his baptism, Picasso served as Jacob's godfather.

This cubist conversion to the religion of order caused some stir even in bohemian Montmartre, since Jacob was at least as well known for his inclinations to 'pederasty' as for his poetry. (As he wrote Jacques Doucet in 1917, Jacob's various inversions – aesthetic, sexual, and now religious – all formed a part of his anti-naturalist mysticism: 'You have already understood, dear sir, that I have a horror of Naturalism, of Realism, and of every work that is worthwhile only in so far as it can be compared to the real.') Jacob's inclinations led to rumours over the exact nature of his relationship with the teenaged Radiguet. For his part, the youth associated inversion and conversion, wryly observing that he lived in an epoch where, 'if one did not marry, one converted.' Or as Stanislas Fumet would write of Jacob, 'He hadn't found a woman, but he had found God.'[15]

Whatever the nature of their own relationship, in February 1919 Jacob told Radiguet, 'I don't know whether you are the future national poet, but you deserve to become it as much as Y or Z.'[16] In June, he introduced the sixteen-year-old to Cocteau, who was passionately overwhelmed by what he saw as Radiguet's genius and charisma. Although the next four years would be tempestuous, Radiguet and Cocteau 'lived out a homosexual friendship that is quite without precedent if appraised in terms of the artistic and aesthetic intensity that each achieved through contact with the other.'[17]

Radiguet's defection from the Dadaist camp (he had corresponded with Dada founder Tristan Tzara and written for André Breton's *Littérature*) to collaborate with Cocteau's *Le Coq* caused a stir. They were bitterly opposed factions, as a letter from Breton to Tzara that December makes clear: 'My completely disinterested feeling, I swear to you, is that [Cocteau] is the most detestable creature of this period.' For his part, Cocteau wrote in May 1920 that 'The articles that call me a dadaist amuse me greatly, because I am the very type of anti-dadaist. The dadaists know it well ... I invented the extreme right ... I feel so far from the left and the right, so close to the extreme left closing the circle with me that they and I are often confused.'[18] Radiguet – who had been eleven years old when the war broke out – was even more persuaded than Cocteau of the need for a new postwar 'order,' and egged him on in the quest for a return to tradition.

In May 1923, after reading Cocteau's Collège de France address entitled 'On Order Considered as Anarchy,' Maritain wrote these alluring lines: 'It is a rare and enviable victory to have succeeded, as you have, in making "order" seem as new and as disturbing as "anarchy" ... the reading of your last book and of your conference ... have increased still more the sympathy which I have already experienced for a long time for their author, for a soul so sought out by the angels.'[19] Accompanied or not by the angels, Cocteau's soul was definitely sought out by Maritain and sympathetic figures like Frédéric Lefèvre.

Lefèvre was editor-in-chief of *Les Nouvelles littéraires*, the foremost weekly literary journal of its day. He published a regular column entitled 'An hour with ...' in which all the celebrities of the day either wrote or were interviewed.[20] On 13 October 1923, Lefèvre published an interview with those two ultimate 'men of order' – Maritain and Massis – that asked, 'But now, where are we going and who will save us?'

To this question Maritain responded, 'I wonder whether Max Jacob and the youth (for whom Jean Cocteau is trying to formulate an aesthetic) do not allow us to hope for an evolution analogous to that of the [Group of Six] about whom I have spoken to you.'[21] (When Cocteau complained that he had been put in second place behind Jacob, Maritain revised his response; Lefèvre published this final draft in which Cocteau and Jacob shared equal billing.)[22] To be sure, Maritain had done his homework and played directly to his audience: it was Lefèvre who (in *Young French Poetry* [1917])[23] had first grouped together Apollinaire, Reverdy, Blaise Cendrars, Cocteau, and Jacob under the name 'Cubist.' Since Lefèvre's account proved controversial – Reverdy himself responded that 'Cubist poetry doesn't exist' – Maritain's choice in some sense affirmed his interviewer's early convictions.[24] In another sense, the incident vividly demonstrated Maritain's strategy. When asked who could 'save' the future, Maritain linked the future of 'order' to sexual 'moderns': Cocteau, Jacob, and (implicitly) Radiguet.

Up until this moment, Maritain's relationship with Cocteau was mediated through the written word; but it would now become intensely personal. Radiguet got sick after eating infected oysters, the ailment was diagnosed by Cocteau's personal physician as pneumonia, and Radiguet treated it as directed with hot toddies. They were mistaken: it was typhoid. After a terrible ordeal, the twenty-year-old Radiguet died in the hospital alone at five o'clock in the morning of 12 December 1923.

Cocteau stayed away from both the deathbed and the funeral, leaving the burial arrangements in Père-Lachaise up to his indulgent patroness, Gabrielle 'Coco' Chanel. Cocteau took off for Monte Carlo, secluding himself in an opium haze and vowing never to write again.

Two days after Radiguet's death, Maritain paid a visit to Cocteau's old mentor, André Gide.[25] Maritain had come to Gide hoping to dissuade him from publishing *Corydon*. Gide had started working on this neo-classical imitation of four Socratic dialogues, written in defence of 'pederasty,' as early as 1907. He had distributed it only among friends because, as a 'firm believer in public decorum,' he was 'quite prepared to conceal [his] views if [he] thought they might jeopardize law and order.' As late as 1920 he authorized a second limited edition of the text but again published it privately. In 1922, though having resolved 'not to keep [the text] secret forever,' he hesitated once more.[26]

Henri Massis had been attacking Gide in *La Revue universelle*, and now he feared that the publication of *Corydon* was intended as a retribution.[27] Maritain conveyed Massis's anxieties to Gide who in turn told Maritain to 'leave Massis all his fears and regrets and remorse.' Gide said he had received a 'wonderful' letter from Paul Claudel that conveyed 'the impulse of a truly Christian thought' not to be found anywhere 'in Massis' articles.' When Maritain suggested that Massis may not have properly understood Gide's thought, Gide countered that Massis was 'too intelligent' and that he considered such 'falsification as conscious and voluntary.'

Surprisingly, as Gide related the conversation, Maritain did not deny the 'truth' of Gide's claims about homosexuality. Granting Gide his premises, Maritain had instead asked: 'But don't you think that that truth, which your book claims to make manifest, can be dangerous?' Steering the conversation towards the subject of authenticity and dissimulation – he was at the time in the midst of writing *The Counterfeiters* (1926) – Gide replied: 'However dangerous that truth may be, I hold that the falsehood that covers it is even more dangerous.' Perhaps digging at Maritain's having traded his childhood Protestantism for Catholicism, Gide pushed even harder: 'I have a horror of falsehood. That is perhaps just where my Protestantism lurks. Catholics cannot understand that ... Catholics do not like truth.' Hoping to spare others the anguish and self-loathing that had driven his fictional Alexis to suicide, Gide resisted Maritain's appeals and finally published *Corydon* in 1924 – to a disastrous reception.

Regrettably, we do not have Maritain's version of this encounter.

However, if Gide's account can be believed, Maritain displayed a perhaps surprising ambivalence. While apparently granting the truth of Gide's book, he still considered it a 'dangerous truth.' Maritain's quarrel with Gide was not about sexual inversion so much as about social subversion – and in this esteem for social order he simply echoed the republican naturalism articulated pseudonymously by Zola: 'An invert is an agent of dissolution for the family, the nation, humanity. Man and woman are certainly only here to have children, and they kill life when they no longer do what is necessary to that end.'[28] Which was more dangerous? The 'invert's' self-loathing and suicidal self-destruction? Or the risk that acceptance would pose to society's 'law and order'? Experience had changed Gide's mind. It would soon affect Maritain's sense of 'order.'

1924–1925: Maritain-Cocteau: An Entente Cordiale

In the wake of Radiguet's death, Cocteau turned to Maritain, the very opposite of his former intellectual guide and father figure, Gide.[29]Opium had rendered Radiguet's body ill-prepared to combat typhoid and Cocteau's mind unready to handle trauma. Two months later, Cocteau was back in Paris feeling desperate. He wrote Maritain, asking, 'Might we not meet together with Georges Auric?' Another letter in April ended by saying, 'As for the rest, our meeting must be more than a visit; I have serious advice to ask of you.' Raïssa recorded their first meeting in July 1924: 'For the first time Auric brought Jean Cocteau to us. Crippled since the death of Radiguet, practically in despair, he comes to Jacques because someone told him that he might help him re-find peace again, and re-find God.'[30]

If the recollections nearly fifty years later of Henri Massis can be believed, Maritain's newly intensified pursuit of Cocteau was extremely self-aware. Radiguet's novel *The Mask of the Count Orgel* was published posthumously in the June 1924 issue of Gide's *Nouvelle Revue française*. According to Massis, Maritain encouraged him (whether before or after Cocteau's July visit is unknown) to review Radiguet for the *Revue universelle*: 'I have just read Radiguet in the *NRF*. I find it quite good and important. Wouldn't this be the occasion to talk about him? In itself, this would seem to me very desirable. In addition, I know that Cocteau and his friends want it very much and this would be very opportune.' Then, Maritain expressed his conviction that Cocteau's anti-surrealist movement more properly belonged to the *Revue universelle* (animated by Thomistic and Action Française principles) where both the Catholic and the neoclassicist shared universal and eternal Latin forms. 'The moment has come, it seems to me, to welcome this whole movement and not to let it be captured by the *NRF* to which it is in reality contrary.'[31]

Massis's hommage to Radiguet appeared on 15 August 1924, concluding with the estimation that Radiguet's work 'assimilates, selects and distills the best of Proust, Gide, and, even more closely, Cocteau and Morand. It is by this modernity that *The Mask of Count Orgel* will win the young and influence them.'[32] The essay achieved its end; Cocteau wrote Maritain at once from his vacation in Villefranche saying that, although he had only been able to see the 'magnificent fragment' reproduced in Lefèvre's *Les Nouvelles littéraires*, he wanted his thanks passed on to Massis. Auric too immediately sent a response to Maritain: 'We read yesterday with emotion the moving and beautiful article of Massis – which redeems to a large extent his silence at the moment of [Radiguet's] *Devil in the Flesh* ... This small portrait of Radiguet is animated with a feeling and a movement in which one senses the sincere impulse of a *heart* and which I would not have expected, I must say, from Massis.'[33] The *Revue universelle* had staked an important yet unstable claim: it would attract and influence 'the young' by means of 'this modernity' – Proust, Gide, Radiguet, and 'even more closely,' Cocteau.

Later that year, Maritain persuaded Cocteau to enter a sanatorium to be treated for his opium addiction. Cocteau entered the Thermes Urbains clinic at the beginning of March 1925 and, as recounted in *The Difficulty of Being*, Maritain visited Cocteau frequently, urging him to return to Catholicism.[34] Three months later, on 15 June, while visiting the Maritains' home in Meudon, Cocteau met Père Charles Henrion and was greatly impressed by him: 'A priest struck me with the same shock as Stravinsky and Picasso ... Picasso and Stravinsky [knew] how to cover the paper with divine signs, but the Host [was] the only masterpiece Charles offer[ed] me.'[35] On Friday, 19 June 1925, Cocteau returned to the fold. He recalled the event: 'the morning of the Feast of the Sacred Heart of Jesus ... in your chapel, [Maritain], in the midst of some of your intimates, Father Charles gave me Communion.' At the death of Radiguet, Max Jacob had counselled Cocteau to confess himself and receive communion. 'What?' exclaimed Cocteau. 'You are recommending the Host to me as you would an aspirin.' Jacob responded solemnly: 'The Host must be taken like an aspirin.' Cocteau swallowed his medicine. In this ironic literal reversal of Marx's infamous figurative observation, religion was taken as the antidote to opium.[36]

Cocteau's conversion back to his childhood faith became a cultural event of that summer 1925 and, as a consequence, a catalyst: the attraction of Maritain for the young literary circle that had already begun to form around him only increased. In late August, Maurice Sachs – whose later reflections entitled *In the Time of the Boeuf sur le Toit (Journal of a Young Bourgeois during the Epoch of Prosperity, 14 July 1919–30 October 1929)* would christen the decade – was baptized at Meudon with Cocteau as godfather and Raïssa (in spite of her misgivings) as godmother. He described Maritain in retrospect as appearing 'to be a bit miraculous ... He drew us like a magnet without intending it.'[37]

The *catholicity* of Cultural Thomism: The *Roseau d'Or*

Already in March 1925, even he was just beginning his cure, Cocteau had collaborated in the foundation of Maritain's new publishing venture, the *Roseau d'Or*. Eventually, the directorship would number three – Maritain, Massis, and Lefèvre – and a secretary, Stanislas Fumet.[38] Like the *Revue universelle*, Maritain consciously intended his new venture to challenge Gide's *N.R.F.* as the centre of élite intellectual life. But the *Roseau d'Or*, a series that included monographs and novels as well as occasional collections or *Chroniques*, would be more overtly literary in its union of 'Thomistic thought' with the intellectual and cultural mainstreams.[39]

Maritain intended the series to realize his vision of a Thomistic realism that would influence every aspect of culture. He had explored this idea in an essay produced the year before – the year of Breton's first *Surrealist Manifesto* – entitled 'The Crisis of the Modern Spirit and the Thomistic Movement.'[40] This essay functioned as Maritain's own manifesto, calling for Thomism to put away its ghetto status as a marginal 'restoration in Catholic schools and in the education of clerics.' (This was partly in service of himself since Maritain's own status as a layman pronouncing on such matters was controversial to some.) Thomism was 'not old in itself but as young as truth,' needing to be taken out of the dusty 'old file cabinet folders' and reclaim its place – 'which is to say the first place' – in the culture beyond the confessional. Having rejected 'the spirit of modern philosophy,' 'a generation would raise itself up' and 'introduce Thomism into the intellectual life of the century.'

Undoubtedly, the 'diffusion of Thomism into the world and into laicist milieus' would require a delicate hylomorphism: 'all the materials of life ... palpitating and precious in their human quality' would need to be assimilated to 'the Thomistic form.' Thus, the 'mission' of the new generation was 'to save everything that is still viable in the modern world' and lead it 'to the perfect order of wisdom.' *Voilà une grande nouveauté*, he exclaimed: Thomism would be taken out from parochial schools and seminaries and brought into the *cité* of 'art, science, and culture.' In this, the words of scripture would be fulfilled once again: '*sapientia foris praedicat, in plateis dat vocem*.'[41] This was the vision undergirding the *Roseau d'Or*.

The first monograph published in early 1925, Maritain's own *Three Reformers*, seemed to many a cry much too shrill.[42] This polemical assault on Luther, Descartes, and Rousseau stirred up a bitter reaction and initially painted the *Roseau d'Or* with the reputation of 'a visceral antimodernism.'[43] In June, Pierre Lasserre accused Maritain in *Les Nouvelles littéraires* of 'archaicism': 'To search for lessons in Saint Thomas, what could be better? But to respond to the difficulties of contemporary thought solely by Saint Thomas, this is archaicism.'[44] The next three issues – *The Comedian and Grace* by Henri Ghéon, *The Love of the World*, a novel by C.-F. Ramuz (librettist for Stravinsky's 'The Soldier's Story' [1918]), and *Saint Francis of Assisi* by G.K. Chesterton – softened the series' reputation. From the very beginning, the *Roseau d'Or* attracted international recognition, extending the Catholic revival's influence beyond the boundaries of France.[45]

In December 1925, the first issue of the *Chroniques* was published. The main attraction was 'Day One' of what would become one of Paul Claudel's most famous works, a play comprised of four days, 'The Satin Slipper' (1929).[46] The piece was a coup for Maritain: Claudel's standing as a grandfather of the *renouveau catholique* anchored the new series in a venerable lineage, and Claudel was published by the *N.R.F.*, the *Roseau d'Or*'s self-defined competitor. (Claudel would reappear in the next volume of the series as well, a collection of his *Correspondence* with the late Jacques Rivière, postwar director of the *N.R.F.* and tragically dead from typhoid fever in 1925.)[47]

If Claudel was the main event, the real innovation of this first collection could be seen in the Thomistic/avant-garde hybrid that Maritain had promised:

Jacques MARITAIN:	Grandeur et misère de la métaphysique
Jean COCTEAU:	Raymond Radiguet
Max JACOB:	Pèlerinages, nage!

In this literary launch, the heights and depths of philosophical ruminations shared top billing with Cocteau's homage to his deceased young muse. The title of Jacob's account of the Holy Year at various pilgrimage sites – a rhyming word-play that might literally translate 'Pilgrimages, Swim!' – wasn't 'made to be taken seriously,' wrote one reviewer. 'Simple mischievousness or word juggling.'[48] Other works included two additional poems by Cocteau ('The Fire of Fire' and 'The Young Girl who Sleeps'), a prose-poem by Pierre Reverdy, Stanislas Fumet's 'Another Idea of Order,' and Hilaire Belloc's 'Catholic Consciousness of History,' translated into French for this volume and giving this issue (like the previous one featuring Chesterton) a connection to British Catholic revivalism.[49] René Johannet had written an extremely negative review of this first *Chroniques*, and *Le Correspondant* responded that Johannet's accusation of 'scornful laughing' had 'perhaps exaggerated' the case. Max Jacob's humour was 'very acceptable,' and it wasn't 'necessary to denounce M. Claudel as a corruptor of French taste.' On the other hand, even *Le Correspondant* found it difficult to 'defend the prose-poem of M. Pierre Reverdy ... In this case we no longer resist M. Johannet.'[50]

The project's aspirations immediately raised eyebrows among traditionalists who did not share Maritain's vision. Again, Johannet expressed irritation: 'What links can there be between a Catholic like Maritain, a Protestant like Ramuz, an atheist, and a Jew, since, if my information is correct, the *Roseau d'Or* is going to publish the works of Jews and atheists.'[51] Others found such diversity a cause for celebration. The venture would provide, said *L'Eclaireur du Soir* of Nice, a meeting place for writers who were 'very different from one another, indeed even opposed, assembled together however by a single spiritual anxiety much superior to all literature. This is the first issue of the *Chroniques*, waited for with an exceptional curiosity.'[52] 'They have grouped together writers of diverse temperaments and made a curious melange of men,' said the *Revue Européene*. 'But with an unanticipated diversity of means of expression, they end up by reuniting themselves and walking in a single direction. The mind is struck by the harmony that prevails between them.'[53] Maritain himself held firm: 'Many of the collaborators of *Roseau d'Or* are Catholic writers,' he wrote. 'However, this collection is not a *confessional* collection. It has published, and it will publish, Orthodox, Jewish, and Protestant writers.'[54]

April 1926 saw Maritain's publication of Georges Bernanos's first novel, *Under Satan's Sun*, in the *Roseau d'Or* series with phenomenal results. This unexpected best seller about a country village stalked by the devil – 'in the very midst of the 20th century,' as Paul Souday mocked – attracted fame and notoriety to the *Roseau d'Or* and turned the unknown Bernanos into a celebrity overnight. Meanwhile, Maritain actively enrolled other novelists for publication, including Julien Green. Maritain had first contacted Green after reading his angry tract, entitled *Pamphlet Against the Catholics of France. Dedicated to Six French Cardinals* (1924), denouncing the embourgeoisement of French clergy and laity. Green was a homosexual convert to Catholicism, and his earliest fiction was marked by a chasm between bodily attractions and the claims of the spirit, producing 'a world condemned to lovelessness and non-communication by an undefined, invisible, malevolent destiny.'[55] On 6 April 1926, responding to a request from Maritain, Green wrote: 'I would like to thank you for having thought of me for the next issue of the *Chroniques*.'[56]

Maritain published both of Green's 'magical realist' novels: *Adrienne Mesurat* (1927) and *Leviathan* (1929).[57] 'Nothing is farther from *naturalism* than the novels of Julien Green,' wrote Maritain. 'The "observation" of things hold little place there. Their force comes from the interior, they rise up from the bottom of the soul ...'[58] Reviewing *Leviathan*, Gabriel Marcel wrote in April 1929 (just one month after his baptism) that, 'after having been initially surprised and even a bit scandalized at seeing *Leviathan* appear in the *Roseau d'Or*,' he had come to think that 'M. Maritain was, on the contrary, guided by a very sure intuition.' 'It is not insignificant,' wrote Albert Thibaudet the same week, 'that *Leviathan*, the work of a Catholic writer, has appeared in the *Roseau d'Or*, which, under the direction of M. Maritain, groups together works of Catholic inspiration.' Thibaudet judged that in 1929, the 'two eminent representatives' of the 'Catholic novel' descended from Barbey d'Aurevilly and Léon Bloy were 'Georges Bernanos and Julien Green, the authors of *Under Satan's Sun* and of *Leviathan*,' both published in the *Roseau d'Or*.[59]

In addition to those already mentioned, Maritain would eventually publish Berdiaeff, Massignon, Mauriac, and Mounier, as well as the enormously popular German theologian Romano Guardini, Graham Greene (England) and Giovanni Papini (Italy), two converts whose somewhat heterodox Catholic works scandalized mainstream Catholics and were at one time or another censured.[60] This line-up gave the *Roseau d'Or* its reputation for youthfulness and contemporaneity. 'Printed by a traditional publishing house, it carries one of the hopes of young literature,' wrote *Études*. 'This avant-garde team is of a high quality, as much for the refinement of form as well as for the elevation of thought.' As for those critics who said it had 'clinkers, obscurities and bizarre pieces' that were a 'bit audacious,' *Études* replied apodictically: 'Certainly not.'[61] The team 'presents itself for the most part as a grouping of young writers,' reported *Les Nouvelles littéraires*, 'all animated by the same faith in the theological sense of the word.'[62]Although *Le Semeur* could see some reservations that one might have about Maritain's 'attitude,' his work nevertheless was 'a fine effort for displaying the essential values of Christianity to this generation.' The *Roseau d'Or*, concluded Jean Morienval, was 'one of the most significant manifestations of the spirit of the time' and deserved 'a long study.'[63]

The *Roseau d'Or* would become enormously successful, as attested to negatively by the Marxist Henri Lefèvre who deplored the place that Maritain had secured in French intellectual life.[64] In a wistful 'obituary' written for the series after its last publication in 1932, *L'Intransigeant* would later reminisce, 'Is it necessary to recall the great movement of interest that the *Roseau d'or* aroused from the moment of its appearance? In the eyes of the public the *Roseau d'or* represented an audacious alliance of the philosophy of Saint Thomas and of all kinds of avant-garde literature.'[65] Maritain's vision had been realized. Wisdom cried out in the *cité*.

1926: *Letter to Jacques Maritain / Response to Jean Cocteau*

In June 1926 appeared the jointly published *Letter to Jacques Maritain* and *Response to Jean Cocteau.*[66] As one of his first post-conversion 'plans for Catholic activity,' Cocteau had begun writing his *Letter* in August 1925, intending it as a public 'edifying document designed to bring other artists into the fold, away from the atheistic Surrealists' whom he despised.[67] In return, Maritain wrote his *Response to Jean Cocteau.* Among many other topics, the exchange recounted Cocteau's opium detoxification and subsequent conversion, both assisted by Maritain's spiritual midwifery. Its association of the *enfant terrible* with the man of prudence made order look like anarchy.

No single image in the exchange accomplished this association more directly (or more poetically) than Antigone. Cocteau wrote, 'Now instinct always pushes me against the law. This is the secret reason why I translated *Antigone*. I would hate to have my love for order benefit from the meaning that is idly lent to that word ... I must salute, in its least high form, an unforeseen force opposed to Creon, to the foreseen mechanism of the law. ' Maritain responded:

> You have an admirably jealous longing for freedom. How well I understand your love for Antigone! Yet she herself tells us, and that is why she is dear to you, that in breaking human law she was following a better commandment – the unwritten and unchangeable laws.
>
> *οὐ γὰρ τι νῦν γε κἀχθες ἀλλ ἀεί ποτε*
> *ζῆ ταῦτα κοὐδεις οἶδεν, ἐξ ὅτου 'φάνη*[68]

Like the *enfant terrible* from antiquity, Cocteau's scandal lay in breaking contingent human customs. But appearances deceive, and his avant-garde outrages might also be interpreted as transgressions of the law's letter in service of its spirit – invisible and eternal law, as primeval as the Greek script that preserved it in pristine purity.

The publication also provided a context in which Maritain could expound his own scandalous theory of 'Christian art' to a broader audience. In *Art and Scholasticism*, Maritain had insisted that 'Christian Art' was not Church Art nor any other 'species of the genus art.' An art was Christian not because of its subject matter but rather because it was produced by a soul in which 'Christ is present through his love.'[69] In his *Response to Jean Cocteau*, Maritain could restate his thesis for the benefit of avant-garde readers: 'The art of the church ... must be religious, theological. Except for this particular (and eminent) case, however, it is very true that God does not ask for a "religious art" or a "Catholic art." The art he wants for himself is art. With all its teeth.' Maritain illustrated what he meant by the art God wanted: Erik Satie's *Socrates*, Stravinsky's *Noces*, 'the figures of Rouault and Picasso, and of your *Orpheus*, my dear Jean.' Certainly, Fra Angelico had been correct to say, '*to paint the things of Christ one must live in Christ* ... But one must first be a painter.'[70]

The new alliance became a lightning rod, attracting both jeers and cheers. On the Catholic right, Bernanos's disgust with Maritain, as remembered years later by Massis, was couched in terms of disguise and masque: 'I wonder by what disgrace, by what curse the Catholic intelligentsia has been so reduced, that in order to instruct its flock, it should find its nourishment among the disciples of Bergson and Cocteau, wearing the clownish whiteface of Thomists [*grimés en thomistes*]? ... Cocteau, the conversion of Cocteau and his little "fairies" from Le Boeuf sur le Toit; come now, is this what they call the Catholic Revival?'[71]

Shots at Cocteau came from the left as well. The English novelist Mary Butts deplored Cocteau's 'scuttling back to the church.' 'He knew of nowhere else to go but to the traditional depository of spiritual comfort,' she wrote. 'Was it ignorance or fear that did not allow him to look into his own heart?' Predictably, the surrealists could (and would) proceed to doubly vilify Cocteau. They hated him for being bourgeois – the March 1926 issue of *La Révolution surréaliste* called Cocteau the 'animal who reeks'[72] – and now they could hate him for being a bourgeois Catholic.

Reviews of the literary exchange itself were also mixed. 'I do not see very clearly the stages' of Cocteau's conversion, confessed *La Liberté*. Referring to the poet's revelation that he had lost seven of his closest friends, the reviewer asked: 'Is M. Cocteau claiming that God has made seven young men suffer and die in order to conquer a single precious soul? We are not able to believe it.'[73] The report of *Carnet de la Semaine* was shot through with irony. 'The mysticism of the author is the result of diverse peregrinations and of a sorrow experienced too vividly. This last was Radiguet's departure in order to lift him up to God. Point of departure and fall. Break.' New paragraph. From then on, Cocteau changed friends 'like one changes shirts. But he no longer changes his shirt. He keeps on his hair shirt.' As for Maritain's response, Cocteau's 'trainer-manager-convertor wrote it in a minor key.' It read like a sermon normally appearing during 'March in Lent,' and only had 'salt' because of 'the letter that provoked it.'[74] Yet another review, noting that Cocteau's *Letter* said 'God is patient because he is eternal' and concluded that 'speed unleashes diabolical things,' came up with this headline: 'According to Jean Cocteau the airplane would be the preferred son of Satan.'[75]

Advocates, however, rejoiced. Gaëtan Bernoville read the Maritain-Cocteau exchange in a way that would vindicate his own efforts at fostering literary revivalism. 'One result of this type of publication,' he enthused, 'is that it loudly proclaims the stupid state of mind which likes to say: "The Church is incompatible with everything that is modern; it is a power of the past." ... The Church has always been, in every epoch, modern in this sense. It has always and in every epoch assimilated that which was capable of being incorporated and renovated [*renouvelé*] by this fertile force which is at the heart of Christian thought – Christianity, that is, liberated from a suffocating academicism and everything else which is contrary to its spirit.'[76] Anti-academic metaphors delegitimated both integralist neoscholastics as well as bourgeois moderates.

Another reviewer and apologist also lauded Catholicism's modernist possibilities when liberated from 'academic' strictures. Appearing in the *Revue Apologétique*, an essay entitled 'The Catholic Renaissance among the Intellectual Elite' combined the wartime metaphor of a political-cultural 'sacred union' and the religious metaphor of a triptych.[77] 'In the left wing' (of the triptych), Art aided Cocteau by calling to its defence 'the philosophy of Saint Thomas incarnated in Maritain.' In the right wing, Maritain's call to order was bolstered by Cocteau's 'order as anarchy.' In his letter, Cocteau opposed his order to the disorder of Dadaists and surrealists: 'Order after a crisis, that is the new order I insist upon. This is why I am hated by the profiteers of disorder ...'[78] The reviewer approvingly quoted Maritain's *Response*: what Cocteau is seeking in art 'is *order* ... obviously, not the academic kind of order which is a false one ... That which scandalizes our contemporaries the most is order: I mean order in spirit and in truth which is just as much the enemy of a stuffed-shirt order ... as it is of disorder.' As an example of such non-stuffy order, the reviewer gleefully glossed Cocteau's reminiscence of Jacob's advice to take the host 'like an aspirin': 'This is the free translation of the doctrine of the Council of Trent,' he wrote, 'reminding us that communion is the remedy for our infirmities of the soul.' Tridentine doctrine as a riff for free improvisation: this was Jazz Age Catholicism.

The reviewer further acknowledged the dowry that Maritain's marriage had brought: his 'doctrine on freedom in art' had won over prestigious in-laws by demonstrating that artists like 'Péguy, Claudel, Max Jacob' could now 'easily find grace for their eccentricities of language and extravagant images.' Cocteau's conversion provided the proof: it had not 'stopped him from admiring a Stravinsky or a Picasso. For him, simplicity in music is called Erik Satie; in poetry, Max Jacob.' His religious conversion would not drive a wedge between him and his Group of Six. The Maritain-Cocteau marriage seemed finally to have reconciled the nineteenth-century divorce between Catholicism and modernity, and the reviewer concluded that this was a 'Touching solidarity where faith has its part.'

However, the essay's subtitle – 'The Call to Order: The Connections between Art and Morality' – was haunted by an unspoken spectre. Using the Biblical image of Pentecost, the reviewer observed that Maritain seemed intent on gathering together people 'from every tribe – from every language, from every nation' in his new Jerusalem. But anxieties lingered: perhaps Maritain's attempt might end up rather more like the Tower of Babel?[79] What 'measuring device' was Maritain using, he asked, to decide who could 'return to the flock' and those to whom one could 'only extend credit' redeemable at some future date? 'The question is of importance,' he anxiously insisted: 'it is a question of nothing less than finding a *terrain d'entente* between Catholic morality and modern art – or perhaps better, between art and morality.'

The fundamental aim of *Art and Scholasticism* in 1920 had been to dispel the prejudice that there was a conflict between 'Art and Prudence.' The Cocteau-Maritain collaboration of 1926 personified this reconciliation. But the reviewer's post-war politico-military metaphor of an *entente cordiale*, conveying the sense of a fragile pact threatened by unspoken motives, suggested that Maritain had not dispelled everyone's anxieties. Fears about the forged alliance between 'art and morality' – that is, Cocteau and Catholicism (with homosexuality as the suppressed middle term) – pointed beyond themselves to another fear: namely, that the Church, beneath the masque that let it pass, might actually still be 'incompatible with all that is modern.'

The year 1926 ended traumatically for French Catholics: following the directive of Pope Pius XI, the Vatican's Holy Office issued a decree on 29 December 1926 condemning the Action Française and Maurras's writings. Integralist Catholics were forced to choose between Maurras and Rome.[80] In three separate publications, Maritain set out his position: *An Opinion About Charles Maurras and the Duty of Catholics* (1926), *The Primacy of the Spiritual* (1927) – as opposed to Maurras's slogan 'Politics First!' – and (in collaboration with Father Paul Doncoeur, S.J.) *Why Rome Has Spoken* (1927). On 1 February 1927, Maritain resigned his position at the *Revue universelle*, which he had founded with Massis.[81] Massis's response to the upheaval was typically curious: in 1927 he would publish a new edition of the collected letters of Bishop Bossuet (the fervent seventeenth-century absolutist), an apparently Gallican response to Rome's never-ending interference in France.[82]

A 1928 letter from Georges Bernanos, previously angered by the publication of the Maritain/Cocteau letters, colourfully conveys the betrayal felt by Maritain's collaborators on the right: 'What bullshit! ... For a long time I have wanted to say this to you: a wager like yours could be made only by a saint. Our souls have already paid for a good part of your illusions. Your work will pay for the rest. It has already been knocked to the ground ... The enthusiastic cries of a small number of esthetes and epileptic Jews are of no avail ... You speak well, you speak too well, you speak like the friends of Job ... with useless palinodes you have dishonored the very notion of obedience and the humble submission of hearts.'[83]

Through their conversion to the Church more than twenty years earlier, the Maritains had established and sustained links to the political right. As these ties were now severed, the loss of friends meant a painful time lay ahead for the couple.[84] However, as doors on the right closed, others opened, and the condemnation freed the Maritains to walk through them, recovering some of their earlier selves and broader horizons.

1927: Maritain on Music: His Debt to Cocteau[85]

In 1927, Maritain published an enormously expanded edition of *Art and Scholasticism* whose many intertextual references solidified his project of Catholic modernism. Among the most important of these was his exaltation of the musicians Erik Satie (d. 1925) and Igor Stravinsky. Maritain's linkage with these musicians gave him access to the broad cultural legitimation that the new music defining the era could bestow. For his few words on music, Maritain – in 1927 as he had been in 1920 – was almost entirely indebted to Cocteau.

In 1920, Maritain had followed Cocteau's use of Wagner to symbolize all that was decadent and 'anti-classical' in German music. *The Cock and the Harlequin* lampooned Wagner: 'There are certain long works which are short. Wagner's works are long works which are long, and *long-drawn-out*, because this old sorcerer looked upon boredom as a useful drug for the stupefaction of the faithful.'[86] By appealing to the authority of Friedrich Nietzsche, Maritain also vilified Wagner as well as the romantic republican Victor Hugo: 'they both prove one and the same thing: that in declining civilisations, wherever the mob is allowed to decide, genuineness becomes superfluous, prejudicial, unfavorable ... With drums and fifes, Wagner marches at the head of all artists in declamation, in display and virtuosity ...'[87]

In the late nineteenth century, the term *néoclassicisme*, superceded by romanticism and Impressionism, had been a pejorative one. Cocteau reversed those values and, pitting Claude Debussy against Erik Satie, turned Satie into an authentically 'Latin' exemplar for a victorious France. Invoking Satie's three *Gymnopédies*, Cocteau contrasted their original arrangements for a simple solo piano with Debussy's orchestral settings of them. Satie's music remained 'intact. Listen to his "Gymnopédies" so clear in their form and melancholy feeling.' But Debussy's orchestration confused them, wrapping 'their exquisite architecture in a cloud.' Debussy played 'in French, but he use[d] the Russian pedal,'[88] creating 'a kind of fuzzy atmosphere favorable to short-sighted ears.' He 'deviated: on account of the German ambush, he fell into the Russian trap,' and the 'thick lightning-pierced fog of Bayreuth' became 'a thin snowy mist flecked with impressionist sunshine.' Whereas Satie musically translated the neoclassicist painter Ingres, Debussy transposed 'Claude Monet *à la russe*.' 'You can't get lost in a Debussy mist as you can in a Wagner fog,' Cocteau quipped, 'but you can still catch cold.'[89]

We have already seen Cocteau's anxious obsession with masks, disguises, and the possibilities of passing in the case of the German Harlequin, and it was most evident in the special venom he reserved for cultural cross-breeding. While Russian music was 'admirable because it is Russian music,' hybridized 'Russian-French music or German-French music' was 'necessarily bastard [*bâtarde*], even if it be inspired by a Stravinsky, a Wagner ... The music I want must be French, of France.' Maritain's 1920 *Art and Scholasticism* echoed Cocteau: 'By reason of its subject and of its roots, [art] is of a particular age and of a particular country ... That is why in the history of free peoples the eras of cosmopolitanism are times of intellectual bastardization [*d'abâtardissement*].'[90]

This was certainly a peculiar line for Maritain to write: born and raised in cosmopolitan Paris, he had married a Russian Jewish emigrée, and devoted his studies to Aquinas – the great medieval synthesizer of Greek, Christian, Jewish, and Islamic thinkers, all in the highly cosmopolitan thirteenth-century Paris. An anxiety over 'bastardization' (i.e., uncertain *paternité*) could have been psychological as well as cultural: like several other well-known writers of the time, Gide, Maritain, and Cocteau all shared 'the bankruptcy of the father ... early disappearance, suicide, deliberate escape ...'[91] Uncertainty about cultural lineage suggested larger genealogical fears around both *paternité* and *patrie* – over the unsettled identities of France and its culture.[92]

Significantly, nationalistic passages softened somewhat in the 1927 edition of *Art and Scholasticism*, likely in response to the papal condemnation of Action Française in late December 1926. For example, in 1920 (as seen above in chapter 4), Maritain had quoted Maurras: 'The classical, the Attic, is the more universal in proportion as it is more austerely Athenian–Athenian of an epoch and a taste better purged of all foreign influence. In the high moment when it was itself alone, Attica was the human race.' Those words reappeared in 1927 unaltered.[93] However, Maritain altered the text to rewrite the meaning of 'universal.' In this revised edition, the gloss on Maurras was deleted – '*French genius has, in modern times, analogous characteristics*' – and replaced by a softer claim: 'It would appear at the present time that French genius might have a similar mission, but one compelling it to serve *a more exalted universality than that of pure reason – [that is, to serve] the full catholicity* of natural and supernatural truth.'[94] The universal was no longer the French national genius but rather Catholicism as catholicity, restating the *Pri-*

macy of the Spiritual in response to Maurras's 'Politics first!' Again in 1920, Maritain had concluded that 'a certain kind of nationalism – *political and territorial nationalism* – is the natural safeguard of ... the very universality of intelligence and art.' In 1927, Maritain rewrote 'nationalism' as 'a vigorous *political and territorial* attachment to the nation.'[95]

In addition to softening its nationalism, the 1927 *Art and Scholasticism* reversed the earlier edition's estimation of Stravinsky. In 1920, referring to what made a work 'classical' in its simplicity, Maritain had associated Stravinsky with bombast: 'Compare, from this point of view, in the order of thought, Aristotle and Saint Thomas Aquinas to Luther or to Jean-Jacques Rousseau, in the order of art the Gregorian melody or the music of Bach to the music of Wagner and Stravinsky.' In 1927, Maritain altered the passage. First, he deleted the non-musicians: 'Compare, from this point of view, Gregorian melody or the music of Bach to the music of Wagner or Stravinsky.'[96] Second, he apologized for lumping Stravinsky in with Wagner by appending the following note – not at the end with the other 160 endnotes, but rather as a retraction statement prominently displayed at the bottom of the page: 'I regret having thus spoken of Stravinsky. All I had heard [in 1920] was *The Rite of Spring*, and I should have perceived then that Stravinsky was turning his back on everything we find distasteful in Wagner. Since then [Stravinsky] has shown that genius conserves and increases its strength by renewing it in light. Exuberant with truth, his admirably disciplined work teaches the best lesson of any today of grandeur and creative energy, and best answers the strict classical "austerity" here in question. His purity, his authenticity, his glorious spiritual strength, are to the gigantism of [Wagner's] "Parsifal" and "Ring Cycle" as a miracle of Moses to the enchantments of the Egyptians.'[97] Maritain's praise continued: after an epoch of decadence, 1920s music was recovering 'respect for genuine subordinations' to the truth, to 'obedience, to sacrifice.' After 'so much sentimentalism' in French music led astray by Wagner, the postwar epoch wanted 'hard contact with the real, denuded and naked.' The 'example of Satie' was 'teaching it once more a chaste honesty' while Stravinsky was teaching it 'grandeur.'[98] (Decades later, this note elicited a grudging acknowledgment from a Stravinsky biographer who credited Maritain for not being above apologizing 'for such stupidity.')[99]

The 1927 reader might have been forgiven for being puzzled: whatever 'chaste' might mean in music, Satie's ballet *Parade* (1917) did not seem like a prime candidate, having been scored for an orchestra that included typewriters, sirens, pistol shots, and a lottery wheel, and incorporating jazz for the first time in Parisian music-making – the 'Steamboat Rag.'[100] As for Stravinsky's own turn to the purity of the 'neoclassical,' Maritain had in mind Stravinsky's *The Soldier's Tale* (1918), a piece containing parodies of a chorale, march, waltz, tango, and ragtime. As Stravinsky himself said, 'Jazz meant, in any case, a wholly new sound in my music, and *Histoire* [Soldier's Tale] marks my final break with the Russian orchestral school.'[101] (Stravinsky's *Ragtime* was published in 1919 and *Piano-Rag-Music* [written for Arthur Rubinstein] in 1920.) What did Maritain mean by having found obedience, sacrifice, subordination, chastity, and classical simplicity in Satie and Stravinsky?

Perhaps all politics, including musical politics, really is personal. First, Maritain's visits to Satie's deathbed in 1925 had catalysed the musician's return to the faith before he died, and this greatly affected Maritain.[102] Second, Cocteau's own 1924 revision of *The Cock* had included a retraction of his 1918 assault on Stravinsky – and Maritain, as he had in 1920, simply followed Cocteau's lead.

In 1918, in a passage curiously infused with seduction metaphors, Cocteau alluded to the Odysseus tale in which the singing of the Sirens enticed young sailors to their deaths on the rocks: 'The theatre corrupts everything, even a Stravinsky ... I should not like this paragraph to affect our faithful friendship, but it is useful to put our young compatriots on their guard against ... these stout golden sirens who caused even so formidable a ship [i.e., Stravinsky] to change its course ... Stravinsky grabs us by means other than Wagner; he does not make a pass at us; he rhythmically hits us over the head ...' Cocteau added insult to injury: 'Wagner cooks us slowly; Stravinsky does not give us time to say "Ouf!"; but both of them upset our nerves. This is music which comes from the bowels; an octopus from which you must flee or else it will devour you.'[103]

Despite Cocteau's expressed desire, Stravinsky took these remarks very personally and their 'faithful friendship' foundered. In the 1924 revised edition of *The Cock*, Cocteau appended a note to his insult of Stravinsky, positioned at the bottom of the page. The retraction read: 'This unjust remark is, of course, nullified by *The Soldier's Tale*, with which I was then unacquainted, as well as by all Stravinsky's later works. See [my] "Stravinsky – Stop-Press" (Appendix 1924).'[104] The appendix included this reassessment: 'Genius cannot be analyzed any more than electricity. You either have or don't have it. Stravinsky has it, and so never bothers about it at all ... He canalizes an elemental force, and, in order to make it serviceable, provides it with appliances ranging from factories to pocket lamps.' Maritain, following Cocteau's 1924 edition, used exactly the same redemptive metaphor in 1927: 'Stravinsky has shown that genius conserves and increases it strength by renewing it in light.'[105](Perhaps 'light' seemed more dignified than 'pocket lamps.')

Maritain's 1927 apotheosis of Stravinsky allowed him to associate Catholicism with the towering musical figure of Jazz Age Paris. For his part, Stravinsky's own philosophy of music, especially with respect to the idea of tradition as a living force, was strongly influenced by Maritain (especially as mediated largely through their mutual friend, Arthur Lourié). In 1927, as Maritain's prominent retraction of his former criticism of Stravinsky appeared, Stravinsky premiered *Oedipus Rex*. The oratorio's libretto (written by Cocteau and translated into Latin by the Jesuit seminarian [later Cardinal] Jean Daniélou) reconstructed Sophocles' tragedy for a new generation. The exotic primitivism of the *Rite of Spring* had perhaps too eerily presaged the horrific blood sacrifice of youth by their elders in 1914–18. In retelling the story of a city polluted by plague-stricken corpses, Stravinsky said, 'I chose the archetypal drama of purification.'[106] Composed in angular rhythms and sung in the timeless cadences of the Latin language, *Oedipus Rex* was, to use Cocteau's words from *The Cock*, 'a case of oriental romanticism (with its uneasiness and savage upheavals) placing itself at the service of Latin order.'[107] The *Symphony of Psalms* (1930) soon followed, also set to Latin texts from the Vulgate. As late as 1945, Stravinsky's *Poetics of Music* directly imitated lines in *Art and Scholasticism*: Stravinsky first quoted Baudelaire, then Poussin, on to Bellay, and finally Montaigne.[108]

In Cocteau's musical rhetoric of nationalistic universalism, the Maritain of 1920 had found a cultural niche into which he might weave his own new 'universality.' But after the December 1926 papal condemnation of Action Française, nationalistic 'universality' became Catholic 'catholicity.' The continuous thread remained modern art: an art whose spirituality progressed proportionately with its abstraction, but whose 'religiosity' – in the absence of religious subject matter – became proportionately problematic.

C/catholicism: A Particularist Universalism

In this time of cataclysmic upheaval for French Catholicism, who were the 'Catholics' and what was the 'catholic'? The reader of the 1927 *Art and Scholasticism* paying close attention to a small orthograpical shift in the first endnote might have been unsure. The quotation from St Albert the Great, Aquinas's medieval master, distinguished the contemplation of 'Philosophers' from that of 'Saints, which is to say the Catholics.' Philosophers ended up in ideas, Catholics in love. The versions from the 1920 and 1927 editions look like this:

> 1920: *sed contemplatio Sanctorum, quae est Catholicorum*
> [but the contemplation of the Saints, that is, of Catholics]
> 1927: *sed contemplatio Sanctorum, quae est catholicorum*
> [but the contemplation of the Saints, that is, of catholics][109]

In the 1927 edition, only the word *catholicorum* had been altered; the rest of the note remained untouched. Typographically the shift was barely perceptible; culturally speaking, it was enormous. In the first version, 'Saints' were identified with 'Catholics,' whereas the second transformed them into a more fluid group with universalist aspirations. Once again, the medium was the message: an impressive array of authorities – from Pseudo-Dionysius to Maurice Denis, Hildegard of Bingen to Baudelaire, and of course Thomas Aquinas to Georges Auric – seemed to prove that *catholicisme* was a particular vision universally realizable in every time and culture. The 1926 papal condemnation had set Maritain free to push the envelope of Catholicism's catholicity.

The means towards this end would continue to be modern 'art,' especially as it became loosened from any 'religious' representational moorings whatsoever. The 1927 edition included 'An Essay on Art' in which Maritain attacked two opposite ends of 'particularism': from the left, laicists who were 'utterly ignorant of the Faith,' from the right, integralists whose 'zeal for souls' turned Catholicism into just one more 'human effort at domination.' Both groups had missed the point: those taking part 'in the works of the mind as Christians' were not engaged in a particular kind of thought – not a '*clerical* philosophy or *clerical* art, or in *confessional* philosophy or *confessional* art.' Catholicism was not one among many particulars, 'not a *particular confession of faith* any more than it is *a* religion.' It was rather, said Maritain, the universal animating the others, '*the* religion, confessing the unique omnipresent Truth.' In this sense, there was 'neither Catholic art nor philosophy.' Instead, those Christians engaged in art and philosophy produced 'C/catholic art and philosophy, that is to say, genuinely universal,' simply because they did so as believers.[110]

'All our values depend upon the nature of our God' – Raïssa's journal had recorded this fundamental starting point in 1919, sketching out a refutation of the notion that Catholicism was incompatible with modern progress. If God is Spirit, she had reasoned, then 'in the scale of values, Spirit will therefore be first ... To progress, therefore, is to go from matter to spirit.'[111] In 1927 Jacques made an analogous argument: if God was universal, and if Truth was Christ, then artists who served truth must serve a universal end. 'Those who by their art desire to serve the Truth which is Christ are not pursuing a particular human end but a divine end, an end as universal as God Himself.' Paradoxically, insofar as God was Spirit, the more particular their denominational affiliation – 'the more rooted they are in the Church' – the more universal their faith – 'the more spiritual their inner life becomes.' As a result, Catholics rose 'higher above human limitations and the conventions, opinions, and special interests of particular social groups.' Ten years earlier Raïssa complained of the 'narrow' confines of Catholicism. Now Jacques could say that Catholics, more fully understanding the 'universality of the action of God in their souls, their art and their thoughts' were 'purged of all human narrowness ...'[112]

Another 'annex' in the 1927 edition, entitled 'Some Reflections Upon Religious Art,' expanded these implications. Borrowing a page from Huysmans's assault on *l'art sulpicien* as the devil's revenge, Maritain too judged 'Saint-Sulpician art' as 'devilish.' He apologized for using the term – it was 'very insulting to an estimable Parisian parish, the more so because the plague is worldwide' – yet he nevertheless considered such kitsch 'an offence to God.' It was all the more 'harmful to the spread of religion than is generally believed' because it encouraged a 'kind of bitter contempt' for true artists and poets.[113]

In Maritain's view, clarifying what 'religious art' meant was not an intramural Catholic concern but rather 'a crisis affecting our whole civilization.' Religious art and contemporary art needed one another in order to express universal truth. On the one hand, if all 'religious art' was equated with *l'art sulpicien*, it remained imprisoned in its marginal particularism, incapable of reaching a wider audience and achieving its universal end. 'Religious art,' wrote Maritain, 'is not a thing which can be isolated from art in general, from the general artistic movement of an age: confine it, and it becomes corrupted, its expression a dead letter.' On the other hand, a 'contemporary art' divorced from genuine religious art could also not achieve its end, since the spirituality it conveyed was 'not infrequently poor indeed and sometimes very corrupt.'[114]

How could religious art and contemporary art be reconciled? Maritain made a revolutionary declaration: 'There is no style *peculiar* to religious art, there is no *religious technique*.' Dismissing the notion that 'religious' art had anything to do with external 'shapes,' he pointed to its capacity for incarnation in any particular culture and epoch: religious art followed 'the example of God Himself who speaks the language of men' and can 'assume ... every means and every form of technical vitality, so to speak, placed at its disposal by the contemporary generation.'[115] To underscore this radical claim, Maritain added an impish exhortation: '(From this point of view, it may be parenthetically observed, it does not seem at all necessary that Christian artists, especially such as have not attained to full possession of their craft, should work in sacred art exclusively. Let them begin by doing still-life studies, accustom themselves to discovering a religious significance in the inevitable apples, jam-jar, pipe and mandolin).'[116] One would have expected the Catholic convert to send aspiring 'sacred artists' to study Fra Angelico or Romanesque masters: scenes of nativities, crucifixions, and the Virgin Mary. But the mandolin?

Maritain theologically justified his rejection of the need for religious subject matter. Since sacred art was 'in a state of absolute dependence upon theological wisdom,' 'this same dogmatic point of view' lead to the conclusion that 'the disgraceful sentimentality of so many commercial products must be an equal source of distress to sound theology.' Theological wisdom clearly did not 'impose any aesthetic *genre*, any style, any particular technique, on sacred art.'

He also justified himself philosophically: 'naturalist imitation of material details and picturesque appearances' was even 'more out of place and execrable' in religious art than elsewhere. If art ought never to represent the outward shapes of material objects, how much more should this be true of divine mysteries to which human means of expression are always inadequate? Thus (echoing Denis), sacred art should probably always retain 'some element of hieratic and so to speak ideographical symbolism, and, in any event, of the strong intellectuality of its primitive traditions.'[117] But Maritain cautioned: 'Nevertheless, let us repeat once more after Maurice Denis,' that a work of art's value 'does not depend on the *subject matter* itself. Nor does it depend, I am convinced, on the formula of a school and a particular technique.' In sum, religious art did not need to be kitsch: 'It would be a great mistake to think that clumsy angles and a cheap material are the necessary means of expressing a Franciscan emotion or that a geometrical rigidity and dull, austere tones are required to stamp a work with the seal of Benedictine dignity.'[118]

Maritain accomplished for the 1920s what Huysmans and Denis had in the 1890s: through the medium of art, and with the help of an avant-garde, he made it possible for intellectual and cultural elites to be Catholic. But Maritain's accomplishment outstretched theirs. The Catholicism of Huysmans and Denis would always be somewhat peripheral to the orthodoxy of institutional Catholicism. In contrast, Maritain's avant-garde aesthetic, situated completely within the framework of neo-scholasticism, and anchored institutionally in the Institut Catholique of Paris, was thoroughly orthodox and institutionally central. Maritain's hylomorphism discredited mimetic resemblance as a deformation of the truly real, thus rewriting the 'contemporary art' of Kandinsky, Picasso, Rouault, and Severini as genuinely 'religious art.'

The fin-de-siècle *renouveau catholique* had represented a halfway house between naturalist culture and ultramontanist Catholicism. Maritain's *renouveau catholique* was not a halfway house. It was a homecoming.

1927: 'This letter closes a loop ...'

In 1927, the Maritain-Cocteau collaboration might have seemed to be the beginning of a long and fruitful venture. Maritain's increasing appeals to the modernity symbolized by homosexuality can be seen in the endnotes of the revised *Art and Scholasticism*: Oscar Wilde's *De Profundis* (192), Arthur Rimbaud's *A Season in Hell* (174), and Henri Ghéon (notes 168 and 181).[119](Curiously, as seen above in Calvet's *Panorama* [1927], Maritain had become imaginatively linked with Ghéon. He had in fact published Ghéon's *The Comedian and Grace* [1925] and would write a dedicatory preface later that year.)[120] Max Jacob was not mentioned in 1920; in 1927 he was referenced six times. Raymond Radiguet had the work's last word (199), quoted (somewhat ironically) from Massis's *Raymond Radiguet* (1927).[121]

As for Cocteau, in 1920, *The Cock and the Harlequin* was cited twice, in 1927 nine times. Art's capacity to access absolute truth was verified by a trinity of authorities – Aquinas ('*ars magis convenit cum habitibus speculativis in ratione virtutis, quam cum prudentia ...*'), Cocteau ('Art is science made flesh'), and Severini ('Art is nothing more than humanized science'). Cocteau and Severini, added Maritain, had returned 'to the ancient notion of *practical science.*'[122] In a gloss on the word 'sacrifice,' Maritain could now quote Cocteau's public letter to him: 'St Therese of Lisieux says: *I prefer sacrifice to any ecstasy*,' said the *Letter*. 'A poet ought to have these words tattooed upon his heart.'[123] The fin-de-siècle girl saint, dead from tuberculosis, heroine of the Catholic integralists, and canonized in 1925, had been transformed into the patroness of misunderstood avant-gardists everywhere.

Yet, the epigraph to Cocteau's *Letter* had declared an end, not a beginning: 'This letter closes a loop which began with *The Cock and the Harlequin.*' Presumably Cocteau meant that the road to order upon which he embarked in 1918 had found its fulfilment in his 1925 conversion. But it would soon mean 'closure' in another sense. The promise of Maritain's project – the sacred union of Catholicism and modernity, Prudence and Art, sacred and profane – had carried within it a perilous corollary, expressed in metaphors of clothing, masks, disguises, *bal masqué*. What if Maritain's Catholicism was not truly modern but only disguised, cross-dressing as modernity? This anxious question had been posed by reviews of the Cocteau-Maritain *Letters*, and it was now acted out in their relationship's unravelling over Cocteau's 'modern' sexuality.

The drama had its prelude in the 'Sachs Affair' during the summer of 1926, just after the publication of the mutual *Letters*. Like that of a number of other drug addicts drawn to Maritain's steadying hand, Maurice Sachs's addiction had left him in financial difficulties which Maritain generously settled for him.[124] After his baptism at Meudon (about which godmother Raïssa had such misgivings), Sachs went as far as entering a Carmelite seminary on 2 January 1926. He spent the following summer vacation at a seaside resort known as a homosexual hangout – in Cocteau's words, 'very *boeuf sur le toit.*' Cocteau wrote Maritain that he had seen the deeply sun-tanned 'Maurice – blacker than his cassock and wearing / preaching [*portant/prêchant*] our works on the beaches.' The seminarian met and instantly fell 'violently in love' with a young American named Tom Pinkerton. Pinkerton borrowed Sach's cassock as a bathrobe in which to walk the beach: unbuttoned, it flowed back in the breeze, providing a vivid contrast with Pinkerton's pink bathing suit, and provoked laughter and scandal.[125] Cocteau 'ordered' Sachs to return to Paris the very next day.

Maritain was infuriated and Cocteau wrote to soothe him: 'I have counseled [Maurice] against the apostolate until he attains a new ORDER.' Five days later, Cocteau wrote Maritain again, but now he himself had become enraged and used language redolent with anxiety over cross-dressing and passing. Calling Sachs a frivolous and gullible *comédien* (i.e., a clown who wears greasepaint), Cocteau said that he and Maritain '*must* publicly reprimand this *pantalonnade*' – a 'slapstick farce' named after Pantalon, the grotesque stock character in *commedia dell'arte* – 'on account of the young souls who listen to us.' The youth lured by this new Catholic modernity might be confused by Sachs's simultaneous performance of two possibly incompatible roles. (Curiously, Sachs actually inscribed this double-signification into the garment itself: he had double-lined his black cassock with a pink Chinese crêpe, acknowledging 'the physical pleasure of being dressed with a robe and ... a chill of pleasure over having to raise it when climbing the steps to his [monastic] cell.' Small wonder that its colour coordination with Pinkerton's pink bathing-suit provoked laughter.) 'Certainly [Maurice] will say that ... he is changing his life *without changing his costume*, etc.,' wrote Cocteau. 'Alas, this is impossible.'[126]

Three days later, the mercurial Cocteau had changed his mind again and apologized for writing 'so severely *à propos* Maurice.' Having heard the story recounted by one of those 'Americans thrilled by a hatred of Catholicism,' he now decided he had overreacted. This 'young Tom, who is Catholic but hates our religion to such a degree that he wants to convert to Protestantism,' had used the cassock to walk the hotel corridors '*déguisé*' – that is, 'dressed up' and/or 'disguised.' Although he could 'appreciate the scandal,' Cocteau now wanted Maurice back in the seminary. 'It is false to believe, as the American colony does,' he wrote with contempt of the postwar Yankees, 'that Maurice is unworthy to wear the cassock.' However, Cocteau still wanted to reprimand Sachs for having worn the cassock in order to 'perform a role' [*jouer un rôle*].'[127]

Throughout *l'Affaire Sachs*, metaphors of performance, passing, and disguise abounded: both Maritain and Cocteau panicked – in this case, perhaps Cocteau moreso. Cocteau had converted in search of order; Catholicism could play at looking anarchic. But in the end, beneath the cassock, what was it really? Inwardly contested, the fragile unity of this *entente cordiale* was about to unravel. Several months later, while the Pope was condemning Action Française, Cocteau would confide to a friend that he had met Jean Desbordes. 'A miracle has happened in heaven,' he wrote, 'Raymond has come back *in another guise*.'[128]

On Palm Sunday, 1927, Cocteau, now several months into his relationship with Desbordes, wrote Maritain regarding the prohibition of receiving communion after same-sex relations: 'Love prevents love. Love prevents the sacraments. This would be monstrous. It is not true ... Love renders the sacraments useless because it is a sacrament: we commune with God by means of one of his creatures.' An infuriated Maritain replied on 6 July 1927 with a long letter. 'Thus the cross [of Christ] is everywhere' he wrote. 'And by the very nature of things.' The strong emphasis on 'nature' with its overtones of materialist determinism said less about

Christianity than about the fatalistic naturalism that dominated Maritain's republican education. This lingering sense of fatalist entrapment had its parallel in another letter to Cocteau written a year later, scolding him for writing *The White Book* (1928). 'Everything about this book comes back to saying that *God is conquered*, that he encloses men in the impossible. This is false ...' The underlined emphasis on the Creator's being *conquered* by created nature was Maritain's, calling to mind his lycée thesis ('What are the Distinctive Traits?') and closely following suicide pact.[129]

A second suggestive term used by Maritain in the July letter was 'sterile': 'Fleshly love is sterile.' The term in itself was not unusual: it was ubiquitous in the 1920s, pervaded by natalist discourse, programs, and legislation. If voluntary – e.g., in the 'man-woman' [*la garçonne*] or in homosexual men – sterility was seen as selfishness, a refusal to procreate for the regeneration of the depopulated *patrie*. Yet, the idea that *all* 'fleshly love' is sterile indicates a Manicheanism (or perhaps Tertullianism) that was far from popular. Moreover, 'sterile' was an odd word for Maritain to use in this vigorously natalist atmosphere: his own marriage, childless as a result of the vow of chastity, must have been the object of speculations about 'onanism' and judgments about selfishness. However, it fit well with his idea that celibacy was the true 'fecundity.' In his *Letter to Jean Cocteau*, Maritain had written about the virgin-martyr Antigone: 'in the things of the spirit it is virginity that is fecund.' Thus, the 'freedom of a virgin obeying the laws of the gods is more beautiful than that of the poet or philosopher. It is to a higher one still that we are called – to the freedom of the souls of whom the Spirit has taken possession.'[130]

Clearly referring to his own relationship with Raïssa, Maritain tried to explain himself: 'I am not speaking here against love. But rather against disfigured love, stolen love. I am convinced that a truly spiritual love, delivered from sex, is possible, even for our fallen nature.' The passage suggests that for Maritain, sexual activity of any kind detracted from the attainment of a 'truly spiritual love': *modesty* as distinct from *prudery* (as Raïssa wrote in 1919). He then implicitly compared same-sex friendships favourably with his own relationship to Raïssa: 'In particular, those friendships between beings of the same sex truly merit the name love if love signifies that a friend is *everything* [*tout*] for the other friend. Such a love may be chaste, preserved by a great ignorance of the flesh.'[131] Again, the emphasis was Maritain's, and the sense seemed to be that sexual or bodily activity gets in the way of a total self-giving to another, whether same-sex or otherwise.

Finally, Maritain's use of the word *l'homosexualité* – a term that had only been invented in 1891 – suggested instability: '*L'homosexualité détruit cet ordre*,' he wrote Cocteau in terms reminiscent of his 1923 visit to Gide. 'Homosexuality destroys this order ... it is for eternal reasons that the Church condemns it ...' The use of *l'homosexualité* was ambiguous: if it meant same-sexual activity ('sodomy'), then it was true that Catholic penitential manuals for many centuries had levied heavy penalties against it. (It is worth noting that the 'eternal reasons' given were the weight of the laws of 'nature' – a materialist, laicist, and implicitly atheist conception.) But if Maritain meant *l'homosexualité* as the recently invented condition, state of being, 'inversion of the genital instinct,' then the Church had not pronounced anything about it – and would not do so for another fifty years, when it eventually accepted the paradigm.[132] Thus, Maritain's indeterminate use of the concept reflected the fact that it was still in the process of being invented: even as he condemned sodomy, he praised those 'friendships between members of the same sex' in which 'a friend is *everything* for the other friend' and merited 'the name of love.'

The verbal confusion – and perhaps Maritain's internal confusion – is even more evident when considering a letter written just one month earlier, at the beginning of June 1927, to Julien Green. Earlier that month, Green apologized for having 'lied' to Maritain: when asked if he intended to live a celibate life, Green had 'said yes when I should have said no.' Maritain responded with both compassion and affection: 'Now that I know you a little better, my dear friend, I love you more than before, and the sense of respect I feel for your soul has grown even greater.' Some days later (29 June), Maritain amplified his acceptance: 'I will never judge you. I do not think you are living in sin. I know nothing about that. What I do know is the depth of your heart, and that you are inclined, as a matter of fact, to push scrupulosity too far, and that at no price would you wish to offend Jesus.'[133] In this case, not only did Maritain accept Green's 'homosexuality' as a condition or state of being; he also refrained from condemning Green's same-sexual activity as 'living in sin,' claiming ignorance about such ultimate matters: 'I know nothing about that.'

Maritain then confessed his extremely odd sense of mission to homosexuals. 'God has led me to understand I *must* help souls like yours to work out the problems in which they find themselves involved. What good am I,' he asked, 'if I do not carry out this service?' Strangely, by June 1927, Maritain had invested a striking amount of his self-identity in his 'service' to homosexuals, and he saw this as intimately connected to his own unorthodox marriage. 'I know some married couples who for the love of Christ have made a vow of continence,' he continued, 'and whose mutual love has divinely deepened because of it. Why could the same *separation* not be possible in other cases?' Apparently, Maritain self-consciously thought of his marriage with Raïssa as an evangelical model for same-sex relationships: lifelong monogamous unions of ever-deepening mutual love by means of sexual abstinence. 'The Gospel nowhere tells us to mutilate our hearts,' said Maritain to Green, 'but it counsels us to make ourselves eunuchs for the Kingdom of God. This is how I think the question must be posed.'[134]

Reading the compassion that suffuses the Green-Maritain correspondence suggests that Maritain's fallout with Cocteau had less to do with 'homosexuality' than with having been lied to and personally betrayed by both Cocteau and Desbordes. 'What caused me the greatest pain in this whole affair,' he confessed to Green in December 1928, 'is that Jean did not have the confidence to show [*The White Book*] to me, when all the while he acted *as if* his confidence were complete.'[135] Cocteau's confidence had not been everything – *tout*.

Still, it is also clear that Cocteau's double-performance – like Sachs's cassock on the beach – panicked Maritain. In one of several heated exchanges during June 1928, Maritain invoked the logical principle of non-contradiction: 'Moreover, you are Catholic and you have said this publicly. However, the position which you take in this book is essentially non-Catholic. Thus it's an equivocation ...'[136] Maritain might have made the same observation of his own endnotes in *Art and Scholasticism*. He had pursued Cocteau (and company) precisely because Cocteau's flamboyant celebrity could make order seem like anarchy and Catholicism seem avant-garde. As Cocteau played out his double role as the Catholic *enfant terrible*, Maritain's self-doubt seems to have surfaced. Was avant-garde Catholicism an 'equivocation'? Mere 'passing' in an age without sexes? Such questions had been brought on by the unstable plays that Maritain himself had scripted.

In the end, although they repaired their relationship and continued their correspondence (some of it quite poignant), Maritain would refuse to authorize a reprint of the mutual *Letter* and *Response* until Cocteau's death in 1963.

1928: *Humani nihil a me alienum puto*

The Maritains' home became an experimental laboratory in which the catholicity of Catholicism might be attempted and tested. In part, this was due to Maritain's increased celebrity after his literary successes of

1926; in part, the Maritains' post-1926 severance from the Action Française crowd, though extremely painful at the moment, freed them up for a broader circle of intimates more closely resembling the friends of their youthful homes.

As one decade passed into the next, notes for the Thomistic Study Circle, originally founded in 1919 in order to study scholastic philosophy and Catholic doctrine, listed the phenomenologist Merleau-Ponty, the Personalist philosopher Emmanuel Mounier (editor of *L'Esprit*), the musician Arthur Lourié (who influenced Stravinsky), the Russian Orthodox philosopher Nicolas Berdiaeff, and the young Olivier Lacombe, a Normalien who became an expert in eastern religion. In 1926, the annual retreat scheduled for 24–8 September discussed topics like 'Faith,' 'Necessity of Supernatural Faith for Salvation,' and 'The Virtue of Religion.' Four years later, topics had changed considerably: 'Olivier on the Vedanta Sara' (7 December 1930); 'Olivier on the Baghavad-Gîta' (18 January 1931); 'Mounier on property' (10 April 1932); 'Berdiaeff at 5 o'clock ... He says very remarkable things concerning the present state of Soviet philosophy' (17 April 1932).[137]

Massis's *Defense of the West* (1927) did not disguise his contempt for Maritain's dressing up Catholic order in exotic orientalist costume. Did one have to 'call the *Summa* of St Thomas the *Baghavât Gita*, turn the Council of Trent into an assembly of Tibetan lamas, dress up St John of the Cross or St Francis of Assisi in a *bhiksu* or the Curé d'Ars in a *cramana*,' he asked; in short, '*disguise our own religion* in "Asiatic rags," for certain aesthetes, in their love of exotic wisdom, to undertake its discovery and to admire its profundities?'[138] Although Maritain had published Massis's *Defense of the West* in the *Roseau d'Or*, he was disturbed at being linked so closely with it and immediately tried to distance himself, turning his face eastward.[139]

This universalist vision was infectious, as shown by the October 1928 inaugural issue of a journal entitled *La Vie intellectuelle*. Its mission statement owed much to Maritain: 'We will encourage intellectual tendencies oriented toward Catholic truth. We will praise the good everywhere we might find it. Catholic thought, we will suggest, according to the self-requirement of its being Catholic, is a thought which is truly universal, and is not like one particular thought among others. We will be interested in everything which preoccupies contemporaries' minds, believers or not, abroad and in France.'[140]

'Catholics must possess a genuinely informed doctrine *concerning everything that is human*.' This was Raïssa's 1919 reformulation of Terence's dictum. A year later, Jacques tweaked the phrase in *Art and Scholasticism* to redefine Catholicism's universality for a realist generation: 'the very *catholicity* of its wisdom that *embraces everything that is real.*' In 1928, the 'genuinely informed doctrine' for which Raïssa had called a decade earlier was institutionalized in *La Vie intellectuelle*'s mission statement: 'Catholic thought has authority over all, and *everything that is human is ours.*'[141]

If ideology's function is to disguise origins and make what is constructed seem naturally transparent, the *renouveau catholique* had succeeded spectacularly. In 1918, no one could have imagined that the most 'straightforward' meaning of the word 'Catholic' might be construed to designate 'anyone in service of truth.' Yet this is what *La Vie intellectuelle* took for granted in 1928: 'We represent no [factional] chapels; we are neither right nor left – simply Catholics. Our light comes from the teaching of the Church, from traditional doctrine and the directives of the Roman Pontiff. All those who wish to serve the truth are able to find their meeting place here. LA VIE INTELLECTUELLE wants simply to be a *catholic* journal, in the most simple, the most straightforward and also, the most vast sense of the word.'[142] Maritain's discursive genius had made the most complex reading of the word seem the most self-evident.

The following year, the mission statement of a companion journal, *Les Documents de la Vie intellectuelle*, reminded its readers that 'We must not forget, in fact – a great Pope reminds us – that *catholicism* means *universalism* ...' The *Documents* would gather together excerpts from Catholic periodicals in Europe, America, and Asia for the benefit of French readers. The editor revealed the idea behind this project: 'the idea of the *unity* of Catholicism. The union between Catholics of every country is inscribed in the very essence of our faith: our religion is not alive, it is not what it must be if the Catholics of the entire world do not feel themselves attracted to one another for a fruitful collaboration.'[143]

One of the first essays appearing in *La Vie intellectuelle* was Maritain's 'Saint Thomas and the Unity of Christian Culture.'[144] In it, he quoted at some length an article about Indian philosophy that concluded with an allusion to the Baroque era Jesuit Robert de Nobili. Following the Order's common strategies of cultural accommodation, when de Nobili went to India in 1605, he wore Brahman robes signifying his status in Hindu terms. 'Without adopting, like Robert de Nobili of yesteryear, the clothing of a Brahman,' said the author quoted by Maritain, 'very modern apologists' had been able to create an extremely subtle psychology that was 'very Thomistic while nevertheless Bengalie.'[145]

Maritain used this synthetic point to propose a global mission: 'This example shows us how Saint Thomas Aquinas prepared the conceptual and notional tools, the metaphysical tools of intelligence that Christian culture needs, and thanks to which we are able to hope that it will realize its unity in the vast world. And it is just this that is the greatest privilege of Western culture, that which makes us precious among all: it is because [Western culture] itself is universal in its very foundation ... It is here that this intellectual cooperation between Catholics of all nations ... is more necessary than ever before.'[146]

The notion that the particularity of 'Western culture' was universally 'human' was an old trope, rooted in France's ideology of a *mission civilisatrice* and a more general 'Orientalism.' Still, Maritain's vision, freed from anxieties over 'bastardization' and cultural cross-breeding, had taken on a genuinely cosmopolitan flavour. His idea of Thomism as the form animating the material of the global world helped him imagine that any culture whatsoever might be the genuine expression of eternally valid principles. Nothing human is alien: this was the logical conclusion of Maritain's hylomorphic theory of culture.

Semi-Cadence: *Homo Sum*

Another increasing preoccupation of Maritain's was human sexuality and contraception. In this area, as seen in correspondence from 1934 onward, his views departed from the Church's official positions articulated from the 1930s through the 1950s.[147] Maritain reflected broader trends among his fellow French Catholic laity and the clerical hierarchy: members of both groups found themselves at odds with the intransigent views on sexuality in general and contraception in particular that emerged from Rome.[148] However, in spite of the natalist offensive, the linkage between human sexuality/erotic love and biological procreation continued to be loosened throughout the 1920s. Maritain's vocation to homosexuals, as well as his own celibate marriage, contributed to this early twentieth-century revolution.

The 1936 publication of *Integral Humanism* marked a significant milestone in Maritain's development. His overtures to the humanistic and existentialist movements of the extreme left, as well as his relationships with anarchists like Saul Alinsky and Dorothy Day, led right-wing critics to call him a 'Christian Marxist.'[149] Because Maritain refused to recognize Franco's war as a religious crusade, some in the Catholic press and institutions were hostile to him: a visit to the American University of Notre Dame in Indiana caused an uproar and left some in doubt about Maritain's orthodoxy.[150] Yet, Maritain's 'turn' in the 1930s was largely a 'return home': he retrieved much of his pre-conversion self nourished by Baudelaire, Jaurès, Péguy, and Bergson.

But one wonders whether the single most powerful influence on his increasing catholicity was not Raïssa's Jewish origins. His right-wing critics thought so, and they reacted bitterly to his increasing outspokenness on the 'Jewish Question' during the 1930s.[151] On 24 September 1937, Maritain recorded a dinner with Père Garrigou-Lagrange, the Maritains' old Thomist friend, that had not gone well. 'Father is very worked up against me, goes so far as to reproach me, a convert, with wanting to give lessons in the Christian spirit to "us who have been Catholics for three hundred years." ... It seems that Raïssa and Véra are being implicated as dragging me along by their influence. (Russian Jewesses, are they not? ...) This puts me in a black rage, which I do not hide ...'[152] In 1938, Georges Bernanos responded to Maritain's lecture, 'The Jews Among the Nations': 'I am perfectly capable ... of honoring Mr. J. Maritain at the same time that I deplore his effeminate daydreams about the Jews ... which win for him public acclaim at the Théâtre des Ambassadeurs.'[153] In April that same year, *Je suis partout* ['I am everywhere'], the Fascist journal that would become collaborationist during the approaching war, published an article attacking Maritain in language filled with fears of 'passing for gentile': 'Jacques Maritain married a Jew. He has jewified [*enjuivé*] his life and his doctrine. His theology, his dialectic are *falsified like the passport of a Jewish spy.* M. Maritain, body and soul, represents what the Germans call with good reason a "*Rassenschander*," a race polluter [*souilleur de race*].'[154]

When war broke out in late 1939, the Maritains were in North America where Jacques had travelled annually throughout the decade, delivering lecture courses at the Institute of Mediaeval Studies in Toronto. On account of Raïssa's Jewish origins, they decided not to return to France and in 1940 moved to the United States where Jacques taught at Princeton University (1941–2) and then Columbia (1942–4). The couple befriended such figures as the artist Marc Chagall and the 'Fugitive Poets' of the South, Caroline Gordon and Allen Tate, and they helped found the École Libre des Hautes Études in New York City.[155]

Jacques committed himself to staying in contact with France, using weekly radio messages transmitted by the BBC. On 8 September 1942, his broadcast deplored the first massive arrests of Jews in France – 20,000 in Paris and 13,000 in the unoccupied zone – as cruelty to 'the women and the men who have the honor of belonging to Jesus Christ's own people.' 'France's soul,' he declared, 'is cast into a state of mortal sin.'[156] After the war, Maritain would participate in the creation of the United Nations' Universal Declaration of Human Rights (1948). Here his universalist vision found its most concrete realization during his lifetime.

On the night of the Liberation of Paris in August 1944, Cocteau heard Maritain's radio broadcast from the BBC announcing deliverance. Cocteau's wartime situation had been ambiguous: in 1942, he wrote a piece praising the Fascist artist, Arno Becker, and many of his contemporaries maintained afterward that he was a collaborator; yet Vichy labelled him 'decadent,' *Je suis partout* condemned his work as 'perverted and Judaic,' and the Germans shut down his theatrical productions.

Shortly before the Liberation, Maurice Sachs, who had acted as an informant in exchange for drugs, was assassinated on a forced march from his Gestapo prison outside Hamburg to Kiel, a single bullet delivered to the back of his skull. In July, Jean Desbordes had died a hero and a martyr, never betraying Resistance names as he was tortured to death, gruesomely beaten into a coma by the Gestapo. Four months earlier, Max Jacob had been arrested and sent to the Drancy transit camp, slated for convoy No. 69 to Auschwitz on 7 March 1944. Having contracted pneumonia and become delirious, he died early in the morning of 5 March, confidently confessing 'I am with God' – *Je suis avec Dieu*.

Je suis partout reported his passing: 'Max Jacob is dead. Jewish by race, Breton by birth, Roman by religion, sodomite by custom [*moeurs*], he became the most characteristic Parisian figure imaginable, of that decadent and corrupt Paris whose most notable disciple, Jean Cocteau, remains equally its symbolic exemplar.'

Jacob, however, interpreted his life within a theological framework deeply indebted to Léon Bloy's *Salvation by the Jews*: 'Creator of the seas and the skies, of the continents, of all that is imponderable ... I thank you for having caused me to be born to the suffering Jewish race, for he alone is saved who suffers and who knows that he suffers and offers his suffering to God.' From her American exile, the Jewish Catholic Raïssa recorded Jacob's death: 'Max gave his life with the humility of a saint.' Jacques concurred in a letter to Julien Green: 'Max Jacob died a saint.' Only months after Jacob's death came the definitive judgment: *Max Jacob. Mystic and Martyr* (1944).[157]

Perfect Cadence: All Tables Are Holy.

What estimation can we make of Maritain's refusal to quarantine the sacred? In the late 1920s, there was something to offend everyone in reading the *Catholic* as the *catholic*. Anticlericalists might have considered it little more than rhetorical cross-dressing; religious conservatives might have seen in it just another dangerous step towards 'secularization.' Maritain urged aspiring young sacred artists to find 'religious significance' in a mandolin. Was the turn from Fra Angelico's *Madonna and Child* to Picasso's *Violin and Guitar* an impoverishment or enrichment of religious language?[158] Was it a reduction of discourse to a single dimension, or was it an expansion into something significantly more complex?

The historian Owen Chadwick once formulated the question of 'secularization' in its simplest terms: 'Was this movement from unusual to usual a deprivation, so that if all the world is supernatural nothing is supernatural and everything is dis-enchanted? Or was it an insight, like seeing that because Sunday is a holy day all days are holy days, or that because an altar is a holy table for a holy meal all tables and all meals are holy?'[159]

In Maritain's sacramental modernism, the turn from the *Madonna and Child* to a *Violin and Guitar* expressed an insight – a world not so much secularized as desecularized – or sacralized. It was an extremely optimistic vision. Some would call it naive. It would be sorely tested in the world events beginning in 1933. But for the postwar generation that had survived the trenches of 1914–18, it offered exactly the synthetic reconciliation that had been needed in a decade of mourning. His aesthetic formulations would be given colour, story, and sound by the artists now to be considered, each one representing a *mystique réaliste*: the masked redemption of Georges Rouault's art, the passionate supernaturalism of Georges Bernanos's literature, and the mystical dissonance of Charles Tournemire's music.

By the end of the postwar decade, sacramental modernism had changed the meanings of both 'Catholic' and 'modern,' not just accidentally but substantially. Less *bal masqué*, more *missa brevis*, this Jazz Age dramaturgy resembled nothing so much as transubstantiation. All tables were holy.

PART THREE

Mystic Modernism: Catholic Visions of the Real

Chapter 6

Georges Rouault: Masked Redemption

> This law extends to the inclusion in Christian beauty of even the Cross and everything else which a worldly aesthetics (even of a realistic kind) discards as no longer bearable ... Our task, rather, consists in coming ... to see his 'formlessness' as a mode of his glory because a mode of his 'love to the end,' to discover in his de-Formation (*Ungestalt*) the mystery of trans-Formation (*Übergestalt*).
>
> – Hans Urs von Balthasar

> The touching entrancing beauty of Christianity depends upon a subtle something which all this fastidiousness ignores ... A soul that is ... dominated ... by such fastidiousness ... is as yet only hovering round the precincts of Christianity, it has not yet entered the sanctuary ... It is really a very hideous thing; the full, truly free, beauty of Christ, completely liberates us from this miserable bondage.
>
> – Baron Friedrich von Hügel[1]

The aesthetics entailed by the Maritains' neoclassical Catholicism nicely accounted for works of art that tended towards formalism and abstraction – Picasso, Severini, or Stravinsky. But could it account for the other dominating strain of postwar art emphasizing nervous anxiety and emotional pathos – that is, the expressionism of Max Beckmann or Arnold Schoenberg?[2] The friendship between Maritain and Georges Rouault was mutually beneficial: Maritain's celebrity would help disseminate Rouault's work; conversely, Rouault's work would help Maritain refine his formalist aesthetics so it could include a broader canvas of twentieth-century artistic practices. Before the war, no critics – not even friends like Léon

Bloy or Maritain – seemed capable of finding 'religious' meaning in Rouault's 'ugly' realist work. After the war, Rouault gradually became known as the main 'religious artist' of the twentieth century. The story of Rouault's reception among critics is not just the story of Rouault. It is also the story of how the category 'religious painter' – and hence 'religious' – acquired new meaning after the Great War.

1895–1910: 'Attracted exclusively to the ugly'

Georges Rouault was born on 27 May 1871 at his grandparents' home in the Parisian district of Belleville.[3] Even before the Franco-Prussian war, the neighbourhood had been marked by radical egalitarian politics: Léon Gambetta, running for election, presented his 'Program of Belleville' in April 1869, calling for universal suffrage, liberty of the press, and the separation of church and state. The district was a revolutionary stronghold during the Paris Siege and Commune of 1870–1, and its name symbolized terror for middle-class Parisians, 'an area occupied by dangerous working-class Reds, one of several arrondissements which were virtually no-go areas to the police.'[4] During the 'Bloody Week' of the Fall of Paris (21–8 May 1871), it became the Commune's last stand and the site of the heaviest bombardments. On the penultimate day of the Commune – just one day after the Belleville massacre of the fifty-one hostages (including Father Olivaint) – Rouault's mother went down into her parents' cellar in order to escape the shelling and gave birth to Georges. Born in blood, Rouault was nicknamed *Obus* ('shell').

Although Georges was baptized Catholic, his family was anticlerical and he was not raised in the faith. His father, an artisan (cabinetmaker) and passionate admirer of the liberal ultramontanist Lamennais, lost faith in the Church whose Pope condemned Lamennais's movement. Initially sent to a Protestant school, Georges was transferred to a state school after his father discovered how severe the religious school's punishments were. In addition to his father's socialism, Rouault was also influenced by his maternal grandfather, a retired postman who loved art and collected reproductions. He passed on to his grandson his preference for realism, especially of Rembrandt, Courbet, and Daumier. From 1885 to 1890, Rouault worked as an apprentice to stained-glass makers, an experience that shaped his trademark bright colours framed within heavy black outlines. In March 1892, Georges passed his entrance examinations and was officially admitted to the École des Beaux-Arts – an opportunity made possible by his mother's taking on extra work to support him financially.

Fortuitously for Rouault, Gustave Moreau, the foremost symbolist painter, was appointed to the atelier that same year. Moreau had first achieved recognition with his *Oedipus and the Sphinx* at the 1864 Salon. Against the realists and naturalists, Moreau followed Stéphane Mallarmé's symbolist dictum that 'reality' could never be represented by direct 'copying' of external details – it could only be 'pointed to.' The ideal, said Mallarmé, 'is to *suggest* the object. It is the perfect use of this mystery which constitutes the symbol. An object must be gradually evoked in order to show a state of soul ...' Jean Moréas simplified this complex understanding in his mechanical 'Symbolist Manifesto' (1886): the ideal was to 'clothe the Idea in a perceptible form.'[5] Invisible realities were to be evoked by employing symbolic or 'literary' subject matter – for example, scenes from Judeo-Christian scriptures, classical antiquity, ancient mythologies, the 'Orient,' and esoterica.[6]

In 1884, Moreau had achieved literary fame by means of his cameo appearance in Huysmans's novel *Against Nature*. Huysmans's protagonist Des Esseintes praised Moreau as the ideal painter, and placed him in his personal pantheon along with the symbolist writers Baudelaire and Mallarmé, and the Catholic literary revivalists, Villiers de l'Isle Adam, d'Aurevilly, and Verlaine. Rouault's profoundly anxious work, in sharp contrast to that of Henri Matisse (his classmate in Moreau's atelier), would continue (albeit in a radically different mode) his master's concern with what constituted 'reality.'[7] 'Art for you is serious, sober and in its essence religious,' Moreau told Rouault. 'And everything you do will bear this stamp.'[8]

In 1895, the twenty-five-year-old Rouault entered his painting entitled *Jesus Among the Teachers* into the Salon des Champs-Élysées. Painted in the official academic style required by the Salon, the 'literary' scene recounted the scriptural story in which the twelve-year-old Jesus goes to the Temple and engages in disputation with the theologians, leaving them confounded in amazement at his wisdom and learning. In the earliest written review of Rouault's work, an article for *La Revue encyclopédique* compared him to Rembrandt who alone 'would be able to decipher the enigmatic form.'[9] The reviewer noted three subjects. First, Christ. Second, 'three men who interrogate him and are astonished by his responses' and whose faces registered 'a badly disguised surprise to be seen in the presence of such precociousness.' Third, 'a crowd of miserable wretches' who stood as onlookers. In contrast to the judges, who were disappointed in the presence of the precocious Christ, one could see that 'both hope and faith' were already awakening in these *misérables*.

The review remarkably summarized themes that would endure throughout the rest of Rouault's work. The worldly wise interrogate Christ, yet these judges are not up to their task of judging accurately. The *seeming* inferior is judged by those below him as being of no esteem, while the socially marginal are the ones capable of perceiving and judging the situation accurately. The reviewer concluded that Rouault owed his work 'to the study of the master of Amsterdam,' Rembrandt. He was an eminently 'religious' painter in the academically approved style.

This judgment quickly changed. In the next year's 1896 Salon des Champs-Élysées, Rouault submitted yet another 'literary' work representing a Biblical event, *Christ Wept Over by the Holy Women*. Writing for the same *Revue encyclopédique*, Claude Roger-Marx noted that the painting had 'caused a huge stir' at the École des Beaux-Arts in its competition for the *Prix de Rome*. Although there was still a trace 'of fervent and frequent visits to the great masters' like Rembrandt, Rouault's gift had faltered in 'the severe layout of the arrangement and in the choice of this rich, greenish tonality spread out everywhere that adds such a dramatic horror.'[10] Roger-Marx, a great enthusiast for Honoré Daumier, complimented Rouault by comparing his realism to Daumier's. This comparison with Daumier would endure for a century, and it placed Rouault in the 'laicist' camp, a social context far removed from – indeed, bitterly opposed to – what was considered to be 'religious' painting.[11]

During this period of painting scriptural themes, Rouault developed two friendship with Catholic religious figures: a Benedictine oblate who had studied at Moreau's studio named Antonin Bourbon, and a Father Vallée. Sometime during the year after the Salon, Rouault received his long-delayed first communion from Vallée. This personal conversion to Catholicism was followed almost immediately by Moreau's death in 1898, a severe blow that provoked a serious depression. In 1901, Rouault followed the oblate Bourbon to Ligugé Abbey, an offshoot foundation of Solesmes. J.-K. Huysmans, also living as an oblate, had set up Maison Notre-Dame there, intended as a community of artists and writers who would produce worthy sacred art. Regrettably, this plan fell through as the 1901 Law of Associations sent the monks into exile soon after. Although the artistic commune never materialized, Rouault faithfully continued to visit Huysmans after he moved back to Paris until the end of his life.

Rouault was about to encounter Léon Bloy. One might have expected him to have done this through his friend Huysmans, but Bloy, in 'misery and solitude,' had severed his relationship with Huysmans in 1889.[12] Rouault thus discovered Bloy by stumbling across his work in Moreau's studio. Moreau had willed the studio to the French government with provisions that it be turned into a museum and that Rouault be appointed its curator. During this particularly dark time in his life, while Rouault performed the morbid task of going through and arranging his deceased master's belongings, he found Bloy's recently published *The Woman Who Was Poor* (1897) in Moreau's library. Rouault's childhood influences – his father's socialist politics, his grandfather's love for realists, his own preference for Daumier's caricatures – had laid the foundation for his favoured depictions of subjects like widows, orphans, the homeless, prostitutes, tragic circus figures, and judges who condemned the innocent. However, Bloy's novel, the story of the poverty-stricken Clotilde (based on Berthe Drumont, the prostitute who became Bloy's mistress) gave such realist subjects a new and profoundly religious meaning. Although they might be mistreated by such bourgeois figures as M. and Mme. Poulot, the poor were those whom God favoured. Discovering Bloy enabled Rouault to travel a significant distance away from Moreau's dandyish world.

On 14 January 1903, the Musée Gustave Moreau officially opened with Rouault as curator.[13] A year later, Bloy first mentioned Rouault in his published diary: 'I learn that the painter Georges Rouault, a student of Gustave Moreau, is enthusiastic about me. He found at Moreau's my book *The Woman Who Was Poor* ... This book struck his heart, wounded him incurably. I shudder to think of the punishment in store for this unhappy wretch.'[14] A week later, Bloy recorded having met Rouault: 'A nice face. Apparently a lot of talent, too much, in fact, not to remain poor. He is the devoted type who naïvely expresses his enthusiasm for me.'[15]

During that autumn 1904, eight years after the 'dark' review at the 1896 Salon des Champs-Élysées, Rouault entered his work at the Salon d'Automne, an event strongly represented by the late Moreau's students. The 'dark' reviews continued. *Le Journal* reported that Rouault 'confounded the sympathy' of the viewer by his '*violently black*' series of canvases done in '*impénétrable pastels.*' 'According to the [salon] catalogue,' although the reviewer could not himself see it, these were allegedly 'circus impressions.' Only a few small landscapes 'in the English style' were capable of 'somewhat redeeming *these dark mistakes*.'[16] *Le Petit*

Parisien agreed: Rouault belonged to 'the school of caricature' but his *Circus Sketches* were simply 'excessive.' He could do better than stifle his 'genuine talent as a colorist in such *exaggeration of the truth*.'[17]

Le Figaro saw Rouault not as a realist but as a symbolist. The review distinguished between *l'informe* – that is, formless, shapeless, misshapen – and *le déformé*, that is, the symbolist's/post-Impressionist's deliberate distortion of outward form in order to suggest 'truer' form, either invisible or geometrical. The formless was simply a product of 'the ignorant and the incapable,' said *Le Figaro*, and Rouault was not ignorant. However, he was also not an 'instinctive' deformer like the post-impressionists Cézanne or Toulouse-Lautrec. Rouault was more like Odilon Redon (Huysmans's preferred satanist painter), Moreau, and all his students: a 'systematic deformer' who brought his 'personal notion of form' to bear on representations of reality. Having said this, Rouault's *déformations* went too far. Among all Moreau's students, Rouault's 'strange visions' were the most curious and 'lost themselves' in an 'unmitigated blackness' – *un implacable noir*.[18]

The reviews devastated Rouault. On 2 October 1904, Bloy responded to a despondent letter. 'Dear friend,' Bloy wrote Rouault, 'you wrote me a beautiful and sorrowful letter. I wish that God had given me words of comfort for you ... You are one of those whom God is seeking ... Tribulation is not given to us without measure and the human villainy of which we despair is not infinite.' With typical self-reference, Bloy added (as if it were consoling), 'You will not be more flagellated than I.'[19]

In 1905, in homage to Bloy's book, Rouault painted an enormous canvas depicting the bourgeois couple, M. and Mme. Poulot, from *The Woman Who Was Poor*. It was an exploratory attempt at synthesizing Moreau and Bloy, the hybridization of a 'literary' scene (the symbolist's method) with mundane reality (the realist's method). One might expect Bloy to have been flattered, but he exploded with rage during his visit to the Salon d'Automne: 'This artist that I thought was capable of painting seraphim seems only able to imagine the most atrocious and avenging caricatures. The meanness of the bourgeois works in him such a violent reaction of horror that his art seems to be a mortally wounded creature. He wanted to do my Poulot couple ... Not for all the money in the world would I accept this *illustration*. Something very tragic was needed: Two bourgeois characters, male and female, guileless, peaceable, merciful ... He has made two assassins from the slums.'[20] The injustice of Bloy's accusations is plain enough. No reader of Bloy's novel, quite vicious in parts, and especially in the colourful descriptions of its petit-bourgeois antagonists, could have appraised M. and Mme. Poulot as 'guileless' or 'merciful.'

Bloy did not yet sever his relationship with Rouault. On 12 November 1905 he recorded a conversation with Raïssa Maritain (whom he had met earlier that June): 'We also spoke about Huysmans whom Rouault has been to see and who is practically blind, attacked by a very rare disease whose name seems to me to sound the death-knell. It is remarkable that this man who has only lived by the eyes would be killed by a sickness of the eyes.'[21] (Huysmans would be killed by mouth cancer. Bloy's need to see symmetrical suffering – as seen above, he prayed that he might lose his mind since it was the possession he most valued – distorted the picture.)

However, Bloy's fury mounted over the next year and a half. On 30 April 1907, just twelve days before Huysmans's death, Bloy recorded his visit to the Salon des Indépendants. 'As for the paintings of *nudes*, they are a hideous hell, and Rouault, alas! his works take first place. I have tried in vain to understand how it can be that an artist who is exactly the opposite of someone who is stupid and despicable – the only one perhaps who can remind you again of a Rembrandt – should dedicate himself to this abominable caricature that deteriorates in a deadly way, in its own person, the most manly painting of our time.'[22]

The following day Bloy wrote a letter extremely significant for the way in which it constructed realism as being incompatible with religious practice.

> My dear friend, I saw the *Salon des Indépendants* yesterday. Independent of what? These slaves of stupidity and absolute ignorance! Naturally I saw your unique and sempiternal canvases: always the same slut [s*alope*] and the same clown, with the single and lamentable difference that each time the worthlessness appears greater.
>
> Today I have two things to say to you, only two, the last! After which you will be no more to me than a mere acquaintance! First, *you are attracted exclusively to the ugly*; you seem to be enthralled by the hideous. Secondly, if you were a man of prayer, a communicant, you would not be able to paint such terrible canvases.[23]

Certainly, the very same accusations might have been levelled against Bloy's own violent writings. More important than his self-blindness, however, was the dualism he perceived between pictorial realism and religiosity. Bloy considered Rouault's realist's sympathies to be incompatible with the religious representations (of 'seraphim') expected from a daily recipient of communion. In this way, Bloy was thoroughly a man of his Banquet Years epoch.

1910: 'The truth is never found in the copy'

By happy serendipity, both the Rouaults and the Maritains moved to Versailles in 1909 and became neighbours. Through their mutual relationship with Bloy, the Maritains had become one of Rouault's very few close acquaintances and this physical proximity deepened their friendship. In late February 1910, Rouault was going to open his first solo exhibition at the Galerie Druet, and he asked Jacques to write the preface to the catalogue. In a letter to Raïssa dated 24 January 1910, Rouault asked whether Jacques might 'look for a name *as signature* relating to the workers of Cathedrals. Example: Jean Le François.'[24] Maritain coined the name 'Jacques Favelle' – a combination of his mother's maiden name (Favre) and the final syllable of *cathédrale* – and wrote the catalogue preface under the pseudonym, leaving its author's identity a mystery for more than half a century.[25]

In early 1910, Maritain was a strange (and perhaps desperate) choice for authoring an art exhibition preface. He had been trained as a biological scientist and, after returning from Heidelberg, in order to have free time for reading philosophy, he earned a living by editing an orthographical lexicon. He had not yet begun reading Aquinas or *L'Action française*, he and Raïssa had not yet made their vow of chastity, and his future celebrity as the anti-modernist Thomist was unimaginable. His godfather Bloy's assaults on Rouault – 'always the same slut and the same clown' – were widely circulated, the diary pages having been published in *The Unsaleable* (*L'Invendable*, 1909). What could Jacques Favelle have to say – and have the courage to say – about Rouault's art?

He began by pointing to the obvious: 'At first sight, the subject matter itself of Georges Rouault's paintings astonishes. This strange assembly of sinister or appalling heads, these fearsome and synthetic puppets, judges, rich bourgeois, honest women, women who think they're smart [*savantasses*]; these poor miserable wretches, distorted by misery, these entertainers, these clowns, these sad cripples, these frightening wounded – is this a wholesale slaughter prepared here to amuse the public and make it laugh?'[26] Maritain's list aimed at being complete, but it tiptoed around the elephant in the living room. 'Honest women who think they're smart,' even laced with irony, hardly answered Bloy's 'always the same slut.' Jacques Favelle circumnavigated the quicksand.

To his own rhetorical question he then replied, 'No, all of this work is serious, absolutely opposed to a mean kind of caricature and derision.' Admitting that the 'gripping simplification' of Rouault's types could sometimes shock and thereby cause the viewer to 'laugh involuntarily,' Maritain maintained they came from 'the deepest and most severe' kind of emotion. With this somewhat tepid defence, Maritain quickly left the problem of Rouault's subjects and headed for safer territory, reading Rouault as a medieval artisan and as a contemporary expressionist.

Maritain first praised Rouault as a medieval artisan, directly descended from those 'patient workers,' those long-lost artisans who loved 'their tools and matter.' Having been a stained-glass maker in his adolescence, and being a ceramicist and lithographer in adulthood, Rouault in fact thought of himself as an artisan. Rouault loved his skill (*métier*) just as the 'workers of another time' loved their own. Rouault's art was 'a popular art' whose 'frank and naive' inspiration resembled that of those 'happy artisans of days gone by.'[27] Reflecting both Rouault's and his own anti-bourgeois contempt for the Academy, Maritain noted that 'the people' always had 'an admirable reserve of rich sensibilities, of spontaneous imagination, of naive and intelligent humor.' However, these gifts were 'generally misunderstood and ridiculed' by the academic and artistic establishment. Considered 'uneducated' by the Academicians, these artisans did not follow 'a science completely in formulae,' but rather 'a living science,' a wisdom passed on by 'a truly professional tradition.' They were trained by 'masters,' not 'pedagogues,' in *ateliers*, not 'schools.' In all these ways, Rouault was 'thus related to the artisans of the Middle Ages.'[28]

Turning to his second theme, Maritain portrayed Rouault as being simultaneously medieval and contemporaneously expressionist: he searched for 'the *most immediate reality*.'[29] What exactly did Maritain mean by the 'real'? In a crucial passage, he wrote: 'As much as it is true that he endeavors to represent the most immediate objects and beings, M. Rouault does not intend to make *a textual transcription* of their traits; he knows that *the truth is never found in the copy*. In addition, he never sees things from the aspect of their ordinariness; he has *an imaginative vision of them*, he *contemplates them immediately in the world of their greatest reality* – and it is in this world that he paints them. Thus the dramatic exaggeration of his forms.'[30] The word 'immediately' suggests Bergson's *Objects Given Immediately to Consciousness* (1899) as well as *Laughter* (1900): the artist has immediate and 'unveiled' access to the deepest reality. Rouault's expressionist theory added to what Maritain had retained from Bergson. The true 'realism' meant expressing objects as they were inwardly experienced and then imaginatively expressed with 'dramatic exaggeration.'

Using the language of 'material' and 'form' – partly from Driesch's vitalism and perhaps also from Raïssa's reading (beginning in late 1909) of Aquinas – Maritain argued for continuity in Rouault's works and against those who said he had 'fallen' from his idyllic 'Rembrandt' days of 1895–6. 'From *The Child Jesus Among the Teachers* (1894) to his ceramics and engravings filled with common subject matter (judges, prostitutes, clowns and peasants),' said Maritain, Rouault struggled 'in the very same sense, attempting to awaken in the material all of its representative virtues, insistently *comparing the material* with every possible means in order to decide how *to assume the form* in *the most exactly evocative way*.'[31]

In portraying matter as 'assuming' or (more literally) 'being reclothed in' (*revêtir*) the form so as to 'evoke' the invisible, Maritain drew on Mallarmé – he would certainly have known him through his immersion in Baudelaire – and Moréas's popularization of him as 'clothing the Idea.' Although the matter/form language was confused, its attempt to unite Mallarmé, Driesch, and (perhaps via Raïssa) Aquinas sowed the seeds of *Art and Scholasticism* that would appear ten years later. Rouault's treatment of 'common subject matter' was realist in method, but his systematic *déformation* of such matter was a symbolist's attempt to get beyond a naturalist 'copy' to the true 'form' – the truly 'real.' Still, Maritain found it difficult (if not impossible) to find aesthetic, ethical, or religious value in the grotesque subject matter. In this regard he was one with his godfather Bloy and most of the critics who read his pseudonymous preface.

1910: 'Rigorous and Exclusive'

Maritain's preface was a story of Paradise rediscovered: the medieval artisan restored a world lost in the Renaissance to the hyper-individualism of the 'artist' and 'genius.' On the whole, however, other reviewers of Rouault saw a story of Paradise Lost – a once-promising student of Moreau had lost his way. During his days in 'the atelier of Gustave Moreau,' wrote *Le Siècle*, his canvases had revealed 'the study of the great Italians, so greatly in fashion at that time.' Since then, however, he had 'escaped into the unformulated, the confused, let us say the word: toward scribbling.' Rouault now carried 'burdens, and they are sad,

sad ...' Jacques Favelle had warned in his preface that Rouault's work was not 'rigged in order to please' and *Le Siècle* concurred: 'we have no trouble believing him. This work doesn't please in the least.'[32] Seeing Rouault's old *Child Jesus* made the *Journal des Arts* lament the loss of a 'high-pitched sensibility, a dillentantism which one unfortunately no longer finds again among the current strange productions by the same painter.'[33]

Les Nouvelles also mourned Rouault as 'one of the most singular artistic cases of our epoch.' From Moreau he had acquired a symbolist's 'taste for subject matter outside of ordinary life.' His 1890s paintings from 'sacred history' were 'sacred works.' But then, 'a deep transformation took place in his mind.' 'Contemporary life attracted him' and he 'regarded it with bitterness.' Going 'from one extreme to the other,' he followed the realists Toulouse-Lautrec and Daumier. Worse yet, whereas these two 'never lost one ounce of their style,' Rouault chose for his 'disillusioned observation' figures who best expressed everything he perceived as 'latent with tragedy' and 'sorrowfully comic.' He 'gave birth to' an entire world of clowns, circus figures, 'judges, lawyers, and automobilists' [*sic*]! All these he drew in 'a violent caricature style with a terrible pessimism.' Most of the pieces on this 'disastrous road' were 'only barbarous images without any rapport whatsoever with true art.' 'In persevering down this road,' concluded the ominous prediction, 'Mr. Rouault will only find disappointments.'[34]

The fall had been so far that *Progrés* wondered whether, were Gustave Moreau to come back from the dead, he would still hand over the Musée Moreau to his protégé. Rouault's '*collection of horrors*' were simply 'babbling,' a 'firefighter who had caught fire.' It was possible that one of these mornings, suddenly possessed by a 'furious madness,' Rouault might 'cut out the canvases and admirable designs of Gustave Moreau, his forgotten master, in order to decorate the frames of the latest impressionists and the most seductive paintings of the Honorable Salon des Indépendants.'[35]

Other reviews also criticized Rouault's perceived lack of form. Did he want 'to begin Daumier all over again?' asked *Le Feu*. 'I am able to admit that perhaps Mr. Rouault creates beautiful things, but I just don't see it.' His oils were 'like puppet-farces' – *guignolesques* – 'without construction,' all 'color and no lines.' Clearly Rouault had the *métier*, but it was impossible to know 'what Rouault wants to do' in 'this painting that does not amuse.'[36] Such 'chaos' was merely the logical terminus of symbolism, wrote *Paris-Journal*. Symbolism, Impressionism, and musical Wagnerism were '*passé* or close to being finished,' and after such 'exasperating disequilibrium of both the brain and the eye,' the time had come to submit to 'order' and 'good posture' under 'the domination and the authority of wise and skilled supervisors.'[37] *Les Marges* also feared that, in spite of 'the very best sincerity,' one would find 'mediocrity itself' hiding 'under this appearance of daring and wild mastery.'[38] In a review of Rouault's watercolors later that year, *Excelsior* found his work 'simply incomprehensible.' His 'slapping paint' on the canvases ended in 'chaotic forms,' resembling – here hovered Lévy-Bruhl's studies on primitivism – more the '*mentalité* of a Caribbean than a Parisian of the Twentieth century.'[39]

In addition to lamenting Rouault's 'fall' and the 'chaos' in his work, some reviewers followed Bloy's lead in judging his work violent and 'exclusive' in its embrace of ugliness. Again using the 'puppet' metaphor to malign what it saw as two-dimensional caricatures of life, *Gazette de la Capitale* published a review entitled 'The Puppet-Farce [*guignol*] of M. Rouault.' Some of his caricatures had 'the atmosphere of being Daumier over-the-top [*outré*],' while his 'unrestrained Cezanne-isms' led to an 'extraordinary style of badly balanced violence.' 'These apparitions of nightmares, judges, gendarmes, clowns, harlots' produced a world that was 'ugly, grimacing, and obscene – *contemporary society as seen by this artist*.' Although Rouault's work might be 'gripping, profoundly faithful' to reality, it was definitely 'not pretty, pretty. You will see all this at the Druet.'[40]

La République's reaction echoed Bloy more closely. Although Rouault's coloration might be 'brutal, yet always excellent,' his 'rigorous and *exclusive*' vision of humanity, so attached '*to defects, to sluts, to monstrosities*,' was intolerable. Rouault complacently shoved such figures in front of the viewer's eyes in order to 'strike us with horror.' He 'secretly desired' that his viewers would follow him in 'detesting and condemning them as he himself does' – a 'Lacedaemonian manner of education' more appropriate to ancient Spartans. 'But look!' exclaimed *La République*. 'No, M. Rouault, I persist in my belief that life is not made *exclusively of hideousness*, that humanity is not *inevitably ugly and repugnant or grotesque*.' For proof he appealed to Rouault's 'very own witness' to be found in his 'paintings from the old days' where 'the search for a noble ideal united to pure truth' had been manifest. 'Isn't all that infinitely respectable?'[41]

In contrast, Louis Vauxcelles's review in *Gil Blas* criticized Rouault for resembling Bloy and Huysmans too much. These '*hallucinants* sketches,[42] traced with a sorrowful fit of rage, this whole romantic and twisted puppet-farce (*guignol*), these obscene negresses, these grimacing judges, these clowns and prostitutes – *voilà* humanity and modern society such as M. Rouault understands and sees it! His pessimism is truly filled with pathos.' In listening to Rouault's 'cries, explosions, and raucous stammerings,' one began to 'dream' of 'a Huysmans, a Bloy, vomiting out their epoch, of some mystic apprehending life in horror and in terror.' However, 'Huysmans and Bloy, being writers, have at their disposal a form which M. Rouault, being a painter, lacks.' It was not a matter of skill or knowledge, but rather that one sensed past several years' works 'an interior trouble, a fevered disequilibrium.'[43]

A minority of reviewers applauded Rouault's realism. *Echos Parisiens* read Rouault's journey not as a fall but as a noble escape. The work he did under Moreau's 'oppression' had lacked interest because of its 'impersonality.' But Rouault's strong constitution forced him 'to shake off the yoke' before too long. 'Deserting the literary painting of his mentor, [Rouault] walked toward *simplification in realism.*' His 'brutality of design' made his 'realism' systematic while he retained a post-naturalist method to 'increase the intensity ... a *déformation* in service of rhythm.' Rouault 'excelled' in the 'dark range' with his 'abrupt violence in the transcription.'[44] His preference for 'ugliness and misery in the choice of subjects' as well as his 'brilliant desire to shock the bourgeois,' wrote *L'Aurore*, ended up becoming 'almost artistic.' Rouault was the 'glory of the Independents': his coloring, though 'the saddest and the dirtiest,' was still 'the most sumptuous.' His forms were 'the least designed, his *déformations* the most staggering and childlike,' yet they possessed an indescribable 'accent of realism and of sincerity.'[45]

In general, reviews of Rouault's work were nearly as depressing as the work they thought they were seeing. However, one notice appearing in *Paris-Journal* on 14 March 1910 was written to make the avant-garde point with humour. 'The Truth Completely Nude' was written for the preview day of the annual spring Salon des Indépendants and predicted once again a time of 'heroic and comic struggles between artists and the bourgeoisie.' There was always some painting 'to stir up and scandalize the crowd,' and in one of the last Salons, a Rouault work had this honor: his 'nude' bodies were 'deformed either by vice or by age.' In either case, they lacked any 'kindness' on the artist's part, eliciting protests and laughter.

Two women staring at the Rouault had howled to their hearts' content – 'two fat women who probably had nothing in common with the virgins of Raphael except Virtue nor with the Venus de Milo except old age.' All of a sudden, an 'exasperated' friend of the artist, 'neglecting even the most elementary principles of gallantry, suddenly planted himself right in front of them' and said: 'But look, Ladies, you have to admit that if someone were to shove you out there completely nude, you'd be a lot more screwed [*plus mal f...*] than that!' Turning to the 'amused crowd' he lamented, 'It's never the pretty women who complain!' Suddenly, someone unnoticed – 'perhaps the husband or a knightly servant of these ladies' – stepped forward. 'Then came the moment for unveiling the truth!' '"He's right," he shouted, completely red from confusion and anger, "those nudes are well made for you! What are you interfering for? Did anyone ask for your opinion? Go on, get out of here!" And the two fat women, after having thought about fainting, decided it was more prudent to slip away.'[46] However, even this humorous piece meant to defend the Independents underscored the widespread view that Rouault's 'violent and satirical art,' in the words of Gustave Kahn, regarded 'his contemporaries with an anxious and hate-filled eye.' Simply put, said Kahn, 'He doesn't like them.'[47]

Two reviews stood out for their sense that Rouault might be on to something. A piece published by Jacques Rivière in the *N.R.F.* (he would become its secretary the following year) seemed to take its cue from Jacques Favelle. 'Rouault is in a wrestling hold with the form as if with a person,' wrote Rivière, 'an unending battle which will never become a triumph.'[48] Less metaphysical in tone was Charles Morice's review in the venerable *Mercure de France.* Morice allowed that Rouault's 'excessive visions' of 'hideous, enormous or skinny prostitutes, odious slanders on the human situation' might betray 'a sad soul,' and that his work expressed 'every sadness of vice and of shame, of fury and of misery.' Yet, there was something true that Rouault had captured about modern life: he had 'seen that life, *at least our life today cannot consent to fables*.' His painting exacted 'revenge for such lies,' and Rouault seemed to be punishing himself for his 'credulity by exaggerating *the disparity he perceives between his hopes and reality*.' It was both 'puerile and great at the same time.'[49]

One year later, on 16 July 1911, Rouault wrote the first of what would be many letters to André Suarès, the friend who perhaps best understood him and on whom he relied heavily for support.[50] 'I carry inside myself a bottomless well of sorrow and melancholy which life has only developed,' he wrote, 'and of which my art of painting, if God allows, will be only an expression (albeit imperfect) and illumination.' Rouault said he had tried to 'love Ingres' – about whom Suarès had just published an essay and who was the paradigm of neoclassical order – but Ingres was 'too full of health' for Rouault. Rouault 'was punished for' this attempt to love order (and implicitly to go against his own nature). However, he had recently been reading Dostoevsky's *Crime and Punishment*, and finding there a tragic sense of beauty that resonated with his own. Rouault summed up this experience: 'Yes, in spite of my infirmity I feel and I discover at every instant new beauties, and what beauties, unknown and marvelous ... in the midst of the most tragic and most base realities transfigured by genius ...'[51]

Rouault's religious realism, a complex *mélange* of beauty and baseness, was not a vision that could easily be accommodated in the Manichean world of the Banquet Years. 'How much I prefer this painting of Rouault, rich only in aborted plans [*avortements*], brutality and dark ardor,' reported *La Cote* later that fall.[52] But this world was about to evaporate, and the survivors would see Rouault with eyes transformed by four years of 'brutality and dark ardor.'

1920: Dialectical Realism at the Galerie Licorne

We have seen how the pages of *Le Petit Parisien* for the final week of November 1920 were permeated with postwar concerns suggesting the need for repatriating the repressed: bodies needing recovery and burial; the building of memorials to the martyred; shortages of milk and coal, rampant inflation, unemployment and social unrest. On 28 November 1920, two days after the big news of the day crowded the front page – 'A Tumultuous Debate in the Chamber on the Vatican Question' – the newspaper published a review of the Rouault exhibition showing at the Galerie Licorne. 'Georges Rouault, a former student of the only modern illuminator, Gustave Moreau,' it announced triumphantly, had proven 'his mastery.'

Rouault had taken 'almost everything from the realism of the nineteenth century' but with a difference: he had 'transported the raw light' from where Toulouse-Lautrec had left it into the 'tempera of his ink, both morbid and compassionate at the same time.' Thus, Rouault's case would 'remain unique': 'the more he fills in black around his subjects, the more their right to existence becomes luminous and evident. *It is the Christianity of a painter enlightened by pure humanism*.'[53] The 'black' that had been *implacable* before the war now made colours luminous. The 'raw light of realism' had become 'enlightened Christianity.' Rouault's vision was a religion that could face the facts.

A comparison of reviews written by André Salmon in 1910 and 1920 illustrates pre-war and postwar differences in perception.[54] In 1910, Salmon had found Rouault to be 'a realist who always sees broadly and who often sees correctly,' not necessarily (as Daumier had been) 'always creating a work of irony.' Rouault had 'a powerful vision of life' that corresponded to 'a very deep sensibility.' Content with the subject matter 'his epoch propose[d] to him,' Rouault simply needed to apply himself as a painter in order 'to condemn them without judging them.' Thus, his judges were 'hideous,' his bourgeoisie 'loathsome,' and his prostitutes emitted 'the stenches of vulgar vice.' His peasants, however, were 'touching'; 'attached to the soil,' their faces were 'the same color as the nourishing ploughed fields.'[55]

In late 1910, having rhetorically asked whether Rouault was a 'caricaturist,' Salmon answered: 'Perhaps, but he is definitely no humorist.' His models were 'from Hell' and they danced 'the most horrible of macabre dances.' Noting that Rouault was 'a skilled ceramicist' who liked to decorate dessert plates with his 'terrible effigies' in order 'to punish us for our sins,' Salmon let his imagination roam. He pictured Baudelaire enjoying his morning 'meditations on human scandals' while 'digesting his pear and cheese.' As for Rouault's imitations of Daumier's caricatures of hypocritical judges, Salmon noted that several observers had registered loud shrieks of protest in front of Rouault's 'horrific puppets in the halls of justice.' But he also related the judgment of an art patron who was also a lawyer: Rouault's representations of the barristers were 'completely faithful.'[56]

These witticisms had been written during the Belle Époque. Salmon's use of Daumier and Baudelaire were quite different in 1920. 'Moving beyond the bonhomie of Daumier (to whom he [was] in debt),' Rouault revealed 'a heroic calm in front of *life's bitterness which must be accepted precisely because it is life.*' He also moved beyond 'the purest lines of Baudelaire: *May you be blessed, my God, who gives us suffering!*' Rouault created 'beauty, without any literature,' out of 'suffering and ugliness' by using 'only the means, only the virtues of painting.' 'The grimness of [Rouault's] talent is identical to its joy,' concluded Salmon; 'the drama it translates is not a despairing one. *It is rather a lesson in stoicism.*'[57]

In 1920, Salmon could juxtapose what had been incommensurable in 1910. The *âpreté* – that is, grimness, pungency, bitterness, harshness, fierceness – was 'identical with' *joie*. The 'suffering and the ugliness' were no longer dead-ends but rather the (literally) God-given material out of which Rouault created his unique 'beauty.' Baudelaire was no longer merely a prop for ridiculing Rouault's ceramics, but rather the retrieved proto-Decadent whose supplication for suffering prefigured both Bloy and Huysmans. Daumier's liberal bonhomie was transformed into ancient stoicism, part of a larger postwar turn to classicism's capacity to mourn with dignity. Bitterness needed to be accepted 'because it is life.'

Rouault's now-recognized compassion for the marginal drew praise from *L'Humanité*, founded by Jaurès in 1904 with prodding by his former professor Lévy-Bruhl (and later the official organ of the French Communist Party [S.F.I.C.]).[58] In 1920, the paper was trying to rekindle France's love for Daumier, and Claude Roger-Marx (who had first compared Rouault to Daumier in 1896) published a piece in mid-December entitled 'Daumier Unknown.' Roger-Marx accused the Third Republic of being 'ungrateful' to Daumier, and he invoked nineteenth-century Republican giants as his witnesses: 'Daumier is the painter of the people,' said Viollet-le-Duc. 'He was the people and he loved the people to the very depths of his being,' wrote Théodore de Banville. 'It is by you that the people are able to speak to the people,' Michelet wrote Daumier in 1851 on the eve of Napoleon III's *coup d'État*. 'The Empire offered the cross to Daumier,' noted Roger-Marx. 'He refused it,' and the price he paid was being classified by posterity as 'merely as a caricaturist.' His home town of Marseille had no monument to him and there was not even a bust on his 'humble tomb in Père-Lachaise.' It was high time, Roger-Marx concluded, for the Republic to honour Daumier with a Louvre retrospective.[59]

With an anticlerical cartoon on nearly every other page, *L'Humanité* was hardly the place one might expect to find praise of Rouault the religious painter. Yet the anonymous reviewer (perhaps Roger-Marx himself?) praised Rouault's work as the expression of a 'pungent [*âpre*] personality undiminished by any concessions to the present.' In a time when artistic fashion tended towards *faux primitifs*, Rouault demonstrated 'the violence of the true primitives, as well as their tenderness.' Beneath Rouault's 'riot of coloration, Daumier is exasperated.' Such 'contrasts' were the key to his art: 'Mystical in its flagellation of sensuality, it is as aggressive as it is sumptuous.'[60] Such evocations from *L'Humanité* must have warmed Rouault and reminded him with pride of his origins: his working-class birth, his father's impassioned anticlerical principles, his grandfather's collected reproductions of Daumier forming his childhood imagination. It also inserted him into a social sphere far removed from, and indeed bitterly opposed to, that usually associated with religious art.

René-Jean, a reviewer for *Comoedia*, noted that Roger-Marx had taken up Rouault's cause and associated him with Daumier. René-Jean found the comparison overstated: whereas Daumier had a 'shrill and critical intellectualism,' Rouault completely lacked this and let his forms be dictated solely by the 'direct impression of his emotions.' The 'liberty' with which Rouault expressed himself came not out of 'ignorance,' as some believed, but rather his 'spontaneous vision, an acuity both singular and almost *hallucinante*.' Rouault used 'the same manner of certain Flemish primitives, clarifying by suppressing the details in order to accentuate characteristic traits,' and these traits were almost always the same: 'the poor human wrecks tossed by the back-wash of life, from the circus to the brothel.'[61]

By loosening up the connection with Daumier and invoking 'certain Flemish primitives,' René-Jean had reframed the discourse and linked Rouault's realism with Huysmans's more complex aesthetic of 'spiritualist naturalism.' A few weeks later, *Le Calepin* followed this lead and made the connection more explicit. Rouault's Christ figures, 'decomposed and grimacing,' had all the 'vigor' of Grünewald's famous 'Christ on the Cross.' In contrast to Grünewald, however, Rouault was 'barely religious' and even then 'only when he feels like it.' Not religion but rather a 'sincere study and deep appropriation of humanity at its most vulgar' inspired his renditions. His 'grotesque – yet how human – physiognomies' of society's poorest showed an intimate knowledge of the humanity 'that haunts the *faubourgs*' (i.e., working-class districts/urban slums). Although Daumier had also 'understood humanity,' he had frequently 'ridiculed' his subjects by making them into 'puppets who became inhuman.' In contrast, Rouault never breached this limit. Rouault was rather 'the Huysmans of the canvas, the Huysmans of the Parisian sketches ...' Somewhat ironically (and inexplicably), this reader acquainted with Huysmans's discourse assumed that Rouault, being so compassionate, must be an atheist. His paintings of Christ had become 'more tormented, more human, and more true because the one who painted them does not have the soul of a believer.'[62]

The catalogue of subjects enumerated by Gaston Varenne in *Bonsoir* demonstrates that this change in evaluation of Rouault was due to perception and not to a change in style or substance. 'After having wandered for a long while through museums – those cemeteries,' began Varenne, 'Rouault suddenly discovered life, modern life, breathless and feverish.' As seen above, in 1910 this 'discovery of modernity' had meant Rouault's original fall. But for Varenne, it meant that the constricting 'scholasticism' of his art had become 'emboldened' and 'liberated itself.' As a result, this once 'wise imitator' of other painters found his own voice and became a 'trembling colorist.' Trading in museums for cabarets at the edge of town, circuses at fairs, and working-class hovels, he found a 'horde of prostitutes, of pimps, of down-and-out clowns.' These are the people 'he loves, those he sees with a cruel truthfulness, just barely caricatured,' these 'lamentable beings who live on the margin of contemporary society.' The reviewer catalogued Rouault's outcasts and then concluded that the painter loved and painted 'all these spoiled beings, cursed, abandoned to their dismal destinies without any stars to guide them.' In a concise example of dialectical realism, Varenne anticipated Breton's surrealist manifesto by four years, calling Rouault the '*hallucinant historiographer*' – a phrase remarkably close to Breton's 'reality and the dream state' – of the downtrodden.

But there was more. Varenne moved beyond this aesthetic hybridization of *hallucinant* realism to an explicitly *religious* realism. 'Weary of the depravity and the mud,' Rouault raised 'his eyes to heaven, to the Christian heaven whose touching images he returns to us.' Rouault was returning to religious 'subjects that he treated as an adolescent,' but now he represented them 'with a more personal piety' that was 'no less orthodox' than before. 'Huysmans would certainly have loved these harmonious faces with which, with a faith exempt from artifice, he models *sorrowful beauty*.' Situating Rouault completely within the nineteenth-century *renouveau catholique* tradition, Varenne connected the links: 'We are far from *Saint-Sulpician* Crucifixions, and also from those of M. Maurice Denis, whose imitation of the Primitives ends up being, too often, slavish. That which is called religious painting today no more resembles [Rouault's painting] than a prayer learned by rote resembles a cry of the heart which rises up to God ...'[63]

This reviewer for *Bonsoir*, a new newspaper (1919) attracting young writers and leaning left, was clearly well-versed in the nineteenth-century *renouveau catholique* tradition.[64] Yet the heterodoxy of Huysmans and the *hallucinant* was reconfigured as something radically new, profoundly ethical, and deeply religious. Former oppositions were overcome: Rouault could now be religious in direct proportion to his humanism. 'Georges Rouault,' concluded Varenne, 'is most definitely one of the most honest and sincere artists in this time lacking both honesty and faith.'

1921: *N.R.F.:* From Puppet-Farce to *Bal Masqué*

1921 marked a milestone for the fifty-year-old Rouault: the first monograph on his work was written by Michel Puy and published in the *N.R.F.* as number eight of the 'New French Painters' series.[65] As opposed to prewar metaphors (especially the 'puppet-farce') that read Rouault's characters as two-dimensional caricatures, Puy emphasized the three-dimensional depth of Rouault's world, underscoring Rouault's fascination with the interplay between external appearances and unseen reality. Drawing on the nineteenth-century discourse of the *fantastical* meant to indicate uncertain causes, Puy said Rouault's 'vision' led him to draw '*fantastical* beings, both sorrowful and terrifying ... the creation of a universe that belongs to him, wild in its imagination, passionate, contorted, caricatured – where, in a tragic atmosphere, the *hallucinatoire* and *irréel* flow over into elements full of reality.'[66] Appearing as it did in 1921, Puy's interpretation echoed the concurrent popularity of Einstein and Freud – visions of relativity, unpredictability, and the uncanny, eery premonitions of a vast unseen universe. Inverting the outdated nineteenth-century positivist's schema, physical or phenomenal reality seemed to be the distinctly subordinate partner in comparison with the overflowing enormity of this mysterious and not-realistic other. This was the cosmic, indeterminate, and sometimes horrifying aspect Puy found in Rouault's creations.

There was also the deeply human aspect symbolized by the masked face that conceals even as it reveals. Rouault's clowns were certainly rooted in the nineteenth-century use of them: the 'sad clown' had became a heroic figure, 'bravely masking a melancholy nature and a difficult, rootless and dependent existence behind a colorful costume and professional mirth.'[67] Moreover, the wandering performer's social status as an outcast had drawn Daumier to use the clown as a central image of the artist.[68] But in addition to the past century, Rouault's clowns also paralleled the 'obsessions with Pierrot' that pervaded modernism both before the war as well as afterward.[69] Puy was able to situate Rouault's clowns within this overall modernist context, calling his figures 'startling on the exterior, made-up faces, faces grimacing in pain, decked out in multicolors, disguised, whose extravagant masks and grotesque traits [Rouault] accentuates.'[70]

Having drawn this distinction between external masques and unseen truth, Puy extended the clown's use in a theological (and implicitly, metaphysical) way: 'Rouault, who has resumed painting religious scenes at various times, is a religious spirit. *Under the human rag, he discerns the soul.*' Perhaps taking a cue from Maritain's *Art and Scholasticism* (which had appeared the previous year), Puy redefined categories. It was not Rouault's occasional employment of religious subject matter that made him 'a religious spirit.' It was rather his interest in the depth-dimensions of human existence, his fascination with a reality masked by appearances.

In both cosmic and human terms, Rouault's spirit was religious because it was interested in things insofar as they both revealed and disguised realities they suggested. Rouault's spirit was sacramental.

Puy drew out the implications of Rouault's love for the tragic possibilities of the masked face. With respect to prostitutes, Puy wrote of the 'contradiction' between the 'profession of these women and their external aspect, between the theatricality of their hand-me-downs and the pitiful nature of the used-clothes shop, between the divine flirtatiousness they try to incarnate and the heaviness of their bodies made up with such labor, disproportionate, fatigued and grown old.'[71] This inconsistency between appearance and reality, concretely manifest in the 'powdered and heavily made-up faces,' was to be found in clowns as well. In clowns' faces Rouault could explore 'a mask whose simplicity is at one and the same time both comic and tragic: comic because it distorts humanity, tragic because, beneath the illusory appearance, *humanity subsists with its true nature*.'[72] (Like Maritain, Puy drew on theological language coming from dogmatic formulations about the incarnation of Christ – that is, the divine and human 'natures' of Christ coming together 'to *form one person and subsistence*.') The dialectical realism of Puy's imagery was thoroughly Catholic: surface comedy and underlying tragedy, appearance and reality, matter and form, accident and substance, sign and reality – *sacramentum et res*.

The same dialectic applied to Rouault's judges in whom Puy found no trace of criticism or outrage. Rouault, seeing that the courts of law had a certain aspect of the *parade* to them, recognized the judicial world's 'requirement to invent a face in front of the public.' Rouault's 'distorted physiognomies of everyone, judges, lawyers, gendarmes, the accused, all appear strained, immobile, outside of themselves.' In the judicial system the viewer saw a human contradiction that stretched far beyond the particular situation of prostitutes or clowns. One sensed 'a life where the essential interests of individuals are at play, that a deep emotion hides itself under all the theatrical apparatus, and that nevertheless the task of the judge is an impossible one: for there is no human justice and the judgments made are no better than compromises and approximations.'[73] Although a dark subversion of appearances motivated the painting of clowns, prostitutes and judges, the courtroom sideshow seemed to be the most humanly tragic: the very possibility of justice – that is, correct judgments based on appearances – seemed unattainable.

Puy glossed these disturbing epistemological and moral questions with two small excerpts from Rouault's own writings: 'Human grandeur is the negation of that which we humans in general call great and admirable. However, a truth hidden at the core of ourselves sometimes makes us have a premonition of true beauty and true grandeur.' This 'negation' of human valuation might be simply depressing were it not for an ancient religious tradition that saw grace as a powerful force capable of inverting the given order: 'The most noble subjects are humbled by a low spirit, but modest and simple realities are able to be raised up and magnified. An art considered inferior is suddenly able to find its redeemer.'[74] Rouault's language played on the verses in the Gospel of Luke known as the *Magnificat* (from magnify/*magnifier*). Upon hearing the angel's announcement that Mary would be the God-bearer, she proclaimed: *Magnificat anima mea Domino* – 'My soul doth magnify the Lord. And my spirit hath rejoiced in God my Saviour ... He hath put down the mighty from their seat, and hath exalted the humble.'[75] Derived partly from Bloy and the Decadents and partly from his evident immersion in scriptures, Rouault's belief in the world's fundamental brokenness was paralleled by his hope in redemption through inversion.

There had been a time when there were 'loud cries of indignation against Rouault' by critics who reproached him for 'enjoying ugliness.' However, having recently reread a series of articles about Rouault's work, Puy noticed that the critics all agreed on something: a 'great drama' took place in his universe. Human beings lived a life half-comic and half-tragic: comic because of the energy invested in clothing, make-up, and public masks; tragic because humans did not recognize what was truly valuable and real. Puy expressed this poignantly: 'How seductive they are in their own eyes, and how their seduction passes unperceived by the eyes of others!'[76] Without fanfare, Puy linked together the complex associations in Rouault's vision: clowns, prostitutes, and the courtroom circus, far from being superficial subjects, led the viewer into epistemological, aesthetic, moral, and theological depths.

Puy's re-evaluation of Rouault as a 'religious spirit' at the half-century mark seems to have marked a definitive turning point in critical evaluations of him. A piece by André Lhote appearing in December 1923 in *L'Amour de l'Art* showed this sea change. During the war, Lhote had made a name for himself by publicly attacking the artistic left and linking Cubism with individualism, obsession, and illness. In the wartime climate during which Cubism was associated with 'Kraut' art, his *rappel à l'ordre* encouraged a retrieval of Ingres, the paradigm of French neoclassicism.[77] Now, in 1923, Lhote felt obliged to admit that even 'Ingres himself did not escape' the 'fatality' of 'Saint-Sulpician vapidness' that, ever since the days of Bartolomé Esteban Murillo (1617–82), had 'conquered' whatever might be considered religious or Catholic art. Observing that Rouault (a 'fervent Catholic and of a Catholicism a bit suspect') had 'only one desire: to become a religious painter,' Lhote did not believe that 'a renaissance in this sense' was possible – although if it were, 'no doubt Rouault would be its elect artisan.'

In 'evoking this curious painter' Rouault, Lhote 'involuntarily' felt compelled to compare him to Hieronymus Bosch, the 'great Flemish' painter. Bosch represented those 'primitive painters' who surrounded their 'saintly subjects' with creatures that were 'monstrous, puerile, and a bit irreverent.' Regrettably, all this 'necessary candor totally disappeared' with the 'classical era,' taking along with it 'the last malleable witnesses to faith.' However, it was possible that 'the beautiful and moving anxieties [*soucis*] of Rouault,' like those of the primitives, 'would bring forth the fruits that he desired.' Perhaps Rouault could be a 'religious painter.'[78]

For those like Lhote who followed Puy, Rouault was religious not because he sometimes painted religious subjects – 'Saint-Sulpician art' was full of that – but rather because of his dialectical juxtaposition of them with the 'monstrous.' By 1924, Rouault's beauty was perceived as being tragic and anxious – in a word, modern. What the world considered profane or even sacrilegious was a masque beneath which dwelled mystery. His was a graced grotesque.

1924: The Druet Revisited – Image of the Lamb

In 1924 Rouault returned to the Druet Gallery and Jacques Maritain once again wrote an essay of review. Life had changed dramatically since the days of 'Jacques Favelle.' Léon Bloy had died in 1917; Maritain had left biology for philosophy and become a professor at the Institut Catholique of Paris; the publications of *Bergsonian Philosophy*, *Art and Scholasticism*, and *Antimodern* had made him infamous; he was in the midst of helping a grieving and addicted Cocteau, and he was preparing to launch the *Roseau d'Or*. Far from writing this review under a pseudonym, he was writing it under his own name for the *Revue universelle* that he had co-founded with Maurras and Massis. Torrents of blood and Psichari's sacrifice separated him from 1910. 'Jacques Favelle' was a distant and hidden memory.

Notably missing in his review of 15 May 1924 was the centrepiece of 1910: the term 'medieval artisan' occurred just once and then only as an end-tag – 'this great artist who has always remained an artisan.'[79] Also missing was any metaphysical discussion of material 'assuming form.' The word 'form' occurred only once – notably, along with Bloy and 'prostitutes' (here Maritain named them) – and here it was subordinate to a larger moral quest: 'Bloy, affectionately but without much consideration, certainly! accused [Rouault] of falling into a demoniacal art, of taking pleasure in ugliness and deformities. [Rouault] listened without moving, blanched and speechless. And how could he have responded? He was obeying a necessity of growth which was stronger than he. Prostitutes [*filles*], clowns, judges, shrews – it is he himself whom he was searching, or I would like to say, his own interior accord in the universe of form and of color. He found it, but that is a path which it is necessary to walk all alone.'[80] What had been anxiously unspoken in the 1910 preface was now merely noted without fanfare. Life had moved on.

In his review, Maritain did not approach Rouault primarily from his own neoclassical inclinations that privileged abstract form over representation. Perhaps he realized that Rouault's uniqueness in his time came from being the only French painter 'not to have abandoned the signification of the subject.'[81] Whatever the reason, Maritain now paid closer attention to Rouault's expressionistic transformations of subject matter. Perhaps alluding to Arnold Schoenberg's *Pierrot Lunaire* (1912), an image made only more powerful by the popularity of Freud and Breton, Maritain began with the quintessential icon of romantics, Decadents, and expressionists: the clown intoxicated by the *hallucinatoire* moonlight. With his 'Pale complexion, an eye always clear and alert, but with a gaze fixed inward rather than on an exterior object,' Maritain found in Rouault's circus figure 'something here of the moonlit clown [*clown lunaire*] – *a surprising mixture of pity and bitterness*, of malice and lack of guile ...'[82] Maritain immediately established Rouault's expressionism, celebrating Pierrot's turn away from daylight's rational falsehoods to the greater truth of the interior gaze, moonlight, and the dream state. He also pointed to its *surprenant mélange* of two apparent opposites, 'pity and bitterness.'

In addition to Rouault's 'curious instinct of moralizing proselytism' and a 'natural incapacity to resign himself to the mediocrity of his neighbor,' Rouault paradoxically also had '*an insatiable sympathy for human things*.' Beneath his brusque and even brutal exterior, Rouault had 'hidden within himself a soul which [knew] neither indifference nor disdain.' From this came his 'ferocious images, much darker than your usual caricature,' his 'most violent exasperations against the bourgeoisie' and against all of 'our social order.' Rouault had 'fallen in love with an interior order,' and he wanted to 'rediscover' it 'in the streets, in the courtrooms, and in the subway.'[83]

Maritain's new ability to find redemption in Rouault stands in stark contrast to the piece by 'Jacques Favelle,' and his image of 'the Divine Lamb' suggested the crucial catalyst behind this aesthetic conversion. There was 'in Rouault a *purity* – an almost Jansenist purity capable of becoming cruel,' wrote Maritain the Tertullian (perhaps with self-awareness), that gave him 'both his force and his freedom.' But this sometimes cruelty coexisted with a deeper drive, 'as if a hidden living spring of water, a profoundly religious sentiment, a stubborn hermit's faith that led him to Huysmans and to Léon Bloy. This faith makes him discover *the image of the Divine Lamb in all the abandoned and all the rejected* whom he pities.'[84] Maritain's attention to 'abandonment' was not new, perhaps because he had been effectively abandoned by his father. After first meeting Bloy he judged that 'Christians have abandoned the poor – and the poor among the nations: the Jews,' and later recalled Bloy as feeling that he was the voice of 'all those who are abandoned or oppressed by the modern world.'[85]

The novelty was not abandonment of the marginal but rather seeing in them the 'image of the Divine Lamb' – or more precisely, the blood of the Lamb. In a long iconographic tradition, the Lamb is a symbol of *sacrifice*. A common object of oblation among the ancient Jews, burnt as a 'holocaust' or sin-offering, it was transformed into the centrepiece of the annual Passover celebration. In the biblical narrative of the *Exodus*, when God delivered the Israelites from the Egyptians, each Hebrew family was instructed to sacrifice a lamb and paint its blood on the front door of the dwelling. In this way the Angel of Death would pass over the Hebrew homes as it slaughtered the first-born sons of the Egyptian captors, forcing them to set the slaves free. Taken over by first-century Christians, the image of the Lamb came to symbolize Jesus Christ, the first-born son who was sacrificed and whose blood was spilled in order that, through baptism, Christians might be in turn liberated from death. The earliest Christian martyrs interpreted their self-sacrifice in this way: 'These are they who are come out of great tribulation,' records the *Apocalypse*, 'and have washed their robes, and have made them white in the blood of the lamb.'[86]

Of the entire iconic store from which Maritain could have chosen his image, this was among the richest. In *Le Sacrifice*, Henri Massis had famously made Ernest Psichari's death on the battlefield a sacrifice: like Christ, Psichari too had been a 'son destined for a mission' of sacrifice; he too immolated himself as 'an authentic holocaust,' 'redeeming' the *patrie*. (Psichari himself had written, in words published posthumously, that the blood spilt in the colonies was 'an image of the Redemption.') Maritain had extended these metaphors in *Antimoderne*: Psichari's priestly vocation of reparation for the sins of his grandfather's generation had been accomplished, not at the altar of the Mass, but on the battlefield in a sacrifice no less priestly in its redemptive efficacy.[87]

Maritain now read Rouault through the postwar lens of the sacrifice of the Lamb, an image of all the abandoned of the world. This allowed him to find meaning in Rouault's subjects that, in spite of his intimate acquaintance with Bloy, he had not seen found before the war. He could now synthesize his Thomistic optimism with Rouault's expressionism: 'Rouault has seized into the real [*saisi dans le réel*] and made a certain splendor burst out of it which *no one up until now has discovered*; these prostitutes and these clowns, this monstrous and miserable flesh, enslaved in these hidden harmonies and these precious transparencies of the most complex matter – this is the wound of Sin, it is the sadness of fallen Nature, penetrated by an observation without complicity and an art which does not bend.' Maritain repeated here what he had said in *Art and Scholasticism* – 'The religious quality of a work does not depend on its subject but rather on its spirit' – and then drew this revisionist conclusion: 'Thus, *this art of pathos* has a *profoundly religious signification*.'[88]

Maritain had redefined 'religious art' as being completely compatible with its expression of existential *pathos*. This dialectical realism still paid attention to Maritain's privileged interior reality, but the unseen form now seemed much less 'eternal' and much more human, historical, and even *hallucinant*.

Guerre et Miserere

Other reviews of the 1924 Druet also found new depths in Rouault. For *Journal des Débats*, Rouault's 'hundred paintings, water-colours, and ceramics, executed between 1897 to 1919,' formed 'one of the most original, the most troubling that one could see.' 'Never is there paint "on the surface," never does the work lack profundity or emotion.'[89] 'Every transposition is permitted in view of revealing to us a bit of the truth,' wrote Louis Léon Martin of *Paris*, and added (using the verb that Maritain might have borrowed for his 'seizing into the real'): 'A canvas of Rouault, whatever might be the originality of the means employed, is gripping in its truth [*saisissant de vérité*].'[90] In *Comoedia*, René-Jean, calling Rouault 'the authentic descendant of Honoré Daumier,' said the two artists shared a mixture of 'marked antipathies' and 'impulses of tenderness towards the disinherited of all categories.'[91] For Louis Vauxcelles, Rouault applied himself 'to transpose humanity' within a context that was 'comical, *hallucinant*, and filled with pathos.' Of the artists of the day, he was perhaps one of those 'whose trace' would remain in the future.[92]

One of the critics who worked hardest to promote Rouault and shape his reception was Waldemar George, an early collaborator on the Dadaist review *Interventions*. In his review of Rouault in the *Bulletin de la vie artistique*, published on the same day as Maritain's in *La Revue universelle*, George emphasized and applauded Rouault's tenacious refusal to abandon realism. Unlike the symbolists, 'that esoteric Redon' as well as Moreau himself, Rouault was not content with either abstraction or 'literary' themes. He resembled more 'all the mystical painters [*peintres mystiques*] of the North' (presumably, both Bosch and Grünewald were intended here). Rouault took 'a part of reality that he transforms, he transposes, he re-creates without idealizing.'[93] George's verbs expressed both genuine *change* in something and a simultaneous *conservation* of that original thing. 'Abstraction' would take reality and change it into something not-real. The appeal to 'transformation' and 'transposition' also evoked 'transubstantiation': that is, a thing's genuine self-transcendence even as it preserves itself; a genuine change made possible because of potential already possessed.

George expanded these ideas later in that autumn 1924 as he proclaimed Rouault 'a great French Romantic painter.'[94] Here again, drawing on a recent essay by Roger Fry in England, George expressed his disapproval of the taste for abstraction fashionable in Paris among 'our generation': Picasso, Matisse, Bonnard, Braque, Derain, and Segonzac. For George, 'classicism' was not 'a historical notion but rather a purely psychological' notion: 'A classic work is self-sufficient in itself. It is an end in itself.' To make his point, George compared Raphael to 'the hands of Christ on the cross of Mathias Grunevald of the Isenheim Triptyque at Colmar.' Raphael was essentially self-sufficient whereas by contrast, 'a hand of Mathias Grunevald is a living symbol.' George claimed Grünewald for the Franco-Italian patrimony: 'the last century produced in France a certain number of artists who can take their place in the great family illustrated in another time by Grunevald ... Rembrandt, Caravaggio,' and others.

Into this setting George placed Rouault. During this epoch in which painters practised 'a vain formalism, banishing the subject from their works and forcing themselves to be classic,' this 'great visionary' dared 'to tackle themes which he magnifies by his sense of the tragic and by his *faculty of transposition of elements taken from life onto the plane of art.*' 'A painter with character, a *mystical painter* [*peintre mystique*], a *religious painter* [*peintre religieux*], Rouault is all of this and is also *a powerful realist* [*réaliste puissant*].' George summarized the dialectic: 'It is this *strange alloy* [*alliage*] *of realism and of spirituality* that constitutes the distinctive trait of Georges Rouault.' Reaching into the past for some kind of predecessor, the 'name of François Villon' came to George's mind. It seemed that 'the soul of the great French poet, *mystic and bawdy at the same time*,' had taken up residence in 'Rouault, this Saint of painting, *the only Catholic painter* produced by our epoch, the only, whose essentially modern work re-clothes [*revête*] the aspect of a genuine Passion.'

George's alchemical formulations, expressed in metaphors (transpose, transform, re-clothe, alloy) and pairings (life/art, mystical/realist, realism/spirituality, mystical/bawdy, Catholic/modern), took the depth-dimensional insights first expressed by Puy and explored their possibilities with enormous sophistication. He had a subtle yet penetrating understanding of Catholic sacramentalism: no doubt it came largely from his attempt to preserve a realist's esteem for subjects taken from mundane life while at the same allowing for their aesthetic 'transformation.'

It is worth remarking that George's disdain for abstraction made the anti-Semitic attacks of his critics both ironic and absurd. 'Unfortunately, like too many Jewish minds,' wrote Marcel Hiver two months later, 'he is an abstractionist who juggles with ready-made concepts ... From a physical point of view, M. Waldemar George would inspire the antipathy even of a dog ...'[95] George responded to such critics in his review the next year of the exhibition 'Fifty Years of French Painting.' *L'Action française* had been vocal in its opposition to some of the pieces and George fought back. '*L'Action française* has covered itself in shame when, under the signature of M. Louis Dimier, it exhales its hatred of modern painting and pursues its deaf campaign against the painters who make up the glory of our School.' Attacking 'the newspaper of M. Charles Maurras which is the organ of classicism' for putting forth 'academic painters' as models, George cited the 'great independents' who opposed 'the royalist gazette: Braque, Picasso, Matisse, Vlaminck, Derain, and Georges Rouault.' So much for 'the pages claiming to assume the defense of the French spirit, of French culture.'[96]

During that same late autumn 1924, after the spring exhibition at the Druet, Rouault was interviewed by Jacques Guenne, director of *Les*

Nouvelles littéraires, and given a chance to explain himself. Guenne asked: 'Is it necessary to see in your work an intention to moralize and be satirical?' Rouault answered, 'No. I have never had the pretension of being either an "avenger" or a moralizer.' Some critics had found certain 'emphases in the heads' of Rouault's prostitutes that they interpreted as a desire to 'show the ignominy of these creatures.' But Rouault reported that he had only seen such ignominy after others had suggested it: 'And I have only felt pity for them.' Saying that he agreed that 'the grotesque and the tragic juxtaposed themselves' in his works, he asked pointedly, 'but aren't they sometimes united that way in life?'

As for his judges, Rouault said that if his renderings of them were 'so lamentable,' it undoubtedly betrayed 'the anguish that I feel in view of a human being who must judge other humans. If I have sometimes ended up confusing the head of a judge with that of an accused, this error only betrays my own confusion. One could give me all the fortune and all the happiness of the world, but I would not be capable of becoming a judge.' Rouault concluded: 'So look, I am not able to condemn even the judges themselves!'[97] The artist continued this theme in one of two poems he published the next year in *L'Amour de l'Art*. In these verses, printed beneath an illustrated Christ (identified as a 'projected monument to the dead of l'Yser'), the judges were now art critics judging Cézanne: 'Far from the microbes criticizing so often with severity / In judging you they are judged, in measuring you they are measured.' Once again, Rouault, steeped in scripture, creatively played with the words of Christ: 'Judge not, that you may not be judged. For with what judgment you judge, you shall be judged: and with what measure you mete, it shall be measured to you again.'[98]

In 1925, the public was given its first glimpses of Rouault's mammoth project of lithographs that he had been working on since the war began – *Miserere et Guerre*.[99] The title (whose two words' endings rhyme in French) combined the Latin verb 'to have mercy' and the French noun 'war,' thus roughly translated as 'Mercy and War.' Pronounced as French, the Latin *miserere* also sounded like *misères* ('miseries'), thus linking Rouault's project to Jacques Callot's large series of etchings from the Thirty Years' War, *Les Misères et malheurs de la guerre* (The Miseries and Misfortunes of War [1633]). The series' subjects recapitulated many of Rouault's most profound themes. The image of a condemned criminal was juxtaposed with that of Christ and connected by the inscription, 'Jesus still flagellated,' illustrating Rouault's (and Bloy's) conviction that Christ suffered in the modern world's abandoned. Another juxtaposed set of images posing the question 'Are we not slaves ... believing ourselves kings?' referred to the human tendency noted by Puy: 'How seductive they are in their own eyes ...' One of the most poignant plates was that of a pale sad clown, his head tilted to one side, asking, 'Who does not wear a mask?' The ensemble, a singular part of Rouault's legacy, would not appear in its completed form until after the Second World War.[100]

However, André Salmon's 1925 article entitled 'Le Miserere de Georges Rouault, published in *L'Amour de L'Art*, contained reproductions of water-colour versions of several *Miserere* plates and announced their upcoming display at the Exposition des Arts Décoratifs. 'The world would rise up if Georges Rouault ... covered the walls of its town halls, its prisons, its schools, its churches' with his 'terrible' figures, wrote Salmon. His was the world of the 'horror of times heavy with crimes ... The Middle Ages!' And yet, there was once again 'unlimited hope, reconquered,' taking hold of 'the souls beneath the mass graves, beneath the cesspool.' To remind his readers that healing and horror were not incommensurable in everyday life, Salmon used a familiar image: 'hope in healing, after all, is in the sick body.' Like Waldemar George, and playing on Rouault's own hybridized title, Salmon concluded with his own alchemical formula: 'Georges Rouault, the artist of *Guerre et Miserere*, is well *the master of this horror and of this hope*.'[101]

Examples from *Miserere* were also reproduced in an article by Georges Charensol appearing in *L'Art vivant* in February 1926: Christ on the Cross and a condemned man were joined by a third figure: 'Clowns.' Charensol, Lefèvre's assistant at *Nouvelles littéraires*, played on the phrase 'art for art's sake' (*l'art pour l'art*) and wrote that Rouault painted '"the horrible for the sake of the horrible" [*l'horrible pour l'horrible*] and this morose delectation reaches an astonishing amplitude and intensity.' Even 'the most violently expressive artists and the most vehement satirists – Bosch, Callot, Daumier, Lautrec – even these know how to temper their compositions from time to time with a little light or a smile. But in Rouault, on the contrary, we find nothing but vice, desolation, and death.'

But then Charensol took a deeper look and came up with his own dialectical formula: 'These are the four themes which have inspired Georges Rouault's greatest *chefs-d'oeuvre* ... One suspects that the women whom he paints are all prostitutes, his clowns are all pitiful, his judges are infamous Pilates. As for his Christs, they are raised up by *a mysticism so exasperating* that one dares to give Rouault the name of *religious painter* which no one, since Delacroix, has been worthy of bearing.'[102] In Rouault, 'mysticism' (and thus 'religious') had lost all connotations of *la paix de l'éternel*, its realist component exhausted to the limit.

In his *Panorama of Contemporary French Painting* (1927), Pierre Courthion said that he had asked himself 'for a long time how to think about this man, the painter of such misery [*misère*],' when all at once 'one fine day, the *Miserere*' appeared. 'All of his previous paintings, these empty creatures, this humanity without a soul, this ridiculous human justice' had been pushed out of the way for 'this *Miserere*, this moving cortège of superior forms.'

This 'spiritual, religious and even profoundly Catholic' art placed Rouault squarely within 'the family of mystics.' In fact, Rouault could not possibly have been 'anything but a religious painter.' How did Rouault accomplish this? It was precisely his 'tendency to mysticism' that allowed him to 'lay bare human misery' [*la misère humaine*]. Echoing Breton, Courthion articulated Rouault's alchemy as an 'atrocious *mélange of reality and of dream.*' This dialectical realism was 'the key to this art.' 'There was no more doubt: I had before me the greatest religious painter of our time.'[103]

Rouault's stature continued to blossom. In 1925, he exhibited for the first time outside of Paris at the Flechtheim Gallery of Berlin and Dusseldorf. Carl Einstein's essay written for the show had no trouble beginning unequivocally: 'Rouault is THE great Catholic painter, and his work seems to be shaped by "the hand of the Father."'[104] Rouault would produce the sets and costumes for the ballet *The Prodigal Son*, scored by Sergei Prokofiev and choreographed by George Balanchine. It was premiered by the Ballets Russes de Diaghliev at the Théâtre Sarah Bernhardt on 21 May 1929. That same year, Rouault exhibited at the Galerie des Quatre-Chemins. Headlines accompanied Waldemar Georges's review entitled 'The Human Evolution of a Great Painter' in *La Presse*: 'Thanks to "Quatre Chemins," the wider public will finally be able to know Georges Rouault.' The same exposition also received coverage from Georges Charensol and Maurice Raynal.[105] In 1930, Rouault would exhibit in New York, Chicago, London, and Munich, as well as Paris; in 1931, in New York, Brussels, and Geneva.

Later that year, André Malraux published notes whose anxiety over the 'absurd' prefigured his later preoccupations in his masterpiece, *The Human Condition* (1933). Speaking of Rouault, Malraux wrote: 'There is not today work that is more stripped of love than the profane work of this Christian painter; as if love, for the one who maintains the kinds of connections with the world that are Rouault's, could only express itself in the figure of Christ.' For Rouault, an abstract God would be meaningless in such a world as this one. Love would have to be manifest in a sacrificial figure. Malraux expressed it thus: 'Christ – and not God – delivers those who believe in him from the absurd.' Comparing Rouault to Rimbaud, Malraux concluded: 'At the heart of his work, Rouault is like Rimbaud at the center of his *Illuminations*. Both tell God that they do not accept his universe. But Rimbaud is large-spirited enough to respect a silence in which the final heroes spit in each other's faces, while Rouault's God answers him that there is *also* Satan.'[106]

Epilogue: Religious Subjects versus Fundamental Fate of Humanity

After 1945, Rouault's reputation as a 'religious painter' only increased. In a work published by the New York Museum of Modern Art in 1947, James Thrall Soby called Rouault 'a devout Catholic and devotional painter in a period when artists have often run the gamut of anti-religious feeling, from indifference to irreverence.' As such, he was 'a man who has long opposed Henri Matisse's peaceful wish that art evoke 'the same sensation as a good arm chair,' by making much of his own painting resemble a seat of moral judgment.'[107] In 1954, the Italian Mia Cinotti agreed: the 'truly dominant trait' of Rouault's personality was his 'deep and inborn religiousness' manifest more 'in the sadness of his clowns, his whores and his melancholy suburban landscapes, than in his earlier pictures of religious subjects.'[108] In 1963, Anthony Blunt wrote that Rouault's identity as 'a fervent Catholic' was 'certainly deducible' from all of his works, 'even the least evidently religious.'[109] As recently as 1988, a German exhibition catalogue called Rouault the artist of the 'fundamental fate of humanity' and suggested that, although the Passion of Christ was Rouault's preferred paradigm for this sorrow, the figure of Christ need not appear in order for a painting to be religious.[110] Rather, the tragic resonances of Rouault's clowns prefigured the 'emergent religious component.'[111]

By the end of the twentieth century, 'religious realism' and religious grotesquerie was taken for granted. It is easy to forget that at the beginning of the century, the hybridization of those two terms, like the idea of a 'Catholic novel' (as we are about to see) had been difficult to imagine. The meaning of 'religion' changed throughout the twentieth century in large part because the epoch's unprecedented horrors forced such revisions. Numerous persons in the art world, both religious and non-religious, collaborated in the effort that produced a new meaning for 'religious painting.' It is unlikely, however, that they could have accomplished it without the tortured, complex, and transcendent personal vision of Georges Rouault's masked redemption.

Chapter 7

Georges Bernanos: Passionate Supernaturalism

> I have found that violence is strangely capable of returning my characters to reality and preparing them to accept their moment of grace. Their heads are so hard that almost nothing else will do the work. This idea, that reality is something to which we must be returned at considerable cost, is one which is seldom understood by the casual reader, but it is one which is implicit in the Christian view of the world ... Our age not only does not have a very sharp eye for the almost imperceptible intrusions of grace, it no longer has much feeling for the nature of the violences which precede and follow them. The devil's greatest wile, Baudelaire has said, is to convince us that he does not exist.
>
> – Flannery O'Connor

> In a word, one might say that the mystical is a reaction against the appropriation of truth by the clerics ... It favored the illuminations of the illiterate, the experience of women, the wisdom of fools, the silence of the child; it opted for the vernacular languages against the Latin of the schools. It maintained that the ignorant have competence in matters of faith ... The mystical is the authority of the crowd, a figure of the anonymous, that makes an indiscreet return in the field of the academic authorities.
>
> – Michel de Certeau[1]

In the first week of April 1926, Maritain's *Roseau d'Or* published Georges Bernanos's novel *Under Satan's Sun* as the series' seventh volume. For supporters and opponents, the work would become a site in which a newly constructed Catholic dialectical realism could be discussed and refined. More singular efforts would be made to promote the 'Catholic novel' or 'mystical novel' by writers such as François Mauriac and Émile Baumann, the (not yet converted) philosopher Gabriel Marcel in the *N.R.F.*, the Sorbonne literary professor Robert Garric in *La Revue des jeunes* (which Garric also directed), and Victor Poucel in the Jesuit *Études*. Above all, Bernanos's unexpected success would have been less likely without its launch by Léon Daudet in *L'Action française*, a book by Frédéric Lefèvre, and coverage offered in *La Revue catholique des idées et des faits*.[2] A variety of persons and venues, including a wide institutional web of journals, publishing houses, associations, and universities, was necessary for the expression of traditional Catholic ideas as a postwar literary dialectical realism.

Georges Bernanos: *Under Satan's Sun*

Georges Bernanos was born in Paris on 20 February 1888.[3] His father's large library included the complete works of Balzac (all of which Bernanos claimed to have read as a youth), and undoubtedly his father's regular reading of *La Libre Parole*, published by the extreme anti-Semite Drumont, affected him during this turbulent epoch of the Dreyfus Affair. From 1904 to 1906, while attending a *collège* at Aire-sur-Lys, Bernanos was introduced to the writings of the Catholic revivalist writer Ernest Hello, developed his sympathies for Action Française, and engaged in street action with its youth auxiliary, the Camelots du roi ('streethawkers of the king').[4] After completing his studies in 1913, he moved to Rouen and became editor-in-chief of the local royalist *L'Avant-Garde de Normandie*.

When war broke out, Bernanos enlisted, fought at both Verdun and the Somme, was seriously wounded, and later decorated. While recovering from injuries in 1917, Bernanos's fiançée, Jeanne Talbert d'Arc, daughter of the president of the Royalist Ladies of Rouen, sent him the works of Léon Bloy. The reading of Bloy so moved the wounded soldier that he literally 'rolled in the grass in fury.'[5] In 1917, he married Jeanne, and the best man at his wedding was Maurras's assistant and co-founder of *L'Action française*, the novelist and literary critic Léon Daudet. After his convalescence, Bernanos returned to the homefront and earned his living as an insurance inspector. In his off hours he wrote *Under Satan's Sun*.

In 1919, Bernanos was introduced to Robert Vallery-Radot, a poet and editor of the Catholic review *L'Univers* (most popularly associated with its nineteenth-century editor, Louis Veuillot). The importance to Bernanos of Vallery-Radot's friendship cannot be exaggerated, including both literary and financial assistance. (Bernanos later said that Vallery-Radot alone was responsible for the eventual publication of *Satan's Sun*, which was dedicated to him.) Bernanos sent the manuscript to his best man, Daudet, but Daudet never read it. He then sent it to Vallery-Radot, who in turn sent it to Henri Massis, one of the directors of the *Roseau d'Or*.[6] Massis championed its publication in the series and it was accepted. Bernanos's considerably darker vision of a world in which Satan stalked country roads gave Maritain pause, and his own more optimistic take on reality led him to insist that Bernanos make significant alterations to the text.[7] In a letter to Maritain dated 14 February 1926, Bernanos articulated his different view from Maritain, especially (implicitly) regarding Cocteau and his circle. 'I wonder whether your charity – that of your heart and that of your intelligence – does not accord too much importance,' wrote Bernanos to Maritain, 'to certain small effeminate souls [*petites âmes femelles*] who search for God, not in order to let themselves be visibly worked by his grace, but in order to clasp him in their arms and cry on his shoulder. I would not avoid scandalizing these souls.'[8] Despite divergent views, Bernanos submitted the corrections to Plon on 20 February 1926.[9] The novel appeared several weeks later in early April.

Under Satan's Sun is divided into three parts: (1) The Prologue. Mouchette's Story, (2) The Temptation of Despair, and (3) The Saint of Lumbres. In a country setting not unlike that of *Madame Bovary*, a sixteen-year-old girl named Germaine Malorthy (nicknamed 'Mouchette' by her adult lovers) is three months pregnant. She goes to the home of the local marquis, with whom she has been having a sexual relationship. After an exchange she grabs his rifle and shoots him. 'The shot was so close,' reported Bernanos in language resembling Flaubert or Zola, 'that the greased felt wad went straight through his neck and was later found in his cravat.' Germaine then pays a visit to the local Doctor Gallet, with whom she has also been having an affair. (The doctor is a radical republican in his politics and, as Malorthy's father says of him, 'a doctor's not supposed to be an ordinary man. He's education and science in person. He's the republican's priest.') Germaine tells the doctor she's pregnant and becomes upset over his cold clinical response. 'It's hyperaesthesia,' says Gallet, quickly diagnosing her 'overwrought' state. 'Quite normal after a nervous shock.' Germaine seduces him in order to regain a sense of power and then tells him she wants an abortion. The doctor refuses to perform it himself. Just as Germaine, in a further attempt to pressure the doctor, confesses to having killed the marquis, Gallet's wife's footsteps in the house signal her unexpected return. Again he diagnoses her: 'It's a type of dementia ... you're a highly-strung girl, with a family history of alcoholism ... and you're in the early stages of pregnancy.' As Germaine goes into a fit that illustrates contemporaneous descriptions of hysteria, Gallet's wife hears the commotion and comes running to help. A handkerchief soaked in ether knocks Germaine out and she is whisked away to a convalescent home. The prologue ends: 'A month later, she came home completely cured, after giving birth to a premature, stillborn child.'[10]

In Part Two, The Temptation of Despair, we meet Father Donissan, a man whose boots are frequently 'muddy,' who has a 'limited intelligence,' and whose parishioners and superiors regard him as useless and of no esteem. During a conversation with an older priest, Donissan faints. As the older priest loosens Donissan's shirt to give him air, he discovers that the younger priest is completely wrapped in a penitential hair shirt. 'In some places, the epidermis had been completely rubbed away,' wrote Bernanos (in prose resembling Huysmans's *Saint Lydwine*), 'while in others it had risen in blisters as wide as a man's hand, forming a single wound of oozing water and blood ...' The older priest sees (quite literally) beneath the surface: there is something of the saint in this young cleric. Later, Donissan offers up to Christ in prayer what little he has: 'What have I to give? What have I to offer? Just this hope. Take it from me ... I would let my own soul be damned to save those that You – in mockery – have entrusted to a wretch like me!'[11] The poverty-stricken Bloy had prayed that his most valuable possession – his considerable intelligence – be taken in order to redeem another's soul. This priest has less than intelligence. He offers up his only possession: hope.

In perhaps the most famous scene of the novel, Donissan becomes lost at night in the unfamiliar countryside. After walking for a long time, he becomes aware – in a moment best described as uncanny – that he is not alone. 'But then, he thought, *he had been alone*. For some time now in fact – why not admit it? – *he had not been alone*. Someone was walking beside him.' He has a conversation with a man who identifies himself as a horse trader but might also be Satan. In a particularly grotesque moment, 'in a mad act of sacrilege,' the mysterious figure's 'unclean mouth was pressed against [Donissan's], leaving him gasping for breath.' '"That's a friend's kiss," the horse dealer said tranquilly,' alluding to Judas's kiss that betrayed Christ. A textbook example of the *fantastical* genre, this scene established Bernanos firmly within the lineage of Barbey d'Aurevilly. 'Was it just a dream then?' asks the priest afterward. 'Have I gone mad?'[12] It also echoed the mythic founding document of the *fantastical* genre in France, Cazotte's *The Devil in Love* (1772): 'was Alvare dreaming or did he really surrender to the devil?'[13]

Almost immediately, Donissan meets Germaine Malorthy on the road. Since he had been given the 'gift of seeing directly into souls,' he was able to recount for Germaine not only her own history – as Christ had done for the Samaritan woman at the well – but her entire family history as well, for generations. He told this story 'not narrated simply as it had happened, in the tangled skein of cause and effect' – that is, as Zola had done in the massive *Rougon-Macquart* series, an endless web of facts – 'but related to one or two major misdeeds, the mainsprings of the action.' In despair, Germaine now turns to Satan: 'So there she lies before our eyes,' wrote Bernanos (echoing Görres and Huysmans), 'this unsophisticated little mystic, Satan's little servant ...' Taking a razor blade and facing the mirror, Germaine slit her throat: 'she did not slash quickly but applied the blade fiercely and consciously to her throat and heard it rasp through her flesh. The last thing she remembered seeing was the jet of warm blood flowing onto her hand and down into the crook of her arm.' Towards the end of a long discussion with Donissan about despair and visionaries, his aging priest-mentor receives news at the door: 'Mademoiselle Malorthy's just killed herself,' reports the old woman at the door, adding with relish, 'She's cut her throat with a razor!' Father Donissan is committed to an asylum after the diagnosis of 'a serious intoxication of the nerve cells, probably due to intestinal causes.' After his cure, he spends five years in a Trappist monastery, and is then sent to the obscure little village called Lumbres, where he acquires the reputation of being 'the new curé d'Ars.'[14]

In Part Three, The Saint of Lumbres, Father Donissan is asked to visit a sick child. By the time he arrives, the child (like Christ's friend Lazarus in the gospel) has already died. Donissan 'lifted the little boy up like a host ... He was not begging for a miracle, but *demanding* it. God owed it to him and would give it to him, or else everything was a dream.' Again, the priest seems to hallucinate and hears mocking voices as he elevates the boy. He runs out of the room convinced he has failed ... But apparently, judging from the later fact that crowds of pilgrims now come on buses to see him, his miracle had succeeded. (Again in the *fantastical* genre, the episode is unstable as written and the reader is left unsure about 'what really happened' due to conflicting accounts of the priest, the mother, and the old priest's third-party report: 'I ... with a mind like mine ... could hardly tell what was real and what wasn't.')[15]

The story ends with a visit by a fictional novelist named Antoine Saint-Marin, in whose character many critics thought they found a thinly veiled Anatole France (who had just died in 1924). A former literary critic for

Le Temps, France had been something like an early-twentieth-century Voltaire: witty, mocking, and thoroughly sceptical. In a discussion with Father Sabiroux, a liberal and literary priest who greets him, the aged Saint-Marin insists on the value of the 'supernatural and miraculous': 'We all hope to see a miracle, Father, and the sad old universe calls for one just as we do. What does it matter whether it comes today or in a thousand centuries, if some liberating event is to drive a breach into the universal mechanism?' When the priest, intended as a type of the younger modern clergy, dismisses such things and tries to show that his eminently bourgeois brand of Catholicism can fully accommodate Saint-Marin's worldliness, the old fox destroys him with his razor-sharp wit. 'At first glance the savage scorn Saint-Marin showed towards fools was surprising, for he also affected a kind of indulgent skepticism, but this was his way of giving expression, with as little risk as possible, to his natural hatred of the infirm and weak.'[16] Although others found the prologue more objectionable, it was this third part of *Satan's Sun* that seems to have most disturbed Jacques Maritain: out of the forty corrections submitted by Bernanos to Plon, twenty-nine were from this section, a combative one somewhat at odds with the *Roseau d'Or*'s own accommodationist agenda.[17]

In the end, Saint-Marin finds only the corpse of Donissan, dead in his confessional. The sceptic sneers at such an uneventful conclusion to the reputed saint's life: 'A fine sort of miracle,' he mutters angrily through clenched teeth. 'The good Father has died quietly here from a heart attack.' However, Donissan seems to have the last word: 'Although there was no sound from the black mouth in the shadow ... the whole body seemed to be miming a dreadful challenge: "You wanted my peace!" the saint cried. "Come and take it!"'[18] This is the novel's final line.

In his many choices of motifs, situations, and style, Bernanos had quite consciously framed the novel as one might expect from a former *Camelot du roi* looking for a street fight. His authorial intention had thrown down the gauntlet. Partisans would take up the fight in its critical reception.

Daudet-Souday: 'Spiritual synthesis' versus 'Mystical hodgepodge'

Before the unknown Bernanos's novel had hit the bookstands, its 'launch' by Léon Daudet in *L'Action française* on Wednesday, 7 April 1926 stirred more than enough publicity. Perhaps Bernanos's best man felt guilty for having ignored his friend's manuscript; perhaps Vallery-Radot and Massis pressured him to help the cause. In any case, Daudet's effusive praise of

Satan's Sun served to link immediately two central themes: the genealogy of 'mystic realism' and the Great War. 'It had been seen,' began Daudet, 'that the literary revival succeeding the convulsions of the war and their immense repercussions – despite ... the mental debilitation of our contemporaries in general, would be of a metaphysical, transcendental, quasi-mystical order in so far as it followed upon a completely diluvial effusion of blood. Because only in that order will an author, who feels vividly and sees broadly, be capable of finding this refuge of peace, of consolation and of justice ...'[19]

By calling to mind the 'diluvial effusion' of the war – literally, a torrent of blood of Biblical proportions – Daudet implied that the war's own facts had rendered a positivist or naturalist literature *dépassé*. This necessitated a turn towards the metaphysical, transcendental, and even *mystique* for a more adequate vision. Although 'many young writers who were very well gifted' had felt it important 'to dominate matter and rise above its fatalism,' none had so far been able to accomplish this with the 'glimmering-red summit of a supernatural light' on which 'the author of *Under Satan's Sun* has just placed himself with a mastery that astonishes.' Daudet's 'supernatural light' was not Maritain's eternal form bursting out with symmetry and proportion. The glowing cinder suggested another supernatural force lingering behind the scenes. To make the demonic link, Daudet established Bernanos's genealogy: 'Let's not mistake ourselves for even a minute. The way in which he treats the subject – even apart from its importance and its universality – immediately classes M. Georges Bernanos on the same plane as a Balzac or a Barbey d'Aurevilly ...'

1926 was the year in which Louvain students declared their generation's 'crazy need for synthesis,' and Daudet celebrated Bernanos's 'synthetic' vision. From the point of view of literature, he had made a 'rare, singular and powerful effort' 'to tear the novelistic plot away from the painting of brutal instincts and sentimental anecdotes' (Flaubert and Zola were implied here) and 'lead it toward the heights.' Daudet recalled that 'one could say of Bernanos' what he had 'only a short while ago said of Marcel Proust' (here interjecting 'alas!' since Proust had died in 1922): Proust, 'a great force, both intellectual and imaginative, has appeared in the firmament of French letters.' (Daudet's rabid anti-Semitism had not kept him from being among the first to promote and publicize Proust, helping him win the Prix Goncourt in 1919.)[20] But Bernanos's force was even greater than Proust's since it was 'one that is synthetic and no longer analytic.'

Daudet observed that throughout its history, when faced with 'the spiritual life – the most important because it is in command at the hour of death and thus of all metaphysical imagination – the novel [had] generally hesitated' and 'the pen lagged behind, a bit out of breath.' Since the 'avatars of the novel' had struggled to be the literary counterparts of the 'avatars of the biological sciences,' trying to perfect the physiological novel, they had been incapable of accurately representing the 'spiritual life.' In contrast to subjects permitting an analytical observation and notation of factual details, the spiritual life was 'synthetic ... This synthesis permitted the construction of *ensemble works* such as the cathedrals, those immense enterprises such as the Crusades, the miraculous existence of a Joan of Arc, the periodic public sphere of a Lourdes, etc.'

Not only was Bernanos's novel 'synthetic,' it was suggestive. 'A novel of the spiritual life, that devotes itself to suggesting [*suggerer*] the invisible by means of the visible, surprises the contemporary reader, accustomed to admire nothing but analysis, analytical refinements, the brilliant dissipation of the mercurial mind under the shock of the metaphor.' The word *suggerer* located Bernanos within a genealogy: Mallarmé had used it to describe the ideal use of the symbol, and Huysmans's Des Esseintes used it to admire Baudelaire's 'suggestiveness' of an invisible line parallel to the written one. Daudet signalled Bernanos's descent from this symbolist-Decadent tradition: Baudelaire, Mallarmé, Huysmans.

For Daudet, *Satan's Sun* was not 'valuable simply as a narrative'; it was 'much more valuable as a symptom.' It announced a postwar aesthetic: 'a new form, a new orientation of French and Latin thought.' Daudet transformed Huysmans's 'parallel routes' of spiritualism and naturalism into a footrace: the metaphysical element was about to 'pass beyond the novel, run alongside the esthetic, catch up with and cross over criticism, and then – hang on tight! – go on to rejoin science on unforeseen riverbanks.' As seen above, during the vote to restore Vatican relations, Daudet had shouted that laicist politics had been the politics of Bismarck. In Bernanos's anti-laicist retrieval of unseen things, French and Latin thought would also be restored to postwar France. Daudet's launch of this literary unknown set the terms of discourse: he was like the great modern Proust (only better); he was descended from the symbolist-Decadent-Catholic family tree; he was the author for whom the postwar had been waiting, the creator of a genuinely Franco-Latin dialectic both *physiologique et mystique*.

Two weeks later, a stinging response to Daudet's launch came from Paul Souday, literary critic for *Le Temps*. A widely read paper that was right-leaning yet moderate in tone, *Le Temps* had been called by Maurras (in a phrase not intended as a compliment) 'the greatest journal of the Republic' prior to 1914.[21] Souday had succeeded the position previously occupied by Gaston Descamps and Anatole France (whom many said was the model for Bernanos's fictional Antoine Saint-Marin). Souday's poison pen lampooned Daudet's launch: 'I had not yet received *Under Satan's Sun*, and I also believe that the volume could not yet be found on the shelves of the bookstores, when M. Léon Daudet announced that it was a *chef-d'œuvre* and that the author – unknown up to this moment – was a genius ... Happy news! We can never have too many *chefs-d'œuvre*, and new geniuses will always be welcome.'[22]

Souday praised the novel's prologue whose pages he considered fine examples of realistic mirror reflections (*vraisemblables*). The heroine, Mouchette, possessed 'an energy and a pride' that were 'almost Stendhalian.' Approving of this 'human part' of the book, Souday judged that the novel didn't 'begin too badly' but added this caveat: the reader was only 'at page 82' in a novel that weighed in at 'three hundred sixty pages.' In opposition to the 'human' part, a 'mystical' part was about to consume more than three-quarters of the total. Since one 'might have hoped for an organization with better equilibrium,' it was 'not yet established that M. Georges Bernanos knows how to compose. It is true that the art of composition is not in fashion today; but a new genius owes it to himself to redress this problem, and not simply follow it like someone in a herd.'

Turning to the second part of the novel, Souday alleged that it both destroyed the overall equilibrium and compromised the mimetic realism (*vraisemblance*) established in the first part. Souday ridiculed the diabolical figure that Bernanos had created to tempt his priestly hero, Father Donissan:

> The strange devil of M. Bernanos evokes absolutely nothing that would tempt the senses, the mind, or the heart of the young cleric ... Let it be understood, I would raise no objection against the [temptation] scene itself, and I do not doubt in the least that it could not be subject to direct observation, nor do I doubt that in the present time one encounters the devil almost daily on the auto-routes. Obviously, *c'est la vie*. All I am saying is that if he is as blundering, boring, and disagreeable as M. Georges Bernanos shows him to be – no doubt modeled on his personal experience – then Satan could not possibly be dangerous, and one is astonished at the terror that he inspires in Fr. Donissan ... At least in the Gospel, the devil effectively offered all the kingdoms of the world to Jesus whom he transported on top of the mountain (*Matt*. IV, 8–9). But he offers nothing to the young vicar. As for me, perhaps I am damning myself, but I would go for a more mouth-watering devil.

Bernanos's Satan provided entertainment, but Souday moved on to a more serious issue. Father Donissan, the protagonist, had 'the gift of reading souls,' and Bernanos's unstable construction ended in unresolved questions: 'Is it a diabolical or a divine gift? Is Satan the author of the gift or merely its announcer? *One doesn't know enough.*' Although Souday did not say so, his words employed the very essence of the *fantastical* discourse nearly a century old. It was precisely the destabilizing introduction of conflicting possible causes and the final uncertainty about what had really happened that had once distinguished the short story from the novel. Souday criticized Bernanos for this mixing of genres: 'There is all the way through this novel a mystical hodgepodge, heterogeneously nonsensical, and frequently incomprehensible.'

Concluding his review of the second part, Souday also ridiculed the priest's visionary gift. After Father Donissan revealed to Mouchette the deepest hidden secrets of her soul, she 'went home, gave herself to the devil, became effectively a demoniac, and slit herself with a razor. The throat open, she dies. What a success for Fr. Donissan's apostolate! He had the time to carry her agonizingly to the parish church and absolve her. Way to go! all the better!'

Arriving at the third and final part of *Satan's Sun*, Souday announced, 'The mystical hodgepodge begins again,' and tried his hand at theology. Recounting the priest's counsel to Mouchette – that having been dominated by Satan, she was not entirely culpable for her actions – Souday objected that here, if he was 'not mistaken,' was 'a negation of free will which still seems to be a heresy.' Later, quoting Bernanos's line saying that God throws human beings 'between Satan and Himself' as 'his last defense,' Souday again suggested heresy: 'This is the devilish blossoming of Manicheanism.'

Concluding his review, Souday faulted the lack of equilibrium between the 'human parts' of the novel and the 'mystical part.' 'In sum, in the *human parts* of this novel there are serious qualities. In the *mystical part*, the style becomes fastidious like terribly tough meat. Huysmans' diableries were more amusing. M. Bernanos will probably make a novelist's career for himself, if he knows how to renew himself. But until that new day, the noise of the apparition of a new genius continues to be a false noise.'

Most striking about Souday's exposition is the way in which it replicated arguments made a century earlier. In September 1833, Charles Augustin Sainte-Beuve (seen above in his use of 'palingenesis') had published a review of George Sand's *Lélia* (1833). 'Since the initial given of *Lélia* is totally real and has its analogues in the society in which we live,' wrote Sainte-Beuve, 'I could not help regretting, despite the prestigious brilliance of this new form, that the author did not confine himself [sic] within the limits of the realistic (*vraisemblable*) novel.' By 'entering into the state of ideal representation or symbol, the characters or the scenes' that had been initially 'grounded' in realism had entered into a 'metamorphosis' during some 'indeterminate moment.' The end result was 'a *mixed and fantastic character* that does not satisfy.'[23] In her preface to the 1839 edition, Sand acknowledged without apology the novel's hybrid nature: '*Lélia* was and remains in my mind a poetic essay, a *fantastical novel* where the characters are *neither completely real ... nor completely allegorical*.'[24] A century later, the terms of discourse remained almost entirely unchanged in Souday's review.

Daudet offered a gleeful counter-attack four days later on the front page of *L'Action française*.[25] Recalling his earlier successful launch of Proust, Daudet happily reported, 'There has come about for the novel of Bernanos ... that which had already come about for the work of Marcel Proust ...: one article was sufficient, signaling to the lettered public something new and great, in order for them to rush out as if to a fire' and empty booksellers' shelves. Now, Bernanos was even out-performing Proust in sheer numbers: 'Six thousand copies of the collection of *Roseau d'or*, published at Plon, were sold out during the day. The new printing has started at 700 copies each day.' Although he was proud of having made a best-seller, Daudet did not want to sound too crassly materialistic: 'You know that I do not think that numbers have an absolute significance in literature as did that idiot in Zola. A *chef-d'œuvre* might well pass by unappreciated at first, and only find its audience very slowly.' For example, 'This was the case for Arthur Rimbaud' (now a Catholic revivalist icon, thanks to Claudel's conversion account).

For Daudet, the instant popularity of Bernanos simply pointed to a postwar fact: 'We've been asking, "Who will be the novelist of the postwar?" And then! He appeared!' Daudet used the phenomenal numbers to verify (and restate) his prophecy two weeks earlier: Bernanos's success had been more extensive than Proust's because of 'the novel being synthetic and not analytic, thus entering into the great category of Balzac and Barbey d'Aurevilly.'

Both Daudet and Souday drew on nineteenth-century heritages in order to analyse Bernanos: Balzac, d'Aurevilly, and (implicitly) Huysmans for one, Flaubert, Zola and (implicitly) Sainte-Beuve for the other. What were in fact two competing visions of reality – Souday's laicist naturalism and Daudet's Catholic dialectical realism – were argued over in terms of the novel's 'construction.' Questions that might normally be thought of as philosophical or theological came to be framed in literary terms. As Joseph Jurt has exhaustively shown, no reader after this exchange could approach *Satan's Sun* as 'a virginal object; it was now laden with the first readers.'[26] The discursive terms in which the novel as a site of contest between two large world-views had been set. In this way, reception by critics (Catholics, non-Catholics, and non-believers) focused on whether 'realism' was compatible with its perceived opposite. This ongoing reception would contribute to the larger project of constructing a postwar Catholic dialectical realism.

Literary Centrists, Political and Catholic Moderates: Manichean Disequilibrium

For politically moderate critics,[27] the analyses tended to follow Souday's lead in seeing an unsuccessful welding of two incompatible world-views. In aesthetic terms, these moderates were extremely traditionalist in their unwillingness to see the genre evolve to include elements not normally associated with mimetic realism (*vraisemblance*).

A week after Daudet's rebuttal of Souday, the 4 May 1926 issue of *Comœ dia* reported that *Satan's Sun* 'lacked one essential thing: celestial light.' It was 'too dark, too bitter, too hostile to humanity.' Its title lied: 'Satan has no sun. He is the night; he is a nocturnal fire, a glimmer portending disaster.' This faint night-time glimmer 'devours, it strays, it strikes with blindness; it clarifies nothing.' Bernanos engaged in false advertising: 'Nothing of the sun comes from Satan. Nothing thrives under his lightning, whether fiery or glacial.' Quoting Bernanos's own description of the novel as a work of 'Catholic steadfastness and of desperate clear-mindedness,' the reviewer retorted: 'A confident Catholic who despairs! Oh! Oh! This demographer who doubles as a hagiographer, doesn't he know any logic? ... It is said that the devil is a logician. Our author studied him up close, but he didn't carry away from him the ability to reason in a rigorous manner.' Like Souday, *Comœ dia* – in the midst of news devoted to music, theater, ballet, and literature – strayed into strangely theological territory: 'A true believer never abandons himself to despair. Hope is the second of the theological virtues, framed by Faith and Charity. If M. Bernanos has no Hope, he has neither Faith nor Charity. He is not Catholic.'

This 'loss of logic' manifested itself as a literary fault, and the novel ended up as a failed construction – an 'assembly' of externally related elements but not an 'ensemble' internally animated: 'Its feverish power contains something one might find in a Stendhal passionate for mysticism *blended with* [*mélangé*] a Balzac tortured by a hidden doubt. This *assembly* allows for a resounding debut. It does not, however, assure that *equilibrium*, that *ensemble* of healthy qualities which, in order to achieve superior ends, unites the rays of light with the shadows, the virtue with the vice, the divine with the human, and moves from the definite that contains us to the infinite that calls us.' 'Melodrama,' writes Peter Brooks, 'starts from and expresses the anxiety brought by a frightening new world in which the traditional patterns of moral order no longer provide the necessary social glue. It plays out the force of that anxiety with the apparent triumph of villainy, and it dissipates it with the eventual victory of virtue.'[28] Although *Comœ dia* attributed Bernanos's problem to a question of construction, the real issue was his transgression of what a religious novel *ought* to look like: namely, a work of melodrama in which virtue (light both infinite and divine) clearly vanquished villainy. *Comœ dia* concluded that this alleged '"Catholic" novel,' winding its way along the 'sulfurous path' where Bernanos seemed as comfortable as a bird in the air, would most certainly 'suffocate his elegant and virtuous clientele.'

Two days later, *Le Journal* for 6 May also found a dualistic vision in Bernanos and suggested this made *Satan's Sun* a 'curious, strange' book with the possibility of causing a shift in 'everyday literary production.' For this reviewer, the novel astonished because it was 'at one and the same time that of a *realist* and that of a *visionary*.' Unfortunately, this *mélange* did not always work: while the realist 'happily came to the help of the visionary in order to render it more acceptable,' it also sometimes happened that the 'visionary damaged the realist.' (We see the nineteenth-century fear again that idealization of a subject 'distorts' reality.) For example, in an effort to 'mystically relate' Mouchette to the priest, Bernanos made the young hysteric say things that, given her lack of catechism training in the Republic's laicist schools, 'she would certainly never have known in reality.' Bernanos's irreconcilable conflict between realist and visionary was a 'weakness of his novel.'

As a consequence, this novel would not appeal to non-believers, nor would it (as *Comœ dia* had predicted) appeal to believers. Curiously, *Le Journal* concluded by echoing Souday's expression of his anxieties in the theological language of 'Manicheanism.' 'But this priest,' asked *Le Journal*, 'who seems to have a greater notion of the presence of Satan than that of God, would he not be considered above all to be Manichean? It has seemed to us that the true saints never have to undergo Desolation except in order to attain very soon Knowledge by Love, so that they might both be more luminous!'[29] In a newspaper otherwise replete with advertisements, economic news, and front-page sensationalist reports of murders, a reader might well have asked what such a theological evaluation (emphasized by 'Desolation, Knowledge, and Love!') was doing in this literary supplement. This recurring trope of Manichean *desolation* and *despair* suggests the articulation in religious language of a larger grief – a culture anxious over the death of an ideological confidence in progress.

On 15 May, *Les Marges* also divided *Satan's Sun* into incompatible components.[30] Here the opposite of the 'novelistic' (*romanesque*) was neither the 'mystical' nor 'supernatural,' but rather the 'apologetic' (*apologétique*). Although the Prologue contained 'excellent novelistic parts,' 'this well-begun novel did not continue. It was arrested.' In the novel's second part, a 'fastidious and absurd' work of 'apologetics' took over. *Les Marges* cautioned the reader not to expect any 'famous books' from Bernanos in the future, for he would write nothing but '*a literature of combat*, without objectivity, without truth, without equilibrium, aggressive and partial,' successful only with a public 'more political than actually religious.' (Ironically, the volume immortalizing Bernanos's prose essays in the French pantheon of the Pleiade series would later be entitled, 'Essays and Writings of Combat.')[31]

Finally, one week later, *L'Intransigeant* praised Bernanos's realistic scenes as signs of his 'genuine talent' as a 'novelist – if not, perhaps, an orthodox hagiographer.'[32] (For hagiography, the reviewer directed the reader to consult the biography of a genuine saint, the Curé d'Ars, for example, as opposed to Father Donissan). But this reviewer also found a 'defect of construction' due to two unresolved positions that caused the book to founder: 'one laicist, one religious' [*l'une laïque, l'une religieuse*] on the theme of Satanic possession.' These 'two absolutely distinct variations' on the theme – the laicist believing that possession could explained physiologically by hysteria, the religious believing that supernatural forces were at work – had 'absolutely no relationship to one another.' The novel faltered in its inability to resolve this gap. Unlike the more sophisticated Souday, this reviewer seemed unaware of the *fantastical* tradition which he had unwittingly just summarized: the text's final indeterminacy and the reader's final uncertainty regarding competing causal explanations.

As the 23–4 May 1926 review in *La Croix* shows, Catholic moderates did not differ significantly from their counterparts in secular publications. The piece, written by Jean Guiraud, editor-in-chief of *La Croix*, and professor of history at Besançon, was entitled 'A Diabolical Novel.'[33] (An infuriated Bernanos wrote Guiraud at the end of May 1926: 'The article in *la Croix* saddened me ... I do not believe that I have written a "diabolical novel." I think that the choice of your title is unfortunate.')[34] Guiraud complained that 'the Christianity which M. Bernanos presents to us is too discouraging, and, in the last analysis, his book is *depressing even for Catholics* and with even greater reason for others.'

Bernanos had not allowed enough time in his novel to speak sufficiently of 'those who counterbalance Satan in the economy of our salvation, namely, the angels and above all the Redeemer' himself. When he was tempted by the devil in the Garden of Gethsemane, Christ had been attended to by angels, yet angels were 'totally absent in the work of M. Bernanos.' When Donissan was made the prey of Evil who 'made himself an illusionist' in order to tempt the priest, 'where was the guardian angel of the priest? Moreover, where was redemptive grace itself?' Of course, one could argue that in the Bible, Christ 'seemed to have been abandoned by his Father' when he cried out in his distress, '*Deus meus, Deus meus, utquid dereliquisti me!*'[35] But this was 'only a moment' which marked the culmination of the powers of darkness – the use of shadow, perhaps, in an overall aesthetic design. Even during his 'bloody agony in Gethsemane,' Christ was consoled by an angel.

Guiraud could not 'see this grace very well in the work of M. Bernanos.' For example, Father Donissan had not been able to stop the suicide of Mouchette. Or again, the priest had immediately assumed that the impulse to raise a young man from the dead was a temptation to pride coming from the devil and not a grace from God. In short (and this seemed to be the crux of the reviewer's problem), the priest was a defeated warrior: 'in this battle [*lutte*] of the priest against Satan, the priest, in spite of his sanctity, is made a *figure of vanquishment.* Even aided by divine grace, his liberty was not able to disengage itself from the diabolical grip and to surmount this test which God only permits in order to better glorify his elected. And there lies a serious reproach which I would make against the novel of M. Bernanos: the action of Satan is presented to us with such power that it *eclipses* the powers of both human liberty and of divine grace.'[36] Curiously, while Souday had not hesitated to employ the theological word 'Manichean,' the confessional *La Croix* held back. Nevertheless, the accusation was implicit: this depressing and discouraging vision of a battle between forces of God and Satan was a Manichean one in which *Satan's Sun* eclipsed free will.

The confessional Dominican *La Revue des jeunes* did not hold back.

Louis Artus, himself a 'Catholic novelist' who had also just published a 'Catholic novel,' concluded that he would be pleased to discover 'reassuring possibilities in a clear soul against Jansenist suggestions' such as those found in the 'Saint of Lumbre.' In the meantime, Artus prayed 'that this hope remain with us who are assisting – accompanied by a jazz-band [*accompagnement de jazz-band*] – at the atrocious end of the world.'[37]

Comœ dia complained that Bernanos portrayed 'the anxious combat between the angels and the demons, with humanity in the middle, but overwhelmed with fatality, consecrated to emptying the cup of bitterness to its dregs.'[38] *La Croix*, in contrast, complained that there were no angels in sight. Starting from different premises they arrived at the same judgment: Bernanos was depressing, discouraging, dark, and worst of all, full of defeat. Both the confessional and secular moderate press strongly resisted Bernanos's implicit yet central point: a culture that had survived the war of 1914–18 needed to abandon its optimistic faith in human agency and progress. Although the reviews used apocalyptic terms, their language suggested thoroughly historical and terrestrial fears. Abbé Charlier summed up this concern: 'Our generation has more need that one should display God rather than Satan, or, if one likes, that one should show God victorious over Satan, even in this world.'[39]

In this sense, the moderates who accused Bernanos of a too-dark heterodoxy seemed unaware of the orthodoxy they claimed for themselves. 'Christianity is an anti-tragic vision of the world,' George Steiner has pointedly observed. 'In the drama of Christian Life, the arrow beats against the wind but points upward. Being a threshold to the eternal, the death of a Christian hero can be an occasion for sorrow but not for tragedy.'[40] Moderate criticisms of Bernanos, undoubtedly colored by postwar grief, were perhaps more neoclassical than Christian.

In summary, if we schematize moderate reviews, we see binary oppositions that allegedly foiled the novel's unified construction:

ASSEMBLY V. ENSEMBLE
DESPERATE CLEAR MINDEDNESS V. GREAT CATHOLIC CONFIDENCE
DISCOURAGING V. CONSOLING
DARK V. LIGHT
ROMANCIER AS A RATIONALIST V. THE SUBJECT-MATTER OF THE *SURNATUREL*
REALIST V. VISIONARY
ROMANESQUE V. *APOLOGÉTIQUE*
LAICIST V. RELIGIOUS

For these moderate reviewers, the antinomies could not be resolved: one and the same novel could not successfully synthesize such radically incompatible approaches to the world. Taking a traditionalist approach to the genre, these writers were unable (or unwilling) to imagine the novel's development beyond *vraisemblance*. Although today's reader, after thinking about what '"reality" in a work of literature can possibly be,' might take for granted the impossibility of maintaining a 'realist' aesthetic, these reviews of *Satan's Sun* let us see just how tenaciously naturalism's grip endured into the 1920s.[41]

Political and Catholic Rightists: Metaphors of Synthesis

In contrast to the traditionalist reviews by moderates, those from the political and Catholic right tended to be more progressive in their capacity (and desire) to expand the genre's inclusion of non- or super-naturalist elements. This apparent paradox echoes 1920s trends already noted above, including the nostalgic attitudes of avant-gardists and today's sense that postwar 'modernism' meant the rejection of 'everything progressive and challenging in the earlier twentieth century.'[42] Right-leaning reviews pushed the evolution of the novel as a realist form that could accommodate the dreamlike, the eternal, and the 'mystical.' In this regard, they shared fundamental concerns with the surrealism of Breton, the neoclassicism of Cocteau, and the High Modernism of Eliot.

On 15 May 1926, the *Revue de France* noted that, on one level, the 'moving and perfect recitation' of the novel's prologue could be read simply as yet one more naturalist chronicle: the 'banal adventure of the daughter of a petit bourgeois,' a 'perverse, vicious, cruel' young girl who comes unhinged by madness. Mouchette's encounters with her lovers reminded one of 'certain episodes from *Madame Bovary* (Emma at the home of Rodolphe de la Huchette) or certain pages from *A Life*' by Maupassant.[43]

But suddenly, 'strange infernal lights and sulphurous fumes' burst out like wildfires in this small country village. Immediately the reader knew that there was more than met the eye. Mouchette's problem was 'not merely madness' but rather 'Satan who was haunting her.' What had begun so predictably as a realist critique of petit-bourgeois life in the countryside – 'these various rural events given to us by analogous stories of realism' – was suddenly raised beyond itself [*surélève au-dessus*].

Far from being an object of ridicule, Father Donissan, evoking in the reviewer 'the great cursed priests of Barbey d'Aurevilly,' was described here as a cross between the saintly Curé d'Ars and Sigmund Freud. Satan had given him 'the gift of seeing' into the hidden depths of souls, a gift of 'discerning, within the blink of an eye, the most secret thoughts, the most intimate of inner reaches.' The priest could read Mouchette's soul 'as if it were a book.' He could 'see' exactly what Mouchette was with a 'superhuman lucidity,' and he revealed to her 'the secret of all this misery.' Scientific psychologists might persist in their belief that such misery could be read as a complex of nineteenth-century biological inheritance, an 'entanglement' (quoting from the novel) 'of effects and causes, of acts and intentions.' But the priest read misery, not from its surface symptoms, but rather as it was 'grasped from within – the most hidden, the best defended.'

Bernanos could 'excavate' or 'dig deeply into life' (*fouiller*), representing it as horribly as the next realist. But he could also 'transpose,' simultaneously excavating and elevating (the musical metaphor of transposition into another key fleshing out the meaning of *surélèver*). The use of 'digging' seemed intended to recall Huysmans: he had used the same metaphor in *Là-bas*, describing the spiritual naturalist as a 'well-digger' getting to the mysterious bottom of hysterical symptoms. Not surprisingly, the reviewer here cited a work that had just been published, Henri Bachelin's *J.-K. Huysmans, from Literary Naturalism to Mystical Naturalism* (1926).[44] Just as Rouault's reviewers turned back to Huysmans's embrace of the Flemish Primitives to give postwar art a futural past, so here the critic interpreted Bernanos as the realization of Huysmans's vision of a synthetic mystical naturalism. In sum, much of Bernanos's plot – unbearable rural boredom, a slit throat, hysterical suicide, blood and gore soaking a poor country curate's cassock, his eventual commitment to an insane asylum – could have been written by any naturalist author. Yet, this plot was raised beyond itself, transposed into a supernatural register by Satan's gift of vision to Donissan, the 'naive mystic' (*mystique ingénue*).

Several days later, *La Revue Bleue* of 19 June continued the search for metaphors that would express transformation and transposition, laying out a vision that 'interwove' disparate elements into 'a single web.'[45] Beginning with an assault on positivistic psychology, the reviewer suggested that Bernanos's Doctor Gallet was a 'medical quack,' a 'simpleton nourished on the bible of Raspail.'[46] He saw nothing in Mouchette but naturalist stereotypes of lower-class inherited degeneration: a 'girl with nerves, from an alcoholic family, tormented by a precocious pregnancy.' But such surface observations missed the unseen motion: 'Do we not already have a premonition that there is something else in this explosion of an insane and cruel adolescence, ignited by the fire of disappointed pride, and that this scene of hysteria, of delirium, is masking over [*déguise*] a "possession"?' Quoting from the novel – 'But the facts are nothing: the tragic is in the heart.' – the reviewer glossed Bernanos: 'It doesn't suffice to read the story and the brutal, disconcerting drama where it is concentrated. What is necessary is to read it in the heart: a difficult task.' Far from an antiquated spirituality, the reviewer concludes: 'Now there's a psychology in the fashion of the day, apparently influenced by Freud.' Father Donissan was perhaps the quintessential therapist for Mouchette: 'With a superhuman lucidity, he could see what she was.'

The ultimate *mélange* of mysticism and realism occurred, however, in the scene recounting the priest's night-time encounter with a *fantastical* figure – either a horse trader or a supernatural demon, it was impossible to be sure which – on the road. Here, the two series of images, the realistic one of a mere mortal, the *hallucinant* other of a demon, seemed to 'follow one another and interweave with one another [*se mêlent*]' so completely that 'they form a single web [*trame unique*].' In this alchemical union the illusory and the real became 'confused with one another' (*se confondent*), for the priest as well as the reader.

In conclusion, *La Revue bleue* explained the financial and literary success of *Satan's Sun* as Daudet did: it revealed how much the postwar generation was 'obsessed' with the 'anxiety over the problem of evil' that had a 'stranglehold' on 'our time' – an 'age of fetters and despair, an age of violence and brutality.' Certainly, Bernanos's novel was horribly realistic, 'violent' and 'brutal,' and reading it induced no small measure of 'suffering' in itself! But the reader who persevered in climbing up its steep slope would arrive at 'a vast extension of the horizon' and a consequently dizzying, 'vertiginous vision of the abyss.' Neither pleasant nor restful, Bernanos's art was sure to 'rattle the nerves' and would be too strong for some to take. Its power was undeniable.

Finally, the mid-summer issue of *Chronique des lettres françaises* admitted that *Satan's Sun* was 'not really a novel according to the rules' of realism. Nevertheless, it responded in its very depths to 'the mystical aspirations with which, in spite of everything, today's minds are obsessed.'[47] Only a dialectical form could adequately express such mystical aspirations while employing literary realism: 'Donissan ... encounters Satan, his enemy, face-to-face *under the human form* of a horse trader over whom he finally triumphs after a tragic battle.' Here, the author who had the 'audacity to imagine the Spirit of Evil *under the most realist form* in the very midst of the twentieth century' attained to '*a pure supernatural beauty* ...' *Satan's Sun* introduced the reader to 'the very highest spheres of spirituality ... mystical souls tormented by moral grandeur.' For this new work, not easily categorized as a novel, confession or *récit*, the customary taxonomies of 'literary language' had not yet invented a name.

To be sure, there were exceptions on the right as there were in every political category. Writing in *Le Petit Journal*, Raymond Escholier humorously cautioned that, given Bernanos's inclination to 'the Manichean error,' had this been thirteenth century, 'we would most certainly watch [Bernanos] burn with the curé of Lumbres – this Perfect One – at the stake of Montségur.'[48] In general, however, reviews from the political right differed most from moderate reviews in their willingness to expand the genre by accommodating non-realism. In them we see the attempts to overcome simple binary oppositions and articulate a dialectical realism:

THE ILLUSORY AND THE REAL
BECOME CONFUSED WITH
ONE ANOTHER

THE TWO SERIES OF IMAGES
INTERWEAVE
A SINGLE WEB

THE SPIRIT OF EVIL
IS IMAGINED UNDER
THE MOST REALIST FORM

ANALOGOUS TALES GIVEN US BY REALISM
ARE ELEVATED ABOVE THEMSELVES
BY THE METAPHYSICAL CHARACTER OF SATAN

EXCAVATES
BUT ALSO
TRANSPOSES

Metaphors of intermingling – to interweave (*se mêler*), to be confused (*se confonder*), to excavate and elevate (*fouiller/surélèver*), to transpose (*transposer*) – attempted to represent surface and depth not as simple oppositions, but rather as two types of reality capable of hybridization, mixture, interpenetration, or mediation. They were an attempt to overcome (again citing Peter Brooks) the 'logic of the excluded middle (the very logic of melodrama).'[49]

The *Chronique des lettres françaises* correctly noted that Bernanos's unorthodox novel defied known categories of conventional 'literary language.' However, there were critics and theoreticians avidly working on constructing a name for this postwar 'Catholic novel.' Each of them exploited the possibilities inherent in traditional Catholic notions of hylomorphism.

Literary Hylomorphism: Émile Baumann, Frédéric Lefèvre, Robert Garric

Beyond short reviews found in the daily press, Bernanos's novel provoked more extended reflections as well. Trying to theorize *Satan's Sun* as fitting within the orthodox parameters of both the 'novel' as well as of Catholicism, boundaries between literary criticism and theology became fluid. As the notion of a 'Catholic novel' evolved into that of a 'mystical novel,' the genre became a site of working out postwar convictions about the largest horizons against which humanity lives out its existence.

Three figures in particular contributed significantly to different literary formulations of the hylomorphic idea. First, Émile Baumann was a writer whose novels dating back to 1906 had gone through several editions by 1926. He also produced several non-fiction works, including *The Golden Ring of Great Mystics from Saint Augustine to Catherine Emmerich* (1924) and *The Life and Works of Several Great Saints* (1926).[50] As *Satan's Sun* appeared, another novel by Baumann had just been published, along with a long study devoted to him as a 'Catholic Novelist' in *La Revue des jeunes*.[51] Second, Frédéric Lefèvre's activity on the front line in promoting Bernanos's novel did not go unnoticed by either supporters or detractors.[52] Presumably he did this not only because he believed in Bernanos's work and used critical reception of the novel as a venue for setting out his own literary vision, but also because he had a personal interest in seeing the novel succeed: along with Maritain and Massis, Lefèvre was one of the *Roseau d'Or*'s directors. Third, Robert Garric was a veteran of the trenches who returned to teach French literature at several venues, including the Sorbonne (one of his students in 1925 was the young Simone de Beauvoir). Evidently a man of enormous energy and talent, Garric also directed *La Revue des jeunes* from 1924 to 1939, maintained a large correspondence with a wide variety of the day's major figures, and won the Grand Prix of the Académie française for his depictions of the working-class district that had terrified middle-class Paris during the Commune, *Belleville, Scenes from Popular Life* (1928).[53] Garric was best known for having founded the Équipes sociales in 1921, a progressivist Catholic social movement for youth. This trio illustrates the complex variety of persons and institutions that helped invent and maintain the 'Catholic novel' of the 1920s.

Baumann published his essay 'The Possibilities of the Catholic Novel' in the May 1926 issue of Bernoville's *Les Lettres*. His dialectical approach to the subject owed a significant debt to Huysmans: 'The Catholic novelist must be together at once a realist and a supernaturalist.' But then Baumann diverged: 'I say "realist" but not at all a "naturalist." "Catholic" and "naturalist": these two words scream when seen together. The naturalist attaches himself to "the fact for fact's sake"; he sets himself up in front of creation as if he were a notary clerk taking inventory of personal property ... What he grasps in the human being is its animality; he takes note of atavistic defects, the meanness of its habits, the hideousness of its vices.' 'Naturalism,' quipped Baumann, 'is so inhuman that even its fanatical followers themselves are barely able to confine themselves to it.'[54]

While both the Catholic realist and the naturalist breathed the same 'common air' – 'the nausea of ugliness' – they attributed different significances to this single factual perception. Baumann made this distinction using traditional sacramental language of substance and accident. The naturalist only recognized in ugliness '*the accidental play* of unconscious forces' while the Catholic realist discovered in it 'the consequences of sin – and at the end of even the most atrocious dramas he sees the Redemption glimmering.' Like Maurice de Wulf, Baumann perhaps alluded to Stendhal when he called the art of the naturalist 'a mirror that reflects gloomy surfaces.' Such a mirror allegedly reflected reality without distortion, but Christianity saw things differently: the art of the Christian realist penetrated '*to the very substance* and to the roots of events.'[55]

Baumann's gloss on the word 'substance' echoed both Maritain and Puy (on 'subsistence'), identifying the Creator as creation's deepest reality. 'The notion of *substance* – only Catholicism possesses it in its fulness. In all the things of the world, [the notion] reveres the divine hand that creates them and saves them.' In contrast to the neoclassicist ultramontanist aesthetic, 'Jesus did not bring to humanity a chimera of perfection. He wanted to suffer and die in a real way [*réellement*].' To justify the orthodoxy of his claim, Baumann quoted a fragment of Aquinas's medieval hymn (later immortalized by Mozart, among others) that linked the doctrine of Christ's Real Presence in the transubstantiated bread with his real presence on the Cross:

Ave verum Corpus natum / de Maria Virgine:
Hail true Body born / of the Virgin Mary:
Vere passum immolatum / in cruce pro homine:
Truly suffered and sacrificed / on the cross for humanity.

Aquinas's hymn not only insisted on Christ's true presence in the bread. It also stood against various heterodox theologians throughout the centuries (e.g., the Docetists) who, in an effort to preserve the divinity from the possibility of undergoing suffering (and hence change), said that it had only 'seemed' from the outward appearances that God had suffered in Christ. Aquinas held the orthodox line: the human being on the Cross had not been a bodily disguise who suffered while the Godhead remained protected from undergoing change; it had truly been Christ, a person of the Godhead, undergoing passion. Orthodoxy entailed a harsh realism. '*Vere passum, immolatum,*' Baumann quoted. 'The faith in the Real Presence remains the foundation of Catholic realism.'[56]

Repeating his own remarks delivered four years earlier at the 1922 'Week of Catholic Writers,' Baumann pushed his claim even further: 'Realism and supernaturalism comprise only one thing.' What the Christian saw 'behind the horizon' of mundane reality made difficult the expression of 'the enlargement of earthly things' provided by such a wider set. Only the 'visionary,' the 'contemplative' or the 'artist with faith' were capable of seeing '*the infinite converging in the poor spark* of our lives.'[57] This synthetic grasp of the finite within an infinite horizon suggested 'the immense possibilities of Christian art' in the novel.

For a traditionalist (like Sainte-Beuve or Souday), a hybridized novel represented an aesthetic monstrosity; for Baumann, the novel as 'the most arduous of all literary forms' was the ideal medium for representing such convergences. Baumann's language suggested Bergsonian distinctions: ordinarily, 'we live in the sphere of appearances.' In order that these phenomena might not overwhelm us by 'the weight of their attractions' and their 'terror and disgust,' we customarily view things with a pragmatic eye. However, the Catholic novelist needed to see them with a different eye, 'under the light of divine regions,' in order to 'represent them faithfully.' No other genre was capable of such a 'complex play' as the Catholic novel: when 'a vast subject interlaces [*entrelace*] characters and settings, making a great vital idea' – *idée vitale* echoed *élan vital* –

'suddenly appear beneath the multiple figures and mass of episodes, this is equivalent to introducing into the plane of the real [*le plan du réel*] a system of forces, almost an uncreated world [*un monde incréé*].' Baumann inverted the traditional terms of realism: for the nineteenth-century realists, the introduction of anything besides observed facts would 'distort' reality. For Baumann, representation without distortion *required* the introduction of the unseen in order to represent reality in its fullness. Thus, the 'Catholic and mystic novelist' needed to know how to 'make hold together in a synthesis [*synthèse*] the relations of the visible and the invisible.'[58]

Baumann concluded his general remarks by defining 'the *integral* Catholic novel' as a form that could 'look at life as closely as one might attain' while simultaneously seeking 'to clarify all those aspects which come from the abysses on high or from below by means of this mysterious flame.' The introduction of non-realistic material did not limit the novel. On the contrary: 'What I want to stress is the enlargement of novelistic horizons by supernaturalism.'[59] Baumann's enlargement echoed contemporaneous movements in surrealism and magical realism.

Applying these reflections to *Satan's Sun*, Baumann praised certain elements. It was able to synthesize (*synthétise*) successfully both 'a strong and condensed realism' and 'a sharp, subtle, bitter penetration of souls.' Even in his realist descriptions, Bernanos maintained a 'continuous intensity, excessive even, of *hallucination*.' He had a talent for painting the 'transcendental glimmers' that were 'projected from within by the exteriors' of things. Bernanos's vision owed its power, for the most part, 'to *the realism supported by supernaturalist terror*.'[60] Baumann's connotations of the supernatural are worth underscoring: the penetration of souls was 'bitter,' real life was marked by 'terror,' and far from being comforting, (invoking Chateaubriand) 'the holy law of sacrifice' ruled. This uncomfortable supernaturalism closely resembled Rudolph Otto's *Idea of the Holy* (1917) as a mystery simultaneously 'terrifying and fascinating' – *mysterium tremendum et fascinans*.[61]

In the end, however, Baumann felt Bernanos's Father Donissan was 'a wild Jansenist, almost a Manichean.' To represent the triumph of Satan was equivalent to despairing of mercy, the unforgivable sin against the Spirit. In Baumann's negative final judgment, the difficulty of dialectic was clear. On the one hand, 'A Catholic novel must never be an insipid false idyll.' On the other hand, 'This expression of disorder, as strong as it might be, is it nevertheless going to inflict despondency on the souls of its readers?' Baumann concluded: 'The possibilities of the Catholic novel are immense; its difficulties equal them. May they not put off young writers ...'[62]

Baumann used explicitly theological language to articulate a literary hylomorphism. In another articulation, Frédéric Lefèvre kept his language within secular parameters that could appeal broadly. On 17 April, just ten days after Daudet's *L'Action française* launch, Lefèvre's 'Interview with Georges Bernanos' appeared in the *Nouvelles littéraires*. (Of all the interviews that Lefèvre published throughout the years, this was the only one whose final version was edited by the interviewee.)[63] On 28 July, Lefèvre published *Georges Bernanos*, a small book that contained the 'Interview,' Bernanos's 'Letter to Frédéric Lefèvre' published earlier in the June *Chroniques* of the *Roseau d'Or*, and Lefèvre's own essay, 'Georges Bernanos and the Contemporary Novel.'[64]

In this essay, Lefèvre examined *Satan's Sun* by comparing it to another blockbuster published that same year, André Gide's *The Counterfeiters*. (Lefèvre's method imitated both Daudet's comparison of Bernanos and Proust and Maritain's juxtaposition of Maurras and Gide. Homosexual celebrities seemed to bestow a certain aura of modernity on men of the right while at the same time serving as foils.) At first glance, a less likely comparison could hardly be made. In contrast to Bernanos's thoroughly metaphysical novel, Gide's exploited an extended metaphor about homosexual passing. (Gide had published *Corydon* two years earlier; in 1926 he also published *Unless the Grain of Wheat Die*, his autobiography that frankly talked about his homosexuality.) The counterfeiting of coins in a private boys' school symbolized everyday falsifications of both students and elders by means of outward conformity and convention.

At second glance, the two novels shared common themes of realism/mysticism and surface/depth. Gide's fictional Edouard jots notes in his journal about the novel he wants to write: 'I am beginning to catch sight of what I might call the "deep-lying subject" of my book. It is – it will be – no doubt, the rivalry between the real world and the representation of it which we make to ourselves. The manner in which the world of appearances imposes itself upon us, and the manner in which we try to impose on the outside world our own interpretation – this is the drama of our lives.'[65]

In his essay on Bernanos, registering his great esteem for Gide's *Counterfeiters*, Lefèvre quoted from another entry in Edouard's journal: 'I lean with a fearful attraction over the depths of each creature's possibilities and weep for all that lies atrophied under the heavy lid of custom and morality.'[66] Within the context of *Corydon*, *Counterfeiters*, and *Unless the Grain*, the 'heavy lid of custom' suggested the suffocating masks that lead homosexuals to leave possibilities unused and hence atrophied. Lefèvre placed Gide's contempt for bourgeois values within the larger framework of the Great War: 'We know well that there are in each being all these possibilities, those for good and those for evil. Take the war, for only one example, but one that makes an impact. It revealed to many the marvelous possibilities of heroism and sacrifice in those whom, before this sorrowful event, one might only have believed capable of mediocrity and indifference.'[67] Having positively framed Gide's work, Lefèvre concluded however that Gide's amoralism was 'monotonous.' By declaring that 'every act has the same importance,' Gide had created a world that suffered 'no sort of anxiety concerning the conduct of existence, whether these anxieties be moral or religious.' His 'closed novel' was a 'negative world, so totally inadequate' to the complex moral world that we know exists 'with all the essential certitude of our souls.'[68]

In contrast, Bernanos had 'reintroduced the sense of the supernatural' into the novel, making it one of those 'few works in our epoch of transition' both 'powerful enough and complete enough' to command total support in 'this anemic postwar time.' To explain Bernanos's novelty, Lefèvre reached for the term '*compénétration*.' The word exploited the ability of the Latin prefix 'com-' to suggest the dialectical transformation of two distinct entities into a third communion greater than the sum of its parts. In *Satan's Sun*, two distinct planes were at play: 'The bitter, spiritual and supernatural reality appears on the first plane even as the exterior contours – the sensible forms that alone reveal both people and objects to us in everyday life – become *hazy in an atmosphere of dream*. Only from time to time does this strange suprasensible life slip out [*s'éclipse*], and thus we perceive *more than the ordinary aspect of beings* ... The most supple, the most nuanced, the most enlivened style – *the style of a great creator* – marvelously renders this *compénétration* of different planes.'[69]

If Lefèvre's definition sounded much like the surrealist's aim of uniting 'reality and the dream state,' it was not coincidental. André Breton's 1924 *Manifesto* (as noted above) had explicitly quoted from Pierre Reverdy's earlier reflections of 1918: '*The image ... cannot be born from a comparison but from a juxtaposition or two more or less distant realities ...*' In 1917, Lefèvre had grouped Reverdy along with Cocteau, Jacob and others as a 'Cubist' – an appellation Reverdy himself rejected. Lefèvre's use of *compénétration* was the product of nearly ten years of reflection involving both Reverdy and Breton, and Bernanos's novel provided an opportunity to articulate the result.

Like numerous other reviewers, Lefèvre chose the scene in which Father Donissan meets the horse dealer on the dark night-time road as a prime example of *compénétration*. At times, the figure seemed to assume the form of Satan – but Bernanos's prose never allowed the reader to be sure. Lefèvre praised this scene that exemplified the 'passage from the supernatural plane to the sensible plane' in which the mind 'genuinely oscillates from the feeling that this really was a case of meeting the devil and that the figure of the human horse dealer is a dream, to the feeling that the dealer is the reality [*la réalité*] and the devil is the unreality [*l'irréalité*].[70] For Lefèvre, this *compénétration* was the effect of Bernanos's 'style,' and style was 'before everything else, *integration and synthesis*, the agreeable ability to weave and unweave an ever-wider web of connections and relationships.'[71] In contrast to Baumann's overtly Catholic language, Lefèvre's contribution to the formation of a literary hylomorphism was a firmly secular language deeply indebted to his reflections on cubism and surrealism, Reverdy and Breton.

In addition to Baumann and Lefèvre, the theorizing of the 'Catholic novel' or 'mystic novel' as a matter of 'planes' owed a third significant debt to Robert Garric, professor of French literature. Writing in *La Revue des jeunes* (of which he was the director) in July 1926, Garric preferred the term 'mystic novel' to 'Catholic novel.'[72] By this he meant one in which 'the supernatural is on the first plane (or foreground: *au premier plan*), and nothing is comprehensible, nor even interesting, if one does not see *le sens fondamental* of this action of God which fills up the entire scene.' (The multivalent denotations of *sens* as 'sense,' 'significance,' or 'direction' could translate *le sens fondamental* as 'the deepest significance' giving the dramatic action its 'fundamental direction.') The primary action of the plot could not be read off the surfaces, but only discerned as the deepest meaning of what was happening 'on the first plane,' that is, the 'plane of eternity.'[73]

Perhaps following Maritain's lead, Garric drew a liberating conclusion: if a novel's fundamental significance could not be read off its secondary plane – that is, the visible plane of outward shapes – then its deepest sense did not depend on its subject matter but rather on its motivating forces. This led Garric to set aside the 'term much abused today, Catholic novels' in favour of his preferred 'mystic novel.' 'There are no Catholic novels any more than there are Catholic finances or Catholic architecture: there are Catholics who write novels,' concluded the literature professor. 'These novels are good or bad, depending on the talent and the temperament of their author, as well as his *métier*, regardless of whether his faith has anything whatsoever to do with this genius and this technique.'[74] Just as an artwork's religious significance for Maritain was not about outward shapes or copies but rather about interior (and invisible) forms, so for Garric, a novel could not 'be called Catholic just because its author is, or because a priest plays a role in the book, or because a religious problem is posed for which the author gives a Catholic solution.' It could be 'called mystic only if the supernatural is the *secret spring of the work* and if divine action continuously moves the souls of the characters.'[75] Like an Aristotelian *entelechy*, the secret spring animated the material on the secondary plane with life, motion, and direction.

For Garric, what made *Satan's Sun* 'mystical' was not that the protagonist was a priest, but rather the drama's subterranean source – especially the unsettled ambiguity over the source of Donissan's gift of vision. This was the *sens fondamental* without which *Satan's Sun* was quite literally senseless, lacking both meaning and dramatic direction.[76] Although they differed among themselves in both style and judgment, Baumann, Lefèvre, and Garric all helped construct a hylomorphic understanding of the Catholic or mystical novel as a dialectical synthesis of both realism and supernaturalism.

Polluted Protagonists: François Mauriac, Victor Poucel, Gabriel Marcel

The dialectical composition of the world was one issue that *Satan's Sun* provoked; the complex structure of Father Donissan's sanctity was another. If Father Donissan was a redemptive figure – and there was a heated debate over whether he was – then redemption came through human failure, not moral action or wilful strength. More disturbing, it seemed that the mysterious crushing of that human will was central to this redemption, and this apparently by the very God to whom Donissan had offered his life. The figure of this Suffering Servant, completely lacking in the world's eyes and 'the most abject of men' (Isaiah 53:3), was thoroughly scriptural and traditional. (Read every Good Friday at Catholic services, the passage and its figure were beloved by Bloy, Rouault, and Bernanos.) Postwar critics understandably recoiled from the neurasthenic figure of a young priest who seemed to be dull-witted, ill-mannered, and in the end, 'vanquished.' Yet to the patient reader, Bernanos passed on his own belief in material limits – finitude, failure, and perhaps worldly defeat – as possible and perhaps even privileged carriers of invisible grace. Like Rouault, Bernanos made the polluted protagonist a masked history of eternity.

Three critics especially contributed to this vision of the unlikely Saint of Lumbres. The first, François Mauriac, had already established himself as a central literary postwar figure (*The Kiss to the Leper* [1922]; *Génitrix* [1923]; *The Desert of Love* [1925]), and he was working on what was to be his classic, *Thérèse Desqueyroux* (1927).[77] Second, Father Victor Poucel, S.J., having taught rhetoric in Alexandria (Egypt) for nine years, lived in Avignon from 1919 to 1930, working as a writer and also as a literary critic for the journal *Études*. Significantly, Poucel had suffered a long psychological depression after five years of Jesuit formation in the Near East and spent seven years recovering (mostly in Switzerland). Undoubtedly, this shaped his religious vision that found kinship in Bernanos's, one described as 'simultaneously symbolist and mystic: the visible, sign of the invisible, worked on the believer in a sacramental manner, in giving him God.'[78] Third, Gabriel Marcel, a disciple of Bergson, was a philosopher (as well as a playwright and music critic) whose rehabilitation of metaphysics would lead him into phenomenology and existentialism. Although Marcel did not formally convert to Catholicism until 1929, his *Metaphysical Journal* (1927) conveys a sense of his immersion in thoughts about mystery during this period.[79] These three would attempt to think through individual sanctity in a way that was not (in Poucel's phrase) 'rectilinear.'

On 19 June 1926, Mauriac published an essay on the front page of *Nouvelles littéraires* entitled 'Mystic Novels.'[80] The reviewer for *Comœ dia* had correctly warned that Bernanos's 'sulfurous path' would 'suffocate his elegant and virtuous clientele.' Mauriac transformed this warning into a bold manifesto, announcing that from now on the Catholic novel would no longer be the comforting palliative it used to be. 'Pascal reminds us with contempt,' began Mauriac, 'how the Jews cried out to Moses: "Tell us agreeable things and we will listen to you." And Pascal adds: "As if agreeability must regulate credibility!" Agreeability does not regulate the credibility of mystical novelists today. The Catholic novel is no longer what it used to be: a book primarily both edifying and consoling. *Under Satan's Sun* has troubled and terrified a number of good souls who, with all their heart, believe in God, but have forgotten that they also believe in the Devil.'

Mauriac did not deny that 'the consolations of religion' still existed. But these consolations were 'not at all that upon which the new religious writers' wanted to elaborate. There was plenty in the works of these new writers 'to confuse that immense crowd of Christians who have never seen anything more in religious law than a certain number of prescriptions meant to assure them of a comfortable eternity.' For this reason, it was not the 'least of M. Bernanos's merits' to have rudely fixed readers' minds on 'the mystery of Evil which has always seemed so simple that we never thought about it.' But now readers realized that '*Satan's Sun*, no more than death, cannot really be looked at directly in the face.' What kind of vision was needed, then, to examine closely what cannot be seen?

Mauriac offered his own version of the required sacramental vision: 'A mystic novelist is a great novelist when – even while painting the *unverifiable* – he does not allow us even a second of leisure to question ourselves about the *reality* of that which he is showing us.' Mauriac's sense of literature was hylomorphic: just as the *entelechy* never existed apart from the matter it informed, so too there could be no representation of the *unverifiable* apart from the verifiable.[81] Thus, a mystic novelist had to walk a tightrope: he must lead us 'barefoot into the realm of the "*surréel*"' – the use of Breton's term was Mauriac's – yet, at the same time, not 'turn our heads' too much.

Since our vision is so seriously limited, we cannot study either God or the Foul One directly. We can only study the human being in its reality, 'neither the solitaire nor the saint, but the man of the herd, the one like us, our brother.' By restricting the subject matter to mundane humanity, even 'the least of readers can verify for themselves whether our painting is a lie or the truth.' This was the way that the *surréel* and the *réel* could be held together: by focusing on the human person who is the site in which both realms intersect. Whereas Baumann, Lefèvre, and Garric were interested in large dramatic stages, Mauriac turned his attention to the *dramatis personae*.

Father Victor Poucel also focused on the dramatic character and responded to the charge that Father Donissan, the 'Saint of Lumbres,' was no saint. 'M. Donissan is not a rectilinear saint,' replied Poucel, 'he is not a saint whom I see being easily canonized. But isn't there something of the saint in him? Are the only existing saints rectilinear ones, besides those in our imaginations which are a bit too geometrical?' For Poucel, Bernanos was right: the world of human motivations is a mixed bag of illusion and clarity, evil and grace, darkness and light. 'Is not the world of religious fervor populated with these incomplete creatures,' asked Poucel, 'half-saints, risqué saints, off-colored, many-colored – in whom two contrary actions, one from the good and one from the evil spirit, visibly share the hours?' Reading Bernanos through the eyes of Loyola, Poucel noted that discerning one strand from another is never easy and sometimes not even possible. ('Read the *Rules for the Discernment of Spirits* of Saint Ignatius,'

Poucel urged, 'they are categorical enough on the subject.') For Loyola, graceful rays were sometimes violent, light appearing as darkness, shaking us out of complacency and encrusted habits. The converse was also true: the 'illusions' of the Prince of Darkness, masked as the Light-bearer (*lux* + *-fer*), were 'mixed-up' or 'muddled' [*mêlées*] with the 'sun-rays of grace': this was 'one of the laws of the spiritual life.'[82]

If Bernanos had represented this confusion in all its gore, then one might 'contest the good taste' of his approach, but one did not have 'the right, at least, to refuse to a novelist the permission to write a novel.' As a pastor, Poucel recognized some danger in representing things so graphically, and on account of Bernanos's 'crudity in the painting of sin,' he admitted he would not 'recommend this novel indiscriminately to every reader.'[83] Having expressed this reservation, Poucel saw in *Satan's Sun* not only a 'remarkably Christian sensibility' beneath its 'incoherent exterior,' but also the answer to an urgent question about art in a time during which existentialism and expressionism – and the keyword *anxiety* – were becoming increasingly salient. 'Can one advance much further in the literary expression of life,' asked Poucel, 'and mix into the invention of the novel *this anxiety which forms the true foundation of human life*?' (Poucel's phrase appeared a year before Heidegger's: '*That in the face of which one has anxiety* [*das Wovor der Angst*] *is Being-in-the-world as such*.')[84] 'The suffering of God, the anxiety of salvation,' asked Poucel, 'will the novel be able to sustain this dangerous worsening of the situation? Many think that it will withstand it,' he responded, evidently agreeing with them. 'I'm not speaking here of what some call the "edifying novel," a genre condemned practically without question based simply on its title. Before everything else, a book must be true, and the truth is rarely edifying, at least in the overly-restricted meaning to which usage has confined the word.'[85]

Poucel's words echoed those employed by Rouault's critics, who found postwar meaning in his work precisely because 'life is bitter.' (In a letter to the director of *la Croix Meusienne*, Bernanos quoted Poucel in support: if Bernanos's work was a bad book, Poucel wrote, 'Keep giving us bad books!')[86] The broader implication of the critique was whether the concept of 'religion' would be confined to 'edification,' or whether it could adapt itself to an age of anxiety that was about to intensify during the next decade. If so, it would have to abandon 'rectilinear' notions about life – simple lines common to both nineteenth-century naturalists and ultramontanists – and come to terms with a 'muddled' world. Poucel advised suspending judgment and remaining open in these unprecedented times: 'Let us also wait,' he cautioned, 'to see our ideas change on the subject of novels.'[87]

Few critics were as suited to grappling with the anxious questions raised by Poucel than Gabriel Marcel. Soon to become known as a 'Christian existentialist' (a term he himself did not accept), Marcel wrestled with the question of a metaphysical anti/hero in his review published in the *N.R.F.* on 1 December 1926.[88] Marcel noted that some had 'spoken of Manicheanism' with respect to *Satan's Sun* and that perhaps it had been 'necessary to expect it.' But he summarily dismissed such a critique: 'the underlying metaphysic which one senses beneath the novel surely won't let itself be reduced to a formula as *artlessly dualistic* as that.'[89]

What distinguished the work for Marcel was precisely the way it led the reader beyond dualism into ambiguity. For example, there was not a single moment in which Donissan was uniformly presented in a materialist way as 'a simple sick man, a matter for a psychiatric examination – or a toxicological one – pure and simple.' Yet on the other hand, there was also never a moment in which he was portrayed supernaturally as 'a mouth-piece charged by the novelist to initiate us into a hidden wisdom.' Both the 'beauty and the obscurity' of the book relied entirely on this relationship between Bernanos and his hero, which was consistently 'a little ambiguous.'[90] Far from constructing simplistic dualisms, Bernanos seemed quite in control of the novel's systematic tension between the physiological and the mystical.

Marcel was drawn to the scene that others had viewed as simple heresy. When Father Donissan, said that he was willing to sacrifice everything to God, including 'My salvation, if God wants it,' the reader had arrived at 'the central nervous system of the book. The paradox of a sanctity which at its limit negates itself and passes over into its contrary, transforms itself into a wild negation of being – you have, it seems to me, the mysterious antinomy that gives *Under Satan's Sun* its true significance.'[91] Marcel's vocabulary reflected his influence, like a number of his contemporaries – including Miguel de Unamuno y Jugo, Karl Barth, Martin Heidegger, and Jean-Paul Sartre – by Søren Kierkegaard.[92] Kierkegaard's rejection of cosmic harmony and his emphasis on humanity confronting the absurd – most famously exemplified theologically in God's directive to Abraham to slay his only son Isaac and negate the promise of posterity – had new appeal for the postwar generation. Far from being 'rectilinear,' a dialectical sanctity demonstrated its logic in Father Donissan's having exhausted the finite limits of reason and will, negating himself (or more biblically, 'denying himself': *se nier*), and thus being open to a transforming synthesis.

In order to illustrate this abstract concept, the philosopher exchanged places with the playwright and drew on a theatrical example, Henrik Ibsen's early verse drama *Brand* (1866). (Ibsen's work had been as important as any French playwright in the history of modernist drama, and *Brand* had premiered at the Théâtre de l'Oeuvre in Paris on 22 June 1895.)[93] The title came from the name of the main character, a Lutheran pastor, and Marcel asked: 'one may wonder whether Bernanos has not enriched our literature with a Catholic Brand.'

Ibsen's Brand was the ideal type of the Kierkegaardian pastor for whom the claims of Christianity were unrelenting and any compromise with worldly philosophies an impossibility. (As a cultural historian commented in 1925: 'Behind Ibsen's *Brand* stands one of the mightiest philosophical figures of the nineteenth century – Søren Kierkegaard, one of the greatest moral anarchists of all time ... He tried to unite the Romantic notion of individuality with radical, personal inwardness in order to *reach the absolute by an act of will through the paradox*.')[94] In a series of episodes illustrating the application of his 'either/or' theology, Pastor Brand, like the Biblical figure Job himself, loses his mother, his child, his wife, and eventually his congregation. As the play draws to a close, voices taunt the ineffectual and powerless pastor with his inability to act like Christ. They enjoin him, against every Lutheran principle attacking works-righteousness, to act on the moral plane – to rely on his power, do God's will, and be saved. Brand is reduced to tears by the taunts, calls upon Christ, and believes that his words are heard. He soliloquizes: 'My life was a long darkness. / Now the sun is shining. It is day. / Until today I sought to be a tablet / On which God could write. Now my life / Shall flow rich and warm. The crust is breaking. I can weep! / I can kneel! I can pray!'

At just this moment when all finally seems to right itself, another character fires a rifle that triggers an avalanche. As cascades of snow rush over Brand on bended knee, he cries out in desperation: 'Answer me, God, / in the moment of death! / If not by Will, / how can Man be redeemed?'[95] The avalanche buries him, filling the whole valley. A voice cries out through the roaring thunder, 'He is the God of Love.' The curtain falls.

On the surface the play is horribly dismal, but in its Kierkegaardian context, the ending is marked by hope. In realizing that he cannot be redeemed by human will, the pastor leaps from the ethical to the religious sphere and is saved (or at least one can hope) by the absolutely free and arbitrary grace of God.

Marcel was drawn to *Brand* because its ending closely resembled that of *Under Satan's Sun*. In a concluding scene (that many reviewers found overly melodramatic),[96] the last words of the 'priest of Lumbres to his Judge' are portrayed as coming from Father Donissan's corpse in the confessional. This ineffectual and ultimately vanquished minister seemingly cries out in anguish: 'As for me, I have reached the place you have led me to, ready to suffer your last blow ... Take everything from me, leave me nothing! After me there will be another, and then another, from age to age, with the same cry on their lips, embracing the Cross! We are not the vermilion and gilt saints with golden beards simple people see in pictures, whose eloquence and sound health the philosophers themselves would envy. Our task is not what the world imagines. Compared with it, even the constraint of genius is a frivolous game. Every beautiful life is a witness for you, oh Lord, but the witness the saints bear is, as it were, torn from their bodies with iron.'[97] Marcel saw this not as melodramatic but rather dialectical. The self-negation of Donissan's will passed over into a third higher synthesis of his willing and not-willing. Redemption was not a naive matter of rectilinear will, but rather about the paradoxical necessity of human will's negation in order to be transformed.

'Certainly it goes without saying,' Marcel added, 'that Abbé Donissan remains as removed as possible from the *ethical* rigorism of Brand. *The drama unfolds on a metaphysical plane, not a moral one*. But in both cases a human will attached as passionately as possible to the salvation of others sees its designs partially foiled by a force of negation.' Marcel's deeply disturbing point echoed Bernanos's: the force that negated the wills of Brand and Donissan, so devoted to the salvation of others, seemed to be, for inscrutable reasons, not the demonic but the divine. Marcel concluded by applauding Bernanos's successful representation of 'this hidden dialectic of the saintly will which negates itself as an efficacious power from the very moment it begins to reflect on itself, and at the same time isolates itself from the supernatural order surrounding and supporting it.'[98]

'*Et voilà*,' Souday had quipped, 'if I am not mistaken, a negation of free will which still seems to be a heresy.' Yet, Marcel's dialectical language rewrote the game entirely: now it was the self-negating 'holy will' that could be efficacious, and the real significance of surface action took place in a manner 'mysterious,' 'hidden' [*occulte*], and irreducibly ambiguous. Mauriac, Poucel, and Marcel all worked to interpret Donissan's redemption by leaving behind earlier notions of sanctity – edifying, rectilinear, and pure (i.e., not muddled). Their efforts laid the groundwork for a religious figure more adequate to the late 1920s soon becoming the 1930s: an anxious world into which human beings were 'thrown' without apparent reason and 'not-being-at-home' [*das Nichtzuhause-sein*]. Polluted protagonists in an existence marked by mêlée were unexpectedly revealed as privileged vessels of divine force. This was a twentieth-century version of Huysmans's nineteenth-century *mystérique* and of scripture's Suffering Servant.

Réalisme intégral: 'Nothing human must remain foreign to it'

The idea that protagonists would be saintly precisely by means of their pollution attracted some and offended others. In the early summer of 1926, an article in *Les Marges* by Denis Saurat on 'The Excesses of Literary Catholicism' complained about the movement's 'exploitation of mysticism.' In a juxtaposition common during the interwar period, Saurat linked Bernanos with literature that had been 'created by pornography, homosexual or not [*la pornographie, homosexuelle ou non*].' Like all realisms, pornography also justified itself by saying 'because it exists, why not describe it?' Saurat placed Bernanos in some scandalous company: 'James Joyce and Bernanos; Proust and Bernanos; Victor Margueritte and Bernanos.' All these 'pornographers [*pornographes*]' saw it as their right to write graphic descriptions, and as a result, the 'phenomena that they describe are more frequent.'[99]

Similar objections continued into the next decade. In his 1933 survey of *The Catholicism of Some Contemporaries* (with chapters on Bloy, Barrès, Bernanos, and Mauriac), Claude Romain revisited the question of Manicheanism and the proper proportions of light and darkness. 'A Catholic writer has the right, certainly, to create "the true, authentic, human." He may expose, discuss, and even resolve, if he has the means, the problem of the flesh. But only that he might measure out grace in proper portion to the spectacle of evil and, above all, that he might know how to extract a little bit of good. Because God himself does not permit evil except in order that it might serve good.'[100]

Romain applied this principle to Mauriac's protagonists such as Thérèse Desqueyroux. (Like Madame Bovary, Desqueyroux is a bored bourgeois country wife; unlike Bovary, Desqueyroux poisons not herself but her husband.) Romain prescribed this remedy: 'In brief, a Catholic writer can very well write Catholic novels, but on condition, first of all, that *the hysterics be abandoned to the medical doctors*. Hysteria is not a matter for literature. This is why M. Mauriac would do well from now on to create above all beings with healthy bodies and minds.' (Romain seems to have been oblivious to the key point: the *fantastical* atmosphere of the Catholic novel had depended precisely on *not* handing mysterious behaviour over completely to the physiologists.) His prescription did not prevent Romain himself from concluding with a medical analogy. 'The Catholic novelist,' he wrote, could open up human wounds as any 'prudent surgeon' would: namely, 'by taking care not to infect himself and not to propagate the contagion to those around him.' This prudential care, he suggested, was severely lacking in the new breed of contemporary Catholics.[101]

In the end, however, Romain usefully focused on the reversal in language that had been made by discourse over the 'Catholic novel' – namely, a revaluation of what was *intégral*. Originally it had been a combative term of integralists against modernity. It evolved into a more inclusive term: as Baumann said, what was wanted was a synthetically *integral* novel, a literary hylomorphism of supernaturalist realism. Romain pointed to more: a vision not only of the novel, but of the human person's existence. 'And it is because the Catholic novel will fashion an integral realism [*réalisme intégral*] and will observe the human being as a whole in its entirety,' wrote Romain, 'that it will be the most complete and the only true [novel]. Natural human being and supernatural human being, sinful humanity and penitent humanity, sin and sanctity, individual and nation, the life of humanity and that of the Church: How can one not construct a powerful a work of art with such materials!'[102] Notions of the integral novel, integral realism, and *Integral Humanism* (to borrow Maritain's title of 1936)[103] refashioned the catholicity of Catholicism's embrace of human reality.

In 1919, Raïssa Maritain had urged Catholics to 'possess a genuinely informed doctrine *concerning everything that is human.*' A year later, Jacques redefined Catholicism's universality as embracing '*everything that is real.*' In 1928, the mission statement of *La Vie Intellectuelle* declared that '*everything that is human is ours.*' Here, in 1933, Romain too concluded with his own version of Terence: 'Literary and novelistic observation must have the human being as its subject, that's understood. But must it concern itself only with *natural* human being to the detriment of *supernatural* human being, if the human being is composed of a body and of a soul? ... If integral realism is the essential law of the novel, then nothing that is human must remain foreign to it.'[104]

After many decades, the idea of a 'Catholic novel' today raises few eyebrows. It is difficult to recover the world of 1920 when it was considered as 'impossible as a squared circle.' Although its creation certainly required the monumental productions of artists like Bernanos, Mauriac, Graham Greene, Evelyn Waugh and others, it could not have happened without the intellectual work of numerous thinkers and critics (many Catholic but many others not), as well as the institutional means that supported them and disseminated their thought. In the end, production of the 'Catholic' or 'mystical' novel was not simply about a literary genre. The claims it made for integral realism – a dialectical realism – redefined notions of Catholicism, religion, and human existence. This discourse happened not primarily in seminaries and pulpits but in novels, journals, and publishing houses. The supernatural could now appear in passionate fashions. Conversely, the often petty passions always played out their dramas against a horizon sometimes *hallucinant*, frequently violent, and finally unfathomed.

Chapter 8

Charles Tournemire: Mystical Dissonance

Tradition is entirely different from habit, even from an excellent habit, since habit is by definition an unconscious acquisition and tends to become mechanical, whereas tradition results from a conscious and deliberate acceptance. A real tradition is not the relic of a past that is irretrievably gone; it is a living force that animates and informs the present ... Far from implying the repetition of what has been, tradition presupposes the reality of what endures. It appears as an heirloom, a heritage that one receives on condition of making it bear fruit before passing it on to one's descendants.

– Igor Stravinsky

The arts, especially music but also literature and painting, allow us to penetrate domains that are not unreal, but beyond reality. For the surrealists, it was a hallucinatory domain; for Christians, it is the domain of faith. 'Blessed are those who have not seen and who have believed.' They haven't seen, but they have a secret intuition about what they don't see. Now, I think music, even more than literature and painting, is capable of expressing this dreamlike, fairy-tale aspect of the beyond, this 'surreal' aspect of the truths of faith.

– Olivier Messiaen

The Mysticity of a work is made of unreality produced according to norms. The work that is real in its form and unreal in its expression is perfect: Léonard.

– Charles Tournemire[1]

Charles Tournemire's monumental organ work, *L'Orgue Mystique* (composed 1927–32; published 1928–36) contributed to a radical reversal of religious musical values. Whereas plainchant in the nineteenth century had been revived in order to stand over and against the fleeting world of passionate music, Tournemire imagined the musical devices representing 'passion' – chromaticism, polytonalism, and the perceived resulting 'dissonance' – as the most appropriate material carriers of the 'eternal' and unchanging Latin forms. Images of dress abounded as ancient chants were imagined to be 'clothed' in 'modern' musical fashions. This musical hylomorphism shared the same general aims as musical neoclassicism and surrealism of the 1920s: traditional motifs were used as a way of nostalgically evoking the surety of the past, of eternity, or what was most deeply 'real,' even as they were subverted to show that modernity had emerged from a traumatic rupture with that same deep reality. Although Tournemire's writing of *L'Orgue Mystique* might have been triggered by intensely private griefs, the mystical-modernism of his musical language would be received by a culture whose musical forms facilitated mourning.

Plainchant Semantics: Anti-Dreyfusard Integralism

The stereotypical image of Charles Tournemire, when there is an image of him at all, usually has him sitting at the organ console on which, in the words of his student Maurice Duruflé, 'the book of Gregorian chant was always on the music rack, open at the liturgical office of the day.'[2] He has become so intimately linked with chant that one must work hard to extricate him from it in order to see just how novel his attitude was and, as a corollary, how creative an innovation was his hybridization of plainchant with modern music. In addition, it is important to understand that plainchant, like its philosophical sibling, Thomism, was inextricably linked with ultramontanism and integralism until the war. Neither ultramontanist nor integralist, Tournemire approached chant in a fresh way. In order to see how his background differed from the language he would transform, we must begin with what plainchant had come to mean.

Gregorian chant's connection with ultramontanism lay already in the 1832 document by which Pope Gregory XVI authorized the founding of Solesmes Abbey, charging it with 'restoring the sound traditions of the pontifical jurisprudence and of the sacred liturgy.'[3] Under the direction of Dom Prosper Louis Pascal Guéranger (later a fervent servant of Gregory's successor, Pope Pius IX, and his anti-naturalist campaigns), Solesmes devoted its resources to paleographical studies, employing historicist methods (somewhat ironically) in order to discover the most authentic versions of eternalist chants.[4] In Paris, Charles Bordes had founded his choir devoted to plainchant and polyphony, Les Chanteurs de Saint-Gervais. Inspired by their success, Bordes, Alexandre Guilmant, and Vincent d'Indy founded the Schola Cantorum in 1894 as a society for promoting and teaching religious music. The foundational manifesto called for a school of music dedicated to seemingly incompatible ideals: the performance of plainchant 'according to the Gregorian tradition'; restoration of polyphonic music in the Catholic Reformation style of Palestrina; the creation of a 'new modern religious music'; and improvement of repertory for organists.[5]

However, as the Dreyfus Affair began to unfold in late 1894, French music became radically politicized, and the *Schola* took on a new meaning as the 'counteridentity' of the Conservatoire Nationale.[6] If the Conservatoire was Republican, laicist, and Dreyfusard, the Schola opposed it by being nativist, religious, and anti-Dreyfusard.[7] For Bordes and d'Indy, the eighteenth-century Conservatoire, rooted in the Enlightenment both historically and ideologically, viewed tonal harmony as 'scientific' and 'natural.' Conversely, it attacked polyphonic counterpoint – epitomized in the work of Palestrina, composer to the papal court of the Catholic Reformation – as 'unnatural' and 'artificial.'

Bordes and d'Indy inverted this discourse: Enlightenment tonal harmony was 'artificial' and 'utopian' and, in contrast, plainchant was a 'free discourse' both 'natural' and 'logical.' This idea of chant's *liberté* flowed from Dom Guéranger's revolutionary *Rational Method of Plainchant* (1859): 'plainsong is an inflected recitation in which the notes have an unfixed value, the rhythm of which, essentially free, is that of ordinary speech.'[8] In contrast to 'the established method of performing plainsong, whereby each note received an accent and was sung in a slow and heavy fashion, the Solesmes method directed the notes to be sung quickly and lightly,' grouped either according to principles of ordinary speech, or in unpredictable groups of two and three.[9]

The Schola extended this Solesmes innovation, and imagined plainchant as a 'free recitative' in a 'free music'; a 'free-flowing chant with infinite variation'; 'freedom' in the musical phrase; a 'cult of nature' and – in a phrase reminiscent of Johann Gottfried Herder's *Voices of the Folk* (*Stimmen der Völker*, 1807) – 'music of the people.' Bordes took the complex ecclesiastical form forged in medieval monasteries and imagined it as something natural, rooted in simplicity, and erupting spontaneously from the heart. Having heard a shepherd sing the song 'Balatsa' in the Basque countryside, Bordes remarked, 'In hearing this theme sung so freely, I sensed the admirable art which is true plain chant ... It was the unexpected confirmation of the logical and natural precepts of Gregorian plain chant, the *basic condemnation of all utopias of measured music.*'[10]

This primitivist discourse might not have had such force were it not for the fact that Bordes's contemporaries – Gustav Mahler, Richard Strauss, Claude Debussy (*Prelude to the Afternoon of a Faun*, 1894; *Pelléas and Mélisande*, 1902), and Arnold Schoenberg (*Transfigured Night*, 1899) – were also trying to emancipate themselves from measured music. Revived plainchant's 'primitive modalism' reverberated with this musical moment: in the midst of writing *Pelléas*, Debussy visited Solesmes in 1893, and also enjoyed going to concerts given by Bordes's Chanteurs de Saint-Gervais.[11] In 1897, Bordes visited Solesmes, later returning with d'Indy and Guilmant.[12] In the archaic modalism of Solesmes, composers found an extension of melodic vocabulary allowing them to go beyond tonalism's strictures. Consequently, when Bordes framed the Schola as an emancipating force in 1903, his argument sounded plausible: 'The Schola thus seeks the triumph of natural music, music as free and supple speech, moving and rhythmic as the ancient dances, basing itself on the monuments of religious art, of the early lyric theater, and on the cult of nature, in the folk tradition, having only one concern, one avowed purpose: the triumph of French music ... the true music of France, the most natural, the most refined there is, the closest to nature and the most filled with life.'[13]

In addition to being 'natural' and 'free,' the Schola also imagined plainchant as both particularly [Roman] Catholic and universally 'catholic.' In his address given at a 1900 symposium, Amédée Gastoué explained that 'the great Aryan family, from which we have issued' formed 'a tight bond between modern nations' with the 'infinite delicacy' of its artistic productions. Alluding to the Biblical passage medievals had used to justify the domination of non-Europeans – one resurrected for Arthur de Gobineau's *Essay on the Inequality of the Human Races* (1853–5) – Gastoué explained the passage from Hebrew chant into Gregorian chant.[14] It was 'the realization of the ancient prophecy reported in the story of Noah: That Shem would dominate Chaim, but that afterward, Japhet – our race – would inhabit these tents.' For this reason, he concluded, 'The purely Jewish phase was in effect extremely short in the history of Christianity.' Playing on the word *catholique*, he added that, 'in order for a religious form to become *universal, catholic – it is the same meaning* – it was necessary that the forms of different arts impregnate it.'[15] One month later, speaking at the opening of the Schola's new location on the Rue St-Jacques, d'Indy would 'declare war' on 'particularism.' Associating it with 'that unhealthy fruit of the Protestant deviation,' he also linked it with 'Jewish art' that did not recognize the 'logical chain of the past': 'This tendency would seem to be yet a last metamorphosis of the Jewish school that retarded the progression of art during a large part of the nineteenth century ...'[16] Although plainchant might have been Semitic in origins, it had quickly escaped the strictures of particularism and become a truly 'catholic' art.

In 1903, Pope Pius X published a letter *motu proprio* ('of his own accord') on the 'reform' of liturgical music. Closely following the agenda laid out by the Schola, it was generally seen as a triumph for the Bordes-d'Indy program. One of the letter's more intriguing points decreed the exclusion of women from singing in choirs. In somewhat bizarre language alluding to the ancient Jewish priestly tribe of Levites, Pius X argued that to sing in the choir was a priestly function: 'all the rest of the liturgical chant *belongs to the choir of levites*, and, therefore, singers in church, even when they are laymen, are really taking the place of the ecclesiastical choir ... On the same principle it follows that singers in church have a real liturgical office, and that therefore *women, as being incapable of exercising such an office, cannot be admitted* to form part of the choir or of the musical chapel. Whenever, then, it is desired to employ the acute voice of sopranos or contraltos, these parts must be taken by boys, *according to the most ancient usage of the Church.*'[17]

This decree might have been quickly forgotten in history's dustbin (since it was nearly impossible to implement) had not it been immortalized in James Joyce's short story 'The Dead,' written four years later. Here, Aunt Kate, turning 'fiercely on her niece,' makes her feelings known about the Pope's new prohibition: 'I know all about the honour of God, Mary Jane, but I think it's not at all honourable for the pope to turn out the women out of the choirs that have slaved there all their lives and put little whippersnappers of boys over their heads. I suppose it is for the good of the Church if the pope does it. But it's not just, Mary Jane, and it's not right ... there's such a thing as common everyday politeness and gratitude.'[18]

The decree was not unprecedented. In 1835, when the ultramontanist movement was first underway, the Archbishop of Paris banned women from the city's choirs. (A century later, Henri Bachelin reported the reaction: 'What a misfortune for the capital of the arts to have as the head of its clergy a crusty mind of such barbarity.')[19] Another Parisian archbishop banned women in the late 1880s, and the strict enforcement of this decree led female singers to leave the Chanteurs de Saint-Gervais, forcing the Schola to begin preparing more boys for the choir beginning in 1893. Classes for women were forbidden at the Schola itself.[20]

The deep anxieties over purity and pollution evident in the 1903 ban tell us something about the traumatic character of the moment. Beginning with the Law of Associations in 1901 and concluding with the Act of Separation in 1905, the church institution felt besieged from without by secular forces. In 1903, the same year as the *motu proprio*, the monks of Solesmes were expelled from France (along with other religious orders) under the anticlerical legislation, and set up their abbey-in-exile on the British Isle of Wight. The integralist papacy felt besieged from within as well: in 1905 and 1906, the works of theologians identified as 'Roman Catholic Modernists' were condemned; in 1907 came the anti-Modernist documents *Lamentabili* and *Pascendi*. Encountering what it perceived as massive chaos, and feeling its stability and identity threatened from both inside and out, church authorities attempted to re-establish order by means of the 'reform' and 'restoration' of its innermost sanctuary. The directives clearly demarcated areas of purity and danger on the ecclesiastical body by inscribing such boundaries on the bodies of women like Aunt Kate.

Thus, by 1903, Gregorian Chant had become a privileged site in the politically charged musical contest after the Dreyfus Affair. In the hands of Solesmes, the Schola, and the papacy, chant became a language representing forces opposed to the Republic's dominant culture and institutions, including the Conservatoire. Charles Tournemire did not share these inclinations. This makes his later innovative use of plainchant all the more intriguing.

1870–1920: Charles Tournemire, Republican Symbolist

Charles Arnould Tournemire was born in Bordeaux on 22 January 1870, nine months before the Franco-Prussian War debacle and the end of the Second Empire. His family background was fairly typical of the provincial petit bourgeois class: he was descended from artisans and farm peasants. His paternal grandfather was a hatter, his maternal grandfather an 'agricultural proprietor,' and his father the co-owner of a small metalworking firm that dealt in tin-plate engravings. Starting at the age of eleven, Tournemire studied at the Conservatoire of Bordeaux. In 1886, at age sixteen, he left the provinces for Paris, studying composition with d'Indy at the Schola Cantorum and taking piano lessons in private. (An indication of his feelings for the Schola is found in the occasional memoir references to the 'Schola "cancro"-rum,' i.e., 'School of Dunces.')[21] In January 1890, having passed his admissions examination, he entered the Conservatoire National in Paris, studying harmony and enrolling in the organ class of César Franck, whom he had first met in early 1889.[22]

César Franck was the organist of the Basilica of Ste-Clotilde in Paris, a church built in the neo-Gothic style during the Haussmann years to accommodate the burgeoning bourgeois neighbourhood of the seventh arrondissement. A native of Belgium, Franck had been named the new church's first organist in 1857 and, although the position was not prestigious like that in the ancient churches of St-Sulpice, Ste-Eustache, or Notre-Dame, his evolution into one of the greatest French musicians of the nineteenth century brought fame to the parish. Although Franck would be portrayed after his death as the incarnation of Aquinas, Dante, and Gothic cathedrals, Franck himself was not responsible for this image, 'remaining to the end of his life a bourgeois professor of music, of limited general culture, typical of his epoch.'[23] His teaching method encouraged improvisation, and this appealed immediately to Tournemire's greatest musical gift. However, it should be emphasized that Franck himself did not use plainchant or other liturgical melodies as the themes upon which he improvised. In the words of d'Indy, Franck 'knew nothing about the erudite and definitive researches of the Benedictines into the subject of Gregorian music,' and those who visited the organ loft of Ste-Clotilde reported that Franck took his themes for improvisation from Bach, Beethoven, Schubert, and popular French, Breton, and Scandinavian tunes, especially Noëls.[24] Tournemire's gift for improvisation flourished under Franck, and he idolized his mentor.

In the spring of 1890, Tournemire was 'first runner up' in the organ department's competition. In November later that year, Franck died, leaving the twenty-year-old Tournemire devastated in very much the same way that his exact contemporary, the painter Georges Rouault, had been left bereft by the death of Gustave Moreau. On 11 December 1890, Charles-Marie Widor, the organist of the prestigious St-Sulpice, took over the organ class. His radically different approach from Franck came as a cold shock to his students. Louis Vierne, Tournemire's fellow student in Widor's class and later organist of Notre Dame of Paris, recalled Widor's opening remarks that served as a changing of the guard: 'In France we too greatly favor improvisation over execution. This is more than a mistake. It is nonsense.'[25]

The transition from Franck to Widor was harsh for Tournemire, who despised his mentor's replacement. Later in life, he would recall his sense that Widor's arrival had been 'catastrophic': 'What shocked me most of all was, in this man, the lack of self-consciousness and the lightness with which he took possession of the illustrious chair! ... The first contact between the new master and myself was disastrous! The words "aquatic music," à propos of my first free improvisation, ring outrageously in my ears. I remember, as if it were yesterday, my riposte: "Aquatic music? You should know that what you have just heard is the reflection of the marvelous teaching of César Franck, my master ..."'[26] In retrospect, Widor's metaphor of 'aquatic music' seems poetically just, calling to mind not only the similarity between so much of Tournemire's music and Debussy's impressionistic evocations of the tempestuous sea and Monet's serene water lilies, but also giving a vivid concretely watery image to Tournemire's trademark 'ambient' sound.[27] Regardless of how we might now evaluate their encounter, Tournemire concluded that it was 'a chill that ... degenerated on the part of Charles-Marie Widor into a profound and absurdly enduring hatred with regard to me.'

Tournemire readily admitted that he gained a great deal in six months from Widor's '*technique formidable*,' and this emphasis on virtuosity paid off as he won first prize in organ and improvisation in the spring of 1891. When Gabriel Pierné resigned the post at Ste-Clotilde in 1898 (which he had held for the eight years since Franck's death), Tournemire competed with thirty other contestants and won. Although he complained that the position meant a drastic cut in his already meager income, it had compensatory pay-offs as he fulfilled a dream by succeeding to Franck's tribune.

These beginnings might give the impression that Tournemire's life as a composer was spent primarily at the organ, but almost the inverse is true. After his *Triple Choral* (1910) in homage to Franck's three great *Chorales*, Tournemire did not return to composition for the organ until 1927. He was, rather, an extraordinarily prolific composer of works for nearly every genre: piano, voice, chamber ensembles, symphony, chorus, and opera.[28] More importantly, Tournemire's music was almost always symbolist or 'literary' in its approach. Just as Mallarmé had theorized that ultimate realities could never be directly represented but only 'suggested,' and just as Moreau used 'literary' themes (from classical and Biblical antiquity, Oriental mythology) in his painting to evoke the invisible, so symbolist composers following Wagner (e.g., *Parsifal*) used music to provide musical exegeses of written texts and 'suggest' the unseen.[29] (Debussy's rendering of Mallarmé's poem 'Prelude to the Afternoon of a Faun' is perhaps the most well-known French example.) No matter what instruments Tournemire composed for, his primary interest lay in exegeting a text via musical material.

Tournemire's association with the Parisian symbolists began soon after his arrival in Paris as he frequented the bookstore of Edmond Bailly (11, rue de la Chaussée d'Antin), publisher of Debussy's 'Cinq Poèmes de Charles Baudelaire.'[30] All the symbolists met there: Verlaine, Bloy, Debussy, Mallarmé, and Péladan. Over the years, Tournemire would also become a highly regarded participant in the Société Baudelaire, officially founded in 1872 for the poet's posthumous rehabilitation after his prosecution as the author of several unacceptably audacious poems in the *Flowers of Evil*.[31] As in the Académie française, words would be investigated and presented in the Société, both as they had been used by Baudelaire as well as in terms of the values they incarnated, and an ever-evolving Dictionary was compiled. Oscar Wilde's contribution to the Dictionary (1898), in the form of brief dictated suggestions, was later expanded by Tournemire, who had been acquainted with them by the artist Léonard Sarluis, one of the composer's few close friends and a former confidant of Wilde. Péladan, another member of the Société, introduced Tournemire to his wife's sister, Alice Taylor. Tournemire and Taylor married in November 1903, making the composer's connection to the symbolists even more concrete. In short, Tournemire's symbolist identity was both personal and theoretical, and he thought of musical composition in a symbolist way, that is, as the exposition of (or commentary on) a text, whether a formal libretto or not.

In 1903, Tournemire also obtained the Grand Prix for composition in that year's musical competition sponsored by the City of Paris. His prizewinning piece, *The Siren's Blood*, was a work for soloists, chorus, and orchestra, employing for its libretto a poem by Marcel Brennure based on a text by Anatole Le Braz.[32] Having obtained Franck's organ position, a prestigious prize that brought with it some relief from constant financial worries, and having contracted a happy marriage, Tournemire had in several ways come into his own at the age of thirty-four. It was at this moment that he began to undergo, as he himself wrote, an intellectual and spiritual crisis.

Perhaps there was a premonition of this crisis in a review of the first performance of *The Siren's Blood* in November 1904. The reviewer judged that Tournemire was a 'sad' personality, 'resembling in this the majority of young men born in the period of the cruel years 1870–1871.' They lived 'in a milieu of despair, of resignation, and their soul, plunged into an atmosphere of grief, cannot conceive of anything but sad subjects.' To those who doubted him, he suggested: 'Look at literature, painting, music, the whole production of works given life by the new generation ... and see for yourself if the sorrow is not profound. The feeling of malaise fermenting in the heart of the young is reflected in their compositions.' In his conclusion, he felt that 'it seemed necessary' to 'point out a case that is perhaps more a matter for pathology than for psychology; it is curious and calls for a medical comparison.' Tournemire's art came out of a great deal of learning and elevated tendencies, and he 'did not fear letting his heart speak.' Hence, the reviewer concluded with hope that Tournemire would write, 'in the near future, a work more developed, more simple, more open, and in a word, more human.'[33]

In Tournemire's memoirs, the reader finds a large parenthesis opened here that lasts for thirty typewritten pages and describes the reading done between 1903 and 1920 that profoundly altered his world-view.[34] As a prelude, Tournemire recalled that, 'like many men' his age, educated in the new Third Republic's schools, he had been 'stuffed with French literature of the 18th century.' 'Very much in love with' the 'seductive and dangerous Jean-Jacques [Rousseau],' the schoolboy Tournemire had 'considered him like a demi-God.' Not having 'yet bitten into other fruits,' the Enlightenment had seemed to be 'the intellectual summit of the world.' However, this 'intellectual orientation – under the healthy, essentially Christian, influence of my wife – was preparing itself to choose another star in the sky of thought ...'

'Books were delicately placed beneath my eyes,' he wrote, and one has an image of Alice Taylor guiding Tournemire's new regime of reading by literally passing books on to him in a systematic order. He began with readings from the ancient Church Fathers, followed by Abbé Jacques-Paul Migne's *Universal Dictionary of Mythology Ancient and Modern* (1855),[35] immersing himself in the history of religions. Tournemire's notes on religion seem nearly endless: Chaldeans, Egypt, Assyria, Greek legends of Thrace, Orpheus, the Argonauts, the Latin classics, Greek tragedies, the four Védas (Rig-Véda, Yadjour-Véda, Sama-Véda, and Arthave-Véda), Persian, Germanic, Slavic, and Scandinavian religions, Chinese Buddhism, Assyro-Babylonian religion, Shintoism, and so on. In 1905, searching for a text upon which to base his next composition, he asked Péladan for advice who sent him to Egyptian mythology. Tournemire worked on *Nittetis* between 1905 and 1907, yet another composition for orchestra, choir, and soloists, including Amasis (king of Egypt), Psamnétès (son of Amasis), and Nittetis, (princess of Egypt).[36]

The year 1907, Tournemire's thirty-seventh, stood as a milestone in his life. '*Nittetis* is like the closure of my first "manner,"' he wrote. At this moment his spirit began to move, and 'a mystical ideal' (*un idéal mystique*) increasingly 'developed in my brain and in my heart,'[37] and another 'manner' seems to have blossomed in 1908. In March he composed *Poème mystique* ('Mystical Poem'), a piece for solo piano exegeting verse texts from Paul Verlaine's collection of poems entitled *Happiness* (1891), and in May he completed *Wisdom*, a work for voice and piano, again based on poems from Verlaine's collection with the same title (1893).[38] His personal library attests to his acquaintance with symbolists, Decadents, and *renouveau catholique* writers.[39] The two most influential of these (probably introduced by Péladan) would eventually be Ernest Hello and Léon Bloy, who believed there was 'a symbolism of History.'[40]

Between 1910 and 1912 Tournemire wrote a 'lyric drama,' more oratorio than opera (to be considered below): *The Gods Are Dead*, a musical setting of a poem by Eugène Berteaux.[41] The manuscript, entitled 'Chryséis' (after the title character), alluded to the fact that this was a 'drama of antiquity,' and its epigraph taken from Ernest Hello showed the influence of Tournemire's interests in antique religions. Hello had suggested that 'pagan art' was filled with such creatures as 'nymphs in the trees' in order to keep open an empty place for the God they were searching. In 1913, Tournemire had a triumphant premiere of his Third ('Moscow') Symphony at the Concertgebouw in Amsterdam. On the side of all this activity, he maintained his duties at Ste-Clotilde and also travelled with Charles Bordes, playing the organ alongside the Chanteurs de Saint Gervais.

In 1914, the forty-four-year-old Tournemire was mobilized as a 'territorial' for a short time. He saw no action, and a postcard sent to his dear friend, Pierre Garanger, suggests that the war was something distant from him: 'Here I am, in gracious nature, occupied with guarding, using bayonette and canon, an inelegant viaduct ... Like a vulgar cow, I watch the passing trains; 4 to 500 every day; what music! A few too many timpani! ... If the military authorities ... [conclude] the peace, I will be able to go to the end of my 'Sixth' by the end of this year.'[42] His Sixth Symphony (1915–18) innovated by adding a 'literary' element paraphrased from the Biblical prophet Jeremiah – 'We hear the cry of war, the sound of the trumpet/ruin upon ruin, the nation is devastated./Do not be angry, Lord! Listen! Pardon!' – allowing for 'a chorus ascending toward God, pleading to stop the horrors of the war.'[43] In 1918, Tournemire began his Seventh Symphony, a work he had been planning for two years and titled *The Dances of Life*. A year later, in November 1919, he was named professor of the Ensemble Class at the Conservatoire Nationale and looked forward to obtaining César Franck's organ chair there in the near future.

In January 1920, Tournemire celebrated his fiftieth birthday and he seemed at the top of his form. However, he was about to undergo a six-year ordeal of bereavement: his wife would die, his career at the Opéra would be short-lived, and he would be passed over for Franck's chair. Although there is little available evidence showing that he had been affected by the war in a deeply personal way, his postwar existence was to be marked by profound disappointment and sorrow, and in this his personal mourning paralleled that of his nation's.

1920–1926: Twilight of the Gods

In May 1920, the death of Tournemire's first wife of seventeen years, Alice Taylor Tournemire, inaugurated a six-year period of losses.[44] Two months later, he signed and dated his 'Don Quichotte' manuscript: 'On a day of great distress. 22 July 1920.' On 6 August, having sought out refuge in a monastery cell, he wrote notes in preparation of his 8th symphony, *The Symphony of the Triumph of Death*: 'I was in the valley ... I wept without end ... I can finally read the life of her whom I will not see again, whom I will not hear any longer on this earth ...'[45]

Shortly after the first-year-anniversary of Alice's death, Tournemire's former student, Joseph Bonnet, gave him a set of Dom Guéranger's fifteen-volume *The Liturgical Year* and inscribed the front cover of the first volume: 'To my Dear Master and friend Ch. Tournemire – in homage of profound admiration and affection. Jos. Bonnet.' The date was 15 June 1921.[46] (Bonnet, a central figure in the postwar plainchant revival, had spent the previous summer at Solesmes' abbey-in-exile on the Isle of Wight.) Whether or not Tournemire actually read the work at the time, certainly his reception of *The Liturgical Year* would have been linked in his mind with the period of grief following Alice's death.

The year 1921 was significant for Tournemire in two other respects. First, he was named a chevalier of the French Legion of Honor. Second, he intensified his involvement in the Société Baudelaire. The year was significant for the Société as well, since 1921 marked the centenary of Baudelaire's birth. The committee overseeing the celebration included the society's president Victor-Émile Michelet, the esoteric poet, and vice-president Gustave Kahn, co-founder (with Jean Moréas) of the journal *Le Symboliste* (1886). The program, taking place on 2 April 1921 at the Salle Malakoff, included an address given by Ernest Raynaud (who had just published the first two volumes of his panoramic *The Symbolist Mêlée, 1870–1910: Portraits and Souvenirs*), the reading of poems by Baudelaire, and music by Claude Debussy – all performed with 'the artistic participation of the Comédie Française, of the Opéra Comique, of the Odéon and the Théâtre de Paris.'[47]

Tournemire would become even more deeply involved in this heady atmosphere when Camille Saint-Saëns's death on 16 December 1921 left vacant his prestigious chair. In 1922, the Société passed over both Gabriel Fauré and Maurice Ravel in naming Tournemire to fill the position. At the Société's meetings, in addition to his close friends, the philosopher Pierre Garanger and the painter Sarluis, Tournemire could have met other participants such as the composer and critic Florent Schmitt, organist and composer Dynam-Victor Fumet (friend of Bloy and Verlaine), his son Stanislas Fumet, Jacques and Raïssa Maritain (whom Stanislas introduced to the Société), and Georges Rouault. (Had he lived longer, Tournemire might also have met Albert Camus, Jean-Paul Sartre, and Simone de Beauvoir, who once wrote, 'The Société has involved the century's most eminent artists and writers.')[48]

One of the Société's editorial boards over which Tournemire acquired the presidency (succeeding Péladan, who had died in 1918) was that defining *la Mystique* – 'The Mystical.' This led him to delve into the seminal nineteenth-century work of Johann Joseph von Görres, author of *Mysticism: Divine, Natural, and Diabolical*. This encyclopedic five-volume survey (used extensively by William James for his *Varieties of Religious Experience* [1902]) collected accounts of 'mysticism' from every age and corner of the globe, recounting manifestations as varied as bloody stigmatics, diabolical witches, and exotic tales from the Hindu Orient.[49] A gifted orator, Tournemire gave a presentation on Görres closely analysing the three manifestations of 'the mystical.' Like the gift from Bonnet of Guéranger's *Liturgical Year*, Tournemire's accession to the late Péladan's chair of *La Mystique* would also have been associated with the recent death of his wife (and that of her brother-in-law through whom they had met). In the score for Tournemire's *Don Quichotte*, 'Prelude to Combats of the Ideal,' dated 7 December 1922, Tournemire inscribed this line from Görres: 'When the soul is, as it were, plunged into a profound desolation, it seems to completely disperse itself in tears.'[50]

The second grief for Tournemire would be the aftermath of the dispiriting reviews he received for *The Gods Are Dead* (1912), produced by Pierre Chéreau and premiered on 19 March 1924 at the Théâtre national de l'Opéra.[51] The opera was widely reviewed, and although Tournemire reported that 'the whole auditorium rose to its feet at the first performance,' the critics, though not necessarily negative, were also not enthusiastic.[52] The reviews must be read in perspective: in 1924, *The Gods Are Dead* was in fact somewhat 'anachronistic' since it had been composed in 1910–12. In addition to the watershed in music that occurred in 1912–13 – Stravinsky's *Rite of Spring* premiered 29 May 1913; Stravinsky himself attended a production of Schoenberg's *Pierrot Lunaire* on 12 December 1912 – there had been Cocteau's *Cock and the Harlequin* (1918), the postwar effort of Les Six to establish Parisian neoclassicism (and not Berlin's atonalism) as modern music's epicentre, and the advent of jazz.[53] Given this broad context, the musical meanings assigned to Tournemire's prewar opera-oratorio reflected at least partially critics' attitudes towards the musical ferment in 1924 Paris.

On the whole, Tournemire was praised for his sturdy academic style and steadfast opposition to fashion – and, by implication, his lack of creative novelty. Paul Souday's review in *Paris Midi* lauded Tournemire: he had been able to write 'an honest score, conscientious and academic' for the libretto text of Eugène Berteaux which was 'as bizarre and illogical as the dramatic work of M. Anatole France is historically and humanely true.' The musical score for 'this incoherent drama' – a handwritten scrawl in Tournemire's own copy of the press clipping preserves his estimation of Souday: 'What an idiot!!!' – was 'exempt from defects properly speaking.' It was not exempt, however, from the 'gravest of all, which is a cruel absence of qualities and a practically constant lack of interest throughout.' Souday concluded that this 'gloomy enough work was remarkably performed' by the ensemble.[54] Souday did not here (as he did in his critique of Bernanos) accuse *The Gods Are Dead* of being a 'hodgepodge,' but *Le Monde Musical* implicitly did: 'This *mélange* of philosophy, religion, poetry and history can only have one justification: the sublime. Lacking the sublime, there remains nobility – and brevity.'[55]

Other reviewers were less overtly negative, but their praise of Tournemire's 'solidity' in the era of Cocteau, Satie, and Stravinsky sounds like the faint praise that damns. Tournemire possessed the 'solidity of a rock' and his form was 'proof of the greatest reliability.' But 'from his religious career' he carried a certain 'severity,' and for his orchestration 'one might hope for a lighter pastry.' He also also seemed to 'nourish' a 'disproportionate taste' for the clarinet in the high registers. It grated the nerves, and the amount of playing confided to this reed 'in the course of these two acts' was 'of an unimaginable quantity!'[56]

For others, monotony was the principal defect. *Le Petit Parisien* judged

Tournemire 'a remarkable musician' whose 'inspiration' was 'always elevated.' Even if 'certain parts seemed sometimes to err by a certain monotony which such a subject' (i.e., the religious evolution from paganism to Christianity), 'however noble it might be, cannot avoid,' the listener could still be consoled by 'reflecting on numerous passages which could be cited in the work as a whole.'[57] *Le Quotidien* similarly praised Tournemire's 'pure ideal, without compromise or weakness,' and the 'imposing work' of his opera was a 'testimony to the profound seriousness' he tried to express. However, such seriousness was bound to end up in 'some monotony,' above all on a subject that had 'such little variety.' The work as a whole thus 'assumed a tone of colorlessness' not broken by 'the possibly intentional sobriety of the instruments.' In spite of this, there was 'nothing in the work unworthy of the warm estimation' that Tournemire never lacked and that his merits continued to attract.[58]

Perhaps it was precisely Tournemire's training and quality as 'one of the most well-known organists of our time,' suggested *La France Théâtrale*, that 'most harmed him' when composing for opera. M. Chéreau, the 'remarkable director' at the Opéra had 'done the impossible by breathing some life into' an action that 'dragged on somewhat,' a languor that 'long musical passages certainly aggravated.' The 'arms raised to the sky and the consternated faces' were 'insufficient to move' the audience emotionally, especially when they only underlined 'a somewhat heavy orchestration occasionally lacking variety.' (Above all, the first act's 'abuse of the harp' was 'especially tedious.') Having expressed these reservations, it was still necessary to recognize that Tournemire was 'a true musician,' 'not unconscious of the resources of his art' and possessing an 'impeccable technique that never failed for even an instant.'[59]

Tournemire was especially praised for his steadfast opposition to fashion, the unalterable character of his artistry, and his use of traditional forms. *La Revue mondiale* was sure that even those who 'might hope from him certain more lively oppositions' and 'a lighter atmosphere in certain episodes' would be 'the first to render homage to his remarkable homogeneity,' to the 'equilibrium of his proportions, to the constant elevation of his feeling.' Although 'so many of his musical confreres' seemed 'above all preoccupied with following the fluctuations of fashion,' Tournemire continued to manifest his 'disinterested cult for the highest forms of musical art.'[60] *Candide*'s Émile Vuillermoz, a Tournemire advocate, agreed. Tournemire possessed both a 'magnificent scorn for contingencies' as well as the 'tranquil temerity of mystics,' and his aesthetic was 'resolutely and courageously "not-contemporary"' [*inactuelle*]. 'In a century in which the lyrical theater' was undergoing 'dangerous assults,' Tournemire maintained 'a touching fidelity to an ideal of dramatic spectacle *whose anachronism seemed to be definitely demonstrated.*'[61] *Beaux-Arts* applauded the stability implicit in Tournemire's choice of a 'subject entailing little action' and a form 'closer to an oratorio than conventional theater.' Precisely because this 'solidly written score' delivered 'no new aesthetic' and its orchestration would 'not surprise anyone,' it was 'the affirmation of an unalterable artistic conscience' and a career 'with rare nobility.'[62] *Le Ménestrel* lauded the 'austerity, simplicity, and grace' of Tournemire's style, 'inspired with a great deal of taste and measure.'[63]

In sum, the 1924 reviews of Tournemire's 1912 opera mostly praised the virtues of dependency and security, academic accuracy, contempt for trends and fashions, and a love for the past up to the point of anachronism. As a consequence, *The Gods Are Dead* effectively killed Tournemire's career at the Opéra, and a series of letters written to librettist Albert Pauphilet (from 30 November 1926 through 13 January 1930), painfully demonstrates the agonizing (and ultimately unsuccessful) attempts to find a venue for *The Legend of Tristan.*[64] In addition, Tournemire's just-completed eighth and final symphony, *The Triumph of Death* – signed and dated '9 July 1924. *Per aspera spera*' (Through difficulty, hope) – would never be performed in his lifetime. In 1925, Vuillermoz would lament the fact that the character of 'Tournemire's vast compositions' did not destine him for 'great success among the crowds.' He also predicted that 'historians in the future will be astonished at the ingratitude of the orchestral conductors who imposed' works on their audiences that were 'infinitely less interesting' than Tournemire's.[65]

In 1926, a third blow struck Tournemire. Eugène Gigout had died on 9 December 1925, leaving Franck's organ chair at the Conservatoire vacant. Ever since Tournemire had become professor of the instrumental ensemble class in 1919, he had assumed he would eventually succeed to Franck's post. Gigout had emphasized improvisation and plainsong accompaniment over virtuosity in performance, and Tournemire's own freedom with respect to rhythm, phrasing, and legato would have continued his approach.

However, as early as 1922, Charles-Marie Widor had urged another of his students, Marcel Dupré, to try for the succession. By 1926, the forty-year-old Dupré, a handsome and photogenic figure sixteen years younger than Tournemire, had become a celebrity with a cult following. His astonishing technique reflected Widor's own preference for virtuosity in execution over improvisation as well as strictness in rhythm, phrasing, and legato.[66] (Dupré's difficult *Three Preludes and Fugues* [1920] were initially deemed unplayable.)[67] Widor began a campaign to promote Dupré's candidacy and prevailed in the end. Dupré was chosen over Tournemire to be Franck's successor.[68]

As an indication of just what a turning point Tournemire considered this to be in his life, his memoirs' long undated summary of his life ends with this episode in 1926. The structure is all the more significant because the dated entries begin on 6 April 1933, which would have been the natural and obvious terminus for the first section. A traumatic moment for him, 6 March 1926 was the fulcrum around which Tournemire structured the narrative of his own life. Speaking of his 1919 appointment, Tournemire recalled that he 'had accepted this post, *without seeking it*, with the quasi-certitude of later obtaining the organ chair of the same Conservatoire. Hélas! I was foiled ...'

Tournemire quoted from an article appearing in the *Cri de Paris* of 7 March 1926: 'M. Marcel Dupré has just been named professor of organ at the Conservatoire. The minister ratified the designation of the candidate made according to the rules by the Conseil supérieur de l'enseignement.' Referring to Tournemire, the notice reported that 'the candidate coming in second place' had applied an 'ingratiating and vigorous pressure' on the minister 'in order to obtain from him the nomination to the chair of organ ...' The 'minister' in question was Edouard Daladier who became prime minister in 1933. Tournemire, remembering this event from the perspective of 1933, attacked 'M. Daladier (who has since become famous!).'

Tournemire unleashed his bitterness on others as well: 'From all the evidence, M. Marcel Dupré was the instigator of this disgraceful act as well as Madame Dupré. Tournemire has *never* known intrigue. In this sad affair, it is only necessary to retain one thing: the lack of decency of my "rival" with respect to an artist of my age *at the very least!*' He also attacked the 'lack of frankness of Rabeau [*sic*], *who had promised me this post for a long time*' and 'the hateful support of Widor.' 'I end with this sad memory,' wrote Tournemire – meaning the undated portion of his memoirs – 'in here consigning the serious reproaches, which I addressed, in the aftermath of this injustice, to Rabeau [*sic*], reproaching him for his lack of speaking out, of *dignity* vis-à-vis one of his professors ...'[69]

For Tournemire at fifty-six, the 1926 event was thoroughly intertwined with generational issues and consequently his identity. His transition from the provinces to Paris as a late teenager had been completely coloured by Franck; Widor, however, had 'ambushed' him. Conversely,

Henri Rabaud, who held Tournemire's life in his hands, was also a former student. With the succession of the relatively youthful Dupré, Tournemire knew this meant the definitive end to his long-time dream of fully replicating Franck's positions. It was, as Freud would say, a moment in which the 'testing of reality' demonstrated 'that the loved object no longer exists.'[70]

Tournemire's response would be the writing of *L'Orgue Mystique*, a composition that would fascinate reviewers in its ability to hybridize antique modes with ultramodern harmonies. In retrospect, *Comœ dia*'s 1924 review of *The Gods Are Dead* seemed proleptic. Like others, the review had both praised and gently parodied Tournemire's 'dark and haughty score' in whose sincere writing style even 'the most morose technician would not be able to discover the slightest deviation in language or the slightest relaxation.' Every measure had been 'reasoned, intentional, imperturbable in its logical march,' 'minutely chiseled and detailed,' fashioned 'according to certain laws, immutable for more than two centuries that form the code of every composer of the highest class.' The reviewer had concluded: 'It follows from all of this that M. Tournemire's score ... does not dream for even an instant of offering sacrifice to the taste of the "cutting-edge" [*avancés*].' Moreover, in his deliberately primitivist work (subtitled *Chryséis*), Tournemire had not made 'the useless and impossible attempt to establish, in our days, a work based entirely upon the antique modes.'[71]

Tournemire's *L'Orgue Mystique* would not be based 'entirely' on modes – but ironically, its innovation and capacity to surprise would come from utilizing them as a futural past. The retrieval of antiquity had not worked well for Tournemire at the Opéra, but at the organ console, it was about to make him *avancé*.

1927: *L'Orgue Glorieux* – Plainchant Unbound

On 4 January 1927, Tournemire played the organ for the wedding of his student, Joseph Bonnet, at Saint-Ferdinand-des-Ternes, Paris. Dom Joseph Gajard, O.S.B., master of the choir at Solesmes Abbey, was in the organ tribune as well. Tournemire used the occasion to announce his intention of composing a mammoth undertaking tentatively entitled *The Glorious Organ*. He had not composed for the organ in over seventeen years, that is, since his 1910 *Triple Choral* in homage to Franck. Although there are conflicting opinions about how long Tournemire had been thinking about this project and why he decided to choose this moment for its launch,[72] it seems reasonable to consider it, like the *Triple Choral*, as being connected to memorializing César Franck. He had lost the Franck chair the year before; and he was about to begin writing a book – *César Franck* (1931) – that would establish his version of Franck for posterity (as opposed to, for example, Dupré's).[73] If the process of memorialization is an act of mourning meant to incorporate a painful past into a new version of one's self; and if monuments are at least partially about one version of the past being asserted over rival versions; then a 1930 review of the project was aptly named: 'A Monumental Work for Organ.'[74]

Tournemire's choice of using the organ tribune at Bonnet's wedding as the place and time to announce *The Glorious Organ*, with Dom Gajard from Solesmes as witness, was masterful. Bonnet himself had proposed the idea four years earlier as part of his active promotion of a postwar plainchant revival for a mystic generation. (In 1917, Bonnet wrote from a concert tour in New York, 'This mystic, young people is thirsty for the Ideal, for Music and Beauty, and the artist who allowed himself to play unworthy music to them would be as culpable as someone corrupting the pure soul of a child.')[75] Gregorian congresses were held in Tourcoing in 1919 and in Toulouse in 1920, and an assembly of 'scholae grégoriennes' in Paris in 1921. On 9 October 1921, Cardinal Dubois of the Archdiocese of Paris issued a directive 'permitting the use' of the 1904 Vatican Edition of plainchant in the Archdiocese of Paris, an internationalizing move that went against the Gallican grain of preserving local traditional rituals, chants, and books. The movement was also catalysed by the return to France of the Solesmes monks from exile in Britain (completed by 1922), an aspect of the 'second ralliement' following the restoration of Vatican relations in December 1920. In 1923, Cardinal Dubois founded an *Institut grégorien* in Paris.[76]

The universalist aims of the Schola-Solesmes ideology extended to the colonies as well as at home. A 1924 article, 'Gregorian Chant in China and in the Lower Congo,' responding to letters from missionaries, asked whether these did not demonstrate that 'there is in the beauty of Gregorian music something human and universal which makes our liturgical chants participate in the *catholicity* of the Church and renders them accessible, not only to an élite of cultivated Latins, but to Christian people everywhere, without distinction in race and latitude?' (The writer also asked, 'if the old Chinese are "filled with wonder" by our antique Western melodies, why believe that Gregorian Chant will forever remain incapable of moving the villagers of our provinces?')[77] In the postwar epoch, the idea of a 'greater France' that spanned the globe was seen as a necessary component of France's ability to survive. 'The French have to become more and more convinced to the marrow of their bones,' explained Marshal Lyautey in an interview regarding the 1931 International Colonial Exposition, 'that the whole nation must line up behind its colonies, and that our future lies overseas.'[78] Plainchant's imagined qualities as being 'natural,' 'primitive' (like *Volkslieder*), and 'universal' made it an ideal cultural language for the postwar colonial project.

It was within this broad revivalist context, yet another aspect of the *renouveau catholique* aim of re-Christianizing France in the wake of its sacrifices, that Bonnet addressed the Congress of Gregorian Chant in December 1922 with his discussion 'The Role of the Liturgical Organist at the Great Organ.'[79] Bonnet too hoped that provincial villagers might be moved by chant, desiring with all his 'heart that our people of France learn again how to sing in our churches' just as he had 'heard the dear people of Alsace in the Cathedral of Strasbourg at the [Gregorian] Congress of 1921, singing with a single voice.' The nostalgic yearning for a mythical medieval unity paralleled the completion and organic wholeness felt by the repatriation of Alsace and Lorraine, symbolized in the Cathedral of Strasbourg, to the French body politic.

Bonnet yearned for even more completion and wholeness: he called for a gifted organist-composer to take the massive text of Dom Guéranger's *The Liturgical Year* (which he had given as a gift to Tournemire the previous year) and use it as a textual libretto: 'If I might dare, Sirs, I would like to express myself on the subject of instrumental pieces – the desire that a sincere and talented artist, utilizing the repertory of Gregorian melodies, compose a "liturgical year" for the organ, in the spirit of that which Dom Guéranger wrote the text. The utilization, in effect, of Gregorian themes in music for the organ by an organist-composer, musically well-endowed and nourished on the liturgy, would be a guarantee of beauty and would assure liturgical musical unity.'[80] Bonnet made his yearning for monumental 'completion' explicit: noting that other 'modern artists' had already broken ground in this sense – Alexandre Guilmant had composed the *Liturgical Organist* for example, and Widor's own 'Roman' and 'Gothic' symphonies both incorporated plainchant motifs – Bonnet specified that what had not yet been accomplished was '*a complete "liturgical year" for the organ*.'[81]

Bonnet's idea of using Dom Guéranger's collection of texts in *The Liturgical Year* would have had great appeal for Tournemire's symbolist world-view and method. The idea was also eminently postwar. The appeal of Biblical tales and Latin texts throughout the 1920s – Honegger's *King David* (1921), T.S. Eliot's *The Waste Land* (1922), Stravinsky's *Oedipus Rex* (1927) – was, in the words of one musicologist, 'indicative not so much of a fashion as of the acknowledgment of a vital resource and its continuing utility in addressing the dilemmas of a weary postwar world.' In particular, Stravinsky came to prefer 'Latin as the language best suited to the expression of universal truths.'[82] All this reflects Tournemire's own proclivities and procedure: it seems that he chose the 'chants' because of their textual content (as found in Guéranger's French-Latin parallel passages), and only afterward did he consult ritual books for the Gregorian melodies that carried the texts.[83]

Sometime after August 1926, Tournemire obtained one of the two books from which he obtained the melodies: his personal copy of the *Liber Antiphonarius* (1897 Solesmes edition) bore a 26 July 1926 imprimatur. He may already have owned a copy of the other book, the *Paroissien romain.* (Although it was the 1920 edition, his personal copy was obtained no earlier than 19 June 1922, the date of the last inserted 'supplement' inserted.)[84] During the summer of 1927, he made his first visit to Solesmes, noting in his memoirs his 'first office improvised at Solesmes' on 14 June 1927.

Among those with whom he spoke at Solesmes was the choirmaster Dom Gajard who was writing (or about to write) an article on rhythmic 'freedom' as the very essence of Gregorian Chant. Gajard promoted the Schola-Solesmes notion of plainchant's 'freedom' (and hence, rhythmic superiority) over 'meter' and cited Maritain's newly revised edition of *Art and Scholasticism* as his authority: 'Thus, the "metered time" disappears as such; the rhythm, of material, becomes a thing of the spirit. And it is because of this condition that it deserves its very definition: *the order of movement.* "All order," says M. Maritain, "and all proportion is a work of intelligence. And thus, to say with the scholastics that beauty is the shining forth of the form upon proportionate parts of matter, is to say that it is a bursting-forth of the intelligence upon matter intelligently disposed."'[85] Gajard's conception of chant as being hylomorphic, an organic interpenetration of matter and its *entelechy*, could also be seen in his reference to a work entitled *Theory of Rhythm in Modern Composition*: '"By rhythm alone," M. Combarieu says excellently in turn, "*sonorous matter takes on form*; by means of it, *matter becomes an organism*, completely ordered, intelligible."' The metaphor continued as listening was compared to the Thomistic notion of connatural knowledge, a genuine identity between the form of the known object and the form known in the mind: '"And the mind of the listener, instead of wandering aimlessly, enjoys itself, as if its own eurhythmy was being revealed."'[86]

Tournemire's ideas resonated with Gajard's and he extended them to a degree which the monk might not have approved. In his review of Tournemire, Dom Maur Sablayrolles would later complain that sometimes 'the transformation of Gregorian rhythm is such that one can barely recognize the theme.' Extending his deepest congratulations to the composer, the monk asked permission 'to add a vow': namely, that Tournemire now 'consecrate his beautiful talent to paraphrase, in pieces no less sumptuous ... Gregorian melodies *in their proper rhythm*.'[87] But Tournemire remained adamant in the face of criticism: 'I had to forcibly free myself from the rhythm of Solesmes,' he asserted. 'I had as an obligation in many cases to modify the rhythm and to make it flexible to the imperious exigencies of the diverse and strongly varied compositions ...'[88] As will be seen, most other reviewers also found liberation in Tournemire's liberties.

If Tournemire's ideas on rhythm needed freeing from Solesmes, this was even more the case with respect to the matter of harmony, chromaticism, and dissonance. Tournemire's idea that eternalist chants could be carried in 'passionate' materials departed radically from Solesmes's ultramontanist aesthetic. This would be his definitive innovation.

Realist Mysticism: Chromatic Modalism as Passionate Eternalism

Tournemire's proposal was bold: each Sunday of the Catholic liturgical year (excepting the penitential Sundays of Advent and Lent during which organ playing was prohibited) and several major feast days would have their own composed 'office.' In turn, each Sunday office would have five 'movements' corresponding to five moments in the Catholic mass: an Introit played between the 'Asperges me' sprinkling rite and the sung 'Kyrie'; an Offertory; an Elevation after the consecration; a Communion; and a *Final*, played as the ministers exited, often offering a *resumé* of the texts that had been used that day.[89] The idea of an 'organ-mass' went back to the seventeenth century, beginning with Frescobaldi in Italy and followed by Titelouze, de Grigny, and Couperin in France.[90] None of them could have conceived, however, writing and publishing fifty-one organ masses for the liturgical year. *L'Orgue Mystique*, when completed, comprised two hundred and fifty-three (Holy Saturday being an anomaly) pieces of varying lengths.

This idea of a sweeping cycle came not from the Catholic tradition but rather the Lutheran one of J.S. Bach. Tournemire explicitly intended to imitate Bach's cycle of cantatas, a complete musical office for a year's Sundays. Bach's cantatas consisted of variations on Lutheran chorales, elaborations of both the hymn's textual 'libretto' as well as its musical themes. Like Bach, Tournemire would write variations on plainchants taken from both the Mass and the monastic Hours for each Sunday, finding in them a textual 'libretto' which he could 'paraphrase' and 'comment on,' as well as musical themes which he could set like gems within modern encasements.

Tournemire would differ from Bach, however, in using pre-eighteenth-century modal language rather than the tonal system that Bach himself perfected. 'The master of masters, J.S. Bach, has done it – and in what a manner – for the Protestant liturgy,' wrote Tournemire. 'I thought it was necessary to endow the Catholic cult with an ensemble work conceived in the same spirit, but with this difference: the greatest of musicians had based his art on the Protestant chorale, and in service of the *tonal system* in the immense part of his work. As for myself, I offered commentary on Gregorian chant in the modal system which, furthermore, did not know how to exclude *chromaticism*.'[91] The almost parenthetical way in which Tournemire wrote this last phrase disguised a key conflict with Solesmes that led to his singular innovation.

The term 'chromatic' denotes an interval that is not part of a diatonic scale.[92] Although it loosely refers to notes marked with accidentals foreign to the key's scale, in a stricter sense it does not apply to notes that are modulating to a chord in the piece's key. Put another way: 'chromatic' notes wander – they are not on their way to a chord with a recognizable relationship to the tonal center. They do not refer the listener back 'home.' Chromaticism flourished in the nineteenth century, and in Wagner's symbolist use, it was still tied to an earlier notion of the Baroque 'Doctrine of the Affections' (*Affektenlehre*) in which prescribed musical devices were used to express fundamental moods or emotional states.[93] In Romantic hands, stepwise chromatic motion could be used to represent emotions such as a sinking into depression, a rising feeling of exhilaration, and mounting sexual tension.

In this context, Dom Gajard saw chromaticism as the musical analogue of the nineteenth-century realistic novel: it was a means of representing the passions and thus excluded by the ultramontanist aesthetic of *la paix de l'éternel*. In the same article written around the time of Tournemire's visit to Solesmes, Gajard proceeded from rhythm to harmony, and explicitly rejected Tournemire's own notion. 'Gregorian melody is before all else *diatonic,*' wrote Gajard, 'which is to say that *it excludes every chromatic succession* ... Thus already we are alerted by this simple detail of that which Gregorian art desires. Chromaticism excels at painting the passions, the extreme feelings that agitate the human heart. But that which Gregorian art desires to paint is not our passions, but rather the love of God and the peace which results from it.' Here Gajard quoted his predecessor, Dom Mocquereau, drawing on the ultramontanist distinction between 'sensual' and 'religious' music: 'The ear habituated to [plainchant's] incomparable straightforwardness is no longer able to sense these flabby airs, *impregnated with sensualism* even in that which ought to be the expression of divine love. *There is something angelic in the inflexibility of its scale which does not undergo any alteration.*'[94] Solesmes's eternalism was the logical conclusion of theological premises: for a perfect being to change would be corruption into the less than perfect; hence perfect beings (God, angels, the Gregorian scale) cannot undergo alteration.

Tournemire rejected this straitjacket and turned back to the ancients in search of both justification and a language that could bridge plainchant and modern harmony. He did not have to look far. At least as early as 1923, he had become engaged in musicological research and published an edition of Dietrich Buxtehude's works.[95] Although Buxtehude followed Matthias Grünewald by nearly two centuries, Tournemire was able to use him in much the same way that Huysmans (and Rouault's critics) used the 'Flemish primitives.' A predecessor of Bach, Buxtehude had not yet completed the transition from modalism to tonalism and was thus in some sense a musical 'primitive.' 'The grand masters of modality,' Tournemire wrote Dom Gajard, had been 'Frescobaldi in Italy, Buxtehude in Germany, Titelouze and Grigny in France,' all of them 'pioneers of ancient modality.'[96] However, just as Racine, Molière, and Corneille (in the 'classical' age of the Sun King) had destroyed the 'incomparable language of Rabelais,' so Bach, 'without taking away anything from his transcendent genius,' had 'killed modal art.'[97]

Since Gregorian lines already contained within themselves the possibility of being 'united' to modern harmonics and polytonalities, Tournemire argued,[98] a 'modern musician' was free to compose using the modal system. (As we have seen, Debussy himself had visited Solesmes while writing *Pelléas.*) Tournemire explicitly acknowledged his intention of forging a hybrid language, preserving the tradition even as he renewed and reclothed it: 'The interest I had in writing this work resided principally in the great modal tradition of the masters anterior to Bach. *Tradi-*

tion renewed in "L'Orgue mystique," after 250 years of oblivion. I tried hard to *continue* these masters while at the same time serving modern polytonality, like *clothing* [*vêtement*]. However, I always respected the lightness of the Gregorian lines, the fluidity of the aerial paraphrases. Didn't Huysmans write: "Plainchant is the aerial and mobile paraphrase of the immovable structure of the cathedrals!"'[99]

Tournemire's return to the sources was thoroughly in accord with postwar trends. In 1920, the Ballets Russes had premiered Stravinsky's *Pulcinella*, allegedly based on themes of the eighteenth-century Giovanni Battista Pergolesi. In 1921, Juan Gris had written, 'now I believe that the "quality" of an artist derives from the quantity of the past that he carries in him – from his artistic atavism.'[100] In 1927, the year Tournemire announced *L'Orgue Glorieux*, Stravinsky's premiere of *Oedipus Rex* (with its libretto by Cocteau) reached back to Greek antiquity. That same year, Abbé Calvet's *Panorama* called the postwar epoch a 'climacteric' in need of a 'palingenesis.'

Reflecting on his teacher, Raymond Petit made these links explicit: 'Admittedly the Middle Ages has always attracted Tournemire ... But I really see nothing incompatible between the fact of his being inspired by the past and yet being "modern." It is probably nothing more than going forward by relying for support upon a renaissance, a palingenesis (in a domain diametrically opposed to that which we occupy; I am thinking for example of *Pulcinella*). And very often the march of evolution is by no means arrested. Many new stages take for their point of departure, not that which has just gone before, but that which lies in a more distant past.'[101] (Petit had very likely spoken with Tournemire who articulated his own palingenesis: 'Thus one sees the interest there was to return to the source of "modality" in order to develop an art that had not, up until this day, blossomed again in full liberty ... It was necessary to reconstruct it.')[102] Like neoclassicism, Tournemire's return to the past was thoroughly avant-garde.

Searching for a noun that would express the kind of hybridization that Lefèvre's *compénétration* of 'planes' had provided for Bernanos, Petit settled on *le conglomérat*: 'The conglomeration of medieval melodic segments and modern harmonies that *L'Orgue mystique* presents appears to me not merely extremely interesting, but even extremely new.' Tournemire's planar juxtapositions, compenetrations, or conglomerations shared aspects of surrealist music as well as neoclassical. By 'paraphrasing' eternal melodies with fashionable 'passionate' clothing, his work was the intersection of incongruities – eternity and history, divinity and humanity, form and matter. If surrealism is marked primarily by 'semantic dislocation and fissure,' a product of having 'tilted the semantic planes of the old language of music,' then Tournemire's intentions shared basic aesthetic ideas with works by Poulenc.[103] Like surrealism, Tournemire's deployment of chant provided 'an intelligible context of familiar sounds in order to develop a system of meanings' at odds with other systems – for example, of Solesmes. The familiar sounds of chant had been constructed to mean 'incapable of alteration.' Tilting their semantic plane by setting them within chromaticism and polytonalism – whose meanings had evolved into 'passionate' and 'dissonant' – Tournemire constructed a 'semantic vertigo,' since the signs he used both meant and did not mean what they seemed to mean. Tournemire's music was profoundly Baudelairean (and sacramental and hylomorphic): eternal verities made incarnate in the passing passions of history.

In addition to its affinities with both neoclassical palingenesis and surrealist semantics, the 'wrapping' metaphors used to describe Tournemire's music suggest a parallel with the colonizing aspect of primitivist modernism as well. Metaphors such as the encasement of 'gems,' swirling 'garlands,' 'clothing,' and 'embroidery' share the same rhetorical method as the colonialist 'wrapping' of native cultures within the high culture of European France. 'Wrapping' both incorporates the other and gives it new meaning.[104] By incorporating chant, Tournemire's music played a dialectical role in the politics of identity. On the one hand, using 'primitive' chant gave Catholic listeners a nostalgic sense of home and identity. On the other, wrapping the chant within a culture-system it did not natively possess altered its meaning, but it also give those same Catholic listeners a sense of being legitimately 'modern.' This process was thoroughly in synch with the colonialist movements of the day, symbolized most spectacularly by the 1931 International Colonial Exposition.[105]

Even experts could find Tournemire's *déformation* of chant excerpts altered beyond recognition, retaining only the vaguest aura of a certain mode. In his review for *L'Informateur musical et théatral des œuvres catholiques*, Edmond Dierickx initially thought he knew which chant was being paraphrased, but he was suddenly washed over by 'a wave of doubt!' Because Tournemire's 'liberty of stylization' had distended the thematic fragment beyond recognition, Dierickx reasoned that the source chant could plausibly have come from 'the *Sanctus* of Mass IV, or from the Vesper antiphons for Holy Saturday, *Et valde mane* from the Lauds of Easter, *Angelus autem* and *Respondens autem* from the Vespers of Easter, or from any other antiphon of the eighth mode.' So that others might know exactly what text was being quoted, Dierickx offered a suggestion: 'M. Tournemire might, at the very least, in the next volumes, discretely indicate the sources at the head of each piece, if he does not want to overly-determine his musical text at the first appearance of each theme.'[106] If even a critic well acquainted with chant was unable to decide which chant texts and themes Tournemire was 'paraphrasing,' then later listeners can forgive themselves for being unable at times to know what the composer intended to 'comment on.'

In retrospect, it is unfortunate that Éditions Heugel, the publisher of *l'Orgue Mystique*, did not follow the practice of Alphonse Leduc, who published Olivier Messiaen's *Ascension Suite* (1934). Messiaen attached programmatic titles and epigraphs to each of his four movements, and the scores fully quoted and cited the texts upon which his music 'commented.'[107] We can wonder whether Messiaen, an occasional assistant at Ste-Clotilde on whose behalf Tournemire wrote an important letter of recommendation for the post at La Trinité, did not receive this idea from Tournemire.[108] In any event, had Tournemire's own editors published the texts on which he provided 'commentary,' the symbolist's intent (and a surrealist effect) might have been more fully realized.

Tournemire's plainchant project was not a nineteenth-century neo-medieval one of 'thinking with history.' It was not interested in reproducing the 'outward shape' of Gothic originals (as Guilmant and Widor had). Rather, like Maritain's retrieval of Aquinas, Tournemire's retrieval of chant was structuralist, an act of 'thinking without history,' interested in reproducing the form not as 'shape' but rather as *entelechy*. Tournemire acknowledged that his use of chromaticism to clothe chant was '*particulière*' ('odd' or 'peculiar'), but he purposely employed it to produce a 'mystical' effect: '"modality" is always observed,' he wrote, 'and creates a constant mystical ambience [*une ambiance mystique*].'[109]

Tournemire's music is always called 'mystical,' but when pressed to articulate the concept, commentators usually find themselves lost for a more concrete definition. One approach might be to consider that Tournemire's conscious combination of chromaticism (a wandering from home) and plainchant (a nostalgic homesickness for that eternal home) produced something akin to Freud's 'uncanny': familiarity haunted by an eerie sense of the unexpected.[110] It was also marked by a sense of 'longing' distinctly off-modern: 'the direction of force in the desiring narrative is always a future-past, a deferment of experience in the direction of origin and thus eschaton ...'[111] In this context of the uncanny, longing for home, and futuristic nostalgia, words applied to Charles Ives might well be said of Tournemire's 'mysticism': 'rigorously conducted experiments into realms beyond tonality, where his shifting note patterns either ache to settle into the comfort of a home base that is denied them or drift with near resignation across the keyless expanse of a brave new world. ... the tug of nostalgia that throbs in the contrast between the familiar (from hymn tunes ...) and the unknown.'[112]

L'Orgue Mystique (1929–1930): *une synthèse rénovatrice*

In the final week of October 1927, Tournemire began the actual composition of *L'Orgue Glorieux* in earnest. Fifteen days later, he had finished the first set of pieces: the office for Easter's celebration of the dead Christ's resurrection. He had begun composing, not at the beginning of the Catholic liturgical year, that is, in December (as he had sketched out in his initial handwritten overview),[113] but rather with spring's capacity to bring back life. Tournemire finished and dated it on 11 November 1927, the ninth anniversary of the armistice. This symbolic effort to assign the 'Resurrection' piece the armistice's date located it alongside other works that represented the fruition of almost a decade of working through the war: in 1927, Heidegger's *Being and Time*, Daniel-Rops's *Our Inquietude*, and Stravinsky's *Oedipus Rex*; in 1928, Stravinsky's *Apollo* and Carl Dreyer's film *The Passion of Joan of Arc*; in 1929, Remarque's *All Quiet on the Western Front*, Hemingway's *A Farewell to Arms*, and Balanchine's work about a mythic homecoming, *The Prodigal Son* (set design by Rouault). Volumes in Tournemire's personal library – *The Memorial of Foch* (1929) and Georges Clémenceau's *Grandeur and Misery of a Victory* (1930) – also suggest that he shared his contemporaries' hunger for reflecting on the catastrophe.[114] Tournemire's handwritten plan for the cycle quoted Dom Guéranger's *Liturgical Year*: the Easter feast was 'the most sacred, the one toward which the entire cycle converges.'[115] In the composition of *L'Orgue Mystique*, the ninth anniversary of the armistice, 11 November 1927, was the cycle's most sacred point of convergence.

Four months later, having worked at a furious pace, Tournemire completed the first six offices: Easter, Christmas, Immaculate Conception, Pentecost, Assumption, and All Saints' Day.[116] On 16 March 1928, in preparation for their going to press, Tournemire changed the title from *L'Orgue Glorieux* to *L'Orgue Mystique* and eliminated the subtitle alluding to Guéranger, that is, 'Liturgical Year.'[117] Later that year, the first volumes were published with *L'Orgue Mystique* boldly displayed in rubrical red ink.[118] What did the change from 'The Glorious Organ' to 'The Mystical Organ' signify for the composer? Tournemire's *César Franck* (1931), also written at approximately this time, contains repeated references to the 'mystical,' quoting both Görres and Hello. (The second chapter was entitled 'Mystical Considerations.') Part of this was a legacy of the nineteenth century for which the 'mystical' was a codeword for symbolist, Catholic, and Decadent anti-positivists, pointing towards deeper unseen realities. Tournemire's quotation of Hello in his unfinished work, 'On the Exalted Mission of the Organist in the Church,' used the word in this sense: 'Higher than reason, orthodox mysticism sees, hears, touches, and feels that which reason is incapable of seeing, hearing, touching, and feeling.'[119]

Perhaps more importantly, however, was the association in Tournemire's mind of Görres's monumental work with his having succeeded his brother-in-law's presidency over the Société Baudelaire's board for *La Mystique* following Péladan's (and his wife's) death. His inscription of Görres at that time – 'When the soul is, as it were, plunged into a profound desolation ...' – suggests his association of the 'mystical' not only with inwardness but especially grief. The gregarious term 'glorious' stands at odds with so much of *L'Orgue Mystique*'s intensely interior ambience; it also conveys an uncomplicated and one-dimensional sense of triumph in sharp contrast to the work's complex alchemy of shadows and light. In addition, Tournemire's use of the word in a 1930 interview suggests not only grief, but also its connections with blood, vicarious suffering, and redemption in the thought of Huysmans and Bloy. 'Nourished by mysticism,' Tournemire replied, 'I aspire to nothing other than to make music participate with all possible piety in the mysteries of Sacrifice.'[120]

No organist who has opened up any one of the score's fifty-one volumes will have missed either Tournemire's 'Notice of the Author' or the following introduction by Bonnet. Both notices were printed inside each fascicle. However, the organist limited only to English would have missed Bonnet's meanings completely. Whereas the English translation read,

> Our modern musical writing is extraordinary [sic] fit
> to adorn the Gregorian Melodies ...

the French original said:

> Our contemporary musical language possesses astonishing aptitudes to paraphrase Gregorian melodies *eternally young.*[121]

'Extraordinary fit' does not capture the 'astonishment' one would experience at seeing the Jazz Age's 'aptitude' for ancient melodies. (Or, as Messiaen later put it succinctly: 'mi-gothique, mi-ultra moderne.')[122] The word 'adorn,' perhaps intended by the translator to convey something of the 'clothing' image, does not translate 'paraphrase' which Tournemire would have meant his symbolist music to do literally: that is, function as a paraphrase, commentary, interpretation, and exegesis of the given textual libretto. Worst of all, the English simply omitted the words 'eternally young.' Bonnet's phrase echoed his 1917 letter from New York about a 'mystic, young people ... thirsty for the Ideal.' Read at the end of a decade filled with building monuments to dead youth, situated alongside the anniversary of the armistice, *A Realist Generation*, *All Quiet on the Western Front*, and 'the mysteries of Sacrifice,' the reader of Bonnet's notice limited to English would have completely missed *L'Orgue Mystique*'s redemptive promise of an invisible world forever young.

Beginning in March 1929, reviews trickling in emphasized Tournemire's surprising hybridization of ancient and modern. When comparing these reviews with those of his work at the Paris Opéra five years earlier, the reader cannot help but notice a remarkable inversion of tone: in 1924, Tournemire had been praised for his adherence to classical forms, his lack of innovation, and his opposition to modernity and fashion. But in reviews of *L'Orgue Mystique*, critics repeatedly lauded his creative 'novelty' and radical 'innovation' by renewing the past in service of the future.

Reviews came first from Belgium and Catalan, places in which Tournemire had contacts and had concertized, and then from Paris.[123] *Vingtième Siècle* praised Tournemire's 'breaking with the cliché genre, the insipid counterpoints on mummified themes, the Gregorian songs treated for such a long time' in complete 'contempt for their rhythm.'[124] The first polyphonists had been like medieval artisans, able to take folk song texts and lines and transform them into something glorious. Similarly, even as *L'Orgue Mystique* enriched itself with 'all the contemporary harmonic and contrapuntal resources,' it also renewed 'the art of musical illuminations.' This 'decisive musical action' would appeal even to 'the most profane enthusiasm.' *L'Éveil Catalan* put it simply: Tournemire had 'succeeded in putting both plain-chant and 20th-century harmony in contact with one another.'[125] *Le Figaro* used the metaphor of a jeweller who sets stones within encasements. Tournemire's 'contrapuntal novelty' and 'harmonic aggregations' were the settings in which he set the fragments of chant. Moreover, Tournemire had a marvellous ability to 'extract' these gems from 'an inexhaustible source,' the world of 'plainchant, which is the very essence of a music dominated by the spirit of faith.' His knowledge and vision had made utterly contemporary materials 'uniquely adequate to the Gregorian melody' encased within them, and *L'Orgue Mystique* would 'mark a date in the annals of French publishing.'[126]

During July 1929, in *Le Courrier Musical* (a central trade journal for French musicians), Béranger de Miramon Fitz-James, president and founder of the 'Friends of the Organ' [Amis de l'Orgue] published an important review. Fitz-James also reached back to early polyphonists, praising Tournemire for having created 'a religious style of organ' for the first time 'since Frescobaldi, Titelouse, Grigny, Fr[ançois] Couperin, etc.'[127] He underscored Tournemire's symbolist method: each Sunday at Ste-Clotilde, the 'feverish inspirations' of his organ improvisations had shown him to be a 'liturgical metaphysician, and illustrator, and a musical preacher.' The 'novelty' of his undertaking resided in both 'a rich modern stylization of "plainchantesque themes"' and in 'a *return to modal art* for free paraphrase.' This 'powerfully original organ style' seemed like a 'crystallization' of apparently incompatible materials: 'primitive Gregorian forms' and the 'systematic audacities of our contemporary musical language.'

Tournemire's art was 'a renewing synthesis [*synthèse rénovatrice*] of the great epochs of religious music,' one in which 'the primitive piece and modern art conjugally unite [*se conjuguent*].' Reproductive metaphors continued in another *Courrier Musical* review. Insofar as the 'modern resources of polyphony and of registration' had been 'happily associated with' the 'supple medieval garlands,' the recent volumes had been 'completely impregnated with a Gregorian ambience.'[128] All these metaphors attempted to convey that antiquity and modernity fit one another in ways that were not accidental or externally related, but rather substantial and interpenetrating.

1929–1930: Salad Concerts?: 'The word *Madame* in the mouth of a Greek hero'

To those who might imagine Tournemire as primarily a church musician unaware of the musical mainstream, a glance at the musical reviews he wrote for *Le Courrier Musical* during this period will surprise.[129] One of the most entertaining, appearing on 1 January 1930, was his review of a

Wiéner 'concert salade' that tossed together George Gershwin and Fletcher Henderson along with J.S. Bach and Beethoven.[130] 'Hey Wood, Van Philips, composers of Jazz,' exclaimed Tournemire, 'it's an impossible attempt! It's obvious that Messrs. Wiéner et Doucet, by their priceless interpretation of this "music" which emanates from the deepest circle of Hell, have succeeded in consigning the two greatest musicians of all time to the background.'[131]

There is a certain irony in Tournemire's calling the 'salad concerts' an 'impossible attempt!' since the concerts that he and others were giving in order to promote his work were, in their own way, tossed salads as well. In 1929, since disk recordings of *L'Orgue Mystique* had not yet been made, the primary means of publicizing his new work would be through concertizing by friends as well as by himself.[132] Not only did such concerts give the music a hearing, but the published reviews shaped public discourse and reception, allowing interpretative schemes to be repeated and built up into an accepted framework.

One of the first of these attempts was Joseph Bonnet's tour reported on 6 December 1929.[133] After having given recitals playing the complete works of Franck, Bonnet had toured England, giving a series of twelve Bach recitals in 'London, Manchester, and other large cities.' Upon returning to France, he concertized Tournemire: 'From Lyon have come reports of the great success achieved by Joseph Bonnet in several recitals,' reported *Le Ménestrel.* During these, Bonnet had 'made a particular effort, making audiences both taste and applaud *l'Orgue mystique* of Charles Tournemire.' Because of Bonnet's schedule, the notice set Tournemire's work within a genealogy of which he would have approved: Bach – Franck – Tournemire.

Not all the reviews were positive. In a recital of Marcel Paponaud given in Saint-Etienne, *Les Amitiés* reported that 'several were not upset to hear a specimen of the latest work of Ch. Tournemire's *l'Orgue mystique* about which specialists are talking a lot.'[134] However, although the virtuoso had played the score 'brilliantly and with conviction,' the work derailed 'the spirit of analysis.' It was filled with 'tormented and incomplete lines, sudden departures, with the taste of an improvisation conducted by a broken baton.' In spite of this, it was still possible to 'recognize the fragments of liturgical themes in the midst of a shimmering of inexplicable dissonances.' Calling the work 'very "smokey with incense"' [*très 'fumée d'encens'*], *Les Amitiés* noted sarcastically that this was the work (quoting Bonnet's preface) for which 'all organists' had been 'waiting many long years.'

Two weeks later, the prestigious *Le Monde Musical* also had words for Tournemire's dissonances and borrowed words from the anti-realist tradition of *fantastical* writing to describe them. Tournemire had 'strongly desired to entrust to his young colleague' Maurice Duruflé the first performance of two pieces still in manuscript. Duruflé gave an 'impeccable interpretation' of both, and the first of these was 'played in an encore with enthusiasm. It was ravishing.' But the second, 'filled with *fantasie*, seemed to describe – in the manner of the gargoyles of our very oldest basilicas – the very worst moral ugliness, nightmares of sins, cursed *hallucinations*.' Even so, Tournemire had succeeded in creating 'sonorous *beauty*.' This was a lesson for those would claim 'to justify musical *ugliness* under the pretext of "expressionism,"' concluded the reviewer, adding this admonition: 'The mind is not moved when the ear is shocked.'[135]

Tournemire himself set out on a series of recitals to publicize and establish the framework of interpretation for his own work. In putting together a recital program, the rhetoric of hybridizing the ancient and the modern could be accomplished not only by means internal to the composition of *L'Orgue Mystique* itself, but by its placement within the overall program of pieces. Tournemire's method can be seen by contrasting it with more typical arrangements of the day given in programs for 'Les Amis de l'Orgue.'[136] Geneviève Mercier's April 1929 recital began with the baroque: Bach's 'Toccata and Fugue in D minor' was followed by two composers from the age of the Sun King. She then departed from chronological order (significantly, her program included no dates) by playing the 'Scherzo' of Eugène Gigout, and then moving back in time for two organ transcriptions (a fashion of the day) of works by Handel and Beethoven. The romantic tradition continued with Franck and early twentieth-century 'moderns' of a symphonic stripe: Barié, Boellmann, Dupré, and Guillemoteau. Tournemire's own work was represented by a quiet piece from *l'Orgue Mystique* and by a Toccata written in his youth. By ending with Vierne's 'Carillon de Westminster,' the recital repeated a pairing (the 'Carillon' and Gigout's *Scherzo*) that has since become standard fare in recordings.[137] In this context, the heavy emphasis on thick romantic textures and the organ's use as a symphonic instrument would have emphasized that aspect of Tournemire's own work, muffling its modal aspects.

A March 1932 recital by Émile Poillot, a student of Widor and Vierne, offers a similar example. Although Poillot kept to a stricter chronological order, his program also established a romantic genealogy of 'modern' music. Once again, Bach stood at the source, followed by the Third Sonata of Felix Mendelssohn, who had rescued the baroque master from oblivion. Next came E. Bernard, followed by Tournemire, who was heard and interpreted within this romantic setting. One interesting feature of Poillot's printed program was this explanatory note inserted as a gloss on the Tournemire piece: 'Today we are listening to the final piece of one of the 52 offices of *l'Orgue Mystique* which M. Tournemire has just completed. The characteristics of this work are as follows: *the union of modern art and primitive piety*; a search for an appropriateness in terms of the setting, time, and significance of [religious] services; a stylization of melodic elements taken from Gregorian chant; *a bias for modality*; the rhapsodic character of certain final pieces such as that which we will hear today.' Although the music's written description reflected Tournemire's intention, its performance within the non-modal ambience of the rest of the program would have conveyed a different musical sense. Ending the program with excerpts from Vierne's Fourth Symphony, the program place *l'Orgue Mystique* firmly within the ambience of the romantic symphonic organ.[138]

Tournemire's own programming of a 1930 recital at the Cathedral of Rouen on 13 March 1930 shows his innovative approach by contrast.[139] The *Journal de Rouen* outlined the order: first, Tournemire had begun 'by the performance of three pieces from the 17th century: the *Point d'Orgue sur les grands jeux*, a piece of great style from the celebrated de Grigny, whose reputation dominated his epoch – the very deeply expressive *Toccata* of Frescobaldi, the "Fra Angelico" of Music – and the delightful "Modal Fugue" of Buxtehude whose grace, distinction and richness confers on it the privilege of resting forever modern.' The second part of the program was then consecrated to eight pieces taken from the *L'Orgue mystique* of M. Tournemire.

The program's order and the critic's exegesis of it laid out an interpretation of music – that is, modernism was the natural successor of modalism. Judging from the program's silence on the subject, one would not know that there had been a 'tonal' period of music from Bach through the nineteenth century. The *Journal de Rouen* could repeat and amplify Tournemire's self-interpretation: 'The compositions of M. Tournemire consciously take their inspiration from this modal music which, by means of plainchant, stretches backward from the 16th century all the way to the Roman epoch and perhaps even much further yet.' In spite of 'his admiration for J.-S. Bach and Franck,' Tournemire was among those who 'deplored the fact that music had only conserved the major and minor modes out of the seven ancient ones.' Thus, he 'loved to plunge back into the works of the composers of the 17th century' who had, at the very end, 'conserved the imprint of music from the Middle Ages in full bloom to the 16th century.' Yet, the 'marvelous' aspect of Tournemire was this: he did not 'pastiche in any way the Gregorian and polyphonic chants that are his models,' and he 'never offered the slightest archaism.' On the contrary, he – like the 'forever modern' Buxtehude – was 'essentially modern' and even 'timeless [*de tous les temps*].'[140] This approach to Tournemire paralleled those critics who made sense of Rouault's visual works by appealing to the 'Flemish primitives.'

A shorter but more widely circulated review of the Rouen program had already appeared in the *Ménestrel* of Paris. In this recital, 'among the most remarkable concerts that have recently taken place in our city,' Tournemire had 'performed with a real mastery three pieces of ancient authors, Nicolas de Grigny, Frescobaldi and Titelouze.' It is possible Tournemire gave two performances at the Rouen Cathedral, or perhaps one of the reviewers had received an advance program that was changed. Or else *le Ménestrel* had projected a wish fulfilment, since Jehan Titelouze, considered by many to be the founding father of the French organ school, had held the organist's position at the Cathedral of Rouen for forty-five years in the late sixteenth and early seventeenth centuries. Tournemire himself had connected the 'mystical thoughts of Frescobaldi, Titelouze, [and] de Grigny' in an article published several months before playing at Rouen.[141] In any case, substituting the older Titelouze for Buxtehude would only have amplified the audience's reaction to this music 'of a completely new conception that deliberately breaks with routine.' At first, the listener experienced 'primarily a feeling of surprise, then one was seduced, and finally, entirely captivated by the admirable suppleness of the melodic line, by the variety and richness of the harmony, and by the nobility and beauty of the language.'[142]

Tournemire gave nearly the same concert with equally positive results later that summer in Brest, including more 'modal' music from Louis-Nicolas Clérambault who became organist at St-Sulpice in Paris beginning in 1715. The *Courrier Musical* enthusiastically reported: 'The organ recital given at Saint-Matthieu de Morlaix, by the eminent organist Charles Tournemire, received unanimous votes of approval. After the execution of beautiful pieces from Clérambault, Frescobaldi, Buxtehude, etc., Ch. Tournemire had us listen to important fragments of his *Orgue mystique*.' A needlepoint metaphor expressed the hybridity: 'The developments are of a great richness of invention and the *embroidery with which he adorns the liturgical chants* is of extreme ingeniousness and finesse.'[143]

Perhaps Tournemire's most important concerts from this period were given at his own Basilica of Ste-Clotilde, showing off both the instrument and his new work. The invitations, printed in heavy neo-Gothic script and asking the bearer to assist at a 'strictly intimate' concert, added to the neo-medieval ambience of the Basilica's architecture.[144] One such recital devoted completely to *L'Orgue Mystique* was given on 16 June 1930.[145] In his enthusiastic review, Maurice Imbert of *Courrier Musical* drew on the same metaphor used by Fitz-James: 'All the pieces [Tournemire] composes are precious garlands coiled around the Gregorian texts.' In a curious image, perhaps alluding to the Biblical account of God's breathing into clay and creating humanity, Imbert said that Tournemire had drawn 'his subject from musical antiquity' and then treated it 'by breathing a life into it that is completely contemporary.' One could use the word 'classical' in calling Tournemire's work a 'classical musical art' just as one did with reference to 'our great writers of the 17th century.' Perhaps having read Petit's article a year earlier referring to 'palingenesis,' Imbert estimated that Tournemire had created 'something extremely new with something extremely old, that which is respectfully conformed to the law of evolution.' Indeed, some of the 'aesthetic audacities' in Tournemire's lines and harmonic aggregates had 'the savor of the word "Madame" as put by Racine into the mouth of Greek heros.'[146]

In sum, the juxtaposition of antiquity and modernity was effected not only by compositional techniques within the pieces themselves, but also by the way they were juxtaposed with ancient music in concert programs. By omitting the period 1700–1929 from his performances, Tournemire made modernity seem to be the logical heir to antiquity. 'Palingenesis,' with its geological and biological overtones, implied that the inheritance was inevitable in the nature of things, and that if there was an aberration, it had been 'modernity' now grown old.

Liberté: On Order Considered as Anarchy

A curious feature of Tournemire reviews was the frequent appearance of varieties of the word 'freedom': *libre*, *librement*, *liberté*. For example, *L'Ami du Peuple*, reporting Tournemire's 1930 concert at Ste-Clotilde, laid out a kind of extended syllogism. 'Liberty is the kingdom of genius, of mysticity [*la mysticité*], and of mastery. This liberty flows from a single source: inspiration. Genius is inspired creation. Mysticism is inspired spiritual life. Mastery is the liberty resulting from an inspiration strong enough to bring its techniques entirely under submission.' 'The Friend of the People' concluded that 'M. Tournemire may claim for himself this triple liberty' and offered this monarch of genius a praise 'formidable in its grandeur.'[147]

'Liberty' and its cognates pervaded references to *L'Orgue Mystique*. In May 1929, Norbert Dufourcq's review in the Schola Cantorum's *Tribune de Saint-Gervais* hinted at palingenesis in its title: 'A Renewed Tradition.' Here Dufourcq praised Tournemire's 'freely paraphrased' composition and its retention of the 'infinite flexibility' of the Gregorian phrase. His unique contribution lay in the ability to 'treat Gregorian themes *à la moderne*.'[148] Raymond Petit's review the next month also noted the 'extraordinary linear beauty of the free medieval songs.'[149] For *Courrier Musical*, 'the mystical elevation' of chant was made possible by 'the liberty of harmonies and the fitness of registration.'[150] For Fitz-James, Tournemire's novelty derived from the '*return to modal art* by means of free paraphrase.'[151] In announcing summer projects of French composers, *Comœdia* reported that Tournemire, the 'eminent professor at the Conservatoire, is giving himself over entirely to a sizable organ work ... based on Gregorian chant but in a free manner.'[152] For the *Journal de Rouen*, 'the Gregorian phrase, exegeted [*commentée*]' by Tournemire was 'treated very freely both in terms of harmony as well as contrapuntally.'[153] *Le Courrier Musical* noted that the composer 'intended to freely paraphrase one-by-one all fifty-one services of the liturgical year,' and that one could respect 'the habitual divisions of the office' without 'losing an extreme liberty of behavior.'[154] The discourse endured for another decade: in 1938, Dufourcq wrote that Gregorian melodies allowed Tournemire 'forms as free as possible' and 'detached from every artificial hindrance.' The 'Gregorian spirit,' with its 'flexible and diverse' possibilities, allowed for 'the birth of these free "musics."'[155] That same year, Messiaen praised the agility, subtlety, and 'rhapsodic liberty' of *L'Orgue Mystique*'s form that defied 'all analysis.'[156]

The discourse of Gregorian chant's 'freedom' certainly came from the founding rhetoric of Bordes's and d'Indy's program for the Schola. Raymond Petit wrote that, if one were looking for the roots of Tournemire's work, it would be 'necessary to search for them among the predecessors of tonal imperialism.'[157] This language strongly echoed Bordes's comparison of the Basque shepherd's folk-song to plainchant's 'basic condemnation of all utopias of measured music.'[158] The discourse of tonality's tyranny had origins in the fin-de-siècle.

But 'liberty' had acquired a new meaning – an off-modern meaning, both progressive and nostalgic – in the postwar period. No one had expressed this better than Cocteau in his 1923 address at the Collège de France, 'On Order Considered as Anarchy.' It was after reading this that Maritain had written Cocteau, congratulating him on his 'rare and enviable victory to have succeeded, as you have, in making "order" seem as new and as disturbing as "anarchy."'[159] In this Jazz Age context, appeals to Tournemire's 'liberty' helped make both his work and the plainchant on which it was based new, disturbing, and tantalizing. Anarchy has been called 'the record of art's inevitable destruction and reconstruction of language' and 'a disparaging word for artistic *extensions* of formal order.'[160] To figures like Dom Gajard, Tournemire's reconstruction of plainchant within modernist chromaticism and polytonalism was simply destruction. But for others, his innovation was an artistic extension of order. The discourse surrounding Tournemire's music played a significant role in re-imagining religious music as being thoroughly compatible with modern 'dissonance,' thus paving the way for a flourishing of twentieth-century religious works in the 1930s through the 1950s.

As the stock market crash of 1929 inaugurated the Great Depression, *les années folles* ('the crazy years') of the postwar decade turned into the 'menacing years' or 'hollow years' of the 1930s.[161] In this anxious time, Tournemire employed the latest technology to promote his vision. In the spring of 1930, he made award-winning 78-rpm recordings of Franck's works (with his own improvisations on the 'B'-sides) for the Polydor label.[162] Émile Vuillermoz, an ardent supporter of both Tournemire and jazz (*la musique nègre*), happily reported two awards from the newspaper *Candide*'s 'Prix Candide' for 1931: Tournemire's recording of Franck's *Chorale in a minor* won the prize for best recording on a solo instrument, and Mlle. Joséphine Baker won in the category of 'light music' [*musique légère*] for 'Suppose,' recorded for Columbia Records.[163] In 1932, *L'Édition Musique Vivante* announced that it was 'tempted to proclaim' that Tournemire's recording of an 'Improvisation on the *Te Deum*' was 'one of his best successes on disk.'[164]

In late April 1932, two months after Tournemire had finished four long years of composing *L'Orgue Mystique* (on 5 February), excerpts were broadcast by Radio-Paris. On 24 April, both *Antenne* and *Radio-Magazine* published a photo of Tournemire with the caption below: 'M. Tournemire from whom you will hear several works for organ tomorrow on Radio-Paris.'[165] Reviewing the broadcast for *Paris Film*, Suzanne Perrot compared Tournemire favourably with the program's first segment, during which a 'mediocre singer' had succeeded in 'discouraging us with banal melodies.' Fortunately, Radio-Paris had redeemed this disaster and 'removed our sadness by its retransmission of an organ recital by Charles Tournemire at Sainte-Clotilde.' Perrot recapped Tournemire's program: *Choral I for the Tenth Sunday After Pentecost*, an *Offertory*, and a *Communion* (which was 'of a mysticism where joy mixed itself in with love') had made for 'a joy without clouds.' Notably, the *Alleluia* that followed was '*a beautiful cry of hope in a fairly modern form.*'[166]

The same evening as the *radio-diffusion* of Tournemire's pre-recorded concert, a concert of fourteen pieces from the finished work was performed at Ste-Clotilde by the greatest organists of the next generation: Maurice Duruflé, André Fleury, Jean Langlais, Noëlie Pierront, and Gaston Litaize, along with Daniel-Lesur (Tournemire's long-time protégé) and Olivier Messiaen, two of the composers who would form 'La Jeune France' in the 1930s.[167] Remarking that its reviews of *L'Orgue Mystique* in the past had rendered any further praise of its artistic and musical worth 'superfluous,' *Le Ménestrel* simply wanted to note the significance of this event: 'the attraction and influence which *l'Orgue mystique* exercises on the young generations of organists ... is that by which it is permitted to predict a future assured of a solid and lasting success for the monumental work of Charles Tournemire.'

1933 was the worst year of the Depression in Europe, and as it brought Adolf Hitler to power, it definitively ended the postwar period and looked ahead to an ominous future. Although it took the Heugel firm until 1936 to publish the entire *L'Orgue Mystique*, for the most part, new critical receptions of the work ended in 1933. An essay by Pierre Giriat appearing that November in the *Lyon républicain*, the mouthpiece of Lyon's political radicals, was among the last. It also seems to have impressed Tournemire deeply, since he transcribed most of it into his memoirs.[168] *L'Orgue Mystique*, 'this astonishing thing,' a 'work with proportions of the Tower of Babel,' a 'sonorous *Summa* [*Theologica*],' was 'renewing the most efficacious of traditions' after 'three centuries of oblivion.' And yet, Tournemire's art was traditionalist without being antiquarian: having absolutely no 'taste for archeology,' it had proved 'its desire to remain alive by the welcome' it extended to 'the very latest acquisitions of musical writing.' In the 'musical history of our time,' one would be hard-pressed to find writing so 'daring' and 'overwhelming.'

Giriat summed up Tournemire's off-modern aesthetic in a magisterial way: 'The art of Ch. Tournemire is one of the most subtle of our time. Traditionalist on account of its return to the spirit and to the modal forms of a past extending even anterior to J.-S. Bach ... evolutionary on account of its adoption of a modern *polytonality* denounced as ... diabolical by conservatives.' His imagery evoked Huysmans and Péladan: Tournemire 'mixes together harmonies like the poetry of cathedrals, alloys mystical perfumes.' Giriat concluded with a prophesy: although neglected during his own time, the initiated knew that posterity, never stingy with *genius*, would 'remember the work of Charles Tournemire as one of the most exceptional and the freest in a petty and troubled epoch.'[169]

Epilogue: Towards Another Postwar Mystical Music

In 1934, Tournemire married his second wife, Alice Espir, who would remain devoted to him and his work for over a half-century after his death. On 14 July 1939, Tournemire wrote his assistant that he was returning to Arcachon for the summer vacation and that he would see him again in October.[170] On 3 September, war broke out with Germany. In anticipation of bombardment, the government closed Ste-Clotilde (situated across from the War Ministry) and told the clergy to move services to the small chapel on the rue Las Cases (where there was no large organ). Tournemire's memoirs end with this passage: 'Hitler, this monster, has put Europe into fire and blood ... Thus we have taken refuge here in Arcachon at my sister's. We have moved in for what will be in all likelihood a prolonged time, because this cursed war threatens to develop to a considerable extent.'

On 31 October, Tournemire's family reported him to the police as missing. On 4 November his body was discovered. Although there has been talk of suicide ever since, the oral inquiry at the time suggested that a 'light cerebral amnesia' may have caused Tournemire to become lost in the wooded area.[171] On 5 November, the body, having been deceased for twenty-four hours before its discovery, was buried without a funeral in the family plot. The Basilica reopened during the summer of 1940 under the German Occupation.

Jehan Alain, who also used plainchant in extraordinarily innovative ways, was one of his generation's most promising geniuses. He died heroically on 20 June 1940, and was posthumously awarded the Croix de Guerre. In May 1940, Olivier Messiaen was captured and incarcerated in a prisoner-of-war camp. During the winter of 1940–1, he composed the *Quartet for the End of Time* and premiered it on 15 January 1941 with fellow inmates.[172] Released later that year, he was appointed to teach harmony at the Conservatoire. During the Occupation of Paris, Tournemire's widow Alice aided the Resistance and the Jewish cause by smuggling papers across the city hidden in stacks of Tournemire's scores.[173]

In spite of Giriat's optimistic prophesy, posterity has not been kind to Tournemire's repertoire. However, the discursive legacy it engendered, imagining a musical capacity for being both deeply Catholic and thoroughly modern, went on to be realized in startling ways. Maurice Duruflé's *Requiem* (1947) and *Four Motets* (1960) most resemble Tournemire in their hybridization of plainchant and Impressionism. Francis Poulenc, an intimate of Max Jacob and one of the original members of The Group of Six, turned back to Catholicism in shock after a car accident gruesomely beheaded a musical rival.[174] His *Litanies to the Black Virgin* (1936), *Stabat Mater* (1950–1), and *Dialogues of the Carmelites* (based on a libretto by Georges Bernanos, premiered in 1957) continue to grow in popularity. Olivier Messiaen's towering stature in the last century needs only be noted.

The acceptance of these works depended on the aesthetics of ultramontanism having been reversed and on the invention of a new musical religious realism, owed in large measure to Tournemire and the critics who received his work. Ultramodern musical language was not merely seen as compatible with musical religiosity; on the contrary, even and especially in its dissonance, contemporary music was seen as possessing an 'astonishing aptitude' to be the sacramental carrier and material representation of unseen mystery: 'real in form, unreal in expression.'[175] (Or more precisely, as Tournemire put it, 'the mysteries of Sacrifice.') Forged in Tournemire's personal griefs, the aesthetic responded to the collective needs of a neoclassical decade steeped in bereavement, and the decade that followed, expressionist and surrealist, *tremendens et fascinans*.

To the present day, the epitaph on Tournemire's tomb concisely expresses this sacramental modernism in unchanging stone:

Per aspera spera.
Through difficulty, hope.

Abbreviations

Rouault-Arch	Rouault Family Archives
Tourn-BN-fM	Le fonds Montpensier: Charles Tournemire; Département de la Musique, Bibliothèque Nationale de France
Tourn-Mém	Charles Tournemire, *Mémoires (1886–1939)*, unpublished
Tourn-SB	Archives, Société Baudelaire
JRM-Arch	Maritain Archives, Cercle d'Études Jacques et Raïssa Maritain
JRM-OC	*Oeuvres complètes / Jacques et Raïssa Maritain*, ed. Jean-Marie Allion, Maurice Hany, Dominique and René Mougel, Michel Nurdin, and Heinz R. Schmitz, 16 vols. (Fribourg [Switzerland]: Éditions universitaires; Paris: Éditions Saint-Paul, 1982–2000)

***

Antimoderne	Jacques Maritain, *Antimoderne* (Paris: Éditions de la Revue des Jeunes, 1922); in *JRM-OC* II: 923–1136
AS 1920 En	Jacques Maritain, *The Philosophy of Art*, trans. John O'Connor (Ditchling, England: St Dominic's Press, 1923)
AS 1920 Fr	Jacques Maritain, *Art et scolastique* (Paris: Librarie de l'Art Catholique, 1920)
AS 1927 En	Jacques Maritain, *Art and Scholasticism: with other essays*, trans. J.F. Scanlan (New York: Scribner's, 1939)
AS 1927 Fr	Jacques Maritain, *Art et scolastique* (Paris: Louis Rouart et fils, 1927)
AS JRM-OC	Jacques Maritain, *Art et scolastique*; in *JRM-OC* I: 615–788.
CarnetJM-Fr	Jacques Maritain, *Carnet de notes* (Paris: Desclée de Brouwer, 1965); in *JRM-OC* XII: 125–427
CarnetJM-En	Jacques Maritain, *Notebooks,* trans. Joseph W. Evans (Albany: Magi Books, 1984)

CorrJC-JM	*Correspondance Jean Cocteau-Jacques Maritain 1923–1963*, ed. Michel Bressolette and Pierre Glaudes (Paris: Gallimard, 1993)
CorrJG-JMFr	Julien Green and Jacques Maritain, *Une grande amitié. Correspondance 1926–1972*, ed. Henry Bars and Eric Jourdan (Paris: *NRF*, Gallimard, 1982)
CorrJG-JMEn	Julien Green and Jacques Maritain, *The Story of Two Souls. The Correspondence of Jacques Maritain and Julien Green*, trans. Bernard Doering (New York: Fordham University Press, 1988)
CoqArlEn	Jean Cocteau, *A Call to Order by Jean Cocteau. Written between the years 1918 and 1926 and including 'Cock and Harlequin,' 'Professional Secrets,' and other critical essays*, trans. Rollo H. Myers (New York: Haskell House Publishers, 1975; repr. of London: Faber and Gwyer, 1926)
CoqArlFr	Jean Cocteau, *Le Coq et l'Arlequin* (Paris: Éditions Stock, 1918); in Cocteau, *Le rappel à l'ordre* (Paris: Éditions Stock, 1926); in Cocteau, *Oeuvres complètes de Jean Cocteau*, 11 vols. (Genève: Marguerat, 1946–51), 9: 9–263
GrndAmiEn	Raïssa Maritain, *We have Been Friends Together and Adventures in Grace; The Memoirs of Raïssa Maritain*, trans. Julie Kernan (Garden City, NY: Image Books [1942 and 1945], 1961)
GrndAmiFr	Raïssa Maritain, *Les Grandes amitiés. Souvenirs* (New York: Éditions de la Maison Française, 1941); *Les Aventures de la grâce* (New York: Éditions de la Maison Française, 1944); in *JRM-OC* XIV: 619–1083
JournRM-En	Raïssa Maritain, *Raïssa's Journal, presented by Jacques Maritain* (Albany, NY: Magi Books, 1974)
JournRM-Fr	Raïssa Maritain, *Journal de Raïssa, publié par Jacques Maritain* (Paris: Desclée de Brouwer, 1963); in *JRM-OC* XV: 141–507
Letter-Resp	Jean Cocteau, *Letter to Jacques Maritain*, and Jacques Maritain, *Response to Jean Cocteau*, in *Art and Faith: Letters Between Jacques Maritain and Jean Cocteau*, trans. John Coleman (New York: Philosophical Library, 1948)
Lettre-Rép	Jean Cocteau and Jacques Maritain, *Lettre à Jacques Maritain, Réponse à Jean Cocteau* (Paris: Librairie Stock, 1926) in *Corr JC-JM*, 252–352

Notes

Introduction

1 Karl Rahner, S.J., 'On the Theology of the Incarnation,' *Theological Investigations*, trans. Cornelius Ernst (Baltimore: Helicon Press, [1961]–1992), vol. 4, 113; 115. Denise Levertov, 'Annunciation,' *A Door in the Hive* (New York: New Directions, 1989), 86–8.

2 Gaëtan Bernoville, 'Vie Religieuse et Vie Littéraire: Les conversions,' *Le Nouveau Siècle* (26 May 1926).

3 The terms *laïque*, *laïcité*, and *laïciste* are sometimes translated as 'secular,' 'secularism,' and 'secularist.' I retain the European usage, which 'differs from the American tradition in that it seeks less to neutralize public authorities in matters of religion than to neutralize religions in matters of public life.' Christopher Caldwell, 'In Europe, "Secular" Doesn't Quite Translate,' *New York Times* (21 December 2003): sect. 4, 10. For concise overview, see Guy Haarscher, *La Laïcité*, 3rd ed. (Paris: Presses Universitaires de France-PUF, 2004).

4 Pius IX, *Syllabus of Errors*, translation in the *Dublin Review* 56 (1865): 513–29; in *Readings in Church History*, rev. ed., ed. Colman J. Barry (1960; repr. Westminster, MD: Christian Classics, 1985), 992–6.

5 The instability of these terms both frustrates and yet permits their usefulness. I use the following provisional definitions: 'modernization' is 'a social practice and state policy that usually refers to industrialization and technological progress' while 'modernity' is a 'critical project' that is 'a response to the condition of modernization and the consequences of progress.' 'Modernity' is characterized by a temporalization of history marked by common elements: a 'peculiar form of acceleration,' a 'destruction of the exemplary nature of past events [i.e., tradition] and, in its place, the discovery of the

uniqueness of historical processes and the possibility of progress.' Svetlana Boym, *The Future of Nostalgia* (New York: Basic Books, 2001), 22; Reinhart Koselleck, *Futures Past: On the Semantics of Historical Time*, trans. Keith Tribe (Cambridge, MA: MIT Press, 1985), 5; 35. See also Darrin M. McMahon, *Enemies of the Enlightenment: The French Counter-Enlightenment and the Making of Modernity* (New York: Oxford, 2001); Jürgen Habermas, *The Philosophical Discourse of Modernity: Twelve Lectures*, trans. Frederick G. Lawrence (Cambridge, MA: MIT Press, 1987).

As customarily used to signify persons or their critical projects, 'modernist' and 'anti-modernist' respectively signify an embrace or rejection of modernization as entailing progress and repudiating tradition. In its specific sense, post–First World War 'modernism' refers to the Anglo-American literary movement known as High Modernism that repudiated 'modernity' itself insofar as it entailed liberal rationalism. More generally, 'modernism' came to be conflated with the term 'avant-garde' and referred to cultural and intellectual forms on the cutting edge of progress. Vincent Sherry, *The Great War and the Language of Modernism* (New York: Oxford, 2003); Robert B. Pippin, *Modernism as a Philosophical Problem: On the Dissatisfactions of European High Culture* (Cambridge, MA: B. Blackwell, 1991); Astradur Eysteinsson, *The Concept of Modernism* (Ithaca, NY: Cornell University Press, 1990).

With respect to religion: as 'secularization' increasingly came to be seen as an integral and necessary part of 'modernization,' religion logically came to be thought of as incompatible with the critical project of modernity. Owen Chadwick, *The Secularization of the European Mind in the 19th Century* (New York: Cambridge University Press, 1975).

6 H. Stuart Hughes, *Between Commitment and Disillusion: The Obstructed Path and The Sea Change, 1930–1965* (1966; 1975; repr., with a new introduction, Middletown, CT.: Wesleyan University Press; Scranton, PA: Harper & Row, 1987), 65–7.

7 J. Derek Holmes, *The Triumph of the Holy See: A Short History of the Papacy in the Nineteenth Century* (London: Burns & Oates, 1978), 134–5; in Joe Holland, *Modern Catholic Social Teaching: The Popes Confront the Industrial Age, 1740–1958* (New York: Paulist Press, 2003), 53.

8 Jeffrey Von Arx, ed., *Varieties of Ultramontanism* (Washington, DC: Catholic University of America Press, 1998); R.W. Franklin, *Nineteenth-Century Churches: The History of a New Catholicism in Württemburg, England, and France* (New York: Garland, 1987); R.F. Costigan, 'Tradition and the Beginning of the Ultramontane Movement,' *Irish Theological Quarterly* 48 (1981): 27–46; Bernard Reardon, *Liberalism and Tradition: Aspects of*

Catholic Thought in Nineteenth Century France (New York: Cambridge University Press, 1975); William Gibson Ashbourne, *The Abbé de Lamennais and the Liberal Catholic Movement in France* (London: Longmans, Green, 1896).

9 Jonathan Barnes, 'Metaphysics,' in *The Cambridge Companion to Aristotle*, ed. Jonathan Barnes (New York: Cambridge University Press, 1995), esp. 77–101; John F. Wippel, 'Metaphysics,' and Norman Kretzmann, 'Philosophy of Mind,' in *The Cambridge Companion to Aquinas*, ed. Norman Kretzmann and Eleonore Stump (New York: Cambridge University Press, 1993), esp. 107–13; 153, n. 149; Frederick Charles Copleston, *A History of Philosophy*, 7 vols. (Garden City, NY: Image Books, 1962-), esp. vol. 1, part 2, 116–19.

10 Joseph Martos, *Doors to the Sacred: A Historical Introduction to Sacraments in the Catholic Church* (Garden City, NY: Doubleday and Company, 1981), esp. 71–2. The term 'sacrament' refers to one of the seven rituals recognized in Catholic practice and theology since the twelfth century: Baptism, Confirmation, Eucharist (i.e., Mass), Reconciliation (i.e., Confession), Marriage, Holy Orders, Anointing of the Sick (i.e., Extreme Unction). The term 'sacramental' refers to venerated items such as holy water, rosaries, scapulars, statues, blessed candles, etc. See also: Benoît-Dominique de la Soujeole, 'Questions actuelles sur la sacramentalité,' *Revue Thomiste* 92 (1999): 483–95; John Macquarrie, *A Guide to the Sacraments* (New York: Continuum, 1997); Louis-Marie Chauvet, *Symbol and Sacrament: A Sacramental Reinterpretation of Christian Existence*, trans. Madeleine E. Beaumont and Patrick Madigan (Collegeville, MN: Liturgical Press, 1995), orig. *Symbole et sacrement: une relecture sacramentelle de l'existence chrétienne* (Paris: Cerf, 1987); Bernard Cooke, *Ministry to Word and Sacraments: History and Theology* (Philadelphia: Fortress Press, 1976) and *Sacraments and Sacramentality* (Mystic, CT: Twenty-Third Publications, 1983); Joseph Martos, *The Catholic Sacraments* (Wilmington, DE: Michael Glazier, 1983).

11 Gary Macy, *The Theologies of the Eucharist in the Early Scholastic Period: A Study of the Salvific Function of the Sacrament According to the Theologians c. 1080–c. 1220* (Oxford: Clarendon Press, 1984); John W. O'Malley, 'The Feast of Thomas Aquinas in Renaissance Rome: A Neglected Document and its Import,' in O'Malley, *Religious Culture in the Sixteenth Century* (Brookfield, VT: Variorum, 1993), 1–27.

12 The Latin *substantia* renders the Greek *hypostasis* (literally, 'that which settles at the bottom, sediment'); a thing's substance is its dynamic inner 'power' [*dynamis*]. The term acquired metaphysical meanings, including the *nature*, *essence*, and *reality* of something, as well as the *ground of hope or*

confidence. Henry George Liddell and Robert Scott, *A Lexicon: Abridged from Liddell and Scott's Greek-English Lexicon* (1871; repr. New York: Oxford University Press, 1977), 743.

13 Andrew Greeley, *The Catholic Imagination* (Berkeley: University of California Press, 2000); Ralph M. McInerny, *Aquinas and Analogy* (Washington, DC: Catholic University of America Press, 1996); Edward T. Oakes, 'Pryzwa's *Analogy of Being*,' in *Pattern of Redemption: The Theology of Hans Urs von Balthasar* (New York: Continuum, 1994); William F. Lynch, *Images of Faith: An Exploration of the Ironic Imagination* (Notre Dame, IN: University of Notre Dame Press, 1973); *Christ and Apollo: The Dimensions of the Literary Imagination* (New York: Sheed and Ward, 1960); 'Theology and the Imagination,' *Thought* 29 (1954–5): 61–86; and 'Theology and the Imagination II. The Evocative Symbol,' *Thought* 29 (1954–5): 529–54; Allen Tate, 'The Symbolic Imagination: The Mirrors of Dante,' and 'The Angelic Imagination: Poe as God,' in *The Forlorn Demon. Didactic and Critical Essays* (Chicago: Regnery, 1953).

14 Harry W. Paul, *The Second Ralliement: The Rapprochement Between Church and State in France in the Twentieth Century* (Washington, DC: Catholic University of America Press, 1967). Although technically speaking there was no 'Vatican' until its establishment by the Holy See's Concordat of 1929 with Benito Mussolini, I retain the term used by contemporaries: 'la Question Vaticane.'

15 Jean Jacques Becker and Serge Berstein, *Victoire et frustrations, 1914–1929* (Paris: Éditions du Seuil, 1990), 394.

16 Robert Wohl, *The Generation of 1914* (Cambridge, MA: Harvard University Press, 1979).

17 Scholars of religion familiar with the seminal work of theologian David Tracy (*The Analogical Imagination: Christian Theology and the Culture of Pluralism* [New York: Crossroad, 1981]) may find my usage confusing. Tracy's taxonomy identifies the 'dialectical imagination' as Protestant and the 'sacramental imagination' as Catholic, and his distinctions derive from defining the term 'dialectical' as a radical disjunction: e.g., in Søren Kierkegaard's 'Either/Or' choice requiring a decision of faith; and in Karl Barth's sense meaning a radical abyss separating God from human history. In identifying Catholic 'sacramental' imagination as a 'dialectical realism,' I use the word 'dialectical' in its more common sense as a 'synthesis' of a 'thesis' and 'antithesis' – in this case, of 'realism' and some version of its 'antithesis' (e.g., dream, magic, hallucination, utopia, etc.).

18 Philippe Bernard and Henri Dubief, *The Decline of the Third Republic 1914–1938*, trans. Anthony Forster (New York: Cambridge University

Press, 1985), 78–9, 93–101, 128–47. See also Jean Jacques Becker, *The Great War and the French People*, trans. Arnold Pomerans (Dover, NH: Berg, 1985), orig. Becker, *Les français dans la grande-guerre* (Paris: Éditions Robert Laffont, 1983); Paul M. Bouju and Henri DuBois, *La Troisième République, 1870–1940* (Paris: Presses Universitaires de France, 1975); Maurice Agulhon and André Nouschi, *La France de 1914 à 1940* (Paris: Nathan, 1971); Alfred Sauvy, *Histoire économique de la France entre les deux guerres*, 4 vols. (Paris: Fayard, 1965–70).

19 Becker and Bernstein, *Victoire et frustrations*, 147–8; and Marc Auffret, *La France de l'entre deux guerres* (Paris: Culture, Arts, Loisirs, 1972).

20 Antoine Prost, *In the Wake of War: Les Anciens Combattants and French Society*, trans. Helen McPhail (Oxford: Berg, 1992), orig. *Les Anciens combattants et la société française, 1914–1939* (Paris: Presses de la fondation nationale des sciences politiques, 1977). For contemporaneous accounts, see Paul Emard, *Dans la nuit laborieuse: Essai sur la rééducation des soldats aveugles* (Paris: Librairie J. Victorion, 1917); Gustave Hirschfield, *Une Ecole de rééducation professionnelle des grands blessés de la guerre* (Paris: Berger-Levrault, 1917).

21 K.W. Swart, *The Sense of Decadence in Nineteenth-Century France* (The Hague: M. Nijhoff, 1964), 210–11.

22 Gail Bederman, *Manliness and Civilization: A Cultural History of Gender and Race in the United States, 1880–1917* (Chicago: University of Chicago Press, 1995), 23–44; Alice L. Conklin, *A Mission to Civilize: The Republican Idea of Empire in France and West Africa, 1895–1930* (Stanford, CA: Stanford University Press, 1997), 4–6.

23 John Cruickshank, *Variations on Catastrophe: Some French Responses to the Great War* (Oxford: Clarendon Press, 1982), 6.

24 Mary R. Habeck, 'Technology in the First World War: The View from Below,' in *The Great War and the Twentieth Century*, ed. Jay Winter, Geoffrey Parker, and Mary R. Habeck (New Haven: Yale University Press, 2000), 99–131.

25 Herbert Read, foreword, *Promise of Greatness: The War of 1914–1918*, ed. George A. Panichas (New York: John Day, 1968), v.

26 J.F.C. Fuller, *The Decisive Battles of the Western World and their Influence Upon History*, vol. 3 (Eyre & Spottiswoode, 1956), 184; in John Terraine, *White Heat: The New Warfare 1914–18* (London: Sidgwick & Jackson, 1982), 41.

27 Admiral Lord Fisher, memorandum, June 1913; in Terraine, *White Heat*, 35.

28 Henri Bergson, *La signification de la Guerre* (Paris: Bloud & Gay, 1915),

19; in Modris Eksteins, *Rites of Spring: The Great War and the Birth of the Modern Age* (Boston: Houghton Mifflin, 1989), 161.

29 Louis Mairet, letter of 29 December 1916; in Eksteins, *Rites of Spring*, 215–16.

30 Barrie Cadwallader, *Crisis of the European Mind: A Study of André Malraux and Drieu La Rochelle* (Cardiff: University of Wales Press, 1981), 7.

31 Arthur G. Neal, *National Trauma and Collective Memory* (Armonk, NY: M.E. Sharpe, 1998), esp. 3–20. See also: Ron Eyerman, *Cultural Trauma: Slavery and the Formation of African American Identity* (New York: Cambridge University Press, 2001); Petar Ramadanovic, *Forgetting Futures: On Meaning, Trauma, and Identity* (Lanham, MD: Lexington Books, 2001); Dominick LaCapra, *Writing History, Writing Trauma* (Baltimore, MD: Johns Hopkins University Press, 2001); Ruth Leys, *Trauma: A Genealogy* (Chicago: University of Chicago Press, 2000); Cathy Caruth, *Unclaimed Experience: Trauma, Narrative, and History* (Baltimore, MD: Johns Hopkins University Press, 1996); and Caruth, ed., *Trauma: Explorations in Memory* (Baltimore, MD: Johns Hopkins University Press, 1995).

On trauma and the Great War see Winter, 'Shell-Shock and the Cultural History of Great War'; Roudebush, 'A Patient Fights Back: Neurology'; Bourke, 'Effeminacy, Ethnicity and the End of Trauma'; Becker, 'Avant-garde, Madness and the Great War'; Eric Leed, 'Fateful Memories'; all in *Journal of Contemporary History* 35, no. 1, Jan. 2000. See also Jay Winter, 'Catastrophe and Culture: Recent Trends in the Historiography of the First World War,' *Journal of Modern History* 64 (September 1992): 525–32.

32 'Collective cultural identity refers not to a uniformity of elements over generations but to a sense of continuity on the part of successive generations of a given cultural unit of population, to shared memories of earlier events and periods in the history of that unit, and to notions entertained by each generation about the collective destiny of that unit and its culture.' Anthony D. Smith, *National Identity* (Reno: University of Nevada Press, 1991), 25; in Rudy Koshar, *From Monuments to Traces: Artifacts of German Memory 1870–1990* (California, 2000), 13. For anthropology, see Marshall Sahlins, *Islands of History* (Chicago: University of Chicago Press, 1985); for psychology, see Gay Becker, *Disrupted Lives: How People Create Meaning in a Chaotic World* (Berkeley: University of California Press, 1997).

33 Daniel J. Sherman, *The Construction of Memory in Interwar France* (Chicago: University of Chicago Press, 1999). See also: Edward Linenthal, *The Unfinished Bombing: Oklahoma City in American Memory* (New York: Oxford University Press, 2001); Mieke Bal, Jonathan Crewe, and Leo Spitzer, eds., *Acts of Memory: Cultural Recall in the Present* (Hanover, NH:

Dartmouth College: University Press of New England, 1999); Dominick LaCapra, *History and Memory after Auschwitz* (Ithaca, NY: Cornell University Press, 1998); Michael J. Hogan, ed., *Hiroshima in History and Memory* (New York: Cambridge University Press, 1996); Edward Linenthal and Tom Engelhardt, eds., *History Wars: The Enola Gay and Other Battles for the American Past* (New York: Metropolitan Books/Henry Holt and Co., 1996); Edward Linenthal, *Preserving Memory: The Struggle to Create America's Holocaust Museum* (New York: Viking, 1995); *American Sacred Space*, ed. David Chidester and Edward Linenthal (Bloomington: Indiana University Press, 1995); John R. Gillis, ed., *Commemorations: The Politics of National Identity* (Princeton, NJ: Princeton University Press, 1994); Dominick LaCapra, *Representing the Holocaust: History, Theory, Trauma* (Ithaca, NY: Cornell University Press, 1994); James E. Young, *The Texture of Memory: Holocaust Memorials and Meaning* (New Haven: Yale University Press, 1993) and *Writing and Rewriting the Holocaust: Narrative and the Consequences of Interpretation* (Bloomington: Indiana University Press, 1988); Michael Perlman, *Imaginal Memory and the Place of Hiroshima* (Albany: State University of New York Press, 1988); Edward Linenthal, *Sacred Ground: Americans and Their Battlefields* (Urbana: University of Illinois Press, 1991).

34 Pierre Nora, *Realms of Memory: Rethinking the French Past*, trans. Arthur Goldhammer, ed. Lawrence D. Kritzman, 3 vols. (New York: Columbia University Press, 1996–8) and *Rethinking France: The State*, trans. Mary Trouille under direction of David P. Jordan (Chicago: University of Chicago Press, 2001–). Originally Pierre Nora, *Les lieux de mémoire*, 7 vols. (Paris: Éditions Gallimard, 1984–1992).

35 Koshar, *From Monuments to Traces*, 1–14; drawing on Susan A. Crane, 'Writing the Individual Back into Collective Memory,' *American Historical Review* 102, no. 5 (December 1997): 1372–85.

36 T.J. Clark, *Farewell to an Idea: Episodes from a History of Modernism* (New Haven: Yale University Press, 1999); quoted in Christopher Prendergast, 'Codeword Modernity,' *New Left Review* 24 (Nov.–Dec. 2003): 95–111. See 96, n.2. Clark alludes to Charles Baudelaire: 'all *modernism* is worthy of becoming antiquity someday.' Baudelaire, 'Le Peintre de la Vie Moderne,' *Curiosités esthétiques, l'art romantique, et autres oeuvres critiques* (Paris: Éditions Garnier Frères, [1868] 1962), 467; in Walter Benjamin, *Charles Baudelaire: A Lyric Poet in the Era of High Capitalism*, trans. Harry Zohn (London: Verso Books, 1983), 81–3.

37 Michael North, *Reading 1922: A Return to the Scene of the Modern* (New York: Oxford University Press, 1999), 3.

38 Theodor W. Adorno, *Aesthetic Theory*, trans. C. Lenhardt (London: Routledge & Kegan Paul, 1984), 31; orig. *Ästhetische Theorie* (Frankfurt am Main: Suhrkamp, 1970). For an opposing view, see Edward Shils, *Tradition* (Chicago: University of Chicago Press, 1981), 160ff.
39 Fredric Jameson, 'Reflections in Conclusion,' in Ernst Bloch et al., *Aesthetics and Politics* (London: New Left Books, 1977), 202.
40 Eysteinsson, *Concept of Modernism*, 8.
41 Kenneth Silver, *Esprit de Corps: The Art of the Parisian Avant-Garde and the First World War, 1914–1925* (Princeton, NJ: Princeton University Press, 1989). On the relationship of the terms 'avant-garde' and 'modernism,' see Eysteinsson, *Concept of Modernism*, 143–78; M. Calinescu, *Five Faces of Modernity: Modernism, Avant-Garde, Decadence, Kitsch, Postmodernism* (Durham, NC: Duke University Press, 1987); and Peter Bürger, *Theory of the Avant-Garde*, trans. Michael Shaw (Minneapolis: University of Minnesota Press, 1984).
42 Martha Hanna, *The Mobilization of Intellect: French Scholars and Writers During the Great War* (Cambridge, MA: Harvard University Press, 1996), 143.
43 Romy Golan, *Modernity and Nostalgia: Art and Politics in France Between the Wars* (New Haven: Yale University Press, 1995), ix.
44 Philippe Dagen, *Le silence des peintres: Les artistes face à la Grande Guerre* (Paris: Librairie Arthème Fayard, 1996).
45 Jay Winter, *Sites of Memory, Sites of Mourning: The Great War in European Cultural History* (New York: Cambridge University Press, 1995), 5; drawing on Martin Jay, 'The Apocalyptic Imagination and the Inability to Mourn,' in *Force Fields: Between Intellectual History and Cultural Critique* (London: Routledge, 1993), 84–97; Sigmund Freud, 'Mourning and Melancholia,' *Collected Papers: Papers on Metapsychology*, trans. Joan Riviere, vol. 4 (New York: Basic Books, 1959), 153, 154.
46 Winter, *Sites of Memory*, 5; referring to Paul Fussell, *The Great War and Modern Memory* (New York: Oxford University Press, 1975).
47 David Harvey, *The Condition of Postmodernity: An Enquiry into the Origins of Cultural Change* (Cambridge, MA: Blackwell, 1990), 20.
48 Ibid., 30; referencing Le Corbusier in the words of Kenneth Frampton, *Modern Architecture: A Critical History* (New York: Oxford University Press, 1980).
49 Brett A. Berliner, *Ambivalent Desire: The Exotic Black Other in Jazz-Age France* (Amherst and Boston: University of Massachusetts Press, 2002); Petrine Archer Straw, *Negrophilia: Avant-Garde Paris and Black Culture in the 1920s* (New York: Thames & Hudson, 2000); Jody Blake, *Le Tumulte*

noir: Modernist Art and Popular Entertainment in Jazz-Age Paris, 1900–1930 (University Park: Pennsylvania State University Press, 1999); Elazar Barkan and Ronald Bush, ed., *Prehistories of the Future: The Primitivist Project and the Culture of Modernism* (Stanford, CA: Stanford University Press, 1995).

50 North, *Reading 1922*, 29.

51 Rita Felski, *The Gender of Modernity* (Cambridge, MA: Harvard University Press, 1995), 2–3.

52 E.g., Homi K. Bhabha, *The Location of Culture* (New York: Routledge, 1994); Trinh T. Minh-ha, *Woman, Native, Other: Writing Postcoloniality and Feminism* (Bloomington: Indiana University Press, 1989); Gayatri Chakravorty Spivak, *In Other Worlds: Essays in Cultural Politics* (New York: Methuen, 1987).

53 Felski, *Gender of Modernity*, 211.

54 Ibid., 212; and quoting Paul Gilroy, *The Black Atlantic: Modernity and Double Consciousness* (Cambridge, MA: Harvard University Press, 1993), 198.

55 North, *Reading 1922*, 10–11; quoting Houston Baker, Jr, *Modernism and the Harlem Renaissance* (Chicago: University of Chicago Press, 1987), xvi; and referencing Sandra Gilbert and Susan Gubar, *No Man's Land*, 3 vols. (New Haven: Yale University Press, 1988).

56 Svetlana Boym, *The Future of Nostalgia* (New York: Basic Books, 2001), 22.

57 Ibid., xvi–xvii.

58 Carl E. Schorske, *Fin-de-Siècle Vienna: Politics and Culture* (New York: Cambridge University Press, 1981), xxii.

59 Carl E. Shorske, *Thinking with History: Explorations in the Passage to Modernism* (Princeton, NJ: Princeton University Press, 1998), 4–5.

60 Philippe Chenaux, *Entre Maurras et Maritain: Une Génération intellectuelle catholique (1920–1930)* (Paris: Cerf, 1999); Annette Becker, *War and Faith: The Religious Imagination in France, 1914–1930*, trans. Helen McPhail (New York: Berg, 1998), orig. Becker, *La Guerre et la foi. De la mort à la mémoire 1914–1930* (Paris: A. Colin, 1994); Frédéric Gugelot, *La conversion des intellectuels au catholicisme en France 1885–1935)* (Paris: CNRS Éditions, 1998); Pierre Colin, ed., *Intellectuels Chrétiens et esprit des années 1920* (Paris: Cerf, 1997).

61 Koselleck, *Futures Past*, 32.

62 Benedict Anderson, *Imagined Communities: Reflections on the Origins and Spread of Nationalism* (London: Verso, 1983). See also Peter Fritzsche, *Reading Berlin 1900* (Cambridge, MA: Harvard University Press, 1996).

63 For an American parallel, see Paul Elie, *The Life You Save May Be Your Own: An American Pilgrimage* (New York: Farrar, Straus and Giroux, 2003).
64 Susan Rosa and Dale Van Kley, 'Religion and the Historical Discipline: A Reply to Mack Holt and Henry Heller,' *French Historical Studies* 21 (Fall 1998): 611–29; Jonathan Sperber, *Popular Catholicism in Nineteenth-Century Germany* (Princeton, NJ: Princeton University Press, 1984), 286–7.
65 Sherry, *The Great War and the Language of Modernism*, 16.
66 Harvey, *Condition of Postmodernity*, 12–13.
67 Peter L. Berger, ed., *The Desecularization of the World: Resurgent Religion and World Politics* (Washington, DC: Ethics and Public Policy Center, 1999); Berger, *A Rumor of Angels: Modern Society and the Rediscovery of the Supernatural* (Garden City, NY: Doubleday, 1969); Bernard Eugene Meland, 'The Significance of Religious Sensibility and Wonder in Any Culture,' in *The Secularization of Modern Cultures* (New York: Oxford University Press, 1966), 116–40.
68 Caroline Bynum writes: 'we all – scholars and ordinary readers alike – must ask about how society constructs, uses, and eclipses the wondrous.' Caroline Walker Bynum, review for the publisher; for William A. Christian, *Visionaries: The Spanish Republic and the Reign of Christ* (Berkeley: University of California Press, 1996).
69 Thomas J. Ferraro, ed., *Catholic Lives, Contemporary America* (Durham, NC: Duke University Press, 1997), 9.

Prologue

1 Stephen Greenblatt, 'The Touch of the Real,' *Representations* 59 (Summer 1997): 14–29; repr. in Catherine Gallagher and Stephen Greenblatt, *Practicing New Historicism* (Chicago: University of Chicago Press, 2000), 20–48. See 34. Flannery O'Connor, 'The Church and the Fiction Writer,' *Collected Works. Flannery O'Connor* (New York: Library of America, 1988), 807–12. See 809.
2 Auguste Comte, *Cours de philosophie positive* (1830–42); in *The Essential Comte*, ed. Stanislav Andreski, trans. Margaret Clarke (London: Croom Helm, 1974), 19–21.
3 For examples from the period 1841–1859, see Bernard Weinberg, *French Realism: The Critical Reaction, 1830–1870* (New York: Modern Language Association of America; London: Oxford University Press, 1937), 98–102.
4 Théophile Silvestre, *Histoire des artistes vivants* (1856); in James Henry Rubin, *Realism and Social Vision in Courbet & Proudhon* (Princeton, NJ: Princeton University Press, 1980), 78.

5 Gustave Courbet, letter to the *Courrier du dimanche*, dated 25 December 1861; in Linda Nochlin, *Realism and Tradition in Art, 1848–1900: Sources and Documents* (Englewood Cliffs, NJ: Prentice-Hall, 1966), 35.
6 Rubin, *Realism and Social Vision*, 76–7.
7 Gustave Flaubert, *Madame Bovary*, in *Oeuvres*, vol. 1, ed. René Dumesnil and Albert Thibaudet (Paris: Gallimard, 1951), 269–683; Flaubert, *Madame Bovary*, trans., ed. Paul de Man (New York: W.W. Norton and Co., 1965). See *Madame Bovary*, 455; 580; 583; 596; *Madame Bovary*, trans. de Man, 129; 231; 233; 244.
8 Gustave Merlet, 'Le Roman physiologique. "Madame Bovary," par M. Gustave Flaubert,' *Revue européenne*, 15 June 1860; repr. in *Portraits d'hier et d'aujourd'hui*, vol. IV, *Réalistes et fantaisistes* (Paris: Didier, 1863); in Weinberg, *French Realism*, 161.
9 Edouard L'Hôte, 'Du laid dans les arts, à propos du dernier livre de Michelet,' *Artiste*, 15 February 1861; Anatole Claveau, '"Salammbô,"' *Artiste*, 15 December 1862; Léon Gautier, 'M. Gustave Flaubert,' *Études littéraires pour la défense de l'Église* (Paris: Poussielgue et fils, 1865); in Weinberg, *French Realism*, 138.
10 Michelle Perrot, *A History of Private Life. Vol. IV: From the Fires of Revolution to the Great War*, ed. Michelle Perrot, trans. Arthur Goldhammer (Cambridge, MA: Belknap Press of Harvard University Press, 1990), 124; drawing on Jean Borie, *Mythologies de l'hérédité au XIXe siècle* (Paris: Galilée, 1981). See also: Thomas W. Laqueur, *Solitary Sex: A Cultural History of Masturbation* (New York: Zone Books, 2003); Jean Stengers and Anne Van Neck, *Masturbation: The History of a Great Terror*, trans. Kathryn A. Hoffmann (New York: Palgrave Macmillan, 2001).
11 Émile Zola, *Les Rougon-Macquart*, ed. Henri Mitterand, 5 vols. (Paris: Gallimard (Pléiade), 1960–7), 1736–7; in Frederick Brown, *Zola: A Life* (New York: Farrar Straus Giroux, 1995), 188–9.
12 For alcoholism, see Susanna Barrows, *Drinking: Behavior and Belief in Modern History* (Berkeley and Los Angeles: University of California Press, 1991) and *Distorting Mirrors: Visions of the Crowd in Late Nineteenth-Century France* (New Haven: Yale, 1981). For prostitution, see Timothy J. Gilfoyle, 'Prostitutes in History: From Parables of Pornography to Metaphors of Modernity,' *American Historical Review*, 104, no. 1 (Feb. 1999), 117–41; Walkowitz, *City of Dreadful Delight: Narratives of Sexual Danger in Late-Victorian London* (Chicago: University of Chicago Press, 1992); Alain Corbin, *Women for Hire: Prostitution and Sexuality in France After 1850*, trans. Alan Sheridan (Cambridge, MA: Harvard University Press, 1990); T.J. Clark, *The Painting of Modern Life: Paris in the Art of Manet and His Followers* (Princeton, NJ: Princeton University Press, 1984), esp.

79–146. For department stores and kleptomania, see Michael Miller, *The Bon Marché: Bourgeois Culture and the Department Store, 1869–1920* (Princeton, NJ: Princeton University Press, 1981); Patricia O'Brien, 'The Kleptomania Diagnosis: Bourgeois Women and Theft in Late 19th-c. France,' *Journal of Social History* 17 (Fall 1983): 65–77; and Leslie Camhi, 'Stealing Femininity: Department Store Kleptomania as Sexual Disorder,' *Differences* 5 (1993): 26–50.

13 Émile Zola, *Germinal* (1885), *Oeuvres complètes*, ed. Henri Mitterand, 15 vols. (Paris: Cercle du livre précieux, 1966), 5: 387–8; 391–2; 393–4; Zola, *Germinal*, trans. Havelock Ellis (1895; repr. New York: Vintage Books, 1994), 533–4; 540; 543.

14 Vanessa R. Schwartz, *Spectacular Realities: Early Mass Culture in* Fin-de-Siècle *Paris* (Berkeley: University of California Press, 1998).

15 Donald Reid, *Paris Sewers and Sewermen: Realities and Representations* (Cambridge, MA: Harvard University Press, 1991).

16 *La daguerréotype français. Un objet photographique*, ed. Quentin Bajac and Dominique Planchon-de Font-Réaulx (Paris: Éditions de la Réunion des musées nationaux, 2003).

17 Letter of Alfred Grévin to Émile Zola, 6 July 1881; *L'Illustration*, 10 December 1881; in Schwartz, *Spectacular Realities*, 121–2.

18 Ibid., 77.

19 Robert A. Nye, *Crime, Madness, & Politics in Modern France: The Medical Concept of National Decline* (Princeton, NJ: Princeton University Press, 1984).

20 Joseph Conrad, *Heart of Darkness*, 3rd ed., ed. Robert Kimbrough (New York: W.W. Norton & Company, 1988), 15.

21 Jennifer Michael Hecht, *The End of the Soul: Scientific Modernity, Atheism, and Anthropology in France* (New York: Columbia University Press, 2003).

22 Maria M. Tatar, *Spellbound: Studies on Mesmerism and Literature* (Princeton, NJ: Princeton University Press, 1978), 35; Adam Crabtree, *From Mesmer to Freud: Magnetic Sleep and the Roots of Psychological Healing* (New Haven: Yale University Press, 1993); William J. McGrath, *Freud's Discovery of Psychoanalysis: The Politics of Hysteria* (Ithaca, NY: Cornell University Press, 1986).

23 Martha Noel Evans, *Fits and Starts: A Genealogy of Hysteria in Modern France* (Ithaca, NY: Cornell University Press, 1991).

24 Georges Didi-Huberman, *Invention of Hysteria: Charcot and the Photographic Iconography of the Salpêtrière*, trans. Alisa Hartz (Cambridge, MA: MIT Press, 2003); orig. *Invention de l'hystérie: Charcot et l'iconographie photographique de la Salpêtrière* (Paris: Éditions Macula, 1982).

25 Paul Richer, *Études cliniques sur la grande hystérie* (Paris: Delahaye & Lecrosnier, 1885).

26 Dmitri Ivanovich Mendeleev (1834–1907) first published his table in 1868–70.

27 Jan Goldstein, *Console and Classify: The Psychiatric Profession in the Nineteenth Century* (New York: Cambridge University Press, 1987). See also Ruth Harris, *Lourdes: Body and Spirit in the Secular Age* (New York: Viking, 1999); Jan Goldstein, 'The Uses of Male Hysteria: Medical and Literary Discourse in Nineteenth-Century France,' *Representations* 34 (Spring 1991): 134–65; and 'The Hysteria Diagnosis and the Politics of Anticlericalism in Later Nineteenth-Century France,' *Journal of Modern History* 54 (1982): 209–39.

28 Éléonore Roy-Reverzy, introduction to Camille Lemonnier, *L'Hystérique* (1885; Paris: Nouvelles Éditions Séguier, 1996), 7.

29 J.-M. Charcot and Paul Richer, *Les démoniaques dans l'art* (Paris: Delahaye et Lecrosnier, 1887).

30 Edmond and Jules de Goncourt, 11 April 1857; in *Journal, Mémoires de la vie littéraire* (Paris: Laffont, 1989), 1: 248.

31 Paul-Maurice Legrain, *Du Délire chez les dégénérés, observations prises à l'asile Sainte-Anne, 1885–1886 (service de M. Magnan)* (Paris: A. Delahaye et E. Lecrosnier, 1886), 266; quoted in Max Nordau, *Degeneration*, trans. from the second edition of the German work (1895) (Lincoln: University of Nebraska Press, 1993; orig. New York: D. Appleton, 1895), 45; orig. *Entartung* (Berlin: C. Duncker, 1892–3). See also Robert A. Nye, 'Degeneration and the Medical Model of Cultural Crisis in the French Belle Epoque,' in *Political Symbolism in Modern Europe: Essays in Honor of George L. Mosse*, ed. Seymour Drescher, David Sabean, and Allan Sharlin (New Brunswick, NJ: Transaction Books, 1982).

32 Janet Beizer, *Ventriloquized Bodies: Narratives of Hysteria in Nineteenth-Century France* (Ithaca, NY: Cornell University Press, 1994); Leo Braudy, *From Chivalry to Terrorism: War and the Changing Nature of Masculinity* (New York: Alfred E. Knopf, 2003), 317–6.

33 John Stuart Mill and Auguste Comte, *Lettres inédites de John Stuart Mill à Auguste Comte*, ed. Lucien Lévy-Bruhl (Paris: F. Alcan, 1899); Lucien Lévy-Bruhl, *La Philosophie d'Auguste Comte* (Paris: F. Alcan, 1900).

34 Lucien Lévy-Bruhl, *The Philosophy of Auguste Comte*, trans. Kathleen de Beaumont-Klein (London: Swan Sonnenschein & Co., 1903), 27, 29–30.

35 Lucien Lévy-Bruhl, *La morale et la science des moeurs* (Paris: F. Alcan, 1904); trans. Elizabeth Lee, *Ethics and Moral Science* (London: Archibald Constable & Co. Ltd., 1905), 3.

36 Lucien Lévy-Bruhl, *Les Fonctions mentales dans les sociétés inférieures* (Paris: F. Alcan, 1910), 30; quoted in Lucien Lévy-Bruhl, *Primitive Mentality*, trans. Lilian A. Clare (London: George Allen and Unwin Ltd., 1923), 7. Emphasis original.
37 Lucien Lévy-Bruhl, *La mentalité primitive* (Paris: F. Alcan, 1922); trans. Clare, *Primitive Mentality*, 5. Emphasis added.
38 Gordon Wright, *France in Modern Times: From the Enlightenment to the Present*, 4th ed. (New York: W.W. Norton, 1987), 233. Léon Gambetta quoted in Wright.
39 Marcelin Berthelot quoted in Gérard Cholvy and Yves-Marie Hilaire, *Histoire religieuse de la France contemporaine, 1880–1930* (Toulouse: Privat, 1986), 143. Emphasis added.
40 Jacques Barzun, *Darwin, Marx, Wagner: Critique of a Heritage* (1941), 2nd ed. (Chicago: University of Chicago Press, 1981), 322.
41 For an American parallel, see T.J. Jackson Lears, *No Place of Grace: Antimodernism and the Transformation of American Culture 1880–1920* (New York: Pantheon, 1981).
42 Eric Hobsbawm, 'Introduction: Inventing Traditions,' in *The Invention of Tradition*, ed. Eric Hobsbawm and Terence Ranger (New York: Cambridge University Press, 1983), 5. See also Robert Rosenblum, *Transformations in Late Eighteenth Century Art* (Princeton, NJ: Princeton University Press, 1967).
43 Schorske, *Thinking With History*, 4–5.
44 Ernst Troeltsch, *The Social Teaching of the Christian Churches*, trans. Olive Wyon, 2 vols. (New York: Macmillan, 1931); orig. *Die Soziallehren der christlichen Kirchen und Gruppen* (1912). Compare Erik Sengers, '"Although We Are Catholic, We Are Dutch" – The Transition of the Dutch Catholic Church from Sect to Church as an Explanation for Its Growth and Decline,' *Journal for the Scientific Study of Religion* 43, no. 1 (2004): 129–39.
45 H. Richard Niebuhr, *Christ and Culture* (New York: Harper, 1951).
46 Jeffrey Chipps Smith, *Sensuous Worship: Jesuits and the Art of the Early Catholic Reformation in Germany* (Princeton, NJ: Princeton University Press, 2002); Leo Steinberg, *The Sexuality of Christ in Renaissance Art and in Modern Oblivion*, 2nd ed. (Chicago: University of Chicago Press, 1996).
47 Michael Paul Driskel, *Representing Belief: Religion, Art, and Society in Nineteenth-Century France* (University Park: Pennsylvania State University Press, 1992), 59–97.
48 Ibid., 227–53; Michael Marlais, *Conservative Echoes in Fin-de-Siècle Parisian Art Criticism* (University Park: Pennsylvania State University Press,

1992); Debora Silverman, *Van Gogh and Gauguin: The Search for Sacred Art* (New York: Farrar, Straus and Giroux, 2000).

49 E.J. Delécluze, 'De l'Art chrétien par M. Rio,' *Journal des Débats*, 11 July 1838; in Driskel, *Representing Belief*, 65.

50 Jules Varnier (reporter), 'Opinion sur le Salon de 1842 par une commission spéciale,' *Annales de la société libre des beaux-arts*, 11, 1841–2, 45; in Driskel, *Representing Belief*, 101.

51 Driskel, *Representing Belief*, 99–163. See also J.B. Bullen, *Byzantium Rediscovered: The Byzantine Revival in Europe and America* (London: Phaidon, 2003).

52 Désiré Raoul-Rochette, *Tableau des catacombes de Rome* (Paris: Bibliothèque universelle de la jeunesse, 1837); in Driskel, *Representing Belief*, 152.

53 Frédéric Ozanam, lectures posthumously collected in *La Civilisation au cinquième siècle* (Paris, 1855); in Driskel, *Representing Belief*, 153.

54 Paul Durand, *Manuel d'iconographie chrétienne grecque et latine traduit du manuscrit byzantin, le Guide de la Peinture* (Paris: Royale, 1845); in Driskel, *Representing Belief*, 154.

55 François Picot, mural for Saint-Vincent-de-Paul, Paris (1853); in Driskel, *Representing Belief*, 145–6.

56 Hippolyte Flandrin, mural for Church of Saint-Martin-d'Ainay, Lyon (1855); in Driskel, *Representing Belief*, 149.

57 Hippolyte Flandrin, *The Crucifixion*, Church of Saint-Germain-des-Près, Paris (ca. 1860); in Driskel, *Representing Belief*, 129.

58 Gerard Manley Hopkins, Sermon for 23 November 1879; in *Gerard Manley Hopkins*, ed. Catherine Phillips (New York: Oxford University Press, 1986), 276.

59 Eugène Delacroix, *Christ on the Cross* (1853), in Driskel, *Representing Belief*, 91–5.

60 David Harvey, *Paris: Capital of Modernity* (New York: Routledge, 2003), 311–40; Raymond Jonas, *France and the Cult of the Sacred Heart: An Epic Tale for Modern Times* (Berkeley: University of California Press, 2000), 177–243.

61 Harris, *Lourdes*, 173–4.

62 Memo of Edmond Turquet to Ernest Hébert, 5 July 1881; in Driskel, *Representing Belief*, 159.

63 Maurice Denis, 'Définition du Néo-Traditionnisme' (1890), and 'Notes sur la peinture religieuse' (1896), *Théories, 1890–1910. Du symbolisme et de Gauguin vers un nouvel ordre classique*, 4th ed. (Paris: Rouaurt et Watelin, 1920), 11; 33; 38; in Driskel, *Representing Belief*, 236.

64 Jane F. Fulcher, *French Cultural Politics & Music: From the Dreyfus Affair to the First World War* (New York: Oxford University Press, 1999); Katherine Bergeron, *Decadent Enchantments: The Revival of Gregorian Chant at Solesmes* (Berkeley: University of California Press, 1998); Philip Michael Dowd, 'Charles Bordes and the Schola Cantorum of Paris: Their Influence on the Liturgical Music of the Late 19th and Early 20th Centuries,' unpublished PhD dissertation, Catholic University of America, 1969.
65 Episcopal letter of 1839, quoted in Guéranger's *Institutions Liturgiques* (1841); in Driskel, *Representing Belief*, 85.
66 Joseph d'Ortigue, 'Musique sacrée,' *Revue des Deux Mondes* (30 November 1846); in Driskel, *Representing Belief*, 83.
67 Paul Scudo, 'Essais et notices; De la musique religieuse,' *Revue des Deux Mondes* (15 August 1861), 1016; a review of Félix Clément, *Histoire générale de la musique religieuse* (1860); in Driskel, *Representing Belief*, 84.
68 Hector Berlioz, quoted in Henri Bachelin, *Les maîtrises et la musique de choeur* (Paris: Heugel, 1930), 47.
69 Richard L. Crocker, *An Introduction to Gregorian Chant* (New Haven: Yale University Press, 2000), 6–9; 86–7; 164–72; and Philip Michael Dowd, 'Charles Bordes and the Schola Cantorum of Paris: Their Influence on the Liturgical Music of the Late 19th and Early 20th Centuries,' unpublished PhD dissertation, Catholic University of America, 1969, 52–65.
70 Bergeron, *Decadent Enchantments*, 39; 49.
71 Dom Joseph Pothier, *Les Mélodies grégoriennes d'après la tradition* (Tournai: Desclée, 1880); in Bergeron, *Decadent Enchantments*, 111.
72 Bergeron, *Decadent Enchantments*, 143–61.
73 Fenner Douglass, *Cavaillé-Coll and the French Romantic Tradition*, 2nd ed. (New Haven: Yale University Press, 1999), 1; Gerard Brooks, 'French and Belgian Organ Music after 1800,' in Nicholas Thistlethwaite and Geoffrey Webber, *The Cambridge Companion to the Organ* (New York: Cambridge University Press, 1998), 263–78. See 263–7.
74 As reported by Aristide Cavaillé-Coll in letter to the editor Jean-Louis-Félix Danjou, 26 February 1847, *Revue de la musique religieuse, populaire, et classique*, 1847; in Douglass, *Cavaillé-Coll*, 59.
75 For Cavaillé-Coll, see Brooks, 'French and Belgian Organ Music,' 267–72.
76 Jean-Louis-Félix Danjou, 'De la facture d'orgue au XIXe siècle,' *Revue de la musique*, October 1846 and November 1846; in Douglass, *Cavaillé-Coll*, 53.
77 Cavaillé-Coll letter to the editor Danjou, 26 December 1846, *Revue de la musique* (1847); in Douglass, *Cavaillé-Coll*, 55.
78 Danjou's editor's response to Cavaillé-Coll, *Revue de la musique* (1847); in Douglass, *Cavaillé-Coll*, 57.

79 Report to the Ministère des Cultes, 23 August 1849; in Driskel, *Representing Belief*, 84.
80 Comte, *Essential Comte*, 20.
81 For account of encyclical's genesis, see Gerald A. McCool, *From Unity to Pluralism: The Internal Evolution of Thomism* (New York: Fordham University Press, 1989), 5–38. For reception in various countries, see: (France): François Picavet, *Esquisse d'une histoire générale et comparée des philosophies médiévales*, 2nd ed. (Paris: Félix Alcan, 1907); (Germany): Franz Ehle, 'Die papstliche Enzyklikal vom 4 August 1879 und die Restauration der christlichen Philosophie,' *Stimmen aus Maria Laach* 18 (1880): 13–28; 292–317; 388–407; 485–98; M. Schneid, 'Die Litteratur über die thomistische Philosophie seit der Enzyklikal *Aeterni Patris*,' *Jahrbuch für Philosophie und Spekulative Theologie* 1 (1887): 269–308; T.M. Wehofer, 'Anordnungen Leos XIII, über das Thomasstudium; zum apostolischen Schreiben *Gravissime Nos*,' *Jahrbuch für Philosophie und Spekulative Theologie* 11 (1896–7): 406–31; (Great Britain): Thomas Harper, 'The Encyclical,' *Month* 37 (November 1879): 356–84; J.B. Hedley, 'Pope Leo XIII and Modern Studies,' *Dublin Review* 86 (January 1880): 190–210; 'Leo XIII on St. Thomas and the Schoolmen,' *Tablet* 54 (23 August 1879): 229–30; 'Pope Leo's Philosophical Movement: Its Relation to Modern Thought,' *Tablet* 102 (15 August 1903): 260–2; (Italy:) 'La regola filosofica proposta nella enciclica *Aeterni Patris*,' *Civiltà Cattolica*, ser. 10, no. 11 (9 September 1879): 657–72; 'La regola filosofica di S.S. Leone P.P. XIII proposta nella enciclica *Aeterni Patris*,' *Civiltà Cattolica*, ser. 10, no. 12 (9 October–25 November 1879): 165–83; 272–90; 425–43; 529–47; 'La missione di Leone XIII rispetto alla filosofia coronata da lieto successo,' *Civiltà Cattolica*, ser. 12, no. 1 (6 March 1883): 641–63; (Poland): B. Dembrowski, 'Reception of the Encyclical *Aeterni Patris* in Poland,' *Collectanea Theologica* (Warsaw) 46 (1976): 187–203; (U.S.A.): J.A. Corcoran, 'Recent Encyclical Letter of Pope Leo XIII on the Necessity of Reinstating the Christian Philosophy of St. Thomas in Catholic Schools,' *American Catholic Quarterly Review* 4 (October 1879): 719–32; John Gmeiner, 'Leo XIII and the Philosophy of St. Thomas,' *Catholic World* 46 (December 1887): 167–76; 'The *Princeton Review* and Leo XIII,' *Catholic World* (June 1880): 380–95; 'The *Princeton Review* and St. Thomas,' *Catholic World* (July 1880): 521–35.
82 Quoted in Paolo Dezza's *Alle origini del neotomismo* (Milan: Fratelli Bocca, 1940), 96; in Alasdair MacIntyre, *Three Rival Versions of Moral Enquiry: Encyclopaedia, Genealogy, and Tradition* (Notre Dame, IN: University of Notre Dame Press, 1990), 72.
83 Gabriel Daly, *Transcendence and Immanence: A Study in Catholic Modern-*

ism and Integralism (New York: Oxford University Press, 1980), 10; drawing on the official history of the Gregorian, *L'Università Gregoriana del Collegio Romana nel primo secolo dalla restituzione* (Rome: [1925], 34.

84 Georges van Riet, *Thomistic Epistemology*, trans. Gabriel Franks, Donald G. McCarthy, and George E. Hertrich, 2 vols. (St. Louis: B. Herder Book Co., 1963–5); orig. van Riet, *L'épistémologie: thomiste recherches sur le problème de la connaissance dans l'école thomiste contemporaine* (Louvain: Éditions de l'Institut supérieur de philosophie, 1946).

85 Scott MacDonald, 'Theory of Knowledge,' in *The Cambridge Companion to Aquinas*, ed. Norman Kretzmann and Eleonore Stump (New York: Cambridge University Press, 1993), 160–95. See 160.

86 MacIntyre, *Three Rival Versions of Moral Inquiry*, 76.

87 Pére Désiré-Joseph Mercier, *Revue néo-scholastique* 1 (1894), 5–18; in Daly, *Transcendence and Immanence*, 11. On Mercier, see: *Cardinal Mercier's Philosophical Essays: A Study in Neo-Thomism*, ed. David A. Boileau (Herent, Belgium: Peeters, 2002); David A. Boileau, *Cardinal Mercier: A Memoir* (Herent, Belgium: Peeters, 1997); Roger Aubert, *Le Cardinal Mercier (1851–1926): un prélat d'avant-garde*, ed. Jean-Pierre Hendrickx, Jean Pirotte, and Luc Courtois (Louvain-la-Neuve, Belgium: Academia: Presses universitaires de Louvain, 1994); Louis de Raeymaeker, *Le Cardinal Mercier et l'Institut supérieur de philosophie de Louvain* (Louvain: Universitaires de Louvain, 1952).

88 Roger Aubert, 'Aspects divers du néo-thomisme sous le pontificat de Léon XIII,' *Aspetti della cultura cattolica nell'età di Leone XIII* (Rome: Edizioni 'Cinque Lune,' 1961), 185; in Daly, *Transcendence and Immanence*, 11.

89 Maurice de Wulf, *Mediaeval Philosophy Illustrated from the System of Thomas Aquinas* (Cambridge, MA: Harvard University Press, 1922) and *Philosophy and Civilization in the Middle Ages* (Princeton, NJ: Princeton University Press, 1922). Etienne Gilson's William James Lectures, given at Harvard in the fall of 1936–7 on the university's 300th anniversary of its founding, were published as *The Unity of Philosophical Experience* (London: Sheed & Ward, 1938). See Laurence K. Shook, *Etienne Gilson* (Toronto: Pontifical Institute of Medieval Studies, 1984).

90 The following taken from Maurice de Wulf, 'Moderate Realism and the Universals,' *The System of Thomas Aquinas* (New York: Dover, 1959), 37–45; repr. of de Wulf, *Mediaeval Philosophy Illustrated*; orig. *Initiation à la philosophie thomiste* (Louvain: Institut Supérieur de Philosophie, 1921?).

91 de Wulf, *System*, 42–3. Emphasis original.

92 Jay, 'The Apocalyptic Imagination and the Inability to Mourn'; William F. Lynch, *Christ and Apollo: The Dimensions of the Literary Imagination*

(New York: Sheed and Ward, 1960); Peter Brooks, *The Melodramatic Imagination: Balzac, Henry James, Melodrama, and the Mode of Excess* (1976; repr. New York: Columbia University Press, 1985).

93 For the standard account in English see Richard M. Griffiths, *The Reactionary Revolution: The Catholic Revival in French Literature, 1870–1914* (New York: F. Ungar Pub. Co., 1965); trans. Marthe Lory, *Révolution à rebours; le renouveau catholique dans la littérature en France de 1870 à 1914* (Paris: Desclée de Brouwer, 1971). See also: Elke Lindhorst, *Die Dialektik von Geistesgeschichte und Literatur in der modernen Literatur Frankreichs: Dichtung in der Tradition des* 'renouveau catholique' *von 1890–1990* (Würzburg: Königshausen & Neumann, 1995); Theodore P. Fraser, *The Modern Catholic Novel in Europe* (New York: Macmillan Publishing Company, Twayne Publishers, 1994); Malcolm Scott, *The Struggle for the Soul of the French Novel: French Catholic and Realist Novelists, 1850–1970* (Washington, DC: Catholic University of America Press, 1990); Robert Bessede, *La Crise de la conscience catholique dans la littérature et la pensée françaises à la fin du XIXe siècle* (Paris: Éditions Klincksieck, 1975); Louis Alphonse Maugendre, *La Renaissance catholique au debut du XXe siècle*, 6 vols. (Paris: Beauchesne, 1963–); Gonzague Truc, *Histoire de la littérature catholique contemporaine* (Paris: Casterman, 1961).

For primary source accounts see: Louis Chaigne, *Anthologie de la renaissance catholique*, 3 vols. (Paris: Éditions «Alsatia», 1938–40); Joseph Ageorges, *Le Manuel de littérature catholique en France de 1870 à nos jours* (Paris: Éditions Spes, 1939); Elizabeth Fraser, *Le Renouveau religieux d'après le roman français de 1886 à 1914* (Paris: Société d'édition 'Les Belles Lettres,' 1934); Hermann Weinert, *Dichtung aus dem Glauben. Ein beitrag zur problematik des literarische* renouveau catholique *in Frankreich* (Hamburg: Hamburg Seminar für Romanische Sprachen und Kultur, 1934); Claude Romain, *Le Catholicisme de quelques contemporains* (Paris: Librairie Aniéré, Victorion Frères & Cie, 1933); Jean-Antoine Calvet, *Le Renouveau catholique dans la littérature contemporaine* (Paris: F. Lanore, 1927) and *D'une critique catholique* (Paris: Éditions Spes, 1927); Louis Rouzic, *Le Renouveau catholique. Les Jeunes avant la guerre*, 2nd ed. (Paris: P. Tequi, 1919); Thomas Mainage, O.P., *Les Témoins du renouveau catholique*, 6th ed. (Paris: G. Beauchesne, 1919); Abbé Julien Laurec, *Le Renouveau catholique dans les lettres* (Paris: P. Feron-Vrau, 1917).

94 Nella Arambasin, 'Conversion Religieuse et Conversion Esthétique au XIXe Siècle,' in *La conversion aux XIXe et XXe siècles*, ed. Nadine-Josette Chaline and Jean-Dominique Durand (Artois: Artois Presses Université, 1996), 59–70. See 60.

95 Raymond Hubert, *Le mysticisme de Baudelaire dans les Fleurs du mal et les Journaux intimes; Baudelaire chantre de l'inversion sexuelle et prétendu poète catholique; Baudelaire réhabilité par la Croix; Baudelaire et le prétendu Renouveau catholique* (Nice: 'Establissements Gaudio,' 1930); *Une cythère mystique: le prétendu renouveau catholique* (Nice: Frey & Trincheri, 1920); *Le procès du prétendu 'renouveau catholique' au tribunal de l'opinion* (Nice: Self-published, 1919); *Léon Bloy et le prétendu renouveau catholique*, 2 vols. (Nice: Frey et Trincheri, 1917); *Néo-christianisme et dilettantisme religieux: L'Annonce faite à Marie de M. Claudel: Polémique de presse: Les antécédents littéraires de l'auteur: Indépendance de la critique et respect des personnes: De la mentalité des démocrates chrétiens* (Nice: V. Berretta & Balestre, 1914).

96 Joséphin Péladan, *Le Salon de 1888* (Paris: C. Dalou, 1888), 26; in Arambasin, 'Conversion Religieuse,' 62.

97 Ora Avni, 'Fantastic Tales,' in *A New History of French Literature*, ed. Denis Hollier et al. (1989; repr. Cambridge, MA: Harvard University Press, (1994), 675–81. Roger Cardinal, 'The Fantastic,' in *The New Oxford Companion to Literature in French*, ed. Peter France (New York: Oxford / Clarendon Press, 1995), 298.

98 Avni, 'Fantastic Tales,' 677.

99 *Hallucinant* can be traced back through Gautier, Hugo, and Balzac: its primary association was with opium, hallucinations, and sense-misperception; its secondary usage was like that of 'dream,' 'idealism,' 'fantasy,' and 'imagination – i.e., terms opposed to 'realism.' Alfred Jarry used *hallucination* in opposition to *perception* as denoting the difference between anti-representation and representation. For *hallucinant*, see *Dictionnaire historique de la langue française: contenant les mots français en usage et quelques autres délaissés, avec leur origine proche et lointaine*, ed. Alain Rey et al., 2 vols. (Paris: Dictionnaires Le Robert, 1995), 1: 940. For anti-realist terms, see Weinberg, *French Realism*, esp. 98–102. For Jarry, see Andrew Hewitt, *Political Inversions: Homosexuality, Fascism, & the Modernist Imaginary* (Stanford, CA: Stanford University Press, 1996), 209; and Roger Shattuck, *The Banquet Years: The Origins of the Avant-Garde in France 1885 to World War I* (1955; repr. New York: Vintage, 1968), 35.

100 W. David Shaw, *Victorians and Mystery: Crises of Representation* (Ithaca, NY: Cornell University Press, 1990).

101 Maryanne Stevens, 'Redon and the Transformation of the Symbolist Aesthetic,'and Fred Leeman, 'Redon's Spiritualism and the Rise of Mysticism,' in *Odilon Redon: Prince of Dreams*, ed. Douglas W. Druick (New

York: H.N. Abrams, 1994), 196–236; Stephen Schloesser, 'From "Spiritual Naturalism" to "Psychical Naturalism": Catholic Decadence, Lutheran Munch, *Madone Mystérique*,' in *Edvard Munch: Psyche, Symbol, and Expression*, ed. Jeffrey Howe (Chestnut Hill, MA: McMullen Museum of Art; Chicago: Distributed by University of Chicago Press, 2001), 71–110.

102 Ellis Hanson, *Decadence and Catholicism* (Cambridge, MA: Harvard University Press, 1997).

103 Charles Bernheimer, *Decadent Subjects: The Idea of Decadence in Art, Literature, Philosophy, and Culture of the* Fin de Siècle *in Europe*, ed. T. Jefferson Kline and Naomi Schor (Baltimore, MD: Johns Hopkins University Press, 2002); David Weir, *Decadence and the Making of Modernism* (Amherst: University of Massachusetts Press, 1995); Jean de Palacio, *Figures et formes de la décadence* (Paris: Nouvelles Éditions Séguier, 1994); Murray G.H. Pittock, *Spectrum of Decadence: The Literature of the 1890s* (New York: Routledge, 1993); Barbara Spackman, *Decadent Genealogies: The Rhetoric of Sickness from Baudelaire to D'Annunzio* (Ithaca, NY: Cornell University Press, 1989); R.K.R. Thornton, *The Decadent Dilemma* (London: Edward Arnold, 1983); Jean Pierrot, *The Decadent Imagination 1880–1900*, trans. Derek Coltman (Chicago: University of Chicago Press, 1981); Noel Richard, *Le Mouvement décadent: dandys, esthétes et quintessents* (Paris: Librairie Nizet, 1968).

104 Donald Lee Leach, *Ideological Order and Erotic Disorder in the Conversion of J.-K. Huysmans from Naturalism to Catholicism* (Ann Arbor, MI: University Microfilms, 1989), 126.

105 Leonard Koos, *Decadence: A Literature of Travesty* (Ann Arbor, MI: University Microfilms, 1990).

106 Alex Owen, *The Place of Enchantment: British Occultism and the Culture of the Modern* (Chicago: University of Chicago Press, 2004); Ruth Brandon, *The Spiritualists: The Passion for the Occult in the Nineteenth and Twentieth Centuries* (New York: Alfred E. Knopf, 1983).

107 Allen Putnam, *Mesmerism, Spiritualism, Witchcraft and Miracle: A Brief Treatise Showing that Mesmerism is a Key which will Unlock Many Chambers of Mystery* (Boston: Colby & Rich, 1890).

108 Daniel Pick, *Svengali's Web: The Alien Enchanter in Modern Culture* (New Haven: Yale University Press, 2000); Derek Forrest, *The Evolution of Hypnotism* (Scotland: Black Ace Books, 1999); Alison Winter, *Mesmerized: Powers of Mind in Victorian Britain* (Chicago: University of Chicago Press, 1998); Robert Darnton, *Mesmerism and the End of the Enlightenment in France* (1968; Cambridge, MA: Harvard University Press, 1995).

109 Judith R. Walkowitz, 'Science and the Séance: Transgressions of Gender

and Genre,' in *City of Dreadful Delight*, 171–89; Robert G. Hillman, 'A Scientific Study of Mystery: The Role of the Medical and Popular Press in the Nancy-Salpêtrière Controversy on Hypnotism,' *Bulletin of the History of Medicine* 39 (1965): 163–82.

110 Winter, *Mesmerized*, 199.

111 Pick, *Svengali's Web*, 142–6.

112 John C. Burnham, *How Superstition Won and Science Lost: Popularizing Science and Health in the United States* (New Brunswick, NJ: Rutgers University Press, 1987); Janet Oppenheim, *The Other World: Spiritualism and Psychical Research in England, 1850–1914* (New York: Cambridge University Press, 1985); Thomas Leahey and Grace Leahey, *Psychology's Occult Doubles* (Chicago: Nelson-Hall, 1983); John J. Cerullo, *The Secularization of the Soul: Psychical Research in Modern Britain* (Philadelphia: Institute for the Study of Human Issues, 1982); Alan Gould, *The Founders of Psychical Research* (New York: Schocken, 1968).

113 Harris, *Lourdes*; David Blackbourn, *Marpingen: Apparitions of the Virgin Mary in Nineteenth-Century Germany* (New York: Alfred A. Knopf, 1994).

114 Harris, *Lourdes*, 331–42; Émile Zola, *Lourdes* (Paris: G. Charpentier et E. Fasquelle, 1894).

115 Ann Taves, *Fits, Trances, & Visions: Experiencing Religion and Explaining Experience from Wesley to James* (Princeton, NJ: Princeton University Press, 1999); William James, *The Varieties of Religious Experience* (New York; London: Longmans, Green, 1902).

116 Edgar Saltus, *The Philosophy of Disenchantment* (New York: Houghton, Mifflin, and Co., 1885); in Edward Foster, ed., *Decadents, Symbolists, & Aesthetes in America: Fin-de-siècle American Poetry* (Jersey City, NJ: Talisman House, 2000), 25–6. See 25.

117 Letter of Emmanuel Goldstein to Edvard Munch, 30 December 1891; in Reinhold Heller, 'Edvard Munch's "Night," the Aesthetics of Decadence, and the Content of Biography,' *Arts Magazine* 53/2 (October 1978): 80–105. See 95.

118 The Editors, 'Aux Lecteurs,' *Le Décadent litteraire et artistique* (10 April 1886); Anatole Baju, *L'École décadente* (Paris: L. Vanier, 1887), 5; in Heller, 'Edvard Munch's "Night,"' 82.

119 Joséphin Péladan, *La décadence latine: éthopée*, 21 vols. (1886–1926; repr. Genève: Éditions Slatkine, 1979).

120 Christophe Beaufils, *Le Sâr Péladan, 1858–1918: biographie critique* (Paris: Aux Amateurs de Livres, 1986); Robert Pincus-Witten, *Occult Symbolism in France: Joséphin Péladan and the Salons de la Rose-Croix* (New York: Garland Publishers, 1976). For the original movement, see

John Matthews et al., *The Rosicrucian Enlightenment Revisited* (Hudson, NY: Lindisfarne Books, 1999).

121 Joséphin Péladan, *Le théâtre complet de Wagner: les XI opéras scène par scène avec notes biographiques et critiques* (1894; repr. Paris: Slatkine, 1981).

122 Hanson, *Decadence and Catholicism*, 5, 11.

123 Henri Bachelin, *J.-K. Huysmans, du naturalisme littéraire au naturalisme mystique*, 2nd ed. (Paris: Perrin, 1926); Abbé Jules Pacheu, *Du Positivisme au mysticisme. Étude sur l'inquiétude religieuse contemporaine* (Paris: Librairie Bloud et cie, 1906); Pacheu, *De Dante à Verlaine; études d'idéalistes et mystiques: Dante, Spenser, Bunyan, Shelley, Verlaine, Huysmans* (Paris: Plon, Nourrit, 1897).

124 Henry M. Gallot, *Explication de J.-K. Huysmans* (Paris: Agence parisienne de Distribution, 1955), 68; George Ross Ridge, *J.-K. Huysmans* (New York: Twayne, 1968), 17; Henry Brandreth, *Huysmans* (New York: Hillary, 1963), 23; in Ruth B. Antosh, *Reality and Illusion in the Novels of J.-K. Huysmans* (Amsterdam: Rodopi, 1986), 14.

125 Gustave Flaubert, *Oeuvres complètes*, 8: 224; in Antosh, *Reality and Illusion*, 24.

126 J.-K. Huysmans, *Lettres inédites à Edmond de Goncourt*, ed. Pierre Lambert (Paris: Librairie Nizet, 1956), 73, n.5. See also Antosh, *Reality and Illusion*, 25–8.

127 Letter of Huysmans to Goncourt, 19 January 1882; in *Lettres*, ed. Lambert, 70.

128 Zola quoted by Huysmans, preface to 1904 edition of *À Rebours*; in J.-K. Huysmans, *Oeuvres complètes de J.-K. Huysmans*, ed. Lucien Descaves, 18 vols. (Paris: G. Crès, 1928–34), 7: xxii; Huysmans, *Against the Grain (À Rebours)*, trans. unknown, introduction by Havelock Ellis (1931; repr. New York: Dover Publications 1969), xlv.

129 Anson Rabinbach, *The Human Motor: Energy, Fatigue, and the Rise of Modernity* (New York: Basic Books, 1990); Daniel Pick, *Faces of Degeneration: A European Disorder, c.1848–c.1918* (New York: Cambridge University Press, 1989).

130 Huysmans, *Oeuvres complètes*, 7: 216–18; *Against the Grain*, 133–5.

131 Huysmans, *Oeuvres complètes*, 7: 275; *Against the Grain*, 170.

132 Andrée Hayum, *The Isenheim Altarpiece: God's Medicine and the Painter's Vision* (Princeton, NJ: Princeton University Press, 1989); Kurt Martin and Matthias Grünewald, *Grünewalds Kreuzigungsbilder in der Beschreibung von Joris-Karl Huysmans* (Mainz, Berlin: Kupferberg, 1966).

133 Hanson, *Decadence and Catholicism*, 122–3.

134 J.K. Huysmans to Jules Destrée, 12 December 1890, in *The Road from Decadence: From Brothel to Cloister. Selected Letters of J. K. Huysmans*, ed. and trans. Barbara Beaumont (London: Athlone Press, 1989), 105.
135 J.K. Huysmans to Abbé Boullan, 7 February 1890; in Robert Baldick, *La Vie de J. K. Huysmans* (Paris: Denoël, 1958), 195; in Marc Eigeldinger, 'Du supranaturalisme au surréalisme,' *Le Surnaturalisme français: actes du colloque organisé à l'Université Vanderbilt les 31 mars et 1er avril 1978*, ed. Jean Leblon and Claude Pichois (Neuchâtel: Éditions de la Baconnière, 1979), 115.
136 B.-H. Gausseron, 'Conférence bibliologique sur la littérature d'actualité,' *Le livre moderne* (10 May 1891): 280–1; in Ted Gott, 'Odilon Redon,' *Paris in the Late 19th Century*, ed. Jane Kinsman (Canberra: National Gallery of Australia; New York: Distributed by Thames and Hudson, 1996), 148.
137 Huysmans, *Oeuvres complètes*, 12, 1: 17–20; Huysmans, *La-Bas: A Journey into the Self*, trans. Brendan King, afterward Robert Irwin (Sawtry: Dedalus; Gardena, CA: Distributed in the United States by SCB Distributors, 2001), 24–6. Emphasis added.
138 Huysmans, *Oeuvres complètes*, 12, 1: 6; *La-Bas*, 17. The phrase 'des mystères qui nous entourent' copied from Huysmans's letter to Abbé Boullan, 7 February 1890, cited above.
139 Huysmans, *Oeuvres complètes*, 12, 1: 233; *La-Bas*, 148–9.
140 Huysmans, *Oeuvres complètes*, 12, 1: 10–11; *La-Bas*, 20. Emphasis added.
141 René Dumesnil, 'J.-K. Huysmans,' *Le Réalisme* (Paris: J. de Gigord, 1936), 433–6.
142 Huysmans, *Oeuvres complètes*, 12, 1: 234; *La-Bas*, 149.
143 J.K. Huysmans, *Trois primitifs, les Grünewald du Musée de Colmar, le Maître de Flémalle et la Florentine du Musée de Francfort-sur-le-Mein*, 2nd ed. (Paris: A. Messein, 1905); J.-K. Huysmans, *Grünewald. With an Essay by J.-K. Huysmans*, trans. Robert Baldick (Oxford: Phaidon, 1976), 12.
144 C.J.T. Talar, 'A Naturalistic Hagiography: J.-K. Huysmans' *Sainte Lydwine de Schiedam*,' in *Sanctity and Secularity during the Modernist Period*, ed. L. Barmann and C.J.T. Talar (Brussells: Société des Bollandistes, 1999), 151–80.
145 Huysmans, *Oeuvres complètes*, 15, 1: 82; Huysmans, *Saint Lydwine of Schiedam*, trans. Agnes Hastings (Rockford, IL: Tan Books, (1923) 1979); in Asti Hustvedt, *The Decadent Reader: Fiction, Fantasy, and Perversion from Fin-de-Siècle France* (New York: Zone Books, 1998), 1034.
146 Huysmans, *Oeuvres complètes*, 15, 1: 102–3.

147 'La mystérique' coined in Luce Irigaray, *Speculum de l'autre femme* (Paris: Éditions de Minuit, 1974); trans. Gillian Gill, *Speculum of the Other Woman* (Ithaca, NY: Cornell University Press, 1985); discussed in Cristina Mazzoni, *Saint Hysteria: Neurosis, Mysticism, and Gender in European Culture* (Ithaca, NY: Cornell University Press, 1996); 150–5; quoted in Hanson, *Decadence and Catholicism*, 108.

148 J. Noury, '*Sainte Lydwine*,' in *Études* 88 (1901), 404–6; in Talar, 'Naturalistic Hagiography,' 168, n. 57. The accusation of immorality also in the review in *Polybiblion* 92 (1901): 316–17.

149 Michel Albaric, 'Le commerce des objets religieux dans le quartier Saint-Sulpice,' in *De pierre et de coeur: l'église Saint-Sulpice 350 ans d'histoire* (Paris: Les Éditions du Cerf, 1996).

150 Huysmans, *Les Foules de Lourdes* (1905); quoted in Jean-Pie Lapierre and Philippe Levillain, 'Laïcisation, union sacrée et apaisement (1895–1926),' in *Société sécularisée et renouveaux religieux. XXe siècle*, vol. 4 of *Histoire de la France religieuse,* ed. René Rémond (Paris: Éditions du Seuil, 1992), 4: 114. Emphasis added.

151 Pierre Bourdieu, *Distinction: A Social Critique of the Judgment of Taste* (Cambridge, MA: Harvard University Press, 1984).

152 René Viviani, quoted in Roger Aubert, *The Church in a Secularised Society*, vol. 5 of *The Christian Centuries*, trans. Janet Sondheimer (New York: Paulist Press, 1978), 80. Originally published as vol. 5 of *Nouvelle histoire de l'Église,* 5 vols., ed. Roger Aubert, M. David Knowles, and Louis J. Rogier (Paris: Éditions du Seuil, 1960–8).

Chapter 1 Cultural Manicheanism: Apocalyptic Melodrama

1 Brooks, *The Melodramatic Imagination*, 15. Mary Douglas, *Purity and Danger: An Analysis of the Concepts of Pollution and Taboo* (1966; repr. New York: Routledge, 2002), 163.

2 The word *intégrisme* and its cognates (*intégristes*, *intégraux*, *organe catholique romain intégral*) originated in a Spanish political party inspired by Pius IX's *Syllabus of Errors* (1864). Ecclesiastically, it later denoted intransigent Catholics opposed to the Roman Catholic Modernists. Politically, Maurrasian positivists used it in a nationalistic sense endorsing an 'integral' or 'organic' unity of nation, society, religion, and culture. Jacques Gadille and Jean-Marie Mayeur, eds., *Libéralisme, industrialisation, expansion européenne (1830–1914)*, vol. 11 of *Histoire du Christianisme des origines à nos jours*, 14 vols., ed. Jean-Marie Mayeur, Charles Pietri, André Vauchez, and Marc Venard (Paris: Desclée-Fayard, 1990–), 11: 536–7.

3 For the following, see Michael Burns, *France and the Dreyfus Affair: A Documentary History* (New York: Bedford/St Martin's, 1999). The standard reference remains Jean-Denis Bredin, *The Affair: The Case of Alfred Dreyfus*, trans. Jeffrey Mehlman (New York: Braziller, 1986), originally *L'Affaire* (Paris: Julliard, 1983). See also: Michael Burns, *Dreyfus: A Family Affair, 1789–1945* (New York: Harper Collins, 1991).
4 Burns, *France and the Dreyfus Affair*, 8.
5 Edouard Drumont, *La Libre Parole*, 23 May 1892; in Burns, *France and the Dreyfus Affair*, 11.
6 Edouard Drumont, *La Libre Parole*, 1 November 1894; in Burns, *France and the Dreyfus Affair*, 33–4.
7 Maurice Barrès, election campaign speech of 1 November 1898, in *Scénes et doctrines du nationalisme* (Paris: Félix Juven, 1902), 432–4; in Burns, *France and the Dreyfus Affair*, 7.
8 Theodor Herzl, *Neue Freie Presse*, 5 January 1895; in Ernst Pawel, *The Labyrinth of Exile: A Life of Theodor Herzl* (New York: Farrar, Straus & Giroux, 1989), 206–7; in Burns, *France and the Dreyfus Affair*, 54.
9 'Coma' metaphor from D.W. Brogan, *The Development of Modern France, 1870–1939*, 2 vols., rev. ed. (Gloucester, MA: Peter Smith (1966) 1970), 1: 288; in Burns, *France and the Dreyfus Affair*, 116.
10 Charles Maurras, *La Gazette de France*, 6–7 September 1898; in Burns, *France and the Dreyfus Affair*, 122–3.
11 The standard work remains Eugen Weber, *Action Française: Royalism and Reaction in Twentieth-Century France* (Stanford: Stanford University Press, 1962). See also René Rémond, *The Right Wing in France from 1815 to De Gaulle*, trans. James M. Laux (Philadelphia: University of Pennsylvania Press, 1966); 9; orig. *La Droite en France de la Première Restauration à la Ve République*, 2nd ed. (Paris: Aubier, 1963).
12 Michael Sutton, *Nationalism, Positivism, and Catholicism: The Politics of Charles Maurras and French Catholics, 1890–1914* (New York: Cambridge University Press, 1982).
13 Pierre Sorlin, *'La Croix' et les Juifs (1880–1899), contribution à l'histoire de l'antisémitisme contemporain* (Paris: B. Grasset, 1967).
14 Harris, *Lourdes*, 274–9.
15 Pierre Albert, Louis Charlet, Robert Rang, and Fernand Terrou, *Histoire Générale de la presse française*, vol. 3 (1871–1940), under direction of Claude Bellanger, Jacques Godechot, Pierre Guiral, and Fernand Terrou (Vendôme: Presses Universitaires de France, 1972), 256.
16 Aubert, *Church in a Secularised Society*, 75.
17 Maurice Larkin, *Church and State after the Dreyfus Affair – The Separation*

Issue in France (London: Macmillan, 1974); Pierre Sorlin, *Waldeck-Rousseau* (Paris: Colin, 1967); Louis Capéran, *L'Invasion laïque. De l'avènement de Combes au vote de la Séparation* (Paris: Desclée de Brouwer, 1935).

18 Aubert, *Church in a Secularised Society*, 75–81; Encrevé, Gadille, and Mayeur, *Histoire du Christianisme*, 11: 536–7.

19 Racine: 'Nourri dans le sérail, j'en connais les détours.' *Bajazet* (1672), Act 4, Scene 7. I am grateful to Dominique Salin for this reference. Émile Combes quoted in Wright, *France in Modern Times*, 257.

20 Émile Combes, *Une campagne laïque* (Paris: H. Simonis Empis, 1904).

21 Unnamed, in Aubert, *Church in a Secularised Society*, 76.

22 Aubert, *Church in a Secularised Society*, 79–80, n. 14; Wright, *France in Modern Times*, 257–8. For dechristianization's origins in the eighteenth century, see Roger Chartier, *The Cultural Origins of the French Revolution*, trans. Lydia G. Cochrane (Durham, NC: Duke University Press, 1991), 92–110.

23 Pierre Colin, *L'audace et le soupçon. La crise du modernisme dans le catholicisme français, 1893–1914* (Paris: Desclée de Brouwer, 1997); Marvin R. O'Connell, *Critics on Trial: An Introduction to the Catholic Modernist Crisis* (Washington, DC: Catholic University of America Press, 1994); David G. Schultenover, *A View From Rome: On the Eve of the Modernist Crisis* (New York: Fordham University Press, 1993); Lester R. Kurz, *The Politics of Heresy: The Modernist Crisis in Roman Catholicism* (Berkeley: University of California Press, 1986).

24 Pope Leo XIII, *Aeterni Patris*, ¶ 27; in Claudia Carlen, ed., *The Papal Encyclicals, 1878–1903* (Raleigh, NC: Pierian Press, 1990), 25.

25 Monsignor Dadolle, quoted in Adrien Dansette, *Religious History of Modern France*, trans. John Dingle, 2 vols. (New York: Herder and Herder, 1961), 2: 306; orig. *Histoire religieuse de la France contemporaine* (Paris: Flammarion, 1948–51).

26 *La Vigie*, 5 December 1912; in Aubert, *Church in a Secularised Society*, 200.

27 David N. Myers, *Resisting History: Historicism and Its Discontents in German-Jewish Thought* (Princeton, NJ: Princeton University Press, 2003).

28 Richard E. Rubenstein, *Aristotle's Children: How Christians, Muslims, and Jews Rediscovered Ancient Wisdom and Illuminated the Dark Ages* (Orlando: Harcourt, 2003).

29 George Tyrrell, *Medievalism: A Reply to Cardinal Mercier* (New York: Longmans, Green and Co., 1908).

30 Émile Poulat, *Intégrisme et Catholicisme intégral. Un réseau secret international antimoderniste: la Sapinière, 1909–1921* (Paris: Casterman, 1969).

31 Meriol Trevor, quoted in Aubert, *Church in a Secularised Society*, 202.

32 Gugelot, *La conversion des intellectuels*, 111.
33 Dr Francus, *Comment je suis arrivé à croire. Confession d'un incroyant* (Paris: Bloud, 1901), 28; in Gugelot, *La conversion des intellectuels*, 27.
34 Gugelot, *La conversion des intellectuels*, 27–37.
35 The following taken from the standard biography: Jean-Luc Barré, *Jacques et Raïssa Maritain. Les Mendiants du Ciel* (Paris: Stock, 1995).
36 Rupert Christiansen, *Paris Babylon: The Story of the Paris Commune* (New York: Viking, 1994), 259–73; 289.
37 Ibid., 264.
38 See Jules Favre, *Mélanges politiques: judiciaires et littéraires*, ed. with a preface and notes by Paul Maritain (Paris: A. Rousseau, 1882).
39 Jacques Maritain, 'Quels sont des Traits Distinctifs de la Nature Humaine?,' thesis of 'J.-H.A. Maritain, élève externe du lycée Henri-IV,' in *Concours généraux. Devoirs donnés au concours général des lycées et collèges de Paris et des départements suivis de copies d'élèves couronnés* (Paris: Delalain Frères, 1900), 56–57; in *JRM-OC*, XVI: 599–610.
40 Maritain, 'Quels sont des Traits Distinctifs,' 601.
41 *GrndAmiFr* 640; *GrndAmiEn*, 23.
42 *GrndAmFr*, 661–2; *GrndAmiEn*, 41.
43 For following, see *GrndAmFr*, 689–94; *GrndAmiEn*, 64–8. Emphasis Maritain's.
44 *Que-sais-je?*, i.e., Michel de Montaigne's sceptical motto: 'What do I know?'
45 Griffiths, *Reactionary Revolution*, 39.
46 Dansette, *Religious History of Modern France*, 2: 315–23. Bergson said that he would have asked for baptism had he not feared appearing as though he had separated himself from Jews being persecuted. *JournRM-Fr*, 428, n. 10; *JournRM-En*, 294–5, n. 10; and Raïssa Maritain, 'Henri Bergson,' *The Commonweal* 33 (17 January 1941): 317–19; 'Concerning Henri Bergson. A letter from Dr. A.S. Oko and a reply from Raïssa Maritain,' *Commonweal* 33 (7 March 1941): 492–4; and letter to the editor, *Commonweal* 34 (29 August 1941): 446–7.
47 Cruickshank, *Variations on Catastrophe*, 7. See also Mark Antliff, *Inventing Bergson: Cultural Politics and the Parisian Avant-Garde* (Princeton, NJ: Princeton University Press, 1993).
48 For the following, see Albert William Levi, *Philosophy and the Modern World* (Bloomington, IN: Indiana University Press, 1959), 63–101.
49 Ibid., 70.
50 Henri Bergson, *Creative Evolution*, trans. Arthur Mitchell (New York: H. Holt and Co., 1911), 302; 304–6; orig. *L'évolution créatrice* (Paris: F. Alcan, 1907); in Levi, *Philosophy and the Modern World*, 91.

51 André Encrevé, 'La pensée protestante,' in Gadille and Mayeur, ed., *Liberalisme, industrialisaton, expansion européenne*, 11: 367–426. See 378.
52 Alexis Philonenko, *Bergson, ou de la philosophie comme science rigoureuse* (Paris: Éditions du Cerf, 1994).
53 Henri Bergson, *Laughter: An Essay on the Meaning of the Comic*, trans. Cloudesley Brereton and Fred Rothwell (New York: Macmillan, 1911), 150–5; orig. *Le rire: essai sur la signification du comique* (Paris: F. Alcan, 1900); in Levi, *Philosophy and The Modern World*, 98.
54 Vladimir Jankélévitch, *Henri Bergson* (1959; repr. Paris: Quadrige/ Presses Universitaires de France, 1989), 28–79.
55 Jacques Maritain, *Creative Intuition in Art and Poetry*, Bollingen Series, 35. The A.W. Mellon lectures in the fine arts (New York: Pantheon Books, 1953).
56 Gugelot, *La Conversion des intellectuels*, 85–94.
57 Roger Shattuck, *The Banquet Years*, 3–4.
58 Following: E.T. Dubois, *Portrait of Léon Bloy* (New York: Sheed and Ward, 1951), 7–16; Griffiths, *Reactionary Revolution*, 139–45; 175–81. See also Richard D.E. Burton, *Holy Tears, Holy Blood: Women, Catholicism, and the Culture of Suffering in France, 1840–1970* (Ithaca, NY: Cornell University Press, 2004). I regret that Burton's work appeared too late for me to incorporate this well-documented and important study.
59 David Sweetman, *Explosive Acts: Toulouse-Lautrec, Oscar Wilde, Felix Feneon, and the Art & Anarchy of the Fin de Siecle* (New York: Simon and Schuster, 2000); Jerrold E. Seigel, *Bohemian Paris: Culture, Politics, and the Boundaries of Bourgeois Life, 1830-1930* (Baltimore, MD: Johns Hopkins University Press, 1999).
60 Léon Bloy, *Letters to His Fiancée*, 27 Nov. 1889; in Dubois, *Portrait of Léon Bloy*, 35.
61 Matthew 21:31.
62 Griffiths, 'Vicarious Suffering,' in *Reactionary Revolution*, 149–222.
63 Jacques LeGoff, *The Birth of Purgatory*, trans. Arthur Goldhammer (Chicago: University of Chicago Press, 1984); Bernard Poschmann, *Penance and the Anointing of the Sick*; trans. and rev. Francis Courtney (London: Burns & Oates, 1964).
64 Griffiths, *Reactionary Revolution*, 149–222; and Talar, 'A Naturalistic Hagiography.'
65 T.J. Jackson Lears, 'From Salvation to Self-Realization: Advertising and the Therapeutic Roots of the Consumer Culture, 1880–1930),' in *The Culture of Consumption: Critical Essays in American History, 1880–1980*, ed. T.J. Jackson Lears and Richard Wightman Fox (New York: Pantheon, 1983), 3–38.

66 Letter of Léon Bloy to Pierre Lambert, 1 September 1871; in Griffiths, *Reactionary Revolution*, 176. Emphasis original.
67 Griffiths, *Reactionary Revolution*, 177–8.
68 Interviews with Jacques Maritain by Max Frantel, in *Comœdia*, undated clippings in the Rouault family archives; in Pierre Courthion, *Georges Rouault* (New York: Harry N. Abrams, 1962), 98. Emphasis added.
69 Gugelot, *La conversion des intellectuels*, 61–5.
70 Léon Bloy, *Celle qui pleure* (1908); in Griffiths, *Reactionary Revolution*, 154. The fascination with stigmatas comes largely from Johann Joseph von Görres, *Die christliche Mystik*, 5 vols. (Regensburg: GJ Manz, 1836–42); trans. M. Charles Sainte-Foi, *La mystique divine, naturelle, et diabolique* (Paris: Mme Vve Poussielgue-Rusand, 1854–5). In the New Testament, Simeon prophesies to Mary: 'and a sword will pierce through your own soul also ...' Luke 2:35.
71 Léon Bloy, *Le Salut par les Juifs* (Paris: A. Demay, 1892). Drumont, *La Libre Parole*, 23 May 1892; in Burns, *France and the Dreyfus Affair*, 11.
72 Griffiths, *Reactionary Revolution*, 180; Isaiah 53:3.
73 Richard Griffiths, *The Use of Abuse: The Polemics of the Dreyfus Affair and Its Aftermath* (New York: Berg, 1991). For Bloy here and following, see 142–53.
74 Léon Bloy, *Je m'accuse ... Vignettes et culs-de-lampe de Léon Bloy* (Paris: Édition de la Maison d'art, 1900).
75 Interviews with Jacques Maritain by Max Frantel, in *Comoedia*; in Courthion, *Georges Rouault*, 98. Emphasis added.
76 Barré, *Jacques et Raïssa Maritain*, 82–108.
77 John M. Dunaway, *Jacques Maritain* (Boston: Twayne Publishers, 1978), 17.
78 Barré, *Jacques et Raïssa Maritain*, 104–5.
79 Léon Bloy, *Le Salut par les Juifs*, rev. ed. (Paris: J. Victorion, 1906).
80 Letter of Léon Bloy to Pierre Termier, 24 February 1906, in *Lettres à Pierre Termier* (Paris: Stock, 1927), 12–13.
81 Barré, *Jacques et Raïssa Maritain*, 111–12.
82 Judith D. Suther, *Raïssa Maritain: Pilgrim, Poet, Exile* (New York: Fordham University Press, 1990), 25.
83 Letter of E. Roubanovitch to the Maritains, 27 July 1907; letter of Geneviève Favre to Ernest Psichari, 24 March 1907; in Barré, *Jacques et Raïssa Maritain*, 111–12.
84 Anne Harrington, *Reenchanted Science: Holism in German Culture from Wilhelm II to Hitler* (Princeton: Princeton University Press, 1996), 48–54. For Maritain's interest in biology, see Jacques Maritain, 'Dialogue entre

Jean-Pierre, Louise et un cousin de Jean-Pierre sur les sciences de la nature,' *Jean-Pierre* 1/23 (1 November 1902): 357–64; and 1/24 (15 November 1902), 372–6; 'Mouches,' *Jean-Pierre* 2/7 (22 February 1903): 486–91; in *JRM-OC*, 16: 617–39.

85 Clérissac, in entry for 14 July 1910; in *CarnetJM-Fr*, 206; *CarnetJM-En*, 64.

86 On Véra, see *CarnetJM-Fr*, 359–401; *CarnetJM-En*, 186–218.

87 Suther, *Raïssa Maritain*, 29.

88 This explanation was deleted from the definitive edition of the *Journal de Raïssa*. Quoted in Julie Kernan, *Our Friend Jacques Maritain* (Garden City, NY: Doubleday, 1975), 46–7; in Suther, *Raïssa Maritain*, 30.

89 Daniel Halévy, 'Les chroniques nationales. Notes sur "Antimoderne,"' *Revue de Genève* (December 1922): 760–2; Peter Brown, *The Body and Society: Men, Women, and Sexual Renunciation in Early Christianity* (New York: Columbia University Press, 1988), 78–81. On vow, see Barré, *Jacques et Raïssa Maritain*, 162; and *JournRM-Fr*, 15: 175, n. 1.

90 Wohl, *The Generation of 1914*.

91 Ibid., 11.

92 Barré, *Jacques et Raïssa Maritain*, 53.

93 Jacques Maritain to Ernest Psichari, 12 December 1899, in Barré, *Jacques et Raïssa Maritain*, 62–4.

94 *GrndAmiFr*, 674; *GrndAmiEn*, 51.

95 On Psichari's homosexual inclinations, see Frédérique Neau-Dufoun, *Ernest Psichari: L'ordre et l'errance* (Paris: Cerf, 2001), 109–15. Cited in Burton, *Holy Tears, Holy Blood*, 266n.5.

96 Alec G. Hargreaves, *The Colonial Experience in French Fiction: A Study of Pierre Loti, Ernest Psichari and Pierre Mille* (London: Macmillan, 1981).

97 Ernest Psichari, *Terres de soleil et de sommeil* (Paris: C. Lévy, 1908); in Hargreaves, *Colonial Experience*, 95.

98 Braudy, *From Chivalry to Terrorism*, 327–37. See 327. For the contrasting position, see Gail Bederman, *Manliness and Civilization: A Cultural History of Gender and Race in the United States, 1880–1917* (Chicago: University of Chicago Press, 1995).

99 Psichari, *Terres de soleil*; in Wohl, *The Generation of 1914*, 12. Emphasis added.

100 17 November 1909; *CarnetJM-Fr*, 198; *CarnetJM-En*, 57–8.

101 For following, see Hargreaves, *Colonial Experience*, 101–5; and Marie-Hélène Ryckmans, 'L'Islam et la conversion de Psichari,' *Les Lettres romanes* 12 (1 November 1958): 389–413; 13 (1 February 1959): 19–44.

102 Ernest Psichari to Jacques Maritain, 15 June 1912, *Lettres du centurion: l'adolescent, le voyageur, le croyant*, introd. by Henriette Psichari, preface

by Paul Claudel (Paris: L. Conard, 1933); in Wohl, *The Generation of 1914*, 13.

103 Wohl, *The Generation of 1914*, 13. See Henriette Psichari, *Les Convertis de la belle époque* (Paris: Éditions rationalistes, 1971).

104 Ernest Psichari, *L'Appel des armes* (Paris: G. Oudin et Cie, 1913); in Hargreaves, *Colonial Experience*, 97.

105 Robert Nye, 'Honor, Impotence and Male Sexuality in 19th-Century French Medicine,' *French Historical Studies* 16 (Spring 1989): 48–71.

106 Psichari, *L'Appel des armes*, 176–8; in Hargreaves, *Colonial Experience*, 97.

107 Ernest Psichari to Charles Péguy, 1 May 1913; Charles Péguy, 'Victor-Marie, comte Hugo' (1910); in Sergio Luzzatto, 'Young Rebels and Revolutionaries, 1789–1917,' *A History of Young People in the West*, 2 vols., ed. Giovanni Levi and Jean-Claude Schmitt; trans. Carol Volk (Cambridge, MA: Belknap Press of Harvard University Press, 1997), 2: 229.

108 Charles Péguy, *Temporal and Eternal*, trans. Alexander Dru (1958; repr. Indianapolis: Liberty Fund, 2001); adaptation of *Notre jeunesse* (1910).

109 For following, see Wohl, *The Generation of 1914*, 11–18.

110 Henri Massis and Alfred de Tarde, *Les Jeunes gens d'aujourd'hui; le goût de l'action, la foi patriotique – Une renaissance catholique, le réalisme politique* (Paris: Plon-Nourrit et cie, 1913).

111 Henri Massis and Alfred de Tarde [pseudonym: Agathon], *L'Esprit de la nouvelle Sorbonne. La crise de la culture classique. La crise du français* (Paris: Mercure de France, 1911). *Agathon* is Greek for 'Good,' the first and most noble of the three Platonic transcendentals, i.e., *the Good*, the True, and the Beautiful. On Agathon's program, see Phyllis H. Stock, 'Students versus the University in Pre-World War Paris,' *French Historical Studies* 7 (Spring 1971): 93–110.

112 Massis and Tarde, *Les Jeunes gens d'aujourd'hui*, 12, 117; in Wohl, *The Generation of 1914*, 8–9.

113 'Vers une renaissance catholique,' *La Vie Nouvelle* (19 April 1914), n.p.

114 Jacques Maritain, opinion for Massis and Tarde, *Les Jeunes gens d'aujourd'hui* (1912); in *JRM-OC*, I: 1033–6.

115 See explanatory note for 20 April 1910; *CarnetJM-Fr*, 204; *CarnetJM-En*, 62. Maritain uses the German *grob*, an adjective meaning 'coarse; thick, rough; rude; grossly negligent.'

116 Barré, *Jacques et Raïssa Maritain*, 176; Philippe Soulez and Frédéric Worms, *Bergson. Biographie* (Paris: Flammarion, 1997), 116.

117 1 March 1910; *Carnet JM-Fr*, 203; *CarnetJM-En*, 61.

118 Jacques Maritain, 'L'Esprit de la philosophie Moderne,' *Revue de*

Philosophie (1 June 1914): 601–25 and (1 July 1914): 53–82; in *JRM-OC*, 1: 823–87.

119 Barré, *Jacques et Raïssa Maritain*, 178–9. For Baudrillart, see Alfred Baudrillart, *Les Carnets du Cardinal Alfred Baudrillart, 1er août 1914–31 décembre 1918*, ed. Paul Christophe (Paris: Cerf, 1994), 7–18 and *Les normaliens dans l'église* (La Chapelle-Montligeon: Impr. de l'Oeuvre expiatoire, 1895).

120 Barré, *Jacques et Raïssa Maritain*, 182.

121 *JournRM-Fr*, 174; *JournRM-En*, 24.

Chapter 2 Trauma and Memorial: Repatriating the Repressed

1 Sigmund Freud, 'Mourning and Melancholia (1917),' in Freud, *Collected Papers: Authorized Translation Under the Supervision of Joan Riviere*, 5 vols. (New York: Basic Books, 1959), 4: 152–70. See 154. Jonathan Franzen, 'My Father's Brain,' in Franzen, *How to Be Alone: Essays* (New York: Farrar, Straus and Giroux, 2002), 7–38. See 38. 'Nostalgie,' from Paul Robert, *Dictionnaire alphabétique et analogique de la langue française*, rev. and enlarged by Alain Rey, 2nd ed., 9 vols. (Paris: Le Robert, 1985).

2 Harvey Goldberg, *Jean Jaurès* (Madison: University of Wisconsin Press, 1968).

3 Poincaré cited in *La Journée du 4 Août. Pages d'histoire. 1914[–15]* (Paris: Berger-Levrault, (1914–15), 6–7; in Silver, *Esprit de Corps*, 25. See François Aubry de la Noë, *La France meillure, l'Union Sacrée* (Dijon: A. Benoist, 1916), and Julien de Nafron, *Que subsistera-t-il de l'union sacrée? Conférence donnée le 28 mai 1916 à la Fraternité de l'Ascension, précédée de l'introduction du pasteur Edouard Soulier* (Paris: 33, rue des Saints-Pères, 1916).

4 David Thompson, *Democracy in France since 1870* (New York: Oxford University Press, 1969), 11–12.

5 Jacques Maritain, 'Ernest Psichari,' *La Croix* (19 November 1914); in *JRM-OC*, 1: 1044–6.

6 Julian Green, introduction to Charles Péguy, *Basic Verities: Prose and Poetry*, trans. Ann and Julian Green (New York: Pantheon Books, 1943), 40–1. On baptism, see preface to *Péguy au porche de l'Église. Correspondance inédite Jacques Maritain Dom Louis Baillet*, ed. René Mougel and Robert Burac (Paris: Cerf, 1997), 7–21.

7 Alain-Fournier and Jacques Rivière, *Alain-Fournier, Jacques Rivière: du Grand Meaulnes à la Nouvelle revue française, 1886–1986* (Paris: Biblio-

thèque de la ville de Paris, 1986), editor name missing; *Correspondance Charles Péguy Alain-Fournier: paysages d'une amitié*, rev. ed., Yves Rey-Herme (1973; repr. Paris: Fayard, 1990).

8 Ronald Thomas Sussex, *The Sacrificed Generation: Studies of Charles Péguy, Ernest Psichari and Alain-Fournier* (Townsville, Australia: James Cook University of North Queensland, 1980); *Alain-Fournier (22 Septembre 1914), Charles Péguy (5 Septembre 1914), Ernest Psichari (22 Aôut 1914)* (Paris: C. Coulet et Faure, 1964), author name missing.

9 Richard Harding Davis, *New York Tribune*, 31 August 1914; in WWI Document Archive; http://www.lib.byu.edu/~rdh/wwi/1914/louvburn.html

10 Becker, *War and Faith;* Griffiths, *The Use of Abuse.*

11 Jacques Rivière, *À la trace de Dieu* (Paris: Gallimard, 1925), 37; in Becker, *La Guerre et la foi*, 15; *War and Faith*, 7.

12 Victor Basch in Jean-François Sirinelli, *Intellectuels et passions françaises* (Paris: Fayard, 1990), 39; in Becker, *La Guerre et la foi*, 13; *War and Faith*, 6.

13 Becker, *La Guerre et la foi*, 44–5; *War and Faith*, 44–6.

14 Excerpt from 'Appeal to the Civilized Nations' in *JRM-OC*, I: 1040. See John Horne and Alan Kramer, *German Atrocities, 1914: A History of Denial* (New Haven: Yale University Press, 2001).

15 Jacques Maritain, 'German Science,' *La Croix* (25–6 October 1914); in *JRM-OC*, 1: 1040–3. See 1041.

16 Maritain, 'Ernest Psichari,' 1044–6.

17 Jacques Maritain, *Le Rôle de l'allemagne dans la philosophie moderne*, complete text or resume (by the author) of lectures given at the Institut Catholique of Paris, published in *La Croix*'s 'Supplément'; in *JRM-OC*, 1: 889–1025. Introduction (9 and 17 December 1914); 'The Origins of the Reformation' (25–6 December 1914); 'Lutheranism' (7 and 20 January; 3 February 1915); 'The Role of Germany in Modern Philosophy' (28–9 March); 'Jean-Jacques Rousseau' (2–3 May); 'The Speculative Philosophy of Kant' (27 May); 'The Religious Philosophy of Kant' (4 June); 'The Official German Pantheism: Fichte, Schelling, Hegel' (20–1 June); 'German Science' (15 July); 'Schopenhauer and Nietzsche' (21 July); 'Conclusion. German Influence in France during the 19th Century' (4 August 1915).

18 Maritain, *Le Rôle de l'allemagne*, 9 and 7 December 1914, 909. Emphasis original.

19 Ibid., 901.

20 Ibid., 26 May 1915, 1018.

21 Ibid., 1025. Emphasis original.

22 Philippe Chenaux, *Paul VI et Maritain: Les rapports du «Montinianisme» et du «Maritainisme»* (Brescia: Istituto Paolo VI, 1994), 26–7.

23 *JournRM-Fr*, 177; *JournRM-En*, 26.
24 Henri Massis, *Le Sacrifice* (Paris: Plon, 1917).
25 Ibid., 7. Emphasis original.
26 Ibid., 148–9. The closing quotation from Maritain, 'Ernest Psichari,' *La Croix*, 19 November 1914. Emphasis added.
27 Matthew 3: 2–3. See Ernest Psichari, *Les Voix qui crient dans le désert; souvenirs d'Afrique* (Paris: L. Conard, 1920); in Psichari, *Oeuvres complètes de Ernest Psichari*, 3 vols. (Paris: L. Conard, 1948), vol. 2.
28 Psichari, *Les voix qui crient*, in *Oeuvres complètes*, 2: 354; in Hargreaves, *Colonial Experience*, 102.
29 Louis Rouzic, *Lettres d'un prisonnier* (Paris: Bloud et Gay, 1917); *Une âme chrétienne et militaire: Le Lieutenant Guillaume de Montferrand (1897–1918)* (Paris: P. Lethielleux, 1920); *Théologie de la Guerre en dix-huit leçons* (Paris: Bloud et Gay, 1916), dedicated to 'all my young *Postards* friends, officers or soldiers.' The nickname 'Postard' refers to alumni of the 'rue des Postes.'
30 Abbé Louis Rouzic (1863–1934) was a priest from the Diocese of Saint-Brieuc. In 1900, he appears in the register of the Diocese of Paris as being assigned to the chaplaincy at Ste-Geneviève, a Jesuit *lycée* that had recently relocated itself from the rue des Postes in Paris to Versailles. Rouzic presumably served at Ste-Geneviève because the laws of 1901–5, having expelled the Jesuits from France, made necessary the employment of diocesan clergy in both teaching and counseling positions. Although the Archdiocese of Paris no longer lists Rouzic after the year 1913, an obituary letter in the archives of the Diocese of Saint-Brieuc (dated 20 October 1934) describes him as an *aumônier* at Ste-Geneviève from 1901 to 1928. See Archives Historiques d'Archêve de Paris: Registre III, no. 4134; and *Semaine Religieuse de Saint-Brieuc* (1934), 672–3. I am grateful to the archivists for the Diocese of Saint-Brieuc and the Archdiocese of Paris for their kindness.
31 Louis Rouzic, *Le Renouveau catholique I. Les Jeunes avant la guerre* (Paris: P. Tequi, 1919); *Le Renouveau catholique II. Les Jeunes pendant la guerre* (Paris: P. Tequi, 1919).
32 Rouzic, *Le Renouveau catholique*, 1: 3–4.
33 Following excerpts from letters of students to Rouzic in 'Comment ils regardent l'avenir,' *Le Renouveau catholique*, 2: 283–91.
34 Christiansen, *Paris Babylon*, 356. I am grateful to Robert Bonfils, S.J., for communicating details of Olivaint's life.
35 Père Olivaint, in Rouzic, *Le Renouveau catholique*, 2: 286–7. Emphasis added.
36 Olivaint's journal of notes from his annual retreats had first been published

in 1872, a year after his death. This journal went through a number of editions, including during the bitter years of Church-State conflict leading up to the war: 6th ed. (1899), 7th ed. (1905), and 8th ed. (1911). In addition, his 'counsels to young people' had gone through its 15th edition by 1894. Like Louis Rouzic, Alfred Baudrillart devoted a great effort to building bridges between the grandes écoles and the church, and he devoted several pages of his book on Normaliens to Olivaint, one of their own. See Pierre Olivaint, *Le R.P. Pierre Olivaint, ... Journal de ses retraites annuelles de 1860 à 1870*, 2 vols., 8th ed. (Paris: P. Téqui, 1911) and *Aux jeunes gens, conseils du R. P. Olivaint*, 15th ed., ed. Charles Clair, (Paris: A. Taffin-Lefort, 1894); Alfred Baudrillart, *Les Normaliens dans l'Église* (Paris: La Chapelle-Montligeon: Impr. de l'Oeuvre expiatoire, 1895), esp. 36–8, 42–51). See also Paul Duclos, 'Olivaint (Pierre),' *Dictionnaire de spiritualité, ascétique et mystique, doctrine et histoire*, directed by Marcel Viller, S.J., assisted by F. Cavallera and J. de Guibert, S.J., et al., 21 vols. (Paris: G. Beauchesne et ses fils, 1932–95), 11: 767–71. I am grateful to Robert Bonfils, S.J., and Dominique Salin, S.J., for this information.

37 See Perrot, *A History of Private Life*; Borie, *Mythologies de l'hérédité*; Laqueur, *Solitary Sex*; Stengers and Van Neck, *Masturbation*; Braudy, *From Chivalry to Terrorism*, 364; all cited above.

38 Rouzic's Latin text quotes from Psalm 29:10: 'What profit is there in my blood, whilst I go down to corruption?'

39 Fussell, *The Great War and Modern Memory*.

40 Karl Barth, *The Epistle to the Romans*, trans. W. Montgomery (New York: Macmillan, 1956); excerpts repr. in Carl E. Braaten and Robert W. Jenson, eds., *A Map of Twentieth-Century Theology: Readings from Karl Barth to Radical Pluralism* (Minneapolis: Augsburg Fortress, 1995), 42–50. Originally published as Barth, *Der Römerbrief* (Munich: Chr. Kaiser Verlag, 1922). See also 'The Protestant Principle and the Proletarian Situation,' chapter 11 in Paul Tillich, *The Protestant Era* (Chicago: University of Chicago Press, 1948).

41 Rouzic, *Le Renouveau catholique*, 2: 158.

42 Ibid., 138.

43 Ibid., 285.

44 Réné Doumic, 'La Victoire,' *Revue des deux mondes* 48 (1918): 481; in M. Brady Brower, 'Strategic Re-membering. The Boundary Politics of Mourning in Post-Great War France,' *Rethinking History*, no. 1 (1997): 21–33. See 30. Emphasis added.

45 Paul Deschanel, *Echo de Paris* (1919), in Brower, 'Strategic Re-membering,' 30.

46 Mary Louise Roberts, *Civilization Without Sexes*, 127.

47 Alfred Baudrillart, entries for 8 and 9 March 1917; in Baudrillart, *Les Carnets du Cardinal Alfred Baudrillart,* 510. See also Yves Marchasson, 'Monseigneur Baudrillart et la Première Guerre mondiale,' in Institut Catholique de Paris, *Le Livre du centenaire, 1875–1975* (Paris: Beauchesne, 1975), 93–131; and Marchasson, 'Monseigneur Baudrillart et la propagande catholique française à l'étranger pendant la Première Guerre mondiale: l'exemple de l'Espagne,' in *Humanisme et foi chrétienne: mélanges scientifiques du centenaire de l'Institut catholique de Paris*, ed. Charles Kannengiesser and Yves Marchasson (Paris: Beauchesne, 1976), 71–90.

48 Alfred Baudrillart, *L'âme de la France à Reims. Discours prononcé en la basilique de Sainte-Clotilde le 30 septembre 1914* (Paris: G. Beauchesne, 1914); Baudrillart and André Michel, *Les villes martyrés: Reims, Soissons, Senlis, Arras*; also trans. into English as *The Martyred Towns: Rheims, Soissons, Senlis, Arras* (Paris: Plon-Nourrit et cie, 1915); *Jeanne la libératrice 1429–1915. Panégyrique prononcé à Notre-Dame de Paris le 16 mai 1915* (Paris: G. Beauchesne, 1915); *La Guerre allemande et le Catholicisme* (Paris: Bloud et Gay, 1915), simultaneously published in English, Italian, Spanish, Portuguese, Dutch, and German translations; François Veuillot, *La Guerre allemande et le Catholicisme. Album no 2. Documents photographiques illustrant la conduite respective des armées allemande et française à l'égard de l'Église catholique*, under direction of Baudrillart (Paris: Bloud et Gay, 1915); *L'Allemagne et les Alliés devant la conscience chrétienne* (Paris: Bloud et Gay, 1916); *Notre propagande* (Paris: Plon-Nourrit et cie, 1916), preface by Baudrillart; Baudrillart, *La France, les catholiques et la guerre: réponse quelques objections* (Paris: Bloud & Gay, 1917); Baudrillart and Joseph Désiré Mercier, *Per crucem ad lucem: Lettres pastorales* (Paris, Barcelona: Bloud et Gay, 1917); Baudrillart, *Crimes et châtiments. L'Amérique avec la France* (Paris, 1917); Baudrillart, *L'effort canadien* (Paris: Bloud & Gay, 1917); Baudrillart, *Jérusalem délivrée. Discours prononcé à Saint-Julien-le-Pauvre en l'honneur de la prise de Jérusalem le 23 décembre 1917* (Paris: Beauchesne, 1918); *La Vie catholique dans la France contemporaine* (Paris: Bloud et Gay, 1918), preface by Baudrillart; Baudrillart, ed., *En Alsace, 1914–1918. Souvenirs photographiques de la guerre en Haute-Alsace* (Masevaux: A. Nico, 1919).

49 Léon-Adolphe Cardinal Amette, preface-letter to *The German War and Catholicism* (Paris: Bloud & Gay, 1915), 5–7.

50 Baudrillart, 'Introduction,' *The German War and Catholicism*, 9.

51 A Missionary, 'The Catholic Rôle of France in the World,' *The German War and Catholicism*, 63–96. See 64.

52 A Missionary, 65–6; translation altered using *La Guerre allemande et le catholicisme*, 50.
53 G. Ardant, 'Religion in the French Army,' *The German War and Catholicism*, 168–208. See 202; 207–8.
54 Baudrillart et al., *La Vie catholique dans la France contemporaine.*
55 Abbé Georges Michelet, 'La Renaissance de la philosophie chrétienne en France,' in Baudrillart et al., *La Vie catholique dans la France contemporaine*, 305–85. See 313–14.
56 Ibid., 310; 311. Emphasis original.
57 Ibid., 312–13. See Pierre Lassieur, *La laïcité est-elle la neutralité? Histoire du débat: depuis 1850 jusqu'aux manuels de philosophies aujourd'hui* (Paris: de Guibert, 1995).
58 See Richard Panek, *The Invisible Century: Einstein, Freud, and the Search for Hidden Universes* (New York: Viking, 2004).
59 Baudrillart, preface, *La Vie catholique dans la France contemporaine*, xvi.
60 Brower, 'Strategic Re-membering,' 25.
61 Maurice Barrès, 'Le poilu sous l'Arc de Triomphe,' *Echo de Paris* (15 July 1919); in Brower, 'Strategic Re-membering,' 26–7.
62 Marcel Prévost, 'Réponse de M. Marcel Prévost,' *Discours de Réception de Monseigneur Baudrillart* (Paris: Bloud & Gay, 1919), 8–9; 47–8; 57–8. Emphasis added.
63 Ibid., 58–9.
64 Ibid., 62.
65 See articles in *Petit Parisien*: '250 millions de marks sont passés en Hollande, à destination des Hohenzollern,' 'L'emploi obligatoire des mutilés' (23 November 1920); 'La Sépulture du Soldat Inconnu. Rien n'est décidé encore!,' 'Le Débat sur le Vatican' (24 November 1920); 'Au Reichstag. Le budget d'exécution du traité de Versailles,' 'Encore des agressions en Allemagne,' 'Aujourd'hui, achetez. Achetez tous. Achetez beaucoup!' (25 November 1920); 'La question du charbon d'après M. Le Trocquer' (26 November 1920); 'Le conseil Municipal s'occupe de la crise du lait,' 'La sépulture des Parisiens morts au front,' 'Le rapatriement du corps de nos soldats inhumés en Allemagne' (27 November 1920); 'LA CRISE DU LAIT. NOUS ATTENDONS TOUJOURS que l'Allemagne nous rende les vaches qu'elle nous a enlevées' (28 November 1920).
66 'Un Débat Tumultueux à la Chambre sur la Question Vaticane,' *Petit Parisien* (26 November 1920).
67 'LA REPRISE DES RELATIONS AVEC LE VATICAN est votée à la Chambre par 397 voix contre 209 après une intervention de M. Georges Leygues,' *Petit Parisien* (1 December 1920).

68 Dominique Avon, *Paul Doncoeur, s.j. (1880–1961). Un Croisé dans le siècle*, preface by Gérard Cholvy (Paris: Éditions du Cerf, 2001), 137–52. See also Hugues Beylard, 'DONCOEUR Paul,' in *Dictionnaire du monde religieux dans la France contemporaine*, 9 vols., ed. Jean-Marie Mayeur and Yves-Marie Hilaire (Paris: Beauchesne, 1985–), vol. 1, *Les Jésuites*, dir. Paul Duclos, 95–6.

69 Paul Doncoeur, '*Nous ne partirons pas!* An open letter of Father Doncoeur to the President of the Conseil, Édouard Herriot ' (October 1924); reprinted in Avon, *Paul Doncoeur*, 365–6.

70 Wright, *France in Modern Times*, 329. See also Paul, *The Second Ralliement.*

71 Jay, 'The Apocalyptic Imagination and the Inability to Mourn.'

Chapter 3 Mystic Realism: A Faith That Faced the Facts

1 Wendell Berry, 'Writer and Region,' *What Are People For?* (San Francisco: North Point Press, 1990), 71–87. See 78. Etty Hillesum, diary entry for 19 June 1942, in Hillesum, *An Interrupted Life: The Diaries, 1941–1943; and, Letters from Westerbork*, intro. and notes by Jan G. Gaarlandt (New York: Henry Holt and Company, 1996), 143. Denise Levertov, 'City Psalm,' *The Sorrow Dance* (New York: New Directions, 1967), 72.

2 Becker and Berstein, *Victoire et frustrations*, 178.

3 Jean-Jacob Fazy, *De la gérontocratie, ou Abus de la sagesse des vieillards dans le gouvernement de la France* (Paris: Delaforest, 1828); Pierre Nora, 'Generation,' *Realms of Memory*, vol. 1: 499–531. For Condorcet and Saint-Just, see 501–2; for Fazy, see 608 n. 46. Nora's notation on the year of Fazy's publication ('1928') is a typographic error.

4 Jean Luchaire, *Une génération réaliste* (Paris: Librairie Valois, 1929), 7–9.

5 Massis, *Le Sacrifice* (1917); Alphonse Mortier, *Le Témoignage de la génération sacrifiée* (Paris: Nouvelle Librairie Nationale, 1919); Lucien Febvre, 'Générations,' *Revue de synthèse historique* (June 1920); François Mentré, *Les Générations sociales* (Paris: Bossard, 1920); Jacques Maritain, *Antimoderne* (1922); Georges Valois to Léon Daudet, 23 August 1922, in M.A. Lamarche, 'À propos d'"Antimoderne,"' *Le Devoir* (Montreal) (7 October 1922); Georges Valois, *D'un siècle à l'autre. Chronique d'une génération (1885–1920)* (Poitiers: Société française d'imprimerie et de librairie; Paris: Nouvelle Librairie nationale, 1924); Martin Heidegger, *Sein und Zeit* (1927); from the French trans. Jean-François Vezin, *Etre et temps* (Paris: Gallimard, 1986), 449; Henri Daniel-Rops, *Notre inquiétude* (Paris: Perrin, 1927), 70; Febvre, Heidegger and Mentré in Nora, *Realms of Memory*, 1: 505, 507.

6 Karl Mannheim, 'The Problem of Generations,' in *Essays in the Sociology of Knowledge* (London: Routledge and Kegan Paul, 1959), 278–322, trans. of 'Das Problem der Generationen' in *Kölner Viertel Jahrshefte für Soziologie* (1928); Erich Maria Remarque, *All Quiet on the Western Front*, trans. A.W. Wheen (1929; repr. New York: Fawcett Columbine, 1996); orig. *Im Westen Nichts Neues* (Berlin: Ullstein, A.G., 1928)
7 Becker and Berstein, *Victoire et frustrations*, 391–5. See 394.
8 Luchaire, *Génération réaliste*, 41.
9 André Breton, *Manifeste du surréalisme* (1924), in Breton, *Oeuvres complètes*, ed. Marguerite Bonnet Philippe Berner, Étienne-Alain Hubert, and José Pierre (Paris: NRF/Gallimard, 1988), 1: 313; in *Manifestoes of Surrealism*, trans. Richard Seaver and Helen R. Lane (Ann Arbor: University of Michigan Press, 1969), 6.
10 Breton, *Manifeste*, 316–18; *Manifestoes*, 10–12.
11 Breton, *Manifeste*, 316; *Manifestoes*, 9–10.
12 Breton, *Manifeste*, 319; *Manifestoes*, 13–14.
13 Breton quoting Reverdy, from *Nord-Sud*, March 1918, *Manifeste*, 324; *Manifestoes*, 20. Italics are Breton's.
14 Breton, *Manifeste*, 327–8; *Manifestoes*, 24–6. Small caps are Breton's.
15 Louis Aragon and André Breton, 'Le Cinquantenaire de l'Hystérie (1878–1928),' *La Révolution surréaliste* 11 (15 March 1928): 20–2. See 22.
16 Franz Roh, *Nach-expressionismus, magischer Realismus: Probleme der neuesten Europäischen Malerei* (Leipzig: Klinkhardt and Biermann, 1925) and *Realismo mágico: Problemas de la pintura Europea mas reciente*, trans. Fernando Vela (Madrid: Revista de Occidente, 1927).
17 Roh, preface to *Nach-expressionismus, magischer Realismus*; in 'Magical Realism: Post-Expressionism,' trans. Wendy B. Faris, *Magical Realism: Theory, History, Community*, ed. Lois Parkinson Zamora and Wendy B. Faris (Durham, NC: Duke University Press, 1995), 15–31. See 15–16.
18 Sigmund Freud, 'The "Uncanny"' (1919), in *Papers on Applied Psychoanalysis. Vol. 4 of Collected Papers*, trans. Joan Riviere (New York: Basic Books, 1959), 368–407.
19 David Mikics, 'Derek Walcott and Alejo Carpentier: Nature, History, and the Caribbean Writer,' in Zamora and Faris, *Magical Realism*, 371–404. See 372. For Dix, see Helen Adkins, 'Neue Sachlichkeit – Deutsche Malerei seit dem Expressionismus,' in *Stationen der Moderne: Die bedeutenden Kunstausstellungen des 20. Jahrhunderts in Deutschland* (Berlin: Berlinische Galerie, 1988), 221; in Irene Guenther, 'Magical Realism, New Objectivity, and the Arts during the Weimar Republic,' in *Magical Realism*, 33–73. See 49.

20 Martin Heidegger, *Being and Time*, trans. John Macquarrie and Edward Robinson (New York: Harper & Row, 1962), 234; Heidegger, *Sein und Zeit*, 17th ed. (Tübingen: Max Niemeyer Verlag, 1993), 189. See also Allan Megill, *Prophets of Extremity: Nietzsche, Heidegger, Foucault, Derrida* (Berkeley: University of California Press, 1985), 118–25.
21 Seymour Menton, *Magical Realism Rediscovered, 1918–1981* (East Brunswick, NJ: Associated University Presses, 1983), 13.
22 Walter Benjamin, *The Arcades Project* (Cambridge, MA: Belknap Press, 1999); quoting Rudolf Borchardt, *Epilegomena zu Dante* (Berlin: E. Rowohlt, 1923); in Vanessa R. Schwartz, 'Walter Benjamin for Historians,' *American Historical Review* (December 2001): 1721–43. See 1721.
23 Walter Benjamin, 'Surrealism,' in *Reflections*, ed. Peter Demetz, trans. Edmund Jephcott (New York: Harcourt Brace Jovanovich, 1978), 179; in Margaret Cohen, *Profane Illumination: Walter Benjamin and the Paris of Surrealist Revolution* (Berkeley: University of California Press, 1993), 3. See also Susan Buck-Morss, *The Dialectics of Seeing: Walter Benjamin and the Arcades Project* (Cambridge, MA: The MIT Press, 1989), esp. 32–4; Richard Wolin, *Walter Benjamin: An Aesthetic of Redemption* (1982; repr. Berkeley: University of California Press, 1994); and Michael Jennings, *Dialectical Images: Walter Benjamin's Theory of Literary Criticism* (Ithaca, NY: Cornell University Press, 1987).
24 Walter Benjamin, 'The Paris of the Second Empire in Baudelaire' (1938), 'Some Motifs in Baudelaire' (1939), and 'Paris – the Capital of the Nineteenth Century' (1935); in *Charles Baudelaire: A Lyric Poet in the Era of High Capitalism*, trans. Harry Zohn (New York: Verso, 1976). 'Some Motifs in Baudelaire' also with 'An Introduction to the Translation of Baudelaire's *Tableaux parisiens*' in Benjamin, *Illuminations: Essays and Reflections*, ed. Hannah Arendt, trans. Harry Zohn (New York: Schocken, 1968).
25 Matthew Cullerne Bown, *Socialist Realist Painting* (New Haven: Yale University Press, 1998), 109–10; and 130–203. For Mayakovski, see 109.
26 In Bown, *Socialist Realist Painting*, 109.
27 In ibid., 109–10.
28 In ibid., 119.
29 In ibid., 143. Emphasis mine.
30 For objections to realist aesthetics, see Cohen, *Profane Illumination*, 133; following Martin Jay, 'The Disenchantment of the Eye: Surrealism and the Crisis of Ocularcentrism,' in *Visual Anthropology Review*, 7, no. 1 (Spring 1991): 15–38. For 'mimetics,' see Hewitt, *Political Inversions*, 206.
31 Eysteinsson, *Concept of Modernism*, 204; and quoting Theodor Adorno,

'Voraussetzungen,' *Versuch, das Endspiel zu verstehen* (Frankfurt am Main: Suhrkamp, 1973), 115–16. See 205.

32 See Nora, 'Generation,' 527; and Daniel Milo, 'Neutraliser la chronologie: 'Génération comme paradigme scientifique,' c. 9 of *Trahir le temps (Histoire)* (Paris: Les Belles Lettres, 1990). Both reference Thomas S. Kuhn, *The Structure of Scientific Revolutions* (Chicago: University of Chicago Press, 1962), 98.

33 Pat Barker, *Regeneration* (1991; repr. New York: Penguin, 1992), 82–3.

34 See Jacques Maritain, 'Rencontre avec Pierre Villard,' chapter 4 of *CarnetJM-Fr*, 253–92; 'Meeting with Pierre Villard,' *CarnetJM-En*, 100–32.

35 Pierre Villard to Jacques Maritain, 4 January 1918; *CarnetJM-Fr*, 279; *Carnet JM-En*, 122.

36 Letter of Abbé Charles Rolin to Jacques Maritain, 30 June 1918; in *CarnetJM-Fr*, 285–6; *CarnetJM-En*, 127–8.

37 Chadwick, *Secularization of the European Mind*, 15.

38 Pierre-Dominique Dupouey, 12 March 1915; in *Lettres et essais* (Paris: Le Cerf, 1935), 180; in Becker, *La Guerre et la foi*, 11; *War and Faith*, 6. Becker's work is dedicated to an investigation of this phenomenon: 'C'est de cette mystique que ce livre entend rendre compte.' ['It is is this *mystique* that I wish to account for here.'] Becker, *La Guerre et la foi*, 13; *War and Faith*, 6.

39 Jacques Rivière, notes of 27 February 1917, in Rivière, *À la trace de Dieu*, ed. Paul Claudel (Paris: Nouvelle Revue Française, 1925), 333.

40 Henri Ghéon, *L'homme né de la guerre. Témoignage d'un converti (Yser-Artois 1915)* (Paris: Nouvelle Revue Française, 1919). See Alan Sheridan, *André Gide: A Life in the Present* (Cambridge, MA: Harvard University Press, 1999).

41 Ghéon, *L'Homme né de la guerre*, 190–1; in Becker, *La Guerre et la foi*, 48; *War and Faith*, 50.

42 *Journal de la Grotte de Lourdes*, 10 January 1915; in Becker, *La Guerre et le foi*, 72; *War and Faith*, 79.

43 Pierre de Lescure, 'Mysticisme et Réalisme,' *La Revue des Jeunes* (10 January 1917), 26.

44 Jules Sageret, *La Vague mystique: Henri Poincaré. – Énergétisme (W. Ostwald). - Néo-thomisme (P. Duhem). – Bergsonisme. – Pragmatisme. – Émile Boutroux* (Paris: E. Flammarion, 1920).

45 Advertisement on back cover, *Almanach catholique français pour 1922*, preface by Mgr. A. Baudrillart, published under the patronage of the Comité Catholique des Amitiés Françaises à l'Étranger (Paris: Bloud et Gay, 1922).

46 *Cahiers de la Nouvelle Journée* (Paris: Bloud et Gay): *Le Témoignage d'une génération* (No. 2, 1924); *Qu'est-ce que la mystique? Quelques aspects historiques et philosophiques du problème* (No. 3, 1925); *Où chercher le Réel?* (No. 9, 1925); and Paul Archambault, *Vers un réalisme intégral. L'Oeuvre philosophique de Maurice Blondel* (No. 12, 1928). See also Paul Archambault, 'Qu'est-ce que la politique? Technique, art et mystique,' *Politique* 4 (April 1929): 388–9.

47 Cholvy and Hilaire, *Histoire religieuse de la France contemporaine*, 98; 317–19; Yves Palau, 'Approches du catholicisme républicain dans la France de l'entre-deux-guerres,' in *Les intellectuels catholiques. Histoires et débats*, annual issue of *Mil Neuf Cent-revue d'histoire intellectuelle* 13 (1995): 46–66; D. Daubioul, *Paul Archambault et les Cahiers de la Nouvelle Journée* (Lille: Ed. Prat-Europa, 1992); John J. McNeill, *The Blondelian Synthesis: A Study of the Influence of German Philosophical Sources on the Formation of Blondel's Method and Thought* (Leiden: E.J. Brill, 1966).

48 11 November 1918; *JournRM-Fr*, 230; *JournRM-En*, 85. St Martin was a soldier.

49 Mid-February 1919; *JournRM-Fr*, 234–5; *JournRM-En*, 89–90. Emphasis added.

50 10 March 1919; *JournRM-Fr*, 237–9; *JournRM-En*, 92–96. Quoting Pius X, *E Supremi* (4 October 1903), paras. 4 and 8 on 'restoring all things in Christ.'

51 25 March 1919; *JournRM-Fr*, 241; *JournalRM-En*, 97–8. Citing Cocteau, *CoqArlFr*, 40; *CoqArlEn*, 35.

52 5 April 1919; *JournRM-Fr*, 243; *JournRM-En*, 100.

53 11 and 16 July 1919; *JournRM-Fr*, 251–2; 253; *JournRM-En*, 107–8; 110. Emphasis original.

54 Between 24 September and 8 November, 1919; *JournRM-Fr*, 257–8; *JournRM-En*, 114–15.

55 Henri Massis, 'Pour un Parti de l'Intelligence,' in 'Supplément littéraire,' *Figaro* (19 July 1919), 1: *JRM-OC*, 1: 1047–53. The fifty signatories included: Paul Bourget (of the Académie française), Louis Bertrand, Camille Bellaigue, Jacques Bainville, Maurice Denis, Henri Ghéon, Daniel Halévy, Francis Jammes, Edmond Jaloux, René Johannet, Pierre Lalo, Pierre de Lescure, Charles Maurras, Massis himself, Jean Psichari, Firmin Roz, René Salomé, Jean-Louis Vaudoyer, Robert Vallery-Radot, Georges Valois – and Jacques Maritain. On influence of Maurras, see Bernard Doering, *Jacques Maritain and the French Catholic Intellectuals* (Notre Dame, IN: University of Notre Dame Press, 1983), 22.

56 Appeal by *Clarté* / Henri Barbusse, in *Journal du Peuple*, 19 May 1919; excerpt in *JRM-OC*, 1: 1047, n. 1.

57 Jacques Rivière, 'Notes,' *La Nouvelle Revue française* 13 (September 1919): 617; in Doering, *Jacques Maritain*, 23.
58 Jacques Maritain, letter to Gaëtan Bernoville, in *Les Lettres* 10 (1 December 1919), 19–21; and a response 'to questions of Colonel R ...' in *Les Lettres* 2 (1 February 1920), 49–53; in *JRM-OC*, 1: 1053–9. In his letter to Bernville, Maritain referred to his study of 'Art et scolastique,' also appearing in installments in *Les Lettres*, on 1 September and 1 October 1919.
59 Recounted by Maritain to Henry Bars; quoted in Barré, *Jacques et Raïssa Maritain*, 217. See Weber, *Action Française*, 25; 190; 220; 224; 248.
60 Anne Rasmussen, 'Revue universelle (La),' in Julliard and Winnock, *Dictionnaire des intellectuels*, 976–7.
61 Doering, *Jacques Maritain*, 17–25.
62 16 January 1920; *JournalRM-Fr*, 261; *JournalRM-En*, 118–19.
63 Jacques Maritain, 'De Quelques Conditions de la Renaissance Thomiste,' 26 January 1920; published as chapter 3 of *Antimoderne* (1922); *JRM-OC*, 2: 1009–45. See 1009.
64 Cholvy and Hilaire, *Histoire religieuse de la France contemporaine*, 402.
65 See note to 'Pour une Semaine des Écrivains Catholiques,' *JRM-OC*, 2: 1991–2.
66 'Ce qu'est la Semaine des Écrivains Catholiques,' *Les Lettres* (October 1926): 130–44. See 133. Emphases original.
67 Joseph Huby, 'La Semaine des Écrivains Catholiques,' *Études*, 59/172 (20 July 1922): 194–200. See 194.
68 Jean Morienval, 'La Littérature catholique d'aujourd'hui,' *Almanach catholique français pour 1922*, 173–80.
69 André Bellessort, *Études et figures, variétés littéraires* (Paris: Bloud et Gay, 1920), 131; in M. Claude Foucart, 'Les Paysages de la Passion chez Green et Mauriac,' *Cahiers de l'Association Internationale des Études Françaises* 45 (May 1993): 119–33. See 119.
70 Morienval, 'La Littérature catholique d'aujourd'hui,' 174.
71 Émile Baumann, 15 June 1922 address to the Semaine des Écrivains Catholiques; in Baumann, 'Les possibilités du roman catholique,' *Les Lettres* (May 1926): 7–21.
72 Alfred Baudrillart, 'Pour que dure le Renouveau catholique,' *Revue Apologétique*, 35/297 (15 November 1922), 193–203. See 202, 203. I have not translated *aînés* as 'elders,' which would imply the students' parents' generation rather than their older siblings.
73 'Ce qu'est la Semaine des Écrivains Catholiques,' 141.
74 Ibid., 142–4.

75 Gaëtan Bernoville, 'L'Actualité de la prochaine "Semaine des Écrivains Catholiques,"' *Les Lettres* (1 November 1926): 255–7.
76 'Ce qu'est la Semaine des Écrivains Catholiques,' 141.
77 Albert Thibaudet, 'Réflexions sur la littérature. Le Roman catholique,' *La Nouvelle Revue française* (1 June 1926): 727–34. See 733.
78 Notice for the Semaine Sociale d'Étudiants in *La Revue des jeunes* (10 January 1924): 99. Emphasis in original.
79 René Salomé, 'Les Revues,' *La Revue des jeunes* (25 December 1919): 700–1. Emphasis original.
80 Pierre Descoqs, *Essai critique sur l'hylémorphisme* (Paris: Beauchesne, 1924), 339.
81 Jacques Maritain, 'Nouveaux débats einsteiniens,' *La Revue universelle* 17/1 (1 April 1924): 56–77; 'A propos de l'article d'André Metz sur Einstein, *Les Lettres* (1 November 1924): 748–9; in *JRM-OC*, 16: 314–15; and exchange by Maritain, Sertillanges, Bremond, and Metz in *Les Lettres*, 1925; in *JRM-OC*, 3: 1280–92. Jules Sageret, *La Révolution philosophique et la science: Bergson, Einstein, Le Dantec, J.-H. Rosny aîné* (Paris: F. Alcan, 1924).
82 Hans Hartmann, 'Von französischen Katholizismus,' *Die Tat: Monatsschrift für die Zukunft deutscher Kultur* 17/12 (March 1926): 881–90; in Hans Ulrich Gumbrecht, *In 1926: Living at the Edge of Time* (Cambridge, MA: Harvard University Press, 1997), 289.
83 'La Renaissance du Catholicisme en France,' *Przegląd Współzesny* 5/17, no. 48 (April 1926): 155–8; in *JRM-OC*, trans. Andrez Bernhart, 16: 336–41.
84 Gonzague Truc, 'Qu'est-ce que le thomisme et pourquoi il renaît,' and 'Le thomisme et l'avenir de la pensée,' *Comoedia* (23 May 1926 and 2 June 1926). Press clipping, *JRM-Arch*.
85 For following: Yvan Lenain and Charles-Ernest Renard, editorial, *Nouvelle Équipe* (15 October 1926): 1–2. Emphasis in original.
86 Jacques Maritain, letter to the editors of *Nouvelle Équipe*, 7 November 1926; in *JRM-OC*, 16: 364.
87 L.-O. Graillet, *La Libre Belgique* (3 May 1926). *JRM-Arch*.
88 Jean Calvet, *Le Renouveau catholique dans la littérature contemporaine* (Paris: F. Lanore, 1927). See 408; 412.
89 See Nora, 'Generation,' 527; and Milo, 'Neutraliser la chronologie: 'Génération comme paradigme scientifique.'
90 Charles Augustin Sainte-Beuve, *Dix ans après en littérature* (1840); quoted in Calvet, *Renouveau catholique*, 409; 411.
91 For 'palingenesis,' see the *Oxford English Dictionary*: (1860): Monsieur

Doy, 'the most ardent palingenesist of the age ... [who] pretends that these animals are able to support ... absolute desiccation, without losing the faculty of resurrection.' (1907): 'The granitic magma, once solidified and, in part, decomposed, undergoes again, when brought into the deeper parts of the earth, a resurrection, or, as the author expresses it, palingenesis.' For '*palingénésie*' see the *Dictionnaire Robert*: 'Apparition de caractères hérités d'ancêtres éloignés que l'on ne retrouve pas chez les ascendants immédiats.'

92 I am grateful to Philippe Buc for this suggestion.

93 Roger Chartier, *On the Edge of the Cliff: History, Language, and Practice*, trans. Lydia G. Cochrane (Baltimore, MD: Johns Hopkins University Press, 1997), 23; quoting Pierre Bourdieu, *La noblesse d'état: Grandes écoles et esprit de corps* (Paris: Éditions de Minuit, 1989), 10. See Chartier, 22.

94 Calvet, *Le Renouveau catholique*, 411. Emphasis added.

95 Carolyn J. Dean, *The Frail Social Body: Pornography, Homosexuality, and Other Fantasies in Interwar France* (Berkeley and Los Angeles: University of California Press, 2000); M. Brady Brower, 'Strategic Re-membering.' For parallels, see Caroline Walker Bynum, *Fragmentation and Redemption: Essays on Gender and the Human Body in Medieval Religion* (New York: Zone Books, 1991); *The Resurrection of the Body in Western Christianity, 200–1336* (New York: Columbia University Press, 1995); and *Metamorphosis and Identity* (New York: Zone Books; Cambridge, MA: Distributed by MIT Press, 2001).

96 Calvet, *Le renouveau catholique*, 411. Emphasis added.

Chapter 4 Ultramodernist Anti-modernism: Neoclassical Catholicism

1 Ingmar Bergman, *Four Screenplays of Bergman*, trans. Lars Malmstrom and David Kushner (New York: Simon and Schuster, 1960), xxii. Jean Cocteau, *Le Mystére laïc* (1928); in Cocteau, *Oeuvres complètes de Jean Cocteau*, 11 vols. (Genève: Marguerat, 1946–51), 10: 9–46. See 31. Vincent Scully, *Architecture: The Natural and the Manmade* (New York: St Martin's Press, 1991), 297; in Hanna, *Mobilization of Intellect*, 146.

2 25 March 1919; *JournRM-Fr*, 241; *JournalRM-En*, 97–8. 'In the course of summer 1918 ... Père Charles Henrion brought them *Le Coq et l'Arlequin*.' *CorrJC-JM*, 62 n. 3. Maritain himself says that Henrion brought them the book 'from Paris by accident in his pocket': *Lettre-Rép*, 307; *Letter-Resp*, 76. However, see Raïssa's entry for 23 April 1919: 'Arrival of Charles Henrion ... It has been nearly five years since we saw him ...' *JournRM-Fr* 245; *JournRM-En*, 102.

3 For following, see Arthur King Peters, *Jean Cocteau and André Gide: An*

Abrasive Friendship (New Brunswick, NJ: Rutgers University Press, 1973), 18–33.

4 Alan Sheridan, *André Gide: A Life in the Present* (Cambridge, MA: Harvard University Press, 1999), xiii, 208–12.

5 Henri Ghéon, review of Cocteau's *La Danse de Sophocle*, in *La Nouvelle Revue française* (September–October 1912); in Peters, *Jean Corteau and André Gide*, 30–1.

6 Weber, *Action Française*, 111.

7 Deborah Menaker Rothschild, *Picasso's Parade. From Street to Stage: Ballet by Jean Cocteau; Score by Erik Satie; Choreography by Léonide Massine* (London: Sotheby's Publications in association with the Drawing Center, 1991), 47.

8 Modris Eksteins, *Rites of Spring* (Boston: Houghton Mifflin, 1989), 9–54.

9 Silver, *Esprit de Corps*, 43–51. See 51.

10 'Nous voudrions vous dire un mot,' *Le Mot* 14 (13 March 1915), n.p.; 'Soyons raisonables,' *Le Mot* 15 (27 March 1915), n.p.; 'Nous voudrions'; in Silver, *Esprit de Corps*, 45–7.

11 Neal Oxenhandler, *Scandal and Parade: The Theatre of Jean Cocteau* (London: Constable and Company, 1958); Rothschild, *Picasso's Parade*.

12 Silver, *Esprit de Corps*, 122–3. Apollinaire, 'L'Esprit nouveau et les poètes,' 1917, *Oeuvres complètes de Guillaume Apollinaire*, ed. Michel Décaudin (Paris: A. Balland et J. Lecat, 1965–6), 3: 900; in Silver, *Esprit de Corps*, 122.

13 Cocteau, *Le Secret professionnel* (1922), in *Oeuvres complètes*, 9: 170; in Bettina L. Knapp, *Jean Cocteau*, rev. ed. (Boston: Twayne, 1989), 27. Apollinaire quoted in Pierre Cabanne, *Le Siècle de Picasso* (Madrid : Ministerio de Cultura, 1982), 1: 308; in Silver, *Esprit de Corps*, 122.

14 Silver, *Esprit de Corps*, 126.

15 Cocteau, *Entretiens avec André Fraigneau* (Paris: Union générale d'éditions, 1965), 23; and Gide, *Journals*, 1: 688; both in Knapp, *Jean Cocteau*, 30.

16 See Jane F. Fulcher, 'The Composer as Intellectual: Ideological Inscriptions in French Interwar Neoclassicism,' *Journal of Musicology* 17/2 (Spring, 1999): 197–230.

17 Jean Roy, *Le Groupe des Six* (Paris: Seuil, 1994).

18 *CoqArlFr*, 13; *CoqArlEn*, 3. Emphasis in original.

19 *CoqArlFr*, 24; *CoqArlEn*, 17.

20 *CoqArlFr*, 22; *CoqArlEn*, 15.

21 Silver, *Esprit de Corps*, 131–2.

22 *CoqArlFr*, 27–8; *CoqArlEn*, 20. Emphasis original.

23 *CoqArlFr*, 16–17; *CoqArlEn*, 8. Emphasis original.

24 *CoqArlFr*, 32; *CoqArlEn*, 26. Emphasis original.
25 *CoqArl Fr*, 33; *CoqArlEn*, 27.
26 *CoqArlFr*, 40; *CoqArlEn*, 35. *JournRM-Fr*, 241; *JournalRM-En*, 97–8; Cf. *AS OC-RJM*, 699.
27 Jacques Maritain, 'Notes sur Saint Thomas et la théorie de l'art,' *La Revue des jeunes* 23/5 (10 March 1920); 584–94; in *JRM-OC*, 16: 13–21.
28 Maritain, 'Notes sur Saint Thomas,' 15. Emphasis original.
29 Ibid., 15; 16.
30 Thomas L. Gwozdz, 'Jacques Maritain and the Centrality of Intuition,' PhD dissertation, Fordham University, 1996.
31 Maritain, 'Notes sur Saint Thomas,' 16–17. Emphasis original.
32 Ibid., 17. Emphasis original. Maritain quotes and cites Maurice Denis, *Théories, 1890–1910.* For Denis and Gauguin, see Driskel, *Representing Belief*; Marlais, *Conservative Echoes*; Silverman, *Van Gogh and Gauguin.*
33 Maritain, 'Notes sur Saint Thomas,' 18.
34 Ibid., 20–1.
35 I am grateful to Philippe Buc for this suggestion.
36 Maritain, 'Notes sur Saint Thomas,' 20–1.
37 Jean Cocteau, *Dante on Our Side*, cover of *Le Mot* (15 June 1915); in Silver, *Esprit de Corps*, 94.
38 Maritain, 'Notes sur Saint Thomas,' 21. Emphasis original. Translation of Dante (sì che vostr' arte a Dio quasi è nepote): 'so that your art is almost God's grandchild.' Dante Alighieri, *Inferno* XI, 105; in *The Divine Comedy of Dante Alighieri*, trans. Allen Mandelbaum (Berkeley: University of California Press, 1980), 94. Later used in *Lettr-Rép*, 316–17; *Letter-Resp*, 89. Translation of Aquinas: 'beauty is the resplendence of form upon parts materially proportioned.'
39 Michel Foucault, 'Nietzsche, Genealogy, History,' in *Hommage à Jean Hyppolite* (Paris: Presses Universitaires de France, 1971), 145–72; trans. Donald F. Brouchard and Sherry Simon, in *Michel Foucault: Aesthetics, Method, and Epistemology*, ed. James D. Faubion, 369–91. See 381.
40 *Art et scolastique* was first published as serial essays in *Les Lettres* (1 September 1919): 485–522; (1 October 1919): 579–620. The first edition of *Art et scholastique* in monograph form was published with the Librairie de l'Art Catholique, Paris, 1920. Second edition: Paris: Louis Rouart et Fils, 1927. Third edition, 1935. Fourth edition: Paris: Librairie de l'Art Catholique, 1947. Translations include *The Philosophy of Art*, trans. John O'Connor (Ditchling, England: St Dominic's Press, 1923, limited handpress edition; London: B. Humphries, 1923); *Kunst en Scholastiek*, trans. C.A. Terburg (Amsterdam: Van Munster, 1924); *Art and Scholasticism*, trans.

J.F. Scanlan (London: Sheed and Ward, 1930; New York: Charles Scribner's Sons, 1930); *Sztuka I Madrosc*, trans. K.I.K. Gorscy (Poznan, Poland: Ksiegarnia sw. Wojciecha, 1936); *Umeni a Scholastika*, trans. V. Stom. Olomouc: Fr. Obzina, 1941 (Slovakian edition); and *Arte y Escolastica*, trans. Juan A. Gonzalez (Buenos Aires: La Espiga de Oro, 1945).

41 Anthony Grafton, *The Footnote: A Curious History*, rev. ed. (Cambridge, MA: Harvard University Press, 1997).

42 *AS 1920 Fr*, 178; *AS 1920 En*, 119–20. Contrast *AS JRM-OC*, 784 n. 160–2; *AS 1927 En* 222–3 n. 151–3.

43 *AS 1920 Fr*, 176–7; *AS 1920 En*, 112–13. Contrast *AS 1927 Fr*, 324–5 n. 142–3; *AS 1927 En*, 220–1 n. 142–3; *AS JRM-OC*, 783 n. 152 [Maurras note deleted].

44 Conklin, *A Mission to Civilize*.

45 *AS 1920 Fr*, 106–7; *As 1920 En*, 112–13. Contrast *AS JRM-OC*, 696; *AS 1927 En*, 79.

46 *AS JRM-OC*, 702; *AS 1927 En*, 86.

47 *AS 1920 Fr*, 160 n. 125; *AS 1920 En*, 157–8 n. 125. See *AS JRM-OC*, 767 n. 131. Emphasis added.

48 *AS JRM-OC*, 735–6 n. 43; *AS 1927 En*, 155–8 n. 42.

49 *AS JRM-OC*, 700–1; *AS 1927 En*, 84–5.

50 *AS JRM-OC*, 619; *AS 1927 En*, 1.

51 *AS JRM-OC*, 620; *AS 1927 En*, 2.

52 *AS JRM-OC*, 619; *AS 1927 En*, 1. Emphasis original.

53 *AS 1927 En*, 1. Emphasis original.

54 *AS JRM-OC*, 624; *AS 1927 En*, 7.

55 *AS JRM-OC*, 629–30; *AS 1927 En*, 12.

56 *CoqArlFr*, 17; *CoqArlEn*, 9.

57 *AS JRM-OC*, 635; *AS 1927 En*, 18. Translated: 'Art seems to be nothing else than a particular structure of reason by which human acts, through specific means, reach a specific end.' *Poster. Analyt.*, lib. I, lect. 1,1.

58 *AS JRM-OC*, 636; *AS 1927 En*, 19. Endnote reads: Jean de Saint-Thomas, *Curs. Theol.*, in Ia-IIae, q.52, disp. 16, a. 4.

59 *AS JRM-OC*, 632 and note 20; *AS 1927 En*, 14. Citation: OSCAR WILDE, 'Pen, Pencil and Poison,' in *Intentions*.'

60 *AS JRM-OC*, 636, 629; *AS 1927 En*, 19, 12.

61 *AS JRM-OC*, 700, 784 n. 163; *AS 1927 Fr*, 83, 223 n. 154.

62 *AS JRM-OC*, 625; *AS 1927 En*, 7.

63 Braudy, *From Chivalry to Terrorism*, 396. For the transformation of 'effeminacy' from being overly attracted to females to being like females, see also 327–8; 334.

64 Maurice Denis, *Journal*, 3 vols. (Paris: La Colombe, 1957), 1:63; in Marlais, *Conservative Echoes*, 204. See also Driskel, *Representing Belief*, 68–9, 71, 72, 74, 113, 144, 211; and Marlais, *Conservative Echoes*, 197, 203.
65 *AS JRM-OC*, 632–3; *AS 1927 En*, 15.
66 Joseph Amato, *Mounier & Maritain: A French Catholic Understanding of the Modern World* (1975; repr. Ypsilanti, MI.: Sapientia Press, 2002), esp. 55–76.
67 *AS JRM-OC*, 639; *AS 1927 En*, 22, 21.
68 *AS JRM-OC*, 639; *AS 1927 En*, 22. NB: the verb 'to shelter' [*abriter*] is Cocteau's quoted by Raïssa: 'NOUS ABRITONS UN ANGE ... ' Cf. *CoqArlFr*, 40; *CoqArlEn*, 35.
69 *AS JRM-OC*, 699–700, 785 n. 163; *AS En 1927*, 83, 223 n. 154. Italicized *catholicity* original; other emphasis added.
70 Barbey d'Aurevilly, *AS 1920 Fr*, 179 n. 155; *AS 1920 En*, 177.
71 *AS OC-RJM*, 676–7; *AS 1927 En*, 59–60. 'While Maritain never abandons his Thomistic realism, his esthetics point to the element of mystery in poetry, that element – spiritual, intuitive, unconscious or divine – which is emphasized by all the more conventional theorists of expressionism.' Oxenhandler, *Scandal and Parade*, 20–1.
72 North, *Reading 1922*, 3.
73 Lucien Roure, 'La Psychanalyse et le "Freudisme,"' *Études* 59/172 (5 July 1922): 44–56; reviewing Sigmund Freud, *Introduction à la Psychanalyse*, trans. S. Jankélévitch (Paris: Payot, 1922). See 44. See also Adhémar d'Alès, 'Relativisme à propos des Théories d'Einstein,' *Études* 59/171 (20 May 1922): 431–8; and Auguste Valensin, 'Un Honnête Homme chez Einstein,' *Études* 59/172 (20 July 1922): 172–93. 'M. Paul Dupont, *la Notion du temps d'après Einstein*, Paris, Alcan, 1921, critiques the notion of Einsteinian time from a point of view that is neither that of absolute realism nor of pure idealism.' d'Alès, 'Relativism,' 447 n. 1. See also Panek, *The Invisible Century.*
74 Anne Dulphy, 'Isabelle Rivière et son temps,' *Bulletin des amis de Jacques Rivière et d'Alain-Fournier* 55/2 (1990), 39; in Gugelot, *La conversion des intellectuels*, 45.
75 André Laveyssiere, 'Antimodern,' *La Croix de Marseille* (8 April 1923).
76 Jacques Maritain, *avant-propos* dated June 1922, to *Antimoderne*, 928. Emphasis original.
77 Raïssa Maritain to Jean Cocteau, 14 July 1926; in *Corr JC-JM*, 118. Emphasis original.
78 *Antimoderne*, 934.
79 *AS 1920 Fr*, 73; *AS 1920 En*, 77; *AS JRM-OC*, 670–1; *AS 1927 Fr*, 53.
80 See Philippe Chenaux, 'La Seconde Vague Thomiste,' in *Intellectuels*

Chrétiens et esprit des années 1920, 139–67; and Chenaux, *Entre Maurras et Maritain*, 17–47; and Chenaux, *Paul VI et Maritain*, esp. 11–32, 97–100.

81 The verb *restituer*, like the noun *palingénésie*, carries the double sense of (a) 'return' (as in the myth of 'the eternal return') and (b) 'reproduce' (as in 'reproduce ancient inherited characteristics').

82 *Antimoderne*, 933–4; *CoqArlFr*, 32; *CoqArlEn*, 26. Emphasis original.

83 One might even say that for Maritain, as for his contemporary, Alfred North Whitehead, eternal forms are the precondition for the possibility of inexhaustible novelty. See Stephen Schloesser, 'The Method of Abstraction: A Musical Analysis,' *Process Studies* 15 (Spring 1986): 19–31.

84 Schorske, *Thinking With History*.

85 *Antimoderne*, 931. Emphasis original.

86 Symbol of the General Council of Chalcedon (451), in J. Neuner and J. Dupuis, eds., *The Christian Faith in the Doctrinal Documents of the Catholic Church*, rev. ed. (New York: Alba House, 1982), 154.

87 Barré, *Jacques et Raïssa Maritain*, 49, 60, 62.

88 Harvey, *Condition of Postmodernity*, 20. For Haussmann, see David P. Jordan, *Transforming Paris: the Life and Labors of Baron Haussmann* (New York: Free Press, 1995).

89 Charles Baudelaire, 'The Painter of Modern Life,' 1863, in *The Painter of Modern Life and Other Essays*, trans. Jonathan Mayne (London: Phaidon Press Ltd., 1964), 3, 13.

90 Harvey, *Condition of Postmodernity*, 30.

91 See Jacques Maritain, preface to Hans Driesch, *La Philosophie de l'organisme*, trans. M. Kollmann (Paris: Marcel Rivière, 1921); in *JRM-OC*, 2: 1253–60.

92 For example, see Louis Rouzic, *Le Renouveau catholique. Les Jeunes avant la guerre*, 26.

93 H. Woroniecki, 'Catholicité du Thomisme,' *Revue Thomiste* (October–December 1921); excerpted in *Antimoderne*, 932–3 n. 3.

94 Heidegger, *Being and Time*, 31; *Sein und Zeit*, 11.

95 *Antimoderne*, 937. Emphasis original.

96 Ibid. Like 'universalist,' the word 'modern' also emphasized by Maritain. For models of 'Christ in opposition to Culture' and 'Christ the Transformer of Culture,' see Niebuhr, *Christ and Culture*.

97 Laveyssiere, 'Antimoderne.'

98 *Antimoderne*, 929. For *éternel* Maritain substitutes the archaic '*éviternel*.' Maritain has added the *accent aigu* [*é*] absent in original orthography. See Frédéric Godefroy, *Dictionnaire de l'Ancienne Langue Française*, 10 vols. (Paris: F. Vieweg, 1881–1902; Vaduz: Kraus Reprint, 1965), 3: 675.

99 *Antimoderne*, 928; 933.

100 Author signed 'Les Cannibales,' 'La Plume entre les Dents,' *L'Internationale* (Paris), 22 June 1922.

101 Halévy, 'Les chroniques nationales.'

102 O. de Carfort, 'Le mouvement philosophique en France et à l'Etranger,' *La Flamme* (Paris) (December 1922).

103 Jean Morienval, review of *Antimoderne*, *La Belle France* (8 October 1922); repr. in *Libre Parole* (31 October 1922).

104 Jacques Maritain, preface dated 22 August 1921, in Amélie-Marie Goichon, *Ernest Psichari d'après des documents inédits* (Paris: Éditions de la 'Revue des Jeunes,' 1921); in *JRM-OC*, 2: 1261–72.

105 Advertisement in *La Revue des jeunes*, 14/1 (10 January 1924), n.p. Opposing page advertises two works in same format: Georges Goyau [pseud. Léon Grégoire], *L'Effort catholique dans la France d'aujourd'hui* (Paris: Éditions de la 'Revue des Jeunes,' 1922) and *Catholicisme et politique*, 4th ed. (Paris: Éditions de la 'Revue des Jeunes,' 1923).

106 *Antimoderne*, 1118.

107 Ibid., 1135, 1136; quoting his own *La Croix* letter 1914, *JRM-OC*, 1: 1045.

Chapter 5 Catholic Catholicity: Nothing Human Is Alien

1 Gerard Manley Hopkins, 'Comments on the *Spiritual Exercises* of St. Ignatius Loyola,' ca. 1880–1882, unpublished; in *The Note-books and Papers of Gerard Manley Hopkins*, ed. Humphry House (New York: Oxford University Press, 1937), 316. Virginia Woolf, *To the Lighthouse*, ed. Susan Dick (Cambridge, MA: Blackwell Publishers, 1992), 170.

2 *Corr JC-JM*, 62 n. 2.

3 Barré, *Jacques et Raïssa Maritain*, 246.

4 Jean Cocteau, Raoul Dufy, and Darius Milhaud, *Le bœuf sur le toit, ou, The nothing doing bar: farce imaginée et réglee par Jean Cocteau* (Paris: La Sirène Musicale, 1920). On the decade, see Jacques Chastenet, *Quand le boeuf montait sur le toit* (Paris: A. Fayard, 1958); Georges Bernier and Henri Sauguet, *Au temps du Boeuf sur le toit, 1918–1928* (Paris: Artcurial, 1981); *Au temps du 'Bœuf sur le toit,' 1918–1928, Exposition May–July 1981*, ed. Monique Schneider-Maunoury and Dominique Le Buhan (Paris: Artcurial, 1981). For the bar, see William A. Shack, *Harlem in Montmartre: A Paris Jazz Story between the Great Wars* (Berkeley: University of California Press, 2001), 48–51; Jeffrey H. Jackson, *Making Jazz French. Music and Modern Life in Interwar Paris* (Durham, NC: Duke University Press, 2003), 116–21.

5 James P. McNab, *Raymond Radiguet* (Boston: Twayne Publishers, 1984), 27; see also Francis Steegmuller, *Cocteau: A Biography* (Boston: Little, Brown, 1970), 281–2.

6 Roger Nichols, *The Harlequin Years: Music in Paris 1917–1929* (Berkeley: University of California Press, 2002), 117.

7 Steegmuller, *Cocteau*, 308.

8 For prostitutes, see Timothy J. Gilfoyle, 'Prostitutes in History: From Parables of Pornography to Metaphors of Modernity,' *American Historical Review* (February 1999): 117–41. For homosexuality, see Michael Sibalis and Jeffrey Merrick, ed., *Homosexuality in French History and Culture* (Binghamton, NY: Harrington Park Press, 2002); Sibalis, 'Homosexuality in France,' *French Politics, Culture & Society*, 19, no. 3 (Summer 2001): 108–19; Florence Tamagne, *Histoire de l'homosexualité en Europe. Berlin, Londres, Paris, 1919–1939* (Paris: Seuil, 2000); Carolyn J. Dean, *The Frail Social Body: Pornography, Homosexuality, and Other Fantasies in Interwar France* (Berkeley and Los Angeles: University of California Press, 2000); Gilles Barbedette and Michel Carassou, *Paris Gay 1925* (Paris: Presses de la Renaissance, 1981); and William Wiser, *The Crazy Years: Paris in the Twenties* (New York: Atheneum, 1983), esp. 18–20; Jeffrey Merrick and Bryant T. Ragan, Jr, eds., *Homosexuality in Modern France* (New York: Oxford University Press, 1996).

9 Catharine R. Stimpson, foreword to Mary Louise Roberts, *Civilization Without Sexes: Reconstructing Gender in Postwar France, 1917–1927* (Chicago: University of Chicago Press, 1994), ix.

10 Pierre Drieu la Rochelle, *La Suite des idées* (Paris: Au Sens Pareil, 1927), 125; in Roberts, *Civilization Without Sexes*, 2.

11 The Jazz Age was marked by 'passing' in class, race, and gender: F. Scott Fitzgerald, *The Great Gatsby* (1925), James Weldon Johnson, *Autobiography of an Ex-Colored Man* (republished under his Johnson's own name, 1927), Nella Larsen, *Passing* (1929). For Josephine Baker and African-Americans as 'modernist primitives,' see Petrine Archer-Straw, *Negrophilia: Avant-Garde Paris and Black Culture in the 1920s* (New York: Thames and Hudson, 2000); Tyler Stovall, *Paris Noir: African Americans in the City of Light* (New York: Houghton Mifflin Co., 1996). See also: *Passing and the Fictions of Identity*, ed. Elaine K. Ginsberg (Durham, NC: Duke University Press, 1996); Gayle Freda Wald, *Crossing the Line: Racial Passing in Twentieth-Century U.S. Literature and Culture* (Durham, NC: Duke University Press, 2000); Siobhan B. Somerville, *Queering the Color Line: Race and the Invention of Homosexuality in American Culture* (Durham, NC: Duke University Press, 2000); M. Giulia Fabi, *Passing and the Rise of the African American Novel* (Chicago: University of Illinois Press, 2001). On anxieties

over homosexual / 'new woman' passing in France, see Dean, *Frail Social Body*, and Roberts, *Civilization Without Sexes*.

12 Hanson, *Decadence and Catholicism*, 25. See also Elaine Marks, 'Lesbian Intertextuality,' in *Homosexualities and French Literature: Cultural Contexts / Critical Texts*, ed. George Stambolian and Elaine Marks (Ithaca, NY: Cornell University Press, 1979), 353–77. For Ghéon, see Ghéon, *L'homme né de la guerre*. For Jouhandeau, see Frank Paul Bowman, 'The Religious Metaphors of a Married Homosexual: Marcel Jouhandeau's *Chronique d'une passion*, in *Homosexualities and French Literature*, 295–311; for Green and other converts see Christopher Robinson, *Scandal in the Ink: Male and Female Homosexuality in Twentieth-Century French Literature* (New York: Cassell, 1995), esp. 74–92; for Gide, see Steegmuller, *Cocteau*, 347. For Catholicism and homosexuality in the 1950s, see Robert Merle, 'Oscar Wilde en Prison,' *Les Temps Modernes* 10 (November 1954): 613–36.

13 For 'performance' as a useful concept in analysing identity-formation, I am indebted to Mary Louise Roberts, *Disruptive Acts: The New Woman in Fin-de-Siècle France* (Chicago: University of Chicago Press, 2002). For discursive instability, see Joan Wallach Scott, *Gender and the Politics of History* (New York: Columbia University Press, 1988), esp. 1–11; and 'Fantasy Echo: History and the Construction of Identity,' *Critical Inquiry* 27 (Winter 2001): 284–304.

14 Jacob cited by Maurice du Gard, *Les Mémorables* (Paris: Flammarion, 1957), 106; in McNab, *Raymond Radiguet*, 15. For Jacob, see Neal Oxenhandler, *Looking for Heroes in Postwar France: Albert Camus, Max Jacob, Simone Weil* (Hanover, NH: University Press of New England, 1996), 77–159; for Jacob and Picasso, see Arthur I. Miller, *Einstein, Picasso: Space, Time, and the Beauty that Causes Havoc* (New York: Basic Books, 2001), 12–16; and Benjamin Ivry, *Francis Poulenc* (London: Phaidon, 1996), 74.

15 Max Jacob to Jacques Doucet, 30 January 1917, in *Max Jacob. Correspondance*, ed. François Garnier, 2 vols. (Paris: Éditions de Paris, 1955), 1: 133; Radiguet quoted by Nadia Odouard, *Les Années folles de Raymond Radiguet* (Paris: Seghers, 1973); in Barré, *Jacques et Raïssa Maritain*, 251; Fumet quoted in *CorrJC-JM*, 17.

16 Max Jacob to Raymond Radiguet, 5 February 1919, *Correspondance*, 1: 183.

17 McNab, 15–17. See 17; and also Knapp, *Jean Cocteau*, 49–51.

18 André Breton to Tristan Tzara, 26 December 1919; Cocteau, *Le Coq* (May 1920): n.p.; in McNab, *Raymond Radiguet*, 144 nn. 43, 46.

19 Jacques Maritain to Jean Cocteau, 26 May 1923, *CorrJC-JM*, 62.

20 Frédéric Lefèvre, *Une heure avec ...* (Paris: Éditions de la 'Nouvelle revue française,' 1924–7): 1re série. MM. Jean Ajalbert, Alexandre Arnoux, Maurice Barrès, Joseph Bédier, Henri Béraud, Henry Bordeaux, Ferdinand Brunot, Francis Carco, Alphonse de Châteaubriant, Gaston Chérau, Jean Cocteau, Georges Courteline, Roland Dorgelès, Claude Farrère, Jean Giraudoux. Georges Goyau, Daniel Halévy, Pierre Hamp, Abel Hermant, Alexandre Kouprine, Alfred Loisy, Mme Jack London, Pierre Mac Orlan, Camille Mauclair, François Mauriac, Henry de Montherlant, Pierre Mille, André Suarès.

2e série. MM. Charles Maurras, Paul Morand, Jacques Maritain et Henri Massis, Pierre Champion, Georges Brandès, Jacques Rivière, Lucien Fabre, Alain, Henri Duvernois, Camille Jullian, Max Jacob, René Boylesve, C.F. Ramuz, Valery Larbaud, Georges Duhamel.

3e série. MM. Ferdinand Ossendowski, Henri Bremond, A. Meillet, Pierre Benoît, René Benjamin, Étienne Gilson, Thomas Hardy, Lucien Romier, Sylvain Lévi, Marcel Prévost, G.K. Chesterton, Paul Claudel, Henri Barbusse, Joseph Delteil, Victor Bérard, Jacques de Lacretelle, Henri Pourrat, Paul Hazard.

4e série. MM. Jehan Rictus, Gaston Leroux, Paul Souday, Charles Silvestre. Drieu La Rochelle, Francis de Miomandre, Jean Giraudoux, Colette, Marcel Arland, Georges Bernanos, André Maurois, Raymond Poincaré, H. d'Ardenne de Tizac et Jean Viollis, R.M. Rilke, Joseph Caillaux.

Lefèvre, *Une heure avec ...* 5e série (Paris: Librairie Gallimard, 1929): M. Francis Carco, Mme la comtesse de Noailles, MM. Jean Brunhes, Emile Meyerson, Lévy-Bruhl, Jacques Copeau, Julien Green, Paul Claudel, Léon Brunschvieg, Georges Clemenceau, Pansït Istrati, Henry de Montherlant, Ramón Gomez de la Serna, Alain, Edouard Herriot, Maurice Maeterlinck, Eugenio d'Ors, Léon-Paul Fargue.

Lefèvre, *Une heure avec ...* 6e série (Paris: Ernest Flammarion, 1933): Anatole de Monzie, Heinrich Marin, Maurice Bedel, Pierre Janet, Somerset Maugham, Luc Durtain, André Thérive, Jacques Chardonne, G. de La Fouchardière, André Chamson, E.-M. Remarque, Aldous Huxley, Marcelle Tinayre, Paul Valéry, Jean-Richard Bloch, Thomas Mann, Pierre Benoit, Maurice Genevoix, Jules Romains, Myriam Harry, André Maurois, Joseph Caillaux.

21 Frédéric Lefèvre, 'Une heure avec MM Jacques Maritain et Henri Massis,' *Les Nouvelles littéraires* (13 October 1923), in *JRM-OC* 2: 1236–47. See 1242. See also Barré, *Jacques et Raïssa Maritain*, 248–50; and Sylvain Guéna, 'Max Jacob et Jacques Maritain: Une dialogue sur la foi et l'art,' *Cahiers Jacques Maritain* 33 (December 1996): 6–20.

22 JC to JM, 14 October 1923; JM to JC, 16 October 1923; in *Corr JC-JM*, 62–4.

23 Frédéric Lefèvre, *La jeune poésie française. Hommes et tendances* (Paris: Rouart, 1917).

24 Peter Nicholls, *Modernisms: A Literary Guide* (Berkeley: University of California Press, 1995), 244.

25 Entry for 21 December 1923, André Gide, *Journals*, trans. Justin O'Brien, 4 vols. (1948; repr. Chicago: University of Illinois Press, 2000), 2: 338–41.

26 André Gide, preface to the second edition of *Corydon* (1920), 12; and Gide to Dorothy Bussy, 30 January 1920; in Martha Hanna, 'Natalism, Homosexuality, and the Controversy over *Corydon*,' in *Homosexuality in Modern France*, 202–24. See 206.

27 See Gide, 29 November 1921: 'Big article by Massis in *La Revue universelle* on (or rather: against) me'; 5 November 1923: 'Great offensive on the part of Massis in *La Revue universelle* – of which the spring offensive was only the prelude.' Gide, *Journals*, 2: 274, 337.

28 Émile Zola, preface to G. Saint-Paul (pseudonym 'Dr. Laupts'), *Tares et poisons: perversion et perversités sexuelles* (1896); in Robinson, *Scandal in the Ink*, 13.

29 Peters, *Jean Cocteau and André Gide*, 17; Neal Oxenhandler, *Scandal and Parade: The Theatre of Jean Cocteau* (London: Constable and Co., 1958), 20–1.

30 JC to JM, 20 February 1924; JC to JM, 30 April 1924; *CorrJC-JM*, 65–66. Raïssa Maritain, [between 1–17 July 1924], *JournalRM-Fr*, 305; *JournalRM-En*, 165–6.

31 Jacques Maritain to Henri Massis, 1924, cited by Henri Massis, *Au long d'une vie* (Paris: Plon, 1967); in Barré, *Jacques et Raïssa Maritain*, 250. On Massis's reliability, see caution in Doering, *Jacques Maritain*, 48–51.

32 Henri Massis, *La Revue universelle*, 15 August 1924; in Steegmuller, *Cocteau*, 337. NB: Henri Massis, *Raymond Radiguet* (Paris: Éditions des Cahiers Libres, 1927).

33 JC to JM, August 1924; unpublished letter of Auric to Maritain, 20 August 1924; *CorrJC-JM*, 67; 68 n. 1.

34 Jean Cocteau, *La Difficulté d'être* (Monaco: Éd. du Rocher, 1957); 49–50; Cocteau, *The Difficulty of Being*, trans. Elizabeth Sprigge (London: Peter Owen, 1966), 31.

35 Cocteau, *Lettre-Rép*, 281; *Letter-Resp*, 41.

36 Cocteau, *Lettre-Rép*, 281; 271; *Letter-Resp*, 41; 27. 'La religion comme antidote à l'opium, à l'errance, au désespoir?' Barré, *Jacques et Raïssa Maritain*, 251.

37 Maurice Sachs, *La Décade de l'illusion* (Paris: Gallimard, 1950), 191. For decade, see Sachs, *Au temps du boeuf sur le toit (Journal d'un jeune bourgeois à l'époque de la prospérité 14 juil. 1919–30 oct. 1929)* (Paris: Nouvelle Révue Critique, 1939). Raïssa Maritain, 29 August 1925: 'Baptism of Maurice. In spite of everything, I am not reassured. This boy has something dark in him which disquiets me.' *JournRM-Fr*, 324; *JournRM-En*, 187.

38 See Philippe Chenaux, 'Fumet Éditeur, ou L'Aventure du "Roseau d'Or,"' in *Stanislas Fumet ou la Présence au temps*, ed. Marie-Odile Germain (Paris: Les Éditions du Cerf/Bibliothèque Nationale de France, 1999), 29–44.

39 Philippe Chenaux, 'Le milieu Maritain,' *Cahiers de l'Institut Histoire du Temps Présents* 20 (March 1992): 160–71.

40 Jacques Maritain, 'La Crise de l'esprit moderne et le mouvement thomiste,' *Acta hebdomadae thomisticae Romae celebratae 19–25 novembris 1924 in laudem S. Thomae Aquinatis* (Rome: Academiae S. Thomae Aquinatis, 1924), 55–79.

41 Maritain, 'La Crise de l'esprit moderne,' 75–9; quoting Proverbs 1:20: 'Wisdom preacheth abroad, she uttereth her voice in the streets.'

42 Jacques Maritain, *Trois réformateurs: Luther – Descartes – Rousseau* (Paris: Plon-Nourrit, 1925), *Le Roseau d'Or, œuvres et chroniques*, vol. 1. For analysis, see Amato, *Mounier et Maritain* 60–71.

43 Philippe Chenaux, *Paul VI et Maritain: les rapports du 'montinianisme' et du 'maritanisme'* (Roma: Edizioni Studium, 1994), 26.

44 Pierre Lasserre, *Les Nouvelles littéraires*, 27 June 1925; in Chenaux, *Paul VI*, 26–7.

45 Josef F. Rafols, 'El Tany d'Or,' *Le Veu de Catalunya* (Barcelona) (7 August 1925); Nino Frank, 'Letteratura francese: Il peccato,' *Il Mondo* [?] (Rome) (9 September 1925); P. Van der Meer de Salcheren, 'Gesijd aan het Katholieke Beschavingsleven. "LE ROSEAU D'OR,"' *De Tijd* (January 1926); 'Le Roseau d'Or,' *Idea Europeana* (Bucharest) (1 March 1926); Waldemar Gurian, 'Unter der sonne satans,' *Kölnische Volkszeitun* (26 September 1926); Georges Legrand, *XXè Siècle* (Brussells) (7 August 1927); *Il Mattino* (Naples) (1 October 1927). *JRM-Arch*.

46 Paul Claudel, *Le soulier de satin; ou, Le pire n'est pas toujours sûr*, 2 vols. (Paris: Gallimard, Éditions de la Nouvelle revue française, 1929).

47 See Jacques Maritain's article announcing the appearance of Rivière's posthumous *À la trace de Dieu*, edited with a preface by Claudel: 'L'Apologétique de Jacques Rivière,' *La Revue universelle* 26, no. 7 (1 July 1926), 101–8; in *JRM-OC* 3: 1387–95.

48 *Revue des Lectures* (Paris) (15 March 1926). *JRM-Arch*.

49 Ian Ker, *The Catholic Revival in English Literature, 1845–1961: Newman, Hopkins, Belloc, Chesterton, Greene, Waugh* (Notre Dame: University of Notre Dame Press, 2003); Patrick Allit, *Catholic Converts: British and American Intellectuals Turn to Rome* (Ithaca, NY: Cornell University Press, 1997).
50 Armand Praviel, *Le Correspondant* (Paris) (10 May 1926). *JRM-Arch.*
51 René Johannet, 'La vie littéraire et le mouvement des idées,' *Les Lettres* (May 1926). *JRM-Arch.*
52 Le Liseux, *L'Eclaireur du Soir* (Nice) (26 December 1925). *JRM-Arch.*
53 Maurice Courtois-Suffit, *Revue Européene* (Paris) (1 March 1926). *JRM-Arch.*
54 Jacques Maritain, response in Maurice Charny, 'Revues et journaux littéraires. IV – Les revues littéraires proprement dites (suite),' *Le Progrès Civique* 482 (10 November 1928), 1506–7; in '*Le Roseau d'Or*. Présentation de la collection du même nom,' *JRM-OC*, 3: 1383–6. See 1384 note.
55 Robinson, 'A Season in Hell,' *Scandal in the Ink*, 85.
56 JG to JM [6 April 1926] (#1), *CorrJG-JMFr*, 51; *CorrJG-JMEn*, 41.
57 Robert de Saint Jean et Luc Estang, 'Le réalisme magique,' *Julien Green* (Paris: Seuil, 1990), 45–51.
58 Jacques Maritain, '*Léviathan*. Roman par Julien Green,' (1929); in *JRM-OC*, 16: 399–400. See 399.
59 Gabriel Marcel, 'Les Lettres. "Leviathan" de M. Julien Green,' *Europe Nouvelle* (20 April 1929), Albert Thibaudet, 'Julien Green: LEVIATHAN (Plon),' *Candide* (25 April 1929). *JRM-Arch.* For Marcel, see Étienne Fouilloux, 'Un Philosophe devient catholique en 1929,' *Gabriel Marcel. Colloque*, ed. Michèle Sacquin (Paris: Bibliothèque Nationale, 1989), 93–114.
60 See 'Autour du Roseau d'Or,' in Frédéric Ripoli, *Les grandes amitiés de Jacques et Raïssa Maritain: catalogue de l'exposition* (Vénasque, Pernes: Éditions du Carmel, 1995), 48–68.
61 Édouard Galloo, *Études* (5 June 1926). *JRM-Arch.*
62 *Les Nouvelles littéraires* (15 September 1928). *JRM-Arch.*
63 *Le Semeur* (n.d., 1926); Jean Morienval, *Les Cahiers Catholiques* (June 1927). *JRM-Arch.*
64 Lefèvre, in Bressolette, *CorrJC-JM*, 13.
65 *L'Intransigeant* (12 October 1932). *JRM-Arch.*
66 Jean Cocteau and Jacques Maritain, *Lettre à Jacques Maritain. Réponse à Jean Cocteau* (Paris: Stock, 1926).
67 Steegmuller, *Cocteau*, 348.

68 *Lettre-Rép*, 284; 325–6; *Letter-Resp*, 47; 100. Greek phrase omitted in English translation. The line is Antigone's to Creon about the precedence of eternal divine law over contingent human law: 'For these [laws] have life, not simply today and yesterday, but forever, and no one knows how long ago they were revealed.' Sophocles, 'Antigone,' in *Antigone, The Women of Trachis*, *Philoctetes*, *Oedipus at Colonus*, ed. and trans. Hugh Lloyd-Jones (Cambridge, MA: Harvard University Press, 1994), Greek: 44, lines 456–57; English, 45. Cocteau's adaptation of Sophocles' *Antigone* was first staged in 1922; in 1927 it was set to music by Arthur Honneger.

69 *AS 1920 En* 98; 100–1; *AS 1920 Fr*, 93; 96. *AS JRM-OC*, 685; 688; *AS 1927 En*, 68; 71.

70 Maritain, *Lettre-Rép*, 323–4; *Letter-Resp* 98.

71 Bernanos quoted in Henri Massis, *Maurras et notre temps* (Paris: La Palatine, 1951), 1: 212; in Doering, *Jacques Maritain*, 47.

72 Mary Butts, in Steegmuller, *Cocteau*, 363; Paul Eluard, 'Le Cas Lautréamont,' *La Révolution surréaliste* (1 March 1926): 3.

73 'M. Cocteau et M. Maritain,' *La Liberté* (Paris) (13 May 1926). *JRM-Arch*.

74 Jacques Darnetal, *Carnet de la Semaine* (16 May 1926). *JRM-Arch*.

75 Octave Ottavi, 'D'Après Jean Coteau [sic] l'avion serait le fils préféré de Satan,' *Le Courrier du Pas-de-Calais* (18 May 1926). *JRM-Arch*. Referring to Cocteau, *Lettre-Rép* 280; *Letter-Resp*, 41.

76 Gaëtan Bernoville, 'Vie Religieuse et Vie Littéraire: Les conversions,' *Le Nouveau Siècle* (26 May 1926). *JRM-Arch*.

77 E. Charles, 'La Renaissance catholique dans l'Élite intellectuelle à propos de trois livres à discuter dans nos Cercles d'Études,' *Revue Apologétique* (15 June 1926): 321–30.

78 Charles, 'La Renaissance catholique,' freely quoting Cocteau and Maritain, *Lettre-Rép*, 285–6; 326; *Letter-Resp*, 48; 101.

79 Charles, 'La Renaissance catholique,' 324.

80 Nicolas Fontaine [pseudonym], *Saint-Siège: 'Action française' et 'Catholiques integraux': histoire critique, suivie, entre autres documents, d'un Mémoire sur le 'Sodalitium Pianum' et de la 'Lettre du Gouverneur Smith'* (Paris: Librairie Universitaire J. Gamber, 1928).

81 Doering, *Jacques Maritain*, 25–36.

82 See Jacques Bénigne Bossuet, *Lettres de Bossuet*, ed. Henri Massis (Paris: J. Tallandier, 1927); and Bossuet, *Sermons: publiés avec une introduction*, ed. Henri Massis (Paris: A la cité des livres, 1929). Massis's Gallicanism did not extend to reviling Jansenists: see Blaise Pascal, *Pensées de Pascal*, ed. Henri Massis (Paris: A la cité des livres, 1929).

83 George Bernanos to Jacques Maritain, 21 April 1928; in *Combat pour la vérité, correspondance inéditée, 1904–34*, ed. Albert Béguin and Jean Murray (Paris: Plon, 1971), 321ff.; in Doering, *Jacques Maritain*, 52–3.

84 Raïssa's journal breaks for five and a half years – from March 1926 to 6 October 1931 – when the first resumed entry reads: 'Jacques asked me to take up my diary abandoned for such a long time.' *JournRM-Fr*, 335; *JournRM-En*, 199.

85 For a fuller account of the following, see Stephen Schloesser, 'Maritain on Music: His Debt to Cocteau,' *Beauty, Art, and the Polis*, ed. Alice Ramos (American Maritain Association; Distributed by: Washington, D.C.: Catholic University of America Press, 2000), 176–89.

86 *CoqArlFr*, 21–2. *CoqArlEn*, 14.

87 '*AS 1927 Fr*, note 116 *ter*, 293; *AS 1927 En*, note 116c, 195.

88 'Debussy a joué en français, mais il a mis la pédale russe.' *CoqArl Fr*, 38; *CoqArl En*, 33. To Gide's fury, this line paraphrases one Cocteau took from him without attribution. See Peters, *Jean Cocteau and André Gide*, 34–88. On wartime classicism, see Martha Hanna, 'The Classicist Revival,' in *the Mobilization of Intellect*, 142–66. For neoclassical discourse in music, see Jay Scott Messing, *Neoclassicism in Music: From the Genesis of the Concept through the Schoenberg/ Stravinsky Polemic* Jean (1988; repr. Rochester, NY: University of Rochester Press, 1996); and Fulcher, 'The Composer as Intellectual.'

89 *CoqArlFr*, 24, 39; *CoqArlEn*, 16–17, 33.

90 *CoqArlFr*, 24; *CoqArlEn*, 17. Contrast *AS 1920 Fr*, 106; *AS 1920 En*, 112; with *AS 1927 Fr*, 182; *AS 1927 En*, 79. 'Par son sujet et par ses racines, il est d'un temps et d'un pays. Voilà pourquoi *dans l'histoire des peuples libres les époques de cosmopolitisme sont des époques d'abâtardissement intellectuel.*' Italicized words are suppressed in the 1927 edition.

91 Barré, *Jacques et Raïssa Maritain*, 27.

92 For attention to this issue of uncertain *paternité* and *patrie* I am indebted to Susan Stewart. For postwar anxieties over paternity and virility, see Roberts, 'Madame Doesn't Want a Child' in *Civilization Without Sexes*, 120–47. For *irrational fantasies* related to *unsettled identities* see Gavin Langmuir, *History, Religion, and Antisemitism* (Berkeley: University of California Press, 1990), esp. 253–5; 291–305.

93 *AS 1920 Fr*, 176–7; *AS 1920 En*, 112–13; *AS 1927 Fr*, 324–5; *AS 1927 En*, 220–1.

94 *AS 1920 Fr*, 177; *AS 1920 En*, 113; *AS 1927 Fr*, 324–5; *AS 1927 En*, 220–1. Emphasis added.

95 *AS 1920 Fr*, 106–7; *As 1920 En*, 112–13. *AS 1927 Fr*, 129; *AS 1927 En*, 79.

96 *AS 1920 Fr*, 83; *AS 1920 En*, 87; *AS 1927 Fr*, 97–8; *AS 1927 En*, 60.
97 *AS 1927 Fr*, 98; *AS 1927 En*, 60. For 'purity' discourse, see Carol S. Eliel, *L'Esprit Nouveau. Purism in Paris, 1918–1925* (New York: Harry N. Abrams, 2001).
98 *AS 1927 Fr*, 185–6; *AS 1927 En*, 120–1.
99 Louis Andriessen and Elmer Schönberger, *The Apollonian Clockwork: On Stravinsky*, trans. Jeff Hamburg (New York: Oxford University Press, 1989), 92.
100 Nichols, *The Harlequin Years*, 17.
101 Igor Stravinsky and Robert Craft, *Expositions and Developments* (London: Faber and Faber, 1962), 92; in Nichols, *The Harlequin Years*, 17.
102 Barré, *Jacques et Raïssa Maritain*, 275–6.
103 *CoqArlFr*, 39; *CoqArlEn*, 33–4.
104 *CoqArlFr*, 40; *CoqArlEn*, 35.
105 *CoqArlFr*, 56; *CoqArlEn*, 60. *AS 1927 Fr*, 98; *AS 1927 En*, 60.
106 Stravinsky, quoted by Wolfgang Dömling, in notes for *Oedipus Rex*, recorded by Esa-Pekka Salonen and the Swedish Radio Symphony Orchestra (Sony Classical, 1991).
107 *CoqArlFr*, 56; *CoqArlEn*, 60.
108 Andriessen and Schönberger, *Apollonian Clockwork*, 86–96. See 96 n. 11.
109 AS *1920 Fr*, 119; *AS 1920 En*, 3. *AS 1927 Fr*, 239; *AS 1927 En*, 149.
110 The word-play depends on the French practice of leaving 'catholique' uncapitalized where English would capitalize 'Catholic': 'de l'art et de la philosophie catholiques, c'est-à-dire authentiquement universels.' *AS 1927 Fr*, 207; *AS 1927 En*, 137.
111 *JournRM-Fr*, 243; *JournRM-En*, 100.
112 *AS 1927 Fr*, 206–7; *As 1927 En*, 136–7.
113 *AS 1927 Fr*, 211–12; *AS 1927 En*, 140.
114 *AS 1927 Fr*, 213; *AS 1927 En*, 142.
115 *AS 1927 Fr*, 215; *AS 1927 En*, 143.
116 *AS 1927 Fr*, 215–16; *AS 1927 En*, 143–4.
117 *AS 1927 Fr*, 219–20; *AS 1927 En*, 147. See Denis, 'Définition du Néo-Traditionnisme' (1890), in *Théories* (1920), 11; 33; 38; in Driskel, *Representing Belief*, 236.
118 *AS 1927 Fr*, 220–1; *AS 1927 En*, 148.
119 For Cocteau: 1920 edition: notes 110, 154; 1927 edition: notes 33b, 110, 135, 142, 153, 175, 177, 180, 191. For Max Jacob: 1920 edition: no notes; 1927 edition: notes 89, 112, 117, 182, 183, 197 (all reference Jacob's *Art Poétique*, 1922).
120 Jacques Maritain, 'Henri Ghéon,' in an issue dedicated to Ghéon of *La*

Revue Fédéraliste 95 (January–February 1927), 42–5; in *JRM-OC*, 3: 1314–17. See Ghéon, *Le Comédien et la Grâce* (Paris: Plon-Nourrit, 1925); trans. Alan Bland, *The Comedian* (London, New York: Sheed & Ward, 1933).

121 Henri Massis, *Raymond Radiguet* (Paris: Éditions des Cahiers Libres, 1927).

122 *AS 1927 Fr*, 244, n.33 *bis*; *AS 1927 En*, 154, n.33b.

123 *As 1927 Fr*, 338 n.191; *AS 1927 En*, 231 n.191.

124 Bressolette, *CorrJC-JM*, 17 n.1.

125 Henri Raczymow, *Maurice Sachs* (Paris: Gallimard, 1988), 129; in *CorrJC-JM*, 122 n.2. JC to JM, letter of July–August 1926, *CorrJC-JM*, 119.

126 JC to JM, postmarked 13 September 1926; JC to JM, 18 September 1926; *CorrJC-JM*, 121; 123–4. For Sachs's robe, see *CorrJC-JM,* 126 n2; quoting Raczymow, *Maurice Sachs*, 114.

127 JC to JM, 21 September 1926, *CorrJC-JM*, 125.

128 Steegmuller, *Cocteau*, 382. Emphasis added.

129 JC to JM, 'Palm Sunday 1927'; JM to JC, 6 July 1927; JM to JC, 15 June 1928; *CorrJC-JM*, 144; 149;167. Emphasis original.

130 *Lettre-Rép*, 322; 326; *Letter-Resp*, 95; 101.

131 JM to JC, 6 July 1927; *CorrJC-JM*, 149. Emphasis original.

132 The category of homosexual person began to be used in marriage/annulment cases by the Roman Rota in the late 1960s. See articles by Jean Vernay and Jacques Grelon in *L'homosexuel(le) dans les sociétés*, ed. Jean Schlick and Marie Zimmermann (Strasbourg: Cerdic Publications, 1985). The first use of the distinction in a Vatican document was *Persona Humana: Declaration on Certain Questions Concerning Sexual Ethics* (Congregation for the Doctrine of the Faith, 29 December 1975; released 1976). On this paradigm shift in Roman Catholic theology, see Brian V. Johnstone, 'From Physicalism to Personalism,' *Studia Moralia* 30 (1992): 71–96.

133 JG to JM [June 1927](#28); JM to JG [June 1927](#29); and JM to JG, 29 June 1927(#31); *CorrJG-JMFr,* 77; 78; 81; *CorrJG-JMEn*, 64; 64; 67.

134 JM to JG [Beginning of June 1927] (#29), *CorrJG-JMFr*, 78–9; *CorrJG-JMEn*, 65. Emphasis original.

135 JM to JG, 14 December 1928 (#41), *CorrJG-JMFr*, 91; *CorrJG-JMEn*, 76. In December 1927, Cocteau began writing *Le Livre blanc*, a semi-autobiographical series of homosexual tales of the city. On 4 February 1928, Cocteau revealed to Maritain that he was editing Jean Desbordes's *J'Adore*. The scandal for the reading public would be *J'Adore*'s explicit references to

masturbation, but for Maritain it would be a treacherous personal betrayal, i.e., Desbordes's several ironic allusions to contents in a personal letter from Maritain to Cocteau. See *CorrJC-JM*, 147–51.

136 JM to JC, 15 June 1928, *CorrJC-JM*, 167.

137 'Les Cercles d'Études Thomistes et leurs Retraites Annuelles,' *CarnetJM-Fr*, 293–358; *CarnetJM-En*, 133–85. For a critical view, see William Bush, 'Bernanosian Barbs,' in *From Twilight to Dawn: The Cultural Vision of Jacques Maritain*, ed. Peter A. Redpath (Mishawaka, IN: American Maritain Association; Notre Dame, IN: Distributed by University of Notre Dame Press, 1990), 81–93.

138 Henri Massis, *Défense de l'Occident* (Paris: Plon, 1927), 186–7; as summarized by Cadwallader, *Crisis of the European Mind*, 123. Emphasis added.

139 Doering, 31; Philippe Chenaux, 'L'Orient et l'Occident,' in *Entre Maurras et Maritain*, 163–95.

140 M.-V. Bernadot, 'A nos lecteurs,' *La Vie intellectuelle* 1, no. 1 (October 1928): 5–6.

141 *JournRM-Fr*, 239; *JournRM-En*, 96. *AS JRM-OC*, 699–700, 785 n163; *AS En 1927*, 83, 223 n154. Bernadot, 'A nos lecteurs,' 6. Emphasis added.

142 Bernadot, 'A nos lecteurs,' 6. Emphasis original.

143 'Notre programme,' *Les Documents de la Vie Intellectuelle* 1, no. 1 (October–December 1929): n.p. Emphasis original.

144 Jacques Maritain, 'Saint Thomas et l'unité de la culture chrétienne,' 1, no. 1, *La Vie intellectuelle* (October 1928): 46–74.

145 M. Louis de la Vallée Poussin, 'Indianism,' 9 May 1928, in *Bulletins de la Classe des Lettres et des Sciences morales et politiques de l'Académie Royale de Belgique*; quoted in Maritain, 'Saint Thomas et l'unité de la culture,' 64–5.

146 Maritain, 'Saint Thomas et l'unité de la culture,' 65.

147 Bernard Doering, 'Jacques Maritain and Charles Journet on Human Sexuality,' *Theological Studies* 62 (2001): 597–606.

148 Martine Sevegrand, *Les enfants du bon dieu*; and Sevegrand, *L'amour en toutes lettres: Questions à l'abbé Voillet sur la sexualité, 1924–43* (Paris: Albin Michel, 1996).

149 For critics, see Louis Salleron, 'Humanisme Intégral? M. Jacques Maritain Marxiste-Chrétien,' *La Revue hebdomodaire* 8 (22 August 1936): 417; and Sidney Hook's chapter on Maritain's *Integral Humanism* entitled 'Integral Humanism,' in *Reason, Social Myths, and Democracy* (New York: Humanities Press, 1950). See also Edgar Leonard Allen, *Christian Humanism:*

A Guide to the Thought of Jacques Maritain (New York: Philosophical Library, 1951); Will Herberg, *Four Existentialist Theologians: A Reader from the Works of Jacques Maritain, Nicolas Berdyaev, Martin Buber and Paul Tillich* (Garden City, NY: Doubleday, 1958); *The Philosopher and the Provocateur: The Correspondence of Jacques Maritain and Saul Alinsky*, ed. Bernard Doering (Notre Dame, IN: University of Notre Dame Press, 1994); and Dorothy Day, *The Long Loneliness* (New York: Curtis Books, 1952).

150 Brooke Williams Smith, *Jacques Maritain: Antimodern or Ultramodern?* (New York: Elsevier Scientific Publishing Company, 1976), 40.

151 For Maritain and 'the Jewish Question,' see Doering, *French Intellectuals*, 126–67. For collected texts of Jacques and Raïssa Maritain on anti-Semitism from 1938–44, see Église de France, *Le repentir: Déclaration de l'Église de France, 30 septembre 1997* (Paris: Desclée de Brouwer, 1997), 37–60. *Le repentir* is the public declaration of repentance by the bishops of France, delivered on 30 September 1997, at Drancy. Drancy, the largest French transit camp for the deportation of Jews to eastern concentration camps – and the site of Max Jacob's death – opened in December 1940.

152 24 September 1937, *CarnetJM-Fr*, 338; *CarnetJM-En*, 169.

153 Bernanos, *Nous autres Français* (Paris: Gallimard, 1939), 68; in Doering, *Jacques Maritain*, 156. See also Bush, 'Bernanosian Barbs.'

154 Lucien Rebatet, *Je suis partout* (1 April 1938); in *Le repentir*, 37. Emphasis added.

155 Aristide R. Zolberg, 'The Ecole Libre at the New School 1941–1946,' *Social Research* 65, no. 4 (Winter 1998): 921–53. *Exiles and Fugitives: The Letters of Jacques and Raïssa Maritain, Allen Tate, and Caroline Gordon*, ed. John M. Dunaway (Baton Rouge: Louisiana State University Press, 1992); on Chagall, see Suther, *Raïssa Maritain*, 117–20.

156 Jacques Maritain, *Messages (1941–1944)* (New York: Éditions de la Maison Française, 1945), 42–6.

157 *Je suis partout*, cited in Pierre Andreu, *Vie et mort de Max Jacob* (Paris: La Table Ronde, 1982), 315; Max Jacob, *Méditations religieuses* (Paris: Gallimard, 1947), 35; both in Oxenhandler, 99–119. Raïssa Maritain, 7 April 1944, *GrndAmiFr*, 1004 n10; *GrndAmiEn*, 330 (date given without gloss). JM to JG, 22 May 1955 (#107); in *CorrJG-JMFr*, 163; *CorrJG-JMEn*, 138; Pierre Lagarde, *Max Jacob. Mystique et martyr* (Paris: Éditions Baudinière, 1944).

158 I owe this question and distinction to Philippe Buc.

159 Chadwick, *Secularization of the European Mind*, 263.

Chapter 6 Georges Rouault: Masked Redemption

1 Hans Urs von Balthasar, *The Glory of the Lord: A Theological Aesthetics*, trans. Erasmo Leiva-Merikakis, ed. Joseph Fessio and John Riches, 7 vols. (San Francisco: Ignatius Press; New York: Crossroad Publications, 1983–91); vol. 1, *Seeing the Form*, 124, 160; orig. *Herrlichkeit: eine theologische Ästhetik* (Einsiedeln: Johannes Verlag, 1961–). Letter of Friedrich von Hügel, quoted in Rosemary Haughton, *The Catholic Thing* (Springfield, IL.: Templegate, 1979), 58–9.
2 See Messing, *Neoclassicism in Music.*
3 For following, see Soo Yun Kang, *Rouault in Perspective: Contextual and Theoretical Study of His Art* (Lanham, MD: International Scholars Publications, 2000), 7–30.
4 Christiansen, *Paris Babylon*, 196.
5 Stéphane Mallarmé and Jean Moréas, in Nicholls, *Modernisms*, 36.
6 Edward Lucie-Smith, *Symbolist Art* (London: Thames and Hudson, 1972); A.G. Lehmann, *The Symbolist Aesthetic in France*, 2nd ed. (Oxford: Basil Blackwell, 1958).
7 Pierre Courthion, 'Gustave Moreau: Inspiration and Guide,' *Georges Rouault* (New York: H.N. Abrams, 1962), 33–72.
8 Sarah Whitfield, *Fauvism* (London: Thames and Hudson, 1991), 89. See also Whitfield on Matisse: 'Picasso's comment on Cézanne, "It is the man's anxiety (*inquiétude*) that concerns us" could well be inverted to fit Matisse because it is his lack of anxiety that is absorbing.' Whitfield, 'Fauvism,' in *Concepts of Modern Art: From Fauvism to Postmodernism*, 3rd ed. (New York: Thames and Hudson, 1994), 24.
9 Raoul Sertat, 'Le Salon des Champs-Élysées,' *La Revue Encyclopédique* (1895): 187–8.
10 Claude Roger-Marx, 'Le Salon des Champs-Élysées,' *La Revue Encyclopédique* (1896): 297–306. See 298–9.
11 For example, see Jean Leymarie, preface to *Honoré Daumier. Georges Rouault* (Milan: Electra Editrice, 1983), 8.
12 Jean Steinmann, *Léon Bloy* (Paris: Éditions du Cerf, 1956), 214. On Rouault and Bloy see Courthion, *Rouault* (1962), 97–106.
13 For following, see William A. Dyrness, 'The Religious Reaction of Léon Bloy,' *Rouault: A Vision of Suffering and Salvation* (Grand Rapids, MI: William B. Eerdmans, 1971), 32–45.
14 Léon Bloy, *Quatre ans de captivité à Cochon-sur-Marne, 1900–1904* (Paris: Mercure de France, 1905); in Dyrness, *Rouault: A Vision*, 41.
15 Bloy, in Courthion, *Rouault*, 97.

16 Marcel Fouquier, 'Le Salon d'Automne,' *Le Journal* (14 October 1904). *Rouault-Arch*. Emphasis added.
17 [n.p.n.] Valensol, 'Le Salon d'Automne,' *Petit Parisien* (14 October 1904): 2. Emphasis added. *Rouault-Arch*.
18 Arsène Alexandre, 'Le Salon d'Automne,' *Le Figaro* (14 October 1904): 2. *Rouault-Arch*.
19 Léon Bloy. *L'Invendable, pour faire suite au 'Mendiant ingrat,' à 'Mon journal' et à 'Quatre ans de captivité à Cochons-sur-Marne.' 1904–1907* (Paris: Mercure de France, 1909), 37–8.
20 Bloy, *L'Invendable*, 132; in Dyrness, *Rouault: A Vision*, 43. Emphasis original.
21 Bloy, *L'Invendable*, 136.
22 Ibid., 288. For 'manly,' see note on Maritain's use above, chapter 4, n63.
23 Ibid., 289–90; in Dyrness, *Rouault: A Vision*, 43.
24 Georges Rouault to Raïssa Maritain, 24 January 1910; in 'Deux Lettres Adressées à Raïssa,' *Cahiers Jacques Maritain* 7–8 (September 1983): 19–22. See 19. See also: Nora Possenti Ghiglia, 'Jacques Maritain et Rouault: Aux sources d'une féconde amitié,' *Cahiers Jacques Maritain* 12 (November 1985): 7–22. See 10 n12.
25 'Who was Jacques Favelle? Was he a critic who is now forgotten, or was he an invented character?' (Courthion, *Rouault* 1962, 379 n98.)
26 'Jacques Favelle,' introduction to the catalogue for *L'Exposition de peintures et céramiques de G. Rouault* (Paris: Galerie E. Druet, 1910), in *JRM-OC*, 1: 1077–81. See 1077. Reprinted in *Rouault. Première période 1903–1920*, ed. Fabrice Hergott (Paris: Éditions du Centre Georges Pompidou, 1992), 200–1.
27 Maritain, 'Druet Préface,' 1077.
28 Ibid., 1078–9.
29 Ibid., 1078. Emphasis added.
30 Ibid., 1080–1.
31 Ibid., 1080. Emphasis added.
32 'Les Artistes et Les Oeuvres: G. Rouault (Druet),' *Le Siècle* (27 February 1910): n.p. *Rouault-Arch*.
33 *Journal des Arts* (23 November 1910): n.p. *Rouault-Arch*
34 Ch. Henri-Gigot, 'Galerie Druet, rue Royale, 20 – Exposition de l'ensemble des oeuvres de M. Rouault,' *Les Nouvelles* (1 March 1910): n.p. Emphasis added. *Rouault-Arch*.
35 *Progrès* (15 March 1910): n.p. Emphasis added. *Rouault-Arch*.
36 Tavier, 'Druet,' *Le Feu* (1 April 1910): n.p. *Rouault-Arch*.

37 'Georges Rouault,' *Paris-Journal* (3 May 1910): n.p. *Rouault-Arch.*
38 L. Rouan, *Les Marges* (March 1910): n.p. *Rouault-Arch*
39 Henri Frantz, 'Quelques Aquarelles [Druet],' *Excelsior* (24 December 1910): n.p. *Rouault-Arch.*
40 'Le guignol de M. Rouault,' *Gazette de la Capitale* (5 March 1910): n.p. *Rouault-Arch.*
41 Georges Frappier, *La République* (March 1910): n.p. Emphasis added. *Rouault-Arch.*
42 For *hallucinant*, *fantastique*, and cognates, see Prologue above, 36.
43 Louis Vauxcelles, 'Exposition Rouault,' *Gil Blas* (27 February 1910). *Rouault-Arch.*
44 'A Travers la Peinture – Exposition Rouault (Galerie Druet),' *Echos Parisiens* (10 March 1910): n.p. Emphasis added. *Rouault-Arch.*
45 *L'Aurore* (7 March 1910): n.p. *Rouault-Arch.*
46 'La Verité toute nue,' *Paris Journal* (14 March 1910): n.p. *Rouault-Arch.*
47 Gustave Kahn, 'Exposition Georges Rouault (Druet),' *Mercure de France* (16 January 1912); repr. Hergott, ed., *Rouault. Première période*, 207.
48 Jacques Rivière, 'Une exposition de Georges Rouault,' *La Nouvelle Revue française* (1910): 49–51; in Rivière, *Études* (Paris: Gallimard, 1924), 52–5; repr. Hergott, ed., *Rouault. Première période*, 202.
49 Charles Morice, *Le Mercure de France* (16 March 1910): n.p. Emphasis added. *Rouault-Arch.*
50 Georges Rouault and André Suarès, *Correspondance [de] Georges Rouault [et] André Suarès* (Paris: Gallimard, 1960). André Gide recruited Suarès as a founding member of the *N.R.F.* in 1912. He was known for his attacks on anti-Semitism during both the Dreyfus Affair and later in the 1930s. Suarès won the Académie française's Grand Prix for literature in 1935. His correspondence with Rouault continued throughout the years, interrupted only by his flight from Paris on 11 June 1940 (at the age of seventy-two) just days ahead of the Nazi arrival. He was unsuccessfully hunted by the Gestapo and then the Milice.
51 Georges Rouault to André Suarès, 16 July 1911, in *Correspondance*, 3–4.
52 'Salon d'Automne,' *La Cote* (4 October 1911), n.p. *Rouault-Arch.*
53 *Petit Parisien* (28 November 1920). Emphasis added. *Rouault-Arch.*
54 Salmon's reviews from March 1910 (without attribution) and October 1910 (signed 'A.S.') may be found in the Rouault Archives. They can be identified as Salmon's by comparing them with the review in André Salmon, 'Hier dans aujourd'hui,' *L'Art vivant* (Paris: Éditions du Crès et Cie, 1920), 30–2; and reprinted in Hergott, ed., *Rouault: Première période,* 218. The

Pompidou catalogue, following Salmon's 1920 edition, places this review, partly written in 1910, in its post-1918 section.

55 Unsigned [André Salmon], 'Georges Rouault,' *Paris Journal* (March 1910): n.p. *Rouault-Arch.*

56 A.S. [André Salmon], 'La Palette,' *Paris Journal* (20 October 1910): n.p. *Rouault-Arch.*

57 André Salmon, *L'Europe Nouvelle* (28 November 1920): 1762–63. Baudelaire emphasis original; other emphasis added. *Rouault-Arch.*

58 Christophe Prochasson, 'Humanité (L'),' Julliard and Winnock, *Dictionnaire des intellectuels*, 597–8.

59 Claude Roger-Marx, 'Daumier Méconnu,' *L'Humanité* (14 December 1920): 2. *Rouault-Arch.* Théodore de Banville (1823–91), French poet; Eugène Emmanuel Viollet-le-Duc (1814–79), architect; Jules Michelet (1798–1874), historian. See Roger-Marx, 'Le Salon des Champs-Élysées.'

60 'La Vie Artistique: Georges Rouault (à la Licorne),' *L'Humanité* (1 December 1920): n.p. *Rouault-Arch.*

61 René-Jean, 'Les Petites Expositions,' *Comoedia* (20 November 1920): n.p. *Rouault-Arch.*

62 *Le Calepin* (15 December 1920): n.p. *Rouault-Arch.*

63 G[aston] Varenne, *Bonsoir* (16 November 1920): n.p. Emphasis added. *Rouault-Arch.*

64 *Bonsoir* was founded in the fall of 1919 by the publishing staff of *l'Œ uvre*, an often anticlerical paper that was open to the left but mistrusted the communists. With a style that was 'lively and impertinent,' *Bonsoir* attracted numerous young talents. From 12 to 27 November 1919 during the labour strike by typesetters, the title read: 'Feuille (La) commune. Publiée avec l'autorisation du comité de grève ... [éd. du soir].' See Bellanger et al., *Histoire générale de la presse française*, 3: 567; and catalogue entry for *Bonsoir* in the Bibliothèque Nationale de France.

65 Michel Puy, *Georges Rouault. Trente reproductions de peintures et dessins, précédées d'un étude critique* (Paris: Éditions de la 'Nouvelle Revue Française,' 1921), no. 8 of Les peintres français nouveaux series.

66 Ibid., 7. Emphasis added.

67 See Francis Haskell, 'The Sad Clown: Some Notes on a Nineteenth-Century Myth,' in *French Nineteenth Century Painting and Literature*, ed. Ulrich Fink (Manchester: Manchester University Press, 1972); in Paula Hayes Harper, *Daumier's Clowns: Les Saltimbanques et Les Parades. New Biographical and Political Functions for a Nineteenth-Century Myth* (New York: Garland Publishing Inc., 1981), 11–12.

68 T.J. Clark, *The Absolute Bourgeois: Artists and Politics in France, 1848–1851* (Greenwich, CT: New York Graphic Society, 1973), 122–3. See also

Bruce Laughton, *Honoré Daumier* (New Haven: Yale University Press, 1996), esp. 127–37.

69 Glenn Watkins, 'Obsessions with Pierrot,' in *Pyramids at the Louvre. Music, Culture, and Collage from Stravinsky to the Postmodernists* (Cambridge, MA: Belknap Press of Harvard University Press, 1994), 277–309. See also Martin Green and John Swan, *The Triumph of Pierrot: The Commedia dell'Arte and the Modern Imagination*, rev. ed. (1986; repr. University Park: Pennsylvania State University Press, 1993).

70 Puy, *Georges Rouault*, 6.

71 Ibid., 9.

72 Ibid., 9–10.

73 Ibid., 10.

74 Rouault, in ibid., 15. No dates given.

75 'Mon âme magnifie le Seigneur ...' Luke 1:46. The translation was standard. See *Le Nouveau Testament de notre Seigneur Jésus-Christ et le livre des psaumes. Revision synodale* (Paris: Société Biblique de France, 1905); *Le Nouveau Testament de notre Seigneur Jésus-Christ* (New York: La Societé Biblique Americaine, 1836), 'Imprimé sur l'édition de Paris, de l'année 1805'; and *Le Nouveau Testament de notre Seigneur Jésus-Christ* (Boston: J.H.A. Frost, 1824), 'Imprimé sur la dernière édition de Paris'; and *The Hexaglot Bible; comprising the Holy Scriptures of the Old and New Testaments in the original tongues, together with the Septuagint, the Syriac (of the New Testament), the Vulgate, the authorized English, and German, and the most approved French versions*, ed. Rev. Edward Riches de Levante (New York: Funk and Wagnalls, 1901).

76 Puy, *Georges Rouault*, 11.

77 Silver, *Esprit de Corps*, 57–8. See also Nathalie Reymond, 'Le Rappel à l'ordre d'André Lhote,' in Université de Saint-Etienne, *Le Retour à l'ordre*; in Silver, *Esprit de Corps*, 417 n58.

78 André Lhote, 'La Peinture, le coeur et l'esprit,' *L'Amour de l'art* (12 December 1923): 779–82; repr. in Lhote, *Parlons peinture* (Paris: Denoël et Steele, 1933), 407–11; excerpt repr. in Hergott, ed., *Rouault: Première période*, 220–1.

79 Maritain, 'Chronique de la Quinzaine: Georges Rouault,' *La Revue universelle* (15 May 1924): 507.

80 Ibid., 508.

81 Fabrice Hergott, 'With Rouault and Braque On the Inner Paths of Painting,' in *Max Beckmann and Paris: Matisse Picasso Braque Léger Rouault*, ed. Tobia Bezzola and Cornelia Homburg (St Louis, MI: Saint Louis Art Museum; New York: Taschen, 1998), 107–32. See 116.

82 Maritain, 'Rouault,' 505. Emphasis added.

83 Ibid., 506. Emphasis added.
84 Ibid., 507. Emphasis on *pureté* original; other emphasis added.
85 Interviews with Jacques Maritain by Max Frantel, in *Comœ dia*; in Courthion, *Rouault*, 98; Barré, *Jacques et Raïssa Maritain*, 104–5.
86 Apocalypse 7:14.
87 Massis, *Le Sacrifice*, 148–9; Psichari, *Les voix qui crient* (1920), in *Oeuvres complètes*, 2: 354; in Hargreaves, *Colonial Experience*, 102. Maritain, *Antimoderne*, 1135; see also Maritain, 'Ernest Psichari,' *JRM-OC*, 1: 1044–6.
88 Maritain, 'Rouault,' 508. Emphasis added.
89 'Les Petites Expositions. Georges Rouault (Galerie Druet),' *Journal des Débats* (28 April 1924). *Rouault-Arch.*
90 Louis Léon Martin, *Paris* (27 April 1924). *Rouault-Arch.*
91 René-Jean, 'Parmi les petites expositions,' *Comoedia* (27 April 1924). *Rouault-Arch.*
92 Louis Vauxcelles, *Excelsior* (28 September 1924). *Rouault-Arch.*
93 Waldemar George, *Bulletin de la vie artistique* (15 May 1924): 229–30. *Rouault-Arch.*
94 Waldemar George, 'Un Grand peintre romantique français: Georges Rouault,' *La Revue Mondiale* (1 September 1924): 78–82. Emphasis added.
95 Marcel Hiver, in *Le CAP* [*Critique, Art, Philosophie*] 4 (November–December 1924); in Yves Chevrefils Desbiolles, *Les Revues d'Art à Paris, 1905–1940* (Paris: Ent'revues: Distributed by Distique, 1993), 123–4.
96 Waldemar George, 'Cinquante ans de Peinture Française,' *L'Amour de l'Art* (1925): 271–6.
97 Jacques Guenne, 'Portraits d'Artistes. Georges Rouault,' *Les Nouvelles littéraires* (15 November 1924): 5.
98 Georges Rouault, 'Chronique: Deux poèmes de Georges Rouault,' *L'Amour de l'Art* (1925): 445–6. Matthew 7:1.
99 Various versions of the completed work are available. See especially Georges Rouault, *Miserere*, rev. ed. (Paris: Éditions Le Léopard d'or; Tokyo: Zauho Press, 1991).
100 The story of what eventually became the *Miserere* series is a complicated and tragic one involving confiscation of the plates by Ambroise Vollard, the Nazi invasion, the Rouaults' exile from Paris, and the lawsuit regaining the plates after Vollard's death in a car accident. See Courthion, *Rouault*, 190, 197, 291, 294, 296 ff., 300, 356, 390, 391.
101 André Salmon, 'Le Miserere de Georges Rouault,' *L'Amour de l'Art* (May 1925): 182–6.
102 Georges Charensol, 'Georges Rouault,' *L'Art Vivant* 2/28 (15 February

1926), 128–30. Excerpted from *Georges Rouault, l'homme et l'œuvre* (Paris: Éditions des Quatre Chemins, 1926). Preface by Rouault. Emphasis added.

103 Pierre Courthion, *Panorama de la peinture française contemporaine* (Paris: Simon-Kra, 1927), 123–31; excerpt repr. in *Rouault. Première période*, 232–3.

104 Carl Einstein, 'Georges Rouault,' *Der Querschnitt* 5 (March 1925): 244 ff.; repr. in Einstein, *Werke, Band 2* (Berlin: Medusa Verlag, 1981), 289–97; repr. in *Georges Rouault (1871–1958). Berlin Kunstamt Wedding, Alte Nazarethkirche auf dem Leopoldplatz, 26. Oktober bis 23. November 1988* (Berlin: Das Kunstamt 1988), 22–4; in Hergott, ed., *Rouault. Première période*, trans. Miguel Couffon, 228–31.

105 Waldemar George, 'L'humaine évolution d'un grand peintre,' *La Presse* (13 March 1929); Georges Charensol, 'Les Expositions,' *L'Art Vivant* (15 March 1929): 267; Maurice Raynal, 'Les Expositions,' *L'Intransigeant* (5 March 1929). *Rouault-Arch.*

106 André Malraux, 'Un homme qui "est." Notes sur l'expression tragique en peinture,' in *Formes* 1 (December 1929): 5–6; repr. in *XXe Siècle*, special issue 'Hommage à Georges Rouault' (1971): 31–2; repr. in Hergott, ed., *Rouault. Première période*, 234–5. Emphasis original.

107 James Thrall Soby, *Georges Rouault: Paintings and Prints* (New York: Museum of Modern Art, 1945), 5.

108 *Rouault*, text by Mia Cinotti, trans. Cesare Foligno (Novara: Uffici Press, 1954), 5.

109 *Georges Rouault: Miserere*, introd. by Anthony Blunt (Boston: Boston Book and Art Shop with the Trianon Press, 1963), 2.

110 Curt Grützmacher, 'Georges Rouault oder Die Vergöttlichung des Niedrigen,' in *Georges Rouault 1871–1958* (Berlin: Kunstamt Wedding von Berlin, 1988), 13.

111 Geneviève Nouaille-Rouault and Waldemar George, *Georges Rouault und seine Welt* (Bayreuth: Gondrom, 1981), 25; in Grützmacher, *Georges Rouault*, 15.

Chapter 7 Georges Bernanos: Passionate Supernaturalism

1 Flannery O'Connor, 'On Her Own Work,' *Mystery and Manners: Occasional Prose*, ed. Sally Fitzgerald and Robert Fitzgerald (New York: Farrar, Straus and Giroux, 1969), 107–18. See 112. Michel de Certeau, interview in *Le Nouvel Observateur* (25 September 1982): 118–21; in Roger Chartier, *On the Edge of the Cliff: History, Language, and Practice*, trans. Lydia G. Cochrane (Baltimore, MD: Johns Hopkins University Press, 1997), 46.

2 See the following in *La Revue catholique des idées et des faits*: Léopold Levaux, 'Le diable dans le roman' (14 May 1926): 6–9; Louis Artus, 'La sainteté de l'abbé Donissan' (18 June 1926): 7–13; Joseph de Tonquédec, 'Autour du "Soleil de Satan." Essai de critique théologique' (6 August 1926): 9–11; Georges Bernanos, 'Lettre à Frédéric Lefèvre' (20/27 August 1926): 10–12; Georges Bernanos, letter to the *Gazette Française* (10 September 1926): 14–15; Robert Valléry-Radot, 'L'esprit du mal dans l'oeuvre de Georges Bernanos' (21 January 1927): 2–6; Georges Bernanos, 'En quittant la Belgique ...' (Letter to Paul Werrie, director of *Dernières Nouvelles*) (25 March 1927): 15–16.

3 For short biographical overview, see William Bush, *Georges Bernanos* (New York: Twayne, 1969), 17–50. For longer treatment, see Robert Speaight, *Georges Bernanos* (London: Collins & Harvill Press, 1973).

4 Robert Soucy, *French Fascism: The First Wave, 1924–1933* (New Haven: Yale University Press, 1986), 16–18.

5 Bush, *Georges Bernanos*, 33.

6 For correspondence with Vallery-Radot, Massis, Fumet, Maritain, and the Plon publishing house regarding *Satan's Sun* (20 June 1923–22 April 1926), see Georges Bernanos, *Correspondance*, 2 vols. (Paris: Plon, 1971), vol. 1, 1904–34: 174–222.

7 See William Bush, 'Avant-Propos,' in Georges Bernanos, *Sous le soleil de Satan: roman. Première édition conforme au manuscrit original*, ed. René Guise, Pierre Gille, and William Bush (Paris: Plon, 1982), 7–23. See also 'Notes et variantes,' 307–50.

8 Letter of Georges Bernanos to Jacques Maritain, 14 February 1926; in Bernanos, *Correspondance*, 1: 211.

9 Letter of Georges Bernanos to Maurice Bourdel of Plon, 20 February 1926; in Bernanos, *Correspondance*, 1: 216–17.

10 Georges Bernanos, *Sous le soleil de Satan* (1926), in *Oeuvres romanesques*, ed. Albert Béguin, notes by Michel Estève (Paris: Gallimard, 1961) (Bibliothéque de la Pléiade v. 155). Bernanos, *Under Satan's Sun*, trans. J.C. Whitehouse (Lincoln: University of Nebraska Press, 2001). See *Sous le soleil*, 92; 72; 99; 110; 115. See *Under Satan's Sun* 34; 14; 41; 52–3; 57.

11 *Sous le soleil*, 131–2; 155. *Under Satan's Sun*, 75; 98. The Gospel allusion is to Christ's crucifixion: 'But one of the soldiers with a spear opened his side, and immediately there came out blood and water.' John 19:34.

12 *Sous le soleil*, 167; 174; 191. *Under Satan's Sun*, 111; 117; 134. Emphasis original. For kiss, see *Matthew* 26:48–9: 'And he that betrayed him, gave them a sign, saying: Whomsoever I shall kiss, that is he, hold him fast. And forthwith coming to JESUS, he said: Hail Rabbi. And he kissed him.'

13 Avni, 'Fantastic Tales,' 677. On Cazotte and origins of the *fantastical*, see Prologue above, 36.
14 *Sous le soleil*, 205; 213; 214; 230–2. *Under Satan's Sun*, 147; 155; 156; 172–4. While St Jean-Baptiste-Marie Vianney, the curé of Ars, had died in 1859, he was not canonized until 1925, just a year before the appearance of *Under Satan's Sun*. For Samaritan woman at the well, see John 4:16–18.
15 *Sous le soleil*, 268; 272. *Under Satan's Sun*, 214; 218. Emphasis in translation. For Lazarus, see John 11:1–44.
16 *Sous le soleil*, 284–5; 291. *Under Satan's Sun*, 231; 237.
17 Nine were in the second part and only two in the first. The Bishop of Barcelona, however, would not give his permission to have the Spanish translation of *Satan's Sun* published unless the entire prologue was removed. See Bernanos, *Correspondance*, 1: 217 n. 1; 237 n. 1.
18 *Sous le soleil*, 306; 308. *Under Satan's Sun*, 254; 257.
19 Léon Daudet, 'Révelation d'un Grand Romancier: *Sous le soleil de Satan*,' *L'Action française* (7 April 1926). Emphasis added.
20 For Proust's complex relationship with Daudet, see Albert Sonnenfeld, 'Marcel Proust: Antisemite? I,' *French Review* 62/1 (October 1988): 25–40. See 31. Isabelle Monette Ebert, '"Le Premier Dreyfusard": Jewishness in Marcel Proust,' *French Review* 67/2 (December 1993): 196–217. See 198. Jean-Yves Tadié, *Marcel Proust: A Life*, trans. Euan Cameron (New York: Viking Penguin, 2000), 706; 712–13.
21 See Bellanger et al., *Histoire générale de la presse française*, 352–6; 560–1. For Maurras, see 352.
22 Paul Souday, 'Les Livres. Georges Bernanos: *Sous le Soleil de Satan*,' *Le Temps* (22 April 1926). Emphasis added.
23 Charles Augustin Sainte-Beuve, 29 September 1833, *Le National*; in Sainte-Beuve, *Portraits contemporains* (Paris: Michel Lévy, 1870), 1: 501; 502; in Naomi Schor, 'The Scandal of Realism,' *A New History of French Literature*, ed. Denis Hollier (Cambridge, MA: Harvard University Press, 1989), 656–61. Schor adds that Sainte-Beuve faulted Sand for 'not having respected the law requiring that a realistic content be matched by a realistic form. The result of this violation is an aesthetic monstrosity, with characters frozen somewhere between verisimilitude and symbolism.' See 660.
24 George Sand, *Lélia*, trans. Maria Espinosa (Bloomington: Indiana University Press, 1978), 350; in Schor, 'The Scandal of Realism,' 660. Emphasis added.
25 Léon Daudet, 'À propos de Georges Bernanos. Le succès littéraire,' *L'Action française* (26 April 1926).
26 Joseph Jurt, *La réception de la littérature par la critique journalistique: lectures de Bernanos, 1926–1936* (Paris: J.-M. Place, 1980), 58.

27 For following, see categories used in Jurt, *La réception*, 53–7: Socialist Left (gauche-socialiste), Radical Left (gauche-radicale), Literary Centrist (centre littéraire), Moderate (modérée), Confessional (confessionelle) Right (droite), Extreme Right (l'extrême-droite).

28 Brooks, *Melodramatic Imagination*, 20.

29 Georges le Cardonnel, 'Magazine Littéraire: *Sous le soleil de Satan*. Par M. Georges Bernanos,' *Le Journal* (7 May 1926). Capitalization original. Emphasis added.

30 Eugène Montfort, 'Chronique des romans,' *Les Marges: Revue de littérature et d'art* 36/143 (15 May 1926): 56–60. See 56–9. Emphasis added.

31 Georges Bernanos, *Essais et écrits de combat*, ed. Yves Bridel, Jacques Chabot, Michel Estève, and Joseph Jurt, 2 vols. (Paris: Gallimard, 1971–95), Bibliothèque de la Pléiade, vols. 232, 423. Following Georges Bernanos, *Écrits de combat* (Beyrouth: Les presses du journal 'La Syrie et l'Orient,' 1943).

32 (Les) Treize, 'Les Lettres. *Sous le soleil de Satan*, par Georges Bernanos,' *L'Intransigeant* (21 May 1926).

33 Jean Guiraud, 'Pages Littéraires. Un roman diabolique,' *La Croix* (23–4 May 1926).

34 Letter of Georges Bernanos to Jean Guiraud, [end of May] 1926; in Bernanos, *Correspondance*, 1: 225–6.

35 'My God, my God, why hast thou forsaken me?' Matthew 27:46.

36 Guiraud, 'Pages Littéraires.' Emphasis added.

37 Louis Artus, 'La Vie littéraire. "Sous le Soleil de Satan,"' *La Revue des jeunes* 16/10 (10 June 1926): 474–93. See 493. Also in *La Revue catholique des idées et des faits* 6/13 (18 June 1926): 10–13.

38 Henri de Noussane, 'La cité des livres. Georges Bernanos: *Sous le soleil de Satan*; Gustave Guiches: *Le Banquet*,' *Comoedia* (4 May 1926).

39 Abbé Charlier, excerpted in René Johannet, 'La vie littéraire et le mouvement des idées,' *Les Lettres*, vol. 13, t. II, no. 4 (1 August 1926): 441–65. This article was the second in which Johannet attacked Bernanos. For preceding piece, see Johannet, 'La vie littéraire et le mouvement des idées,' *Les Lettres*, vol. 13, t. II, no. 2 (1 June 1926): 193–218.

40 George Steiner, *The Death of Tragedy* (1961; repr. New York: Oxford University Press, 1980), 331; 332.

41 Alison Finch, 'Reality and its representation in the nineteenth-century novel,' in *The Cambridge Companion to the French Novel: From 1800 to the Present*, ed. Timothy Unwin (New York: Cambridge University Press, 1997), 36–53. See 37. See also Michel Raimond, *La Crise du roman, des lendemains du naturalisme aux années vingt* (Paris: J. Corti, 1966).

42 North, *Reading 1922*, 11.
43 Fernand Vandérem, 'Les Lettres et la vie,' *La Revue de France* 6/10 (15 May 1926): 350–77. See 369–73.
44 Henri Bachelin, *J.-K. Huysmans, du naturalisme littéraire au naturalisme mystique*, 2nd ed. (Paris: Perrin, 1926).
45 Firmin Roz, 'Un roman du surnaturel,' *Revue bleue* 64/12 (19 June 1926): 380–3.
46 François-Vincent Raspail (1794–1878), biologist, chemist, and socialist politician. Condemned to prison in 1849 and then exiled, he returned to France and was elected Deputé in 1869 and again from 1876 to 1878.
47 Bouzinac-Cambon, 'Chronique des Livres. *Sous le Soleil de Satan*, roman, par Georges Bernanos,' *Chronique des lettres françaises* 22 (July–August 1926): 532–6.
48 Raymond Escholier, '*Sous le soleil de Satan*, par Georges Bernanos,' *Le Petit Journal* (27 April 1926).
49 Brooks, *Melodramatic Imagination*, 18.
50 Émile Baumann, *L'immolé* (Paris: Plon, 1906); *La fosse aux lions: roman* (Paris: Grasset, 1911); *La paix du septième jour* (Paris: Perrin et cie, 1918); *Le fer sur l'enclume, roman* (Paris: Perrin, 1920); *L'anneau d'or des grands mystiques de saint Augustin à Catherine Emmerich* (Paris: Grasset, 1924); *La Vie et les oeuvres de quelques grands saints* (Paris: Librairie de France, 1926).
51 Émile Baumann, *Le signe sur les mains: roman* (Paris: Grasset, 1926); Pierre Mesnard, 'Baumann, Romancier Catholique,' *La Revue des jeunes* (10 May 1926): 241–58.
52 Jean Soulairol, 'Frédéric Lefèvre et le roman contemporain,' *La Revue catholique des idées et des faits* 6/25 (10 September 1926): 7–9; Paul Souday, 'Lefèvre et Bernanos,' *Le Temps* (10 December 1926), 1.
53 Pascal Bousseyroux, 'Garric,' in *Dictionnaire des intellectuels français*, ed. Jacques Julliard and Michel Winock (Paris: Éditions du Seuil, 1996), 525–6. Robert Garric, *Belleville, scènes de la vie populaire* (Paris: Grasset, 1928).
54 Émile Baumann, 'Les possibilités du roman catholique,' *Les Lettres* (May 1926): 7–21. See 7–9.
55 Ibid., 8. Emphasis added.
56 Ibid., 9. Emphasis original.
57 Ibid., 9–10. Quoting his own address given 15 June 1922. Emphasis added.
58 Ibid., 7.
59 Ibid., 17–18. Emphasis original.
60 Ibid., 19. Emphasis added.
61 Rudolph Otto, *Le Sacré. L'Élément non-rationnel dans l'idée du divin et sa*

relation avec le rationnel, trans. André Jundt (Paris: Payot, 1929); orig. Otto, *Das Heilige: über das Irrationale in der Idee des Göttlichen und sein Verhältnis zum Rationalen* (Breslau: Trewendt und Granier, 1917).

62 Baumann, 'Les possibilités,' 20, 21.

63 Anne Simonin, 'Nouvelles littéraires, artistiques et scientifiques (Les),' in *Dictionnaire des intellectuels*, ed. Julliard and Winock, 843–4. See 843. See Georges Bernanos, 'Interview de 1926 par Frédéric Lefèvre,' in Bernanos, *Essais et écrits*, 1: 1038–48.

64 Frédéric Lefèvre, *Georges Bernanos* (Paris: La Tour d'Ivoire, [28 July] 1926). This book includes the 'Interview' with Bernanos, *Les Nouvelles littéraires* (17 April 1926); Bernanos's 'Lettre à Frédéric Lefèvre,' *Chroniques du Roseau d'Or* (June 1926); and Lefèvre, 'Georges Bernanos et le Roman Contemporain.' See Bernanos, 'Lettre,' in *Essais et écrits*, 1: 1048–55.

65 André Gide, *Les Faux-Monnayeurs* (1926), in *Romans, récits et soties; oeuvres lyriques*, notices and bibliography by Yvonne Davet et Jean-Jacques Thierry (Paris: Gallimard, 1958), 931–1248; Gide, *The Counterfeiters with Journal of 'The Counterfeiters,'* trans. Dorothy Bussy and Justin O'Brien (1927; repr. New York: Vintage, 1973). See *Faux-Monnayeurs*, 1096; *Counterfeiters*, 205.

66 Lefèvre, *Georges Bernanos*, 52; quoting Gide, *Faux-Monnayeurs*, 1023; *Counterfeiters*, 114.

67 Lefèvre, *Georges Bernanos*, 52.

68 Ibid., 53–54; 56–57.

69 Ibid., 8. Emphasis original.

70 Ibid., 8–9.

71 Ibid., 31. Emphasis added.

72 Robert Garric, 'Les lettres. Le roman mystique: Émile Baumann et Louis Artus,' *La Revue des jeunes* 16/12 (25 July 1926): 212–18. See 212. This essay primarily reviewed Artus's *La Chercheuse d'amour* (Paris: Grasset, 1926) and Baumann's *Le Signe sur les mains* (Paris: Grasset, 1926). *La Revue des jeunes*' review of Bernanos was given to Artus. See Artus, 'La Vie littéraire. "Sous le Soleil de Satan."'

73 Garric, 'Le roman mystique,' 213.

74 Ibid., 212.

75 Ibid.

76 Ibid.

77 François Mauriac, *Le baiser au lépreux* (Paris: B. Grasset, 1922); *Génitrix* (Paris: B. Grasset, 1923); *Le désert de l'amour* (Paris: B. Grasset, 1925); *Thérèse Desqueyroux* (Paris: B. Grasset, 1927).

78 Paul Duclos and Auguste Demoment, 'POUCEL, Victor,' in *Dictionnaire du monde religieux*, 218–19. See 218.
79 Gabriel Marcel, *Journal métaphysique* (Paris: Gallimard, 1927). See *The Philosophy of Gabriel Marcel*, ed. Paul Arthur Schilpp and Lewis Edwin Hahn (La Salle, IL: Open Court Pub. Co., 1984). See also Fouilloux, 'Un Philosophe devient catholique en 1929.'
80 François Mauriac, 'Les Romans mystiques,' *Les Nouvelles littéraires* (12 June 1926): 1.
81 In 1929, Mauriac assessed Maritain and Thomism at a conference in Madrid: 'Catholic philosophy is, today, in France, in the forefront of an anti-Bergsonian and anti-pragmatic movement, and this is so thanks to a rebirth of Thomism of which, among laymen, not to speak of eminent theologians both Dominican and Jesuit, Jacques Maritain remains the most illustrious representative. No doubt if I had been a philosopher by profession, it is on this Thomist renascence that I would have insisted.' François Mauriac, *Paroles catholiques* (Paris: Plon, 1954), 32; in Doering, *Jacques Maritain*, 94.
82 Victor Poucel, '*Sous le soleil de Satan*,' *Études* 63/187 (5 May 1926): 339–47. See 343.
83 Ibid., 343–4.
84 Heidegger, *Being and Time*, 230; *Sein und Zeit*, 186. Emphasis original.
85 Poucel, 'Sous le soleil,' 343; 344; 340. Emphasis added.
86 Letter of Georges Bernanos to M. le Directeur of *la Croix Meusienne*, Bar-le-Duc, 27 May 1926; Bernanos, *Correspondance*, 227–8.
87 Poucel, 'Sous le soleil,' 346.
88 Gabriel Marcel, '*Sous le soleil de Satan*, par G. Bernanos (Plon),' *La Nouvelle Revue française* 26/153 (1 December 1926): 754–7.
89 Ibid., 754. Emphasis added.
90 Ibid., 755.
91 Ibid., 756–7. Emphasis added.
92 Alastair Hannay, *Kierkegaard: A Biography* (New York: Cambridge University Press, 2001), 428–9; 436–8.
93 George B. Bryan, *An Ibsen Companion: A Dictionary-Guide to the Life, Works, and Critical Reception of Henrik Ibsen* (Westport, CT: Greenwood Press, 1984), 29–39; and Charles R. Lyons, 'Introduction: Ibsen's Drama and the Course of Modern Criticism,' in *Critical Essays on Henrik Ibsen*, ed. Lyons (Boston: G.K. Hall & Co., 1987), 1–21.
94 Harry Fett, *Vort nationale Enevœlde. Ethos og Eros* (Oslo: H. Aschehoug & Co. [W. Nygaard], 1925), 62; in Hannay, *Kierkegaard*, 440. Emphasis added.

95 Henrik Ibsen, *Brand*, Act 5, Scene 3; trans. Michael Meyer, with a foreword by W.H. Auden (Garden City, NY: Anchor Books, 1960), 156–7.
96 'Why not have given to a saint an ending less theatrical and less tragic?' Edmund Jaloux, 'L'esprit des Livres, *Sous le soleil de Satan*, par Georges Bernanos; *Les Dames de Bois-Brulon*, par François Fosca,' *Les Nouvelles littéraires* (8 May 1926).
97 *Sous le soleil*, 308; *Under Satan's Sun*, 256.
98 Marcel, '*Sous le soleil*,' 757.
99 Denis Saurat, 'Propos. Excès du catholicisme littéraire,' *Les Marges* 36/144 (15 June 1926): 128–33; repr. in Saurat, *Tendances* (Paris: Les éditions du monde moderne, 1928). For association of pornography and homosexuality, see Dean, *The Frail Social Body*. Victor Margueritte was the author of *La Garçonne* (1922). See Patrick de Villepin, 'Garçonne (La),' in Julliard and Winock, *Dictionnaire des intellectuels*, 524–5; and Roberts, *Civilization without Sexes*, 46–62.
100 Claude Romain (pseudonym of Canon Claude-Romain Bastide), *Le Catholicisme de quelques contemporains* (Paris: Victorion frères, 1933), 48.
101 Ibid. Emphasis added.
102 Ibid., 47.
103 Jacques Maritain, *Humanisme intégral*.
104 Romain, *Le Catholicisme*, 46; 47. Emphasis original. See *JournRM-Fr*, 239; *JournRM-En*, 96. *AS JRM-OC*, 699–700, 785 n. 163; *AS 1927 En*, 83, 223 n. 154. Bernadot, 'A nos lecteurs,' 6.

Chapter 8 Charles Tournemire: Mystical Dissonance

1 Igor Stravinsky, Charles Eliot Norton Lectures (1939–1940), published as Stravinsky, *Poetics of Music: in the Form of Six Lessons*, trans. Arthur Knodel and Ingolf Dahl (n.p.: Oxford University Press, 1947), 56–7; orig. *Poétique musicale sous forme de six leçons* (Cambridge, MA: Harvard University Press, 1942). Olivier Messiaen, interview with Claude Samuel, in Messiaen, *Music and Color: Conversations with Claude Samuel*, trans. E. Thomas Glasgow (Portland, OR: Amadeus Press, 1994), 233. Originally published as Claude Samuel, *Entretiens avec Olivier Messiaen* (Paris: Belfond, 1967). Charles Tournemire, notes made during the long summer vacation period of 1934. *Tourn-Mém*, 110. The 'Léonard' from whom Tournemire quotes is most likely his close friend, the painter Léonard Sarluis. For her kind permission to consult Tournemire's *Mémoires*, I am deeply grateful to Mme. Odile Weber, the niece of Tournemire's widow, the late Mme. Alice (née Espir) Tournemire.

2 Maurice Duruflé, 'My recollections of Tournemire and Vierne,' trans. Ralph Kneeram, *The American Organist* (November 1980), 54; in Nichols, *The Harlequin Years*, 193.
3 Quoted in Benjamin Van Wye, 'The Influence of the Plainsong Restoration on the Growth and Development of the Modern French Liturgical Organ School,' unpublished PhD dissertation, University of Illinois at Urbana-Champaign, 1971, 74; in Charles Stanley Phillips, *The Church in France, 1848–1907* (New York: Macmillan, 1936), 19.
4 Dom Guy-Marie Oury, *Dom Guéranger. Moine au coeur de l'Église* (Solesmes: Éditions de Solesmes, 2000), esp. 301–13; 332–9; 411–21. For Solesmes and chant, see Prologue above, 30–3.
5 In Dowd, 'Charles Bordes and the Schola Cantorum of Paris,' 30; 51–2.
6 Jane Fulcher, *French Cultural Politics and Music: From the Dreyfus Affair to the First World War* (New York: Oxford, 1999). See especially 15–63. See also: 'La Schola et le Conservatoire,' *Mercure de France* 16 (September–October 1909): 234–43; Vincent d'Indy, ed., *La Schola Cantorum: Son histoire depuis sa fondation jusqu'en 1925* (Paris: Librairie Bloud et Gay, 1927).
7 See Fulcher, *French Cultural Politics*, 31–5. See also Fulcher, 'In Preparation for Vichy: Anti-Semitism in French Musical Culture between the Two World Wars,' *Musical Quarterly* 79/3 (Autumn, 1995): 458–75; Fulcher, 'Vincent d'Indy's "Drame Anti-Juif" and its Meaning in Paris, 1920,' *Cambridge Opera Journal* 2/3 (November, 1990): 295–319.
8 Dom Guéranger and Canon Gautier, *Méthode raisonée de plainchant* (1859) in John Rayburn, *Gregorian Chant: A History of the Controversy Concerning its Rhythm* (1964; repr. Westport, CT: Greenwood Press, (1964) 1981), 10; 75; in Van Wye, 'The Influence of The Influence of the Plainsong Restoration,' 75.
9 Van Wye, 'The Influence of the Plainsong Restoration,' 75.
10 Bordes cited by André Coeuroy, *La Musique et le peuple en France* (Paris: Stock [Delamain et Boutelleau], 1941), 95; in Dowd, 'Charles Bordes and the Schola Cantorum of Paris,' 50. Emphasis added.
11 See letters of attestation in Julia d'Almendra, *Les Modes Grégoriennes dans l'oeuvre de Claude Debussy*, rev. ed. (Paris: G. Énault, 1950), 183–7; cited in Bergeron, *Decadent Enchantments*, 168n54.
12 d'Almendra, *Les Modes grégoriens*, 24.
13 *La Tribune de Saint-Gervais* 9 (1903): 307–8; in Dowd, 'Charles Bordes and the Schola Cantorum of Paris,' 50.
14 'May God enlarge Japheth, and may he dwell in the tents of Sem, and Chanaan be his servant.' Genesis 9:27. For the use of this story in racial discourse, see Ivan Hannaford, *Race: The History of an Idea* (Washington,

DC: Baltimore, MD: Woodrow Wilson Center Press; distributed by the Johns Hopkins University Press, 1996), 264–70.

15 Amédée Gastoué, 'L'Art Grégorien: Les Origines premières,' in *Mémoires de Musicologie Sacrée lus aux assises de musique religieuses les 27, 28, et 29 Septembre 1900 à la Schola Cantorum* (Paris: Bureaux d'Édition de la 'Schola,' 1901), 3–17. See 9–11. Emphasis added.

16 Vincent d'Indy, 'Une École d'art répondant aux besoins modernes,' *La Tribune de Saint-Gervais* 6 (November 1900): 303–14. See 310–11; in Fulcher, *French Cultural Politics*, 34.

17 Pope Pius X, *Tra le sollecitudini* (22 November 1903), in R. Kevin Seasoltz, *The New Liturgy: A Documentation, 1903–1965* (New York: Herder and Herder, 1966), 3–10. See 8. Emphasis added.

18 James Joyce, 'The Dead' (1907), in *The Dead*, ed. Daniel R. Schwarz (New York: Bedford/St Martin's, 1994), 36–7.

19 Bachelin, *Les maîtrises et la musique de choeur*, 49; in Dowd, 'Charles Bordes and the Schola Cantorum of Paris.' 3. See Bachelin, *J.-K. Huysmans*; and J. Barbey d'Aurevilly, *Les oeuvres complètes*, ed. Henri Bachelin, 17 vols. (Paris: Bernouard, 1926–7).

20 See *La Tribune* 3 (1897): 130; and 8 (1902): 231; and Dowd, 'Charles Bordes and the Schola Cantorum of Paris.' 3; 15–16; 25; 56; 128.

21 Tournemire, 3 June 1933: 'Received a "jesuitical" letter (which would have made Pascal happy), from M.X., professor at the Schola "cancro"-rum.' *le cancre* = 'dunce' *Tourn-Mém*, 69.

22 Pascal Ianco, *Charles Tournemire* (Geneva: Éditions Papillon, 2001), 27–35. For date of meeting Franck, see 35.

23 Andrew Thomson, 'Les enregistrements de Charles Tournemire,' trans. Jacqueline Englert-Marchal, in Leersnyder, 57–9. See 57.

24 Vincent d'Indy, *César Franck*, trans. Rosa Harriet Jeaffreson Newmarch (London: J. Lane, 1909), 131; Amédée Gastoué, 'César Franck et Paul Poujard, à propos d'un thème de folklore, le "Chant de la Creuse,"' *Revue de musicologie* 21 (nouvelle série; May–August 1937), 37; in Van Wye, 'The Influence of the Plainsong Restoration,' 76.

25 Louis Vierne, 'Mes Souvenirs,' quoted in Michael Murray, *French Masters of the Organ* (New Haven: Yale University Press, 1998), 114.

26 *Tourn-Mém*, 7.

27 Mark Prendergast, *The Ambient Century: From Mahler to Trance – The Evolution of Sound in the Electronic Age* (New York: Bloomsbury, distributed by St Martin's Press, 2000).

28 For chronology of Tournemire's works, see Joël-Marie Fauquet, *Catalogue de l'œuvre de Charles Tournemire* (Geneva: Éditions Minkoff, 1979), 15–20.

29 The *Révue Wagnérienne*, begun in 1885, had been a principal instrument in creating the symbolist movement in Paris. On French musical symbolism, see Louis Marvick, *Waking the Face That No One Is: A Study in the Musical Context of Symbolist Poetics* (Amsterdam: Rodopi, 2004); Josceyln Godwin, *Music and the Occult: French Musical Philosophies, 1750–1950* (Rochester, NY: University of Rochester Press, 1995); David Michael Hertz, *The Tuning of the Word: The Musico-Literary Poetics of the Symbolist Movement* (Carbondale: Southern Illinois University Press, 1987); Margaretha Müller, *Musik und Sprache: zu ihrem Verhältnis im französischen Symbolismus* (New York: Peter Lang, 1983).

30 I am grateful to Richard-Isée Knowles of the Société Baudelaire for communicating this and following information in conversation. For the Société, see also Ianco, *Charles Tournemire*, 83–4.

31 For chronology of trial, see the Société Baudelaire-authorized translation of *Baudelaire: The Complete Poems*, ed. Dr Philip Higson, the society's current president (Chester, UK: Limouse Museum Publications, 1992), xxxiv–xxxv. Baudelaire's case was newly interesting after the war. See Dufay, 'Le Procès des *Fleurs du Mal*,' *Mercure de France* (1 April 1921); cited in Joanna Richardson, *Baudelaire: A Biography* (New York: St Martin's Press, 1994), 532.

32 Charles Tournemire, *Le Sang de la Sirène* (Paris-Brussels: Henry Lemoine, 1904); Anatole Le Braz, *Le Sang de la Sirène* (Paris: Calmann-Lévy, 1901); in Fauquet, *Catalogue*, 85–7.

33 H. Imbert, '*Le Sang de la Sirène*, première audition au théâtre de la Gaîté, le 17 novembre 1904,' *Le Guide Musical* (27 November 1904): 893–6. *Tourn-BN-fM*.

34 *Tourn-Mém*, 16–45.

35 Tournemire's memoir is filled with pages of notes on ancient religions from what he cites as 'Abbé Migne's *History of Ancient Religions*.' Most likely he means Jacques-Paul Migne, *Dictionnaire universel de mythologie ancienne et moderne* (Paris: J.P. Migne, 1855). Migne was a priest as well as the proprietor of a large publishing house, the Imprimerie Catholique, during the mid-nineteenth century.

36 Fauquet, *Catalogue*, 87–8.

37 *Tourn-Mém*, 19; 16.

38 Fauquet, *Catalogue*, 27–8; 76–7. Paul Verlaine, *Bonheur* (Paris: L. Vanier, 1891); and *Sagesse* (Paris: L. Vanier, 1893).

39 Several handwritten pages list what appears to have been Tournemire's library – possibly written out by his widow, the late Mme. Alice Espir Tournemire. Among the works listed are: Villiers-de-l'Isle-Adam (2 vols.);

Görres's *Mystique* (5 vols.); Th. Gautier (18 vols.); Barbey d'Aurevilly (13 vols.); Huysmans's *La Cathédrale*; Ernest Hello (6 vols.); L. Bloy, *Le Révélateur du globe*; a collection of writings by *The Fathers of the Church* (15 vols.); Guéranger, *L'Année liturgique* (15 vols.) Mâle, *L'Art religieux*; Edouard Schuré, *Évolution divine du Sphinx au Christ. Tourn-SB*. I am grateful to Richard-Isée Knowles for communicating these documents.

40 Ianco, *Charles Tournemire*, 47.

41 Fauquet, *Catalogue*, 88–9.

42 Letter of Tournemire to Pierre Garanger, quoted in Raymond Petit, 'Introduction à l'étude de l'œuvre de Charles Tournemire,' *L'Orgue* 115 (July–September 1965): 111–37. See 114.

43 Henry Eymieu, 'Nos grands organistes: Charles Tournemire,' *Revue pratique de liturgie et de musique sacrée*, 7/83–4 (May–June 1924): 412–16. See 416. On 'literary,' see Petit, 'Introduction,' 114. See Jeremiah 4:19–21: 'I will not hold my peace, for my soul hath heard the sound of the trumpet, the cry of battle. Destruction upon destruction is called for, and all the earth is laid waste: my tents are destroyed on a sudden, and my pavilions in a moment ... how long shall I hear the sound of the trumpet?'

44 Petit, 'Introduction,' 118.

45 Charles Tournemire, 'Don Quichotte,' BN Rés Vma., Ms. 995. Cited in Pierre Vidal, 'Les manuscrits de Charles Tournemire de la donation Daniel Lesur à la Bibliothèque Nationale,' in *Charles Tournemire (1870–1939)*, ed. Brigitte de Leersnyder, *Cahiers et Mémoires de l'Orgue* 41 (Paris: Les Amis de l'Orgue, 1989), 99–110. See 103. For 8th Symphony, see Petit, 'Introduction,' 119.

46 Robert Sutherland Lord, 'La liturgie et le chant grégorien dans "L'Orgue mystique" de Charles Tournemire,' in Leersnyder, ed., *Charles Tournemire (1870–1939)*, 35–52; translated from Lord, 'Liturgy and Gregorian Chant in L'Orgue Mystique of Charles Tournemire,' *The Organ Yearbook* 15 (1984): 60–97. See Lord, 'La liturgie,' 39; 'Liturgy,' 64.

47 Details are from an invitation dated March 1921 with letterhead reading 'Société Baudelaire, Siège Social: 26, rue Monsieur le Prince, Paris (5e).' A similar invitation is for a commemoration of Baudelaire's death (31 August 1867) to be held at the poet's tomb on 28 October 1927. The program included an address by Paul Bourget of the Académie française, and poems of Baudelaire to be read by theatre performers from the Œuvre, Odéon, and Comédie Française. Guests were asked to gather 'at 10 a.m., at the main entrance to Cimetière Montparnasse, Boulevard Edgar Quinet.' Both documents are preserved in the W.T. Bandy Center for Baudelaire and Modern French Studies at the Jean and Alexander Heard Library of Vanderbilt

University. I am grateful to Mary Beth Raycraft of the Bandy Center for locating and communicating these documents. See Gustave Kahn, *Symbolistes et décadents* (Paris: L. Vanier, 1902); Ernest Raynaud, *La mêlée symboliste (1900–1910): portraits et souvenirs*, 3 vols. (Paris: La Renaissance du Livre, 1920–2); Richard-E. Knowles, *Victor-Emile Michelet, poète ésotérique* (Paris: J. Vrin, 1954).

48 Stanislas Fumet held the presidency of the board dealing with the word 'Grandeur' between 1945 and 1959 – his predecessors had been Barbey d'Aurevilly (1876–89), Paul Bourget (1889–1921), Edouard Schuré (1923–6) and Tournemire (1927–39). Upon his accession, he discovered a number of contributions by Jacques Maritain spanning many years. Stanislas Fumet's version of Baudelaire was published as volume 8 of the *Roseau d'Or, oeuvres et chroniques* series for which he was Maritain's secretary. See Stanislas Fumet, *Notre Baudelaire* (Paris: Plon-Nourrit et cie, 1926); compare date of publication with Fumet, *Ernest Hello, ou, Le drame de la lumière* (Paris: Éditions Saint-Michel, 1928). I am grateful to Richard-Isée Knowles for communicating this information in conversation and correspondence. See also Ianco, *Charles Tournemire*, 82–4.

49 Johann Joseph von Görres (1776–1848), *Die christliche Mystik*, 5 vols. (Regensburg: G.J. Manz, 1836–42); trans. M. Charles Sainte-Foi, *La mystique divine, naturelle, et diabolique* (Paris: Mme Vve Poussielgue-Rusand, 1854–5). See also Griffiths, *Reactionary Revolution*, 122–46.

50 Charles Tournemire, 'Prélude aux combats de l'Idéal,' dated Thursday, 7 December 1922. B.N., Mus., Ms. 18919; in Fauquet, *Catalogue*, 72.

51 Charles Tournemire, 'Les Dieux sont morts (Chryséis),' op. 42. Composed between 1910 and 27 September 1912. B.N., Mus., Ms. 18916 (1–2); in Fauquet, 88–9. Charles Tournemire, *Les dieux sont morts: drame lyrique en deux actes*, libretto by Eugène Berteaux (Paris: Choudens, 1924). For the Paris Opera between the wars, see Nichols, *The Harlequin Years*, 59–77. For *Les Dieux sont morts*, 67.

Tournemire's 'Don Quixote' was also premiered during this time on 18 January 1924 at the Conservatoire. Tournemire's handwritten list of reviews for the 18 January 1924 performance includes: Th. Lindenlaub, *Temps* (10 Feb.); L. Schneider, *Gaulois* (22 Jan.); A. Bruneau, *Matin* (21 Jan.); A. Bosehof, *Echo de P[aris]* (21 Jan.); P. Daubly, *P[etit] Journal* (21 Jan.); E. Vuillermoz, *P[etit] Parisien* (21 Jan.); R. Dézarnaur, *Liberté* (22 Jan.); M.A., *Act[ion] Fran[çaise]* (21 Jan.); R. Charpentier, *Comœ dia* (21 Jan.); G. Pioch, *Paris Soir* (22 Jan.). In *Tourn-BN-fM*.

52 Tournemire's handwritten list of reviews for March 1924 performances of 'The Gods Are Dead' includes: n.n., *Echo de P[aris]* (21 Mar.); Adolphe

Jullien, *J[ournal] des Débats* (30 Mar.); Edouard Fonteyne, *Bonsoir* (20 Mar.); Alfred Camdessus, *Courrier de Bayonne* (31 Mar.); Jean Gandrey-Rety, *Comœdia* (11 Apr.); G.F., *J[ournal] des Débats* (22 Mar.); n.n., *Intransigeant* (20 Mar.); n.n., *Action Fr[ançaise]* (25 Mar.); Charles Montclar, *Information* (29 Mar.); André Rigaud, *Comœdia* (21 Mar.); Henry Matherbe, *Temps* (19 Mar.); Robert Dézarnaux, *Liberté* (19 Mar.); Ch. Pons, *L'Echo National* (19 Mar.); Emile Vuillermoz, *Excelsior* (19 Mar.); G. De Paw-lowski, *Journal* (19 Mar.); n.n., *N.Y. Herald* (18 Mar.); Georges Pioch, *Paris-Soir* (19 Mar.); Fernand Le Borne, *P[etit] Parisien* (18 Mar.); n.n., *Figaro* (19 Mar.); n.n., *P[etit] Journal* (19 Mar.); Charles Pons, *Eclair* (19 Mar.); n.n., *Liberté* (16 Mar.); n.n., *P[etit] Parisien* (15 Mar.); n.n., *Gorriere d. Sera* [Italian] (18 Mar.); n.n., *Excelsior* (15 Mar.); n.n., *P[eti]t Bleu* (18 Mar.); n.n., *Bonsoir* (15 Mar.); Raoul Brunel, *Oeuvre* [?] (18 Mar.); n.n., *Comœdia* (17 Mar.); Raymond Charpentier, *Comœdia* (18 Mar.). In addition to these reviews of the Paris production, numerous reviews are also cited for the Strasbourg production one year later. See *Tourn-BN-fM*.

53 See Messing, *Neoclassicism in Music*; and Fulcher, 'The Composer as Intellectual.'

54 Paul Souday, *Paris Midi* (18 March 1924). *Tourn-BN-fM*.

55 Maurice Boucher, *Le Monde Musical* (n.d., 1924). *Tourn-BN-fM*.

56 Raymond Balliman, *Lyrica*, (n.d., 1924), 260. *Tourn-BN-fM*.

57 Fernand le Borne, *Le Petit Parisien* (18 March 1924). *Tourn-BN-fM*.

58 Unsigned, *Le Quotidien* (26 March 1924). *Tourn-BN-fM*.

59 Jules Mazellier, *La France Théâtrale* (12 April 1924). Press clipping, *Tourn-BN-fM*

60 Gustave Samazeuilh, 'La Musique,' *La Revue mondiale* (ancienne *Revue des Revues*) 25/158 (15 April 1924): 415–20. *Tourn-BN-fM*.

61 Émile Vuillermoz, *Candide* (27 March 1924). *Tourn-BN-fM*. Emphasis added.

62 Arthur Hoérée, 'Chronique Musicale,' *Beaux-Arts (Revue d'information artistique paraissant deux fois par mois, Paris)* 11 (1 June 1924): 175–6. *Tourn-BN-fM*.

63 n.n., *Le Ménestrel* (1924), 127. *Tourn-BN-fM*.

64 See letters: Charles Tournemire to Albert Pauphilet (30 November 1926): 'I am going to see my friend Wolff, orchestral conductor of the Opéra-Comique – and speak to him about our ['Tristan'] ... If I do not succeed in Paris, it will be necessary to think about Lyon'; CT to AP (21 March 1927): 'As for "Tristan," I am waiting for a rendezvous with Wolff, orchestral conductor of the Opéra-Comique to play our work for him ...'; Pierre Chereau [Théatre National de l'Opéra] to CT (11 May 1928): 'Do not be

discouraged. It is necessary to fight for your Tristan which I would produce if I were the director'; CT to AP (30 May 1928): 'You will find included here a letter from Chereau, the admirable general stage manager of the Opera. <Would that he were director?!> ... the Opéra-Comique is impossible at the moment. It is a commercial firm that is selling cheap products ... Let's see, why couldn't we try Lyon?'; CT to AP (3 November 1928): 'M. Maurice Wilmotte who has great admiration for you ... is the rector of the University of Liège ... He asks me to tell you that he is going to apply himself *with ardor* on our work and speak seriously about it with the École des Bx Arts de Liège' ... He asks you to send him *immediately* a single-page *resume* of your text ... I am counting on you – because it is a matter of the future of our child'; CT to AP (12 October 1929): 'Our Tristan is despairing. At Liège there is nothing to be done ... As for M. W[ilmotte], he is hardly serious and does not know the joy of keeping one's promises!'; CT to AP (30 June 1929): 'M. Wilmotte is not the man I believed him to be. He has done absolutely nothing for our "Tristan." So, let's forget about Liège!'; CT to AP (30 November 1929): 'I saw [Georges Martin] Witkowski in Paris ... He talked to me about the 'Quest.' It's settled for either the 22 December or ... January'; CT to AP (7 January 1930): 'Quick, quick, *very quickly*, a word. It's a matter of proposing to [Jacques] Rouché, Director of the Opéra, a title other than "The Legend of Tristan and Iseult." It's a piece of advice which my friend P. Chereau, general stage manager of the Opera has just given me. He is trying, by means of mischievous innuendos to our great national Director, to reconsider his first decision ... Let's still keep hoping! Thus, I ask you to send me a title or several titles within the next 48 hours'; CT to AP (13 January 1930): 'I accept with pleasure ... your kind invitation for *Sunday evening*, after the concert ... You are going to hear three times *our* work.' *Tourn-SB*. I am grateful to Richard-Isée Knowles for communicating these documents.

The 'Quest for the Holy Grail' premiered in Lyon two weeks later, on 26 January 1930, played by Witkowski's orchestra of the Grands Concerts de Lyon and conducted by Tournemire. 'The Legend of Tristan' was never produced. Tournemire records (with parenthetical comments) having received a letter dated 21 November 1933 from Jacques Rouché: 'I beg you to please excuse me, it seemed to me that I had responded to your first letter. (Joker!) ... Please send me the text in order that I might take better account of it with a second reading of the subject. (Another pleasantry no less bitter).' *Tourn-Mém*, dated 'From 19 October to 23 November [1933],' 96. For 'Tristan' and the 'Grail,' see Fauquet, *Catalogue*, 85; 94–5.

65 Émile Vuillermoz, 'La Symphonie, Charles Tournemire,' *Cinquante ans de*

musique française de 1874 à 1925, 2 vols., ed. L. Rohozinski (Paris: Éditions musicales de la Librairie de France, 1925), vol. 1, 338–9.

66 Murray, *French Masters*, 83, 114–18; 160; 169.

67 Brooks, 'French and Belgian Organ Music,' 276.

68 Murray, *French Masters*, 160.

69 *Tourn-Mém*, 63. The rest of the memoir (pages 63–194) covers 1933–9. Note discrepancy on the name [Henri] Rabeau / Rabaud, director of the Paris Conservatoire 1920–41. See Nichols, *The Harlequin Years*, 177.

70 Freud, 'Mourning and Melancholia,' 154.

71 Raymond Charpentier, *Comœdia* (18 March 1924). *Tourn-BN-fM*.

72 For conflicting assessments, see: Norbert Dufourcq, 'Panorama de la musique d'orgue française au XXe siècle,' *La Revue Musicale* 19/184 (June 1938): 368–76; Flor Peeters, 'L'Oeuvre d'orgue de Charles Tournemire (1870–1939), *La Revue Musicale*, 21/197 (April 1940); trans. as 'In Memoriam Charles Tournemire,' *The Organ*, 45/221 (July 1977): 22–34; Maurice Duruflé, 'Mes souvenirs sur Tournemire et Vierne,' in *L'Orgue* 162 (1977); trans. Ralph Kneeream, 'My Recollections of Tournemire and Vierne,' *American Organist* 14 (1980): 54–7; Lord, 'La liturgie,' 39–41; 'Liturgy,' 64–6.

73 Charles Tournemire, *César Franck* (Paris: Delagrave, 1931). See also Marie-Louise Jaquet-Langlais, 'The Organ Works of Franck: A Survey of Editorial and Performance Problems,' in Lawrence Archbold and William J. Peterson, *French Organ Music from the Revolution to Franck and Widor* (Rochester, NY: University of Rochester Press, 1995), 143–88; esp. 151–5. Dupré's version of Franck would be passed on by his recordings and his edition of the complete works. See César Franck, *Oeuvres complètes pour orgue; revues, annotées et doigtées*, ed. Marcel Dupré (Paris: Durand and cie, 1955); and Marcel Dupré, 'The Music of Franck,' on the Mercury label, 1960. Recorded in midsummer 1959 by Dupré playing the gallery organ in the Church of Saint-Sulpice, Paris.

74 Door Marius Monnikendam, 'Een monumentaal orgelwerk. "L'Orgue Mystique" van Ch. Tournemire,' *De Musiek* 4/8 (1930): 345–51.

75 Letter of Joseph Bonnet to Alfred Cortot, New York, 11 March 1917; in Nichols, *The Harlequin Years*, 195.

76 Nichols, *The Harlequin Years*, 195–6. The text of Dubois's 1921 directive published in *La Petite Maîtrise* 104 (1922): 2–3; citation in Lord, 'La liturgie,' 47 n26; 'Liturgy,' 83 n26.

77 A.C., 'Le Chant grégorien en Chine et au Bas-Congo,' *La Vie et les arts liturgiques* 110 (February 1924): 186–7. See 187. Emphasis original.

78 Marshal Lyautey, interview in a special issue of *Monde & Voyage* dedicated to the exposition (Archives Nationales, sec. Outre-mer, Br 7700D); in Herman Lebovics, *True France: The Wars Over Cultural Identity, 1900–1945* (Ithaca, NY: Cornell University Press, 1992), 53.
79 Joseph Bonnet, 'Le rôle de l'organiste liturgique du grand orgue,' *Revue Grégorienne* 8 (January 1923): 3–11.
80 Ibid., 6.
81 Ibid., 9. Emphasis added.
82 Watkins, *Pyramids at the Louvre*, 355, 357.
83 Lord, 'La liturgie,' 39, 41; 'Liturgy,' 63–4; 65–6.
84 Lord, 'La liturgie,' 41; 'Liturgy,' 65.
85 Dom Joseph Gajard, O.S.B., 'La Musicalité du Chant Grégorien,' *Le Courrier Musical* 30, n. 2 (15 January 1928): 41–6. Here: 44, quoting Maritain, *Art et Scholastique* (1927).
86 Gajard, 'La Musicalité,' 43; quoting Jules Combarieu, *Études de philologie musicale. Théorie du rythme dans la composition moderne d'après la doctrine antique, suivie d'un essai sur l'archéologie musicale au XIXe siècle et le problème de l'origine des neumes* (Paris: A. Picard et fils, 1897). Emphasis added.
87 Dom Maur Sablayrolles, O.S.B., 'L'Orgue Mystique,' *La Musique Sacrée* 31/7–8 (July–August 1932): 57–9. See 58, 59. Emphasis added.
88 *Tourn-Mém*, 56.
89 Lord, 'La liturgie,' 37; 'Liturgy,' 63.
90 Dufourcq, 'Panorama' (1938), 373.
91 *Tourn-Mém*, 56. Emphasis original.
92 George Dyson, William Drabkin: 'Chromatic,' *Grove Music Online*, ed. L. Macy, http://www.grovemusic.com (accessed 9 May 2004).
93 George J. Buelow: 'Affects, theory of the'; and Christopher D.S. Field, E. Eugene Helm, William Drabkin: 'Fantasia,' *Grove Music Online*, ed. L. Macy, http://www.grovemusic.com (accessed 9 May 2004).
94 Dom Joseph Gajard, O.S.B., 'La Musicalité du Chant Grégorien,' *Le Courrier Musical* 30/2 (15 January 1928): 41–6. See 41; quoting Dom André Mocquereau, *L'Art grégorien, son but, ses procédés, ses caractères, conférence prononcée à l'Institut catholique de Paris, le 14 mars 1896* (Solesmes: Impr. Saint-Pierre, 1896). Emphasis added except for *diatonic.* Gajard continued: 'For the rest, the principle of diatonism is not completely unknown in our contemporary music: Debussy and others have given it a place of honor: they have even pushed it to the extreme in recommending the "whole-tone scale."'

95 Dietrich Buxtehude, *Passacaile, chacones, préludes et fugues, toccatas, canzonette: pour orgue*, ed. Charles Tournemire (New York: Éditions Salabert, 1923).
96 Tournemire to Dom Gajard; in Bernadette Lespinard, *L'Orgue mystique' de Charles Tournemire, impressions plain-chantesques* (Paris: 'L'Orgue,' 1971), 4.
97 Tournemire to Dom Gajard; in Lespinard, *L''Orgue mystique,'* 4. Also copied into memoir. See also Tournemire, 'La Musique modale à l'orgue,' *La Tribune de Saint-Gervais* 26/12 (November 1929): 165–7.
98 Charles Tournemire, 'Des possibilités harmoniques et polytonales unies à la ligne grégorienne,' *Revue grégorienne* (September–October 1930): 172–4.
99 *Tourn-Mém*, 56. Quotation is from Joris-Karl Huysmans, *En Route*, vol. 13 (in two parts) of *Oeuvres complètes*; trans. C. Kegan Paul (New York: Howard Fertig, 1976), 7; in Bergeron, *Decadent Enchantments*, 23. Tournemire had a copy of Huysmans's *La Cathédrale* in his private library. See list in *Tourn-SB*.
100 Juan Gris to Daniel-Henry Kahnweiler, 27 November 1921; *Letters of Juan Gris (1913–1927)*, collected by D.-H. Kanweiler, ed. Douglas Cooper (London: n.n., 1956), 128; in Silver, *Esprit de Corps*, 251.
101 Raymond Petit, 'L'Orgue Mystique,' *Le Ménestrel* 91/25 (21 June 1929): 281–2. See 281.
102 *Tourn-Mém*, 57.
103 For this and following, see Daniel Albright, *Untwisting the Serpent: Modernism in Music, Literature, and Other Arts* (Chicago: University of Chicago Press, 2000), 289–91.
104 Lebovics, *True France*, 57. Lebovics follows Fredric Jameson, *Politics of Post-Modernity; or, The Cultural Logic of Late Capitalism* (Durham, NC: Duke University Press, 1991), 101–29.
105 Lebovics, *True France*, 51–97.
106 Edmond Dierickx, 'Musique pour la fête de Pâques et le temps pascal,' *L'Informateur musical et théatral des œuvres catholiques* 8/3 (May 1929): 42–4. See also Dierickx, 'Bibliographie. Musique Religieuse. Orgue,' *L'Informateur musical et théatral des œuvres catholiques* 8/5 (May 1929): 73–4.
107 For example, see epigraph to first movement: 'Majesty of Christ praying that His Father should glorify Him. "Father, the hour is come: glorify Thy Son, that Thy Son also may glorify Thee." (*Prayer from Christ, The Gospel according to St John*).' Olivier Messiaen, *L'ascension, quatre méditations symphoniques pour organ* (Paris: Alphonse Leduc, 1934).
108 See letters of Olivier Messiaen to Charles Tournemire, 30 August 1930–end

of September 1933; in Joël-Marie Fauquet; 'Correspondance inédite. Lettres d'Olivier Messiaen à Charles Tournemire,' in Leersnyder, ed. *Charles Tournemire (1870–1939)* 80–5. Messiaen performed two pieces from *L'Orgue Mystique* – the 'Offertory' for *Assumption* and 'Paraphrase' from *Noël* – at Ste-Clotilde on 25 April 1932. See reproduction of Tournemire's handwritten outline in Daniel Lesur, 'Charles Tournemire et l'orgue de Sainte-Clotilde (Correspondance inédite),' in Leersnyder, *Charles Tournemire (1870–1939)*, 27–34; see 28–9. For review of concert, see M.P., 'Eglise Ste-Clotilde (25 avril) – *L'Orgue mystique*,' *Le Ménestrel* (6 May 1932).

109 *Tourn-Mém*, 57.

110 Freud, 'The "Uncanny"' (1919), 368-407.

111 Susan Stewart, *On Longing: Narratives of the Miniature, the Gigantic, the Souvenir, the Collection* (Durham, NC: Duke University Press, 1993), x. For 'off-modern,' see Boym, *Future of Nostalgia.*

112 Anne Midgette, 'A Radical in a Suit and Tie: The One and Only Charles Ives,' *New York Times* (7 May 2004): B13.

113 See Tournemire's handwritten working plan for *L'Orgue Glorieux*, BN Ms. 18932 (Don 77-326 Mus.)

114 Raymond Recouly (pseud. Jean Léry), *Le Mémorial de Foch. Mes entretiens avec le maréchal* (Paris: Éditions de France, 1929); Georges Clémenceau, *Grandeurs et misères d'une victoire* (Paris: Plon, 1930). *Tourn-SB*. On Tournemire's library, see above: I am grateful to Richard-Isée Knowles for communicating these documents.

115 Lord, 'Liturgy,' 72; 'Liturgie,' 43.

116 For analyses of the themes, structures, and harmonic language of *L'Orgue Mystique*, see Lespinard, *L''Orgue mystique*,' 8–43; expanded and revised in Lord, 'Liturgy,' 78–82. For order of composition, see Lord, 'La liturgie,' 51–2; 'Liturgy,' 73–4.

117 See Lord, 'La liturgie,' 43; 'Liturgy,' 72.

118 Charles Tournemire, *L'orgue mystique: 51 offices de l'année liturgique inspirés du chant grégorien et librement paraphrasés pour grand orgue*, 51 vols. (Paris: Heugel, 1928–36). For a recording of the complete cycle, see Charles Tournemire, 'L'orgue mystique. Le cycle de Noël, op. 55,' perf. Georges Delvallée, 3 disks (Levallois: Musidisc; Levallois: distrib. Musidisc, 1996); Tournemire, 'L'orgue mystique. Le cycle de Pâques op. 56,' perf. Georges Delvallée, 3 disks (Levallois: Musidisc; Levallois: distrib. Musidisc, 1997); Tournemire, 'L'orgue mystique. Le cycle après la Pentecôte op. 57,' part one, perf. Georges Delvallée (Levallois: Musidisc; Antony: distrib. Universal music distribution, 1999); Tournemire, 'L'orgue mystique Le

cycle après la Pentecôte op. 57,' part two, perf. Georges Delvallée (Levallois: Musidisc; Antony: distrib. Universal licensing music, 2000). For excerpts, see Charles Tournemire, 'L'Orgue Mystique,' perf. Marie-Bernadette Dufourcet, 2 disks (Bedfordshire: Priory Records Ltd, 2003). For the work interspersed with the chants, see Charles Tournemire, 'Office de l'Assomption,' perf. Susan Landale and Ensemble grégorien Magnus Liber (N.p.: Calliope Records, 2001); and 'The Mystic Organ,' perf. Frederick Swann (Tustin, CA: Gothic Records, 1992).

119 Charles Tournemire, *César Franck* (Paris: Delagrave, 1931). For Tournemire, 'De la haute mission de l'organiste à l'église' (unfinished manuscript), see Lord, 'La liturgie,' 43; 'Liturgy,' 72.

120 Charles Tournemire, interview with Jose Bruyr, 'Un entretien avec ... Charles Tournemire,' *Guide du Concert* (18 April 1930): 791–3. See 793. Capitalization of 'Sacrifice' original.

121 'Notre langue musicale actuelle possède des aptitudes surprenantes à paraphraser les mélodies grégoriennes éternellement jeunes.'

122 Olivier Messiaen, '"L'Orgue Mystique" de Tournemire,' *Syrinx: revue musicale indépendante* (May 1938): 26–7.

123 For example, Tournemire knew Joan Thomàs in Mallorca and dedicated No. 39 of *l'Orgue Mystique* (1934) to him. Thomàs assisted in publicizing the work's appearance: see Joan M.ª. Thomàs, 'El místics de l'orgue,' *Revista Musical Catalana* 26/311 (1929): 461–8. *Tourn-BN-fM*.

124 Paul de Maleingreau, 'La Semaine Musicale,' *Vingtième Siécle* [Bruxelles] (22 March 1929). *Tourn-BN-fM*.

125 'Chronique Musicale: Bibliographie,' *L'Éveil Catalan* [Perpignan] (29 June 1929). *Tourn-BN-fM*.

126 Stan Golestan, 'A travers la Musique. *L'orgue mystique*. Cycles inspirés du chant grégorien,' *Le Figaro* (20 May 1929). *Tourn-BN-fM*.

127 Béranger de Miramon Fitz-James, '"L'Orgue Mystique" de Charles Tournemire,' *Le Courrier Musical* (1 July 1929). *Tourn-BN-fM*.

128 A. Lir, 'Musiques Nouvelles,' *Le Courrier Musical* (1 April 1930): 223. *Tourn-BN-fM*.

129 See the following concert reviews by Tournemire published in *Le Courrier Musical* between April 1929 and March 1932: SSC: Mozart, Debussy (1 April 1929); Les Amis de L'Orgue (15 April 1929); Beethoven, Ibert, Rodrigo, Debussy (15 April 1929); Schumann: *Le Paradis et la Péri* (15 April 1929); Marcel Dupré organ concert; and Stravinsky, *Feu d'artifice* (15 May 1929); Joseph Bonnet at Ste-Clotilde (1 July 1929); OSP: Haendel; Bourguignon, *Esquisses sud-américaines* Debussy; d'Albeniz (15 November 1929); OSP: Vaughan Williams, 'London

Symphony'; Mussorgsky; Debussy (1 December 1929); Music for Harp: Vierne; Tournier (15 December 1929); OSP: Stravinsky, Haydn, Debussy, Moussorgsky 'Pictures at an Exhibition' orchestration by Ravel (1 January 1930); OSP: Verdi, Rimsky-Korsakoff, Reger, Borodin, Liszt (15 January 1930); OSP: Weber; Beethoven; Glück; Wagner; Schubert; Ravel (15 March 1930); OSP: Schubert, Scriabine (1 April 1930); OSP Coppola, Wiéner, Honneger, Gershwin (15 June 1930); Amis de l'orgue [concert of Joseph Bonnet] (1 July 1930); Concerts Poulet: Beethoven, Liszt, M. Henri Casadesus (1 November 1931); SCC: Bruneau; Franck; Chopin; Borodine (1 December 1931); Beethoven, Aubert, d'Inghelbrecht, J. du Bellay (1525–1560) (1 December 1931); OSP: Brahms, Richard Strauss (1 February 1931); SCC: Lalo, Mozart, Dvorak, Rimsky, Fauré (1 February 1932); Berlioz; Glazounoff, Debussy's *Iberia* (1 March 1932); SCC: Beethoven, Profokieff, Respighi, Saint-Saëns (15 March 1932). *Tourn-BN-fM*. (OSP = Orchestre Symphonique de Paris; SSC = Société des Concerts du Conservatoire; on these orchestras, see Nichols, *The Harlequin Years*, 41–58.)

130 Nichols, *The Harlequin Years*, 117; Jackson, *Making Jazz French*, 120–1.

131 Charles Tournemire, review of 'A mixture [*mélanger*] of J.-S. Bach and Beethoven to MM. Gershwin, Irgraham, and Henderson,' *Le Courrier Musical* (1 January 1930). See also Jackson, *Making Jazz French*: George Gershwin: 10, 95, 107, 110, 174, 195; Fletcher Henderson: 68, 126; Sam Wooding: 23, 159, 172; Jean Wiéner: 30, 104, 119–21; Clément Doucet: 119–20.

132 In his memoirs, Tournemire writes that the 'diffusion [of *L'Orgue Mystique*] was rapidly made in a number of foreign countries: Spain, Switzerland, Italy, Belgium, Holland, U.S.A., Canada, Sweden, England, Poland, Pennsylvania [*sic*], Australia, Scotland, Czechoslovakia, Argentina, Ireland, etc. The studies and articles that appeared in the French press and abroad were numerous, and the letters innumerable!' *Tourn-Mém*, 57–8. The following is transcribed from a handwritten list of 1929 publications (reproduced here in original order) that very likely mention either the publication of *L'Orgue Mystique* or of concerts in which it figures. (1929 is the only year for which such a list is provided in the fonds Montpensier Daniel-Lesur donation.)

The Diapason (1 May); *New York Herald* (5 September); *Correo de Mallorca* (17 October); *Revista Parroqiual de Musica Sagrada* (Barcelona) (1 November); *Echo de Paris* (25 November); *La veu de Catalunya* (14 November); *La vie Catholique* (8 June); *Correo de Mallorca* (4 May); *La veu de Catalunya* (24 August); *L'Ami du Peuple du soir* (2 April); *Figaro* (20 May); *Ouest-eclair* (29 July); *Le courrier du Finistére* (3 August); *Le Monde Musical* (31 July); *The Musical Times* (1 August); *Bulletin de l'union des Maîtres de Chapelle et organistes* (15 av. du Maine) (July); *Le 20e siècle de Bruxelles* (23 March); *La veu de Catalunya* (27 October); 'Notre Carnet' Lyon (10 November); *L'écho Paroissial de Brest* (21 July); *Musica Sacra* (Desclée (Bruges)) (September); *Bulletin de St Martin et de St Benoît* (Ligugé abbey in Vienna) (June); *The Catholic Choirmaster* (St. Gregory Society, 170 Rittenhouse Street, Philadelphia – Nicole A Montani, Editor (December); *The Organ* (London) (July); *L'informateur musical et théatral des œuvres catholique* Lyon (March 29); *Caecilia* Strasbourg (November–December); *La Musique d'Eglise* (Hérelle) Paris (May); *La Tribune de St Gervais* (May); *Revista Parroquiall de Musica Sagrada* (Barcelona) (June); *Musical Times* (England/London) (August); *Musique* (252 Faubourg St Honoré) (15 June); *Petite Maîtrise* (June and October); *Revista Musical Catalana* (October). *Tourn-BN-fM*.

133 *Le Ménestrel* (6 December 1929), n.p. *Tourn-BN-fM*.

134 André Létang, review of concert of M. Marcel Paponaud, *Les Amitiés* [Saint-Etienne] (15 April 1930). *Tourn-BN-fM*.

135 J.H., 'Deux œuvres nouvelles de Ch. Tournemire,' *Le Monde Musical* (30 April 1930). *Tourn-BN-fM*. Emphasis original.

136 Tournemire was an influential member of this 'Friends of the Organ,' co-founded by Norbert Dufourcq and Count Bérenger de Miramon Fitz-James in order to revitalize organ studies for a new generation of musicians, and for which Tournemire played the inaugural concert in June 1927. See 'Charles Tournemire et les Amis de l'Orgue,' in Leersnyder, ed., *Charles Tournemire (1870–1939)*, 60–3; and Pierre Denis, 'Naissance des "Amis de l'Orgue,"' in Marcelle Benoit, ed., *Norbert Dufourcq (1904-1990)* (Paris: Association des Amis de l'Orgue, 1993), 53–63.

137 Mlle. Geneviève Mercier, program for recital of 29 April 1929: 1) Bach: Toccata and Fugue in d-minor; 2) G.-A. Calviere, Récit de cromorne en taille; Marchand: Basse de Trompette; 3) Eugène Gigout: Scherzo in E-major; 4) G.-F. Handel: Air from the Passion; L.-V. Beethoven: 'Song of Penitence'; 5) César Franck: Prelude, Fugue, and Variation; 6) Augustin Barié (1883–1915): Intermezzo from the Symphony 7); Léon Boellmann: Allegretto from the Second Suite 8); Marcel Dupré: Berceuse (excerpt from the Suite Bretonne) 9); Gustave Guillemoteau: Three religious melodies; 10) Tournemire: Communion [from *L'Orgue Mystique*, 'Immaculate Conception'] and Toccata [from his youth]; 11) Louis Vierne: Naiades; Carillon de Westminster. *Tourn-BN-fM*.

138 Émile Poillot, program for recital of 19 March 1932: 1) J.S. Bach (1685–

1750): Fantasy and Fugue in g-minor; 2) MENDELSSOHN (1809–47): Third Sonata; 3) E. Bernard (1845–1902): Scherzo-Caprice; 4) Ch. Tournemire: Paraphrase-Carillon for 'Assumption' [*L'Orgue Mystique*]; 5) Improvisation on a submitted theme 6) L. Vierne: Allegro and Menuet from the Fourth Symphony. *Tourn-BN-fM.*

139 Charles Tournemire, recital of 17 March 1930, announced in *Dépêche* [Rouen], 13 March 1930: 'Here is the program of an organ recital which M. Charles Tournemire, professor at the National Conservatory, organist of Sainte-Clotilde, will give this Saturday evening, at 8:30, at the Cathedral.' 1) Nicholas de Grigny: Point d'orgue sur les Grands jeux; 2) Frescobaldi: Toccata per Elevazione; 3) Buxtehude: Modal Fugue; 4) Ch. Tournemire: *L'Orgue mystique* excerpts: a) Diptyque from Feast of the Purification; b) Triptyque from Feast of the Holy Trinity; c) Choral from the Feast of All Saints; d) Offertory from Feast of the Giving of the Name of Jesus; e) Two Communion pieces; f) Toccata; and g) Paraphrase. *Tourn-BN-fM.*

140 H.H., 'Récital d'orgue de M. Tournemire,' *Journal de Rouen* (17 March 1930). *Tourn-BN-fM.*

141 Charles Tournemire, 'De l'utilité des manifestations organistiques ailleurs qu'à l'Église,' *Le Monde Musical* (31 December 1929): 402–3.

142 J. de C., *Ménestrel* (4 April 1930). *Tourn-BN-fM.*

143 Jean d'Arvor, 'M. Ch. Tournemire, à Morlaix' [Brest], *Le Courrier Musical* (1 August 1930). Emphasis added. *Tourn-BN-fM.*

144 For a reproduction of the invitation and program for 17 June 1929, see Daniel-Lesur, 'Charles Tournemire et l'orgue,' 33–4.

145 Charles Tournemire, program for recital of 16 June 1930. All except the final improvisation are from *L'Orgue Mystique*: 1) *Window*, Quinquagesima Sunday; 2) Offertory, Feast of Holy Name of Jesus; 3) *Variations*, Feast of Holy Name of Jesus; 4) Offertory, Feast of Epiphany of the Lord; 5) Fantaisie-Paraphrase, Second Sunday after Epiphany; 6) Communion, Second Sunday after Epiphany; 7) Offertory, First Sunday after Epiphany; 8) *Postlude-Choral*, Feast of St Joseph, Spouse of the Blessed Virgin Mary; 9) *Prelude and Praises*, Feast of the Birth of the Blessed Virgin Mary; 10) *Clamors and Choral*, Septuagesima Sunday; 11) *Improvisation on the 'Te Deum.'* *Tourn-BN-fM.*

146 Maurice Imbert, 'L'Orgue Mystique de M. Ch. Tournemire,' *Le Courrier Musical* (1 July 1930). *Tourn-BN-fM.*

147 Jacques Janin, 'Les Grands Concerts. Musiques d'orgue,' *L'Ami du Peuple* (24 June 1930). *Tourn-BN-fM.*

148 Norbert Dufourcq, 'Une tradition renouvellée: L'Orgue Mystique, de Charles Tournemire,' *La Tribune de Saint-Gervais*, 26 (May 1929): 83–6. See 86.
149 Raymond Petit, 'L'Orgue Mystique,' *Le Ménestrel*, 91/25 (21 June 1929): 281–2.
150 Anonymous, *Le Courrier Musical* (1 May 1929). *Tourn-BN-fM*.
151 Miramon Fitz-James, '"L'Orgue Mystique."'
152 n.n., 'Les projects de M. Charles Tournemire,' *Comœdia* (23 August 1929). *Tourn-BN-fM*.
153 H.H., 'Récital d'orgue' (17 March 1930).
154 A. Lir, 'Musiques Nouvelles,' 223.
155 Norbert Dufourcq, 'Panorama de la musique d'orgue française au XXe siècle (part two),' *La Revue Musicale* 19/185 (July–August 1938): 35–44. See 39–40.
156 Messiaen, '"L'Orgue Mystique,"' 26–7.
157 Petit, '*L'Orgue Mystique*,' 281.
158 Coeuroy, *La Musique et le peuple*, 95; in Dowd, 'Charles Bordes and the Schola Cantorum of Paris,' 50. Emphasis added.
159 JM to JC, 26 May 1923, *CorrJC-JM*, 62.
160 Thomas Harrison, *1910: The Emancipation of Dissonance* (Berkeley: University of California Press, 1996), 59.
161 Suzanne Pagé, *Années 30 en Europe: le temps menaçant 1929 1939: exposition du 20 février au 25 mai 1997, Musée d'art moderne de la ville de Paris* (Paris: Paris musées: Flammarion, 1997); Eugen Weber, *The Hollow Years: France in the 1930s* (New York: Norton, 1994).
162 Thomson, 'Les enregistrements,' 47–59.
163 Émile Vuillermoz, 'Le Grand Prix du Disque,' *Candide* (n.d., 1931). *Tourn-BN-fM*. See Jackson, *Making Jazz French*: for Josephine Baker: 28, 68, 85, 87, 94, 106, 112–14, 125; for Vuillermoz: 30, 89, 127, 157. For Baker, see also Shack, *Harlem in Montmartre*, esp. 27–38; and Blake, *Le Tumulte noir*, esp. 92–9.
164 *L'Édition Musicale Vivante* (April 1932), 17. For other reviews of Tournemire's recordings, see: René Bizet, 'Disques,' *L'Intransigeant* (29 November 1931); Henri Petit, 'Les Disques,' *Courrier Musical* (1 December 1931); Henri Petit, 'L'Édition Phonographique,' *Semaine Musicale* (4 December 1931), 235; Dominique Sordet, 'Le Phonographe. Bons et mauvais disques,' *L'Action française* (26 February 1932); Marcel Farges, 'Les Disques. Musique religieuse et musique profane,' *Ami du Peuple* (21 March 1932). *Tourn-BN-fM*.

165 The broadcast was announced in both *Antenne* (24 April 1932) and *Radio-Magazine* (24 April 1932). *Tourn-BN-fM.*
166 Suzanne Perrot, *Paris Film* (17 June 1932). *Tourn-BN-fM.* Emphasis added.
167 M.P., 'Eglise Ste-Clotilde (25 avril) – *L'Orgue mystique.*'
168 For *Lyon républicain*, see Bellanger et al., *Histoire générale de la presse française*, 3: 238, 402, 517, 604. Tournemire writes: 'Monsieur Giriat, student of d'Indy, has written the following study of me which appeared in the *Lion Républicain* [*sic*] dated 1 November 1933, entitled: 'A great French musician: Charles Tournemire.' *Tourn-Mém*, dated 'from 19 October to 23 November,' 96–8.
169 Pierre Giriat, 'Un grand musicien français: Charles Tournemire,' *Lyon républicain* (1 November 1933). Emphasis original. *Tourn-BN-fM.*
170 Bernard Schulé, 'Souvenir d'un Suisse à Paris,' in Leersnyder, ed., *Charles Tournemire (1870–1939)*, 20–2. See 22.
171 Ianco, *Charles Tournemire*, 95.
172 Rebecca Rischin, *For the End of Time: The Story of the Messiaen Quartet* (Ithaca, NY: Cornell University Press, 2003).
173 I am grateful to Richard-Isée Knowles for communicating this detail in conversation.
174 Benjamin Ivry, *Francis Poulenc* (London: Phaidon Press, 1996), 90.
175 Tournemire quoting 'Léonard,' *Tourn-Mém*, 110. See chapter epigraph above.

Index

www.ingramcontent.com/pod-product-compliance
Lightning Source LLC
Jackson TN
JSHW020249220525
84496JS00001B/1/J

* 9 7 8 0 8 0 2 0 8 7 1 8 8 *